Portrait of

America

PORTRAIT OF
AMERICA

SIXTH EDITION

VOLUME I

*From Before Columbus
to the End of Reconstruction*

STEPHEN B. OATES

UNIVERSITY OF MASSACHUSETTS, AMHERST

HOUGHTON MIFFLIN COMPANY
BOSTON   TORONTO   GENEVA, ILLINOIS
PALO ALTO   PRINCETON, NEW JERSEY

Again, for Greg and Stephanie with my love

Sponsoring editor   Sean W. Wakely
Senior associate editor   Jeffrey Greene
Senior project editor   Rosemary Winfield
Production/design coordinator   Jennifer Waddell
Senior manufacturing coordinator   Priscilla Bailey
Marketing manager   Rebecca Dudley

Cover image: John V. Bloom, "Shucking Corn," Mural WPA, DeWitt, Iowa Post Office, photograph by William Luse Photography © 1994.

Cover design: Edda V. Sigurdardottir.

Printed in the U.S.A.
Library of Congress Catalog Card Number: 94-76537
ISBN: 0-395-70887-7
  3456789-DH-97   96   95

CONTENTS

of the most visible spokesmen of the nascent abolitionist movement, thundering against slavery and slaveowners in a stunning display of moral outrage and seeking to win converts through moral pressure. Korngold not only brings Garrison brilliantly alive in the context of his time, but also introduces other important figures in the abolitionist crusade.

Jackson's arch foe is just a name in most American history textbooks. This portrait resurrects Clay's fascinating personality and recounts his remarkable career as one of the great political figures of the first four decades of the nineteenth century. Speaker of the House, senator, compromiser, Jackson hater, perennial presidential contender, and an antislavery slaveowner, Clay championed Jefferson's scheme of gradual emancipation and colonization and stood as the foremost spokesman of the "American system," which became a casualty of the sectional controversy.

The first planned industrial community in America, Lowell, Massachusetts, became a model of the "paternalistic factory system," employing farm girls in a relatively clean and uncrowded working environment that contrasted starkly with the wretched working conditions in Europe. Klein stresses the tension between democratic ideals and the profit motive in the Lowell mills, and he describes the paternalism that, ironically, sowed early seeds of feminism.

Smith's rollicking narrative describes the advent of the steam-powered locomotive and the railroad age in Jacksonian America, a time when go-ahead Americans devised engines and laid track across the country. The railroads, which accelerated the westward movement and generated an often blind American passion for progress, were America's principal form of transportation until they were replaced by the interstate highway system of the twentieth century.

A prolific Western historian describes one of the most disgraceful chapters of American history: the theft of Cherokee land in Georgia and the brutal resettlement of the Cherokees in the Indian

Territory, along a "trail of tears" where one out of four died. Brown shows how a political split within the Cherokee nation and the duplicity of one faction contributed to the Cherokees' misfortune.

Drawing on contemporary diaries and letters, the authors reconstruct the conditions of life for women and their families heading west on the Oregon and California trails. They raise provocative questions about the differences between men's and women's attitudes and experiences and about how the overland migration altered eastern conventions about family structure and "proper" women's roles.

A former slave who authored the first novel, first play, and first black history by an African American describes his experiences in bondage in the South. His account makes clear the utter vulnerability of African Americans to the whim of every white person they encountered.

In antebellum Dixie, preachers, planters, novelists, and other molders of opinion were fanatical in idealizing and idolizing Southern women. This spirited essay examines the myth of the Southern lady as it flourished in the patriarchal South and explains that the need to preserve the slave system contributed to the insistence on perfect, yet submissive, women.

A Pulitzer Prize-winning historian discusses how the issue of slavery in the territories, revived by the Kansas-Nebraska Act, eroded "the traditional bonds of Union," exacerbated sectional tensions, and hurtled the country toward civil war. Donald stresses how peoples' perception of events dictated the course of the North and the South over the territorial issue.

A Lincoln biographer profiles America's greatest president, pulling back the myths and legends to reveal the man who really lived. Here is both the eloquent public figure who damned slavery as "a vast moral evil" and the troubled private man who was plagued by romantic difficulties and obsessed with death. Oates also traces the evolution of Lincoln's emancipation policy, one of the least understood facets of his presidency.

PREFACE

Like its predecessors, the Sixth Edition of this anthology stresses the human side of history, suggesting how the interaction of people and events shaped the course of the American past. As I compiled selections for *Portrait of America*, my primary criteria were that they be well written and suffused with human interest and insight. I chose essays, narratives, and biographical portraits that humanize American history, portraying it as the story of real people who actually lived, who struggled, enjoyed triumphs, suffered failures and anxieties, just like people in our own time. I hope that the anthology is an example of humanistic history at its best, the kind that combines scrupulous and engaging scholarship with a compelling narrative style. My feeling is that, since college survey audiences are not professional ones, they might enjoy reading history if it presents the past in an exciting and readable form.

There is another reason why students will find *Portrait of America* edifying: it showcases the writings of some of America's most eminent historians. The prizes their work has won testifies to their important places in the galaxy of American letters. Laurel Thatcher Ulrich's *A Midwife's Tale* and James M. McPherson's *Battle Cry of Freedom: The Civil War Era*—sections of both works are excerpted here— received the Pulitzer Prize for history; *A Midwife's Tale* also garnered the Bancroft Prize, the John L. Dunning Prize, and several other awards. Robert V. Remini's biography of Andrew Jackson won the American Book Award and the Carl Sandburg Award for nonfiction, and Eric Foner's extraordinary new study of Reconstruction won the Bancroft Prize and the Francis Parkman Prize of the Society of American Historians. Carl N. Degler has won the Pulitzer Prize and the Bancroft Prize. David Herbert Donald has twice

won the Pulitzer Prize for biography. James MacGregor Burns has received the Pulitzer Prize for history, plus the National Book Award and the Francis Parkman Prize. Page Smith and Richard B. Morris have won Bancroft Prizes, and Walter LaFeber has won the Albert Beveridge Prize. Many of the other contributors have also received significant literary and scholarly awards. Thus *Portrait of America* offers readers a unique opportunity to learn from a lineup of nationally recognized historians and writers.

The Sixth Edition of Volume I has been more extensively revised than any previous edition. It has thirteen new selections and a revised former selection. Some of the new readings—Lewis Lord and Sarah Burke's discussion of the Native American cultures that flourished before European contact, Gary B. Nash's account of the slave trade and the development of slavery in colonial North America, and James M. McPherson's analysis of why the Confederacy lost the Civil War—replace and improve upon earlier selections on similar subjects. Other new selections focus on topics not previously covered:

Gary B. Nash's essay on the transformation of European society in North America,

Douglas L. Wilson's analysis of Thomas Jefferson and the Declaration of Independence,

Laurel Thatcher Ulrich's "A Midwife's Tale,"

Walter LaFeber's discussion of the Louisiana Purchase as a dangerous precedent,

Vincent Harding's lyrical narrative of the black quest for freedom in the young Republic,

Robert V. Remini's provocative interpretation of Andrew Jackson and the Jacksonian Revolution,

Stephen B. Oates's biography of Henry Clay,

David Herbert Donald's account of why the Civil
   War came,
Oates's article on Clara Barton's "finest hour" as a
   Northern battlefield nurse and relief worker,
and Eric Foner's discussion of the birth of the modern
   black community during Reconstruction.

Although the Sixth Edition retains the best and
most popular selections of the previous edition, I have
rewritten the introductions to nearly all of them. I
hope that *Portrait of America* remains as balanced as
ever, for it offers samplings of virtually every kind of
history—men's and women's, black and white, social
and cultural, political and military, urban and economic, national and local—so that students can appreciate the rich diversity of the American experience.

The Sixth Edition offers an important new feature.
Each selection is preceded by a glossary of important
people, events, and concepts that appear in the reading. Introductions set the selections in proper context
and suggest ways to approach studying them. They
also tie all the selections together so that they can be
read more or less as connected episodes. Study questions following the selections are designed to raise significant issues and to help students make comparisons
and contrasts between the selections. The questions
also help students review the readings and suggest
points for class discussion.

The anthology is intended for use largely in college
survey courses. It could be utilized as a supplement to
a textbook or to a list of paperback readings. Or it
could serve as the basic text. The book is organized
into fourteen parts according to periods or themes;
each part contains two or three related selections.
This organization allows readers to make comparisons
and contrasts between different events or viewpoints.

In preparing the Sixth Edition, I drew on the ex-
pertise of many enthusiastic colleagues across the
country. I owe a special thanks to Professor Charles J.
Errico of Northern Virginia Community College,
who has provided constructive critiques of both volumes through many editions. I am indebted to my
research assistant, Anne-Marie Taylor, for writing the
study questions to the new selections and offering excellent critical advice. Dr. Karen Smith and Professor
Betty L. Mitchell of the University of Massachusetts,
Dartmouth, wrote the study questions for the other
selections and gave me helpful suggestions about
readings on women's and social history. Professor
Joyce Berkman of the University of Massachusetts,
Amherst, also counseled me on women's history. I
want to thank the following professors for reviewing
one or both volumes:

Glenn C. Altschuler
Cornell University

James F. Cook
Floyd College

Jean E. Friedman
University of Georgia

James W. Hill
Riverside Community College

Robert Ireland
University of Kentucky

Monroe H. Little, Jr.
Indiana University–Purdue

Lessing H. Nohl
American River College

My gratitude, too, to Rebecca Watson, who
brought me countless articles and books, photocopied
materials, and performed many other indispensable
tasks. Finally, I am grateful to the many students who
have offered praise and suggestions for *Portrait of
America*, for they are invaluable arbiters of how effectively it teaches them about the past.

S.B.O.

Portrait of

America

I

THE EUROPEAN DISCOVERY

1

America Before Columbus

LEWIS LORD AND SARAH BURKE

For many people, as Lewis Lord and Sarah Burke point out, American history began in 1492 when Columbus "discovered" the New World. Every Columbus Day we commemorate the myth of the bold, visionary hero who defied superstition, plunged across a storm-tossed Atlantic against all odds, landed in America, and made the United States possible. In reality, of course, Columbus did not "discover" America; prehistoric people from Asia, the ancestors of the Native Americans, or Indians, had done that about 14,000 years before when they began migrating from Siberia to Alaska across the land bridge of the Bering Strait. Over the centuries, the first Americans fanned out across North and South America and the islands of the Caribbean, until by Columbus's time they numbered approximately 40 million. These "pre–European" inhabitants spoke hundreds of different languages and created remarkably diverse cultures — there were 2 million people and a thousand different tribes in North America alone, ranging from nomadic bands on the Plains to collectivist, corn-growing pueblos in New Mexico and highly developed, agricultural towns in the Southeast.

Who knows what this thriving, complex population of indigenous Americans might have become had Columbus not stumbled onto America in his search for the fabled Orient. What we do know is that the European arrival in the "New World" had profound consequences for the Western Hemisphere, Europe, and Africa. On his second voyage, as Lord and Burke say, Columbus established the first outpost of European civilization in the New World and inaugurated "the Columbian Exchange" — "a global swap of animals, plants, people, ailments and ideas" that altered the course of human history. Among other things, this exchange sent American corn to Africa and American tobacco, potatoes, beans, squash, tomatoes, and peanuts to Europe, and brought horses, cows, chickens, pigs, honeybees, coffee, wheat, and rice to the Americas.

For the first Americans, to whom Columbus gave the name Indios, the introduction of European animals and plants was salutary. The horse, for example, spread rapidly among the buffalo-hunting tribes of the Plains, increasing their speed and range of locomotion and becoming their chief symbol of wealth. But in almost every other respect, the European invasion of the Indian world was a catastrophe. Columbus himself set the example for subsequent Europeans, initiating a policy of enslavement and killing that was to contribute to the near extermination of the first Americans. Even Columbus's otherwise sympathetic biographer, Samuel Eliot Morison, acknowledged that the "cruel policy" begun by Columbus and pursued by his successors amounted to genocide. To make matters worse, the Indians were not immune to the communicable diseases the Europeans carried to the New World. Epidemics of measles, typhoid, smallpox, and tuberculosis, not to mention dysentery and alcoholism, were to sweep through the original Americans, killing them by the countless thousands. By 1890, after four centuries of white conquest, only about 250,000 Indians remained in all of North America.

In the selection that follows, Lord and Burke offer a vivid portrait of the complex world of the Native Americans before Europeans appeared. The authors will introduce you to the mound builders of Cahokia, part of a highly developed, corn-growing civilization that flourished in the eastern woodlands between 700 and 1500 A.D. In the words of W. Michael Gear and Kathleen Gear, "This civilization embraced not only the most complex religious ceremonialism, social organization, and economic sophistication ever seen in prehistoric North America, but also the most expansive political influence heretofore known," with trade routes that extended across the entire continent. The Mississippians, as they are called, built towns of earthen mounds that could reach heights of a hundred feet, and they had sufficient grasp of astronomy and math to "align each of their mounds according to the exact position of the sun when it rose and set on the equinox and solstice." When the Europeans came, however, this once powerful civilization had disappeared, wiped out by droughts and famine. Their temple mound towns were empty now, leaving European immigrants to contemplate their mysteries. In addition to the mound builders, "Columbus Before America" will introduce you to numerous other Indian tribes and cultures, many of them identified in the sidebar, "The Indian Homeland." The authors describe what happened to them as a result of the European invasion and place major emphasis on the significance of the "Columbian Exchange." As a Smithsonian historian says, "The Columbus story is not an Old World, New World story. It is two old worlds that linked up, making one new world."

GLOSSARY

ACOMA   Pueblo Indian town in New Mexico that was first inhabited in the twelfth century; it is twice as old as St. Augustine, Florida.

CAHOKIA   Mound-builder civilization of the thirteenth century, situated along the Mississippi, across from present-day St. Louis.

COLUMBIAN EXCHANGE   "A global swap of animals, plants, people, ailments and ideas that began after Columbus's second voyage and altered the course of history."

LEWIS, MERIWETHER, AND LEWIS CLARK   Led a United States expedition across the continent to the Pacific, 1804–1806.

POVERTY POINT   3,500-year-old mound-builder site in Louisiana.

Most vacationers on Interstate 70 speed right by ancient Cahokia and its 15-acre ceremonial mound, the one that's 2 acres bigger than the Great Pyramid of Egypt. Only a curious few pull off to learn how a feather-crowned dictator known as the Great Sun used to kneel atop the earthen temple every morning and howl when the real sun came up. At its peak, the town across the Mississippi from present-day St. Louis boasted a trade network that stretched from the Gulf of Mexico to the Dakotas and probably had as many residents as did London at that time. But modern textbooks barely take notice. Cahokia's problem is that American history, in the minds of many, started just 500 years ago, back when Columbus discovered the New World. By 1492, Cahokia was an Illinois Babylon, a city that had thrived and vanished.

Like many 20th-century metropolises, 13th-century Cahokia could not handle growth, even though its developers were sharp enough to grasp geometry and astronomy. Besides building more than 100 neatly proportioned mounds, they constructed a circle of tall poles — archaeologists call it "Woodhenge" — that aligned with the sun at equinox and solstice. Despite this evidence of advanced thinking, however, no Cahokian appears to have anticipated the consequences of ecological change and environmental degradation. Cornfields that fed 20,000 to 40,000 urbanites gradually lost their fertility. Forests were stripped of trees not only to fuel thousands of daily household fires but also to form a 2½-mile stockade wall. As hard times set in, Cahokians moved or perished. Centuries later, the French arrived and found only grown-over mounds. The Europeans who peopled America in Columbus's wake believed the land had never been settled, much less civilized. "North America was inhabited only by wandering

Lewis Lord and Sarah Burke, "America Before Columbus," *U.S. News & World Report*. Copyright, July 8, 1991, U.S. News & World Report.

tribes who had no thought of profiting by the natural riches of the soil," wrote Alexis de Tocqueville in 1835. It was, the French observer concluded, "an empty continent, a desert land awaiting its inhabitants." Tocqueville's "empty continent" phrase endures today in Fourth of July speeches that hail the building of the nation, but in fact the New World was anything but empty in Columbus's day. Give or take several million, the Western Hemisphere in 1492 had as many people as Europe. It was the teeming and majestic civilizations of Mexico's Aztecs and Peru's Incas that awed the Spanish conquistadors initially — some gawked like country bumpkins at Montezuma's capital, with its several hundred thousand people — but ancient societies had also been rising and falling for centuries above the Rio Grande. More than 1,000 tribes — with upward of 2 million people — still inhabited the northern forests, prairies and mesas when whites arrived.

Newcomers from Europe, though accustomed to people being burned or beheaded, were shocked at what went on in America. Columbus claimed he had to take hundreds of Carib Indians to Spain for their own good and that of their Arawak neighbors, whom they were eating. (He had a harder time explaining why he also enslaved the gentle Arawaks.) While cannibalism and human sacrifice were rare among Indians north of Mexico, people in some tribes killed unwanted infants, had multiple wives and, in the case of the Hurons, wiped their hands on dogs that ambled by. Other traits seemed alien as well: an awed reverence of nature, a desire to share and, for many, societies free of oppression and class stratification. In addition, most took a daily bath, a practice the Europeans abhorred. America was not new, but it was different.

As whites moved westward across what is now the United States, they encountered a familiar question among tribesmen in their path: "Why do you call us Indians?" The answer, of course, was that Columbus was mistaken. He thought he was in the distant Indies, somewhere between Japan and India, and labeled his hosts los Indios. The Indians had no word for their race. They called their own tribes "people" or "real people," and other tribes names like "friend," "enemy" or "poisonous snake."

The diversity that Americans relish today actually existed long before Columbus arrived. Most of the hundreds of languages the Indians spoke were as different from one another as Farsi is from French. Some Indians loved war. Others hated it. After every reluctant fight, Arizona's Pimas subjected their warriors to a 16-day cure for insanity. Some tribes banned women from their councils. Others were ruled by female chiefs, like Georgia's "Lady of Cofltachequi," who greeted Hernando De Soto with pearls from the Savannah River. (He ungraciously kidnapped her.) Puppies were a gourmet's delight in some huts. Elsewhere, Indians would rather die than eat dog meat. Premarital sex was unthinkable among the Cheyenne. But Mississippi's Natchez tribe encouraged teenagers to have flings while they could. Once a Natchez girl wed, an extramarital affair could cost her her hair or even an ear.

Every American Indian, from the Abenakis of Maine to the Zunis of New Mexico, descended from immigrant stock. Asian-Americans were the first Americans, and they came over 12,000 to 20,000 years ago, probably crossing a glacial land bridge between Siberia and Alaska. For some time, they hunted the mastodon and the long-horned bison, perhaps speeding their extinction. As long ago as 5,000 years, people in Mexico may have cultivated maize, better known as corn, and early residents of Arizona were growing it in A.D. 1. Many people in what is now the United States existed the next 10 or 15 centuries as nomads, moving about in search of game, fish and wild plants for food, but some accomplished much more.

Pioneers who found thousands of abandoned mounds in the Ohio and Mississippi valleys refused to believe they had been built by Indians. "The natural indolence of the Indian and his averseness to any kind of manual labor are well known," wrote author

Five hundred years before Herman Melville wrote Moby Dick, *Makah whalers return to their village in present-day Washington* *state. (Illustration by Greg Harlin/Wood Ronsaville Harlin, Inc.)*

William Pidgeon in 1858. Other 19th-century writers speculated that the mound builders were stray Vikings, Phoenicians or a lost tribe of Israel — obviously an intelligent people who were annihilated by Indian savages. Settlers liked that theory, because it seemed to justify the treatment they inflicted on the Indians on the frontier. Not until the 1890s did educated people agree that the mounds in fact were built by the Indians' ancestors.

The genius of the mound builders has become even more evident in recent years. Just west of the Mississippi in northeast Louisiana lies Poverty Point, a 3,500-year-old collection of concentric semicircles of earth, the biggest nearly three quarters of a mile long. Visitors can stand atop a mound just west of Poverty Point's rings during the spring and fall equinox and see the sun rise over what was the town's central plaza — a view like that at England's Stonehenge during similar conjunctions of earth and sun. On Moundbuilders Golf Course in Newark, Ohio, stands an earthen ring that is 15 centuries old. Its diameter is the same, 1,050 feet, as those of two more circles within 50 miles of Newark. Other precisely measured mounds in central Ohio include three 1,200-foot circles and five 27-acre squares. "Such nice equivalences of shapes and sizes are not the work of savages," says

Roger Kennedy, director of the Smithsonian's Museum of American History, who is writing a book entitled "Medieval America." "I doubt that the Harvard freshman class would be capable of similar intellectual achievement."

Every explorer and early settler seemed to notice the aroma of America. Robert Beverley was awed by "the pleasantest Smell" of Virginia's giant magnolias. De Soto's men admired Georgia's "very savoury, palatable and fragrant" strawberries. Henry Hudson paused in New York's harbor to enjoy the "very sweet smells" of grass and flowers on the New Jersey shore. But the visitors also smelled smoke. Many soon concluded that Indian women did all the work, while the men idled away their time hunting, fishing and setting the woods on fire.

The native men, it turned out, were practicing a form of forest management that put food in their wigwams and longhouses. With torches and stone hatchets, the Nootkas and Haidas of the Pacific Northwest toppled giant redwoods and turned them into whaling canoes. In the eastern forests, Indians slashed and burned to clear the way for cornfields fertilized by the ashes and to create meadows for grazing deer and elk. Every autumn, Indians burned huge chunks of woodland to clear away underbrush. The sprouts that poked each spring through the charred ground boosted populations of game animals, which the Indians could easily spot in the open forests. The trees that survived flourished, too. Sycamores in Ohio grew seven feet in diameter, and the white pines of New England towered 200 to 250 feet. Governor's Island, now in the shadow of Manhattan's skyscrapers, had so many big hickory and walnut trees that the Dutch settlers called it Nut Island.

Colonists enjoyed describing the country they settled as a "howling wilderness" — a phrase from the Book of Jeremiah — and in many places it was. Bamboo canebrakes, 20 to 30 feet high and impenetrable, stretched in parts of the Southeast for 100 miles or more, and tangles of brier and grapevines crowded the cottonwoods of the river bottoms. The forests were so boundless, the settlers liked to say, that a squirrel could travel from Maine to the Mississippi and never touch the ground. But wherever Indians hunted, the forest floor was usually clear, reminding one observer of "our parks in England."

Early English settlers, accustomed to woods with only a few doves, were startled by the spectacle in America's skies. The colonists especially admired the green-and-gold Carolina parakeet, "a fowle most swift of wing [and] very beautiful." Passenger pigeons passed in flocks "for three or foure houres . . . so thicke they have shaddowed the skie from us." Out west, Meriwether Lewis and William Clark would see huge flocks of pelicans and sandhill cranes along the Missouri and dense clouds of geese over the Columbia River.

Animals were bigger then. Pennsylvania trout, nearly 2 feet long, were easy targets for Algonquian arrows. Virginia sturgeon stretched 6 to 9 feet, and Mississippi catfish topped 120 pounds. Off Cape Cod, a few Indians could catch 30 lobsters in a half hour, some weighing 20 pounds, and many Massachusetts oysters had to be sliced into thirds to be swallowed.

Bison roamed not only the Great Plains but also the meadows and open forests of Ohio, Pennsylvania and Virginia. The western bison were infinitely more numerous, thundering along in herds 25 miles long, but the woods buffalo was bigger and blacker with shorter hair and no hump. A few still remained in George Washington's time; he considered crossing them with domestic cattle.

The white man's Bible taught that it is better to give than to receive, and the Indians couldn't agree more. Long after the Arawaks showered Columbus with birds, cloth and "trifles too tedious to describe," natives were offering Europeans virtually anything they had, from fish and turkeys to persimmon bread and the companionship of a chief's daughter. Colonists interpreted the Indians' generosity as evidence they were childlike. That they had no desire to accumulate wealth was seen as a symptom of laziness. The Indians, concluded one New Englander, must develop a love of property. "Wherever this can be established, Indians may be civilized; wherever it cannot, they will still remain Indians."

The Indians felt quite civilized with what they did own, often things a Puritan wouldn't appreciate. Colorado's Pueblos kept parrots that came from Mexico. The Cayuse of Eastern Oregon swapped buffalo robes for the shells of coastal Indians. The Ottawas, whose name meant "to trade," traveled the Great Lakes exchanging cornmeal, herbs, furs and tobacco. The Chinooks of the Northwest even developed their own trade jargon. Their word *hootchenoo,* for homemade liquor, eventually became the slang word "hootch."

Above all else, Indians were religious. They saw order in nature and obeyed elaborate sets of rules for fear of disturbing it. Land was to be shared, not owned, because it was sacred and belonged to everyone, like the air and sea. Animals also were precious. A hunter risked stirring the spirits if he killed two deer when one was all his tribe needed. Europe's view of nature, though rooted in religion, was much different. Man should subdue the Earth, Genesis dictated, "and have dominion . . . over every living thing."

Rituals surrounded each important Indian event. To prove their courage, the Arikara of North Dakota danced barefoot on hot coals and, with bare hands, retrieved and devoured hunks of meat from pots of boiling water. Timucuan leaders started council meetings in Florida with a round of emetics brewed from holly leaves. The Hurons of the Great Lakes carried smoldering coals in their mouths to invoke a spirit to cure the sick. But often the rituals were painless. From New York to New Mexico, tradition allowed a woman to end her marriage by putting her husband's belongings outside their door — a sign for him to live with his mother.

Three centuries before the U.S. Constitution took shape, the Iroquois League ran a Congress-like council, exercised the veto, protected freedom of speech and let women choose officeholders. The New Yorkers ran a classless society, as did many tribes across America. But ancient caste systems also endured. The Great Sun of the Natchez, a mound dweller like Cahokia's Great Sun, used his feet to push his leftovers to his noble subordinates. The nobles were not about to complain; below them was a class known as "Stinkards." Besides, the chief's feet were clean. He was carried everywhere, a French guest reported, and his toes never touched the ground.

Columbus's second voyage — the one in which Europeans came to stay — began the process that changed nearly everything. Instead of 90 sailors on the Nina, the Pinta and the Santa Maria as in 1492, Columbus set out in '93 with 1,200 men in 17 ships. In addition to starting the world's most significant movement of people, he delivered a Noah's Ark of animals unknown to the New World — sheep, pigs, chickens, horses and cows — plus a host of Old World diseases. What the Admiral of the Ocean Sea created was the Columbian Exchange, a global swap of animals, plants, people, ailments and ideas that historian Alfred Crosby calls "the most important event in human history since the end of the Ice Age."

For the Old World as well as the New, the event was both salubrious and calamitous. Twenty years after Columbus colonized Hispaniola — the island now shared by Haiti and the Dominican Republic — diseases and taskmasters reduced its Arawaks from a quarter million down to 14,000. Within two centuries, Old World diseases killed probably two thirds of the New World's natives, and America did indeed seem empty. Africans also were dying by the thousands. They were brought to the New World to grow sugar, another import from the Old World.

Yet, thanks to Columbus, Africa's population boomed. Corn, an American staple for thousands of years, augmented African diets, boosting the continent's birth rates and life spans. The same thing happened in Europe with the potato, also from America. The Columbian Exchange thickened Italy's sauces with tomatoes, seeded Kentucky with European bluegrass and covered the gullies of Georgia with Chinese kudzu. China, in return, became the globe's No. 1 consumer of the American-born sweet potato. "The Columbus story is not an Old World, New World story," explains Smithsonian historian Herman Viola, who heads the Museum of Natural History's Columbus Quincentenary programs. "It is two old worlds that linked up, making one new world."

It is also a story of winning and losing, with many of the losers gone before the winners ever showed up. When whites first penetrated the fertile Ohio Valley, they found many mounds but few Indians. The Southeast also seemed vacant when the French came to stay around 1700. As they moved into lands that abounded in natural food resources, the settlers kept wondering where the Indians had gone. Some scholars believe they were wiped out or chased away by epidemics of European diseases that moved north along Indian trade routes in the century after Columbus. Two years before DeSoto visited Cofitachequi's female chief in the 1540s, pestilence swept her province, decimating her town and emptying others nearby. In one village, the Spaniards found nothing but large houses full of bodies. It was the same medical disaster the conquistadors at that time were discovering in Mexico and Peru and the Pilgrims would notice much later in Massachusetts. Four years before the Mayflower landed, disease killed tens of thousands of Indians on the New England coast, including the inhabitants of a village where Plymouth would stand. John Winthrop, admiring the abandoned cornfields, saw the epidemic as divine providence. "God," he said, "hath hereby cleared our title to this place."

Indians in the forests shuddered every time they found honeybees in a hollow tree. The "English flies" moved 100 miles ahead of the frontier — a sign that the white man was on his way. The smart tribes moved west, pushing whatever band was in their way. The Chippewas pushed the Sioux out of the woods of Minnesota into the Dakotas. The Sioux pushed the Cheyenne into Nebraska. The Cheyenne pushed the Kiowas into Oklahoma. Yet not every Indian fled. The Comanches, with horses descended from Columbus's stock, thwarted Spain's colonial designs on Texas with frequent raids on Spanish outposts. Apaches did the same thing in Arizona and New Mexico. Parts of Pennsylvania and New York today might be part of Quebec had the Iroquois rolled over for the French.

Many who didn't move perished. A generation after their gifts of corn saved England's toehold settlement at Jamestown, the Powhatan Indians were systematically wiped out, their crops and villages torched by settlers who wanted more land to grow tobacco. Florida's Timucuas — of whom it was said "it would be good if among Christians there was as little greed to torment men's minds and hearts" — vanished in the early 19th century, victims of epidemics and conflicts with the Spanish, English, and Creeks. Natchez's Great Sun wound up with his feet on the ground, enslaved in the West Indies by the French, who eradicated his tribe. California's Chumash shrank from 70,000 to 15,000 toiling for the friars. Soon after the Gold Rush, the tribe, like most in California, ceased to exist. The four-century clash of cultures made 2 of every 3 tribes as extinct as the Carolina parakeet.

The land they left is different now. The white pines that towered over New England became masts for the Royal Navy's sailing ships. The redwoods that stretched from the Rockies to the Pacific, like the cypresses that crowded the Mississippi Valley, exist in pockets smaller than the Indians' shrunken reservations. The hours-long thunder of bison hooves no longer shakes Kansas or Nebraska, where only a few stretches of grassland remain like the prairie John Muir described a century ago — "one sheet of plant gold, hazy and vanishing in the distance." The prairie now feeds the nation with Old World food like wheat and pork.

Yet at least one ancient American community endures. Shunning electricity, 3,000 Pueblo Indians live today in Acoma atop a mesa in the high New Mexico

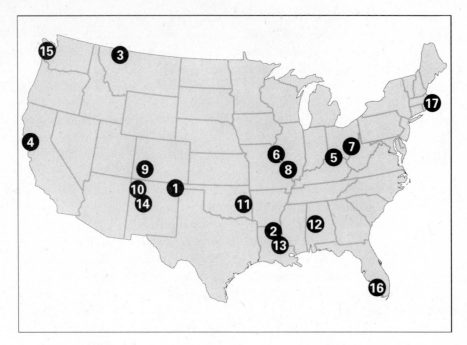

The continental United States is rich in sites of cultures that existed from the Ice Age to the coming of the Europeans.

desert. The town's adobe apartments have been inhabited since the 12th century, through droughts, Apache raids and a brutal occupation in which the enslaving Spaniards chopped off one foot of each adult male. Acomans are reluctant to promote the fact that their settlement is nearly twice as old as St. Augustine, Fla., the Spanish-settled city that is generally considered the nation's oldest community. The people of Acoma figure they have had enough visitors.

☆

THE INDIAN HOMELAND

1. Folsom 9000 B.C. Excavations in New Mexico in 1927 revealed the stone point of a spear beside a skeleton of the extinct long-horned bison — evidence that American hunters existed 11,000 years ago.

2. Poverty Point 2000 B.C.–700 B.C. The biggest town above the Rio Grande 3,000 years ago was a Louisiana community with six giant earthen semicircles, evident now in infrared photographs from the air. Poverty Point's trade network extended 1,000 miles along the Mississippi and its tributaries.

3. Two Medicine River 1000 B.C.–A.D. 1800. Western tribes hunted buffaloes by frightening herds into stampedes over cliffs. The practice ended only when Indians acquired horses and guns. . . .

4. Santa Rosa Island 600 B.C.–A.D. 1817. The Chumash moved along California's coast in boats made of brightly painted cedar planks. They ate fish and acorns, lived in domed houses and used sea-lion bristles as needles. An 1812 earthquake drove most of Santa Rosa's Chumash into Catholic missions on the mainland.

5. Serpent Mound 500 B.C.–A.D. 300. In seven

giant coils, the Great Serpent Mound stretches a quarter mile from tail to jaw along a creek bluff near Cincinnati. Its builders were members of either the Adena or the Hopewell Culture.

6. Bedford Mound 100 B.C.–A.D. 200. Buried near a man who smoked tobacco in Illinois 2,000 years ago was a stone pipe shaped like a beaver, with freshwater pearls for eyes and bone for teeth.

7. Mound City 100 B.C.–A.D. 300. Ohio was the home of the mound-building Hopewell people, hunters and fishers who traded with people from Montana to Florida. Many corpses buried in the mounds were bedecked from head to toe in pearls and surrounded with sculptures and pottery.

8. Cahokia 700–1500. In its 13th-century heyday, 30,000 people of the Mississippian Culture resided in this 6-square-mile city across the Mississippi from present-day St. Louis. Monk's Mound, the biggest of Cahokia's 120 mounds, stands 10 stories high with a base larger than that of the Great Pyramid of Egypt. Atop Monk's Mound lived the Great Sun, Cahokia's godlike leader.

9. Mesa Verde 700–1300. The Anasazis, or "ancient ones," lived for centuries on mesa tops. Later they moved into cliff dwellings with protective overhangs, like Colorado's Cliff Palace.

10. Chaco Canyon 950–1200. Apartments were popular in the Southwest. Pueblo Bonito, Chaco Canyon's most impressive ruin, had 800 rooms. . . .

11. Spiro Mounds 950–1400. The first Mississippian artisans in Oklahoma's Spiro community created images of animals. Humanlike figures, carved from stone, wood, and copper, were popular later.

12. Moundville 1000–1500. On a bluff overlooking Alabama's Black Warrior River stood the South's largest town and 20 pyramidal mounds. Moundville was the center of a chiefdom with perhaps 10,000 members of the Mississippian Culture.

13. Natchez 1000–1729. The Natchez, the last Indians to use temple mounds, were described by the

(Courtesy of the Montana Historical Society, Museum Collection)

French as "the most civilized of the native tribes." Yet the 1725 death of the chief's brother, Tattooed Serpent, touched off a sacrificial orgy. To keep him company, several aides and servants plus his two wives joyously agreed to be strangled.

14. Acoma 1100–present. Atop a 375-foot-high mesa stands one of the two oldest continuously inhabited towns in the United States. The other, Oraibi, is nearby. Acoma's residents gave Francisco Coronado's men corn, turkeys, and deerskins in the 1540s.

15. Ozette 1200–1400. The Makahs of the Olympic Peninsula used dugout canoes and 18-foot-long harpoons to hunt whales in the Pacific. A mudslide from a steep cliff buried the Makah settlement at Ozette more than 500 years ago, dooming the villagers but preserving their tools, baskets and sculptures.

16. Key Marco 1400–1750. The Calusas ... traveled widely. With their dugout canoes, some even visited the Arawaks, the first Indians Columbus met in the Caribbean. The tribe disintegrated in the 18th century when the British took many members to the Carolinas as slaves.

17. Plymouth 1616. The Pilgrims, landing in Massachusetts in 1620, chose a cleared site that had been planted in corn. Only four years earlier, a Wampanoag village existed there. The community, like many on the New England coast, was wiped out by a European disease probably spread by visiting fishermen. Some of the surviving Wampanoags helped the Pilgrims get through their first year in America.

QUESTIONS TO CONSIDER

1. What kinds of Indian cultures existed in the New World before the arrival of Columbus? Were they homogenous or diverse? in what way? Describe some of the Indian communities discussed in the article. How did those cultures and communities compare with Europe?

2. What did the European settlers in South and North America generally think of the Indians and their cultures? why? How did Europeans and Indians misunderstand each other and treat each other at their meetings?

3. Describe some basic principles of Indian religions. What was the Indians' relationship with the land, forests, and animals?

4. Why does this article put particular stress on Columbus's second voyage? What is meant by the "Columbian Exchange"? What was exchanged? among what people? What parts of the globe were affected? with what consequences, good and bad?

5. How have the land and the animals in North America changed since the Europeans first arrived? What animal had a particular influence on North America? why?

2

From These Beginnings

PAGE SMITH

The European arrival in the Americas brought about a clash of imperial energies as Spain, Portugal, France, and eventually England vied with one another in staking claims to the "New World." For a time, it seemed that Spain would become the dominant imperial power in the New World. While Portugal received Brazil, thanks to an edict from the Pope in 1493, Spain claimed the rest of South and Central America and sent out explorers to look for gold and silver there. By the 1550s powerful Spain had a sprawling colonial empire that comprised most of South America, Central America, Mexico, the Caribbean islands, Florida, and the American Southwest from Texas to California.

Meanwhile French explorers searched eastern Canada for the Northwest Passage, a legendary waterway that was supposed to connect the Atlantic and Pacific oceans and that, under France's control, would give France access to the luxuries of Asia. Unable to find such a passage, France was content to establish a fur-trading empire in Canada, with French explorers, traders, and missionaries advancing west to the Great Lakes and then southward down the Mississippi to New Orleans.

England, however, was slow to join the race for colonies, although John Cabot's voyage to North America in 1497 had given England a claim to the New World. Finally, under Queen Elizabeth, the English challenged Spain's rule of the oceans and domination of the New World. Adventurous "sea dogs" under John Hawkins raided Spanish commerce on both the Atlantic and the Pacific, and in 1588, in a dramatic sea battle, the English navy defeated the Spanish armada, a victory that gave England virtually undisputed control of the seas. Thanks to the persuasive arguments of Sir Walter Raleigh, Sir Humphrey Gilbert, and Richard Hakluyt, all champions of colonization, England at last began to build a New World empire. After an abortive attempt to found a colony on Roanoke Island, North Carolina, Queen Elizabeth and her successor James I authorized private corporations called joint stock companies to establish the Virginia (first known as Jamestown) Plymouth, and Massachusetts Bay colonies.

From the outset, the Indians, from the Pequot of Massachusetts to the Powhatan of Virginia, posed the biggest obstacle to English conquest and settlement in North America. How to deal with them? The London-based leaders of Massachusetts and Virginia directed their settlers to treat the Indians "humanely," to christianize, feed, and clothe them, instruct them in "the manual arts and skills," and to incorporate them into "the English community" so that they could enjoy the amenities of "civilization."

These instructions, of course, were based on the European misconception of the Indian as a savage. Although the Indians possessed a culture as old, as rich, and as religious as any in Europe, whites typically thought of them as "bad people, having little of humanity but shape, ignorant of civility or arts, or religion; more brutish than the beasts they hunt, more wild and unmanly than that unmanned wild country, which they range rather than inhabit." Racial prejudice fed that hostile attitude. In white eyes, these dark-skinned people were "pernicious creatures" and barbarians. Only violence would keep them in line. As one white man said, "Unless we bang the Indians stoutly, and make them fear us, they will never love us, nor keep the peace long with us."

And bang the Indians they did, killing off whole tribes and driving others into the interior, where they had to force their way into areas inhabited by other tribes. Some Indians — the Powhatan and Pequot, among them — resisted the colonists and were wiped out. Others, like the Piscataway Indians of Maryland, managed to accommodate themselves to the invaders and thus to preserve "their cultural integrity." Those Indians who did convert to Christianity and adopt the white man's way remained second-class citizens.

Writes historian James Freeman Hawke, "The white man took from the Indian what he could use. The Indian paths through the woods eventually became the settlers' ways and roads. Like the natives, they girdled trees to open up the forest to sunlight. They planted, harvested, and cooked native crops as the Indians did. The Indian taught them how to use snowshoes, how to convert animal pelts into warm winter clothing, how to make a dugout canoe and a pair of moccasins. . . . These borrowings helped to speed the white man's adjustment to the strange new world but did not fundamentally alter his culture." As we saw in the first selection, most of what the Indians got from the Europeans, especially their deadly diseases, virtually destroyed the Indian way of life.

As the number of colonies increased in the seventeenth century, a great migration began to English North America. That migration is the subject of this selection by historian Page Smith, who writes from the standpoint of the European immigrants, thus giving you a different perspective from that in the opening selection. With a vivid pen and an eye for *telling detail, Smith discusses the remarkable hodgepodge of humanity that streamed into the English colonies from more than a dozen European countries. Among them, of course, were hardy farmers, aspiring merchants, indentured servants, and visionary religious groups in search of better secular and spiritual lives. But the unfortunate and the disreputable came as well, ranging from English boys who were stolen and sold into bondage, to convicted felons and "rogues and vagabonds" shipped out to the colonies by the British government. As Smith explains, "rogues and vagabonds" included a variety of outlawed folk — beggars, prostitutes, drunkards, dancers, fiddlers, fencers, actors, jugglers, dice players, minstrels, fortunetellers, charlatans, tinkers, peddlers, and loiterers, all of whom played some part in the drama of colonization. From farmers to felons, this diverse assortment of individuals went on to seize the eastern coast of North America and to forge a new nation in the wilderness.*

GLOSSARY

CALVINISTS   Those who subscribed to the religious teachings of John Calvin (1509–1664), a French theologian and a leader in the Protestant Reformation, who stressed God's sovereignty, the supremacy of the Scriptures, and predestination — the notion that one's fate was already determined by an all-powerful God and that human beings could do nothing to achieve their salvation or alter their fate.

DURAND   French Protestant who described the love-making of indentured servants during a passage to colonial America.

GREAT AWAKENING   Religious revival that swept the English colonies in the 1730s and 1740s. Treated in detail in selection 5.

HUGUENOTS   European Protestants who fled from persecution in Catholic countries such as France.

INDENTURED SERVANT   A man or woman bound over to a master for a period of servitude; in exchange, the master paid the servant's way to the colonies and provided food and shelter.

MITTELBERGER, GOTTLIEB   German immigrant from Enzweiningen who provided a dramatic account of his voyage to America.

PENN, WILLIAM (1644–1718)   English Quaker who founded the colony of Pennsylvania as a refuge for Quakers.

REDEMPTIONERS   Bound servants similar to indentured servants, "they were carried to America by a ship captain with the understanding that after they reached the colonies, they would undertake to sell themselves to the highest bidder and then pay the captain the cost of their passage."

The American Colonists came from a variety of backgrounds. . . . What united them was the wilderness to which they came, a vast land . . . [that] was, literally, incomprehensible; it reached beyond the mind's imagining, threatening and promising, larger than all of Europe: coastal shelf and then mountains and endless plains and more mountains and, finally, the Pacific. No one could measure its extent. The English settlers for their part clung to its eastern margins, to the seacoast strip that faced the ocean highway to the Old World. Even here there were terrains, climates, and topographies as dramatically different as one could imagine — from the rocky, frigid shores of New Hampshire to the sunny beaches of South Carolina.

There was a kind of mad presumption about the whole venture: a few thousand, and then a few hundred thousand, and finally a few million souls scattered along almost two thousand miles of coastline. And in truth it could be said that those who made this strange odyssey to the New World were as diverse as the land they inhabited. Those from England itself represented every class and condition of men. And then there were the Swedes, who settled on the Delaware long before William Penn and his followers arrived, and the stolid and intractable Dutch, reputed to have bought Manhattan from the [Indians] for a few strings of beads — the most famous real estate deal in history. And the French Huguenots, Protestants fleeing from persecution in a Catholic country; the Catholics of Maryland, fleeing persecution in a Protestant country; the Quakers, fleeing the harassments of the Anglican establishment, the Church of England; and Germans from innumerable principalities, fleeing military draft and the various exactions of petty princes.

Within the British Isles themselves — Ireland,

Scotland, England and Wales — there was striking diversity among the New World emigrants. The Separatists — the Pilgrims under William Bradford — wanted, in essence, to be separate; the Puritans wanted to found a Bible Commonwealth and redeem a fallen world. When Cromwell and the Puritans dominated England and beheaded Charles I, certain Royalists found refuge in Virginia and New York. When the restoration of the monarchy brought Charles II to the English throne and re-established the Stuart line, the regicides — those involved in the execution of Charles I — found refuge in Puritan New England. When the Scottish Covenanters, or Presbyterians, so akin in spirit to the Puritans of New England, rose against the highhanded and tyrannical actions of the re-established monarchy, they were crushingly defeated . . . and cruelly repressed. Many, in consequence, came to America. And they continued to come for a hundred years. . . .

And then there were the Irish. They were a special case. They fled famine and rent-wracking landlords. . . . A Catholic people, they fled their Protestant masters. But above all they fled poverty, the poverty of a ruthlessly exploited peasantry. Generation after generation, the Irish came to the American colonies, primarily to Maryland and Pennsylvania, where they gravitated to the frontier areas. In addition to the Catholic Irish, Scotch-Irish Presbyterians came in substantial numbers to the colonies throughout the eighteenth century. The Scotch-Irish were those Covenanters, or militant Presbyterians, who had been forced by the bitter divisions in Scotland itself to seek the protection of the English armies in Northern Ireland (hence Scotch-Irish). For many of them, Ireland was little more than a way station to the colonies, where they showed a marked preference for Pennsylvania and settled, typically, on the frontier. . . .

So the immigrants came in an ever-growing tide — the hungry, the oppressed, the contentious, the ambitious, those out of power and out of favor, the losers, whether in the realm of politics or of economics. And America could accommodate them all: Irish

---

Extracts from *A People's History of the American Revolution*, Vol. II: *A New Age Begins*, pages 28–47, copyright McGraw-Hill Publishing Company. Used by permission of the author.

German Immigrants in Georgia. "The immigrants came in an ever-growing tide," Page Smith writes, "the hungry, the oppressed, the contentious, the ambitious, those out of power and out of favor, *the losers, whether in the realm of politics or of economics." (New York Public Library, Rare Book Room, Astor, Lenox and Tilden Foundations)*

peasant and his land-poor master, Scottish Highlander and Lowlander, persecuted Protestant and persecuted Catholic, fortune-seeker and God-seeker, they found their places, their kinfolk, the familiar accents of their home shires or counties or countries.

But the essence of them all, of all that human congress, the bone and marrow, the unifying principle, the prevailing and pervasive spirit was English. Like the others who came, the English came . . . for a number of reasons. Most of them shared some partic-

ular expectation, whether for spiritual or material betterment or, happily, both. Many of those who came later shared, of course, the hopes of the original settlers. Many more came because conditions were desperately hard in England and Ireland for poor people, even for those who had not yet sunk into the pit of abandoned hopelessness that was the lot of the most wretched.

It has been estimated that London in the eighteenth century had 6,000 adult and 9,300 child beggars. In the entire country of some 10,000,000 persons, there were estimated to be 50,000 beggars, 20,000 vagrants, 10,000 idlers, 100,000 prostitutes, 10,000 rogues and vagabonds, 80,000 criminals, 1,041,000 persons on parish relief. Indeed, over half the population was below what we would call today "the poverty line," and many, of course, were profoundly below it — below it to the point of starvation. An estimate of the different classes — and class lines were almost impassable — in 1688 suggests that nobility, gentry, merchants, professionals, freeholders (those who held land on their own), craftsmen, and public officials constituted 47 per cent of the population; while common sailors and soldiers (recruited, for the most part, from the lowest levels of British society and enduring desperately hard conditions of service), laborers, servants, paupers, and all those other remarkable subdivisions that we have listed above such as rogues and vagrants made up 53 per cent of the population. The colonies, for their part, had a virtually inexhaustible demand for labor. Anyone willing to work could be put to worthwhile labor, and might (and often did) in a few years establish himself as an independent farmer or artisan.

Yet it was one thing to be an undernourished London apprentice who hated his master and another to find a way to get to America. Some indication of the situation of the working class in the larger cities may be discerned from the condition of pauper children in London in the early eighteenth century. Orphaned, or more frequently illegitimate and abandoned at birth, they were sent to workhouses and to parish nurses. A Parliamentary study found that of all such infants born or received in London's workhouses in a three-year period, only seven in every hundred were alive at the end of that time. As part of the "surcharge of necessitous people," orphaned and impoverished children who were public charges were sporadically dispatched to the colonies as indentured servants. People worked, typically, from six in the morning until eight at night for a pittance that barely supported life. They had no holidays except at Christmas, Easter, and on hanging days, when everyone might be enter-

tained and edified by watching wretches hanged for crimes that, in many instances, would be classed as misdemeanors today.

Despite the cruelty of punishments, London had a large criminal class and was infested with prostitutes. The working class drowned its miseries in bad gin and beer. There were some 7,000 ginshops in the suburbs of London and, by 1750, 16,000 in the city itself (only 1,050 of which were licensed); most of them were in the poorest sections of the city, whose horrors are vividly recorded in Hogarth's etchings of Gin Lane. The hard liquor consumed in one year (1733) in London alone amounted to 11,200,000 gallons, or some 56 gallons per adult male.

Next to public hangings, the principal entertainments available to the poor — and enjoyed by the rich as well — were cockfighting, bullbaiting, and badger baiting. In such circumstances there was ample incentive to emigrate almost anywhere. . . . But to the penniless, the question was: How? The growing need for labor in the colonies supplied the answer, and a system of indenture, based on the long-established apprenticeship, was devised. Agents paid for the ship's passage of improvident men and women who were willing to contract themselves in America to work off the cost of their transportation. By this means, tens of thousands of English and Irish workers of both sexes found their way across the ocean.

The system was easily and often abused. A class of men "of the lowest order," called spirits and crimps, arose, who spirited away unwilling lads and sold them into bondage. . . . One spirit boasted that he had been spiriting persons for twelve years at a rate of five hundred persons a year. He would give twenty-five shillings to anyone who would bring him a likely prospect, and he could sell such a one to a merchant at once for forty shillings. Often spiriting was a profitable sideline for a brewer, hostler, carpenter, or tavern keeper. The tavern keeper was in an especially advantageous position, since a drunken patron was an easy victim. So dreaded were these dismal agents that mothers frightened their children into obedience by warning them that a spirit would carry them off if they were bad. It was no idle threat. In 1653 Robert Broome secured a warrant for the arrest of a ship's captain charged with carrying off his son, aged eleven, who had been spirited aboard. A few years later, a commission going aboard the *Conquer* found that eleven out of nineteen servants had been "taken by the spirits." Their average age was nineteen. Not all spirits were depraved men, however, and even the worst of them often performed a useful service in arranging transportation for a servant who wished to emigrate to the colonies against the wishes of parents or a master. . . .

For a time it proved easier to get women servants than men servants. . . . Mathew Cradock, captain of the *Abraham*, sailing for Virginia, made elaborate preparations for carrying a shipload of servants, men and women alike, to Virginia on a four-year indenture. On his ship's arrival in various English ports, . . . he rounded up forty-one men and twenty women, the latter "from 17 to 35 yeares and very lustye and strong Boddied. . . ."

Clothing, "peppar and Gingar," and three-and-a-half pounds of tobacco for the men were all purchased before the ship set sail, and a midwife was hired to make sure none of the women were pregnant. Soon after the ship sailed it was driven into the harbor of Cowes, and it was a month before it got favorable winds. By that time, three of the women were pregnant and were sent home; some who were put ashore to do the washing ran away and had to be tracked down at a cost of ten shillings; and another was found "not fette to be entertained haveing the frentche dizeas [gonorrhea]" and was sent packing.

If a female indentured servant became pregnant during her service, her misdeed represented a loss to her master, so that an indentured servant guilty of bastardy was required to pay the usual charges levied against unwed mothers as well as to indemnify her master for the loss of her services during the later stages of her pregnancy and her lying-in. Not infrequently, the master was the culprit. In Maryland,

Jacob Lumbrozo [of Portugal] . . . alias Dr. John, was charged with having made persistent overtures to his maid, Elisabeth Weales, and when rebuffed, "hee tooke her in his armes and threw her upon the bed she went to Cry out hee plucked out his handerchif of his pocket and stope her mouth and force her whether shee will or noe when hee know that she was with Child he gave her fickes to distroy it and for anything shee know hee would distroy her too. . . ." By the time the case came to court, Lumbrozo had married Elisabeth Weales, who became a prominent if contentious figure in the affairs of the county. In Virginia, a statute was passed to prevent a master who had impregnated his servant girl from claiming extra service from her beyond her indenture: "Late experiments shew that some dissolute masters have gotten their maides with child, and yet claime the benefitt of their service." However, the maid got off no better. After the end of her indenture she was to be sold by the church wardens for the use of the parish for two years. . . .

The terms of indenture required the master to provide food and clothing for his servants and, often in the case of German or Swiss servants, to take the responsibility for seeing that they learned English during the term of their indenture. At the end of their terms they were to be provided with a stated sum of money and a suit of presentable clothes so that they could make a proper start in life. South Carolina required that a female servant at the expiration of her service be given a waistcoat and petticoat, a new shift of white linen, shoes and stockings, a blue apron and two white linen caps. In some colonies, indentured servants received land at the end of their term of indenture. Thus in North Carolina during the proprietary period a servant's "freedom dues" were fifty acres of land and afterward three barrels of Indian corn and two new suits of a value of at least five pounds. . . ."

Whether wickedly abused or treasured and rewarded — and certainly they experienced both cruelty and kindness — indentured servants made up more than half the immigrants to the middle and southern colonies. During the twenty-five-year period between 1750 and 1775, some 25,000 servants and convicts entered Maryland, and a comparable number arrived in Virginia. Abbott Smith estimates that during the same period at least twice as many servants and redemptioners entered Pennsylvania, of whom perhaps a third were German and the rest, in large part, Irish. The Irish . . . were Catholics. To Protestants, this fact made the Irish the least desirable of all immigrant groups. The more substantial class of immigrants, especially the Germans and the Swiss, came as redemptioners. Redemptioners were carried to America by a ship captain with the understanding that after they reached the colonies, they would undertake to sell themselves to the highest bidder and then pay the captain the cost of their passage. Most of the redemptioners were craftsmen whose skills were much in demand in the colonies and who could thus sell themselves on favorable terms to a master. If they could not sell themselves, it was the shipmaster's right to undertake to sell them, often at highly disadvantageous terms. Since a master could buy much cheaper from a ship captain, collusion between prospective buyers and the captain was not uncommon.

The story of indentured servants is one of the most dramatic in colonial America. While many of those who came under indenture were the "scum and offscourings of the earth" — convicts, paupers, runaway apprentices, prostitutes and the like — many, particularly among the non-English, were respectable and decent people who had fallen on hard times or simply wished to improve their fortunes. We also know that in the rude conditions of colonial life, many of the dissolute were redeemed.

In seventeenth- and eighteenth-century England, crime was endemic. The alarm of the more prosperous classes was expressed in cries for law and order. The penalty of death was prescribed for all felonies. In seventeenth-century England, almost three hundred crimes were classed as felonies; a conviction for anything, indeed, from housebreaking and the theft of goods worth more than a shilling must result in the sentence of death by hanging, since the judge had no discretionary power in felony cases. The benefit of clergy and royal pardon were the only mitigations. A convicted felon could "call for the book," usually a Bible, and if he could read it, he was freed of the penalty of death, branded on the thumb, and released. The practice stemmed from medieval times, when generally speaking only those in holy orders were able to read, and they were subject to their own ecclesiastical courts. The benefit of clergy was undoubtedly a great incentive to the development of a literate criminal class, but in a time when a vast majority of the poor were illiterate, it had little else to recommend it. The simple fact was that if you were poor and illiterate you might be hanged for stealing a few shillings' worth of cloth, while a villainous cutpurse who could decipher a simple text would be branded and then would go free. . . .

The royal pardon was the only amelioration of a murderous system. Again in a typically English accommodation, judges who thought sentences too severe could send up a list of those convicted felons they considered worthy of mercy, and these would be pardoned by the king. For many years more than half of those sentenced to hang were pardoned, and increasingly it came to be the practice to issue such pardons on the condition that the culprit agreed to leave the country. From the middle of the seventeenth century until early in the eighteenth, thousands of convicts left England under this arrangement. Of these, a substantial majority found their way to the English colonies in the West Indies and in North America. In 1717, Parliament passed a law permitting the "transportation" out of the realm of certain classes of offenders "in clergy." From 1619 to 1640 all felons reprieved by royal pardon were transported to Virginia to help make up the toll of those settlers lost by disease, and between 1661 and 1700 more than 4,500 convicts were dispatched to the colonies. In the years from 1745 to 1775, 8,846 convicts, 9,035 servants, and 3,324 slaves landed at Annapolis, Maryland.

Convicts were certainly not ideal settlers. In one

contingent, twenty-six had been convicted for stealing, one for violent robbery, and five for murder. . . . The character of such settlers is indicated by the career of Jenny Voss, who was eventually hanged at Tyburn after having been transported to the colonies, where "she could not forget her old Pranks, but used not only to steal herself, but incited all others that were her fellow Servants to Pillfer and Cheat," so that her master was glad to be rid of her, the more so since "she had wheadled in a Son of the Planters, who used to Lye with her and supply her with Moneys. . . ."

Virginia and Maryland, which had been the principal outlets for transported felons, had passed laws forbidding their importation by the end of the seventeenth century. . . . But despite such [laws], Parliament in 1717 passed a statute that overrode colonial efforts to stem the tide of undesirables. A total of thirty thousand convicted felons were shipped from England in the fifty-year period prior to the Revolution, of whom the greater number apparently went to Maryland and Virginia. Since convicts were bound into servitude for seven or fourteen years, which often proved to be a lifetime, the colonists usually bid actively for the most likely ones. The men sold for from eight to twenty pounds or, roughly, twenty-five to fifty dollars. Women brought slightly less, while the old and infirm were given away or, if no taker could be found, a subsidy was paid to anyone who would take them in.

It was not a humane or enlightened system, and the most that can be said for it is that the majority of the transported felons who were sold into white semislavery were slightly better off alive than dead. For those who escaped their masters, fled to other colonies, and established themselves as respectable citizens, it was a handsome bargain. Those willing to work and fortunate enough to have a kind master, had a far better life than the one they had left behind in England. It is safe to surmise that a substantially higher proportion of women than men were redeemed to a decent life — from which it would presumably follow that a substantial number of Americans who trace their line of descent back to colonial times have an ancestress or two who arrived here as a convicted felon, a sneak thief, or a prostitute.

Three or four times a year, the convicts to be transported were marched in irons through the streets of London from Newgate Prison to Blackfriars. This procession provided, like hangings, a popular form of entertainment for mobs who would hoot at the convicts and, when the convicts replied with obscene epithets, sometimes pelt them with mud and stones. The more prosperous convicts could buy special privileges. Thus in 1736, four felons rode to the point of embarkation in two hackney coaches, and another, "a Gentleman of Fortune, and a Barrister at Law," convicted of stealing books from the Trinity College library, had a private coach to carry him in style. These men paid their own passage and shared a private cabin.

Besides the large number of convicted felons, there were many other Englishmen who fell in the rather commodious category of "rogues and vagabonds." Although they came from a very different economic stratum, these were the hippies and dropouts of seventeenth- and eighteenth-century English society, the men and women so alienated from the dominant culture that they had devised their own. They lived on the margins of the law, devoted to preying in a thousand ingenious ways on the public. A statute of Parliament defined them as [beggars, drunkards, prostitutes, dancers, fiddlers, fencers, actors, jugglers, dice players, minstrels, fortunetellers, charlatans, tinkers, peddlers, and loiterers]. . . . Punishments were meant to be exemplary and painful. All beggars were to be stripped to the waist and whipped until they were bloody, then sent home or to the grim confines of a house of correction. Moreover, any rogue who appeared to be a hardened and dangerous character would be sent to such places beyond the seas as the Privy Council might designate.

By these provisions, incorrigible lawbreakers could be shipped out of the mother country even more readily than convicts throughout the colonial period.

How "manie Drunkards, Tossepottes, whore-moisters, Dauncers, Fidlers and Minstrels, Diceplaiers, & Maskers" were dispatched to the colonies is not revealed by British court records. On the other hand, we know of enough charlatans, fortunetellers, minstrels, jugglers, tinkers, and actors in the colonies to assume that a good many of these roguish varieties made their way to America and provided lively if not always discreet entertainment for the less sophisticated colonists. What seems remarkable is that the colonies (like Virginia and Maryland) receiving the largest numbers of indentured servants and convicted felons were not utterly submerged and demoralized by these successive waves of human flotsam. Vicious and depraved as many of them must have been, the great majority made the adjustment to colonial life with reasonable success. Otherwise it is hard to see how these colonies could have survived, let alone prospered in their material and spiritual endeavors.

The transatlantic voyage from England to America was a terrible ordeal for most of those who made the crossing. Indentured servants signed up by crimps and spirits embarked on small, poorly equipped, and often dirty sailing vessels that took from one to as much as five months, depending on prevailing winds, to make the crossing. The *Sea-Flower*, with 106 passengers aboard, took sixteen weeks; forty-six of her passengers died of starvation, and of these, six were eaten by the desperate survivors. The long crossing meant bad food; the water stank and grew slimy, meat spoiled, and butter turned rancid. If the captain or owner was a profiteer, the food was often rotten to begin with. In small boats tossed by heavy seas, seasickness was commonplace. One passenger on such a crossing wrote a crude verse describing the effects of a storm on his fellow voyagers: Soon after the storm began, "there was the odest scene betwixt decks that I ever heard or seed. There was some sleeping, some spewing . . . some damning, some Blasting their legs and thighs, some their liver, lungs, lights and eyes. And for to make the scene the odder, some curs'd Father, Mother, Sister, and Brother."

A French Protestant named Durand sailed for Virginia after the revocation of the Edict of Nantes and the resumption of active persecution of the Huguenots. There were fifteen prostitutes on board ship, headed, hopefully, for a new life in the New World. During the passage, they spent their time singing and dancing and making love with the sailors and the indentured servants aboard. Durand, kept awake by their revels, wrote: "Certainly their insolence wrought a change in my nature, for my acquaintances would no doubt impute to me, as my greatest failing, an exaggerated love of the fair sex, & to tell the truth I must admit that in my youth there was no injustice in this accusation. Not that I was ever low enough or coarse enough to feel an affection for prostitutes, but I am obliged to confess I did not abhor their debauchery as I should have. . . . But when I saw those wenches behave so shockingly with the sailors and others, in addition to the distress caused by their songs and dances, it awakened within me so intense a hatred of such persons that I shall never overcome it." Durand's wife died at sea, the food ran out, and the captain proved to be a knave and a bully. Their voyage took nineteen miserable weeks, long enough for weakness and hunger to quiet the gaiety of the prostitutes.

In the German principalities, the counterparts of the English "spirits" were the Newlanders, agents who tried to persuade guileless countryfolk to set sail for America. Gottlieb Mittelberger, a German immigrant from Enzweiningen who arrived in Philadelphia in 1750, gave a vivid account of his crossing of the Atlantic. He was bitter about the "sad and miserable condition of those traveling from Germany to the New World, and the irresponsible and merciless proceedings of the Dutch traders in human beings and their man-stealing emissaries — I mean the so-called Newlanders. For these at one and the same time steal German people under all sorts of fine pretexts, and deliver them into the hands of the great Dutch traffickers in human souls." The trip meant "for most who undertake it the loss of all they possess, of freedom and peace, and for some the loss of their very lives and, I can even go so far as to say, of the salvation of their souls." Mittelberger's journey took six months, the people "packed into the big boats as closely as herring...." The water distributed to thirsty passengers was often "very black, thick with dirt and full of worms." Mittelberger's description of conditions on the ship refers to "smells, fumes, horrors, vomiting . . . boils, scurvy, cancer, mouthrot . . . caused by the age and the highly-salted state of the food, especially of the meat.... Add to all that shortage of food, hunger, thirst, frost, heat, dampness, fear, misery, vexation, and lamentation . . . so many lice . . . that they have to be scraped off the bodies. All this misery reaches its climax when in addition to everything else one must suffer through two or three days and nights of storm . . . all the people on board pray and cry pitifully together." Under such circumstances, what little civility there might have been collapsed completely. People grew so bitter "that one person begins to curse the other, or himself and the day of his birth, and people sometimes come close to murdering one another. Misery and malice are readily associated, so that people begin to cheat and steal from one another." It is hardly surprising that America, when the immigrants reached it, seemed a land of deliverance; "When at last after the long and difficult voyage the ships finally approach land," Mittelberger wrote, "for the sight of which the people on board had longed so passionately, then everyone crawls from below to the deck, in order to look at the land.... And the people cry for joy, pray, and sing praises and thanks to God. The glimpse of land revives the passengers, especially those who are half-dead of illness. Their spirits, however weak they had become, leap up, triumph, and rejoice...."

As difficult as were the conditions under which indentured servants and redemptioners crossed the Atlantic, the circumstances of the prisoners were, as might be imagined, substantially worse. They were chained below decks in crowded, noisome ranks. One observer who went on board a convict ship to visit a prisoner wrote: "All the states of horror I ever had an idea of are much short of what I saw this poor man in; chained to a board in a hole not above sixteen feet long, more than fifty with him; a collar and padlock about his neck, and chained to five of the most dreadful creatures I ever looked on." Living conditions were little better than those obtaining on slave ships, and before the voyage was over it was not uncommon to lose a quarter of the human cargo, most frequently to the ravages of smallpox. (Only half as many women as men died on these hell ships, a fact attributed by merchants in the convict trade to their stronger constitutions.) Convicts so often arrived in the colonies more dead than alive that Parliamentary statutes finally set minimum allowances of bread, cheese, meat, oatmeal, and molasses per passenger — with two gills of gin issued on Saturdays.

The feelings of the colonists concerning the apparently endless stream of transported felons and vagabonds are indicated by a passage in the *Virginia Gazette* of May 24, 1751: "When we see our Papers fill'd continually with Accounts of the most audacious Robberies, the most cruel Murders, and infinite other Villanies perpetrated by Convicts transported from Europe," the correspondent wrote, "what melancholy, what terrible Reflections must it occasion! What will become of our Posterity? These are some of thy Favours, Britain! Thou are called our Mother country; but what good Mother ever sent Thieves and Villains to accompany her children; to corrupt some with their infectious Vices and murder the rest? . . . In what can Britain show a more Sovereign contempt for us than by emptying their Jails into our Settlements. . . ." Whatever the colonists' feelings, the English were delighted with the practice of transporting their convicts to America. By such a procedure, the criminal was separated from evil companions and from the usually deplorable conditions that had induced him to take up a life of crime.

Not all convicts appreciated, by any means, the opportunity afforded them to start life over in the colonies. Not a few found their way back home (risking certain death, if caught) and declared that they would rather be hanged than return to America.

Servants and convicts who had served out their indentures often drifted to the frontier areas of the colonies, particularly to the southern frontier. Some took up cattle ranching in western Carolina, where the cattle were turned loose to graze, rounded up yearly into pens (hence Cowpens, South Carolina), and driven to the seacoast markets for meat and hides. Some, like the Hatfields and the McCoys, would in time feud with each other for decades; others lived lives of lawlessness and banditry, preying on staid planters in more settled areas and becoming, in some instances, the ancestors of the southern mountain folk, who for successive generations resisted the incursions of tax collectors.

A number, of course, gathered in the seaport towns of Baltimore, Philadelphia, New York, Charles Town, and Boston, where they drank excessively, did occasional labor, committed petty crimes, rioted, and formed the nucleus of revolutionary mobs. The truth was that with few exceptions, they belonged to that class of people whose feelings lie very close to the surface. Violent and passionate by nature, they were peculiarly susceptible to both religious conversion and revolutionary ardor. Restless and rootless, they were readily swept up by any emotional storm. Many of them were converted at the time of the Great Awakening [a series of Protestant revivals lasting from about 1725 to 1770] into pious Presbyterians, Methodists, and, somewhat later, Baptists. These denominations, with their emphasis on personal experience, were perfectly suited to the psychological needs of such individuals. Thus a substantial number of servants and ex-convicts accommodated themselves to the Protestant Ethic and became in time indistinguishable from their orthodox neighbors.

Less colorful, but equally important, were those settlers who came on their own initiative and at their own expense. By a process of natural selection, such individuals were usually aggressive, ambitious, and, as we would say today, highly motivated. Prominent

among them were the Scotch-Irish. . . . [They were] independent yeoman farmers who were stout Presbyterians, often shared a common Scottish aversion to the British, and were now removed in turn to the congenial atmosphere of the colonies, particularly Pennsylvania. Hardy, enterprising Calvinists, they made their way in large numbers westward, where land was plentiful and cheap. There, serving as "the guardians of the frontier," they were constantly embroiled with eastern land speculators or various Indian tribes over ownership of land.

There was a special affinity between native Lowland Scots and the inhabitants of the middle and eastern colonies. This led to a substantial immigration of Scotch-Irish in the middle years of the eighteenth century preceding the Revolutionary crisis. Never large in numbers, the Scots nonetheless, like the Jews and Huguenots, played a disproportionately important role in colonial affairs and were prominent in the patriot cause.

The Rhineland country in present-day Germany was in the eighteenth century divided into a number of principalities, including the Rheinpfalz or Rhenish Palatinate, Württemberg, Baden, and Brunswick. These petty states were constantly embroiled in European conflicts, and many German peasants, most of them pious Lutherans, fled from the exactions of their princes: from conscription, heavy taxes, and a condition of chronic insecurity. The majority came to Pennsylvania, with some in New York, Virginia, and the Carolinas. In Penn's colony, they established tight-knit, self-contained farming communities, where they clung to their language and their folk traditions. Travelers noted that they were stolid, hardworking, and usually more tidy than their English or Scotch-Irish neighbors. From *Deutsch*, they became Pennsylvania Dutch, developing their own patois and, by clinging stubbornly to their folk traditions, making their villages into small fortresses of cultural separatism. The most conspicuous and long-lived of the German immigrant groups that came to America were the Moravians, a pietist sect. . . . This group settled primarily in Salem, North Carolina, and Bethlehem, Pennsylvania, and to this day they preserve a rich tradition of church music, especially that of Johann Sebastian Bach. The Dunkers, who excelled in choral singing and bookmaking, and their close cousins the Mennonites also came largely to Pennsylvania. Today, forbidden by their religion to wear clothes with buttons, to drive cars, to use electricity, radios, or television, the Mennonite men with their chin hair, plain black clothes, and broad-brimmed black hats, and the women with their long skirts and bonnets, still farm the rich and carefully tended soil of central Pennsylvania and [have been] frequently embroiled with the state over their determination not to send their children to public schools. . . .

As Protestant England had persecuted its Catholics, so Catholic France persecuted its Protestants (known as Huguenots). In consequence many Huguenots looked to the New World. Since they were denied entry into New France, a number were strung out from Boston to Charles Town, favoring the toleration and commercial opportunities offered by these port towns. Peter Faneuil, the rich merchant who built Faneuil Hall, Boston's "Cradle of Liberty," and who was both a good patriot and a public benefactor, was of Huguenot ancestry, as were Paul Revere and — in South Carolina — the Rhetts, the Gadsdens, the Ravenels, the Laurenses, the Deveaux and the L'Enfants.

A handful of Jews came to the American colonies in the seventeenth and eighteenth centuries, with Pennsylvania and Rhode Island as the preferred locations. The first American synagogue was built in Providence, Rhode Island. Aaronsburg, Pennsylvania, was founded by Jewish settlers, and in Philadelphia the wealthy Gratz family contributed generously to the patriot cause. A Jewish scholar taught Hebrew at Harvard in the middle of the eighteenth century.

[Ultimately] . . . this collection of astonishingly diverse individuals, from a dozen countries and twice as many religious sects and denominations, spread out over a vast territory and coalesced into a nation and eventually into a united people. . . .

QUESTIONS TO CONSIDER

1. Sixteenth-century immigrants to the American colonies came from England, Scotland, Ireland, France, Germany, Holland, and Sweden. What characteristics does Page Smith suggest they had in common?

2. How did conditions in seventeenth- and eighteenth-century England fuel emigration to the colonies? Describe the system of indenture. How did convicted felons, rogues, and vagabonds end up coming to America?

3. Describe the ordeal of the ocean crossing for indentured servants and for convicts. If they arrived safely, how did these immigrants make their way in American society? In what ways did the system of indenture discriminate against women?

4. By the mid-eighteenth century, established colonists had begun to protest the dumping of England's human refuse on American shores. Why do you suppose the colonies were not simply overwhelmed by the flood of undesirables? Where did these and other colonial protests against English highhandedness eventually culminate?

5. Page Smith says that many of the felons, rogues, and vagabonds were converted to solid citizens in the religious revivals of the mid-eighteenth century. In what ways were these immigrants particularly susceptible to conversion?

II

The First Century

3

Were the Puritans Puritanical?

CARL N. DEGLER

The original Puritans were sixteenth-century English Christians who sought to "purify" the Anglican church, England's sole established church, by forcing it to adopt the tenets of Calvinism (see the glossary in selection 2). Some Puritans, called Separatists, defied English law and formed their own churches in order to worship as they wished. Because they were ruthlessly persecuted, were imprisoned, and even put to death, many Puritans sought refuge in North America. One Separatist group settled in Virginia. Another — the celebrated Pilgrims — came over on the Mayflower *in 1620 and established Plymouth Plantation just north of present-day Cape Cod. Ten years later, a third Puritan group founded Massachusetts Bay Colony, comprising most of what is now Massachusetts and New Hampshire.*

Led by even-tempered John Winthrop, their first governor, the Massachusetts Puritans sought to create a model Christian commonwealth — "a city on a hill" — that would stand as a beacon of inspiration for others to emulate. Each town had its own congregation and its own minister, whose sermons rang with Calvinist precepts. The system of local congregations that selected their ministers and ran their own affairs became known as the Congregational church. In their wilderness Zion, ministers and government officials worked together to maintain holiness, purity, and order. Only church members — the elect — could vote and hold political office. The government, in turn, protected the church by levying taxes to support it on members and nonmembers alike and by making church attendance compulsory. The Puritans, as Edmund S. Morgan said, "not only endeavored themselves to live a 'smooth, honest, civil life,' but tried to force everyone within their power to do likewise."

The Puritans were pious, sedate folk, but were they puritanical? Alas for them, they have received a bad rap in American popular culture. In Playboy *some years ago, Hugh Hefner summed up the popular misconception, referring to the Puritans as grim bigots who hated pleasure in any form and who turned America into a land of rigid sexual repression, censorship, and conformity. As do many others, Hefner confused the Puritans with the custodians of the Victorian moral code of the nineteenth and early twentieth centuries. They were the ones who forbade discussion of sexual matters. They were the ones who cringed at the very notion of sex for pleasure and demanded that it be restricted to the marriage bed solely for purposes of procreation. Those who subscribed to the Victorian moral code were so prudish that they referred to piano legs as* limbs, *because the word* legs *was too licentious for them.*

In the selection that follows, Carl N. Degler, an eminent social historian, sets the record straight as far as the Puritans were concerned. As he points out, they proscribed excesses of enjoyment, not enjoyment itself. What was more, Puritan Massachusetts had the highest educational standard in the English colonies. Bay Colony Puritans were the first to attempt public-supported and -controlled local schools, and their innovation, as Degler says, was "the American prototype of a proper system of popular education."

GLOSSARY

ANABAPTISTS Widely persecuted Christian sects that opposed infant baptism, holding that only believers should be baptized.

COMSTOCK, ANTHONY American moral crusader of the late nineteenth and early twentieth centuries who organized the New York Society for the Suppression of Vice and secured federal laws against obscene material.

COTTON, JOHN Puritan clergyman and leader in Massachusetts who played a part in the expulsion of Roger Williams and Anne Hutchinson.

HUTCHINSON, ANNE Brilliant Puritan who emigrated to Massachusetts Bay in 1634, she was branded a heretic and expelled for preaching what the religious and secular authorities deemed unorthodox doctrine.

LAUDIANS Following of Archibishop William

Laud of England, who believed in the supremacy of the Church of England and who persecuted and imprisoned religious nonconformists.

MASSACHUSETTS CODE OF 1648 Puritan measure requiring that children be taught to read.

MENCKEN, H. L. Baltimore journalist, author, and social critic, 1880–1956, who lampooned middle-class complacency.

MORISON, SAMUEL ELIOT Twentieth-century Harvard historian who wrote a history of the institution.

REFORMATION Sixteenth-century religious revolution in Western Europe, which began as a movement to reform the Roman Catholic Church and led to the rise of Protestantism.

WILLIAMS, ROGER Puritan minister who was banished from Massachusetts Bay in 1633 for asserting that the king of England had no authority to seize Indian land without paying for it; Williams went on to found the colony of Rhode Island, where he established the separation of church and state and welcomed religious dissenters.

WINTHROP, JOHN   Principal lay leader of Massachusetts Bay, he served as its first governor for ten years and as deputy governor for nine; he presided over Anne Hutchinson's trial and approved of her expulsion.

WINTHROP, MARGARET   The governor's wife, "a very gracious woman" who "epitomized the Puritan marital ideal."

To most Americans — and to most Europeans, for that matter — the core of the Puritan social heritage has been summed up in [English historian Thomas Babington] Macaulay's well-known witticism that the Puritans prohibited bearbaiting not because of torture to the bear, but because of the pleasure it afforded the spectators. And as late as 1925, H. L. Mencken defined Puritanism as "the haunting fear that someone, somewhere, may be happy." Before this chapter is out, much will be said about the somber and even grim nature of the Puritan view of life, but quips like those of Macaulay and Mencken distort rather than illumine the essential character of the Puritans. Simply because the word "Puritan" has become encrusted with a good many barnacles, it is worth while to try to scrape them off if we wish to gain an understanding of the Puritan heritage. Though this process is essentially a negative one, sometimes it is clarifying to set forth what an influence is *not* as well as what it is.

Fundamental to any appreciation of the Puritan mind on matters of pleasure must be the recognition that the typical, godly Puritan was a worker in the world. Puritanism, like Protestantism in general, resolutely and definitely rejected the ascetic and monastic ideals of medieval Catholicism. Pleasures of the body were not to be eschewed by the Puritan, for, as Calvin reasoned, God "intended to provide not only for our necessity, but likewise for our pleasure and delight." It is obvious, he wrote in his famous *Institutes,* that "the Lord have endowed flowers with such beauty . . . with such sweetness of smell" in order to impress our senses; therefore, to enjoy them is not contrary to God's intentions. "In a word," he concluded, "hath He not made many things worthy of our estimation independent of any necessary use?"

It was against excess of enjoyment that the Puritans

"Were the Puritans Puritanical?" from Carl N. Degler, *Out of Our Past: The Forces That Shaped Modern America.* Copyright © 1959, 1970 by Carl N. Degler. Reprinted by permission of HarperCollins Publishers, Inc.

Puritan women in Sunday dress. As Degler points out, Puritan dress was not drab and severe, but was rather "in the English Renaissance style." Puritan ladies like those above wore masks to protect their faces from the sun and wind, and wore chicken skin gloves in bed to keep their hands white. (Reproduced from Hollar, Ornatus Muliebris Anglicanus, 1640; Courtesy of the Trustees of the Boston Public Library)

cautioned and legislated. "The wine is from God," Increase Mather warned, "but the Drunkard is from the Devil." The Cambridge Platform of the Church of 1680 prohibited games of cards or dice because of the amount of time they consumed and the encouragement they offered to idleness, but the ministers of Boston in 1699 found no difficulty in condoning public lotteries. They were like a public tax, the ministers said, since they took only what the "government might have demanded, with a more *general imposition* . . . and it employes for the welfare of the publick, all that is raised by the *lottery*." Though Cotton Mather at the end of the century condemned mixed dancing, he did not object to dancing as such; and his grandfather, John Cotton, at the beginning saw little to object to

in dancing between the sexes so long as it did not become lascivious. It was this same John Cotton, incidentally, who successfully contended against Roger Williams' argument that women should wear veils in church.

In matters of dress, it is true that the Massachusetts colony endeavored to restrict the wearing of "some new and immodest fashion" that was coming in from England, but often these efforts were frustrated by the pillars of the church themselves. [John] Winthrop reported in his *History*, for example, that though the General Court instructed the elders of the various churches to reduce the ostentation in dress by "urging it upon the consciences of their people," little change was effected, "for divers of the elders'

31

wives, etc., were in some measure partners in this general disorder."

We also know now that Puritan dress — not that made "historical" by Saint-Gaudens' celebrated statue — was the opposite of severe, being rather in the English Renaissance style. Most restrictions on dress that were imposed were for purposes of class differentiation rather than for ascetic reasons. Thus long hair was acceptable on an upper-class Puritan like [Oliver] Cromwell or Winthrop, but on the head of a person of lower social status it was a sign of vanity. In 1651 the legislature of Massachusetts called attention to that "excess of Apparell" which has "crept in upon us, and especially amongst people of mean condition, to the dishonor of God, the scandall of our profession, the consumption of Estates, and altogether unsuitable to our poverty." The law declared "our utter detestation and dislike, that men and women of mean condition, should take upon them the garb of Gentlemen, by wearing Gold or Silver Lace, or Buttons, or Points at their knees, or to walk in great Boots; or Women of the same rank to wear Silk or Tiffany hoods, or Scarfes, which tho allowable to persons of greater Estates, or more liberal education, is intolerable in people of low condition." By implication, this law affords a clear description of what the well-dressed Puritan of good estate would wear.

If the Puritans are to be saved from the canard of severity of dress, it is also worth while to soften the charge that they were opposed to music and art. It is perfectly true that the Puritans insisted that organs be removed from the churches and that in England some church organs were smashed by zealots. But it was not music or organs as such which they opposed, only music in the meetinghouse. Well-known American and English Puritans, like Samuel Sewall, John Milton, and Cromwell, were sincere lovers of music. Moreover, it should be remembered that it was under Puritan rule that opera was introduced into England — and without protest, either. The first English dramatic production entirely in music — *The Siege of Rhodes* — was presented in 1656, four years before the Restoration. Just before the end of Puritan rule, John Evelyn noted in his diary that he went "to see a new opera, after the Italian way, in recitative music and scenes. . . ." Furthermore, as Percy Scholes points out, in all the voluminous contemporary literature attacking the Puritans for every conceivable narrow-mindedness, none asserts that they opposed music, so long as it was performed outside the church.

The weight of the evidence is much the same in the realm of art. Though King Charles' art collection was dispersed by the incoming Commonwealth, it is significant that Cromwell and other Puritans bought several of the items. We also know that the Protector's garden at Hampton Court was beautified by nude statues. Furthermore, it is now possible to say that the Puritan closing of the theaters was as much a matter of objection to their degenerate lewdness by the 1640's as an objection to the drama as such. As far as American Puritans are concerned, it is not possible to say very much about their interest in art since there was so little in the seventeenth century. At least it can be said that the Puritans, unlike the Quakers, had no objection to portrait painting.

Some modern writers have professed to find in Puritanism, particularly the New England brand, evidence of sexual repression and inhibition. Though it would certainly be false to suggest that the Puritans did not subscribe to the canon of simple chastity, it is equally erroneous to think that their sexual lives were crabbed or that sex was abhorrent to them. Marriage to the Puritan was something more than an alternative to "burning," as the Pauline doctrine of the Catholic church would have it. Marriage was enjoined upon the righteous Christian; celibacy was not a sign of merit. With unconcealed disapprobation, John Cotton told a recently married couple the story of a pair "who immediately upon marriage, without ever approaching the *Nuptial* Bed," agreed to live apart from the rest of the world, "and afterwards from one another, too. . . ." But, Cotton advised, such behavior was "no other than an effort of blind zeal, for they are the dictates of a blind mind they follow therein and not of the Holy Spirit which saith, *It is not good that man should be alone.*" Cotton set himself against not only Catholic asceticism but also the view that women were the "unclean vessel," the tempters of men. Women, rather than being "a necessary Evil are a necessary Good," he wrote. "Without them there is no comfortable Living for Man. . . ."

Because, as another divine said, "the Use of the Marriage Bed" is "founded in man's Nature" the realistic Puritans required that married men unaccompanied by wives should leave the colony or bring their wives over forthwith. The Puritan settlements encouraged marriages satisfactory to the participants by permitting divorces for those whose spouses were impotent, too long absent, or cruel. Indeed, the divorce laws of New England were the easiest in Christendom at a time when the eloquence of a Milton was unable to loosen the bonds of matrimony in England.

Samuel Eliot Morison in his history of Harvard has collected a number of examples of the healthy interest of Puritan boys in the opposite sex. Commonplace books, for example, indicate that Herrick's poem beginning "Gather ye rosebuds while ye may" and amorous lines from Shakespeare, as well as more erotic and even scatological verse, were esteemed by young Puritan men. For a gentleman to present his affianced with a pair of garters, one letter of a Harvard graduate tells us, was considered neither immoral nor improper.

It is also difficult to reconcile the usual view of the stuffiness of Puritans with the literally hundreds of confessions to premarital sexual relations in the extant church records. It should be understood, moreover, that these confessions were made by the saints or saints-to-be, not by the unregenerate. That the common practice of the congregation was to accept such sinners into church membership without further punishment is in itself revealing. The civil law, it is true, punished such transgressions when detected among the regenerate or among the nonchurch members, but this was also true of contemporary non-Puritan Virginia. "It will be seen," writes historian Philip A.

Bruce regarding Virginia, "from the various instances given relating to the profanation of Sunday, drunkenness, swearing, defamation, and sexual immorality, that, not only were the grand juries and vestries extremely vigilant in reporting these offences, but the courts were equally prompt in inflicting punishment; and that the penalty ranged from a heavy fine to a shameful exposure in the stocks . . . and from such an exposure to a very severe flogging at the county whipping post." In short, strict moral surveillance by the public authorities was a seventeenth-century rather than a Puritan attitude.

Relations between the sexes in Puritan society were often much more loving and tender than the mythmakers would have us believe. Since it was the Puritan view that marriage was eminently desirable in the sight of God and man, it is not difficult to find evidence of deep and abiding love between a husband and wife. John Cotton, it is true, sometimes used the Biblical phrase "comfortable yoke mate" in addressing his wife, but other Puritan husbands come closer to our romantic conventions. Certainly John Winthrop's letters to his beloved Margaret indicate the depth of attachment of which the good Puritan was capable. "My good wife . . . My sweet wife," he called her. Anticipating his return home, he writes, "So . . . we shall now enjoy each other again, as we desire. . . . It is now bed time; but I must lie alone; therefore I make less haste. Yet I must kiss my sweet wife; and so, with my blessing to our children . . . I commend thee to the grace and blessing of the lord, and rest. . . ."

Anne Bradstreet wrote a number of poems devoted to her love for her husband in which the sentiments and figures are distinctly romantic.

> To my Dear and loving Husband
> I prize thy love more than whole Mines
> of gold
> Or all the riches that the East doth hold.
> My love is such that Rivers cannot quench,
> Nor aught but love from thee give recompense.

In another poem her spouse is apostrophized as

> My head, my heart, mine Eyes, my life, nay more
> My joy, my Magazine of earthly store

and she asks:

> If two be one, as surely thou and I,
> How stayest thou there, whilst I at Ipswich lye?

Addressing John as "my most sweet Husband," Margaret Winthrop perhaps epitomized the Puritan marital ideal when she wrote, "I have many reasons to make me love thee, whereof I will name two: First, because thou lovest God and, secondly, because thou lovest me. If these two were wanting," she added, "all the rest would be eclipsed."

It would be a mistake, however, to try to make these serious, dedicated men and women into rakes of the Renaissance. They were sober if human folk, deeply concerned about their ultimate salvation and intent upon living up to God's commands as they understood them, despite their acknowledgment of complete depravity and unworthiness. "God sent you not into this world as a Play-House, but a Work-house," one minister told his congregation. To the Puritan this was a world drenched in evil, and, because it truly is, they were essentially realistic in their judgments. Because the Puritan expected nothing, Perry Miller has remarked, a disillusioned one was almost impossible to find. This is probably an exaggeration, for they were also human beings; when the Commonwealth fell, it was a Puritan, after all, who said, "God has spit in our faces." But Professor Miller's generalization has much truth in it. Only a man convinced of the inevitable and eternal character of evil could fight it so hard and so unceasingly.

The Puritan at his best, Ralph Barton Perry has said, was a "moral athlete." More than most men, the Puritan strove with himself and with his fellow man to attain a moral standard higher than was rightfully to be expected of so depraved a creature. Hence the di-

aries and autobiographies of Puritans are filled with the most tortuous probing of the soul and inward seeking. Convinced of the utter desirability of salvation on the one hand, and equally cognizant of the total depravity of man's nature on the other, the Puritan was caught in an impossible dilemma which permitted him no rest short of the grave. Yet with such a spring coiled within him, the Puritan drove himself and his society to tremendous heights of achievement both material and spiritual.

Such intense concern for the actualization of the will of God had a less pleasant side to it, also. If the belief that "I am my brother's keeper" is the breeding ground of heightened social conscience and expresses itself in the reform movements so indigenous to Boston and its environs, it also could and did lead to self-righteousness, intolerance, and narrow-mindedness, as exemplified in another product of Boston: Anthony Comstock. But this fruit of the loins of Puritanism is less typical of the earthy seventeenth-century New Englander than H. L. Mencken would have us think. The Sabbatarian, antiliquor, and anti-sex attitudes usually attributed to the Puritans are a nineteenth-century addition to the much more moderate and essentially wholesome view of life's evils held by the early settlers of New England.

To realize how different Puritans could be, one needs only to contrast Roger Williams and his unwearying opponent John Cotton. But despite the range of differences among Puritans, they all were linked by at least one characteristic. That was their belief in themselves, in their morality and in their mission to the world. For this reason, Puritanism was intellectual and social dynamite in the seventeenth century; its power disrupted churches, defied tyrants, overthrew governments, and beheaded kings.

The Reformation laid an awesome burden on the souls of those who broke with the Roman Church. Proclaiming the priesthood of all believers, Protestantism made each man's relationship to God his own terrifying responsibility. No one else could save him; therefore no one must presume to try. More concerned about his salvation than about any mundane matter, the Puritan was compelled, for the sake of his immortal soul, to be a fearless individualist.

It was the force of this conviction which produced the Great Migration of 1630–40 and made Massachusetts a flourishing colony in the span of a decade. It was also, ironically, the force which impelled Roger Williams to threaten the very legal and social foundations of the Puritan Commonwealth in Massachusetts because he thought the oligarchy wrong and himself right. And so it would always be. For try as the rulers of Massachusetts might to make men conform to their dogma, their own rebellious example always stood as a guide to those who felt the truth was being denied. Such individualism, we would call it today, was flesh and bone of the religion which the Puritans passed on. Though the theocracy soon withered and died, its harsh voice softened down to the balmy breath of Unitarianism, the belief in self and the dogged resistance to suppression or untruth which Puritanism taught never died. Insofar as Americans today can be said to be individualistic, it is to the Puritan heritage that we must look for one of the principal sources.

In his ceaseless striving for signs of salvation and knowledge of God's intentions for man, the Puritan placed great reliance upon the human intellect, even though for him, as for all Christians, faith was the bedrock of his belief. "Faith doth not relinquish or cast out reason," wrote the American Puritan Samuel Willard, "for there is nothing in Religion contrary to it, tho' there are many things that do transcend and must captivate it." Richard Baxter, the English Puritan, insisted that "the *most Religious*, are the *most* truly, and *nobly rational*." Religion and reason were complementary to the Puritan, not antithetical as they were to many evangelical sects of the time.

Always the mere emotion of religion was to be controlled by reason. Because of this, the university-trained Puritan clergy prided themselves on the lucidity and rationality of their sermons. Almost rigorously their sermons followed the logical sequence of "doctrine," "reasons," and "uses." Conscientiously they shunned the meandering and rhetorical flourishes so beloved by Laudian preachers like John Donne, and in the process facilitated the taking of notes by their eager listeners. One of the unforgivable crimes of Mistress Anne Hutchinson was her assertion that one could "feel" one's salvation, that one was "filled with God" after conversion, that it was unnecessary, in order to be saved, to be learned in the Bible or in the Puritan writers. It was not that the Puritans were cold to the Word — far from it. A saint was required to testify to an intense religious experience — almost by definition emotional in character — before he could attain full membership in the Church. But it was always important to the Puritans that mere emotion — whether it be the anarchistic activities of the Anabaptists or the quaking of the Friends — should not be mistaken for righteousness or proper religious conduct. Here, as in so many things, the Puritans attempted to walk the middle path — in this instance, between the excessive legalism and formalism of the Catholics and Episcopalians and the flaming, intuitive evangelism of the Baptists and Quakers.

Convinced of reason's great worth, it was natural that the Puritans should also value education. "Ignorance is the mother (not of Devotion but) of Heresy," one Puritan divine declared. And a remarkably well-educated ministry testified to the Puritan belief that learning and scholarship were necessary for a proper understanding of the Word of God. More than a hundred graduates of Cambridge and Oxford Universities settled in New England before 1640, most of them ministers. At the same date not five men in all of Virginia could lay claim to such an educational background. Since Cambridge University, situated on the edge of Puritan East Anglia, supplied most of the graduates in America, it was natural that Newtown, the site of New England's own college, would soon be renamed in honor of the Alma Mater. "After God had carried us safe to New-England," said a well-known tract, some of its words now immortalized in metal in Harvard Yard, "one of the next things we longed and looked after, was to advance learning, and perpetuate it to posterity; dreading to leave an illiterate ministry to the churches, when the present ministers shall lie in the dust." "The College," founded in 1636, soon to be named Harvard, was destined to remain the only institution of higher learning in America during almost all the years of the seventeenth century. Though it attracted students from as far away as Virginia, it remained, as it began, the fountainhead of Puritan learning in the New World.

Doubt as one may Samuel Eliot Morison's claims for the secular origins of Harvard, his evidence of the typically Renaissance secular education which was available at the Puritan college in New England is both impressive and convincing. The Latin and Greek secular writers of antiquity dominated the curriculum, for this was a liberal arts training such as the leaders had received at Cambridge in England. To the Puritans the education of ministers could be nothing less than the best learning of the day. So important did education at Harvard seem to the New Haven colony in 1644 that the legislature ordered each town to appoint two men to be responsible for the collection of contributions from each family for "the mayntenaunce of scolars at Cambridge. . . ."

If there was to be a college, preparatory schools had to be provided for the training of those who were expected to enter the university. Furthermore, in a society dedicated to the reading of the Bible, elementary education was indispensable. "It being one chief project of that old deluder Satan to keep men from the knowledge of the Scriptures" began the first school laws of Massachusetts (1647) and Connecticut (1650). But the Puritans supported education for secular as well as religious reasons. The Massachusetts Code of 1648, for instance, required children to be taught to read inasmuch "as the good education of children is of singular behoof and benefit to any Commonwealth."

The early New England school laws provided that each town of fifty families or more was to hire a teacher for the instruction of its young; towns of one hundred families or more were also directed to provide grammar schools, "the master thereof being able to instruct youths so far as they may be fitted for the University." Though parents were not obliged to send their children to these schools, if they did not they were required to teach their children to read. From the evidence of court cases and the high level of literacy in seventeenth-century New England, it would appear that these first attempts at public-supported and public-controlled education were both enforced and fruitful.

No other colony in the seventeenth century imposed such a high educational standard upon its simple farming people as the Puritans did. It is true, of course, that Old England in this period could boast of grammar schools, some of which were free. But primary schools were almost nonexistent there, and toward the end of the seventeenth century the free schools in England became increasingly tuition schools. Moreover, it was not until well into the nineteenth century that the English government did anything to support schools. Primary and secondary education in England, in contrast with the New England example, was a private or church affair.

Unlike the Puritans, the Quakers exhibited little impulse toward popular education in the seventeenth and early eighteenth centuries. Because of their accent on the Inner Light and the doctrine of universal salvation, the religious motivation of the [Quakers] for learning was wanting. Furthermore, the Quakers did not look to education, as such, with the same reverence as the Puritans. William Penn, for example, advised his children that "reading many books is but a taking off the mind too much from meditation." No Puritan would have said that.

Virginia in the seventeenth century, it should be said, was also interested in education. Several times in the course of the century, plans were well advanced for establishing a university in the colony. Free schools also existed in Virginia during the seventeenth century, though the lack of village communities made them inaccessible for any great numbers of children. But, in contrast with New England, there were no publicly supported schools in Virginia; the funds for the field schools of Virginia, like those for free schools in contemporary England, came from private or ecclesiastical endowment. Nor was Virginia able to bring its several plans for a college into reality until William and Mary was founded at the very end of the century.

Though the line which runs from the early New England schools to the distinctly American system of free public schools today is not always progressively upward or uniformly clear, the connection is undeniable. The Puritan innovation of public support and control on a local level was the American prototype of a proper system of popular education.

QUESTIONS TO CONSIDER

1.   Discuss the reality of the widely held belief that Puritan society was grim, colorless, bigoted, and repressed. How would Degler respond to H. L. Mencken's 1925 definition of Puritanism as "the haunting fear that someone, somewhere, may be happy"? How did Puritan social and moral standards and ideals compare with those of Catholics, Quakers, and others in the seventeenth century?

2.   What does Degler mean by saying the Puritan at his or her best was a "moral athlete"? How did Puritanism and Quakerism embody the bourgeois spirit that historian Max Weber called the "Protestant Ethic"? Was this ethic merely a religious justification for ruthless materialism, or was it something more? How was the Protestant ethic transformed into the American work ethic?

3.   How did the Puritans' belief in their duty to God influence their view of the responsibility of individuals to themselves and to society? What have been the lasting influences of this view on American attitudes as they have developed since the seventeenth century?

4.   What was the Puritan position on the traditional juxtaposition of emotion and reason? How did they compare in this matter with their contemporaries of different religions?

5.   What was the educational background of the Puritans who settled in New England, and how did it compare with that of the Virginians? What did the New England Puritans see as the role and importance of education in society? How did they go about realizing their ideal, and how did their achievements compare with those of England and Virginia? What has been their lasting influence on the American educational ideal and system?

4

Black People in a White People's Country

GARY B. NASH

In 1619, a year before the Pilgrims landed at Plymouth Rock, a Dutch ship deposited "twenty Negars" on the wharf of Jamestown Colony, in what became Virginia. These were the first Africans to enter colonial America, but their exact status is unknown. Like Africans subsequently imported until 1660, they were probably indentured servants whose period of servitude was temporary. After 1660, however, most Africans who came to America were slaves, purchased through a heinous business operation, the international slave trade. By the eighteenth century, every English colony from Carolina to Massachusetts had enacted "slave codes," bodies of law that stripped black people of all rights and reduced them to pieces of property, or "chattel," with their children inheriting that status.

The troubling question is why the Africans were enslaved and white indentures were not. In the selection that follows, Gary B. Nash, one of the leading experts on colonial America, argues that the answer lies in a combination of racial prejudice and labor needs in early America, particularly in the southern colonies. When faced with the problem of cultivating labor-intensive crops, Nash writes, English settlers "turned to the international slave trade to fill their labor needs." That white colonists viewed Africans as uncivilized barbarians only made it easier "to fasten chains upon them." The Africans, of course, were no more barbaric than were the Native Americans. As Nash observes, the Africans had been stolen from richly complex and highly developed cultures. The English settlers, of course, knew nothing about such cultures beyond that they were neither white nor Christian and were therefore "uncivilized."

As more and more Africans were imported to the English colonies, racial fears intensified in direct proportion to the number of blacks in a given area. Such fears were worse in the southern colonies, where the extensive cultivation of labor-intensive crops necessitated the purchase of large numbers of slaves. In the northern colonies, as Nash points out, "slavery existed on a more occasional basis," because labor-intensive crops were not so widely grown there and far fewer Africans were imported. This is a crucial point. It helps explain why slavery later disappeared in the North, during and after the Revolution.

In the colonial period, meanwhile, every colony in North and South alike enacted laws that severely regulated black people and made them slaves for life. Thus from the very outset, slavery served a twofold purpose: it was both a labor system and a means of racial control in a white people's country. This "mass enslavement of Africans," Nash points out, only reinforced racial prejudice in a vicious cycle. "Once institutionalized, slavery cast Africans into such lowly roles that the initial bias against them could only be confirmed and vastly strengthened."

To provide a fuller understanding of slavery in North America, Nash discusses the origins of African slavery itself and offers a graphic and painful portrait of the Atlantic slave trade, which involved "the largest forced migration in history" and was thus "one of the most important phenomena in the history of the modern world." Greed and profit kept the trade booming for four hundred years, with European entrepreneurs reaping fortunes at the expense of millions of human beings. The captain and crew of a slave ship, whether British, Dutch, Portuguese, or colonial American, had to be monstrously depraved and utterly inured to human suffering in order to carry out this brutal business. One such slave trader, Englishman John Newton, later repented, became a minister and an abolitionist, and wrote a hymn about his salvation, "How Sweet the Name of Jesus Sounds," popularly known as "Amazing Grace." Grace was indeed amazing, he said, to have saved "a wretch" like him.

The horrors of the middle passage, warns one historian, were "so revolting that a writer of the present day hesitates to give such details to his readers." On one slaver, said an eyewitness, "400 wretched beings" were chained and "crammed into a hold 12 yards in length. . . . and only 3½ feet in height." Because of the hold's "suffocating heat" and stench, the Africans panicked and in their torment tried in vain to escape. The next morning, the crew lifted "fifty-four crushed and mangled corpses up from the slave deck." To keep the survivors in line, the crew beat and murdered other Africans. Such atrocities were commonplace on slave ships, and the captains could not have cared less, because "insurance companies bore part of the loss, and profits were so high that heavy risks were cheerfully assumed."

Driven to madness in the rat-filled, claustrophobic bowels of the slave ships, many Africans maimed themselves or committed suicide. Others starved to death or died of some white man's disease. And the women, too many of them, were humiliated in unspeakable ways by their white captors. If the Africans somehow survived the Atlantic passage, they found themselves dumped into some fly-infested slave pen in a port of the New World.

We can imagine such a group in chains on the wharves of colonial New York City or Baltimore. Sick, starving, and frightened, they had to find some way to endure the unendurable in a strange new land. That such Africans salvaged much of their heritage, transforming it into a distinctly African American heritage, was a tribute to their power "to keep on keeping on."

"Thus," writes historian Carl Degler, "began in the seventeenth century the Negro's life in America. With it commenced a moral problem for all Americans which still besets us at the close of the twentieth century." As Nash observes, the emergence of slavery in colonial America was "one of the great paradoxes in American history — the building of what some thought was to be a utopia in the wilderness upon the backs of black men and women wrenched from their African homeland and forced into a system of abject slavery." That paradox, as we shall see, would persist through the American Revolution, the early Republic, and well into the nineteenth century, causing sectional tensions between the North and the South that finally plunged America into the most destructive war in its history.

GLOSSARY

BLACK GOLD   The European expression for slaves.

DUTCH WEST INDIA COMPANY   A leading "international supplier of slaves."

GONÇALVEZ, ANTAM   The first European to set foot on Africa, he brought "the first kidnapped Africans to Portugal in 1441."

MACKRONS   Africans considered too old or too infirm to make good slaves.

MIDDLE PASSAGE   The route across the Atlantic from the African coast to the New World.

ROYAL AFRICAN COMPANY   An English joint stock company chartered by the Crown to carry slaves to the English colonies.

SEQUEIRA, RUY DO   The Portuguese captain who began the European slave trade in 1472.

SLAVE CODES   Colonial laws that legalized and enforced slavery, depriving Africans of all rights and reducing them to pieces of property.

The African slave trade, which began in the late fifteenth century and continued for the next 400 years, is one of the most important phenomena in the history of the modern world. Involving the largest forced migration in history, the slave trade and slavery were crucially important in building the colonial empires of European nations and in generating the wealth that later produced the Industrial Revolution. But often overlooked in the attention given to the economic importance of the slave trade and slavery is the cultural diffusion that took place when ten million Africans were brought to the western hemisphere. Six out of every seven persons who crossed the Atlantic to take up life in the New World in the 300 years before the American Revolution were African slaves. As a result, in most parts of the colonized territories slavery "defined the context within which transferred European traditions would grow and change." As slaves, Africans were Europeanized; but at the same time they Africanized the culture of Europeans in the Americas. This was an inevitable part of the convergence of these two broad groups of people, who met each other an ocean away from their original homelands. In addition, the slave trade created the lines of communication for the movement of crops, agricultural techniques, diseases, and medical knowledge between Africa, Europe, and the Americas.

Just as they were late in colonizing the New World, the English lagged far behind their Spanish and Portuguese competitors in making contact with the west coast of Africa, in entering the Atlantic slave trade, and in establishing African slaves as the backbone of the labor force in their overseas plantations. And among the English colonists in the New World, those on the mainland of North America were a half century or more behind those in the Caribbean in

converting their plantation economies to slave labor. By 1670, for example, some 200,000 slaves labored in Portuguese Brazil and about 30,000 cultivated sugar in English Barbados; but in Virginia only 2,000 worked in the tobacco fields. Cultural interaction of Europeans and Africans did not begin in North America on a large scale until more than a century after it had begun in the southerly parts of the hemisphere. Much that occurred as the two cultures met in the Iberian colonies was later repeated in the Anglo-African interaction; and yet the patterns of acculturation were markedly different in North and South America in the seventeenth and eighteenth centuries.

☆

THE ATLANTIC SLAVE TRADE

A half century before Columbus crossed the Atlantic, a Portuguese sea captain, Antam Gonçalvez, made the first European landing on the west African coast south of the Sahara. What he might have seen, had he been able to travel the length and breadth of Africa, was a continent of extraordinary variation in geography and culture. Little he might have seen would have caused him to believe that African peoples were naturally inferior or that they had failed to develop over time as had the peoples of Europe. This notion of "backwardness" and cultural impoverishment was the myth perpetuated after the slave trade had transported millions of Africans to the Western Hemisphere. It was a myth which served to justify the cruelties of the slave trade and to assuage the guilt of Europeans involved in the largest forced dislocation of people in history.

The peoples of Africa may have numbered more than 50 million in the late fifteenth century when Europeans began making extensive contact with the continent. They lived in widely varied ecological zones — in vast deserts, in grasslands, and in great forests and woodlands. As in Europe, most people farmed the land and struggled to subdue the forces of nature in order to sustain life. That the African popu-

From Gary B. Nash, *Red, White, and Black: The Peoples of Early North America* (3rd ed), pp. 144–161, 208–225. Reprinted by permission of Prentice-Hall, Englewood Cliffs, NJ.

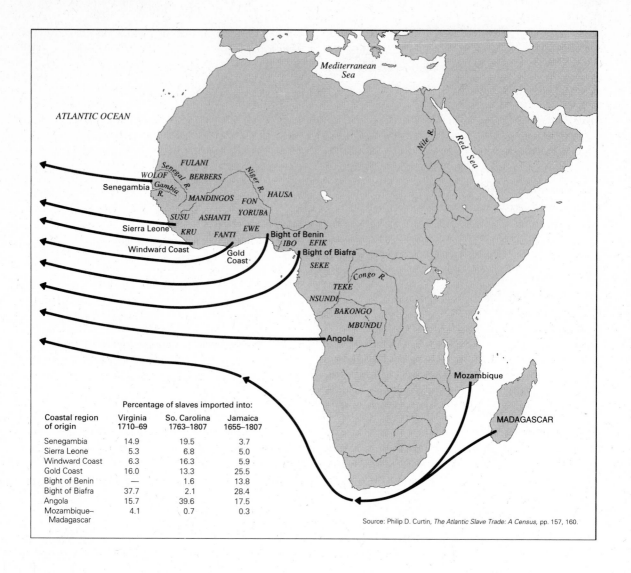

ATLANTIC OCEAN

Mediterranean
Sea

FULANI
WOLOF   BERBERS
Senegambia   Gambia
R.   MANDINGOS   FON   HAUSA
SUSU   ASHANTI   YORUBA
Sierra Leone   KRU   FANTI   EWE
Windward Coast   Bight of Benin
Gold   IBO   EFIK
Coast   Bight of Biafra
                    SEKE
                    Congo R.
                    TEKE
                    NSUNDI
                    BAKONGO
                    MBUNDU
                    Angola

Nile R.
Red Sea

Mozambique

MADAGASCAR

Coastal region of origin	Percentage of slaves imported into:		
	Virginia 1710–69	So. Carolina 1763–1807	Jamaica 1655–1807
Senegambia	14.9	19.5	3.7
Sierra Leone	5.3	6.8	5.0
Windward Coast	6.3	16.3	5.9
Gold Coast	16.0	13.3	25.5
Bight of Benin	—	1.6	13.8
Bight of Biafra	37.7	2.1	28.4
Angola	15.7	39.6	17.5
Mozambique– Madagascar	4.1	0.7	0.3

Source: Philip D. Curtin, *The Atlantic Slave Trade: A Census*, pp. 157, 160.

lation had increased so rapidly in the 2,000 years before European arrival suggests the sophistication of the African agricultural methods. Part of this skill in farming derived from skill in iron production, which had begun in present-day Nigeria about 500 B.C. It was this ability to fashion iron implements that triggered the new farming techniques necessary to sustain larger populations. With large populations came greater specialization of tasks and thus additional technical im-

provements. Small groups of related families made contact with other kinship groups and over time evolved into larger and more complicated societies. The pattern was similar to what had occurred in other parts of the world — in the Americas, Europe, the Middle East, and elsewhere — when the "agricultural revolution" occurred.

Recent studies of "pre-contact" African history have showed that the "culture gap" between European and African societies when the two peoples met was not as large as previously imagined. By the time Europeans reached the coast of West Africa a number of extraordinary empires had been forged in the area. The first, apparently, was the Kingdom of Ghana, which embraced the immense territory between the Sahara Desert and the Gulf of Guinea and from the Niger River to the Atlantic Ocean between the fifth and tenth centuries. Extensive urban settlement, advanced architecture, elaborate art, and a highly complex political organization evolved during this time. From the eighth to the sixteenth centuries, it was the western Sudan that supplied most of the gold for the Western world. Invasion from the north by the Moors weakened the Kingdom of Ghana, which in time gave way to the Empire of Mali. At the center of the Mali Empire was the city of Timbuktu, noted for its extensive wealth and its Islamic university where a faculty as distinguished as any in Europe was gathered.

Lesser kingdoms such as the kingdoms of Kongo, Zimbabwe, and Benin had also been in the process of growth and cultural change for centuries before Europeans reached Africa. Their inhabitants were skilled in metal working, weaving, ceramics, architecture, and aesthetic expression. Many of their towns rivaled European cities in size. Many communities of West Africa had highly complex religious rites, well-organized regional trade, codes of law, and complex political organization.

Of course, cultural development in Africa, as elsewhere in the world, proceeded at varying rates. Ecological conditions had a large effect on this. Where good soil, adequate rainfall, and abundance of minerals were present, as in coastal West Africa, population growth and cultural elaboration were relatively rapid. Where inhospitable desert or nearly impenetrable forest held forth, social systems remained small and changed at a crawl. Contact with other cultures also brought rapid change, whereas isolation impeded cultural change. The Kingdom of Ghana bloomed in western Sudan partly because of the trading contacts with Arabs who had conquered the area in the ninth

century. Cultural change began to accelerate in Swahili societies facing the Indian Ocean after trading contacts were initiated with the Eastern world in the ninth century. Thus, as a leading African historian has put it, "the cultural history of Africa is . . . one of greatly unequal development among peoples who, for definable reasons such as these, entered recognizably similar stages of institutional change at different times."

The slave trade seems to have begun officially in 1472 when a Portuguese captain, Ruy do Sequeira, reached the coast of Benin and was conducted to the king's court, where he received royal permission to trade for gold, ivory, and slaves. So far as the Africans were concerned, the trade represented no strikingly new economic activity since they had long been involved in regional and long-distance trade across their continent. This was simply the opening of contacts with a new and more distant commercial partner. This is important to note because often it has been maintained that European powers raided the African coasts for slaves, marching into the interior and kidnapping hundreds of thousands of helpless and hapless victims. In actuality, the early slave trade involved a reciprocal relationship between European purchasers and African sellers, with the Portuguese monopolizing trade along the coastlands of tropical Africa for the first century after contact was made. Trading itself was confined to coastal strongholds where slaves, most of them captured in the interior by other Africans, were sold on terms set by the African sellers. In return for gold, ivory, and slaves, African slave merchants received European guns, bars of iron and copper, brass pots and tankards, beads, rum and textiles. They occupied an economic role not unlike that of the Iroquois middlemen in the fur trade with Europeans.

Slavery was not a new social phenomenon for either Europeans or Africans. For centuries African societies had been involved in an overland slave trade that transported black slaves from West Africa across the Sahara Desert to Roman Europe and the Middle East. But this was an occasional rather than a systematic trade, and it was designed to provide the trading nations of the Mediterranean with soldiers, household servants, and artisans rather than mass agricultural labor. Within Africa itself, a variety of unfree statuses had also existed for centuries, but they involved personal service, often for a limited period . . . rather than lifelong, degraded, agricultural labor. Slavery of a similar sort had long existed in Europe, mostly as the result of Christians enslaving Moslems and Moslems enslaving Christians during centuries of religious wars. One became a slave by being an "outsider" or an "infidel," by being captured in war, by voluntarily selling oneself into slavery to obtain money for one's family, or by committing certain heinous crimes. The rights of slaves were restricted and their opportunities for upward movement were severely circumscribed, but they were regarded nevertheless as members of society, enjoying protection under the law and entitled to certain rights, including education, marriage, and parenthood. Most important, the status of a slave was not irrevocable and was not automatically passed on to his or her children.

Thus we find that slavery flourished in ancient Greece and Rome, in the Aztec and Inca empires, in African societies, in early modern Russia and eastern Europe, in the Middle East, and in the Mediterranean world. It had gradually died out in Western Europe by the fourteenth century, although the status of serf was not too different in social reality from that of the slave. It is important to note that in all these regions slavery and serfdom had nothing to do with racial characteristics.

When the African slave trade began in the second half of the fifteenth century, it served to fill labor shortages in the economies of its European initiators and their commercial partners. Between 1450 and 1505 Portugal brought about 40,000 African slaves to Europe and the Atlantic islands — the Madeiras and Canaries. But the need for slave labor lessened in Europe as European populations themselves began to grow beginning late in the fifteenth century. It is possible, therefore, that were it not for the colonization of the New World the early slave trade might have ceased after a century or more and be remembered simply as a short-lived incident stemming from early European contacts with Africa.

With the discovery of the New World by Europeans the course of history changed momentously. Once Europeans found the gold and silver mines of Mexico and Peru, and later, when they discovered a new form of gold in the production of sugar, coffee, and tobacco, their demand for human labor grew astonishingly. At first Indians seemed to be the obvious source of labor, and in some areas Spaniards and Portuguese were able to coerce native populations into agricultural and mining labor. But European diseases ravaged native populations, and often it was found that Indians, far more at home in their environment than white colonizers, were difficult to subjugate. Indentured white labor from the mother country was another way of meeting the demand for labor, but this source, it soon became apparent, was far too limited. It was to Africa that colonizing Europeans ultimately resorted. Formerly a new source of trade, the continent now became transformed in the European view into the repository of vast supplies of human labor — "black gold."

From the late fifteenth to the mid-nineteenth centuries, almost four hundred years, Europeans transported Africans out of their ancestral homelands to fill the labor needs in their colonies of North and South America and the Caribbean. The most recent estimates place the numbers who reached the shores of the New World at about ten to eleven million people, although many million more lost their lives while being marched from the interior to the coastal trading forts or during the "middle passage" across the Atlantic. Even before the English arrived on the Chesapeake in 1607 several hundred thousand slaves had been transported to the Caribbean and South American colonies of Spain and Portugal. Before the slave trade was outlawed in the nineteenth century far more Africans than Europeans had crossed the Atlantic Ocean and taken up life in the New World. Black slaves, as one eighteenth-century Englishman put it became "the strength and the sinews of this western world."

Once established on a large scale, the Atlantic slave trade dramatically altered the pattern of slave recruitment in Africa. For about a century after Gonçalvez brought back the first kidnapped Africans to Portugal in 1441, the slave trade was relatively slight. The slaves whom other Africans sold to Europeans were drawn from a small minority of the population and for the most part were individuals captured in occasional war or whose criminal acts had cost them their rights of citizenship. For Europeans the African slave trade provided for modest labor needs, just as the Black Sea slave trade had done before it was shut off by the fall of Constantinople to the Turks in 1453. Even in the New World plantations, slaves were not in great demand for many decades after "discovery."

More than anything else it was sugar that transformed the African slave trade. Produced in the Mediterranean world since the eighth century, sugar was for centuries a costly item confined to sweetening the diet of the rich. By the mid-1400s its popularity was growing and the center of production had shifted to the Portuguese Madeira Islands, off the northwest coast of Africa. Here for the first time an expanding European nation established an overseas plantation society based on slave labor. From the Madeiras the cultivation of sugar spread to Portuguese Brazil in the late sixteenth century and then to the tiny specks of land dotting the Caribbean in the first half of the seventeenth century. By this time Europeans were developing an almost insatiable taste for sweetness. Sugar — regarded by nutritionists today as a "drug food" — became one of the first luxuries that was transformed into a necessary item in the diets of the masses of Europe. The wife of the poorest English laborer took sugar in her tea by 1750 it was said. "Together with other plantation products such as coffee, rum, and tobacco," writes Sidney Mintz, "sugar formed part of a complex of 'proletarian hunger-killers,' and played a crucial role in the linked contribution that Caribbean slaves, Indian peasants, and European urban proletarians were able to make to the growth of western civilization."

The regularization of the slave trade brought about by the vast new demand for a New World labor supply and by a reciprocally higher demand in Africa for European trade goods, especially bar iron and textiles, changed the problem of obtaining slaves. Criminals and "outsiders" in sufficient number to satisfy the growing European demand in the seventeenth century could not be found. Therefore African kings resorted to warfare against their neighbors as a way of obtaining "black gold" with which to trade. European guns abetted the process. Thus, the spread of kidnapping and organized violence in Africa became a part of maintaining commercial relations with European powers.

In the forcible recruitment of slaves, adult males were consistently preferred over women and children. Primarily this represented the preference of New World plantation owners for male field laborers. But it also reflected the decision of vanquished African villagers to yield up more men than women to raiding parties because women were the chief agriculturalists in their society and, in matrilineal and matrilocal kinship systems, were too valuable to be spared.

For the Europeans the slave trade itself became an immensely profitable enterprise. In the several centuries of intensive slave trading that followed the establishment of New World sugar plantations, European nations warred constantly for trading advantages on the West African coast. The coastal forts, the focal points of the trade, became key strategic targets in the wars of empire. The great Portuguese slaving fort at Elmina on the Gold Coast, begun in 1481, was captured a century and a half later by the Dutch. The primary fort on the Guinea coast, started by the Swedes, passed through the hands of the Danes, the English, and the Dutch between 1652 and 1664. As the demand for slaves in the Americas rose sharply in the second half of the seventeenth century, European competition for trading rights on the West African

coast grew intense. By the end of the century monop-
olies for supplying European plantations in the New
World with their annual quotas of slaves became a
major issue of European diplomacy. The Dutch were
the primary victors in the battle for the West African
slave coast. Hence, for most of the century a majority
of slaves who were fed into the expanding New
World markets found themselves crossing the Atlantic
in Dutch ships.

Not until the last third of the seventeenth century
were the English of any importance in the slave trade.
Major English attempts to break into the profitable
trade began only in 1663, when Charles II, recently
restored to the English throne, granted a charter to
the Royal Adventurers to Africa, a joint-stock company headed by the king's brother, the Duke of York.
Superseded by the Royal African Company in 1672,
these companies enjoyed the exclusive right to carry
slaves to England's overseas plantations. For thirty-
four years after 1663 each of the slaves they brought
across the Atlantic bore the brand "*DY*" for the Duke
of York, who himself became king in 1685. In 1698
the Royal African Company's monopoly was broken
due to the pressure on Parliament by individual merchants who demanded their rights as Englishmen to
participate in the lucrative trade. Thrown open to individual entrepreneurs, the English slave trade grew
enormously. In the 1680s the Royal African Company had transported about 5,000 to 6,000 slaves annually (though interlopers brought in thousands
more). In the first decade of free trade the annual average rose above 20,000. English involvement in the
trade increased for the remainder of the eighteenth
century until by the 1790s England had become the
foremost slave-trading nation in Europe.

☆

Capture and Transport of Slaves

No accounts of the initial enslavement of Africans, no
matter how vivid, can quite convey the pain and de-

moralization that must have accompanied the forced
march to the west coat of Africa and the subsequent
loading aboard ships of those who had fallen captive
to the African suppliers of the European slave traders.
As the demand for African slaves doubled and redou-
bled in the eighteenth century, the hinterlands of
western and central Sudan were invaded again and
again by the armies and agents of both coastal and
interior kings. Perhaps 75 percent of the slaves transported to English North America came from the part
of western Africa that lies between the Senegal and
Niger rivers and the Gulf of Biafra, and most of the
others were enslaved in Angola on the west coast of
Central Africa. Slaving activities in these areas were
responsible for considerable depopulation of the region in the eighteenth and nineteenth centuries.

Once captured, slaves were marched to the sea in
"coffles," or trains. A Scotsman, Mungo Park, described the coffle he marched with for 550 miles
through Gambia at the end of the eighteenth century.
It consisted of 73 men, women, and children tied together by the neck with leather thongs. Several
captives attempted to commit suicide by eating clay,
another was abandoned after being badly stung by
bees; still others died of exhaustion and hunger. After
two months the coffle reached the coast, many of its
members physically depleted by thirst, hunger, and
exposure, where they were herded into fortified en-
closures called barracoons.

The anger, bewilderment, and desolation that accompanied the forced march, the first leg of the
5,000-mile journey to the New World, was only increased by the actual transfer of slaves to European
ship captains, who carried their human cargo in small
wooden ships to the Americas. "As the slaves come
down to Fida from the inland country," wrote one
European trader in the late seventeenth century,
"they are put into a booth or prison, built for that
purpose, near the beach . . . and when the Europeans
are to receive them, they are brought out into a large
plain, where the [ships'] surgeons examine every part
of every one of them, to the smallest member, men

and women being all stark naked. Such as are allowed good and sound, are set on one side, and the others by themselves; which slaves so rejected are called Mackrons, being above 35 years of age, or defective in their lips, eyes, or teeth, or grown grey; or that have the venereal disease, or any other imperfection." Such dehumanizing treatment was part of the commercial process by which "merchandise" was selected and bargained for. But it was also part of the psychological process that attempted to strip away self-respect and self-identity from the Africans.

Cruelty followed cruelty. After purchase, each slave was branded with a hot iron signifying the company, whether Spanish, Portuguese, English, French, or Dutch, that had purchased him or her. Thus were members of "preliterate" societies first introduced to the alphabetic symbols of "advanced" cultures. "The branded slaves," one account related, "are returned to their former booths" where they were imprisoned until a full human cargo could be assembled. The next psychological wrench came with the ferrying of slaves, in large canoes, to the waiting ships at anchor in the harbor. An English captain described the desperation of slaves who were about to lose touch with their ancestral land and embark upon a vast ocean that many had never previously seen. "The Negroes are so wilful and loth to leave their own country, that they have often leap'd out of the canoes, boat and ship, into the sea, and kept under water till they were drowned, to avoid being taken up and saved by our boats, which pursued them; they having a more dreadful apprehension of Barbadoes than we can have of hell." Part of this fear was the common belief that on the other side of the ocean Africans would be eaten by the white savages.

The kind of fear that inspired suicide while still on African soil was prevalent as well on the second leg of the voyage — the "middle passage" from the West African coast to the New World. Conditions aboard ship were miserable, although it was to the advantage of the ship captains to deliver as many slaves as possible on the other side of the Atlantic. The preservation

rather than the destruction of life was the main object, but brutality was systematic, both in pitching overboard any slaves who fell sick on the voyage and in punishing offenders with almost sadistic intensity as a way of creating a climate of fear that would stifle insurrectionist tendencies. John Atkins, aboard an English slaver in 1721, described how the captain "whipped and scarified" several plotters of rebellion and sentenced others "to cruel deaths, making them first eat the Heart and Liver of one of them killed. The Woman he hoisted up by the thumbs, whipp'd and slashed her with Knives, before the other slaves, till she died." Though the naval architects of Europe competed to produce the most efficient ships for carrying human cargoes to the New World, the mortality on board, for both black slaves below decks and white sailors above, was extremely high, averaging between 10 and 20 percent on each voyage.

That Africans frequently attempted suicide and mutiny during the ocean crossing provides evidence that even the extraordinary force used in capturing, branding, selling, and transporting them from one continent to another was not enough to make the captives submit tamely to their fate. An eighteenth-century historian of slavery, attempting to justify the terroristic devices employed by slavers, argued that "the many acts of violence they [the slaves] have committed by murdering whole crews and destroying ships when they had it in their power to do so have made these rigors wholly chargeable on their own bloody and malicious disposition which calls for the same confinement as if they were wolves or wild boars." The modern reader can detect in this characterization of enslaved Africans clear proof that submissiveness was not a trait of those who were forcibly carried to the New World. So great was this resistance that special techniques of torture had to be devised to cope with the thousands of slaves who were determined to starve themselves to death on the middle passage rather than reach the New World in chains. Brutal whippings and hot coals applied to the lips were frequently used to open the mouths of recalci-

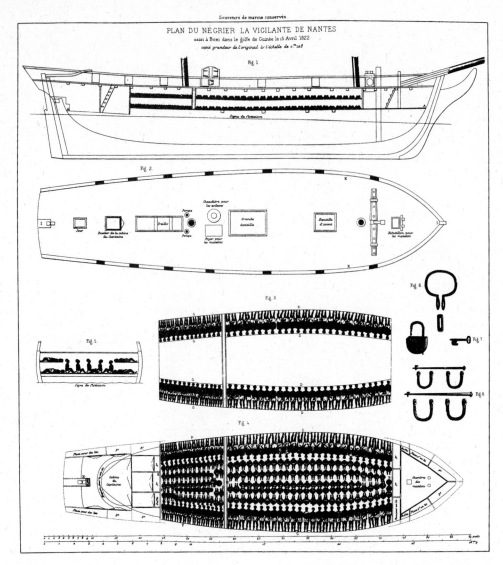

The international slave trade was such an unspeakably brutal business — especially the trip across the Atlantic — that even Southern slaveholders were anxious to outlaw it. Above is a diagram of a slave ship, showing arrangement and padlocks. In recounting a single night on such a ship, an eyewitness wrote of "400 wretched beings . . . crammed into a hold 12 yards in length . . . and only 3½ feet in height." He described how "the suffocating heat of the hold" drove the Negroes to panic in their attempts to escape to the upper air. The next day, he saw 54 "crushed and mangled corpses" lifted up from the slave deck. (Courtesy of The New York Public Library, The Arents Collection)

trant slaves. When this did not suffice, a special instrument, the *speculum oris,* or mouth opener, was employed to wrench apart the jaws of a resistant slave.

Taking into consideration the mortality involved in the capture, the forced march to the coast, and the middle passage, probably not more than one in two captured Africans lived to see the New World. Many of those who did must have been psychologically numbed as well as physically depleted by the experience. But one further step remained in the process of enslavement — the auctioning to a New World master and transportation to his place of residence. All in all, the relocation of any African brought westward across the Atlantic may have averaged about six months from the time of capture to the time of arrival at the plantation of a European slave master. During this protracted personal crisis, the slave was completely cut off from most that was familiar — family, wider kinship relationships, community life, and other forms of social and psychological security. Still facing these victims of the European demand for cheap labor was adaptation to a new physical environment, a new language, new work routines, and, most important, a life in which bondage for themselves and their offspring was unending.

☆

The Development of Slavery in the English Colonies

Even though they were long familiar with Spanish, Dutch, and Portuguese use of African slave labor, English colonists did not turn immediately to Africa to solve the problem of cultivating labor-intensive crops. When they did, it could have caused little surprise, for in enslaving Africans the English were merely copying their European rivals in attempting to fill the colonial labor gap. No doubt the stereotype of Africans as uncivilized made it easier for the English to fasten chains upon them. But the central fact remains that the English were in the New World, like the Spanish, Portuguese, Dutch, and French, to make a fortune as well as to build religious and political havens. Given the long hostility they had borne toward Indians and their experience in enslaving them, any scruples the English might have had about enslaving Africans quickly dissipated.

Making it all the more natural to employ Africans as a slave labor force in the mainland colonies was the precedent that English planters had set on their Caribbean sugar islands. In Barbados, Jamaica, and the Leeward Islands (Antigua, Monserrat, Nevis, and St.

Christopher) Englishmen in the second and third quarters of the seventeenth century learned to copy their European rivals in employing Africans in the sugar fields and, through extraordinary repression, in molding them into a slave labor force. By 1680, when there were not more than 7,000 slaves in mainland North America and the institution of slavery was not yet unalterably fixed, upwards of 65,000 Africans toiled on sugar plantations in the English West Indies. Trade and communication were extensive between the Caribbean and mainland colonists, so settlers in North America had intimate knowledge concerning the potentiality of slave labor.

It is not surprising, then, that the North American colonists turned to the international slave trade to fill their labor needs. Africans were simply the most available people in the world for those seeking a bound labor force and possessed of the power to obtain it. What is surprising, in fact, is that the North American colonists did not turn to slavery more quickly than they did. For more than a half century in Virginia and Maryland it was primarily the white indentured servant and not the African slave who labored in the tobacco fields. Moreover, those blacks who were imported before about 1660 were held in various degrees of servitude, most for limited periods and a few for life.

The transformation of the labor force in the Southern colonies, from one in which many white and a relatively small number of black indentured servants labored together to one in which black slaves served for a lifetime and composed the bulk of unfree labor, came only in the last third of the seventeenth century in Virginia and Maryland and in the first third of the eighteenth century in North Carolina and South Carolina. The reasons for this shift to a slave-based agricultural economy in the South are twofold. First, English entry into the African slave trade gave the Southern planter an opportunity to purchase slaves more readily and more cheaply than before. Cheap labor was what every tobacco or rice planter sought, and when the price of slave labor dipped below that of indentured labor, the demand for black slaves increased. Also, the supply of white servants from England began to dry up in the late seventeenth century, and those who did cross the Atlantic were spread among a growing number of colonies. Thus, in the late seventeenth century the number of Africans imported into the Chesapeake colonies began to grow and the flow of white indentured servants diminished to a trickle. As late as 1671 slaves made up less than 5 percent of Virginia's population and were outnumbered at least three to one by white indentured servants. In Maryland the situation was much the same. But within a generation, by about 1700, they represented one-fifth of the population and probably a majority of the labor force. A Maryland census of 1707 tabulated 3,003 white bound laborers and 4,657 black slaves. Five years later the slave population had almost doubled. Within another generation white indentured servants were declining rapidly in number, and in all the Southern colonies African slaves made up the backbone of the agricultural work force. "These two words, *Negro* and *slave*," wrote one Virginian, had "by custom grown Homogenous and Convertible."

To the north, in Pennsylvania, New Jersey, and Delaware, where English colonists had settled only in the last third of the seventeenth century, slavery existed on a more occasional basis, since labor-intensive crops were not as extensively grown in these areas and the cold winters brought farming to a halt. New York was an exception and shows how a cultural preference could alter labor patterns that were usually determined by ecological factors. During the period before 1664 when the colony was Dutch, slaveholding had been practiced extensively, encouraged in part by the Dutch West India Company, one of the chief international suppliers of slaves. The population of New York remained largely Dutch for the remainder of the century, and the English who slowly filtered in saw no reason not to imitate Dutch slave owners. Thus New York became the largest importer of slaves north of Maryland. In the mid-eighteenth century, the areas of original settlement around New York and Albany remained slaveholding societies with about 20 percent of the population composed of slaves and 30 to 40 percent of the white householders owning human property.

As the number of slaves increased, legal codes for strictly controlling their activities were fashioned in each of the colonies. To a large extent these "black codes" were borrowed from the law books of the English West Indies. Bit by bit they deprived the African immigrant — and a small number of Indian slaves as well — of rights enjoyed by others in the society, including indentured servants. Gradually they reduced the slave, in the eyes of society and the law, from a human being to a piece of chattel property. In this process of dehumanization nothing was more important than the practice of hereditary life-time service. Once servitude became perpetual, relieved only by death, then the stripping away of all other rights followed as a matter of course. When the condition of the slave parent was passed on to the child, then slavery had been extended to the womb. At that point the institution became totally fixed so far as the slave was concerned.

Thus, with the passage of time, Africans in North America had to adapt to a more and more circumscribed world. Earlier in the seventeenth century they had been treated much as indentured servants, bound to labor for a specified period of years but thereafter free to work for themselves, hire out their labor, buy land, move as they pleased, and, if they wished, hold slaves themselves. But, by the 1640s, Virginia was forbidding blacks the use of firearms. In the 1660s marriages between white women and black slaves were being described as "shameful Matches" and "the Disgrace of our Nation"; during the next few decades interracial fornication became subject to unusually severe punishment and interracial marriage was banned.

These discriminatory steps were slight, however, in comparison with the stripping away of rights that began toward the end of the century. In rapid succession slaves lost their right to testify before a court; to engage in any kind of commercial activity, either as buyer or seller; to hold property; to participate in the political process; to congregate in public places with more than two or three of their fellows; to travel without permission; and to engage in legal marriage or parenthood. In some colonies legislatures even prohibited the right to education and religion, for they thought these might encourage the germ of freedom in slaves. More and more steps were taken to contain them tightly in a legal system that made no allowance for their education, welfare, or future advancement. The restraints on the slave owner's freedom to deal with slaves in any way he or she saw fit were gradually cast away. Early in the eighteenth century many colonies passed laws forbidding the manumission of slaves by individual owners. This was a step designed to squelch the strivings of slaves for freedom and to discourage those who had been freed from helping fellow Africans to gain their liberty.

The movement to annul all the slave's rights had both pragmatic and psychological dimensions. The greater the proportion of slaves in the population, the greater the danger to white society, for every colonist knew that when he purchased a man or woman in chains he had bought a potential insurrectionist. The larger the specter of black revolt, the greater the effort of white society to neutralize it by further restricting the rights and activities of slaves. Thus, following a black revolt in 1712 that took the lives of nine whites and wounded others, the New York legislature passed a slave code that rivaled those of the Southern colonies. Throughout the Southern colonies the obsessive fear of slave insurrection ushered in institutionalized violence as the means of ensuring social stability. Allied to this need for greater and greater control was the psychological compulsion to dehumanize slaves by taking from them the rights that connoted their humanity. It was far easier to rationalize the merciless exploitation of those who had been defined by law as something less than human. "The planters," wrote an Englishman in eighteenth-century Jamaica, "do not want to be told that their Negroes are human creatures. If they believe them to be of human kind, they cannot regard them . . . as no better than dogs or horses."

Thus occurred one of the great paradoxes in American history — the building of what some thought was to be a utopia in the wilderness upon the backs of black men and women wrenched from their African homeland and forced into a system of abject slavery. America was imagined as a liberating and regenerating force, it has been pointed out, but became the scene of a "grotesque inconsistency." In the land heralded for freedom and individual opportunity, the practice of slavery, unknown for centuries in the mother country, was reinstituted. Following other parts of the New World, North America became the scene of "a disturbing retrogression from the course of historical progress."

The mass enslavement of Africans profoundly affected white racial prejudice. Once institutionalized, slavery cast Africans into such lowly roles that the initial bias against them could only be confirmed and vastly strengthened. Initially unfavorable impressions of Africans had coincided with labor needs to bring about their mass enslavement. But it required slavery itself to harden the negative racial feelings into a deep and almost unshakable prejudice that continued to grow for centuries. The colonizers had devised a labor system that kept the African in the Americas at the bottom of the social and economic pyramid. Irrevocably caught in the web of perpetual servitude, the slave was allowed no further opportunity to prove the white stereotype wrong. Socially and legally defined as less than people, kept in a degraded and debased position, virtually without power in their relationships with white society, Afro-Americans became a truly servile, ignoble, degraded people in the eyes of the Europeans. This was used as further reason to keep them in slavery, for it was argued that they were worth nothing better and were incapable of occupying any higher role. In this long evolution of racial attitudes in America, nothing was of greater importance than the enslavement of Africans.

QUESTIONS TO CONSIDER

1. How did conditions in the New World transform the traditional character of the slave trade? why? What crop had a particular effect, and why did it become so important in international trade?

2. What effects did the sudden growth of the slave trade in the seventeenth century have on conditions in Europe? in Africa? What had African culture been like before the seventeenth century? How had it compared with European culture?

3. Describe the conditions of the Atlantic slave trade. What was the purpose of physical cruelty in the slave trade? What do you think it would have been like to be an African stolen from his or her native land and taken across the middle passage? What might be the physical and psychological effects of such an experience?

4. By what process did black slavery gradually become established in the British North American colonies? How were the colonies unusual in this? Why did it develop less in the North than in the southern colonies? Why was New York an exception?

5. How does Gary Nash believe that slavery and racial prejudice influenced each other? What are the implications of his conclusions for the subsequent history of America up to the present day?

TRANSFORMATIONS

5

The Transformation of European Society

Gary B. Nash

In all, Americans lived for 169 years under British rule. To place the colonial era in chronological perspective, this is the number of years that elapsed between John Quincy Adams's election to the presidency in 1824 and Bill Clinton's inauguration as president in 1993. In this selection, Gary Nash examines some of the momentous economic, social, and religious changes that occurred in North America during the last decades of British rule. In 1650, as Nash points out elsewhere, the population of the English colonies ran to about fifty thousand — "about the same as the daytime population of a large university campus today." But by 1750, thanks to a continuous stream of immigration from Europe and Africa, the colonial population had leaped to 1,125,000, including 240,000 blacks. As Nash says, this remarkable growth, unparalleled anywhere in the world at that time, encouraged Benjamin Franklin to speculate that one day the population of colonial America would surpass that of England itself.

By the eighteenth century, as Nash says, the colonists had transformed the European attitudes and social structures they had brought with them into something uniquely American. This "transformation of European society" had much to do with the abundance and availability of land in North America, which allowed quite ordinary people to acquire real estate and aspire to fortunes and higher stations in life. As Nash points out, two different forms of agricultural society emerged in eighteenth-century English America. There was the farming and artisan society of the North, where slaves were few and most free men — those who were not indentured servants — could boast of owning at least a fifty-acre farm. Here the Protestant work ethic, which celebrated hard work, thrift, and individual economic enterprise, took hold. In the South, by contrast, a slave-based, planter-dominated society emerged. "But," Nash warns us, "the usual picture of a Southern plantation society made up of immensely wealthy men exploiting the labor of huge gangs of black slaves is badly overdrawn." He observes that perhaps 40 percent of southern white men were nonslave-holding farm workers or tenant farmers — those who rented or leased their land. Any many more were independent small farmers, often called yeomen, who raised the same crops as the planters did. Only about 5 percent of southern white landowners were wealthy planters — those who owned twenty or more slaves and sizable plantations. Even so — and this is a crucial point — owning slaves was a potent status symbol, and the slave-holding planter was the role model in the South, the "ideal" to which other white men aspired. And planters and yeomen alike "were as avid in the pursuit of wealth and material comfort" as were their neighbors in the North.

The remarkable growth of the English colonies, as Nash says, had dramatic consequences. First, it destroyed "the utopian dream" of the seventeenth-century colonists that communities should consist of people who worked for the common good, not simply for individual success. Driven by the Protestant work ethic and apparently unlimited opportunity, eighteenth-century colonists celebrated the individual pursuit of wealth, the idea of every man for himself. As a result, Nash says, "the individual replaced the community as the conceptual unit of thought." Thus was born the "democratic personality, brash, assertive, individualistic, and competitive." And that personality would shape the entire course of American history and thought.

Second, Nash says, economic and population growth — and the emphasis on aggressive individualism — altered the very structure of colonial society. The traditional notion of a God-ordained "hierarchy in human affairs" gave way to a more fluid social structure and the ideal of egalitarianism, that is, of "the equality of all men." As Nash points out, most Americans "below the elite free whites" believed that they were creating a society free of class rule. But this, as Nash says, was the ideal, not the reality, of eighteenth-century colonial America. In reality, the abundance of opportunity allowed the rich to get richer at the expense of the poor and led to a concentration of wealth in the hands of the few. Such "aggrandizement of wealth" was to haunt America's capitalist system for generations to come.

In the last section of his essay, Nash analyzes the great religious and social upheaval in the 1730s and 1740s known as the Great Awakening, which he sees as a cultural crisis that resulted from decades of economic and social change and from the fear that American churches, as William McLoughlin put it, "no longer met the spiritual needs of the people." The Awakening was thus a rebellion against religious authority and dogma. As another historian said, it was "a search for new sources of authority, new principles of action, new foundations of hope." It unleashed "the greatest flow of religious energy since the Puritan movement" in Europe in the sixteenth and seventeenth centuries and transformed the structure and attitudes of colonial religion into something uniquely American.

Among the "middling sort," or middle class, the Awakening represented something more. It represented "a groundswell of individualism" and skepticism of authority that anticipated the American Revolution.

GLOSSARY

DAVENPORT, JAMES   Itinerant preacher during the Great Awakening.

EDWARDS, JONATHAN   Massachusetts Congregational minister who rejected the new religious ideas of "easy salvation for all" and preached traditional Calvinist doctrine — the sovereignty of God, the innate depravity of people, the notion of the elect, and predestination.

EGALITARIANISM   The doctrine of "the equality of all men."

FREEHOLDER   One who owned a landed estate for life.

INNER LIGHT   The Quaker belief that one can find spiritual understanding and guidance through the light within one's self, which the Holy Spirit provides.

ITINERANT PREACHER   One who traveled from place to place, spreading the word of God.

PLANTER   Wealthy southerner who owned a sizable plantation and twenty or more slaves.

WHITEFIELD, GEORGE   English Methodist leader who helped ignite the Great Awakening in America.

YEOMAN FARMER   Small farmer, or lesser freeholder.

☆

LAND, GROWTH, AND CHANGING VALUES

Out of the combination of fertile land; a pool of bound laborers, white, black, and red; and the ambition of thousands of small farmers and artisans who labored independently, two variants of agricultural society emerged in eighteenth-century North America. In the North, small communities made up of farmers and artisans dotted the landscape. New Englanders engaged in mixed farming, which included farming the forests for timber used in barrels and ships, and farming the offshore waters for fish that provided one of the staples in the diet of the fast-growing slave population of the West Indies. The Middle Colonies specialized in producing corn, wheat, beef, and pork. By mid-eighteenth century they were provisioning not only the West Indies but also parts of Spain, Portugal, and England. Slaves were few in number in most of the Northern communities, rarely representing more than 5 percent of the population. A large percentage of free men owned land; and, though differences in ability and circumstances led gradually to greater social and economic stratification, the truly rich and abjectly poor were few in number and the gap between them was small in comparison to European society. Most men lived to acquire a farm of at least fifty acres. They ex-

From Gary B. Nash, *Red, White, and Black: The Peoples of Early North America* (3rd ed., Prentice-Hall 1992), 201–225.

tracted from the soil a modest income that allowed for security from want and provided a small inheritance for their children.

In the Southern colonies, where tobacco, rice, indigo, and timber products predominated, many yeomen farmers also struggled independently, although they were more frequently dispersed across the land than clustered in villages. These men have been far less noticed by historians than the plantation owners with slaves and indentured servants who lived along the rivers and streams that flowed from the Piedmont through the coastal plain to the ocean. But the usual picture of a Southern plantation society made up of immensely wealthy men exploiting the labor of huge gangs of black slaves is badly overdrawn. Perhaps as many as 40 percent of the Southern white males worked as tenant farmers or agricultural laborers, and of the remaining men who owned land, about two out of every three in the Chesapeake region worked farms of two hundred acres or less. In North Carolina farms were even smaller and men of real wealth rarer. In South Carolina the opposite was true; slaveholding was more widespread, plantations tended to be larger, and planters of substantial wealth represented a larger proportion of the population. As early as 1726 in St. George's Parish 87 of 108 families held slaves. . . .

On the whole, probably not more than 5 percent of the white landowners were wealthy enough by the mid-eighteenth century to possess a plantation worth £1,000 — not too different from the North. Similarly, those owning large numbers of slaves were not as numerous as we commonly think. The number of Southern slaves increased rapidly in the eighteenth century, rising from about 20,000 in 1700 to 240,000 in 1750. But a majority of white adult males held no slaves at all at mid-century, and those who operated plantations with more than twenty slaves probably did not exceed 10 percent of the white taxables. South Carolina excepted, the South throughout the pre-Revolutionary period was dominated numerically by small landowners whose holdings, if perhaps twice the size of the average New England farm, were not more

In eighteenth-century British America, "the individual replaced the community as the conceptual unit of thought." When a European first arrived, wrote a New York resident, "he no sooner breathes our air than he forms schemes, and embarks in designs he never would have thought of in his own country." This portrait by John Singleton Copley captures the individualistic spirit of eighteenth-century colonial America. (Courtesy of the Museum of Fine Arts, Boston)

than half again as large as the typical farm in Pennsylvania, New Jersey, or New York.

Nonetheless, the ideal in the South, if not the reality, was the large plantation where black slaves would make the earth yield up profits sufficient to support the leisured life. Statistically speaking, not many white colonists in the South achieved the dream. But that is what people worked for, and they came to identify the quest for material comfort with the exploitation of African slave labor in an era when the Northern colonists were beginning to phase out white bound labor and turning to a market economy where both goods and labor were freely exchanged.

The Protestant work ethic, which purportedly propelled people upward by inculcating a life of frugality, industriousness, and highly rationalized economic activity, perhaps operated less compellingly in the psyches of Southern colonists than in their Northern counterparts. But the abundant, fertile land of the South and the wider availability of slaves after 1690 provided all the incentive necessary for an aggressive, competitive society to develop. Much folklore about Southern cavaliers reposing under magnolia trees has been handed down in the history books, but in the eighteenth century European colonizers in the South were as avid in the pursuit of wealth and material comfort as European colonizers in the North. If the warm climate of the South bred languor, it was also true that farmers in the South had no long frozen winters when there was little to do but mend harness and chop wood. The typical New England farm produced just one crop each year; but a South Carolina rice or indigo plantation produced two. Moreover, the restraints of a New England community orientation and the Puritan bias against the accumulation of wealth which was not disposed of in socially useful ways never hindered entrepreneurial activity in the South. Organized religion was only shallowly rooted in most of the Southern colonies and the community orientation never took hold because communities themselves were few and far between.

Paradoxically, one of the effects of the growth and success of the colonies in eighteenth-century British America was to shatter the utopian dream of the first generation that communities could be built where men and women worked for the commonweal, not only for themselves. The Puritan work ethic and an atmosphere of seemingly limitless opportunity encouraged men to work arduously at their callings. That was to the good. And their labors had generally been rewarded with success. So was that. But living where the ratio of people to land was so favorable compared to the societies from which they came, many colonists developed an aggressive outlook that patterned their behavior. What was to hold a man

back in these uncharted expanses of land and unclaimed river valleys, as soon as the Indians were gone? In Europe, the absence of uncultivated lands ripe for exploitation and the grinding poverty that enshrouded the lives of the great mass of people produced in the peasant consciousness a very low level of expectations. "The frontier zone between possibility and impossibility barely moved in any significant direction, from the fifteenth to the eighteenth century," writes Fernand Braudel. But it moved in North America. The new concept was of a society where anything was possible. A competitive, entrepreneurial spirit began to take hold.

Religion and commitment to community, which acted as brakes on competitive, individualistic behavior, were by no means dead in the eighteenth century. But in general, piety, in terms of defining one's life as a preparation for the afterlife, declined greatly. Even in the seventeenth century Roger Williams had deplored the "depraved appetite after the great vanities, dreams, and shadows of this vanishing life, great portions of land, land in this wilderness, as if men were in as great necessity and danger for want of great portions of land, as poor, hungry seamen have, after a sick and stormy, a long and starving passage." In the eighteenth century land became ever more regarded not simply as a source of livelihood but a commodity to be bought and sold speculatively as a means of building a fortune. It was Franklin's little how-to-do-it best-seller, *The Way to Wealth,* that caught the spirit of the aggressive entrepreneurial eighteenth century. The brakes on economic ambition had been suddenly removed and with the decline of fervid Puritanism in the eighteenth century there was little left to restrain predatory instincts in those who were eager to pit themselves against their fellows in the pursuit of material gain. "Every man is for himself," lamented a prominent Philadelphian in 1706, only a generation after Penn had planted the seed of his "holy experiment." Two generations later the lieutenant-governor of New York, who had grown up in the colony, put it more explicitly: "The only principle of life propagated among the young people," wrote Cadwallader Colden, "is to get money and men are only esteemed according to what they are worth — that is the money they are possessed of." A contemporary in Rhode Island echoed the thought when he wrote "A Man who has Money here, no matter how he came by it, he is Everything, and wanting [lacking] that he's a meer Nothing, let his Conduct be ever so ereproachable."

As these acquisitive values took hold, the individual replaced the community as the conceptual unit of thought. The advice of the ancestors, such as the Puritan minister John Cotton, to "goe forth, every man that goeth, with a public spirit, looking not on your owne things only," or Winthrop's maxim that "the care of the publick must oversway all private respects," carried less and less weight in eighteenth-century society. The conquest of the wilderness and its inhabitants had proceeded far enough, men had shown enough adaptability and endurance for a hundred years, and the future possibilities seemed so great that a mental set developed in which colonial Americans appeared bent upon proving wrong the Elizabethan poet, John Donne, who counseled that no man could survive as an island unto himself. Having gained something, the typical colonist wanted more. A French visitor, who took up residence in New York, described this psychological reorientation:

An European, when he first arrives, seems limited in his intentions, as well as in his views; but he very suddenly alters his scale. . . . He no sooner breathes our air than he forms schemes, and embarks in designs he never would have thought of in his own country. . . . He begins to feel the effects of a sort of resurrection; hitherto he had not lived, but simply vegetated; he now feels himself a man, because he is treated as such;. . . . he begins to forget his former servitude and dependence. . . .

Paradoxically, this transformation of attitudes, while it helped promote phenomenal growth and unleashed economic energies, led toward material success that contained within it the seeds of social strain. The demand for land east of the Appalachian Mountain barrier grew rapidly after 1740, as the population rose rapidly through immigration and natural increase. Especially in New England, ungranted land in the coastal region was a thing of the past, and the division and redivision of original land grants among sons and grandsons had progressed as far as it could go without splitting farms into unviably small economic units. New land — on the Maine frontier, in western Massachusetts and Connecticut, across the Appalachians in Pennsylvania, Virginia, Maryland, and the Carolinas — was the obvious solution to the problem of overcrowding. With the saturation of the Eastern coastal plain making the lands of the interior more attractive, land companies were formed in the mid-eighteenth century. They laid claim, however flimsy, to the valuable Western lands, their investors understanding the enormous appreciation in value that would occur as the next generation came of age and sought *lebensraum* to the west.* But before a westward movement could begin, interior Indian peoples, as well as the French and Spanish, had to be overcome. . . .

☆

CHANGING SOCIAL STRUCTURE

Population growth and economic development, carried on for a century and a half by aggressive and opportunistic individuals, changed both the structure of colonial society and the attitudes of the people toward social structure — but changed them in opposite directions. Seventeenth-century Europeans on both sides of the Atlantic accepted the naturalness of hierarchy in human affairs, the inevitability of poverty, and the right of those in the upper stratum of society to rule those below them. The belief was general that

---

Lebensraum means territorial expansion to extend trade — Ed.

social gradations and internal subordination were not only sanctioned by God but were also essential to the maintenance of social stability and cohesion. Therefore care was taken to differentiate individuals by dress, by titles, in social etiquette, and even in penalties imposed in criminal proceedings. Puritans, for example, did not simply file into church on Sunday mornings and occupy the pews in random fashion. Instead, each seat was assigned according to the social rank of the person in the community. "Dooming the seats," as the assignment process was aptly called, was the responsibility of a church committee, which used every available yardstick of social respectability — age, parentage, social position, service to the community, and wealth — in drawing up a seating plan for the congregation. Puritans never entered their church without being reminded where they stood in the ranks of the community.

In spite of the philosophical commitment to hierarchy, the early European immigrants in North America were notably undifferentiated in their social makeup. Immigrant society was strongly lower-middle class in its composition, and the wide availability of land, combined with the lack of opportunities to amass great fortunes (when one had only his own labor and that of his wife, children, and a servant or two) kept the spectrum of wealth relatively narrow throughout most of the seventeenth century. Even in the cities, where the redistribution of wealth proceeded the fastest, the dawn of the eighteenth century witnessed a colonial society that was overwhelmingly middle class in character. In the Hudson River Valley and in the Southern colonies a handful of large plantation owners had made their mark, but the largest slave owners in Virginia at the beginning of the eighteenth century still owned fewer than one hundred slaves and not more than a handful of men had as much as £2,000 to leave to their heirs. As late as 1722 one of Philadelphia's richest merchants died with personal possessions worth just over £1,000 — a sizeable estate but unimpressive by European standards.

In the eighteenth century, and especially in the half century before the Revolution, the customary commitment to hierarchy and deference waned at the same time that stratification in society was increasing. Social attitudes and social structure were moving in opposite directions. Below the elite free whites developed the ideal of egalitarianism. The middling sort of people, wrote a Philadelphian in 1756, "enjoy and are fond of freedom, and the meanest among them thinks he has a right to civility from the greatest." Such comments were common. The Frenchman, Crèvecoeur, was surprised to see hired workers who "must be at your table and feed . . . on the best you have," and the schoolteacher Philip Fithian wrote of "labourers at the tables and in the parlours of their betters enjoying the advantage, and honour of their society and conversation."

Europeans judged what they saw against what they had known at home and thus sometimes exaggerated the degree of egalitarianism that they thought they saw. But it was true that most American colonists believed they were creating a society where a wealthy aristocracy did not dominate and no masses of poor whites were ground into the dust. The ideal was a rough economic equality where each person would have enough and a social equality "in which invidious discriminations would be abolished." When Benjamin Franklin toured the English countryside in 1772 he was appalled at what he saw and raised thanks that America was different. He described "landlords, great noblemen, and gentlemen, extremely opulent, living in the highest affluence and magnificence" alongside "the bulk of the people, tenants, extremely poor, living in the most sordid wretchedness, in dirty hovels of mud and straw, and clothed only in rags." Franklin could only shake his head and take solace in the knowledge that North America was different. Ignoring Indians and Africans, he wrote: "I thought often of the happiness of New England, where every Man is a Freeholder, has a Vote in publick Affairs, lives in a tidy, warm House, has plenty of good Food and fewel, with whole cloaths from Head to Foot, the

Manufacture perhaps of his own Family." The German Mittelberger summed up the twin ideals of economic equality and democratic scorn for authorities and authoritarian institutions. Pennsylvania, he said, was "heaven for farmers, paradise for artisans, and hell for officials and preachers."

All these commentators occupied favorable positions in society, which may account for the fact that they were describing not the reality but the ideal of colonial life. The reality, in fact, was that eighteenth-century society, even for white colonists, was moving away from the ideal. As the old deferential attitudes gave way to brash, assertive, individualistic modes of thought and behavior — what would become known as "the democratic personality" — society became more stratified, wealth became less evenly distributed, and impressively rich and truly impoverished classes emerged. Population growth and economic development in the eighteenth century made rich men of those with capital to speculate in land, buy slaves and servants, or participate in trade. The aggrandizement of wealth became clearly apparent in all sections of the country — North and South, rural and urban. In Boston, Newport, New York, Philadelphia, and Charleston stately townhouses rose as testimony to the fortunes being acquired in trade, shipbuilding, and land speculation. Probably the last of these was the most profitable of all. "It is almost a proverb," wrote a Philadelphian in 1767, "that Every great fortune made here within these 50 years has been by land." By the late colonial period it was not unusual to find merchant-land speculators with estates valued at £10,000–£20,000. Even in the rural areas of the North wealthy farmers amassed estates worth £4,000–£5,000. In the South, plantation magnates built even larger fortunes, for the rapid importation of African slaves after 1720 accelerated the rate at which profits could be extracted from the cultivation of tobacco or rice. By the eve of the Revolution the great planters of the Chesapeake region, men such as Charles Carroll, Robert "King" Carter, and William Byrd, had achieved spectacular affluence. Their estates, valued at £100,000 or more, were equivalent in purchasing power to a fortune of about six million dollars in 1990. It was not unusual to see 300 to 400 slaves toiling on such plantations, whereas in the late seventeenth century the largest slaveholder on the continent had no more than 50 bound laborers.

While the rapid increase in population and large-scale capital investment in land and slaves enabled a small number of men to accumulate fortunes that would have been noteworthy even in English society, the development of colonial society also created conditions in which a growing number of persons were finding it difficult to keep bread on the table and wood in the fireplace. This was especially true in the cities, where the social stratification proceeded most rapidly. All the major cities built almshouses and workhouses in the second quarter of the century to provide for those who could not care for themselves — the aged, indigent, sick, insane, and orphaned. Between 1725 and 1760, however, the poor in the cities increased more rapidly than the urban population as a whole, and after about 1750 poverty was no longer confined to the old or physically depleted. . . .

Inexorably the expanding economy and the individualistic values incorporated in the society tended to favor the aggressive and able in their drive toward material success. The greater the opportunities — a primary characteristic of a democratic society — the greater the gulf became between the rich and the poor. The growth of cultural and political egalitarianism was accompanied by, and indirectly sanctioned, the decline of economic equality. An open society with ample opportunities in the eighteenth century for entrepreneurship, and with relatively few restraints imposed by government, led, paradoxically, to a concentration of economic power in the hands of a thin upper layer of society. Becoming a society in which the individual and not the common weal was the central concern, the white population of colonial North America was transforming what they thought to be uniquely American into what resembled more and more the European conditions they had fled.

The differing abilities of men to manipulate their economic environment, capitalize on the freedom to exploit white and black labor, and obtain title to Indian land were eventually recorded on the tax lists of the community where each man's wealth was set alongside that of his neighbors. Colonial historians have scrutinized those tax lists that have survived and have found that population growth and economic development led toward a less even distribution of wealth and an increase in the proportion of those without property in virtually every community. The change occurred slowly in rural areas and proceeded more rapidly in the seaboard centers of commercial activity.

In the rural town of Northampton, Massachusetts, for example, the upper 10 percent of property owners controlled 25 percent of the taxable wealth in 1676 and slowly increased their control of the community's assets to 34 percent in 1759. At the same time the proportion of the community's taxable property owned by the bottom third of the society remained steady at about 10 percent. . . .

In the cities the rate of change was far greater. Boston's upper tenth in 1687 held 46 percent of the taxable property while the lowest 30 percent had a meager 2.6 percent of the wealth. Four generations later, in 1771, the top tenth had 63 percent of the wealth; the lowest three-tenths had virtually nothing — a mere tenth of one percent of the community's taxable resources. Economic polarization in Boston, where the population was static after 1735 and economic recession hit hard at many elements of the community, was duplicated in vigorously expanding Philadelphia. In 1693, little more than a decade after settlement, the wealthiest tenth laid claim to 46 percent of the city's wealth. Three quarters of a century later, in 1772, they possessed 71 percent of the taxable wealth. As in Boston, these gains were not made at the expense of those in the bottom third of society, who possessed only a meager 2.2 percent of the wealth in 1693, but were accomplished at the expense of those in the middling elements of society.

If poverty touched the lives of a growing part of the urban laboring class, it was the usual condition on the frontier. Here the gap between rich and poor hardly existed because the rich were nowhere to be found. In its social order the frontier of the mid-eighteenth century was even cruder than rural society on the edge of the continent a century before. Whether in the towns of western Massachusetts and Connecticut, founded in the second and third quarters of the eighteenth century by the sons of Yankee farmers; or the lands along the Mohawk River in New York and the Susquehannah River in Pennsylvania, which represented the hopes of the German and Scots-Irish immigrants; or the backcountry of Maryland, Virginia, and the Carolinas, which sponged up some 250,000 souls in the late colonial period, frontier society was composed of small farmers and rural artisans who all stood roughly on the same plane. They purchased land cheaply, often for as little as four shillings an acre, and struggled to carve farms from the wilderness. Many hoped to get enough land under cultivation within a few years to produce surplus crops for market. But with only the help of one's sons and a few farm animals this often took most of a man's life. Others struggled only to make enough improvements on a piece of land so that other settlers pushing westward on the next wave of settlement would find it attractive enough to pay a price that rewarded one's labor.

On the New England frontier, where people pushed westward in groups, they founded new towns and churches as they went, quickly reproducing the institutions of eastern society. While poor, these simple villagers and farmers lived a life where institutional ligaments had not been altogether severed. But southward from New York on the east side of the Appalachian slopes frontier society existed in what many observers took to be a semibarbarous state. William Byrd described one of the largest plantations on the Virginia frontier in 1733 as "a poor dirty hovel, with hardly anything in it but children that wallowed about like so many pigs." Charles Woodmason, an itinerant Anglican minister who spent three years tramping from settlement to settlement in the Carolina backcountry in the 1760s, was appalled at what he found. "For thro' want of Ministers to marry and thro' the licentiousness of the People, many hundreds live in Concubinage — swopping their Wives as Cattel, and living in a State of Nature, more irregularly and unchastely than the Indians." As an English Anglican, Woodmason carried with him all the prejudices that were usually harbored against the Presbyterian Scots-Irish, the main inhabitants of the region. But there is little reason to doubt that the crudeness of life he described actually existed. After preaching at Flat Creek to "a vast Body of people . . . Such a Medley! such a mixed Multitude of all Classes and Complexions," he paled at their afterservice "Revelling Drinking Singing Dancing and Whoring" and threw up his hands that "most of the Company were drunk before I quitted the Spot — They were as rude in their Manners as the Common Savages, and hardly a degree removed from them." Some of what he saw made him close his eyes in horror, but he kept them open long enough to observe the young women who "have a most uncommon Practise. . . . They draw their Shift as tight as possible to the Body, and pin it close, to shew the roundness of their Breasts, and . . . their Petticoat close to their Hips to shew the fineness of their Limbs — so that they might as well be in Puri Naturalibus — Indeed Nakedness is not censurable or indecent here, and they expose themselves often quite Naked, without Ceremony — Rubbing themselves and their Hair with Bears Oil and tying it up behind in a Bunch like the Indians — being hardly one degree removed from them."

THE GREAT AWAKENING

Nowhere did the line between social and economic change on the one hand and religion on the other crumble more swiftly than in the experiential and ideological upheaval called the Great Awakening.

The Great Awakening erupted in full force when the English evangelist George Whitefield barnstormed the coast of North America, evoking an unprecedented mass response. This painting shows his spellbinding effect on congregations. (By courtesy of the National Portrait Gallery, London)

More than a solely religious movement, this period of sustained religious enthusiasm must be seen as a profound cultural crisis that had been building for several generations.

At its core the Great Awakening was "a search for new sources of authority, new principles of action, new foundations of hope" among people who had come to believe that the colonial churches "no longer met the spiritual needs of the people." The Awakeners preached that the old sources of authority were too effete to solve the problems of the day, too encrusted with tradition, hypocrisy, and intellectualism to bring hope and faith to a generation that was witnessing the rapid transformation of the world of their fathers. A new wellspring of authority was needed, and that source, the evangelists preached, was the individual himself. Like the Quaker "inner light," which dwelled in every man and woman, the "new light" within the awakened would enable them to achieve grace through the conversion experience. When enough people were "born again," as the evangelists of the Great Awakening phrased it, a new sense of community would be forged, a new brotherhood of man achieved, and the city on the hill restored. The Awakening, in its way, was a "revitalization movement," similar to those that would occur periodically in Indian societies, as attempts were made to reject corrosive new ways and return to the traditions of the past.

The Awakening had its first stirrings in the colonies in the 1720s in New Jersey and Pennsylvania and then in the 1730s in Jonathan Edwards' church in Northampton, Massachusetts. But it was not until 1739, with the arrival of George Whitefield from England, that it struck with full force. Whitefield was a master of open-air preaching and had trekked across the English countryside for several years preaching the word of God. A diminutive man with a magnificent voice, he began a barnstorminig trip along the coast of North America in 1739 that evoked a mass response of a sort never witnessed before in the colonies. Thousands turned out to see him, and with each success his fame grew. Especially in the cities, which were the crucibles of social change, his effect was extraordinary, as people fought for places in the churches to hear him or congregated by the thousands in open fields to receive his message.

Some of Whitefield's appeal can be attributed to his genius for dramatic performances, his perfection of the art of advanced publicity, and his ability to simplify theological doctrine and focus the attention of masses of people on one facet of religious life — the conversion experience. In his electrifying performances, where written sermons were cast away, where spastic body movements and magnificent voice control replaced dry, logical, rigidly structured sermons, thousands experienced the desire to "fly to Christ." But it was the message as well as the medium that explains why people flocked to hear Whitefield. He frontally assaulted traditional sources of authority, called upon people to become the instruments of their own salvation, and implicitly attacked the upper-class notion that the simple folk had no minds of their own.

When Whitefield began his American tour in 1739, the social dynamite buried deep in his message was not yet clearly perceived by the elite. After all, his preaching produced thousands of conversions and filled the churches that had been languishing for more than a generation. Whitefield magnified the importance of religion in almost everyone who heard him, so it is no wonder that he was welcomed as "an angel of God, or as Elias, or John the Baptist risen from the dead." But Whitefield's popularity soon waned among the gentry because he was followed by itinerant Awakeners whose social radicalism was far less muted and because of the effects the evangelists' message had on the lower orders. Roaming preachers like Gilbert Tennant infused evangelical preaching with a radical egalitarianism that left many former supporters of Whitefield sputtering. Tennant attacked the established clergy as unregenerate and encouraged people to forsake their ministers. "The sapless Discourses of such dead Drones" were worthless, he proclaimed. James Davenport, another itinerant preacher, told huge crowds that they should drink rat poison rather than listen to the corrupt clergy. Even more dangerous, Davenport indicted the rich and powerful, criticized the growing gap between rich and poor, and exhorted ordinary people to resist those who exploited and deceived them. Only then, he cried, would the Lamb Jesus return to earth.

Crowds followed Davenport through the towns, singing and clapping so that "they look'd more like a Company of *Bacchanalians* after a mad Frolick, than sober Christians who had been worshipping God," as one distressed Boston newspaper complained. Respectable people were convinced that revivalism had gotten out of hand and that social control of the lowest layers of society was crumbling. Revivalism had started out as a return to religion among backsliding Christians but now was turning into a social experience that profoundly threatened the established culture, which stressed order, discipline, and submissiveness from laboring people. The fear of the Awakeners' attacks on genteel literate culture, on wealth and ostentatious living, was epitomized in New London, Connecticut in 1743 when Davenport scandalized the gentry by inducing a huge crowd

to burn "sundry good and useful treatises, books of practical godliness, the works of able divines," as well as "hoop petticoats, silk gowns, short cloaks, cambrick caps, red heeled shoes, fans, necklaces, gloves, and other such apparel." While psalms and hymns were sung over the pile, the preacher added his own pants, "a pair of old, wore out, plush breaches." This, commented one critic, would have obliged him "to strutt about bare-arsed" had not the fire been extinguished.

By 1742 New England and the middle colonies were being criss-crossed by a procession of itinerant gospelers and haranguers, all of them labeled social incendiaries by the established clergy. Of all the signs of social leveling that conservatives saw springing from evangelicalism, the one they feared the most was the practice of public lay exhorting. Within the established churches there was no place for lay persons to compete with the qualified ministry in preaching the word of God. Nor was there room for "self-initiated associations of the people meeting outside of regularly constituted religious or political meetings," for to do so was to relocate authority collectively in the mass of common people. Lay exhorting shattered the monopoly of the educated clergy on religious discourse, put all people on a plane in the area of religion, gave new importance to the oral culture of common people, whose spontaneous outpourings contrasted sharply with the literary culture of the gentry, established among them the notion that their destinies and their

souls were in their own hands instead of the hands of the elite clergy, and turned the world upside down in allowing those who had traditionally been consigned to the bottom of society to assume roles customarily reserved for educated, adult men. In lay exhorting, class lines were crossed and sexual and racial roles were defied, as ordinary men, women, and even children, servants, and slaves rose before throngs to testify emotionally to their own conversion and exhort others to a state of religious ecstasy by preaching extemporaneously the Lord's truth.

The Great Awakening thus represented far more than a religious earthquake. Through it, ordinary people haltingly enunciated a distinctive popular ideology that challenged inherited cultural norms. To some extent, as many historians have noted, the Awakening represented a groundswell of individualism, a kind of protodemocratic spirit that anticipated the Revolution. This was true, especially among the middling people of colonial society for whom the revival years involved an expansion of political consciousness and a new feeling of self-importance, as they partook of spontaneous meetings, assumed new power in ecclesiastical affairs, and were encouraged by the evangelists to adopt a skeptical attitude toward dogma and authority. But among the lowliest members of society, including impoverished city dwellers, servants, slaves, and those who struggled to gain a foothold on the treacherous slopes of economic security, the Awakening experience implied not a movement forward toward democratic bourgeois revolution but backwards to an earlier age when it was conceived that individuals acted not for themselves, always striving to get ahead at the expense of their neighbors, but pulled together as a community. Hence the dispossessed harked to the anti-entrepreneurial, communalistic tone permeating the exhortations of the radical evangelists such as Tennant, who preached that in any truly Christian community "mutual *Love* is the *Band* and *Cement*. . . . For men, by the Neglect of its Exercise, and much more by its Contrary, will be tempted, against the *Law of Nature,* to seek a *single* and independent State, in order to secure their Ease and Safety."

The radical Awakeners were not preaching class revolt or the end to wealth-producing commerce. What they urged was "a thorough reconsideration of the Christian ethic as it had come to be understood in the America of the 1730s." Nor were those who harked to the Awakeners inspired to foment social revolution, for in fact the seeds of overt political radicalism were still in the germinative stage. But the multitudes who were moved by the message of the revivalists, in the North in the 1740s and in the South during the next decade, began to believe that it was justifiable in some circumstances to take matters into their own hands. This is why Jonathan Edwards, a highly intellectual, latter-day Puritan minister, was seen by the commercial elite and their clerical allies as "the grand leveler of Christian history," even though sedition and leveling were not what he had in mind. The Great Awakening produced the greatest flow of religious energy since the Puritan movement a century before, but this outpouring was intimately connected with the tensions in colonial society that had grown from generations of social and economic change.

QUESTIONS TO CONSIDER

1. To what conditions does Gary Nash ascribe the growth of individualism in eighteenth-century America? What emphasis does he place on land and its availability?

2. Gary Nash says that in the eighteenth century, American social structure and ideas about social structure changed in opposite directions. How did they change and why? How did seventeenth- and eighteenth-century American social and economic conditions compare with those of Europe and why?

3. How did social conditions vary from one region to another? What influences led to these variations?

4. According to Gary Nash, how did social and economic conditions and religion influence each other in the seventeenth and eighteenth centuries?

5. What does Gary Nash think the Great Awakening reveals about the tensions in eighteenth-century American society? Did the experience mean the same thing to all parts of society? What implications would the Great Awakening have for subsequent American history?

6

Meet Dr. Franklin

Richard B. Morris

Benjamin Franklin, who called himself "the printer of Philadelphia," was one of the most remarkable human beings colonial America ever produced. As Richard B. Morris says, Franklin was America's first pragmatist: he believed that "what was moral was what worked and what worked was moral." He also celebrated the Protestant work ethic in his bestselling Poor Richard's Almanack, *the advice in which became the maxims of Franklin's generation: "Early to bed, and early to rise, makes a man healthy, wealthy, and wise." "He that riseth late must trot all day, and shall scarce overtake his business at night." "Sloth makes all things difficult, but industry all easy." "Laziness travels so slowly, that poverty soon overtakes him." "Women and Wine, Game and Deceit, Make the Wealth Small and his Wants Great." Franklin not only personified the frugality, hard work, restlessness, and occasional irreverence of colonial Americans but came to symbolize their growing sense of nationality as well.*

In his long lifetime, Franklin tried his hand at virtually every trade and profession young America had to offer — among other things, he was a farmer, a printer, a scientist, an author, a philosopher, a statesman, a diplomat, and a connoisseur of women. In the last capacity, he composed an article on the cultivation of a mistress and became a legendary womanizer. According to one anecdote, he fathered so many children that a colleague was moved to quip that it was not Washington but Benjamin Franklin who was "the real father of our country." Franklin would have appreciated the anecdote, for he had a consummate sense of humor. But above all, he had an unflagging love for liberty and the natural rights of people.

Still, Franklin was a complex and often contradictory person. As Morris demonstrates

67

in his lively and candid portrait, Franklin went through identity crises as anyone else, indulged in literary pranks, and had ambivalent attitudes about women. Although he abhorred violence, he was a devious individual who rebelled against convention and authority and in time became a leading American revolutionary. At the same time, Franklin regarded himself as truly a citizen of the world who hoped one day "that not only the love of liberty, but a thorough knowledge of the rights of man, may pervade all the nations of the earth, so that a philosopher may set his foot anywhere on its surface, and say, 'This is my country.'"

On the issue of slavery and race, however, Franklin was not always enlightened. In the 1730s, he held a low opinion of black people's intellectual abilities and even traded in slaves at his Philadelphia printing shop, either selling them for others or buying them as an investment. He once advertised that he had for sale "a breeding Negro woman about twenty years of age. Can do any household work." He also owned a slave couple, who worked with white servants in his home. By 1751, however, he had come to regard slavery as an economically unsound labor system. Twenty-one years later, a visit to an African American school was a revelation for him. What he saw convinced him that the schoolchildren were the equal of their white peers in intellectual capacity. That same year, Franklin publicly condemned the slave trade as "a detestable commerce" and damned slavery as a crime against humanity. After the Revolution, at the age of eighty-one, Franklin became the president of the Pennsylvania Society for the Abolition of Slavery. His evolution from slave trader to prominent American abolitionist demonstrated that people can be enlightened, can grow out of their prejudices.

GLOSSARY

BRILLON, MME   One of Franklin's French mistresses.

CARROLL, JOHN   Franklin had him appointed as the first Roman Catholic bishop in the United States.

DEISTS   Eighteenth-century rationalists who rejected formal religion and the idea of "supernatural revelation." Deists argued that God created all nature, then allowed it to operate by natural laws.

GRAND OHIO COMPANY   Land-speculating operation with which Franklin was associated.

HELVÉTIUS, MME   Widow with whom Franklin "carried on a long flirtation."

HUTCHINSON-OLIVER LETTERS   A series of injudicious epistles sent to English authorities by the Massachusetts Bay governor and lieutenant governor. The letters recommended that England severely restrict liberties in the Bay colony.

LOCKE, JOHN (1632–1704)   Preeminent English philosopher of the Enlightenment who contended that all human beings were innately good and equal and were entitled to "life, health, liberty, and possessions."

PENNSYLVANIA ABOLITION SOCIETY   America's first antislavery society; Franklin became its president.

PLAN OF UNION OR ALBANY PLAN
Franklin's 1751 plan to unite the colonies.

POLLY BAKER STORY   One of Franklin's
"outrageous" inventions that illustrated his "liberal
sexual code."

POOR RICHARD   Fictional character in
Franklin's immensely popular almanac who offered
aphorisms and proverbs for Franklin's colonial
readers.

Deceptively simple and disarmingly candid, but in reality a man of enormous complexity, [Benjamin] Franklin wore many masks, and from his own time to this day each beholder has chosen the mask that suited his fancy. To D. H. Lawrence, Franklin typified the hypocritical and bankrupt morality of the do-gooder American with his stress upon an old-fashioned Puritan ethic that glorified work, frugality, and temperance — in short, a "snuff-coloured little man!" of whom "the immortal soul part was a sort of cheap insurance policy." Lawrence resented being shoved into "a barbed wired paddock" and made to "grow potatoes or Chicagoes." Revealing in this castigation much about himself and little insight into Franklin, Lawrence could not end his diatribe against the most cosmopolitan of all Americans without hurling a barbed shaft at "clever America" lying "on her muck-heaps of gold." F. Scott Fitzgerald quickly fired off a broadside of his own. In *The Great Gatsby,* that literary darling of the Jazz Age, he indicted *Poor Richard* as midwife to a generation of bootleggers.

If Lawrence and Fitzgerald were put off by Franklin's commonsense materialism which verged on crassness or if Max Weber saw Franklin as embodying all that was despicable in both the American character and the capitalist system, if they and other critics considered him as little more than a methodical shopkeeper, they signally failed to understand him. They failed to perceive how Franklin's materialism was transmuted into benevolent and humanitarian ends, how that shopkeeper's mind was enkindled by a ranging imagination that set no bounds to his intellectual interests and that continually fed an extraordinarily inventive and creative spark. They failed to explain how the popularizer of an American code of hard work, frugality, and moral restraint had no conscien-

From pp. 6–30 in *Seven Who Shaped Our Destiny* by Richard B. Morris. Copyright © 1973 by Richard B. Morris. Reprinted by permission of the author.

tious scruples about enjoying high living, a liberal sexual code for himself, and bawdy humor. They failed to explain how so prudent and methodical a man could have got caught up in a revolution in no small part of his own making.

Franklin would have been the first to concede that he had in his autobiography created a character gratifying to his own vanity. "Most people dislike vanity in others, whatever share they have of it themselves," he observed, "but I give it fair quarter wherever I meet it." Begun in 1771, when the author had completed a half-dozen careers and stood on the threshold of his most dramatic role, his autobiography constitutes the most dazzling success story of American history. The penniless waif who arrived in Philadelphia disheveled and friendless, walking up Market Street munching a great puffy roll, had by grit and ability propelled himself to the top. Not only did the young printer's apprentice manage the speedy acquisition of a fortune, but he went on to achieve distinction in many different fields, and greatness in a few of them. In an age when the mastery of more than one discipline was possible, Franklin surpassed all his contemporaries as a well rounded citizen of the world. Endowed with a physique so strong that as a young man he could carry a large form of type in each hand, "when others carried but one in both hands," a superb athlete and a proficient swimmer, Franklin proved to be a talented printer, an enterprising newspaper editor and publisher, a tireless promoter of cultural institutes, America's first great scientist whose volume on electricity turned out to be the most influential book to come out of America in the eighteenth century, and second to none as a statesman. Eldest of the Founding Fathers by a whole generation, he was in some respects the most radical, the most devious, and the most complicated.

From the available evidence, mainly provided by the subject himself, Franklin underwent two separate identity crises, when, as modern-day psychoanalysts suggest, the subject struggles for a new self and a new conception of his place in the world. In adolescence

Joseph Duplessis painted Franklin from life in 1787 and later made this copy from it. Franklin was a complex, contradictory individual, now witty and self-confident, now deceitful and given to literary pranks. Even so, he succeeded in everything he tried, from publishing a Philadelphia newspaper and Poor Richard's Almanack *to charming the women of Paris. (New York Public Library)*

Franklin experienced a psychological crisis of the kind that Erik Erikson has so perceptively attributed to personages as disparate as Martin Luther and Mahatma Gandhi. Again, Franklin, the middle-aged man seeking a new image of himself, seems the prototype of Jung's classic case. As regards the first crisis, Franklin's autobiography reveals a sixteen-year-old rebelling against sibling rivalry and the authority of his household, using a variety of devices to maintain his individuality and sense of self-importance.

Born in Boston in 1706, the tenth son of Josiah and Abiah Folger Franklin, and the youngest son of the youngest son for five generations, Franklin could very easily have developed an inferiority complex as one of the youngest of thirteen children sitting around his father's table at one time. Everything about the home reduced Franklin's stature in his own eyes. When his father tried to make a tallow chandler and soap boiler out of him, he made it clear that his father's trade was not to his liking. His father then apprenticed the twelve-year-old lad to his brother James, who had started a Boston newspaper, the *New England Courant,* in 1721. For the next few years Benjamin was involved in one or another kind of rebellion.

Take the matter of food. Benjamin, an omnivorous reader, devoured a book recommending a vegetarian diet. Since his brother James boarded both himself and his apprentices at another establishment, Franklin's refusal to eat meat or fish proved an embarrassment to his elder brother and a nuisance to the housekeeper. Franklin, to save arguments which he abhorred, worked out a deal with his brother, who agreed to remit to him half the money he paid out for him for board if he would board himself. Concentrating on a frugal meatless diet, which he dispatched quickly, Franklin, eating by himself, had more time to continue his studies. While eating one of his hastily prepared meals he first feasted on Locke's treatise *On Human Understanding.*

A trivial episode, indeed, but this piece of self flagellation forecast a lifelong pattern of pervasive traits. Benjamin Franklin did not like to hurt anyone, even nonhuman creatures. He avoided hostilities. Rather than insisting upon getting the menu he preferred, he withdrew from the table of battle and arranged to feed himself. This noncombative nature, masking a steely determination, explains much of Franklin's relation with others thereafter. Even his abandonment of the faddish vegetarian diet provides insights into the evolving Franklin with his pride in rational decision. On his voyage from Boston to Philadelphia, he tells us, his ship became becalmed off Block Island, where the crew spent their idle moments catching cod. When the fish were opened, he saw that smaller fish came out of the stomachs of the larger cod. "Then, thought I," he confessed in his autobiography, "If you eat one another, I don't see why we

mayn't eat you." With that, he proceeded to enjoy a hearty codfish repast and to return at once to a normal flesh-eating diet. With a flash of self-revelation, he comments, "So convenient a thing it is to be a *reasonable creature,* since it enables one to find or make a reason for everything one has a mind to do."

Franklin's rebellion against authority and convention soon assumed a more meaningful dimension. When, in 1722, his brother James was jailed for a month for printing critical remarks in his newspaper about the authorities, the sixteen-year-old apprentice pounced on the chance to achieve something on his own. He published the paper for his brother, running his own name on the masthead to circumvent the government. Continually quarreling with his overbearing brother, Franklin determined to quit his job, leave his family and Boston, and establish himself by his own efforts unaided. The youthful rebel set forth on his well-publicized journey to Philadelphia, arriving in that bustling town in October, 1723, when he was little more than seventeen years of age.

To carve out a niche for himself in the printing trade, Franklin had to keep a checkrein on his rebellious disposition. For weeks he bore without ill temper the badgering of his master Keimer. When the blow-up came, Franklin, rather than stay and quarrel, packed up and lit out. Once more he was on his own. "Of all the things I hate altercation," he wrote years later to one of his fellow commissioners in Paris with whom he was continually at odds. He would write sharp retorts and then not mail the letters. An operator or negotiator *par excellence,* Franklin revealed in his youthful rebellion against family and employers the defensive techniques he so skillfully utilized to avoid combat. Yet there was little about Franklin's behavior which we associate with neurotics. He was a happy extrovert, who enjoyed the company of women, and was gregarious and self-assured, a striking contrast to Isaac Newton, a tortured introvert who remained a bachelor all his life. Suffice it to say that Franklin never suffered the kind of nervous breakdown that Newton experienced at the height of his powers, and as a result his effectiveness remained undiminished until a very advanced age.

If Franklin early showed an inclination to back away from a quarrel, to avoid a head-on collision, if his modesty and candor concealed a comprehension of his own importance and a persistent deviousness, such traits may go far to explain the curious satisfaction he took in perpetrating hoaxes on an unsuspecting and gullible public. The clandestine side of Franklin, a manifestation of his unwillingness to engage in direct confrontation, hugely benefited by his sense of humor and satirical talents. An inveterate literary prankster from his precocious teens until his death, Franklin perpetrated one literary hoax after another. In 1730, when he became the sole owner of a printing shop and proprietor of the *Pennsylvania Gazette,* which his quondam boss Keimer had launched a few years earlier, Franklin's paper reported a witch trial at Mount Holly, New Jersey, for which there is no authority in fact.

Franklin's greatest hoax was probably written in 1746 and perpetrated the following year, when the story ran in London's *General Advertiser.* Quickly it was reprinted throughout England, Scotland, and Ireland, and in turn picked up by the Boston and New York papers. This was his report of a speech of Polly Baker before a Massachusetts court, in defense of an alleged prosecution for the fifth time for having a bastard child. "Can it be crime (in the nature of things I mean) to add to the number of the King's subjects, in a new country that really wants people?" she pleaded. "I own it, I should think it as praiseworthy, rather than a punishable action." Denying that she had ever turned down a marriage proposal, and asserting that she was betrayed by the man who first made her such an offer, she compared her role with that of the great number of bachelors in the new country who had "never sincerely and honourably courted a woman in their lives" and insisted that, far from sinning, she had obeyed the "great command of Nature, and of Nature's God, *Encrease and Multiply."* Her compassionate judges remitted her punishment, and, according to this account, one of them married her the very next day.

How so obviously concocted a morality tale as that one could have gained such wide credence seems incredible on its face. Yet the French sage, the Abbé Raynal, picked it up for his *Histoire Philosophique et Politique,* published in 1770. Some seven years later, while visiting Franklin at Passy, Raynal was to be disabused. "When I was young and printed a newspaper," Franklin confessed, "it sometimes happened, when I was short of material to fill my sheet, that I amused myself by making up stories, and that of Polly Baker is one of the number."

When some years later Franklin's severe critic John Adams listed Polly Baker's speech as one of Franklin's many "outrages to morality and decorum," he was censoring not only Franklin's liberal sexual code but the latter's ability to throw off bad habits in old age. Franklin's penchant for pseudonymous writing was one side of his devious nature and evidenced his desire to avoid direct confrontation. He continued in later life to write a prodigious number of letters under assumed names which appeared in the American, English, and French press, some still undetected. His sly "Edict by the King of Prussia," appearing in an English newspaper in 1773, was a parody, in which Frederick the Great threatened reprisals against England for failing to emancipate the colonists from Germany that originally settled the island. As commissioner in Paris Franklin reputably wrote a vitriolic hoax, *The Sale of the Hessians,* in which a Count de Schaumbergh expressed delight that 1605 of his Hessians had been killed in America, 150 more than Lord North had reported to him. This was a windfall, since he was entitled to a sum of money for every fatality suffered by the mercenaries he had sold to George III. In the midst of delicate negotiations with the British to end the war of the American Revolution the irrepressible Franklin fabricated a hoax about the scalping of Americans by Indians in the pay of the British, and then printed it in the guise of a *Supplement to the Boston Independent Chronicle.* Gruesome propaganda in-

Drive thy businefs, let not that drive thee. Sloth makes all things difficult, induftry all eafy.

Early to bed, and early to rife, makes a man healthy, wealthy and wife.

Poor Richard, *which brought Franklin fame and fortune, offered readers a broad range of aphorisms and proverbs. The ones shown here are fairly tame. Others reflected Franklin's bawdy sense of* humor *and taste for pungent language. (Yale University Art Gallery)*

deed, but Franklin justified his deception to the censorious Adams by remarking that he believed the number of persons actually scalped "in this murdering war by the Indians to exceed what is mentioned in invoice."

The image of himself Franklin chose to leave us in his unfinished autobiography was of a man on the make, who insincerely exploited popular morality to keep his printing presses running. Yet he himself, perhaps tongue in cheek, would have said that the morality of *Poor Richard* was foreshadowed by the plan of conduct Franklin had put down on paper on a return

voyage in 1726 to Philadelphia from London, where he had spent almost two years in an effort to be able to buy equipment to set himself up as a printer. Later in life Franklin praised the plan as "the more remarkable, as being formed when I was so young, and yet being pretty faithfully adhered to quite through to old Age." The plan stressed the practice of extreme frugality until he had paid his debts, as well as truthfulness, industry, and the avoidance of speaking ill of others.

Franklin, the sixteen-year-old apprentice, absorbed the literary styles of his brother James and other New

England satirists running their pieces in the *Courant,* and he clearly used the *Spectator* as his literary model. He produced the Silence Dogood letters, thirteen in a row, until, he admitted, "my small fund of sense for such performances was pretty well exhausted." Until then even his own brother was not aware of the identity of the author. Typical was No. 6, which criticized pride in apparel, singling out such outlandish fashions as hoop petticoats, "monstrous topsy-turvy *Mortar-Pieces* . . . neither fit for the Church, the Hall, or the Kitchen," and looming more "like Engines of War for bombarding the Town, than Ornaments of the Fair Sex."

If the Dogood letters satisfied Franklin's itch for authorship, *Poor Richard* brought him fame and fortune. Lacking originality, drawing upon a wide range of proverbs and aphorisms, notably found in a half-dozen contemporary English anthologies, Franklin skillfully selected, edited, and simplified. For example, James Howell's *Lexicon Tetraglotton* (London, 1660), says: "The greatest talkers are the least doers." *Poor Richard* in 1733 made it: "Great talkers, little doers." Or Thomas Fuller's *Gnomolonia* (London, 1732): "The way to be safe is never to be secure"; this becomes in *Poor Richard*, 1748: "He that's secure is not safe." Every so often one of the aphorisms seems to reflect Franklin's own views. Thus, *Poor Richard* in 1747 counseled: "Strive to be the *greatest* Man in your Country, and you may be disappointed; Strive to be the *best,* and you may succeed: He may well win the race that runs by himself." Again, two years later, *Poor Richard* extols Martin Luther for being "remarkably *temperate* in meat and drink," perhaps a throwback to Franklin's own adolescent dietary obsessions, with an added comment, *"There was never any industrious man who was not a temperate man."* To the first American pragmatist what was moral was what worked and what worked was moral.

If there was any priggish streak in the literary Franklin it was abundantly redeemed by his bawdy sense of humor and his taste for earthy language. Thus, to *Poor Richard,* foretelling the weather by as-

trology was "as easy as pissing abed." "He that lives upon Hope dies farting." The bawdy note of reportage guaranteed a good circulation of Franklin's *Gazette.* Thus in 1731:

We are credibly inform'd, that the young Woman who not long since petitioned the Governor, and the Assembly to be divorced from her Husband, and at times, industriously solicited most of the Magistrates on that Account, has at last concluded to cohabit with him again. It is said the Report of the Physicians (who in Form examined his *Abilities,* and allowed him to be in every respect *sufficient*) gave her but small Satisfaction; Whether any Experiments *more satisfactory* have been try'd, we cannot say; but it seems she now declares it as her Opinion, That *George is as good as de best.*

Franklin's ambivalent views of women indubitably reflected his own personal relations with the other sex. In his younger days he took sex hungrily, secretly, and without love. One of his women — just which one nobody knows for sure — bore him a son in 1730 or 1731. It was rumored that the child's mother was a maidservant of Franklin's named Barbara, an accusation first printed in 1764 by a political foe of Franklin's, reputedly Hugh Williamson. Whether it was this sudden responsibility or just the boredom of sowing his wild oats, Franklin came to realize that "a single man resembles the odd half of a pair of scissors." Having unsuccessfully sought a match with a woman who would bring him money, Franklin turned his thoughts back to Deborah Read, the girl he had first courted in Philadelphia and then jilted. Rebounding from that humiliation, Deborah married a potter named Rogers who quickly deserted her. Then she did not even bother to have the marriage annulled, relying instead on the rumor that her husband had left behind him a wife in England. Franklin, so he tells us in his autobiography, conveniently overlooked "these difficulties," and "took her to wife, September 1st, 1730." The illegitimate child, William, whether born before or after Franklin's common-law marriage to Deborah, became part of the household, a convenient arrangement for Franklin while a constant reminder to Deborah of her spouse's less than romantic feeling about her. Soon there arose between Deborah and William a coldness bordering on hostility.

The married Franklin's literary allusions to women could be both amicable and patronizing; he could treat them as equals but show downright hostility at times. He portrayed the widow Silence Dogood as frugal, industrious, prosaic, and earthy, but somehow retaining her femininity. Such inferiority as women appeared to have must be attributed to their inferior education. While believing in the moral equality of the sexes, Franklin did not encourage women to enter unconventional fields of activity. He stuffed his *Almanack* with female stereotypes, perhaps charging off his own grievances to the sex in general. He frequently jabbed at "domineering women," with Richard Saunders the prototype of all henpecked husbands and Bridget, his "shrewish, clacking" wife. Scolding, gossipy women and talkative old maids are frequent targets of Franklin's jibes. A woman's role in life, he tells us, is to be a wife and have babies, but a man has a more versatile role and therefore commands a higher value.

Franklin's bagatelles "On Perfumes" and "On Marriages," frequently if furtively printed, kept under wraps for years by the Department of State, attained a clandestine fame, but few in the nineteenth century dared to print either. With the sexual revolution of the twentieth century and the penchant for scatological vocabulary, Franklin's letter on marriage and mistresses attained respectability and wide circulation. In essence, Franklin, in a letter dated June 25, 1745, commended marriage as the state in which a man was "most likely to find solid Happiness." However, those wishing to avoid matrimony without foregoing sex were advised to choose "*old Women to young ones.*" Among the virtues of older women he listed their more agreeable conversation, their continued amiability to counteract the "Diminution of Beauty," the absence of a "hazard of Children," their greater pru-

dence and discretion in conducting extra-marital affairs, and the superiority of techniques of older women. "As in the dark all Cats are grey, the Pleasure of corporal Enjoyment with an old Woman is at least equal, and frequently superior, every Knack being by Practice capable of Improvement." Furthermore, who could doubt the advantages of making an old woman *"happy"* against debauching a virgin and contributing to her ruin. Finally, old women are *"so gratefull!!"*

How much this advice reflected Franklin's own marriage of convenience remains for speculation. *Poor Richard* is constantly chiding cuckolds and scolding wives, and suggesting that marital infidelity is the course of things. "Let thy maidservant be faithful, strong, and homely." "She that paints her Face, thinks of her Tail." "Three things are men most liable to be cheated in, a Horse, a Wig, and a Wife." Or consider poor Lubin lying on his deathbed, both he and his wife despairing, he fearing death, she, "that he may live." Or the metaphor of women as books and men the readers. "Are Women Books? says Hodge, then would mine were an *Almanack,* to change her every Year."

Enough examples, perhaps, have been chosen to show that Franklin's early view of women was based on a combination of gross and illicit sexual experiences and a less than satisfying marriage with a wife neither glamorous nor intellectually compatible.

Abruptly, at the age of forty-two, Franklin retired from active participation in his printing business. He explained the action quite simply; "I flattered myself that, by the sufficient tho' moderate fortune I had acquir'd, I had secured leisure during the rest of my life for philosophical studies and amusements." These words masked the middle-age identity crisis that he was now undergoing. Seeking to project himself on a larger stage, he did not completely cut his ties to a less glamorous past, including a wife who was a social liability, but conveniently eluded it. Now he could lay aside the tools of his trade and the garments of a petit bourgeois and enter the circles of gentility. Gone were the days he would sup on an anchovy, a slice of bread and butter, and a half-pint of ale shared with a companion. His long bouts with the gout in later life attest to his penchant for high living, for Madeira, champagne, Parmesan cheese, and other continental delicacies. Sage, philanthropist, statesman, he became, as one critic has remarked, "an intellectual transvestite," affecting a personality switch that was virtually completed before he left on his first mission (second trip) to England in 1757. Not that Franklin was a purely parochial figure at the time of his retirement from business. Already he had shown that passion for improvement which was to mark his entire career. Already he had achieved some local reputation in public office, notably in the Pennsylvania Assembly. Already he had displayed his inventive techniques, most notably his invention of the Pennsylvania fireplace, and had begun his inquiries into the natural sciences.

Now, on retirement from private affairs, he stood on the threshold of fame. In the subsequent decade he plunged into his scientific investigations and into provincial politics with equal zest. Dispatched to England in 1757 to present the case of the Pennsylvania Assembly against the proprietor, he spent five of the happiest years of his life residing at the Craven Street residence of Mrs. Margaret Stevenson. Mrs. Stevenson, and especially her daughter Mary, provided for him a pleasant and stimulating home away from home. Reluctantly he returned to Philadelphia at the end of his five-year stay, so enraptured of England that he even contemplated settling there, "provided we can persuade the good Woman to cross the Seas." Once more, in 1764, he was sent abroad, where he stayed to participate in all the agitation associated with the Grenville revenue measures. Snugly content in the Stevenson ménage, Franklin corresponded perfunctorily with his wife back in Philadelphia. Knowing that Deborah was unwilling to risk a sea voyage to join him in London, Franklin did not insist. And although he wrote his wife affectionate letters and sent her gifts, he never saw her again. She died of a stroke in December, 1774, without benefit of Franklin's presence.

It was in France after the American Revolution had broken out that Franklin achieved more completely that new identity which was the quest of his later years. There the mellow septuagenarian, diplomat, and peacemaker carried out a game with the ladies of the salon, playing a part, ironic, detached but romantic, enjoying an *amitié amoureuse* with his impressionable and neurotic neighbor, Mme. Brillon in Passy, flirting in Paris with the romantically minded Comtesse d'Houdetot, and then in the rustic retreat of Auteuil falling in love with the widow of Helvétius, whom he was prepared to marry had she been so inclined. In the unreal world of the salon Franklin relished the role of "papa." Still he avoided combat or confrontation even in his flirtation. Where he scented rejection, he turned witty, ironic, and verbally sexual.

He found time, while engaged in the weighty affairs of peacemaking during the summer of '82, to draw up a treaty of "eternal peace, friendship, and love" between himself and Madame Brillon. Like a good draftsman, Franklin was careful to preserve his freedom of action, in this case toward other females, while at the same time insisting on his right to behave without inhibitions toward his amiable neighbor. Some months before he had written her:

I often pass before your house. It appears desolate to me. Formerly I broke the Commandment by coveting it along with my neighbor's wife. Now I do not covet it any more, so I am less a sinner. But as to his wife I always find these Commandments inconvenient and I am sorry that they were ever made. If in your travels you happen to see the Holy Father, ask him to repeal them, as things given only to the Jews and too uncomfortable for good Christians.

Franklin met Mme. Brillon in 1777, and found her a beautiful woman in her early thirties, an accomplished musician, married to a rich and tolerant man, twenty-four years her senior. To Mme Brillon Franklin was a father figure, while to Franklin she combined the qualities of daughter and mistress. Part tease, part prude, Mme. Brillon once remarked: "Do you know, my dear papa, that people have criticized the sweet habit I have taken of sitting on your lap, and your habit of soliciting from me what I always refuse?" In turn, Franklin reminded her of a game of chess he had played in her bathroom while she soaked in the tub.

If Franklin was perhaps most passionately fond of Brillon, other ladies of the salon set managed to catch his eye, among them the pockmarked, cross-eyed Comtesse d'Houdetot, who made up in sex appeal what she lacked in looks. Unlike Rousseau, who cherished for the Comtesse an unrequited passion, which he widely publicized in his posthumous *La Nouvelle Héloise,* Franklin's relations with her never seemed to border on close intimacy. Contrariwise, Franklin carried on a long flirtation with the widowed Mme Helvétius. Abigail Adams, John's strait-laced wife, was shocked at the open intimacies between the pair. Franklin complained that since he had given Madame "so many of his days," she appeared "very ungrateful in not giving him one of her nights." Whether in desperation or because he really felt the need to rebuild some kind of family life, he proposed to her. When she turned him down, he wrote a bagatelle, recounting a conversation with Madame's husband in the Elysian Fields, as well as his own encounter with his deceased wife Deborah. He then dashed into print with the piece, an odd thing to do if he were deadly serious about the proposal. As Sainte-Beuve remarked of this episode, Franklin never allowed himself to be carried away by feeling, whether in his youth or in old age, whether in love or in religion. His romantic posture was almost ritualistic. He almost seemed relieved at the chance to convert an emotional rebuff into a literary exercise.

Franklin's casual attitude toward sexual morality was shared by his son and grandson. Himself illegitimate, William, who sought to efface the cloud over his origin by becoming an arrant social climber and most respectable Tory, also sired an illegitimate son, William Temple Franklin, whose mother remains as much a mystery as William's own. Temple, engaged at Franklin's behest by the American peace commissioners as secretary in Paris, had an affair with Blanchette Caillot, a married woman by whom he had a child and whom he abandoned on his return to America.

If Temple was a playboy, that charge could never fairly be leveled at his grandfather. The Old Doctor, an irrepressible activist and dogooder, embodied in his own career that blend of practicality and idealism which has characterized Americans ever since. Convinced from early youth of the values of self-improvement and self-education, Franklin on his return to Philadelphia from his first trip to England organized the Junto, a society half debating, half social, attesting both to the sponsor's belief in the potentialities of continued adult education and to his craving for intellectual companionship not provided in his own home. Then came the subscription library, still flourishing in Philadelphia. Franklin's plans for an academy, drawn up in 1743, reached fruition a decade later, and were a positive outgrowth of his conviction that an English rather than a classical education was more suitable to modern man and that most colleges stuffed the heads of students with irrelevant book knowledge. Then, too, the Pennsylvania Hospital project drew upon his seemingly inexhaustible fund of energy, hospitalization being defended by him as more economical than home care. So did his organization of a local fire company, and his program for a tax-supported permanent watch, and for lighting, paving, sweeping, draining, and deicing the streets of Philadelphia. Convinced of the virtues of thrift and industry, Franklin could be expected to take a dim view of poor relief, and questioned "whether the laws peculiar to England which compel the rich to maintain the poor have not given the latter a dependence that very much lessens the care of providing against the wants of old age." Truly, this revolutionary, if he returned to us today, might well be aghast at the largess of the modern welfare state with its indifference to the work ethos.

Franklin evolved what he called his "moral algebra" to explain his code of ethics, a system which clearly anticipated Jeremy Bentham. In a letter to Joseph Priestley written in 1772 he outlined his method of marshaling all the considerations pro and con for a contemplated decision, setting them down in parallel columns, and then pausing for a few days before entering "short hints" for or against the measure. Subtracting liability from assets, one would come up with a moral or political credit or debit. Franklin never narrowed down the springs of human conduct to pain and pleasure, as did Bentham, but assumed a more complex set of motives. Franklin's moral algebra stemmed in part from his bookkeeping mentality, in part from his desire to reduce life to an orderly system.

That the oldest of American Revolutionaries should be committed to controlled, orderly change takes on larger significance when one seeks explanations as to why the American Revolution did not pursue the violent, even chaotic, course of the French. Nowhere is this better illustrated than in Franklin's evolving view about the Negro and slavery, in neither of which subjects did he show any active interest until well after middle life (after due allowance for the fact that as printer he published a few antislavery tracts in his earlier years). By shrewd calculation he demonstrated that the labor of a slave in America was dearer than that of an iron or wool worker in England. Embodying these calculations in what turned out to be a seminal paper on American demography, written when he was forty-five, Franklin did not let himself get actively drawn into the Negro question for another twenty years, and then he agreed to serve as a trustee for an English fund to convert Negros. As a Deist he could hardly have been passionately aroused by the prospect of saving souls, but may have consented to serve because of the degree of respectable public exposure involved. Earlier, in 1764, he was prepared to concede that some Negroes had "a strong sense of justice and honour," but it was not until 1772, when he was sixty-six years old, that he became aroused about the slave trade, that "detestable commerce." By the next year he was on record sympathizing with the movement to abolish slavery, and in 1787 he became president of the Pennsylvania Abolition Society, the oldest society of its kind in the world. He soon proposed a program for the education of free blacks in trades and other employment to avoid "poverty, idleness, and many vicious habits."

Franklin's last public act before his death was the signing of a memorial to Congress from his own Abolition Society asking for justice for the blacks and an end in the "traffic in the persons of our fellowmen." When Southern congressmen denounced the measure he sent to the press one of the last writings to come from his pen, a fictional account of an observation by an official of Algiers in 1687 denying a petition of an extremist sect opposing the enslaving of Christians. Accordingly, the divan resolved, in Franklin's tongue-in-cheek reporting, "The doctrine that plundering and enslaving the Christians is unjust, is, at best, problematical; but that it is the interest of the state to continue the practice, is clear: therefore let the petition be rejected."

A man of the Enlightenment, Franklin had faith in the power and beneficence of science. In moments snatched from public affairs during the latter 1740's and early 1750's — moments when public alarms interrupted his research at the most creative instant — he plunged into scientific experimentation. While his lightning kite and rod quickly made him an international celebrity, Franklin was no mere dilettante gadgeteer. His conception of electricity as a flow with negative and positive forces opened the door to further theoretical development in the field of electromagnetism. His pamphlet on electricity, published originally in 1751, went through ten editions, including revisions, in four languages before the American Revolution. Honors from British scientists were heaped upon him, and when he arrived in England in

1757 and again in 1764, and in France in 1776, he came each time with an enlarged international reputation as a scientist whom Chatham compared in Parliament to "our Boyle" and "our Newton."

Pathbreaking as Franklin's work on electricity proved to be, his range of scientific interest extended far beyond theoretical physics. He pioneered in locating the Gulf Stream, in discovering that northeast storms come from the southwest, in making measurements of heat absorption with regard to color, and in investigating the conductivity of different substances with regard to heat. A variety of inventions attested to his utilitarian bent — the Franklin stove, the lightning rod, the flexible metal catheter, bifocal glasses, the glass harmonica, the smokeless chimney. Indefatigable in his expenditure of his spare time on useful ends, he made observations on the nature of communication between insects, contributed importantly to our knowledge of the causes of the common cold, advocated scientific ventilation, and even tried electric shock treatment to treat palsy on a number of occasions.

To the last Franklin stoutly defended scientific experimentation which promised no immediate practical consequences. Watching the first balloon ascension in Paris, he parried the question, "What good is it?" with a characteristic retort, "What good is a newborn baby?"

Committed as he was to discovering truth through scientific inquiry, Franklin could be expected to be impatient with formal theology. While not denigrating faith, he regretted that it had not been "more productive of Good Works than I have generally seen it." He suggested that, Chinese style, laymen leave praying to the men who were paid to pray for them. At the age of twenty-two he articulated a simple creed, positing a deistic Christian God, with infinite power which He would abstain from wielding in arbitrary fashion. His deistic views remained unchanged when, a month before his death, Ezra Stiles asked him his opinion of the divinity of Jesus. Confessing doubts, Franklin refused to dogmatize or to busy himself with

the problem at so late a date, since, he remarked, "I expect soon an opportunity of knowing the truth with less trouble."

Unlike the philosophers who spread toleration but were intolerant of Roman Catholicism, Franklin tolerated and even encouraged any and all sects. He contributed to the support of various Protestant churches and the Jewish synagogue in Philadelphia, and, exploiting his friendship with the papal nuncio in Paris, he had his friend John Carroll made the first bishop of the Catholic Church in the new United States. He declared himself ready to welcome a Muslim preacher sent by the grand mufti in Constantinople, but that exotic spectacle was spared Protestant America of his day.

Although he fancied the garb of a Quaker, a subtle form of reverse ostentation that ill-accorded with his preachments about humility, Franklin was no pacifist. During King George's War he urged the need of preparedness upon his city and province, praising "that *Zeal* for the *Publick Good,* that *military prowess, and* that *undaunted Spirit,"* which in past ages had distinguished the British nation. Like most of the Founding Fathers he could boast a military experience regardless of its brevity, and in Franklin's case it lasted some six weeks. Following Braddock's disastrous defeat in December, 1755, Franklin as a civilian committeeman marched into the interior at the head of an armed force, directing an improvised relief program for the frontier refugees who had crowded into Bethlehem and seeing about the fortifying of the Lehigh gap. Back in Philadelphia he organized a defense force known as the "Associators," of which he was elected colonel. As in his other projects, he entered into these military arrangements with gusto, all to the annoyance of the proprietor, who regarded Franklin as a dangerous political rival and who regularly vetoed all tax bills which included military levies on the proprietary estate of the Penn family.

Once again, almost a decade later, he took command of a military force — this time to face down a frontier band known as the Paxton Boys who in 1764 set out on a lawless march to Philadelphia to confront the government with a demand for protection against the Indians. Franklin issued a blazing pamphlet denouncing the Paxton Boys for their attacks on peaceful Indians and organized and led a force to Germantown, where he confronted the remonstrants and issued a firm warning. The Paxton Boys veered off, and order was finally restored. "For about forty-eight hours," Franklin remarked, "I was a very great man, as I had been once some years before in a time of public danger."

Franklin's brief exposure as a military figure, combined with his leadership of the antiproprietary party, and his general prominence and popularity had by now made him anathema to proprietors and conservatives alike. Standing out against the Establishment, Franklin was heartened by the enemies he had made. A thorough democrat, Franklin had little use for proprietary privileges or a titled aristocracy. In his Silence Dogood letters written as far back as 1723 he had pointed out that "Adam was never called *Master* Adam; we never read of Noah *Esquire,* Lot *Knight* and *Baronet,* nor the *Right Honourable* Abraham Viscount Mesopotamia, Baron of Carian; no, no, they were plain Men." Again, *Poor Richard* engaged in an amusing genealogical computation to prove that over the centuries it was impossible to preserve blood free of mixtures, and "that the Pretension of such Purity of Blood in ancient Families is a mere Joke." With perhaps pardonable inconsistency Franklin took the trouble to trace his own family back to stout English gentry, but his basic antiaristocratic convictions stood the test of time. When, in the post-Revolutionary years, the patrician-sounding Society of the Cincinnati was founded in America, Franklin in France scoffed at the Cincinnati as "hereditary knights" and egged on Mirabeau to publish an indictment of the Order which set off an international clamor against its hereditary character.

For courts and lawyers, defenders of property and the status quo, Franklin reserved some of his most vitriolic humor. His *Gazette* consistently held up to ridicule the snobbery of using law French in the courts, excessive legal fees and court costs, and the prolixity and perils of litigation. For the lawyers who "can, with Ease, Twist Words and Meanings as you please," *Poor Richard* shows no tolerance. Predictably, Franklin took the side of the debtor against the creditor, the paper-money man against the hard-currency man.

Franklin's support of paper money did not hurt him in the least. As a matter of fact, the Assembly gave him the printing contract in 1731 for the £40,000 in bills of credit that it authorized that year. This incident could be multiplied many times. Franklin ever had an eye for the main chance. Whether as a poor printer, a rising politician, or an established statesman-scientist, he was regarded by unfriendly critics as a man on the make of dubious integrity. One of the improvements Franklin introduced as deputy postmaster general of the colonies was to make the carrying of newspapers a source of revenue and to compel his riders to take all the papers that were offered. On its face a revenue producer and a safeguard against monopoly, the ruling could hardly damage Franklin, publisher or partner of seven or eight newspapers, a chain stretching from New York to Antigua, and even including a German-language paper in Pennsylvania.

Accumulating a tidy capital, Franklin invested in Philadelphia town lots, and then, as the speculative bug bit him, plunged into Nova Scotian and western land ventures. His secretive nature seemed ideally suited to such investments, in which he followed a rule he laid down in 1753: "Great designs should not be made publick till they are ripe for execution, lest obstacles are thrown in the way." The climax of Franklin's land speculations came in 1769 when he joined forces with Samuel Wharton to advance in England the interests of the Grand Ohio Company, which was more British than colonial in composition. This grand alliance of speculators and big-time politicians succeeded in winning from the Privy Council of July 1, 1772, a favorable recommendation supporting their fantastic dream of a colony called Vandalia, to be fitted together from pieces of the present-day states of Pennsylvania, Maryland, West Virginia, and Kentucky. There Franklin's love of order would replace that frontier anarchy which he abhorred.

Standing on the brink of a stunning success, the Vandalia speculators were now put in jeopardy by Franklin's rash indiscretion in turning over to his radical friends in Massachusetts some embarrassing letters of Governor Thomas Hutchinson which had been given to him in confidence. Indignant at Franklin's disloyalty, the Crown officers refused to complete the papers confirming the grant to the Grand Ohio Company. With his usual deviousness, Franklin, in concert with the banker Thomas Walpole, publicly resigned from the company. In reality Walpole and Franklin had a private understanding by which the latter would retain his two shares out of the total of seventy-two shares of stock in the company. As late as April 11, 1775, Franklin, Walpole and others signed a power of attorney authorizing William Trent to act on their behalf with respect to the grant, hardly necessary if Franklin was indeed out of the picture. In the summer of 1778 Franklin had a change of heart and decided to get back his original letter of resignation. When Walpole complied, Franklin added thereto a memorandum asserting: "I am still to be considered as an Associate, and was called upon for my Payments as before. My right to two shares, or two Parts of 72, in that Purchase still continues . . . and I hope, that when the Trouble of America is over, my Posterity may reap the Benefits of them." Franklin's posterity, it should be pointed out, stood a much better chance were England to retain the Old Northwest and the Crown validate the Grand Ohio claim than were title thereto to pass to the new United States, whose claim to that region Franklin would be expected by Congress to press at the peacemaking. Such an impropriety on Franklin's part was compounded by his casual attitude about his carrying on a correspondence with a British subject in wartime while officially an American commissioner to France.

Franklin's critics denounced his penchant for nepotism, his padding the postmastership payroll with his relatives, the pressure he exercised on his fellow peace commissioners to have the unqualified Temple Franklin appointed as secretary to the Commission, and his willingness to have his grandnephew Jonathan Williams set up as a shipping agent at Nantes. Franklin's conduct of his office in France continued to supply grounds for ugly charges. What is significant is not that Franklin was guilty as charged but rather that the suspicion of conflict of interest would not die down despite his own disclaimer. At best, Franklin in France was untidy and careless in running his office. What can be said about a statesman whose entourage numbered a secretary who was a spy in British pay, a maître d'hôtel who was a thief, and a grandson who was a playboy! Only a genius could surmount these irregularities and achieve a stunning triumph. And Franklin had genius.

Because of Franklin's prominence in the Revolutionary movement it is often forgotten that in the generation prior to the final break with England he was America's most notable imperial statesman, and that the zigzag course he was to pursue owed more to events than to logic. As early as 1751 he had proposed an intercolonial union to be established by voluntary action on the part of the colonies. Three years later, at Albany, where he presented his grand design of continental union, he included therein a provision for having the plan imposed by parliamentary authority. A thorough realist, Franklin by now saw no hope of achieving union through voluntary action of the colonies, and, significantly, every delegate to the Albany Congress save five voted in favor of that provision. Twenty years later a number of these very same men, chief of them Franklin himself, were to deny Parliament's authority either to tax or to legislate for the colonies.

Franklin's Plan of Union conferred executive

power, including the veto, upon a royally appointed president general, as well as the power to make war and peace and Indian treaties with the advice and consent of the grand council. That body was to be chosen triennially by the assemblies of the colonies in numbers proportionate to the taxes paid into the general treasury. Conferring the power of election upon the assemblies rather than the more aristocratic and prerogative-minded governor's councils constituted a notable democratic innovation, as was his proposal for a central treasury for the united colonies and a union treasury for each colony.

Each intensely jealous of its own prerogatives, the colonial assemblies proved cool to the plan while the Privy Council was frigid. As Franklin remarked years later, "the Crown disapproved it as having too much weight in the democratic part of the constitution, and every assembly as having allowed too much to the prerogative; so it was totally rejected." In short, the thinking of the men who met at Albany in 1754 was too bold for that day. In evolving his Plan of Union Franklin had shown himself to be an imperial-minded thinker who placed the unity and effective administration of the English-speaking world above the rights and rivalries of the separate parts. Had Franklin's Plan of Union been put in operation it would very likely have obviated the necessity for any Parliamentary enactment of taxes for the military defense and administration of the colonies.

If Britain did not come up with a plan of union of her own soon enough to save her own empire, the Americans did not forget that momentous failure of statesmanship. Franklin's plan constituted the basic core of that federal system that came into effect with the First Continental Congress and, as proposed in modified form by Franklin in 1775, provided a scheme of confederation pointing toward national sovereignty. While the Articles of Confederation drew upon notions embodied in the Albany Plan, such as investing the federal government with authority over the West, it rejected Franklin's proposal to make representation in Congress proportional to pop-

ulation, a notion which found recognition in the federal Constitution. Writing in 1789, Franklin was justified in his retrospective judgment about his Albany Plan of Union. His was a reasonable speculation that had his plan been adopted "the different parts of the empire might still have remained in peace and union."

Franklin's pride in the Empire survived his letdown in 1754. In April, 1761, he issued his famous Canada pamphlet, "The Interest of Great Britain," wherein he argued the case for a plan which would secure for Great Britain Canada and the trans-Appalachian West rather than the French West Indian islands, arguments upon which Lord Shelburne drew heavily in supporting the Preliminary Articles of Peace of 1762 that his sponsor Lord Bute had negotiated with France.

For Franklin, 1765 may be considered the critical year of his political career. Thereafter he abandoned his role as imperial statesman and moved steadily on a course toward revolution. Some would make Franklin out as a conspirator motivated by personal pique, and while one must concede that Franklin's reticence and deviousness endowed him with the ideal temperament for conspiracy and that his public humiliation at the hands of Crown officials provided him with all the motivation that most men would need, one must remember that, above all, Franklin was an empiricist. If one course would not work, he would try another. Thus, Franklin as agent for Pennsylvania's Assembly in London not only approved the Stamp Act in advance, but proposed many of the stamp collectors to the British government. To John Hughes, one of his unfortunate nominees who secured the unhappy job for his own province, Franklin counseled "coolness and steadiness," adding

. . . a firm Loyalty to the Crown and faithful Adherence to the Government of this Nation, which it is the Safety as well as Honour of the Colonies to be connected with, will always be the wisest Course for you and I to take, whatever may be the Madness of the Populace or their blind Leaders, who can only bring themselves and Country into Trouble and draw on greater Burthens by Acts of rebellious Tendency.

But Franklin was a fast learner. If the violence and virtual unanimity of the opposition in the colonies to the Stamp Act took him by surprise, Franklin quickly adjusted to the new realities. In an examination before the House of Commons in February, 1766, he made clear the depth of American opposition to the new tax, warned that the colonies would refuse to pay any future internal levy, and intimated that "in time" the colonists might move to the more radical position that Parliament had no right to levy external taxes upon them either. Henceforth Franklin was the colonists' leading advocate abroad of their rights to self-government, a position grounded not only on his own eminence but on his agency of the four colonies of Pennsylvania, New Jersey, Massachusetts, and Georgia. If he now counseled peaceful protest, it was because he felt that violent confrontations would give the British government a pretext for increasing the military forces and placing the colonies under even more serious repression. A permissive parent even by today's lax standards, Franklin drew an interesting analogy between governing a family and governing an empire. In one of his last nostalgic invocations of imperial greatness, Franklin wrote:

Those men make a mighty Noise about the importance of keeping up our Authority over the Colonies. They govern and regulate too much. Like some unthinking Parents, who are every Moment exerting their Authority, in obliging their Children to make Bows, and interrupting the Course of their innocent Amusements, attending constantly to their own Prerogative, but forgetting Tenderness due to their Offspring. The true Act of governing the Colonies lies in a Nut-Shell. It is only letting them alone.

A hostile contemporary, the Tory Peter Oliver, denounced Franklin as *"the instar omnium* of Rebellion" and the man who "set this whole Kingdom in a flame." This is a grotesque distortion of Franklin's role. While he was now on record opposing the whole Grenville-Townshend North program as impractical and unrealistic, the fact is that his influence in government circles declined as his reputation in radical Whig intellectual circles and in the American colonies burgeoned. It must be remembered that, almost down to the outbreak of hostilities, he still clung to his post of absentee deputy postmaster general of the colonies, with all the perquisites thereto attached. All that dramatically changed in the years 1773–74, a final turning point in Franklin's political career.

Franklin had got his hands on a series of indiscreet letters written by Thomas Hutchinson and Andrew Oliver, the governor and lieutenant governor of Massachusetts Bay respectively, and addressed to Thomas Whately, a member of the Grenville and North ministries. The letters, which urged that the liberties of the province be restricted, were given to Franklin to show him that false advice from America went far toward explaining the obnoxious acts of the British government. Tongue in cheek, Franklin sent the letters on to Thomas Cushing, speaker of the Massachusetts House of Representatives, with an injunction that they were not to be copied or published but merely shown in the original to individuals in the province. But in June, 1773, the irrepressible Samuel Adams read the letters before a secret session of the House and later had the letters copied and printed.

The publication of the Hutchinson-Oliver letters, ostensibly against Franklin's wishes, caused an international scandal which for the moment did Franklin's reputation no good. Summoned before the Privy Council, he was excoriated by Solicitor General Alexander Wedderburn. The only way Franklin could have obtained the letters, Wedderburn charged, was by stealing them from the persons who stole them, and, according to one account, he added, "I hope, my lords, you will mark and brand the man" who "has forfeited all the respect of societies and of men." Henceforth, he concluded, "Men will watch him with a jealous eye; they will hide their papers from him, and lock up their escritoires. He will henceforth esteem it a libel to be called a man of letters; *homo trium literarum!*" Of course, everyone in the audience knew Latin and recognized the three-lettered word Wedderburn referred to as *fur,* or thief.

Discounting Wedderburn's animosity, the solicitor general may have accurately captured the mental frame of mind of Franklin at this time when he remarked that "Dr. Franklin's mind may have been so possessed with the idea of a Great American Republic, that he may easily slide into the language of the minister of a foreign independent state," who, "just before the breaking out of war . . . may bribe a villain to steal or betray any state papers." There was one punishment the Crown could inflict upon its stalwart antagonist, and that was to strip him of his office as deputy postmaster general. That was done at once. Imperturbable as was his wont, Franklin remained silent throughout the entire castigation, but inwardly he seethed at both the humiliation and the monetary loss which the job, along with his now collapsed Vandalia scheme, would cost him. He never forgot the scorching rebuke. He himself had once revealingly remarked that he "never forgave contempt." "Costs me nothing to be civil to inferiors; a good deal to be submissive to superiors." It is reported that on the occasion of the signing of the treaty of alliance with France he donned the suit of figured blue velvet that he had worn on that less triumphal occasion and, according to an unsubstantiated legend, wore it again at the signing of the preliminary Peace Treaty by which Great Britain recognized the independence of the United States.

Believing he could help best by aiding Pitt in his fruitless efforts at conciliation, Franklin stayed on in England for another year. On March 20, 1775, he sailed for America, convinced that England had lost her colonies forever. On May 6, 1775, the day following his return to Philadelphia, he was chosen a member of the Second Continental Congress. There he would rekindle old associations and meet for the first time some of the younger patriots who were to lead the nation along the path to independence.

An apocryphal story is told of Franklin's journey from Nantes to Paris, to which he was to be dispatched by Congress. At one of the inns in which he stayed, he was informed that the Tory-minded Gibbon, the first volume of whose *History* had been published in the spring of that year, was also stopping. Franklin sent his compliments, requesting the pleasure of spending the evening with the historian. In answer he received a card stating that notwithstanding Gibbon's regard for the character of Dr. Franklin as a man and a philosopher, he could not reconcile it with his duty to his king to have any conversation with a rebellious subject. In reply Franklin wrote a note declaring that "though Mr. Gibbon's principles had compelled him to withhold the pleasure of his conversation, Dr. Franklin had still such respect for the character of Mr. Gibbon, as a gentleman and a historian, that when, in the course of his writing a history of the *decline and fall* of empires, the *decline and fall* of the British Empire should come to be his subject, as he expects it soon would, Dr. Franklin would be happy to furnish him with ample materials which were in his possession."

QUESTIONS TO CONSIDER

1. In what ways was Benjamin Franklin a representative man of his time, a man who reflected and helped to shape the values of his culture?

2. Morris says that Franklin was an enormously complicated man who wore many masks, which disguised the real Franklin from his contemporaries as well as from future scholars and biographers. What were these masks, and how successful is Morris in uncovering the man behind them?

3. How does the available evidence support or detract from Morris's thesis that Franklin underwent two separate identity crises? What do you think are the strengths and weaknesses of trying to apply twentieth-century psychoanalytic theories to eighteenth-century lives?

4.   Morris calls Franklin "the first American pragmatist," a person who defined morality by what worked
and concluded that what worked must be moral. In
what sense does Franklin embody the seventeenth-
century Puritan ethic described by Degler in selection
3? In what important ways did Franklin alter the
ethic?

5.   In what ways, if any, would you consider Franklin a revolutionary? Do you agree with Morris that if
Franklin "returned to us today" he would be "aghast
at the largess of the modern welfare state with its indifference to the work ethos"?

IV

"WHEN IN the COURSE OF HUMAN EVENTS . . ."

7

A New Kind of Revolution

CARL N. DEGLER

Until 1765, as we saw in the previous selection, Benjamin Franklin remained an ardent defender of the British Empire. Most other colonists shared his pride in the empire and saw no reason to break away from it. But after 1765 — and the date is significant, as we shall see — Franklin and many others marched steadily down the path toward revolution. By 1775, as one historian has noted, the relationship between the American colonials and their English rulers had become "so strained, so poisoned, so characterized by suspicion and resentment that the once seemingly unbreakable bonds of empire were on the verge of dissolution." That same year, in fact, Minutemen at Lexington and Concord fired the opening shots of the war that resulted in American independence.

What were the causes of the American Revolution? What had so poisoned American-English relations that armed conflict broke out? Most experts agree that the roots of the Revolution are to be found in the previous century, when American colonists began developing their own institutions and ideas — particularly ideas about constitutions, taxation, and representation — that significantly diverged from those in England. This "first American revolution," as Clinton Rossiter called it, took place during a period of "salutary neglect," when the British imperial government allowed the colonies to develop without rigid and consistent government control. After 1763, however, all that changed. Reacting to new circumstances inside England and to the enormous cost of a recent war with France (the French and Indian War) for supremacy in North America, the imperial government abandoned salutary neglect and attempted to do what it had every legal right to do: rule the empire, including the North American colonies, forcefully and consistently for the benefit of the mother country. Among other measures, the Stamp Act of 1765 reflected the new imperial approach: it taxed newspapers, pamphlets, and other printed documents in the colonies, for the purpose of making them pay a third of the cost of protecting them. Unaccustomed to such interference from faraway London, colonial Americans protested, first with restraint, then with rising anger and bitterness, every new measure imposed on them from abroad. By 1775, a sizable and outspoken group of colonists had become profoundly disillusioned with imperial rule, and in 1776 they struck for independence.

In this selection, historian Carl N. Degler describes the "ways of governing" that had evolved in colonial America before 1763 and how those ways were threatened by the new imperial policies. Degler goes on to explain, through an imaginative use of metaphor, how the final break with England was a new kind of revolution, a "conservative revolution" to save colonial ideas and habits of governing. What happened in 1775–1776, he argues, was "no heedless, impetuous overthrow of an oppressor; rather it was a slowly germinating determination on the part of Americans to counter and thwart a change in their hitherto established and accepted ways of governing. . . . These men had been satisfied with their existence, they were not disgruntled agitators or frustrated politicians; they were a strange new breed — contented revolutionaries."

GLOSSARY

ADAMS, JOHN   Massachusetts lawyer who attacked the Stamp Act in 1765 but defended British soldiers involved in the Boston Massacre; he was a delegate to the Second Continental Congress and later served as second president of the United States.

BURKE, EDMUND   Member of Parliament who warned against excessive taxes on the North American colonies and advocated conciliation.

CRÈVECOEUR, J. HECTOR ST. JOHN   French-born American Agriculturist and author of *Letters from an American Farmer* (1782), which described American rural life.

FIRST CONTINENTAL CONGRESS   Delegates from all colonies except Georgia attended this assembly in Philadelphia in 1774; it pledged not to obey the Coercive acts and, while promising obedience to the king, denied Parliament's right to tax the colonies.

GAGE, GENERAL THOMAS   Commander of the English garrison in Boston who in 1775 sent the detachment that fought the Minutemen at Lexington and Concord.

GREAT WAR FOR THE EMPIRE (THE FRENCH AND INDIAN WAR)   Anglo-French and Iroquois war (1754–1763) fought for control of North America. In the treaty ending the war, the French ceded Canada to Great Britain, along with all other French possessions east of the Mississippi except New Orleans.

GRENVILLE, GEORGE   English prime minister who led the new imperial policy, begun in 1763, that imposed the sugar and stamp taxes on the colonies.

HAMILTON, ALEXANDER   Born in the British West Indies, he migrated to the New York colony in 1773 and as a college student wrote pamphlets defending the colonial cause; he served as George Washington's aide-de-camp during the Revolution and later became his secretary of the treasury.

HAMILTON, ANDREW   Philadelphia lawyer who defended John Peter Zenger in his trial for libel.

NORTH, LORD   Named prime minister in 1767, North secured the repeal of all the Townsend duties save that on tea. After the Boston Tea Party, he orchestrated the passage of the Coercive acts (one closed the Boston harbor) to bring the troublesome colonials into line.

OTIS, JAMES   Massachusetts pamphleteer who wrote *The Rights of the British Colonies Asserted and Proved,* which protested the Sugar Act of 1764 and argued the principle of no taxation without representation. He also challenged the Stamp Act, demanding an actual colonial representation in Parliament.

SUGAR ACT (1764)   British law that lowered duties on molasses and raised them on sugar in an attempt to stop the illegal sugar trade between the colonies and the French and Spanish West Indies.

TEA ACT (1773)   British law that allowed the British East India Company to monopolize the tea business by exporting tea directly to the colonies without paying the taxes imposed on colonial merchants.

TOWNSHEND DUTIES (1767)   Parliamentary law, named after the chancellor of the exchequer, that imposed new taxes on glass, tea, printer's supplies, and paper in the colonies.

ZENGER, JOHN PETER   New York editor arrested for criticizing the colonial governor and tried for libel. He and his lawyer, Andrew Hamilton, pleaded for freedom to publish criticisms of the government if the accounts were factually true. Zenger was acquitted, and his case became a landmark in the evolution of freedom of the press.

☆

AMERICANS HAVE NEW RIGHTS

"It is . . . to England that we owe this elevated rank we possess," remarked Crèvecoeur, "these noble appellations of freemen, freeholders, citizens; yes it is to that wise people we owe our freedom. Had we been planted by some great monarchy, we should have been mean slaves of some distant monarch." It was for sound historical reasons that during the Revolutionary crisis the colonials stoutly asserted their claims to the "rights of Englishmen." Yet despite the English substance at the core of colonial political forms, the colonists departed in a number of ways from the example of the mother country. Frequently these deviations were merely novel twists given to English institutions; sometimes they were new institutions called into being by the new conditions in America. But whatever the nature of the changes, by the middle of the eighteenth century the forsaking of English practices was in evidence and the American constitutional system of the future was visible.

A common political vocabulary can certainly serve to bind together a colony and a mother country. But when the meaning behind the words is different, then the stage is set for misunderstanding, recrimination, and conflict. During the 1850's, the North and the South found themselves in this dangerous position; the colonists and the English in the years immediately preceding the American Revolution also fell into this predicament. Steeped as they were in the English political language, the colonials spoke in what they thought was the common intellectual idiom of the Empire, neglecting to observe that the American experience had given the words a content quite different from that accepted by the Englishmen with whom they debated. That Americans and Britons were saying different things when they employed the same words did not become apparent until after 1765, but the actual differences in political and constitutional practices of the two peoples were there long before the Stamp Act.

It is true, of course, as Crèvecoeur implied, that in many respects the political institutions of England were reproduced in close detail in the colonies. By the middle of the eighteenth century, for instance, all of the mainland colonies except four were headed by a Royal Governor, appointed by the King and therefore bearing a relation to the people of the colony similar to that of the King to the British people. Moreover, each of the thirteen colonies enjoyed a representative assembly, which was consciously modeled, in powers and practices, after the British Parliament. The resemblance to the English example was carried still further in the division of the colonial assemblies into upper and lower houses in emulation of the House of Commons and the House of Lords. In both England and the colonies, furthermore, the suffrage was exercised only by property holders; in all the colonies, as in England, it was an axiom, as an act of South Carolina put it in 1716, that "none but such persons who have an interest in this Province shall be capable to elect or be elected."

Though in the letter the English and colonial constitutions were similar, in the spirit they were moving in different directions. For example, English constitutional development from the earliest years of the seventeenth century had been sometimes drifting, sometimes driving, but always moving in pursuit of the absolute power of Parliament. The most unmistakable sign of this tendency was the assertion that the King was under the law, as exemplified in the Petition of Right in 1628, the judgment and execution of Charles I in 1649, and finally the *de facto* deposition of James II in 1689. Together with this resolute denial of the divine right of kings went the assertion that Parliament was unlimited in its power; that it could change even the Constitution by its ordinary acts of legislation, just as it had created the Constitution by its past acts. By the eighteenth century, as today, the British accepted the idea that the representatives of the people were omnipotent; that, as the aphorism has it, "Parliament can do anything except change a man into a woman and a woman into a man."

The colonials did not look upon the English Parliament with such fond eyes, nor — equally important for the future — did they concede that their own assemblies possessed such wide powers. There were good historical reasons for this. Though to the English the word "Constitution" meant nothing more nor less than the whole body of law and custom from the beginning of the kingdom, to the colonials it meant a written document, enumerating specific powers. This distinction in meaning is to be traced to the fact that the foundations of government in the various colonies were written charters granted by the Crown. These express authorizations to govern were tangible, definite things. Over the years the colonials had often repaired to the timeless phrases and sonorous periods in their charters to justify themselves in the struggle against rapacious Governors or tyrannical officials of the Crown. More than a century of government under *written* constitutions convinced the colonists of the necessity for and efficacy of protecting their liberties against government encroachment by explicitly defining all governmental powers in a document.

Even before the Stamp Act was passed, James Otis of Massachusetts articulated the striking difference between the colonial and British conceptions of Parliamentary power and the nature of constitutions. "To say the Parliament is absolute and arbitrary is a contradiction," he asserted. Parliament cannot alter the supreme law of the nation because "the Constitution is fixed; and . . . the supreme legislative . . . cannot overlap the Bounds of it without destroying its own foundation." Here, long before the Revolution, was a succinct expression of what was to become the cardinal principle of American constitutionalism, clearly setting it off from the English in both practice and theory.

It is worth emphasizing that it was English practice which was moving away from colonial. Earlier in the seventeenth century, in the minds of jurists like Sir Edward Coke, Otis's arguments would have carried much weight, but now the mutability of the Constitution was widely accepted in England. The colonials in the middle of the eighteenth century, as we shall have occasion to notice during the Revolutionary crisis, were following the old-fashioned and more conservative line.

There was another way in which English and colonial constitutional developments were drifting apart. The intimate relation between the executive and Parliament, so characteristic of English and continental democracies today, was already taking shape in the middle of the eighteenth century. The executive was the cabinet of ministers, who were drawn from the Parliament itself; as a result there was no separation of powers, the executive and legislative branches being merely different manifestations of the same body. This development, however, did not take place in America. The existence, for one thing, of a royally appointed Governor made such a development impossible; he could not be readily supplanted by a cabinet or ministerial council. Moreover, by having written constitutions or charters, the colonies were limited to the forms provided in earlier days. Under such circumstances it is not surprising that the colonial leaders entirely overlooked what was happening in England. From their distance they remained convinced that the King — like their own Royal Governors — was the real executive. Thus, because of the peculiarly American experience, the colonists were committed to a conception of government quite at variance with the English.

An important corollary to the English doctrine of parliamentary absolutism was the assumption that the colonies were subject to the legislative power of that body. For most of the seventeenth century the doctrine was no more than an assumption, and so the colonies did not feel it. This was partly because parliamentary supremacy was achieved late in the century — in 1689 — and partly because the British government, embroiled in successive wars with Holland and France, did not seek to test its authority with the colonies.

This practice of "salutary neglect," as [Edmund] Burke named it, provided a long period during which the colonies developed self-reliance and their own ideas of government. The representative assembly in each of the provinces was widely viewed as the focus of government, peculiarly American, and constitutionally competent for all internal legislative purposes. The sole political tie of any consequence between the colonies and England was through the Royal Governor, and in four of the thirteen provinces there was not even this connection. It was to be expected, therefore, that the colonies should grow to think of their little assemblies as bearing the same relation to the Crown as the Parliament of Great Britain. Such a conception of colonial equality with England, however, ran counter not only to the strong current of parliamentary absolutism we have already noticed; it also flew in the face of a growing movement to centralize the government of the Empire in London.

There is irony in the growing divergence between England and the colonies regarding the power of representative assemblies. No institution introduced into the New World was probably more English than the representative assembly; yet it was this very political form, transformed by the American experience, which, more than anything else, served to bring about a break between the colonies and the Mother of Parliaments.

With the franchise, as with the parliamentary power, the colonists took a typically English institution and remade it into a wedge which drove the two peoples apart. Though both England and the colonies based the franchise on property holding, in the mother country this practice produced a small electorate. In America, however, the same requirement resulted in a quite different effect. Since property was widely distributed, even the use of property qualifications identical with those in England resulted in the colonies in a large electorate, occasionally even approaching univeral manhood suffrage. The studies of Robert Brown in the history of colonial Massachusetts, for example, have made it clear that in both provincial and town elections well over a majority of men — perhaps 80 per cent — could vote. When Thomas Hutchinson was defeated in Boston in 1749 he said of the 200 votes he received: "they were the principal inhabitants, but you know we are governed not by weight but by numbers." At another time Hutchinson remarked with obvious distaste: "The town of Boston is an absolute democracy. . . ." Even allowing for some exaggeration on the part of a defeated politician, these statements of a contemporary indicate that large numbers of men could vote in colonial Massachusetts.

Though some of the other colonies probably could not boast as wide a franchise as Massachusetts or other New England provinces, the franchise in the eighteenth century in all the colonies was considerably wider than is often supposed. Richard McCormick, for example, has shown that in New Jersey the property qualifications were quite easy for the great majority of the adult males to meet. Indeed, he has uncovered instances where the regulations at the polls were so lax that women, boys, and even Negroes voted. Milton Klein has shown that in New York as many as 55 per cent of the adult white males actually voted, suggesting that the eligible actually reached proportions close to 100 per cent. In Pennsylvania, Albert McKinley has estimated, at least one half of the males in a farming area outside Philadelphia could vote, though the figure would be lower in the city itself. Robert and Katherine Brown have found a wide participation in elections in Virginia, often taken as an aristocratically inclined province in the colonial period and after. In a general survey of the colonial suffrage, Chilton Williamson has found that in virtually all areas, where figures are available, the proportion of

adult white males who could vote was at least 50 per cent. In some places, as we have seen, it reached 75 per cent. Furthermore, unlike Virginians and other colonists, South Carolina voters also enjoyed the democratic device of the secret ballot. In short, the forms of political democracy were already beginning to appear in the colonial period. . . .

Related to both the political and constitutional innovations of the colonials was their defense of freedom of the press against the arbitrary power of government. The trial of John Peter Zenger in New York in 1735 is justly considered a landmark in the history of freedom. Under the English and colonial law of that time, the sole responsibility of a jury in a trial for seditious libel was to determine whether the accused had in fact written the alleged libel. Whether the material was in fact libelous was left up to the judge to decide. Since, in Zenger's case, Judge De Lancey was a creature of the Governor against whom the alleged libel was directed, the results of the trial seemed a foregone conclusion. This high probability was further enhanced when Zenger and his attorneys announced that they conceded Zenger's responsibility for writing and printing the article in question.

The drama and long-range significance of the case, however, turns upon the action of Andrew Hamilton, who assumed the leadership of the defense. Contending that the truth of Zenger's charges was the crux of the case, Hamilton argued that a press, unfettered by official control, was indispensable in a society claiming to be free. Truth, he said, was a legitimate, nay, a necessary defense in a libel suit. Almost casually he conceded Zenger's authorship of the offending piece. But then he turned to the jury and, in a masterful presentation, urged upon the jurors a new course. Disregarding the law and appealing to their love of liberty, Hamilton challenged the jurors to decide the larger question of whether the charges Zenger levied against the Governor were true or not. If they were, Hamilton advised, then the jury should acquit the printer. Despite its sure knowledge that it was affronting a powerful and partisan judge, the jury nobly matched Hamilton's boldness and found Zenger not guilty.

It is true that censorship of the press, particularly by the assemblies, and even trial for libel in which truth was not accepted as a defense, occurred after the Zenger case. But there were no more trials for seditious libel in New York for the rest of the colonial period. Moreover, the trial and its outcome produced repercussions in England. Radicals and Whigs, won over by the brilliant colonial innovation in behalf of a free press, began a campaign in support of American liberty which was to reach its full power at the time of the Revolution in the voices of Burke, [Charles] Fox, John Wilkes, Dr. [Richard] Price, and Colonel [Isaac] Barré.

The principle inherent in the Zenger decision was not quickly implemented in America, as Leonard Levy has pointed out. It was not until 1798, during the Jeffersonians' powerful attacks upon the theory of the Sedition Act that the modern view of freedom of the press was worked out. Heretofore, all sides to the question, including the Jeffersonians themselves, had accepted the idea that a government had a right to suppress statements critical of its officials. The new view, going beyond that set forth in Zenger, asserted that if a society was to be considered free it could not suppress criticism under the old rubrics of "seditious libel" or "a licentious press." In fact, the crime of seditious libel, *i.e.,* bringing government into disrepute by attacking its officials, was abandoned. The concept that truth was a defense in a libel suit — the central principle in the Zenger case — was established in New York law in the case of Henry Coswell in 1804 through the joint efforts of Alexander Hamilton and James Kent. The doctrine was reinforced by legislative act in 1805 and inserted, for good measure, in the state constitutions of 1821 and 1846. [But] it was not until 1791, however . . . that English juries were granted the right to determine whether the writing in question was libelous or not, and it was not until 1843 that truth was accepted as a defense in a libel suit under English law.

"ALL OF US AMERICANS"

In the course of the Zenger trial Andrew Hamilton had chided the attorney general for his constant citing of English precedent. "What strange doctrine is it to press everything for law here which is so in England," the clever Philadelphian exclaimed. Hamilton knew full well that the law of England prevailed in the colonies, but he was playing upon the colonials' growing pride of country.

In the years after 1740 the colonials became increasingly conscious of themselves as Americans. To be sure, there were very few outright demands for independence. It would take a good number of years, during which a consciousness of kind was only dawning, before the idea of independence would be thought of, much less advocated. Nevertheless, for two decades or more before the Revolutionary crisis of the late 1760's, Americans were expressing the feeling that they were different from Europeans, that they had a destiny of their own.

Ironically enough, the most obvious manifestations of this budding sense of Americanism appear in the course of the wars with France in the 1740's and 1750's, when colonials fought side by side with the English. During most of the century-long struggle against France in the seventeenth and eighteenth centuries, Britain had not demanded that the American colonies contribute anything more than the defense of their home areas and perhaps an occasional foray into adjacent French-held Canada. But beginning with the so-called War of Jenkins' Ear in 1739, which was first waged against Spain and then (as King George's War) against France, Britain stepped up her expectations of colonial military support. In 1741 the home government succeeded in goading the colonials to assist in the mounting of an offensive against Cartagena, the great port of the Spanish Main.

In part because the enterprise was a colossal fiasco,

but largely because American and European soldiers were thrown together under novel circumstances, the differences between Americans and Europeans were sharply illuminated for both sides. Admiral Vernon, the British commander of the expedition, for example, consistently referred to the colonials as "Americans." The colonials, in turn, referred to their supposed blood brothers, the English, as "Europeans." The words, of course, had been used before, but never so generally or consistently as at this time. The failure of the Cartagena expedition added its bit to the splitting apart of the two national groups. The Americans came away convinced that the English were callous and cruel in their treatment of colonials, and the English soldiery and officers were disgusted with what they stigmatized as the cowardice and ineffectiveness of the colonial soldier.

When the New Englanders under Sir William Pepperell succeeded in capturing the French fortress at Louisbourg [on the Atlantic coast of Nova Scotia] in 1745, the colonials' incipient pride of country burst forth. To some it seemed to prove, as one bit of doggerel put it, that in valor

> . . . the British Breed
> In Western Climes their Grandsires far exceed
> and that New England Schemes the Old
>   Surpass.
>   As much as Gold does tinkling Brass;
> And that a Pepp'rell's and a Warren's name,
> May vie with Marlb'rough and a Blake for
>   Fame.

With the fall of Quebec in 1759, there was loosed a flood of prophecies that the star of American destiny was in the ascendant. "A new world has arisen," exulted the *New American Magazine,* "and will exceed the old!" It is noteworthy, considering its nationalistic name, that the magazine was then in its first year of publication. One scholar, Richard Merritt, in examining the colonial press of the mid-eighteenth century, found a remarkable increase in the early 1760's in references to "America" and "Americans" at the same time that there was a falling off in references to the connection with England. He finds, in short, a rise in American self-awareness prior to the catalyst of the Stamp Act crisis in 1765.

Meanwhile a developing American nationality was evident — perhaps less spectacularly, but nonetheless profoundly — in other ways. Under the influences of distance and the new environment, the mother tongue of the colonists was undergoing change. New words from the Dutch and Indian languages, for example, were constantly being added to the speech of the English in America; words like "boss," "stoop," "cruller," "crib," "scow," and "spook" came from the Dutch. The Indian names were all over the land, and they made America exotic for Englishmen as they still do for Europeans.

Americans also made up words, some of which reflected the new environment. "Back country" and "backwoods" were designed to describe the novelty of the frontier. Bullfrog, canvasback, lightning bug, razorback, groundhog, potato bug, peanut, and eggplant are similar colonial name tags for new natural phenomena.

Familiar English words sometimes assumed new meanings in America. "Lumber" in eighteenth-century England meant unused furniture, but in the colonies it was applied to the raw wood — and so it has remained. "Pie" in England, to this day, means a meat pie, but in the colonies that was a "potpie"; "pie" was reserved for fruit pastry. Dry goods in England included all nonliquids, like corn or wheat; the colonials, however, changed the meaning to textiles only. The same alteration took place with the word "rock," which in England denoted a large mass; in America as early as 1712 it was being applied to a stone of any size. "Pond" was an English word meaning an artificial pool, but in unkempt America it came to mean any small lake. Certain words obviously attached to the English environment were lost in America, where their referents did not exist: fen, heath, moor, wold, bracken, and downs. It is not to be wondered, therefore, that in 1756 lexicographer Samuel Johnson was talking of an American dialect.

The burgeoning sense of Americanism was reflected also in the colonials' image of themselves. When Eliza Pinckney of South Carolina was presented at King George's Court in 1750, she insisted upon being introduced as an "American." That same year an advertisement in a Boston paper advertised beer as "American" and urged that Bostonians should "no longer be beholden to Foreigners for a Credible [sic] Liquor, which may be as successfully manufactured in this country." It is not the self-interest which is important here, but the fact that the advertiser obviously felt he could gain by making an appeal to a sense of American pride among his potential customers. This feeling among Americans that they were different from Europeans was put forth explicitly by a Carolinian in 1762. Speaking about the question of sending young colonials to England for their education, he said it would be most surprising if a British education should suit Americans, "because the Genius of our People, their Way of Life, their circumstances in Point of Fortunes, and Customs, and Manners and Humours of the Country, difference us in so many important Respects from Europeans. . . ." Such an education could not be expected to fit Americans, he went on, any more "than an Almanac, calculated for the Latitude of London, would that of Williamsburg."

As relations between the colonies and the mother country worsened after 1765, expressions of Americanism became more explicit and sometimes belligerent. Colonial students at Edinburgh University before 1765 commonly designated themselves as from the various provinces, but at the time of the Stamp Act, Samuel Bard wrote, he and several others began to style themselves "Americans" and the precedent was followed by many in subsequent years. About the same time Ezra Stiles of New Haven drew up a plan for an "American Academy of Science," which was designed, he said, "for the Honor of American Literature, contemned by Europeans." He stipulated that only native-born Americans should be members. And

at the Stamp Act Congress, Christopher Gadsden of South Carolina urged the gathered colonial leaders to take cognizance of their common nationality. "There ought to be no New England man, no New Yorker, known on the Continent," he advised, "but all of us Americans. . . ."

The magic of the moment and the atmosphere in the new country were so potent that John Morgan, newly arrived at Philadelphia from London in 1765, declared, only a year later, "I consider myself at once as a Briton and an American." Such an ambivalent attitude must have been common among colonials in the early stage of the crisis between the colonies and the mother country. But regardless of Morgan's own ambiguous feelings, his work in helping to establish the new medical school at Philadelphia was hailed by Benjamin Rush as an aid to the growing self-consciousness of the people of America. Pointedly calling Britain an alien land, Rush wrote Morgan that no longer would the colonial student have to tear "himself from every tender engagement" and brave the dangers of the sea "in pursuit of knowledge in a foreign country."

One of the most curious but very clear manifestations of a growing American awareness of differences between the peoples of the Old and New Worlds was the widespread belief that English society was morally inferior, even decadent, when compared with the social character of the colonies. As early as 1735 Lewis Morris, visiting England, wrote in his diary that he and his party "wish'd ourselves in our own Country, far from the deceits of a court." London appeared to Ebenezer Hazard as at once a wonderful "little World" and a "Sink of Sin." In 1767, English social conditions appeared shocking to William S. Johnson, who found the extremes of wealth and misery "equally amazing on the one hand and disgusting on the other." Benjamin Rush wrote from Edinburgh in 1767 that "every native of Philadelphia should be sent abroad for a few years if it was only to teach him to prize his native country above all places in the world."

Standing out against the decadence of England in the minds of colonials and of some Englishmen was the example of America as the hope of the world. In 1771, John Penn, who was certainly no radical, wrote that he considered Great Britain "as an Old Man, who has received several strokes of the Palsy, and tottering upon the brink of the Grave, whereas America was growing daily toward perfection." In 1745 a writer in the *Gentleman's Magazine* drew the lesson from the American success at the siege of Louisbourg that the colonials were truly in the classical tradition so dear to the men of the eighteenth century. He saw the colonists in "the great image of the ancient Romans leaving the plow for the field of battles, and retiring after their conquests to the plow again." For many Englishmen, America seemed to be utopia in actuality. But it was the Americans who above all were convinced of the moral superiority of their society. Colonials returned from Europe overflowing with tales of the iniquities they had witnessed in London or commenting on the manifest corruption of British politics. As early as 1748, Josiah Quincy was saying he was fearful that the venality of English political life would ruin the country. The self-righteousness of Americans toward Britain in the 1750's and 1760's reminds one of nothing so much as an adolescent's indignant strictures against his parent's timeworn but now suddenly recognized foibles. The American people were coming of age.

Along with adolescent carping, assertions of moral superiority, and self-righteousness in the years before 1765, there were also a few strong hints that independence was coming. The war against the French in Canada prompted some Americans to anticipate separation from England. Peter Kalm, for example, traveling through the colonies in 1748, was told that after the French were expelled from the western borders of the colonies, independence would come in a matter of thirty to fifty years. Once the "Gallicks" are removed, John Adams thought in 1755, the colonies would be able to go it alone. "The only way to keep us from setting up for ourselves," he wrote, "is to disunite us."

In 1760 and after, when the British government was wrestling with the question of whether or not the French should be expelled completely from the North American continent, there was much speculation as to the effect such expulsion would have upon the restive colonies. Though the canny Franklin blandly assured Parliament that the removal of the French would bind the colonies still closer to Britain, less suspect parties, like Comptroller Weare, pointed out that never before in history had an industrious and favored people like the Americans hesitated to break away from their mother country when they had the power to do so. It is highly likely, he added, "that a thousand leagues distance from eye and strength of government" would suggest just that "*to a people accustomed to more than British liberty*." Also of this opinion was a correspondent of the *Gentlemen's Magazine* in 1760. "If the people of our colonies find no check from Canada, they will extend themselves, almost without bounds into the inland parts. . . . What the consequences will be," he added ominously and prophetically, "to have a numerous, hardy, independent people possessed of a strong country, communicating little, or not at all with England, I leave to your own reflections."

There was more behind the thought of independence than the removal of the French threat. There was the coming to climax of the whole history of a geographically separate and different people in America. English traveler Andrew Burnaby noticed it in 1759 when he pointed out that the growing cities of the coast were already turning their citizens into "great republicans" and that the farm dwellers too had "fallen into the same errors in their ideas of independency. . . ."

In sum, by the early 1760's the colonists were ready in a vague cultural sense for the parting of the ways with Britain. What remained was for something to happen that would cause them to be sharply aware of those vague differences and to force them to develop consciously those "country" ideas they had been ruminating over for years. The occasion came after 1763, when Britain sought to find a new basis for its relations with the continental colonies. Then the differences between the two peoples were translated into political and ultimately into military terms. That is the story of the coming of the American Revolution.

☆

A New Kind of Revolution

Though the colonists had long been drifting away from their allegiance to the mother country, the chain of events which led to the Revolutionary crisis was set in motion by external factors. The shattering victory of the Anglo-American forces over the French in the Great War for the Empire (1754–63), as Lawrence Gipson has rechristened the French and Indian War, suddenly revealed how wide the gulf between colonists and mother country had become. The very fact that the feared French were once and for all expelled from the colonial backdoor meant that another cohesive, if negative, force was gone. At least one friend of Britain, looking back from the fateful days of 1776, thought that "had Canada remained in the hands of the French, the colonies would have remained dutiful subjects. Their fears for themselves in that case," he reasoned, "would have supplied the place of the pretended affection for this nation. . . ." What actual effect the removal of the French produced upon the thinking of the colonists is hard to weigh, but there can be little doubt that the Great War for the Empire opened a new era in the relations between the colonies and the mother country.

Great Britain emerged from the war as the supreme power in European affairs: her armies had swept the once-vaunted French authority from two continents; her navy now indisputably commanded the seven seas. A symbol of this new power was that Britain's ambassadors now outranked those of France and Spain in the protocol of Europe's courts. But the cost and continuing responsibilities of that victory were staggering for the little island kingdom. Before the war the annual expenditures for troops in America and the British West Indies amounted to £110,000; now three times that sum was needed to protect the western frontier, suppress Indian revolts and maintain order. Furthermore, the signing of the peace found Britain saddled with a debt of £130 million, the annual charges of which ran to another £4 million. Faced with such obligations, the British government was compelled to reassess its old ways of running an empire, particularly in regard to the raising of new revenues.

Before the war, the administration and cost of the Empire were primarily, if not completely, a British affair. Imperial defense on the high seas was in the hands of the Royal Navy, and though the colonies were called upon from time to time to assist in the war with France, the bulk of the fighting was sustained by British troops. In return, the colonies had acquiesced in the regulation of their trade through a series of so-called Navigation Acts, which were enacted and enforced by the British authority; no revenues, however, except those collected as import or export duties, were taken from the colonies by Britain.

Under the pressure of the new responsibilities, the British authorities began to cast about for a new theory and practice of imperial administration into which the colonies might be fitted as actively contributing members. Prior to the war the government had been willing to protect the West Indian sugar interests at the expense of the rest of the Empire. But now, in the interest of increased revenue, the old protective duty, which was much too high to bring any return, was cut in half, thus permitting French molasses to compete with British West Indian in the English and colonial markets. In 1766, this molasses duty, in a further effort to increase revenue, was cut to two-thirds of what it had been before the war. In short, the need for imperial revenues, not private interests, was now dictating legislation. The Stamp Act of 1765 and the Townshend duties of two years later were similar efforts to spread the financial burdens of the Empire among the beneficiaries of the British triumph over the French.

It seemed only simple justice to London officialdom that the colonies should share in the costs as well as the benefits to be derived from the defeat of the ancient enemy. At no time, it should be noticed, were the colonies asked to contribute more than a portion of the price of their own frontier defense. The stamp duty, for instance, was envisioned as returning no more than a third of the total military expenditures in America; the remainder would be borne by the home government. And because the colonists had difficulty scraping together the specie with which to pay such duties, the British government agreed to spend all the revenue obtained from the stamp tax in the colonies in order to avoid depleting the scanty colonial money supply. Nor were Americans heavily taxed; it was well known that their fiscal burden was unique in its lightness. In 1775 Lord North told the House of Commons that the per capita tax payments of Britons were fifty times those of the Americans. It was not injustice or the economic incidence of the taxes which prompted the colonial protest, it was rather the novelty of the British demands.

The new imperial policies of the British government caught the Americans off guard. Reveling in the victory over the French, the colonists confidently expected a return to the lax, uninterested administration of the prewar years and especially to their old freedom from any obligation to support the imperial defenses. Therefore, when the first of the new measures, the Sugar Act of 1764, became law, the Americans protested, but on a variety of grounds and without sufficient unity to command respect. By the time of the Stamp Act in the following year, however, the colonists were ready.

The essential colonial defense, from which the colonies never deviated, was a denial that the British Parliament had any right in law or custom to lay taxes upon the colonies for revenue purposes. Such taxes, the colonials insisted, could only be levied by the colonial legislatures. Actually, this expression of the colonial constitutional position was as novel as the imperial policy. Never before had there been an occasion for such an assertion simply because England

had heretofore confined her colonial legislation to the regulation of trade. It is true that the Pennsylvania Charter of 1681 specifically reserved to the British Parliament the right to tax the colony; but since Parliament had never used this power, the colonists had a case when they said the new British taxes were historically unknown and therefore unconstitutional. The details of this controversy, in which merit is by no means the exclusive possession of either side, do not concern us here. The important fact is not whether the Americans or the British were right in their respective readings of imperial constitutional history, but that the colonials believed they were right and acted accordingly. Regardless of the constitutional niceties involved, it is patent that the English had waited too long to assert their authority. Too many Americans had grown accustomed to their untrammeled political life to submit now to new English controls. In brief, the colonists suddenly realized that they were no longer wards of Britain, but a separate people, capable of forging their own destiny.

This conviction runs all through the polemics of the Revolutionary crisis. For underlying the constitutional verbiage which Englishmen and Americans exchanged were two quite different assumptions about the nature of the British Empire and the character of the American people. Whereas Englishmen saw America as a part of an Empire in which all elements were subordinate to Britain, the Americans, drawing upon their actual history, saw only a loose confederation of peoples in which there were Britons and Americans, neither one of whom could presume to dictate to the other. The colonials, in effect, now felt themselves Americans, not displaced, subordinate Englishmen. Jefferson suggested this to the King himself when he wrote in his *Summary View of the Rights of British America*: "You are surrounded by British counsellors. . . . You have no minister for American affairs, because you have none taken from us." Furthermore, even after 1776 many a Loyalist exiled in Britain found the English annoying and strange — evidence of the fact that residence in America had worked its

On July 2, 1776, as this painting shows, a committee consisting of Thomas Jefferson, Benjamin Franklin, Robert Livingston, Roger Sherman, and John Adams submitted a draft of the Declaration of Independence to the Second Continental Congress. Jefferson (second from the right) is laying the document before John Hancock. Franklin stands to Jefferson's left, Livingston, Sherman, and Adams to his right. (Oil painting by John Trumbull, copyright Yale University Art Gallery)

influence even upon those loyal to the Crown. "It piques my pride, I must confess," wrote one expatriated Loyalist, "to hear us called 'our colonies, our plantations,' in such terms and with such airs, as if our property and persons were absolutely theirs, like the [villeins] in their cottages in the old feudal system."

The imperial view so confidently advanced by Grenville and others of the British administration came too late; the Americans were not interested in making a more efficient Empire to be manipulated from Whitehall. Because of this basic conflict in assumptions, American demands continued to leapfrog ahead of British concessions right up to the Carlisle Peace Mission in the midst of the Revolutionary War. Even ministerial assurances in 1769 that there would be no further imperially imposed taxes failed to divert the colonial drive toward equality with Britain. The child was truly asserting himself, and, as so often happens, the parent was reluctant to strike him down.

Measured against the age of Hitler and Stalin, the British overlords of the eighteenth century appear remarkably benign in their dealings with the colonies in the years after 1763. For it is a fact that the colonies were in revolt against a potential tyrant, not an actual one. As the American Tory Samuel Seabury wrote in 1774, the colonists were convinced that the ministers of the Crown "have laid a regular plan to enslave America; that they are now deliberately putting it in execution. This point has never been proved," Seabury added, "though it has been asserted over, and over, and over again." As Bernard Bailyn has pointed out in a survey of some 400 tracts from the Revolutionary era, Americans were convinced that a conspiracy was afoot in Britain to deprive them of their liberties. Historians, however, can find no real basis for such fears. To the politically sensitive colonists, who had steeped themselves in the "country party" philosophy of the early-eighteenth-century pamphleteers, the intention behind the British legislation of the pre-Revolutionary years seemed all too clear. For in the country party philosophy, which, after the Revolution, would become the philosophy of republicanism, any government of power was a constant danger to individual liberty. And England with a court party of wealth, power, and corruption was perceived by Americans as a growing and obvious threat to liberty. On the other hand, the British could never bring themselves to enforce, with all the power at their command, what they believed was the true nature of the Empire, that is, the subordinate position of the colonies. More than once General Thomas Gage, commanding the British troops in America, reported that his forces were too scattered to preserve proper order and government in the colonies. "I am concerned to find in your Lordship's letters," he wrote from New York in 1768, "that irresolution still prevails in our Councils; it is time to come to some determination about the disposition of the troops in this Country."

Part of this irresolution was born of British confusion as to what should be the government's purpose, as the hasty repeals of the stamp and Townshend duties testify on the one hand, and the remarkably inept Tea Act reveals on the other. Part of it stemmed from the fact that within their own house, so to speak, were Americans: at times Lord Chatham himself, at all times Edmund Burke, Colonel Issac Barré, John Wilkes, and Dr. Price, who insisted that Americans possessed the rights of Englishmen. "The seditious spirit of the colonies," George Grenville wryly complained on the floor of Commons in 1776, "owes its birth to the factions in this House."

Divided as to aims and devoid of strong leadership, the British permitted the much more united colonists, who were blessed with superb and daring leadership, to seize and hold the initiative. Not until the very end — after the destruction of the tea at Boston Harbor in 1773 — did the patience of the British ministry run dry. By then, however, the years of acrimony, suspicion, and growing awareness of the differences between the two peoples had done their work, and the harsh coercive measures taken against Massachusetts only provoked counterviolence from all the colonies. Lexington and Concord, Bunker Hill and Independence Hall, were then not far behind.

By implication, the interpretation of the coming of the Revolution given here greatly subordinates the role of economic factors. Since the economic restrictions imposed upon the colonies have traditionally played a large role in most discussions of the causes of the Revolution, they deserve some comment here. Those who advance an economic explanation for the Revolution argue that the series of economic measures enacted by Britain in the century before 1750 actually operated to confine, if not stifle, the colonial economy. Therefore, it is said, the colonies revolted against Britain in an effort to break through these artificial and externally imposed limits. On the surface and from the assumptions of twentieth-century economic life, the mercantilistic system appears severe and crippling and worthy of strong colonial opposition.

Yet empirical investigations of the effects of the system by modern historians do not find much merit in the argument. Lawrence Harper and others have conclusively shown that the limitations placed on colonial manufactures by British laws did not seriously harm American interests or restrict American economic aspirations. The Navigation Laws, it is true, placed a burden upon colonial trade, especially of staples like tobacco and rice, perhaps amounting to as much as $7 million a year, according to one calculation. Yet very few objections to the Navigation Laws appear in the voluminous literature thrown up by the crisis. In fact, so acceptable did the system seem to that jealous American, Benjamin Franklin, that in 1774 he suggested to Lord Chatham that all the basic Navigation Laws be re-enacted by the colonial legislatures as an earnest of colonial loyalty. Furthermore, in October of that year, the first Continental Congress publicly declared the colonies willing to "cheerfully consent to the operation of such acts of the British Parliament, as are bona fide, restrained to the regulation of our external commerce, for the purpose of securing the commercial advantages of the whole empire to the mother country, and the commercial benefits of its respective members. . . ." In short, the navigation system was acceptable. Certainly laws the repressive nature of which no one was disturbed about can hardly be accepted as the grounds for a revolution.

No better economic argument can be made for taxation as a cause for the Revolution. Despite the tradition of oppressive taxation which the myth of the Revolution has spawned, the actual tax burden of the colonies was much heavier in the seventeenth century than in the years immediately before the conflict. On a per capita basis, taxes were five times greater in 1698 than they were in 1773. The lightness of the British taxes in the pre-Revolutionary period is also shown by the fact that the duty on molasses in 1766 was only a penny a gallon, or less than the duty the federal government imposed in 1791. As Lord North pointed out in 1775, taxation of the Americans was neither excessive nor oppressive.

From the unconvincing character of the economic explanations for the coming of the Revolution, it would appear, therefore, that the underlying force impelling the break was the growing national self-consciousness of the Americans. "The Revolution was effected before the war commenced," John Adams remarked years afterward. "The Revolution was in the minds and hearts of the people. . . ." The origins of the "principles and feelings" which made

the Revolution, Adams thought, "ought to be traced back . . . and sought in the history of the country from the first plantations in America." For a century and a half the Americans had been growing up and now they had finally come of age. Precisely because the Revolution was the breaking away of a young people from a parent, the substance of the Revolution was political. The argument concerned the question of parental authority, because that is the precise point at which tension appears as the child approaches maturity and seeks to assert his independence. Unfortunately for Britain, but like so many modern parents, the mother country had long before conveniently provided the best arguments in favor of freedom. And the colonists had learned the arguments well. For this reason, the rhetoric of the Revolutionary argument was in the language of British political and constitutional thought, though not, significantly, that of the ruling "court party."

As children enjoying a long history of freedom from interference from their parent, the Americans might well have continued in their loose relationship, even in maturity, for they were conservative as well as precocious. History, however, decreed otherwise. Britain's triumph in the Great War for the Empire put a new strain on the family relationship, and so intense was the pressure that Americans could not fail to see, as the argument increased in acrimony, that they were no longer members of the English family, but rather a new people, with their own separate destiny. Some Americans saw it earlier than others; a good many saw it by 1776. John Penn, while in England in 1773, was struck by the English ignorance "with respect to *our* part of the world (for I consider myself more American than English). . . ." To South Carolinian Henry Laurens, the Boston Port Act hit at "the liberty of all Americans," not just at that of the people of Massachusetts. Once they were convinced of their essential difference as a people and that British obduracy would not melt, Americans could not accept the old familiar arrangements. Anything less than their independence as a people was unacceptable; it would take Englishmen another generation to realize that the disagreement was as deep as that.

At no time during the ten-year crisis, however, were most Americans spoiling for a rupture with England merely for the sake of a break. Indeed, no one can run through the constitutional arguments of that day without being struck with the reluctance — almost misgivings — with which Americans reached the conclusion of independence. After attending the Continental Congress in 1774, Washington, for example, was "well satisfied that" independence was not "desired by any thinking man in all North America." And, as late as July 6, 1775 — over two months after the embattled farmers made their stand at the "rude bridge" — Congress denied any "designs of separation from Great Britain and establishing independent states."

This was no heedless, impetuous overthrow of an oppressor; rather it was a slowly germinating determination on the part of Americans to counter and thwart a change in their hitherto established and accepted ways of governing. Except for the long-deferred assertion of independence, the whole corpus of Revolutionary rhetoric — and nothing lends itself more to radicalism than words — was conservative, expressive of the wish to retain the old ways as they understood them. The demands made upon Britain were actually pleas for a return to the old relationship: repeal the Stamp Act, the Townshend Acts, the Mutiny Acts; restore trial by jury as abrogated by the expanded admiralty courts; remove the restrictions recently placed upon western migration. One needs only to run through that famous list of grievances in the Declaration of Independence to be forcefully reminded that what these revolutionaries wanted was nothing but the *status quo ante bellum*.

"We have taken up arms," the Continental Congress carefully explained in July, 1775, two months after Lexington, "in defense of the freedom that is our birth-right, and which we ever enjoyed till the late violation of it. . . ." These men had been satisfied with their existence, they were not disgruntled agitators or frustrated politicians; they were a strange new breed — contented revolutionaries.

QUESTIONS TO CONSIDER

1.   During the revolutionary crisis, colonials asserted their "rights" as English people and claimed that Parliament had violated these rights. Parliament and the king just as adamantly denied any violation of rights. Explain the roots of this misunderstanding between American colonists and the mother country.

2.   Compare the similarities and differences between English and colonial American political institutions and constitutional practices. How did the American experience shape the colonists' political institutions and give new meaning to commonly shared English political language?

3.   Examine the reasons American colonists in the eighteenth century felt a sense of mission, a sense that America was "the hope of the world." Compare this feeling with the seventeenth-century Puritan notion of building "a city upon a hill." Do you see any traces of such missionary zeal today in America?

4.   Comment on the appropriateness of Degler's metaphor comparing American colonists in the 1750s and 1760s with rebellious adolescents who are "coming of age."

5.   Why did the first American revolution — the social and cultural revolution — lead ultimately to the second (and final) political and military revolution? Consider the influence of both external and internal forces.

8

Thomas Jefferson and the Meanings of Liberty

DOUGLAS L. WILSON

The United States was conceived in idealism and in paradox. America joined the family of nations dedicated to the proposition that "all men are created equal," that all are endowed with the inalienable rights of life, liberty, and the pursuit of happiness, and that they have a natural right to rebel when those rights are denied. So said Thomas Jefferson in the American Declaration of Independence, summing up truths that Americans had learned in the eighteenth-century Enlightenment, or Age of Reason, a time of momentous intellectual and scientific advancements that began in Europe and spread to America. Enlightenment thinkers in Europe stressed a belief in natural law, human progress, and government as a rational instrument, ideas that profoundly influenced Jefferson, Benjamin Franklin, and most other American patriots. The ringing prologue of Jefferson's Declaration, in fact, drew much of its inspiration from English philosopher John Locke, who had held that all human beings were innately equal and good and were entitled to "life, liberty, and possessions."

Yet in 1776, enlightened America held some 500,000 Africans in chains. Jefferson himself and George Washington, the commander of the patriot army, were large slave holders. Indeed, slavery existed in all thirteen states and was an indispensable labor force for the patriot cause. Even so, many northerners, in a burst of revolutionary idealism, moved to abolish the institution in their states. Vermont was the first to do so, in 1777. Massachusetts outlawed it by a judicial decision six years later. New Hampshire removed it by "constitutional interpretation," and Pennsylvania, Rhode Island, and Connecticut all adopted gradual emancipation programs. When New York and New Jersey finally freed their slaves, the institution of bondage became peculiar to the South — hence the term peculiar institution.

The story was dramatically different in the South. True, some individual masters, swept up in the spirit of the Revolution, voluntarily manumitted their slaves. But most southern planters and political leaders refused to follow the lead of the northern states. Because those states had so few slaves in relation to their white population, white southerners liked to ask what the northerners had to lose in adopting emancipation. Southern whites did not see how they could abolish slavery, not with their heavy concentration of slaves (in some places they outnumbered whites) and their correspondingly large investments. For white southerners of the revolutionary generation, however, slavery was more than a labor system, more even than a means of race control in a region brimming with blacks. It was the foundation of an entire patrician way of life, so interwoven with the fabric of southern society — as a potent status symbol, as personal wealth, as inheritances and dowries — that it did not seem possible to remove it.

And what of Jefferson, perhaps the most enlightened southerner of his day? In Jefferson, we meet an American anomaly: the antislavery slaveholder. Jefferson truly hated slavery; he damned it as "this blot in our country," this "great political and moral evil," and he devised a specific plan to get rid of it in Virginia — by gradual emancipation and colonization of the freed blacks outside the state. Yet Virginia never adopted his plan, and Jefferson himself was so much a part of his slave-holding culture — and so much in debt — that he felt unable to free his own slaves while he was alive (he did, however, provide for the liberation of five of his skilled slaves upon his death). It is not unfair to point out that Jefferson's illustrious political career — among other things, he was revolutionary governor of Virginia, United States minister to France, Washington's secretary of state, and the third president of the United States — was made possible by slave labor.

In this selection, a distinguished Jefferson scholar reflects on this "many-sided and multi-talented man," especially on his contradictions concerning slavery and race. In doing so, Douglas Wilson raises a crucial point about the perils of presentism — that is, of intruding today's values and attitudes upon the past. To do that, he warns, risks distorting history. What annoys him is that too many Americans today seem unable to discuss the past in its own terms, unable "to make appropriate allowances for prevailing historical conditions." As an example of presentism, Wilson discusses the story of Jefferson's alleged liaison with his house slave, Sally Hemings. The author denies the story as wholly out of character for Jefferson. But even if it were true, does it matter? This leads Wilson to a profound question that all of us ought to ponder. "How should we remember the leading figures of our history?" he asks. "By their greatest achievements and most important contributions or by their personal failures and peccadilloes?" Wilson emphatically sides with the first position.

Of Jefferson's many achievements, Wilson contends that his "pre-eminent contribution to the world was the Declaration of Independence." In discussing that contribution,

Wilson confronts even worse examples of presentism: the view of Jefferson as a ranting hypocrite for trumpeting liberty and equality, yet failing to free his own slaves, and as an inveterate racist for his observations about the traits of black people in his Notes on the State of Virginia. Frankly, those observations are offensive to read today. Yet Wilson reminds us that they were speculative, "a suspicion only," and maintains that Jefferson would have readily discarded them had he encountered an outspoken, literate African American such as Frederick Douglass (whom we will meet in later selections). Addressing the question of why Jefferson did not free his slaves, Wilson observes that the great Virginian faced formidable obstacles in the context of his time and place. Then Wilson turns the whole question around. Instead of asking why Jefferson continued to hold slaves, the question ought to be, "How did a man who was born into a slaveholding society, whose family and admired friends owned slaves, who inherited a fortune that was dependent on slaves and slave labor, decide at an early age that slavery was morally wrong and forcefully declare that it ought to be abolished?"

As for the Declaration of Independence, Wilson makes a convincing case that Jefferson meant to include both blacks and women in his philosophical conception of equality. The author goes on to establish a powerful connection between Jefferson's Declaration and Lincoln's address at Gettysburg during the Civil War. The Gettysburg Address, Wilson points out, "invested Jefferson's eighteenth-century notion of equality with an essentially new meaning and projected it onto the future of the nation." As a result, Americans today have a different view of the prologue of the Declaration than did Jefferson's generation.

This is a powerful, thought-provoking essay. Now that you are aware of the problem of presentism, how would you evaluate the other readings in Portrait of America? Do they judge the past through the lens of the present, or do they assess historical figures and societies on their own terms, within the context of their times?

GLOSSARY

HEMINGS, SALLY   Jefferson's mulatto house slave, by whom he supposedly fathered seven children.

MONTICELLO   Jefferson's Virginia estate.

NOTES ON THE STATE OF VIRGINIA (1785) Jefferson's only published book in which he made observations about the racial traits of blacks and also offered a plan of gradual emancipation and colonization; later, Henry Clay and Abraham

Lincoln (in his pre–Civil War career) would endorse that approach.

PRESENTISM   The imposition of present-day values and assumptions on individuals and societies of the past.

SOCIAL DARWINISM   A belief, based on Charles Darwin's theories of biological evolution, that only the fittest individuals and societies survive.

"Today, makes yesterday mean." Emily Dickinson's gnomic utterance contains at least one undoubted truth — that the perspectives of the present invariably color the meanings we ascribe to the past. Nothing confirms this so readily as the changing reputations of historical figures, whose status often appears indexed to present-day preoccupations. It may be inevitable that every age should refashion its historical heroes in a contemporary idiom, but doing so carries with it an obvious and inherent danger. In imposing Today's meanings on Yesterday, we run the risk of distorting it — whether willfully, to suit our own purposes, or unintentionally, by unwarranted assumptions and because of meager information. In this way we lose track of what might be considered the obverse of Emily Dickinson's remark: that Yesterday has meanings of its own that are prior to and necessarily independent of Today's.

Thomas Jefferson is one of the few historical Americans who need no introduction. Even the most abbreviated knowledge of American history, at home or abroad, includes the author of the Declaration of Independence. Identified around the world with democracy and human rights, Jefferson's name and words have been invoked for two hundred years in the cause of freedom and political reform. But here in his own country, where the name synonymous with democracy is exhibited everywhere — on counties, cities, schools, streets, and every imaginable form of institution, business, and product — it sometimes seems that the man himself is receding from view, and that what is commonly thought and said about him gets harder and harder to reconcile with the great national hero. With the . . . two hundred and fiftieth anniversary of his birth, in 1743, it seems appropriate to note some of the ways in which Thomas Jefferson is remembered by the American public and to exam-

Thomas Jefferson, an oil painting done in 1805 by Rembrandt Peale. Jefferson was tall and slender, with a freckled face, gray eyes, and short, powdered, red hair. The color of his hair inspired one correspondent to salute him as "You red-headed son of a bitch." Despite his aristocratic upbringing, he was largely indifferent about his clothes, which rarely fit him. A Federalist senator once mistook Jefferson for a servant, observing with a sniff that his shirt was dirty. (New York Historical Society)

ine the historical lens through which the man and his contributions are seen.

Only a generation ago Jefferson was still considered to be and treated as an object of veneration, so closely identified with the spirit of America as to constitute a problem for the historian. In 1960 Merrill D. Peterson confronted this problem in one of the most revealing works of Jefferson scholarship, The Jefferson Image in the American Mind, which surveys what Jefferson has meant to succeeding generations of Americans. "Where the object is Jefferson," Peterson wrote,

Originally published in the November 1992 issue of The Atlantic Monthly. Reprinted by permission of the author.

the historian's obligation to historical truth is compromised, in some degree, by his sense of obligation to the Jefferson symbol. Jefferson occupies such an important place in the symbolical architecture of this nation that the search for the elusive *himself* from the vaunted summit, Objectivity, must not be allowed to empty the symbol of meaning for "Jefferson's children."

It is a measure of the change that has occurred in the past thirty years that the one thing Jefferson's children nowadays are most likely to associate with him, apart from his authorship of the Declaration of Independence, is a sexual liaison with one of his slaves, Sally Hemings. College teachers are often dismayed to discover that many if not most of their students now regard this as an accepted fact. But this is not all. In the prevailing ethos of the sexual revolution, Jefferson's supposed liaison is widely received with equanimity and seems to earn him nothing more reproachful than a knowing smile. For most, such a liaison is apparently not objectionable, and for some, its presumed reality actually seems to work in his favor, showing him to have been not a stuffy moralist but a man who cleverly managed to appear respectable while secretly carrying on an illicit relationship. In effect, something that before the 1960s would have been universally considered a shameful blot on Jefferson's character has become almost an asset. Confirming this state of affairs is the case of a prominent black civil-rights leader who complained not long ago that Jefferson's alleged relationship with Hemings is not forthrightly acknowledged by the proprietors of Monticello, Jefferson's residence, and who frankly confessed that this liaison had for him a positive effect in showing that, though a slaveholder, Jefferson was well disposed toward black people.

Although the charge that Jefferson had fathered several children by one of his slaves was first made public in his lifetime, by a vindictive journalist and office-seeker, James Callender, it was believed mainly by those who disparaged Jefferson for political reasons and was not credited by Jefferson scholars or the pub-

lic at large. But that began to change in 1974, when Fawn M. Brodie published a widely read book on Jefferson in which she attempted to establish the truth of Callender's charge as a prime biographical fact. Brodie's thesis about Jefferson and Hemings is an embellished and controversial reading of the evidence, but what is more significant in the present context is that her story was well geared to the dispositions of her audience. She insisted that her object was not to pillory Jefferson or to make him out as a moral monster but merely to depict him as a man. If, as a widower, he fell in love with a beautiful slave girl and took her as a mistress when she was fourteen years old, it was "not scandalous debauchery with an innocent slave victim," she assured us, "but rather a serious passion that brought Jefferson and the slave woman much private happiness over a period lasting thirty-eight years." Brodie's benign version of the story has proved persuasive, and where previous versions had depicted such behavior as scandalous, hypocritical, or shameful, Jefferson and Hemings are represented as a pair of happy lovers, bravely defying the conventions of a sexually puritanical and racist society.

Compelling as this picture has proved to the American public, most Jefferson scholars and historians have remained unpersuaded. It is true that Jefferson was extremely protective of his personal life and went to considerable lengths to keep it private, but it does not follow, as Brodie would have us believe, that he must therefore have had something to hide. In accounting for Jefferson's behavior in the context of his own time, rather than ours, it is difficult for knowledgeable authorities to reconcile a liaison with Hemings with much else that is known about him. Jefferson implicitly denied the charge, and such evidence as exists about the paternity of Heming's children points not to Jefferson but to his nephews. It is, of course, impossible to prove a negative, but the real problem with Brodie's interpretation is that it doesn't fit Jefferson. If he did take advantage of Hemings and father her children over a period of twenty years, he was acting completely out of character and violating his own standards of honor and decency. For a man who took questions of morality and honor very seriously, such a hypocritical liaison would have been a constant source of shame and guilt. For his close-knit family, who worshipped him and lived too near to him to have been ignorant of such an arrangement, it would have been a moral tragedy of no small dimensions.

But haunted as he was by other troubles and difficulties, there is no sign of this sort of shame or guilt in Jefferson's life. That is why Brodie must present Jefferson and Hemings as a happy couple and their supposed life together as giving satisfaction and lasting pleasure. And whereas there are grounds for suspecting a liaison, such as the terms of Jefferson's will and the testimony of Hemings's son Madison, there are no grounds whatever for believing in what Brodie called the "private happiness" enjoyed by Jefferson and Hemings. That is pure speculation. Because Brodie's thesis deals in such unwarranted assumptions, the great Jefferson biographer Dumas Malone regarded it as "without historical foundation." But what makes it possible for the American public to take the Sally Hemings story to heart, even more than the suspicious circumstances, seems to be a prevailing presentism.

"Presentism" is the term that historians use for applying contemporary or otherwise inappropriate standards to the past. An awkward term at best, it nevertheless names a malaise that currently plagues American discussions of anything and everything concerning the past: the widespread inability to make appropriate allowances for prevailing historical conditions. The issue of presentism is hardly new, but it has perhaps been amplified of late by the debunking and revisionist spirit of the times and the effect this has had on public perceptions. As the uncritically positive and unabashedly patriotic approach that for so long characterized the teaching of American history in the public schools has abated, the emphasis has steadily shifted to the problems and failures of the past. The saga of the glories of the old West has thus given way to a saga of exploitation and greed. Pride in conquering the wilderness has yielded to the shame of despoiling the land and dispossessing the indigenous peoples. What seems to have happened is that a laudably corrective trend has predominated to such an extent that the emphasis seems somehow reversed, and parents complain that they scarcely recognize the history their children are taught.

With a built-in emphasis on what had previously been ignored or suppressed, it is hardly surprising that almost all the revisionist news, at least where traditional American heroes are concerned, is bad. A question that was once reasonably clear has become a muddle: How should we remember the leading figures of our history? By their greatest achievements and most important contributions or by their personal failures and peccadilloes? Can one category cancel out the other? In a sense these reversals of fortune are inevitable, inasmuch as nothing ever keeps its place in a world of incessant change. It is perhaps an instance of what the historian Henry Adams called the law of acceleration — the tendency of change to come faster and faster — that John F. Kennedy and Martin Luther King Jr., whose murders elevated them to martyrdom, should both come in for reappraisal while their memories and legacies are still fresh. Do the revelations about such things as Kennedy's womanizing, his not-so-heroic war record, and his non-authorship of a book for which he accepted the Pulitzer Prize detract from his positive accomplishments as President? Do the revelations about King's philandering and his plagiarism as a graduate student have any bearing on his conspicuous achievements as a civil-rights leader? Or is this a case of asking the question backward? Is it perhaps more appropriate and revealing to ask, Are the significant contributions of Kennedy and King, which affected the lives of millions of Americans, in any way diminished by subsequent revelations about their shortcomings and failings in other areas?

In this climate the difficulties of judging a figure like Thomas Jefferson by an appropriate standard are considerably compounded. One who writes voluminously over a long time may easily have his own words quoted against him or cited to prove that he held views later modified or abandoned. Jefferson was pre-eminently such a person. On this point Merrill D. Peterson has observed,

His speculative and practical sides were frequently confused. Few men took into account that Jefferson's private self, as expressed in his letters, might not coincide with his public self. Or that his opinion at one time might not represent his opinion under different circumstances. Or that a man of his intellectual temperament did not often bother to qualify felicitous generalizations.

In some ways that are little recognized, Jefferson is surprisingly modern and accessible to the present age. His pronounced notions about health, for example, which seemed somewhat odd to previous generations, appear nowadays in an entirely different light. He believed strongly that regular exercise was essential to physical and mental well-being. As a college student, he developed a regimen of daily running to keep himself fit, and he came to believe in later life that walking was the most salutary form of exercise for the ordinary person. On the subject of diet he also held strong views, which minimized meat and animal products and emphasized instead the prime importance of vegetables. For our own time, at least, Jefferson turns out to have been something of a health-food prophet.

Whether his leading ideas on politics and government will prove as resilient remains to be seen. In spite of his great reputation as a statesman, many of these have proved as counter to the prevailing currents of American history as his prejudice against large cities and manufacturing. He could never reconcile himself, for example, to the Supreme Court's deciding the constitutionality of laws and acts of the executive — a development he regarded as unwarranted and disastrous. His preference for a small central government and his insistence on the prerogatives of the states have been strongly rebuffed, if not virtually obliterated, by decisive turns in our national develop-

ment. Although history cannot be reversed, the relative size and power of the central government is once more (or still) at issue, as is the proper scope and authority of the Supreme Court. Even Jefferson's views on the disadvantages of large cities have today a resonance that was unheard or unheeded by previous generations.

Because he was attracted to laborsaving devices and was an ingenious adopter and adapter of new gadgets, Jefferson has gained a reputation as an inventor, but aside from a few items — an innovative moldboard for a plough, a revolving book stand — he probably invented little. Though he used and enthusiastically promoted the polygraph, a machine for making simultaneous copies of a written document, he did not invent it, and could not even keep his own in repair. But the fact that Jefferson is perceived as an inventor tells us something about the way he is valued. Abraham Lincoln was much interested in inventions and even went so far as to have one of his own patented, but this fact has made little impression on his admirers and is entirely absent from the legend.

President Kennedy paid a famous tribute to the multiplicity of Jefferson's talents, but they have always been regarded as astonishing. James Parton, one of Jefferson's nineteenth-century biographers, gave his dazzling range of abilities a dramatic accent when he characterized his subject as a man who "could calculate an eclipse, survey an estate, tie an artery, plan an edifice, try a cause, break a horse, dance a minuet, and play the violin." And Parton was describing a young Jefferson who had not yet written the Declaration. When the world's leading scientist and explorer, Alexander von Humboldt, came to visit Jefferson in Washington in 1804, he came to see not the President of the United States so much as the president of the American Philosophical Society and the author of *Notes on the State of Virginia* (1785). Had he visited the President at his home in Virginia, he would have seen what was perhaps the finest private library in America, which later became the foundation of the Library of Congress.

Not all of Jefferson's extraordinary talents are fully recognized by the public at large. One that is not is his great achievement as an architect. Self-taught from books and, until he went abroad, almost without worthy architectural models to observe, Jefferson managed to design a number of memorable structures. The residence of his that crowns (and names) a small mountain in the Virginia Piedmont has become one of the most familiar objects in American iconography. And Jefferson can claim credit for not just one Monticello but two: the domed structure represented on the back of the nickel is his second version of the house, which superseded the first one on the same site, and is dramatically different.

Part of the evidence for Jefferson's distinction as an architect is found in his beautifully detailed drawings, some of which reveal fanciful structures that were never built. But his most original and most imaginative design, and the one recognized by professional architects as among the greatest of all American architectural achievements, is his "academical village" — the campus of the University of Virginia. In forming his conception Jefferson effectively reinvented the idea of the university, from the innovative curriculum to the unique arrangement and design of the buildings. Here those seeking his monument have only to look about them.

Although he was a many-sided and multi-talented man who left a lasting imprint on a number of endeavors, there seems to be little doubt that Jefferson's pre-eminent contribution to the world was the Declaration of Independence — particularly its enduring affirmations of liberty and equality. In the prologue of the Declaration these affirmations were made the axioms from which the rights of revolution and self-government could confidently be deduced. The idea of individual liberty was not, of course, original with Jefferson, or exclusively an American invention. It was fostered in Western Europe by philosophers, religious dissidents, and political rebels, but it took root tenaciously among transplanted Europeans in the New World and, with the founding of the American re-

public, received its most durable expression in the Declaration of Independence. To the Declaration's studious and deeply learned author, many of what had passed in the history of the world for the prerogatives of governmental power were arbitrary and intolerable restraints on individual freedom. In fact, it is not too much to say that Jefferson's reigning political passion was a hatred of tyranny. And although his fear of the tyrannous abuse of power has sometimes been judged excessive, it is hard to argue that tyranny has ever been, or is even now, in short supply.

If it is possible to reduce so complex an issue to its simplest terms, one might venture that for Jefferson the paramount political issue in the American Revolution was what he called liberty and what we now call personal freedom, or choice. It was and remains the virtual sine qua non of American culture, something that Americans from the first have been strongly conscious of and willing to fight for. But what has become the most familiar and the most quoted phrase in the Declaration — "all men are created equal" — is about something else. It is an intriguing fact that although Americans generally understand that the prologue to the Declaration is their charter of freedom, even more indelibly impressed upon their imagination is its affirmation of the ideal of human equality.

How could the man who wrote, that "all men are created equal" own slaves? This, in essence, is the question most persistently asked of those who write about Thomas Jefferson, and by all indications it is the thing that contemporary Americans find most vexing about him. In a recent series of some two dozen radio talk shows, I was asked this question on virtually every program, either by the host or by a caller. Most often, those who point to this problem admire Jefferson, and they appear as reluctant to give up their admiration as they would be to give up the principle of equality itself. But they are genuinely baffled by the seeming contradiction.

The question carries a silent assumption that because he practiced slaveholding, Jefferson must have

Isaac Jefferson, born in 1775, was a skilled slave on Jefferson's Monticello plantation. This daguerreotype was taken by John Plumbe circa 1845. (Tracy W. McGregor Library, Special Collections Department, University of Virginia Library)

somehow believed in it, and must therefore have been a hypocrite. My belief is that this way of asking the question. as in the cases of Kennedy and King, is essentially backward, and reflects the pervasive presentism of our time. Consider, for example, how different the question appears when inverted and framed in more historical terms: How did a man who was born into a slaveholding society, whose family and admired friends owned slaves, who inherited a fortune that was dependent on slaves and slave labor, decide at an early age that slavery was morally wrong and forcefully declare that it ought to be abolished?

Though stating the same case, these are obviously different questions, focusing on different things, but one is framed in a historical context and the other ignores historical circumstances. The rephrased question reveals that what is truly remarkable is that Jefferson went against his society and his own self-interest to denounce slavery and urge its abolition. And, crucially, there is no hidden assumption that he must in some way have believed in or tacitly accepted the morality of slavery.

But when the question is explained in this way, another invariably follows: If Jefferson came to believe that holding slaves was wrong, why did he continue to hold them? This question, because of its underlying assumptions, is both harder and easier than the first. It is harder because we are at such a great remove from the conditions of eighteenth-century Virginia that no satisfactory explanation can be given in a nutshell. To come to terms with the tangle of legal restrictions and other obstacles faced by the eighteenth-century Virginia slaveholder who might have wished freedom for his slaves, together with the extraordinary difficulties of finding them viable places of residence and means of livelihood, requires a short course in early American history. But the question is easier in that there is no doubt that these obstacles to emancipation in Jefferson's Virginia were formidable, and the risk was demonstrably great that emancipated slaves would enjoy little, if any, real freedom and would, unless they could pass as white, be more likely to come to grief in a hostile environment. In short, the master whose concern extended beyond his own morality to the well-being of his slaves was caught on the horns of a dilemma. Thus the question of why Jefferson didn't free his slaves only serves to illustrate how presentism involves us in mistaken assumptions about historical conditions — in this case that an eighteenth-century slaveholder wanting to get out from under the moral stigma of slavery and improve the lot of his slaves had only to set them free.

The inevitable question about slavery and equality partly reflects the fact that most Americans are only vaguely familiar with the historical Jefferson, but delving into his writings and attempting to come to terms with the character of his thought, though illu-

Twenty-nine slaves are listed on this roll of Jefferson's slaves at Monticello in 1774. In fact, Jefferson owned a total of 180 slaves and three large plantations, in addition to several smaller land holdings. The slaves listed on the roll without a footnote designation were under the age of ten. (Massachusetts Historical Society)

minating, can create further consternation. The college student confronting Jefferson's one published book, *Notes on the State of Virginia,* is nowadays unprepared for and often appalled at what the author of the Declaration of Independence had to say about race. Thirty years ago college students were shocked to find Jefferson referring to the slave population as "blacks," a term that to them suggested racial insensitivity. But to those born after the civil-rights acts of the 1960s, it comes as a shock to discover that Jefferson, while firmly in favor of general emancipation, held out no hope for racial integration. Believing that an amalgamation of the races was not desirable and would not

work, he advocated a plan of gradual emancipation and resettlement. Present-day students are even more shocked to find Jefferson concluding, albeit as "a suspicion only," that the blacks he had observed were "inferior to the whites in the endowments both of body and mind." Even his positive finding that blacks appeared to be superior to whites in musical ability rankles, for it comes through to students of the current generation as an early version of a familiar stereotype.

At a time like the present, when relations between the races are in the forefront of public discussion and desegregation is the law of the land, it is not surprising that college students should be sensitive to discrepancies between what they understand to be the prevailing ideals of their country and the views of its most prominent Founding Father. National ideals, however, spring not only from the beliefs and aspirations of founders but also, as this essay attempts to show, from the experience and efforts of subsequent generations. Though he foresaw that slavery could not prevail ("Nothing is more certainly written in the book of fate than that these people are to be free"), Jefferson can hardly be counted bigoted or backward for seriously doubting that a racially integrated society of white Europeans and black Africans was truly feasible. As the Harvard historian Bernard Bailyn has written, "It took a vast leap of the imagination in the eighteenth century to consider integrating into the political community the existing slave population, whose very 'nature' was the subject of puzzled inquiry and who had hitherto been politically non-existent." Interestingly, the reasons that Jefferson gave for doubting the possibility of integration — "deep rooted prejudices entertained by the whites; ten thousand recollections, by the blacks, of the injuries they have sustained; new provocations; [and] the real distinctions which nature has made" — are the same reasons often cited by black separatists, who entertain the same misgivings.

But if Jefferson's being a separatist can be accounted for, what can be said about his invidious comparison of the natural endowments of blacks with those of whites, or with those of American Indians, whom he found to be on a par with whites? His own testimony suggests an answer, for he admitted that his acquaintance with blacks did not extend to the African continent and embraced only black people who had been born in and forced to live under the degrading conditions of slavery. "It will be right to make great allowances for the difference of condition, of education, of conversation, of the sphere in which they move," Jefferson wrote, but it is evident in the hindsight of two hundred years that his estimate of the capabilities of blacks failed to make sufficient allowances, particularly for the things he himself named. It is perhaps poetic justice that posterity should be liable to the same kind of mistake in judging him.

But if Jefferson's beliefs add up to a kind of racism, we must specify two important qualifications. First, that Jefferson offered his conclusions as a hypothesis only, acknowledging that his own experience was not a sufficient basis on which to judge an entire race. Had he lived long enough to meet the ex-slave Frederick Douglass or hear the searing eloquence of his oratory, he would have recognized intellectual gifts in a black man that were superior to those of most whites. Douglass's oratory brings us to the second qualification, which is a telling one. Attacking the justifications for slavery in 1854, Douglass observed,

Ignorance and depravity, and the inability to rise from degradation to civilization and respectability, are the most usual allegations against the oppressed. The evils most fostered by slavery and oppression are precisely those which slaveholders and oppressors would transfer from their system to the inherent character of their victims. Thus the very crimes of slavery become slavery's best defence. By making the enslaved a character fit only for slavery, they excuse themselves for refusing to make the slave a freeman.

Although we may find Jefferson guilty of failing to make adequate allowance for the conditions in which blacks were forced to live, Jefferson did not take the next step of concluding that blacks were fit only for slavery. This rationalization of slavery was indeed the common coin of slaveholders and other whites who condoned or tolerated the "peculiar" institution, but it formed no part of Jefferson's thinking. In fact, he took the opposite position: that having imposed the depredations of slavery on blacks, white Americans should not only emancipate them but also educate and train them to be self-sufficient, provide them with necessary materials, and establish a colony in which they could live as free and independent people.

But if going back to original sources and historical contexts is essential in discerning the meanings that Today has imposed on Yesterday, it is equally important in determining how Yesterday's meanings have colored Today's. The concept of equality that is universally recognized in our own time as a fundamental principle of American society only had its beginnings in the eighteenth century; it did not emerge full-blown from the Declaration of Independence.

Whenever he sent correspondents a copy of the Declaration, Jefferson transcribed the text in such a way as to show what the Continental Congress had added to his draft and what it had cut out. The process of congressional emendation was clearly a painful memory for him, and the deletion about which he probably felt the most regret was also the most radical of the passages, for it undertook to blame the King of England directly for the African slave trade. It begins,

He has waged cruel war against human nature itself, violating it's most sacred rights of life and liberty in the persons of a distant people who never offended him, captivating & carrying them into slavery in another hemisphere, or to incur miserable death in their transportation thither. . . . Determined to keep open a market where MEN should be bought & sold, he has prostituted his negative for suppressing every legislative attempt to prohibit or to restrain this execrable commerce.

Had this passage been ratified as part of the official Declaration, then a question often raised in the nineteenth century — Did Jefferson mean to include blacks in the language of the Declaration? — would have been susceptible of a clear-cut and demonstrable answer. For, as the political scientist Jean Yarbrough has recently pointed out, this passage says unmistakably that the Africans captured into slavery were not a separate category of beings but men, with the sacred rights of life and liberty that are said in the prologue of the Declaration to be the natural endowments of all men. It is precisely in having these same rights that the prologue asserts that all men are created equal.

This deleted passage also provides an answer to a question often raised in the twentieth century: Did Jefferson mean to include women in the phrase "all men are created equal"? Implicit in the passage is that "men" is being used in the broader sense of "mankind," for those who were cruelly transported to be "bought & sold" on the slave market were certainly female as well as male.

That blacks and women were meant to be included in the affirmations of Jefferson's Declaration at a time when they enjoyed nothing remotely like political and social equality underscores a source of continuing confusion for contemporary Americans — the difference between a philosophical conception of natural rights and a working system of laws and societal values which allows for the fullest expression of those rights. In our own time the stubbornly persistent disparity between these two is often a source of cynicism and despair, but a Jeffersonian perspective would put more emphasis on the considerable progress made in closing the gap. Jefferson himself was sustained by a profound belief in progress. His unshakable conviction that the world was steadily advancing, not only in the material but also in the moral sphere, is abundantly evident in his writings. Though sometimes criticized as being naive in this regard, he was fully aware that his belief embraced the prospect of recurrent political and social transformations. Writing from

retirement at the age of seventy-three, he told a correspondent that "laws and institutions must go hand in hand with the progress of the human mind."

As that becomes more developed, more enlightened, as new discoveries are made, new truths disclosed, and manners and opinions change with the change of circumstances, institutions must advance also, and keep pace with the times. We might as well require a man to wear still the coat which fitted him when a boy, as civilized society to remain ever under the regimen of their barbarous ancestors.

One way of looking at American history from Jefferson's day down to our own is as the series of changes and adjustments in our laws and institutions necessitated by the ideals implicit in Jefferson's Declaration. Sometimes the effect of these ideals has been simply to prevent other, incompatible ideals from gaining ascendancy, as in the case of Social Darwinism, whose notions of the natural inferiority of certain racial and social groups were impeded by the prevalence and familiarity of the Declaration's precepts. But without doubt the most important event in the development of the American ideal of equality, after Jefferson's Declaration, was Abraham Lincoln's address at Gettysburg. Without any warrant from the founders themselves or from subsequent interpreters or historians, Lincoln declared that not only the essential meaning of the Civil War but also the national purpose itself was epitomized in Jefferson's phrase "all men are created equal."

As Garry Wills has cogently argued, Lincoln at Gettysburg was practicing not presentism but futurism. In the most stunning act of statesmanship in our history, he invested Jefferson's eighteenth-century notion of equality with an essentially new meaning and projected it onto the future of the nation. Transfigured in the context of civil war, and transformed by Lincoln into a larger and more consequential ideal, Jefferson's formulation would never be the same. Thanks in large part to Lincoln, Americans no longer understand the prologue of the Declaration as a philosophical expression of natural rights, but rather take it to be a statement about the social and political conditions that ought to prevail.

Jefferson's Declaration is thus remarkable not only for its durability — its ability to remain meaningful and relevant — but also for its adaptability to changing conditions. At a time when natural rights are widely proclaimed a nullity, the language of the Declaration is universally understood as affirming human rights, and is resorted to even by those who do not consciously associate their ideas or aspirations with Jefferson. When the black separatist Malcolm X underwent a change of heart about white people and publicly renounced the "sweeping indictments of one race," he told an audience in Chicago, "I am not a racist and do not subscribe to any of the tenets of racism. In all honesty and sincerity it can be stated that I wish nothing but freedom, justice, and equality; life, liberty, and the pursuit of happiness — for all people." Simply to name the most basic American ideals is to invoke the words of Jefferson.

QUESTIONS TO CONSIDER

1. Compare Thomas Jefferson and the Benjamin Franklin you met in selection 6. In what ways were they both representative of their time? Are there ways in which they were not?

2. How did the story of Jefferson and Sally Hemings first surface? What was the purpose of its publication?

This story has been treated and interpreted in very different ways at different times. What do the varying interpretations say about the periods in which they originated?

3. Wilson says that one should not ask why Jefferson, author of the Declaration of Independence, did not free his slaves but rather how Jefferson, member of a slaveholding society, came to hate slavery. Do you agree with Wilson's point of view? During the Revolution and influenced especially by the Declaration of Independence, a number of southern slaveholders as well as the northern states did in fact free their slaves in the name of the liberty for which the American Revolution was being fought. So why did Jefferson not free his own? Is this question necessarily presentist?

4. The anthology entitles this selection "Thomas Jefferson and the Meanings of Liberty." What are the different meanings of liberty embodied in the Declaration of Independence? Which were most current in the eighteenth century? Which are most current today, and why have they changed?

5. Douglas Wilson raises the question of whether figures from the past should be remembered for their "greatest achievements" or for their "personal failures." What are the good sides and bad sides of revisionism that often stress the faults of great figures? What does this trend in historical writing say about the present?

V

BIRTH OF THE REPUBLIC

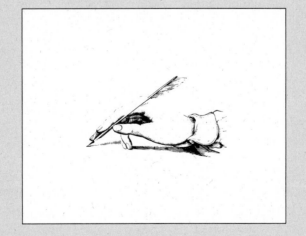

9

Sunrise at Philadelphia

Brian McGinty

Once the Revolution began, Americans set about creating the political machinery necessary to sustain an independent nation. The Second Continental Congress, called in 1775, continued as an emergency, all-purpose central government until 1781, when the Articles of Confederation were finally ratified and a new one-house Congress was elected to function as the national government. Wary of central authority because of the British experience, Americans now had precisely the kind of government most of them wanted: an impotent Congress that lacked the authority to tax, regulate commerce, or enforce its own ordinances and resolutions. Subordinate to the states, which supplied it with funds as they chose, Congress was powerless to run the country. Indeed, its delegates wandered from Princeton to Annapolis to Trenton to New York, endlessly discussing where they should settle.

Patriots such as James Madison of Virginia, Alexander Hamilton of New York, and the venerable George Washington fretted in their correspondence about the near paralysis of the central government and the unstable conditions that plagued the land. "An opinion begins to prevail, that a General Convention for revising the Articles of Confederation would be expedient," John Jay wrote Washington in March 1787. Washington agreed that the "fabrick" was "tottering." When Massachusetts farmers rose in rebellion under Daniel Shays, Washington was horror stricken. "Are your people getting mad? . . . What is the cause of all this? When and how is it to end? . . . What, gracious God, is man! that there should be such inconsistency and perfidiousness in his conduct? . . . We are fast verging to anarchy and confusion!"

Many of his colleagues agreed. There followed a series of maneuvers and meetings that culminated in the great convention of 1787, a gathering of fifty-five notables sent to Philadelphia to overhaul the feeble Articles of Confederation. Without authority, they proceeded to draft an entirely new constitution that scrapped the Articles, created a new government, and undoubtedly saved the country and America's experiment in popular government. As James MacGregor Burns has noted, it was a convention of "the well-bred, the well-fed, the well-read, and the well-wed." Most delegates were wealthy, formally educated, and youngish (their average age was the early forties), and more than a third of them were slave owners. The poor, the uneducated, the backcountry farmers, and women, blacks, and Indians were not represented. Throughout their deliberations, moreover, they compromised on the volatile slavery issue. "For these white men," wrote one scholar, "the black man was always a brooding and unsettling presence (the black woman, even more than the white woman, was beyond the pale, beyond calculation)." For most of the framers of the Constitution, order and national strength were more important than the inalienable rights of blacks or women. Like their countrymen, most could simultaneously love liberty, recognize the injustice of slavery, yet tolerate bondage as a necessary evil.

As we enter our third century under the Constitution, we need more than ever to remember that the framers were not saints but human beings — paradoxical, complex, unpredictable, and motivated by selfishness as well as high idealism. Yet, as Brian McGinty shows in his account of "the miracle of Philadelphia," the founders were able to rise above petty self-interest to fashion what remains the oldest written national constitution, which in turn created one of the oldest and most successful federal systems in history. McGinty tells the full story of the great convention; he describes the remarkable personalities gathered there, the debates and the compromises that shaped the new Constitution, the battle for ratification, and the forging of the Bill of Rights in the form of the first ten amendments.

GLOSSARY

ARTICLES OF CONFEDERATION
(1781–1789)   First American union in which a weak central government was subordinate to the states; it consisted of a one-house Congress that exercised all judicial, executive, and legislative functions but that lacked the power to tax or regulate currency.

THE FEDERALIST (OR FEDERALIST PAPERS)   Eighty-five letters written by Alexander Hamilton, James Madison, and John Jay defending the Constitution during the ratification process.

HENRY, PATRICK   Fiery opponent of the Constitution in Virginia.

MADISON, JAMES   Convention delegate from Virginia; planter, slaveholder, and brilliant political theorist who was "responsible for much of the substance" of the new Constitution.

MORRIS, GOUVERNEUR   Convention

delegate from Pennsylvania who assumed the chief responsibility for drafting the new Constitution; the preamble, which began, "We the people," was his inspiration and was "one of the single most important acts of the Constitutional Convention."

NECESSARY AND PROPER CLAUSE
Provision in the Constitution empowering Congress to enact all laws that were "necessary and proper" for executing its enumerated powers; the clause "would later become one of the chief building blocks of a strong central government."

NEW JERSEY PLAN
Proposed by *William Paterson,* it called for a one-house legislature comprised of members chosen by the state legislatures.

SHERMAN, ROGER
Convention delegate from Connecticut who proposed the first major compromise: it called for a lower house of Congress in which representation was based on population, and an upper house in which the states would be represented equally.

SUPREME LAW OF THE LAND CLAUSE
Provision in the Constitution designating it and the national laws made under it as the supreme law of the land.

THREE-FIFTHS CLAUSE
By this provision in the Constitution, each slave was counted as three fifths of a person when it came to apportioning representation in the lower house on the basis of population; the clause gave the white South disproportionate power in the House of Representatives (the slaves, while counted thus, had no political rights whatever).

VIRGINIA PLAN
Proposed by *Edmund Randolph,* it called for a national executive with veto power, a national judiciary, and a two-house legislature, with the lower house "elected by the people and the upper chosen by the lower."

A s Benjamin Franklin looked over the roster of delegates at the start of the Constitutional Convention, he confessed that he was well pleased. "We have here at present," Franklin wrote a friend, "what the French call *une assemblée des notables,* a convention composed of some of the principal people from the several states of our Confederation." [Thomas] Jefferson, examining the same roster in Paris, proclaimed the convention "an assembly of demi-gods."

Most prominent among the "demi-gods" was George Washington. Early on the morning of May 9, 1787, he had left Mount Vernon in his carriage. Washington was no stranger to the road from the Potomac to Philadelphia, for he had traveled it often during the days of the First and Second Continental Congresses, oftener still while he was leading the military struggle for independence. He would have liked to travel with Martha this time, but the mistress of the plantation on the Potomac had "become too domestic and too attentive to her two little grandchildren to leave home." The retired general's progress was impeded more than a little by the joyful greetings he received at every town and stage stop along the way. When he arrived in Philadelphia on May 13, the biggest celebration of all began. Senior officers of the Continental Army greeted him on the outskirts of the city, and citizens on horseback formed an escort. Guns fired a salute and the bells of Christ Church pealed as the great man rode into the city.

Washington had reflected carefully before deciding to attend the Philadelphia convention. He was fifty-five years old now, and his once-powerful physique was wracked with rheumatism. He was far from certain that the Philadelphia convention would find a solution to the nation's political problems and had little

From "Sunrise at Philadelphia" by Brian McGinty, *American History Illustrated* (Summer 1987), excerpted from pp. 22–47. Reprinted through the courtesy of Cowles Magazines, Inc., publisher of *American History Illustrated.*

A view of the Philadelphia State House (Independence Hall), where the delegates to the Constitutional Convention assembled in May 1787. During these meetings, the United States government, as we know it, took shape. In the tower of the State House hung the Liberty Bell, which tolled the news of the signing of the Declaration of Independence and of American victories in the Revolution. An impassioned motto girdled the bell: "Proclaim Liberty throughout the land, and to all the inhabitants thereof." But given all the inhabitants excluded from the blessings of liberty, the motto seems more than a little ironic. (By permission of the Houghton Library, Harvard University)

wish to risk his reputation in an effort that might be doomed to failure. More important, when he had resigned his military commission in December 1783 he had clearly stated his intention of spending the rest of his days in private life. But his friends had urged him to reconsider his decision and lend his commanding influence and prestige to the Philadelphia assembly.

Despite his lingering doubts about the convention's ultimate outcome, Washington had no reservations about its purpose. "The discerning part of the community," he wrote a friend, "have long since seen the necessity of giving adequate powers to Congress for national purposes; and the ignorant and designing must yield to it ere long." What most troubled the Virginian was the realization that his failure to go to Philadelphia might be interpreted as a rejection of the convention. And so he decided, more out of a sense of duty than with any enthusiasm, to make the long trip to Philadelphia. Although Washington arrived there the day before the assembly was set to convene, he found that some delegates were already in the city. The Pennsylvania delegates, who all lived in Philadelphia, were there, of course, headed by the venerable Dr. Benjamin Franklin. Franklin received Washing-

121

ton in the courtyard of his home just off Market Street above Third, after which the general repaired to the luxurious home of Robert Morris on Market just east of Sixth, where he was to be a guest during the convention.

Franklin was eighty-one years old and beset by infirmities (gout and gall stones) that made it all but impossible for him to walk. But his mind was bright and alert, and he continued to play an active role in the affairs of his city and state. He had returned in 1785 from Paris, where he had been American minister to France, to enjoy comforts of a well-earned retirement, but relented when members of the Supreme Executive Council of Pennsylvania asked him to accept the post of president, an office that corresponded to the position of governor in other states. By late March, on the motion of Robert Morris, Franklin had accepted a commission to attend the upcoming convention as a Pennsylvania delegate. . . .

Although Washington was the most celebrated of the Virginia delegates, he was not the first to arrive in Philadelphia. Thirty-six-year-old James Madison of Montpelier in the Old Dominion's Orange County arrived in Philadelphia on May 3, 1787, from New York, where he had been serving in Congress. A slight man, barely five feet, six inches tall, Madison was shy and bookish. What he lacked in force and dynamism, the little Virginian more than made up in thought and scholarship. After graduating from the College of New Jersey (later Princeton), he had returned to his home state to take an active interest in public affairs. He served in the Virginia House of Delegates and Council of State before accepting election to Congress, where he served twice (in 1780–83 and again in 1786–88). A close friend of Thomas Jefferson, Madison came to the convention with well-developed ideas about democratic processes and republican institutions. . . .

In all, seventy-four delegates were selected to attend the convention, and fifty-five actually appeared in Philadelphia. Although not all of the fifty-five would attend all of the sessions, it was a sizable group — large enough to give the spacious, panelled assembly room on the east side of the ground floor of the Pennsylvania State House (the same room in which the Declaration of Independence had been signed in 1776) an air of excitement when the convention was in session.

In some ways the convention was as notable for the men who were not there as for those who were. The absence of John Adams and Thomas Jefferson was sharply felt, for both of these veterans of 1776 were widely regarded as American giants. Important diplomatic assignments kept them away from Philadelphia: Jefferson was American minister in Paris, while Adams filled the same post in London. Both were apprised of developments in the Pennsylvania city by faithful correspondents on the scene. Adams's intellectual presence was strongly felt at the convention, for he had recently published *A Defence of the Constitutions of Government of the United States of America,* a treatise that explained and analyzed the constitutional structures of a half-dozen American states. Jefferson exchanged letters with James Madison and, at the younger man's request, sent him books on constitutional theory and history, for Madison was particularly interested in the histories of ancient confederacies. . . .

George Washington's presence in Philadelphia was enough to reassure all those who worried about the absence of Adams, Jefferson, [Richard Henry] Lee, [Patrick] Henry, and [John] Jay. When the hero of the Revolution entered Philadelphia at the head of a parade of cheering well-wishers, nearly everyone in the city was able to breathe more easily. If anyone could guarantee the results of the Philadelphia assembly, surely the Squire of Mount Vernon could. New York's Henry Knox wrote the Marquis de Lafayette: "General Washington's attendance at the convention adds, in my opinion, new lustre to his character. Secure as he was in his fame, he has again committed it to the mercy of events." "This great patriot," said the *Pennsylvania Herald,* "will never think his duty performed, while anything remains to be done."

It is not surprising that so many of the delegates (more than half) were lawyers, for members of the legal profession had long led the struggle for independence. Nor was it remarkable that many were present or former public officials. Fully four-fifths of the delegates were serving in or had been members of Congress, while even more had been involved, at one time or another, in colonial, state, and local governments. Many had helped draft their states' constitutions, and about half were veterans of military service. There were merchants, farmers, and one or two men who described themselves as "bankers" in the group. Three of the delegates were physicians, and one, Franklin, was a printer.

On the whole, the delegates were remarkably young: The average age was forty-three. Jonathan Dayton of New Jersey, at twenty-six, was the youngest; Franklin, at eighty-one, the oldest. Many had humble origins. Franklin had once been an indentured servant, and [Roger] Sherman of Connecticut had begun his working life as a cobbler's apprentice. But most delegates had acquired comfortable positions in life. A few ranked among the richest men in the country.

In a letter to Jefferson, Franklin expressed cautious optimism about the convention. The delegates were men of character and ability, Franklin said, "so that I hope Good from their meeting. Indeed," he added, "if it does not do good it must do Harm, as it will show that we have not Wisdom enough among us to govern ourselves; and will strengthen the opinion of some Political writers, that popular Governments cannot long support themselves." . . .

George Washington appeared regularly in the State House (the historic building would not be known as Independence Hall until the nineteenth century) at the appointed time each day, waiting patiently for the stragglers to appear and be recorded as present. When on May 25, the delegates of seven states were at last in their chairs, the convention was ready to begin.

First, a presiding officer had to be selected. Nobody in attendance had any doubt that the honor would be conferred on Washington; the only uncertainty was who would nominate him. Benjamin Franklin had planned to do so, but it was raining on May 25 and he was not well enough to make the trip from his home to the State House in poor weather. The motion was made in his stead by Robert Morris (Pennsylvania) and seconded by John Rutledge (South Carolina). Without discussion, the question was put to a vote, and Washington was unanimously elected president of the convention. Morris and Rutledge escorted the Virginian to the President's Chair. The chair belonged to the Pennsylvania Assembly and had been used by all the presidents of the Continental Congress when it had met in Philadelphia. Surmounting its back was the carved and gilded image of a sun that, before the assembly was concluded, would become a symbol for the convention and its work.

Second, rules for the convention's proceedings had to be adopted. One rule . . . was readily approved. It provided that "no copy be taken of any entry on the journal during the sitting of the House without the leave of the House. That members only be permitted to inspect the journal. That nothing spoken in the House be printed, or otherwise published, or communicated without leave." . . .

To impress on the delegates the seriousness with which the rule of secrecy was to be enforced, armed sentries were posted in the hall beyond the assembly chamber and on the street outside the State House. . . .

The delegates, on the whole, were scrupulous in their observance of the "rule of secrecy"; so scrupulous, in fact, that for nearly a generation after the convention the positions taken during the debates were still largely unknown to the public. Washington even refused to write about the debates in his diary. A few delegates kept private records that found their way into print long after the events at Philadelphia had become history. The best record was kept by James Madison. "I chose a seat," the Virginian later explained, "in front of the presiding member, with the other members on my right hand and left hand. In this favorable position for hearing all that passed I noted in terms legible and abbreviations and marks intelligible to [no one but] myself what was read from the Chair or spoken by the members; and losing not a moment unnecessarily between the adjournment and reassembling of the Convention I was enabled to write out my daily notes during the session or within a few finishing days after its close. . . . I was not absent a single day, nor more than a casual fraction of any hour in any day, so that I could not have lost a single speech, unless a very short one." Published in 1840, Madison's notes form the single best record of the convention's proceedings.

The Virginia delegates came to the convention's first deliberative session on May 29 equipped with a comprehensive plan for a new charter of government. Although the "Virginia Plan" had been discussed at length by members of that state's delegation, it bore the mark of Madison's careful thought and planning on every page. Edmund Randolph, who, as governor of the state, was titular leader of the Virginia delegation, presented the plan to the convention. The Virginia Plan proclaimed that it was designed to "correct and enlarge" the Articles of Confederation, but it was actually a blueprint for a whole new structure of government. Under it, the "national legislature" would consist of not one, but two houses, with the lower elected by the people and the upper chosen by the lower. There would be a "national executive," with veto power over legislative acts, and a "national judiciary," with authority to decide cases involving "national peace or harmony."

The Virginia plan was a tempting subject for debate, but the convention's leaders believed more fundamental questions had to be decided first — questions upon which all other as yet undecided questions depended.

First among these threshold questions was whether the convention ought to content itself with revising the Articles of Confederation or propose an entirely new government with truly national purposes and powers. Delegates from at least four of the states had been sent to Philadelphia with strict instructions to consider revisions of the Articles and nothing else; and Congress, in its resolution approving the convention, had purported to limit the convention to revising the old charter.

Next the delegates resolved to organize into a Committee of the Whole. The purpose of this parliamentary maneuver was to keep discussions informal and to allow the representatives to change their votes until near the end of the convention. The device promoted open minds and frank speech.

As discussion began, South Carolina's Charles Pinckney expressed concern that, if the convention proposed a national government, the states might cease to exist. But Edmund Randolph (Virginia) assured him that a national government would not prevent the states from continuing to exercise authority in their proper spheres. John Dickinson (Delaware) and Elbridge Gerry (Massachusetts) admitted that the Articles of Confederation were defective, but they thought that the convention should correct their defects, not toss them aside.

Gouverneur Morris (Pennsylvania) expressed his belief that a national government was essential to the future of the country. "We had better take a supreme government now," Morris warned his fellow-delegates, "than a despot twenty years hence — for come he must." Agreeing with Morris, George Mason (Virginia) argued that the country needed a government that could govern directly, without the intervention of the states.

On May 30, on the motion of Gouverneur Morris, the convention decided, by a vote of six states to one, that "a *national* government ought to be established consisting of a *supreme* Legislative, Executive and Judiciary." Almost before they knew it, the delegates had decided what was to be the single most important issue of the convention. From that day forward, the convention would be irrevocably dedicated to the construction of a national government for the United States.

On May 31 the Committee of the Whole (the convention delegates) proceeded to consider other potentially explosive questions: whether the "national legislature" should have two houses or one; whether either or both houses should be elected by the people; and how the national government should function in terms of the citizens and the states. . . . Surprisingly, the delegates quickly agreed that there should be two houses in the legislature, that the lower house should be popularly elected, and that the legislature should have broad powers "to legislate in all cases to which the separate States are incompetent."

After deliberating for two weeks, the Committee of the Whole presented its recommendations to the convention. The proposed form of government followed the terms of the "Virginia Plan" closely — too closely, some delegates thought. Elbridge Gerry (Massachusetts) protested that some decisions might have been made too hastily, "that it was necessary to consider what the people would approve." Taking his cue from Gerry, William Paterson (New Jersey) proposed an alternative to the "Virginia Plan." Introduced on June 15, Paterson's "New Jersey Plan" suggested an entirely different frame of government: a unicameral legislature with members chosen by the state legislatures but with powers to "pass Acts for the regulation of trade and commerce." . . .

The delegates now decided to refer both the New Jersey Plan and the Virginia Plan to the Committee of the Whole for discussion.

The debates were now becoming contentious. The large states, led in size by Virginia, believed it was essential to do away with the old principle embodied in the Articles of Confederation of "one state, one vote." Under this rule, voters in the large states were effectively disfranchised by those in the small states. For their part, the small states insisted they could never consent to any rule that would deprive them of an equal voice in the federal government. If such a resolution were passed, Delaware's George Read announced, he would have no choice but to leave the convention, for his credentials forbade him to consent to such a measure.

Washington had been pleased when, in the early days of the convention, the delegates quickly and readily reached agreement on difficult questions. Now, it seemed, they were arguing about every issue that came before them. Discouraged, he wrote home for additional clothing, explaining that he saw "no end to my staying here." The sweltering heat (some Philadelphians thought the summer of 1787 was the worst since 1750) added to the bad humor of the delegates. Franklin, noting the rancor of the debates, suggested the representatives invite clergymen to attend their sessions and offer daily prayers. Roger Sherman (Connecticut) seconded the motion, but Alexander Hamilton (New York) doubted the wisdom of calling for "foreign aid." Many different faiths were represented among the delegates, and it would have been difficult to meet the demands of them all. Besides, a call for prayer might signal to the public outside the hall that all was not well inside. After some discussion, Franklin's proposal was dropped.

Sensing that the convention was approaching an impasse, Roger Sherman (Connecticut) rose to propose the convention's first important compromise. Representation in the lower house, Sherman suggested, should be based on population, while representation in the upper house should be equal. Sherman's proposal was ingenious. Its chief virtue was that it satisfied neither the large states nor the small states. Hamilton called it a "motley measure," and Madison said it was a "novelty & a compound." Because it met the demands of neither interest, however, it was acceptable to both. On July 16, by a vote of five states in favor, four states against, and one (Massachusetts) evenly divided, the "Connecticut Compromise" was passed. Another major hurdle to agreement had been overcome.

But many difficult questions still remained to be resolved. After spirited debate, the convention decided that each state would be allotted two representatives (senators) in the upper house of the national legislature and that the senators would vote "per capita," that is, individually. Additional debate prompted the delegates to decide that the "national executive" (the president) would be chosen neither by the national legislature nor by the people directly, but by a body of men (the electoral college) specially chosen for the purpose. George Mason (Virginia) proposed that membership in the national legislature be limited to "citizens of the United States," and no one objected.

By July 26, the convention felt it had made enough progress on the broad questions that faced it to safely proceed to more particular issues. To this end, it referred the proposed Constitution to a Committee of Detail with instructions to report back on August 6 with specific proposals to implement the convention's broad intentions. Its five members, John Rutledge (South Carolina), Edmund Randolph (Virginia), James Wilson (Pennsylvania), Oliver Ellsworth (Connecticut), and Nathaniel Gorham (Massachusetts) represented all sections of the country; the committee constituted a kind of "miniature convention."

From July 26 to August 6, the committee proposed, debated, revised, and, finally, resolved a host of important questions. It spelled out the powers of the national legislature, including a power that the Articles of Confederation had never given the old Congress: "to lay and collect taxes, duties, imposts and excises." The committee proposed to grant the national legislature the power to make all laws that should be "necessary and proper" for carrying out its specific powers. The "necessary and proper" clause would later become one of the chief building blocks of a strong central government. The committee decided the Supreme Court should have jurisdiction to decide all "Cases arising under the Laws passed by the general Legislature." And, significantly, the Committee

of Detail provided that acts of the national legislature, treaties, and "this Constitution" should all be the "supreme Law of the Land."

With the basic structure of the proposed government now agreed upon, the convention appointed a Committee of Style and Arrangement to draft the Constitution. Some of the best penmen of the convention were appointed to the committee — James Madison (Virginia), Alexander Hamilton (New York), William Samuel Johnson (Connecticut), and Rufus King (Massachusetts). But the chief responsibility for drafting the document fell to the talented Gouverneur Morris (Pennsylvania). Years later, Morris would write that the Constitution "was written by the fingers, which write this letter." Madison, who was responsible for much of the substance of the document, admitted "the finish given to the style and arrangement of the Constitution fairly belongs to the pen of Mr. Morris."

Morris worked quickly and apparently with inspiration. One of the last sections he composed was the Preamble. As originally drafted by the Committee of Detail, the Preamble had stated:

"We the People of the States of New-Hampshire, Massachusetts, Rhode-Island and Providence Plantations, Connecticut, New-York, New-Jersey, Pennsylvania, Delaware, Maryland, Virginia, North Carolina, South-Carolina, and Georgia, do ordain, declare, and establish the following Constitution for the Government of Ourselves and our Posterity."

The Committee of Style and Arrangement rewrote the same passage to read:

"We the People of the United States, in Order to form a more perfect Union, to establish Justice, insure domestic Tranquility, provide for the common defence, promote the general Welfare, and secure the Blessings of Liberty to ourselves and our Posterity, do ordain and establish this Constitution for the United States of America."

The change from "We the People" of named states to "We the People of the United States" did not seem particularly significant to the delegates when they read and considered Morris's draft. To history, however, it became one of the single most important acts of the Constitutional Convention. It would signify that the Union was the product, not of thirteen states, but of more than three million citizens. It was not a compact between sovereign governments, but a contract to which the citizens were parties.

When the Committee of Style presented its draft to the convention, there was a flurry of last-minute objections. Some delegates thought that Congress's right to overrule presidential vetoes should be by a vote of two-thirds rather than three-fourths of both houses. Others thought the document ought to guarantee the right of trial by jury in all civil cases. George Mason (Virginia) demanded that a bill of rights (similar to the precedent-setting Bill of Rights he drafted for the Virginia Constitution in 1776) be appended to the Constitution. But the hour was late, and the delegates were opposed to making major revisions. All states on the convention floor (including Mason's own Virginia) voted "no" to adopting a bill of rights.

Some delegates left the convention before the final copy of the Constitution was prepared. Others remained in Philadelphia, but only to express their opposition to the final version of the charter. George Mason, obstinate on the point of a bill of rights, announced that he "would sooner chop off his right hand than put it to the Constitution." Another Virginian, Edmund Randolph, who had first proposed the "Virginia Plan" that had formed the basis for many of the Constitution's major provisions, now doubted whether the people of his state would approve the document, and announced that he could not sign it. Elbridge Gerry (Massachusetts) thought that members of the Senate would hold their offices too long, that Massachusetts would not be fairly represented in the House of Representatives, and that a Supreme Court without juries would be a "Star-Chamber as to civil cases." He announced that he would not sign.

Word was circulating in Philadelphia that Pennsylvania's Benjamin Franklin also objected to the Constitution, but the philosopher-statesman soon put an end to such speculation. On Monday morning, September 17, after the secretary of the convention read a newly engrossed copy of the document, Franklin asked for permission to present a speech he had written. Because it was painful for him to stand, he asked James Wilson to read it for him:

"I confess that there are several parts of this constitution which I do not at present approve, but I am not sure I shall never approve them: For having lived long, I have experienced many instances of being obliged by better information or fuller consideration, to change opinions even on important subjects, which I once thought right, but found to be otherwise. . . . Thus I consent, Sir, to this Constitution because I expect no better, and because I am not sure, that it is not the best."

Before the Constitution could be signed, Nathaniel Gorham (Massachusetts) proposed that one final change be made in the document. Where the charter provided that each member of the House of Representatives would represent 40,000 citizens, Gorham suggested that the number be changed to 30,000. Several of the delegates felt that 40,000 was too large a constituency to be represented by one man. Rufus King (Massachusetts), Daniel Carroll (Maryland), and, finally, George Washington announced their agreement with Gorham. Although Washington had previously maintained a rigorous silence on disputed questions, he felt that he should express his opinion on this matter. He hoped that grounds for objection to the Constitution would, wherever possible, be eliminated. He believed that 40,000 was too large a constituency, and, although the hour was late, he still favored the change. Without objection, the word "forty" was erased and the word "thirty" written in its place on the engrossed copy.

The question now arose as to the manner in which the Constitution should be signed. Quorums in all of the represented states (although not all of the delegates in those states) were in favor of submitting the document to ratification. Most delegates wished to present the document to the public in the most favorable light possible and, to that end, hoped to give the impression of unanimity. Accordingly, Franklin moved that the signature clause be made to read: "Done in Convention by the Unanimous Consent of the States present." The motion was passed by a vote of eleven states to one. (South Carolina was divided on the issue. Charles Pinckney and Pierce Butler thought the clause too ambiguous.)

That same day, September 17, nearly four months after the convention began, the engrossed copy of the Constitution was signed. Proceeding in the traditional order of states from north to south, the delegates walked to the front of the room, bent over the table in front of the President's Chair and, with quill pen dipped in iron gall ink, signed their names on the last of the four pages of parchment. There were thirty-eight delegates and thirty-nine signatures (George Read of Delaware, who had overcome his earlier opposition to the document, signed both for himself and for John Dickinson, who was feeling ill and had gone home to Wilmington). Only three members present — Edmund Randolph (Virginia), George Mason (Virginia), and Elbridge Gerry (Massachusetts) — abstained. Thirteen members had left the convention before the final day.

Appropriately, Benjamin Franklin had a few last words. While the other delegates signed their names, the old patriot looked thoughtfully toward the President's Chair. He told a few delegates near him that painters had found it difficult "to distinguish in their art a rising from a setting sun. I have," said he, "often and often in the course of the Session, and the vicissitudes of my hopes and fears as to its issue, looked at that behind the President without being able to tell whether it was rising or setting: But now at length I have the happiness to know that it is a rising and not a setting Sun."

After the Constitution was signed and the last gavel fell, the delegates filed out of the State House, then proceeded to the City Tavern on Second Street near Walnut. The City Tavern was one of old Philadelphia's most enjoyable gathering places and had been a favorite haunt of the delegates during the convention. The members shared a last dinner together, complete with toasts and speeches, then bade each other a fond farewell. George Washington's mind was still excited when he returned to his room at Robert Morris's house. Washington tended to some business matters and then, in the words of his diary, "retired to meditate on the momentous work which had been executed."

The newspapers were full of news from the convention. The delegates' self-imposed "rule of secrecy" had heightened the air of mystery surrounding the meeting, and now it seemed as if the public could not hear enough about what had happened during the convention. In Philadelphia on September 19, the *Pennsylvania Packet and Daily Advertiser* published the full text of the Constitution. Just under the newspaper's masthead, in boldface type, were the words of the Preamble, beginning with the soon-to-be memorable phrase: "We, the People of the United States." Within weeks, the Constitution was reprinted in newspapers, pamphlets, and booklets all over the country. . . .

Article VII of the Constitution prescribed the process by which the charter was to be ratified. When conventions in at least nine states had approved the document, the Constitution would be "established" between the ratifying states. Until ratifying conventions had assembled, deliberated, and expressed their approval, however, the document would be nothing more than a hope for a better future. . . .

When Congress received the document, some of its members were baffled. The Articles of Confederation, from which Congress derived its authority, did not authorize it to do away with the Confederation and replace it with a *national government*. Those members of Congress who had also attended the Philadelphia assembly argued strongly that Congress should follow the wishes of the convention and submit the

Constitution to state ratifying conventions. Richard Henry Lee, a Congressman from Virginia, objected. Lee thought the "Federalists" (as proponents of the Constitution were now being called) were trying "to push the business on with dispatch . . . that it might be adopted before it had stood the test of reflection and due examination." But a majority of Congress favored the document, paving the way for passage of a resolution referring the Constitution to the legislatures, by them to be "submitted to a convention of Delegates chosen in each state by the people thereof in conformity to the resolves of the Convention. . . ."

[Meanwhile], proponents and opponents of the Constitution began to argue their cases. James Madison [noted:] "The advocates for it come forward more promptly than the adversaries. . . . The sea coast seems everywhere fond of it."

Indeed, many were "fond" of the Constitution — but hardly anyone entertained the notion that it was "perfect." The charter was the work of different men with various ideas, the product of a long string of concessions and compromises. To be sure, it called for the establishment of some notable features: three autonomous branches of government, each invested with power and authority to check the excesses of the others; a Congress consisting of two houses with specifically enumerated powers; a national judiciary; and a strong executive. And it provided the framework for a federal government that combined national supremacy with state autonomy and made both subservient to the popular will.

But the document was not free of anomalies. For instance, members of the House of Representatives were to be apportioned among the states "according to their respective numbers," but the "numbers" were to be calculated in a curious way: all "free persons" were to be counted, as were persons "bound to service for a term of years," but "Indians not taxed" were to be excluded, and only three-fifths of "all other persons" were to be counted. The delegates knew, of course, that the words "all other persons" referred to slaves and that, by allowing the southern states to count three-fifths of their slaves, the document gave tacit recognition to slavery. But the Constitution by no means *approved* slavery; indeed, many delegates believed the institution should be abolished throughout the country. The document did require enforcement of fugitive slave laws, but it also empowered Congress to forbid the importation of new slaves into the country after the year 1808. In its curious and conflicting references to slavery, the Constitution was reflecting the concessions and compromises by which it was produced.

In many ways, the charter was a hodgepodge. And yet it was bound together by common values: dedication to the ideals of American independence and liberty, and a conviction that a strong federal government was the best way to safeguard those ideals. . . .

By the end of October, however, Madison could see that the tide of opinion in the country was beginning to turn away from the Constitution. In Virginia, Richard Henry Lee and Patrick Henry announced their intention to work against ratification. In Massachusetts, James Winthrop (writing under the pseudonym of "Agrippa") published letters that charged that the Constitution gave too much power to the central government and not enough to the states. In New York, Melancton Smith published an *Address to the People of the State of New York* in which he warned that the Constitution would create an "aristocratic tyranny." Meanwhile, in Pennsylvania, Samuel Bryan published a broadside predicting that, under the Constitution, the United States would be "melted down into one empire" with a government "devoid of all responsibility or accountability to the great body of the people."

Richard Henry Lee's views were recorded in his *Letters from the Federal Farmer*. Forgetting for the moment his own privileged background, Lee said that the Constitution was the work of "the artful and ever active aristocracy." He agreed with George Mason that the Constitution should include a bill of rights. He also thought that it should provide for a council to assist and advise the president and guarantee the right of jury trial. "If our countrymen are so soon changed," Lee charged, "and the language of 1774 is become odious to them, it will be in vain to use the language of freedom, or attempt to rouse them to free inquiries."

Patrick Henry warned Virginians who lived in the region called Kentucky (it would not become a state until 1792) that the Constitution favored the eastern part of the country at the expense of the west and that it would inevitably lead to loss of navigation rights on the Mississippi. Henry was angered by the Preamble's reference to "We the People" and challenged the right of the Philadelphia delegates to use such an all-encompassing term. "[W]ho authorized them to speak the language of *We the people*," Henry demanded, "instead of, *We the states*? States are the characteristics and the soul of a confederation. If the states be not the agents of this compact, it must be one great consolidated national government, of the people of all the states."

In New York on September 27 the newspapers began to publish a series of articles attacking the Constitution and the Philadelphia convention. Signed with the pseudonym "Cato," the letters were widely supposed to have been written by New York's staunchly antifederalist governor, George Clinton. Other letters, similar in tone and content, appeared under the names of "Sydney" and "Brutus" and were widely recognized as pseudonyms for Clinton's supporters. Alarmed by the vigor of the "anti-Federalist" letters, Alexander Hamilton decided to mount a reply.

Hamilton had been the only New Yorker to sign the Constitution. He now tried to use the influence he had with other New York politicians. Hamilton was one of the state's most brilliant lawyers and effective writers. His home and law office on Wall Street were not far from the residences of John Jay and James Madison. The three soon joined forces to answer the attacks of "Cato," "Sydney," and "Brutus" with a series of letters [to various newspapers] signed with the name of "Publius." . . .

There were eighty-five letters from "Publius" — fifty-five written by Hamilton, twenty-nine by Madison, and five by Jay. Never one to lose the opportunity to publicize his views, Hamilton arranged with a printing firm to publish the letters in book form, and on May 28, 1788, a two-volume edition bearing the title of *The Federalist* was issued by J. and A. McLean in New York. . . . The book was both a reasoned defense of the Constitution and a ringing call for its ratification. "The establishment of a Constitution," Hamilton wrote in his last *Federalist* paper, "in time of profound peace, by the voluntary consent of a whole people, is a prodigy, to the completion of which I look forward with trembling anxiety." . . .

The demand for a bill of rights had become a clarion call of the antifederalists. In his speeches and letters, George Mason, who had written the Virginia Bill of Rights, argued that the people needed protection against a strong and powerful central government and that they could secure that protection only by specifically limiting the government's powers. Supporting Mason, Richard Henry Lee complained of the Constitution's lack of provisions to protect "those essential rights of mankind without which liberty cannot exist."

Prominent supporters of the Constitution generally opposed a bill of rights. Hamilton thought such a declaration not only unnecessary, but "dangerous." Under the Constitution, the federal government would have only the powers that the people granted it. Therefore, Hamilton argued, the government could have no power to abridge the people's rights unless they *gave it* that power. He pointed out that the Constitution already contained many provisions guaranteeing basic civil rights: protection of the writ of *habeas corpus,* a prohibition against bills of attainder and *ex post facto* laws, strict proof requirements in all prosecutions for treason, and a guarantee of the right of trial by jury in all criminal cases except impeachments. A bill of rights, Hamilton said, would inevitably "contain various exceptions to powers which are not granted; and on this very account would afford a colourable pretext to claim more than were granted. For why declare that things shall not be done which there is no power to do?"

South Carolina's Charles Cotesworth Pinckney pointed out that bills of rights "generally begin with declaring that all men are by nature born free." "Now, we should make that declaration with a very bad grace," Pinckney said, "when a large part of our property consists in men who are actually born slaves." Connecticut's Roger Sherman said, "No bill of rights ever yet bound the supreme power longer than the honeymoon of a new married couple, unless the rulers were interested in preserving the rights." And Pennsylvania's James Wilson sneered: "Enumerate all the rights of men? I am sure that no gentlemen in the late Convention would have attempted such a thing."

James Madison at first agreed with Hamilton that a bill of rights was unnecessary and potentially dangerous. But, by the fall of 1788, he had become convinced that such a declaration was not only desirable but essential to ratification of the Constitution. On October 17, 1788, Madison expressed his belief that an enumeration of the "fundamental maxims of free Government" would be "a good ground for an appeal to the sense of community" and "counteract the impulses of interest and passion." Madison pledged that, if the new Constitution went into effect, he would do everything in his power to see that it was amended in such a way as to protect basic human rights from federal infringement. . . .

[The ratification process began in Delaware, whose convention voted unanimously to endorse the new Constitution. The conventions of several other states did likewise. New Hampshire was the ninth and deciding state to ratify. The federalists found themselves hard-pressed in Virginia, where Patrick Henry and other antifederalists resisted tenaciously. "Whither is the spirit of America gone?" Patrick Henry cried. "Sir, the American spirit, assisted by the ropes and chains of consolidation, is about to convert this country into a powerful and mighty empire." Virginia nar-

rowly approved the Constitution, as did New York. North Carolina was the twelfth state to ratify, but tiny Rhode Island, the only state that had refused to send a delegation to Philadelphia, held out until May, 1790, when it finally approved the Constitution and joined the new Union. Meanwhile, Congress had adopted] an "ordinance" setting March 4, 1789, as the date and New York City as the place for the first meeting of the first Congress under the Constitution. Members of the electoral college were chosen, and on February 4 they cast their ballots. To nobody's surprise, their unanimous choice as the first president under the Constitution was George Washington.

James Madison attended the new Congress as a member of the House of Representatives from Orange County, Virginia. He was denied a Senate seat by a vindictive Patrick Henry, who declared him "unworthy of the confidence of the people." In the House, Madison took responsibility for introducing the Bill of Rights that Henry, George Mason, and other antifederalists had demanded. . . . [This took the form of seventeen amendments to the new Constitution; Congress approved most of them and sent them to the states for ratification. By the end of 1791, the requisite three-fourths of the states had approved ten of the amendments, which afterward became known as the American "Bill of Rights."] Now United States citizens everywhere could be sure that their most valued civic rights — freedom of speech and of the press, freedom of assembly and of religion, freedom from unreasonable searches and seizures, the right to bear arms, the privilege against self-incrimination, the right to due process of law, the right to trial by jury, and the right to representation by counsel — would be protected from federal abridgment.

The process was complete. . . . The United States had become a nation.

QUESTIONS TO CONSIDER

1. James Madison was not destined to be a happy president (1809–1817), but he was a brilliant states-

man and the true father of the Constitution. In what ways did he shape the drafting and passage of the Constitution? How did he overcome his own prejudices and the pressures exerted on him by his fellow Virginians in order to ensure the final success of the document?

2. In selection 7, Carl Degler concluded that Americans fought a conservative revolution to preserve the status quo. Discuss what might have been revolutionary or counterrevolutionary in nature about the Constitutional Convention, the delegates to which, instead of revising the Articles of Confederation as they were charged to do, scrapped that document and came up with an entirely new plan of government.

3. The framers of the Constitution were all well-to-do, socially prominent Americans. Did they produce a document that was fundamentally democratic or undemocratic? How did they feel about the will of the majority? What steps did they take to control that majority?

4. In many ways, as author McGinty says, the charter was a hodgepodge, a collection of ideas based on northern or southern biases, agricultural or commercial interests, federalist or antifederalist sentiments. What kinds of compromises did the representatives of these divergent interests finally accept?

5. How did the framers deal with the issue of slavery? Where, in particular, did they find it an embarrassment? Wherein did they sow the seeds of future discord?

6. The Constitution nearly failed the battle for ratification. What was the most significant area of dissension? What forms of suasion and compromise did both federalists and antifederalists employ?

10

George Washington and the Use of Power

EDMUND S. MORGAN

In polls taken in 1948, 1962, and 1982, American historians and presidential scholars ranked George Washington as the second-best president in American history (the first in all three surveys was Abraham Lincoln). More than any other statesman, specialists contend, Washington defined the presidency and set the standard for executive leadership. "It is no exaggeration to say that but for George Washington, the office of president might not exist," one historian maintains. Washington was so respected in his day, so much above factional bickering and regional jealousies, that he was probably the only leader behind whom the country could unite. "One of the problems with Washington," says writer Garry Wills, "is that we think of him in the wrong company, as a peer of Franklin and Jefferson, when he belongs in the select company of Caesar, Napoleon and Cromwell as a charismatic nation-builder who personified an epoch."

Not that Washington was a saint. As historian Edmund S. Morgan makes clear, the first president had human flaws — among them, an aloofness that made him a hard man to know. Uncomfortable among learned men, he developed the habit of listening carefully to what was being said, pondering it, but rarely expressing his own opinion. His reticence struck some as arrogance, what an Englishman described as "repulsive coldness." His formidable size contributed to his seeming aloofness: standing a "ramrod straight" six-feet, three inches, which made him a giant in his day, he looked down at everybody. A man of robust health and energy, he nevertheless suffered from chronic dental problems and had to wear false teeth made of ivory and wood.

Adapting himself to the slave-owning world in which he was born and raised, Washington became a wealthy Virginia planter who owned as many as 317 slaves and shared the racial prejudice of most whites of his time. He even brought slave "servants" to the president's house in Philadelphia. He said he regretted that slavery existed and wished it could be abolished but was unable to do anything about it beyond providing for the manumission of his own slaves upon his death.

In The First of Men *(1988),* the best biography of Washington yet written, historian John E. Ferling reveals that Washington had a complex and contradictory character. He suffered from low self-esteem, struggled all his life to overcome feelings of worthlessness, and had a pathological need for the admiration and affirmation of other people. Yet, as Ferling reminds us, Washington was also a man of extraordinary personal courage. He demonstrated a rare ability for self-criticism, strove hard to better himself, proved to be an excellent organizer, and gave his family "tender love and abiding steadfastness." But his most significant trait, Edmund Morgan believes, was his understanding of the use of power, both as commander in chief of the Continental Army and as president of his infant nation. When it came to understanding power, Morgan contends, Washington was unsurpassed among his contemporaries.

GLOSSARY

CORNWALLIS, LORD   Commander of the British forces in the southern colonies who surrendered to Washington in the Battle of Yorktown (1781), which ended the fighting in the Revolution.

HAMILTON, ALEXANDER   Washington's aide-de-camp during the Revolution and the nation's first secretary of the treasury, he served in the latter capacity under both Washington and second president John Adams.

JAY'S TREATY (1795)   Treaty which provided, among other things, that Great Britain would evacuate its posts in the Northwest Territory and that commissions would resolve boundary disputes.

PINCKNEY'S TREATY (1795)   Treaty with Spain that established the United States' southern boundary at the 31st parallel and that granted Americans free navigation rights on the Mississippi River.

When a crowd of American farmers opened fire on the regular troops of the British army some 200 years ago, the action must have seemed foolhardy to any impartial observer. Such an observer might have been a little surprised at the events that immediately followed, when the farmers put the regulars to rout, chased them from Concord to Boston, and laid siege to that town. But however impressive this performance, it did not alter the fact that the British army was probably the most powerful in the world, having succeeded scarcely a dozen years before in defeating the armies of France, England's only serious rival. For a handful of colonists, unorganized, without any regular source of arms or ammunition, with no army and no navy, to take on the world's greatest power in open war must still have looked like a foolhardy enterprise.

Somehow or other it proved not to be. Yet it remains something of a puzzle that the farmers were able to bring it off. With the benefit of hindsight we can offer a number of explanations. For one thing, the generals whom the British sent to put down the rebels proved to be somewhat less than brilliant in using the immense force at their disposal. For another thing, the colonists got a great deal of assistance from England's old enemy, France. But perhaps most important, the American Revolution seems to have elicited from those who participated in it a response that no other event or situation in American history has been able to do.

It was not that extraordinarily large numbers of people were ready to sacrifice their lives or their fortunes for the common good. That has often happened in times of crisis. And the revolution did not in fact induce this kind of sacrifice very widely. It was always difficult to fill up enlistments in the Continental Army. What was extraordinary about the revolution was the talent it generated, the number of men of genius who stepped out of farmyards and plantations, out of countinghouses and courtrooms, to play a leading role in winning the war and then in building a national government. Prominent among them was George Washington, who more than any other single man was responsible for bringing success to this seemingly foolhardy enterprise. Since there was nothing in his previous career to suggest that he could play so large a role, it may be worth asking what there was in him that enabled him to do what he did.

This is not an easy task, for George Washington is and was a hard man to know. Part of the difficulty in approaching him comes from the heroic image in which we have cast him and which already enveloped him in his own lifetime. But it is not simply the plaster image that stands between him and us. We have other national heroes who also became legendary figures in their own lifetimes, a Benjamin Franklin, an Andrew Jackson, an Abraham Lincoln; and yet with them we

Reprinted from *The Genius of George Washington* by Edmund S. Morgan, with the permission of W. W. Norton & Company, Inc. Copyright © 1980 by Edmund S. Morgan.

find no great difficulty in pushing past the image to find the man. In their letters and other writings, in the countless anecdotes they inspired, we can meet them on familiar terms and feel comfortable in their company.

But not George Washington. The familiar anecdotes about Washington tell us to keep our distance. The most arresting one is told about a gathering at the time of the Constitutional Convention in 1787. One evening during the sessions of the convention a group of Washington's old friends from wartime days were remarking on the extraordinarily reserved and remote manner he maintained, even among his most intimate acquaintances. One of them, Gouverneur Morris, who was always full of boldness and wit, had the nerve to disagree with the rest about Washington's aloofness. He could be as familiar with Washington, he said, as with any of his other friends. Alexander Hamilton called his bluff by offering to provide a dinner with the best of wine for a dozen of them if Morris would, at the next reception Washington gave, simply walk up to him, gently slap him on the shoulder, and say, "My dear general, how happy I am to see you look so well." On the appointed evening a substantial number were already present when Morris arrived, walked up to Washington, bowed, shook hands, and then placed his left hand on Washington's shoulder and said, "My dear General, I am very happy to see you look so well." The response was immediate and icy. Washington reached up and removed the hand, stepped back, and fixed his eyes in silence on Morris, until Morris retreated abashed into the crowd. The company looked on in dismay, and no one ever tried it again.

It seems today a rather extravagant reaction on the part of our national hero, a bit of overkill. It makes us almost as embarrassed for Washington as for poor Morris. Yet it may serve as an appropriate starting place for our inquiry, because Washington's dignity and reserve, the aloofness that separated him from his contemporaries and still separates him from us, were,

"Washington's genius," says Edmund S. Morgan, "lay in his understanding of power, both military and political. . . . But he accepted the premises of a Republican government as an Oliver Cromwell never did . . . [and] he never sought power on any other terms than those on which he had initially accepted it, as servant of the people." (The Metropolitan Museum of Art, Bequest of Charles Allen Munn, 1924)

I believe, an integral part of the genius that enabled him to defeat the armies of Great Britain and to establish the United States as an independent world power.

Washington's genius lay in his understanding of power, both military power and political power, an understanding unmatched by that of any of his contemporaries. At a time when the United States needed nothing quite so much as military power but had very little, this hitherto obscure Virginia planter knew how to make the best possible use of what there was. And after securing independence, when the United States was trying to establish itself in a war-torn world, he knew how to deal with foreign countries to the maximum advantage of his own. He was

not a bookish man. He contributed nothing to the formal political thought of the American Revolution, nor did he produce any treatises on military strategy or tactics. But he did understand power in every form.

At the simplest level Washington's understanding of power showed itself in the ability to take command. Some men have the quality; others do not. Washington had it, and in exercising it he nourished the aloofness that became his most conspicuous trait. That aloofness was deliberate, as it may be in many men who have the gift of command. In Washington it may have grown around a nucleus of inborn native reserve, but Washington purposely cultivated it. We should not mistake it for arrogance. Washington did crave honor and pursued it relentlessly, but he did not deceive himself with that spurious substitute for honor which is arrogance. His aloofness had nothing to do with arrogance. It had to do with command.

He explained the matter in a letter to a fledgling colonel in the Continental Army in 1775: "Be easy and condescending in your deportment to your officers," he wrote, "but not too familiar, lest you subject yourself to a want of that respect, which is necessary to support a proper command."

Washington practiced what he preached, and as his talents for command developed there were fewer and fewer persons with whom he could allow himself to be familiar. As commander in chief and later as president, he could scarcely afford it with anyone. The remoteness that still surrounds him was a necessary adjunct of the power he was called upon to exercise.

But Washington's understanding of power went far beyond mere posture. Although he had not had a great deal of military experience before he took charge of the Continental Army in 1775, his participation in the French and Indian War from 1754 to 1758 had exposed him to the geographical conditions of warfare on the American continent and the way in which they must affect the exercise of military power. As commander of the revolutionary army he was quick to perceive the significance of geographical factors that his opponents seem never to have grasped. At the outset of the war, when the British almost caught him in the Battle of Long Island, he learned the danger of allowing his forces to be bottled up in any location where their retreat might be cut off. Having learned that lesson, he did not make the same mistake again. Though he was not always able to prevent his subordinates from making it, his constant alertness to it enabled him to keep his precarious army in existence. In September 1777, for example, he sent a letter on the subject to Brigadier General Thomas Nelson in Virginia. In the light of future events it was a remarkable letter. Nelson had proposed to station his forces at Hampton and Yorktown, which lay at the end of the peninsula between the James and the York rivers. Here, of course, they would be in a position to observe the movement of any British troops into the area by sea. But the location, Washington perceived at once, was one where they could be trapped, and he quickly warned Nelson against it. The troops, he said,

by being upon a [narrow] neck of land would be in danger of being cut off. The Enemy might very easily throw up a few Ships into York and James's river, as far as Queens Creek; and land a body of men there, who by throwing up a few Redoubts, would intercept their retreat and oblige them to surrender at discretion.

Four years later Lord Cornwallis made the mistake that Washington warned Nelson against, and Washington pounced. It was almost like taking candy from a child. For Cornwallis it was the world turned upside down, but for Washington it was a lesson learned long before in the geography of power.

Of course, if the British navy had been on hand in sufficient strength Cornwallis might have escaped by sea. But Washington did not move until he had the French navy to dominate the seas nearby. He had realized early in the war that without local naval superiority to stand off the British warships, he could not capture a British army at any point on the coast. Washington understood this better than his more ex-

perienced French helpers. The Comte de Grasse, in command of the French navy, seems to have missed the whole point of the Yorktown strategy, complaining to Washington that he would prefer to cruise off New York where he might encounter the main British fleet, rather than be an idle spectator in the Chesapeake. Washington knew, however, that even with de Grasse on hand, he was not strong enough to attack the main British force in New York. But by picking off Cornwallis at Yorktown he could deal the British a crippling blow.

Washington's appreciation of geographical factors made him not only wary of being trapped like Cornwallis but also averse to defending any particular point, including cities. The British armies were much more powerful than his and capable of taking any place they wanted. It was therefore not worthwhile to erect elaborate stationary defenses. When General Howe was approaching Philadelphia and Congress wanted Washington to divert troops to the preparation of fortifications for the city's defense, he refused. If he could defeat Howe in the field, he said, the defenses would be unnecessary. If he could not, then the time and labor spent on them would be lost, for the fortifications would sooner or later fall to Howe's superior forces and could then be used against the Americans. It was imperative, he believed, to keep his small force concentrated and mobile, so that he could strike effectively when opportunity presented. "It would give me infinite pleasure," he assured the Congress, "to afford protection to every individual and to every Spot of Ground on the whole of the United States." But that was not the way wars were won. Wars were won by destroying or disarming the enemy, not by trying to spare civilians from occupation. And Washington was bent on winning.

Washington, in other words, was or became a good field general. But his understanding of military power did not stop at the ability to command troops and deploy them effectively. He also understood that the power he could wield in battle depended on the willingness of the civil government to supply him with men and money. He understood the political basis of military power, and he also understood that in the new United States this was a very precarious basis. His army was the creature of a Congress that never quite dared to act like a government. Congress declared independence. It authorized the creation of the army. It even authorized the creation of a navy. But it did not attempt to levy taxes to pay for these things. Instead, it recommended to the states that they make contributions, specifying the amount for each state. Whether a state followed the recommendation depended on public opinion. And public opinion was as fickle then as now. Rumors of peace and of British surrender came with every skirmish, and each one produced a debilitating effect on the willingness of taxpayers in the different states to advance money for a war that might soon be over.

Men were almost as hard to get as the money to pay and clothe and feed them. As a result Washington was never able to build an army strong enough to face the British on even terms. At the outset of the war he had hoped to enlist soldiers for the duration. Instead, Congress provided for enlistments of a year only. It took almost that long to collect and build a disciplined fighting force, even from men who already knew how to fire a gun. By the time he had them trained, their terms would be up, and off they would go, frequently taking with them the guns he had issued them. In their place would often come raw militia on even shorter terms, men who were not used to obeying commands and who did not take kindly to them, men who were ready to head for home and tend the crops the moment they were offended by some officer's efforts to bring them in line. In 1780, after the war had dragged on for five years, Washington was still trying to get Congress to place the army on a more lasting basis. If they had done so at the beginning, he reminded them, his forces would

not have been the greatest part of the War inferior to the enemy, indebted for our safety to their inactivity, enduring

frequently the mortification of seeing inviting opportunities to ruin them, pass unimproved for want of a force which the Country was completely able to afford.

Although Washington's complaints to Congress were fruitless, he never appealed over the heads of Congress to their constituents. He refrained from doing so in part because the very effort to explain the situation to the public would also have explained it to the enemy. He did not dare to advertise the weakness of his force, when the only thing between him and defeat was the fact that the enemy did not realize how weak he was. But his restraint was also based on principle. In spite of the imperious manner with which he bolstered his ability to command, Washington was a republican. He had been fully persuaded that the king of England and the minions surrounding him were conspiring to destroy the liberties of Americans. More than that, he was persuaded that kings in general were a bad lot. He welcomed Thomas Paine's devastating attack not only on George III but on monarchy itself. He never doubted that the United States must be a republic. And the principles of republican liberty as he saw them dictated that the military must be forever subordinate to the civil power. Although he could lament the short-sightedness exhibited by Congress and the state legislatures, he never even suggested that he and his army should be anything but their servants.

Washington realized that he could have commanded an immense popular following in defiance of the do-nothing Congress and that he could have counted on the backing of his officers and troops in such an adventure. But he accepted the premises of republican government as an Oliver Cromwell never did. Although it meant submitting to a body that became increasingly incompetent, irresponsible, and corrupt, he never sought power on any other terms than those on which he had initially accepted it, as servant of the people. And when his men grew exasperated with the failure of the government to feed, arm, or pay them, he stood between them and Congress and thwarted every threat against the civil power. Enlisted men mounted mutinies, and he faced them down with his steely authority. Some of his officers conspired to seize power, and he nipped the movement in the bud.

Washington was fighting not simply for independence but for an independent republic. He was fighting a people's war, and he knew that he would lose what he was fighting for if he tried to take more power than the people would freely give. One of the difficulties of republican government, as he explained later to uncomprehending foreigners, was that the people must always feel an evil before they can see it. "This," he admitted, "is productive of errors and temporary evils, but generally these evils are of a nature to work their own cure." In the end, he believed the people would do the right thing.

Washington's patience in waiting for the people to do the right thing is the more remarkable because he knew that the ineffectiveness of Congress not only prolonged the war needlessly but also exposed the country to needless perils. Because Congress lacked the nerve to vote him the needed men and money, he had to rely on assistance from the French in order to bring the war to a successful conclusion. And reliance on the French could have meant the loss of the very independence Americans were fighting for. Once French forces were engaged on the American continent, Washington feared that they would wish to invade and occupy Canada. Ostensibly the United States would be the sole beneficiary of such a move, for the French agreed to forgo any territorial claims on the continent in their treaty of alliance with the United States. But Washington had no illusions about the binding power of treaties.

Unfortunately Congress did have illusions. At the beginning of the war Americans had hoped that Canada would join them in rebellion against England, and Washington himself thought it highly desirable to eliminate this bastion of British power. He had sent an expedition to effect the liberation of the province, but the inhabitants had not responded in the manner hoped for, and the expedition was a disaster. With the arrival of French troops, congressmen developed an enthusiasm for trying again with French forces. The population of Canada was mainly French, and it was plausible to suppose that they would welcome their countrymen more warmly than they had the Americans. But Washington was alarmed. He would not have been in a position to refuse if the French had decided to employ their troops in this way, but he did not want Congress encouraging them to do so. He wrote out all the tactical reasons he could think of against the expedition and sent them in an official communication to Congress. Then he wrote out a private, confidential letter to Henry Laurens, the president of Congress, explaining his real objection. The letter remains one of the more striking examples of the quick perception of political realities that lay behind Washington's understanding of power.

The expedition, he explained to Laurens, would mean

the introduction of a large body of French troops into Canada, and putting them in possession of the capital of that Province, attached to them by all the ties of blood, habits, manners, religion and former connexions of government. I fear this would be too great a temptation to be resisted by any power actuated by the common maxims of national policy.

He went on to outline all the economic and political benefits that France would gain by holding on to the province in violation of the treaty. It would not be difficult to find a plausible pretext. The United States had borrowed funds from France on a large scale; and the United States government, if one could dignify Congress by that name, had no power to tax its citizens in order to repay the debt. The United States could scarcely object if France retained Canada as security for the payment. "Resentment, reproaches, and submission" would be the only recourse left to the United States. And Washington went on to read a gentle lecture to the gullible members of Congress: "Men are very apt," he said,

to run into extremes; hatred to England may carry some into an excess of Confidence in France; especially when motives of gratitude are thrown into the scale. Men of this description would be unwilling to suppose France capable of acting so ungenerous a part. I am heartily disposed to entertain the most favourable sentiments of our new ally and to cherish them in others to a reasonable degree; but it is a maxim founded on the universal experience of mankind, that no nation is to be trusted farther than it is bound by its interest; and no prudent statesman or politician will venture to depart from it.

☆   2   ☆

With the victory at Yorktown and the peace that followed, the United States had no further need of the military wisdom of which it had made such poor use. But Washington as a civilian was no less cogent in his understanding of power than he had been as commander in chief. His response to the postwar vicissitudes of the nation matched that of the most constructive political thinkers on the scene, and his influence may have been greater than theirs because of the enormous prestige he now carried.

The ineffectiveness of Congress that had hampered Washington's prosecution of the war continued to threaten the viability of the new republic in peacetime. Having submitted to the military loss of her mainland colonies, England set about to regain them by economic warfare, or so it seemed. In the early years of peace English merchants, offering liberal credits, sent shiploads of goods to their old customers in America, and Americans rang up a huge debt. But when Americans tried to ship their own goods to their old prewar markets in the British West Indies and elsewhere, England closed the ports to them. Be-

fore the Americans could gain new outlets for their produce many found themselves bankrupt. Washington's reaction was that power should be met with power. If England barred American ships, Americans should bar English ships until England relented. But for some states to do so and others not would defeat the strategy, and Congress had no authority to regulate trade for the whole nation. Washington supported every move to give it such authority, but at the same time he despaired of putting power in the hands of men who had demonstrated again and again their timidity in using it. What was the use of giving them more powers, he asked, when "the members seem to be so much afraid of exerting those which they already have, that no opportunity is slipped of surrendering them, or referring the exercise of them, to the States individually?"

Washington had been convinced, long before the war ended, that the national government as it operated under the Articles of Confederation was not adequate to carry out its functions; and he feared it had in effect written its own death warrant by failing to exercise what powers it had. "Extensive powers not exercised," he once observed, ". . . have I believe scarcely ever failed to ruin the possessor." But he hoped against hope that this would not be the case with the United States. When the inhabitants of western Massachusetts rose in arms against their own elected government in Shays' Rebellion, and neither the state nor the national government seemed ready to do anything about it, it looked as though the case was hopeless. Henry Lee urged Washington to use his influence to quiet the troubles, but Washington snapped back, "Influence is no Government. . . . If they have *real* grievances, redress them. . . . If they have not, employ the force of government against them at once." It was mortifying to see the new American republic exhibiting the weakness that doctrinaire European political philosophers had always attributed to republics. "How melancholy is the reflection," Washington wrote to James Madison, that in so short a space, we should have made such large strides towards fulfilling the predictions of our transatlantic foe! 'Leave them to themselves, and their government will soon dissolve.' . . . What stronger evidence can be given of the want of energy in our governments than these disorders? If there exists not a power to check them, what security has a man for life, liberty, or property?

But the weakness of the American republic did not diminish Washington's republican ardor. He was outraged by the very idea of rebellion against a republican government, but he was also outraged by the reaction of Americans who talked without horror of substituting a monarch for the ineffective Congress. And after the Massachusetts government finally succeeded in putting down the rebels, he objected to the fact that they had been disfranchised. To deprive them of political rights was as much an abuse of power as the failure to use power effectively against them in the first place.

When Washington became the first president of the United States, he brought to the office a determination to establish what he called "a national character," by which he meant something like national reputation. It was essential, in his view, that the country gain a reputation that would oblige other countries to respect it. "We are a young Nation," he had written in 1783, "and have a character to establish. It behooves us therefore to set out right for first impressions will be lasting, indeed are all in all." And in the years that followed the winning of independence, as the power of Congress continued to wane, his great worry had been that the failure of the states to support the union would "destroy our National character, and render us as contemptible in the eyes of Europe as we have it in our power to be respectable." With an effective national government in operation at last, it became possible to establish a proper national character, a reputation that would command respect both at home and abroad. And in his conduct of the presidency Washington bent his every effort toward that end.

He recognized that he was on trial, that the character of the government and the respect accorded it would be measured by the respect that he himself demanded and commanded. As president of a republic he aimed at an elegant simplicity in his style of living, sumptuous enough to escape any imputation of ostentatious poverty, but restrained enough to avoid outright splendor. At the same time he cultivated his characteristic aloofness, even to the point where his critics charged that his condescension smacked of monarchy.

Washington identified the national interest so closely and so personally with the new national government that he could scarcely recognize the validity of any kind of dissent. It is all too easy at the present day to see his impatience with public criticism as intolerance bordering on paranoia. But Washington had borne the brunt of a war that was needlessly prolonged because of the supineness of the central government. He had watched the nation approach the point of dissolution in the 1780s, a development that threatened everything he had fought for. And in the 1790s it was by no means clear that the new government was there to stay. If he greeted criticism with distrust, it was because domestic dissent might belie the character he was seeking to establish for his government, might return the nation to the impotence of the 1780s, might signal to the watching world the predicted collapse of the republic.

In spite of his determination to establish a strong character for the nation, Washington had no yearning for personal power, nor did he want any military adventures of the kind that so often infatuate men who are obsessed with power for its own sake. He did want the United States to grow in strength, for strength must be the ultimate basis of respect. And strength, he was sure, would not come to the United States by going to war. He had had ample experience that war was the way to poverty, and poverty meant impotence. The way for the country to grow strong, he believed, was to eschew internal dissension and steer clear of the quarrels which he saw were about to envelop the nations of Europe. The United States was encumbered with a French alliance, but as Washington read the terms of it, it did not require the United States to become involved in any quarrel that France might have with other countries, including England. And although he was grateful for the assistance received from France in the winning of American independence, he did not think that gratitude had a place in the determination of national policy. As he had pointed out some years earlier to Henry Laurens, the nation, like other nations, should not be counted on to act beyond its own interest. France in helping Americans during the Revolution had acted out of self-interest — her interest to have England weakened by loss of the colonies. Now, as Washington saw it, the main interest of the United States was to recover from the economic exhaustion incurred, however needlessly, in the Revolutionary War. The means of recovery, he thought, lay in exploiting the American land to produce as much as possible for sale to nations less fruitfully engaged in quarreling with one another.

Washington had no difficulty in persuading the new Congress or the advisers whom he appointed to his cabinet that a policy of neutrality was the way to let the United States develop its powers. But his advisers never understood the operation of the policy as well as Washington did. Jefferson was bent on making a weapon of neutrality, on wringing concessions, especially from England, in return for American neutrality. Hamilton, on the other hand, was highly conciliatory in trying to restore commercial relations with England, and went almost past the limits of neutrality in his obsession with the ideological dangers presented by the French Revolution. Although Washington was closer to Hamilton than to Jefferson, neither of the two men fully grasped the sophistication of their chief's policy for the nation.

Washington realized that the people of the United States would benefit from high prices for their agricultural exports while European farmers were distracted by war. But other than this benefit, he did not propose to take advantage of the distress of any country in order to wring concessions from it, because he was convinced that benefits thus obtained would not last. In 1791, when he was about to appoint Gouverneur Morris (he of the slap on the back) as minister to France, he warned him against seeking to obtain favorable treaties from countries in distress, "for unless," he said, "treaties are mutually beneficial to the Parties, it is in vain to hope for a continuance of them beyond the moment when the one which conceives itself to be over-reached is in a situation to break off the connexion." A treaty had to match the powers and interests of the parties making it. Otherwise it would be indeed a scrap of paper. Washington signed two treaties as president of the United States. The first one, Jay's Treaty with England, was extremely unpopular; and Washington himself did not think well of it. But he signed it because he thought that commercial relations with England would be worse with no treaty than with this one. The popular outcry against it did not move him and indeed struck him as senseless, because he believed that the United States in 1795 was not sufficiently powerful and England was not sufficiently weak to have negotiated a better treaty. And even if Jay had been able to get a better treaty, Washington thought there was no reason to suppose that it would have been better kept than the peace treaty, in which England had agreed to give up her posts in the Northwest Territory. The fact that England had not yet given up the posts and the fact that Jay had not secured any further agreement for her to give them up was no surprise to Washington. The American negotiators at the peace conference had got more from England than America's bargaining powers really entitled her to. England's retention of the northwest posts was therefore to be expected and was no reason for rejecting Jay's treaty if it might improve the commercial situation of the United States in any way.

Washington could afford to be equally calm about Pinckney's Treaty with Spain. That treaty was almost as popular with the American people as Jay's had been unpopular, and it had generally been hailed as a triumph because it secured the American right to navigate the Mississippi. Yet it merely obtained what Washington was certain the United States would get anyhow. After the Revolutionary War settlers had poured into the western country in such numbers that by 1795 Spain could not safely have denied them the right to export their produce down the Mississippi. What prompted the concession was not Pinckney's negotiating skill but the expanding American strength in the west and the strong character that Washington had conferred on the national government. Treaties, in Washington's view, were not important. What was important was power.

Washington was not a man of many talents. He had none of the range of the brilliant men around him, the intellectual curiosity of a Jefferson, the fiscal genius of a Hamilton. But in his understanding of power he left them all behind, as he did the British generals who opposed him and the French who assisted him. When he retired from the presidency after eight years, he had placed the United States on the way to achieving the power that he had aspired to for it. In the years that have followed, that power has grown until there are those who wonder whether it has been a good thing for the world. But at the time it looked like a very good thing indeed. And for better or for worse, it was the work of George Washington, the man who still keeps us all at a distance.

QUESTIONS TO CONSIDER

1. Contrast the image of George Washington with the reality of the man. In what ways does Morgan's biographical portrait demythologize Washington and restore his humanity?

2. How much credit should we give to individuals, particularly to one man — George Washington — for achieving what at first must have seemed impossible: the defeat of the most powerful army in the world, winning independence from England, and establishing a viable national government in the former colonies?

3. Do you agree with Morgan that Washington was a genius in his understanding of the use of power? On that score, how does he compare with such modern presidents as George Bush and Bill Clinton?

4. In what ways did Washington, as president, help to establish the national reputation of the new Republic? What were his greatest fears for the new nation?

5. Washington's goal as president was to make the new Republic strong. Today the United States is the most powerful country in the world. If Washington could speak to us now, what advice do you think he might offer?

VI

PATTERNS OF DAILY LIFE

11

A Midwife's Tale:
The Life of Martha Moore Ballard
1785–1812

LAUREL THATCHER ULRICH

The study of everyday life is one of the most fascinating new fields of American history. Like biography, it is firmly grounded in specific experience; it allows us to see ordinary people of the past going about the daily business of living, and it invites us to compare their patterns of behavior with our own. By allowing us to reach back and touch the people of a bygone time, and be touched by them, the new social history does much to preserve the human continuum.

The next selection is an example of the new social history at its best. Here, a gifted historian uses a seemingly mundane document, the daily diary of a woman who lived in Maine during Jefferson and Washington's time, as the basis for recreating her life and neighborhood. While previous historians dismissed the diary as nothing but trivia, Laurel Thatcher Ulrich finds it an extraordinary chronicle, an "earnest, steady, gentle, and courageous record" that affords us a window into another way of life that no longer exists. The diary contains no profound meditations, no notes about sensational murders, no trenchant reactions to national events. But there is drama here and a quiet dignity. "It is in the very dailiness," Ulrich believes, "the exhaustive, repetitious dailiness, that the real power of Martha Ballard's book lies." By explicating Ballard's entries and sketching in rich background detail, Ulrich reconstructs both a woman and a mood, a sense of time and place, that is the very antithesis of the presentism Douglas Wilson laments in his discussion of

Jefferson (selection 8). Ballard's diary transports us back into "'a lost substructure of eighteenth-century life," where we meet her on her own terms, without the intrusion of present-day assumptions and moralizing.*

We can appreciate Ballard all the more if we remember that women in her day were excluded from the republican idea of government for "the people" and were denied legal and political rights. Indeed, republican theory relegated women to the home. To solve the problem of female citizenship, the idea of Republican Motherhood came into vogue. That concept linked motherhood to the state by summoning women to raise virtuous, patriotic, republican sons. Ballard, however, did not identify with political ritual and never subscribed to Republican Motherhood. As Ulrich writes, her values belonged "to an older world, in which a woman's worth was measured by her service to God and her neighbors rather than to a nebulous and distant state." Within her neighborly activities, she found a deep sense of personal fulfillment and left a mark on the history of her community through the traditional woman's role of midwife. In her day, the midwife was one of the most important figures in American family and social life. Summoned to the bedside of a woman in labor, the midwife took full charge, with the assistance of other women. The midwife comforted the expectant woman, gave her hard liquor or wine, and helped her as she gave birth, which she did by squatting on a midwife's stool, kneeling on a pallet, or sitting on another woman's lap. In addition to her work in childbirth, the midwife might serve as the mother's confidante and even attend her child's baptism. In those days, people regarded childbearing as something that women must suffer through with the help and encouragement of other women while the menfolk stayed away.

As Ulrich emphasizes, Ballard's diary corrects the implications of male records — that by 1787 the new science of obstetrics had replaced the midwife in Hallowell. The diary shows that the physicians (all physicians were male in her day) merely supplemented the midwives — Ballard alone delivered more than half the local babies that year. What is more, the midwives "provided much of the medical care as well."

Ballard's diary also reveals the important role that she, her daughters, and other women played in Hallowell's economic life beyond the home. As Ulrich points out, the diary "forces us to consider midwifery in the broadest possible context, as one specialty in a larger neighborhood economy, as the most visible feature of a comprehensive and little-known system of early health care, as a mechanism of social control, a strategy for family support, and a deeply personal calling." As you read Ballard's story, think of her as "an archetypical pioneer," a frontier heroine who brought nobility to the unyielding dailiness of her life. For her, as Ulrich says, "living was to be measured in doing. Nothing was trivial."

GLOSSARY

BALLARD, CYRUS   Son of Martha Ballard.

BALLARD, DOROTHY "DOLLY"   Daughter of Martha Ballard.

BALLARD, EPHRAIM   Husband of Martha Ballard.

BALLARD, JONATHAN   Son of Martha Ballard.

BALLARD, LUCY   Only one of Martha Ballard's first four daughters to survive.

BARTON, CLARA   Granddaughter of Stephen Barton; pioneering battelfield nurse in the Civil War and founder of the American Red Cross (and the subject of a later selection).

BARTON, DOROTHY   Younger sister of Martha Ballard.

BARTON, STEPHEN   Brother-in-law of Martha Ballard, the husband of her sister Dorothy; a physician.

CONY, DANIEL   Hallowell's most prominent physician.

HOWARD, WILLIAM   Town's richest man, a trader.

LEARNED, EBENEZER   Cousin of Martha Ballard; resident of Maine.

LEARNED, HANNAH   Grandmother of Martha Ballard.

MOORE, ABIJAH   Uncle of Martha Ballard; a Yale graduate and a physician.

MOORE, DOROTHY   Mother of Martha Ballard.

MOORE, JONATHAN ("BROTHER JONATHAN")   Harvard-educated younger brother of Martha Ballard.

MOORE, RICHARD AND MARY MOORE   Uncle and aunt of Martha Ballard.

TORY   An American who sided with England during the Revolution.

Map of New England, 1789

Map of Hallowell, 1789

E ight months of the year Hallowell, Maine, was a seaport. From early April to late November, ocean-going vessels sailed up the Kennebec, forty-six miles from the open Atlantic, bringing Pennsylvania flour, West Indian sugar, and English cloth and hardware, returning with shingles, clapboards, hogshead and barrel staves, white ash capstan bars, and pine boards destined for Boston or Bristol or Jamaica. In late autumn, ice blockaded the river, sometimes so suddenly that though a man had been expecting it for weeks, he was caught unprepared. One year, on November 25, after the last ships had sailed from the town, Jonathan Ballard pushed off from his father's sawmill with a raft of boards destined for Long Reach on the coast. He got no farther than

KENNEBEC
RIVER
REGION

Winslow

Vassalboro

Sidney

Hallowell

KENNEBEC RIVER

Pittston

Bowdoin-
ham

Pownal-
boro

Merry
Meeting
Bay

Swan
Is.

Long Reach

Casco Bay

Portland

ATLANTIC OCEAN

Map of Kennebec River Region

corn and pork to the straitened town. People both welcomed and feared the opening of the river. In bad years ice jams made ponds of fields and rafts of fences, backing up water in the mill creeks that cut through the steep banks on both sides. In good years, the opening water sent mill hands flying through April nights, ripping logs and securing lumber unlocked by the spring thaw. Sometimes the greatest danger was not from the river itself, though high water might pitch a man from a raft to his death before his fellows could reach him, but from the raging creeks on the shore.

In 1789, the river opened on April 7 in a heavy rain that took away the bridge over Ballard's brook, made a breach in the mill dam, and washed out the under-pinning of the north side of the house. "But we are yet alive & well for which we ought to be thankful," Martha Ballard told her diary. She was fifty-four years old, a midwife. She and her family had lived at the mills since 1778, seven years after the incorporation of the town. Though she knew little of the sea, she had traveled much on the Kennebec, by water, by ice, and, during those treacherous seasons when the river was neither one nor the other, by faith.

The year Old Lady Cony had her stroke, Martha Ballard crossed the river in a canoe on December 2, pushing through ice in several places. On December 30 of another year, summoned by a woman in labor, she walked across, almost reaching shore before breaking through to her waist at Sewall's Eddy. She dragged herself out, mounted a neighbor's horse, and rode dripping to the delivery. Necessity and a fickle river cultivated a kind of bravado among Hallowell folks. "People Crost the river on a Cake of ice which swong round from the Eddy East side & stopt at the point below Mr Westons," Martha wrote on December 15 of one year. On April 1 of another she reported walking across on the ice after breakfast, adding drily in the margin of the day's entry, "the river opened at 4 hour pm."

Martha Moore was born in 1735 in the small town of Oxford, near the Connecticut border in Worcester

Bumberhook Point, three miles below, before the Kennebec closed around him. It didn't open again until April 1.

Hallowell folks remembered openings and closings of the river the way people in other towns remem-bered earthquakes or drought. In 1785, the year of the long winter, the ice was still firm enough on April 22 to hold a sleigh bearing the body of Samuel How-ard, one of the original settlers of the town, to his burying place at Fort Western. Not until May 3 did the first vessels arrive from "the westward," bringing

County, Massachusetts, but the real story of her life begins in Maine with the diary she kept along the Kennebec. Without the diary her biography would be little more than a succession of dates. Her birth in 1735. Her marriage to Ephraim Ballard in 1754. The births of their nine children in 1756, 1758, 1761, 1763, 1765, 1767, 1769, 1772, and 1779, and the deaths of three of them in 1769. Her own death in 1812. The *American Advocate* for June 9, 1812, summed up her life in one sentence: "Died in Augusta, Mrs. Martha, consort of Mr. Ephraim Ballard, aged 77 years." Without the diary we would know nothing of her life after the last of her children was born, nothing of the 816 deliveries she performed between 1785 and 1812. We would not even be certain she had been a midwife.

In the spring of 1789, Martha faced a flooding river and a rising tide of births. She attended seven deliveries in March and another seven before the end of April, twice her monthly average. On April 23 she went down the Kennebec to visit several families on the west side of the river opposite Bumberhook. This is how she told her story:

[*April 23*] Clear & very Pleasant. I sett out to go to Mr Bullins. Stept out of the Canue & sunk in the mire. Came back & Changd my Cloaths. Maid another attempt & got safe there. Sett out for home. Calld at Capt Coxes & Mr Goodins. Was Calld in at Mrs Husseys. Tarried all night. A sever storm before morn.

[*April 24*] A severe Storm of rain. I was Calld at 1 hour pm from Mrs Husseys by Ebenzer Hewin. Crosst the river in their Boat. A great sea A going. We got safe over then sett out for Mr Hewins. I Crost a stream on the way on fleeting Loggs & got safe over. Wonder full is the Goodness of providence. I then proseeded on my journey. Went beyond Mr Hainses & a Larg tree blew up by the roots before me which Caused my hors to spring back & my life was spared. Great & marvillous are thy sparing mercies O God. I was assisted over the fallen tree by Mr Hains. Went on. Soon Came to a stream. The Bridg was gone. Mr Hewin took the rains

waded thro & led the horse. Asisted by the same allmighty power I got safe thro & arivd unhurt. Mrs Hewins safe delivd at 10 h Evn of a Daughter.

After great deliverances came small annoyances. In the margin of that day's narrative, she wrote, "My Cloak was burnt while there so that it is not wareable." In all the excitement, someone had apparently allowed the midwife's sodden wrap to hang too near the fire. The story continued:

[*April 25*] Rainy. I came from Mr Hewins to Mr Pollards. My hors mired & I fell off in the mud but blessed be God I receivd no hurt. Mr Hewins attended me to Mrs Husseys. We arivd at 11 hour morning. Mrs Norcross was in Travill. Her women were immediately Calld & Shee was Safe Delivd at 5 hour 30 minutes Evening of a fine son. Her Husband & Mrs Delino & her Childn went on board bound for Nantucket Early this morn.

[*April 26*] A very Cold morn. Snowd. I took my leav of Mrs Hussey & family. Came to Mr Herseys. He & William Howard brot me from fort Western by water. I left my patients Cleverly & found my famely well. It is the greatest freshet in this river that has been this many years.

Reading such a story, we can easily imagine Martha as an archetypical pioneer. Indeed, the rhythms of her story echo the seventeenth-century captivity narratives that gave New England its first frontier heroines. One thinks of Mary Rowlandson crossing the Ware River in Vermont on a makeshift raft in the early spring of 1676 or of Hannah Swarton traveling into Maine "over Steep and hideous Mountains one while, and another while over Swamps and Thickets of Fallen Trees." The religious language in Martha Ballard's diary strengthens the affinity with her Puritan progenitors. Dramatizing the dangers of her journey, she both glorified God and gave meaning and dimension to her own life. Mr. Hewins led her horse and Mr. Hains walked beside her, but Providence rescued her from the violence of the spring freshet.

"A great sea A going" — Martha knew how to suggest an entire landscape, or in this case a riverscape, in a phrase. Her description of the river crossing is part psalm, part tale. She understood instinctively, if not self-consciously, the importance of repetition and the uses of convention. Notice how in the April 24 passage she alternated spare, but vivid, action sentences with formulaic religious phrases:

I Crost the stream on the way on fleeting Loggs & got safe over. *Wonder full is the Goodness of providence.* I then proseeded on my journey. Went beyond Mr Hainses & a Larg tree blew up by the roots before me which Caused my hors to spring back & my life was spared. *Great & marvillous are thy sparing mercies O God.* I was assisted over the fallen tree by Mr Hains. Went on. Soon Came to a stream. The Bridg was gone. Mr Hewin took the rains waded thro & led the horse. *Asisted by the same allmighty power* I got safe thro & arivd unhurt.

Here the religious sentiments become a kind of refrain, punctuating and accentuating each stage in the narrative. Such a passage reveals a storyteller, if not a writer, at work.

There are other passages of similar quality in the diary. Yet most of Martha's entries are more mundane. The structure of her diary derives from two workaday forms of record-keeping, the daybook and the interleaved almanac. In eighteenth-century New England, farmers, craftsmen, shopkeepers, ship's captains, and perhaps a very few housewives kept daybooks, running accounts of receipts and expenditures, sometimes combining economic entries with short notes on important family events and comments on work begun or completed. Other early diarists used the blank pages bound into printed almanacs to keep their own tally on the weather, adding brief entries on gardening, visits to and from neighbors, or public occurrences of both the institutional and the sensational sort. Martha Ballard did all these things.

The extant diary, which begins in January of 1785, may have been preceded by an almanac of some sort, since she ruled the margins of her homemade booklets and numbered the days of the month and week, using a "dominical letter" for Sundays, according to the almanac form. Whatever its origins, the diary functioned as a kind of daybook. Martha recorded debts contracted and "rewards" received, and some of the time she noted numbers of yards "got out" of the loom and varieties of beans put into the ground. Her midwifery accounts are even more methodical. She carefully labeled and numbered each delivery, adding an XX to the margin when the fee was paid.

Those few historians who have known about the diary have not known quite what to do with it. In his *History of Augusta* published in 1870, James W. North quoted several passages, including the one for April 24, 1789, but he pronounced most of the entries "brief and with some exceptions not of general interest." Although Charles Elventon Nash devoted more than a third of his 600-page *History of Augusta* to an abridgment of the journal, carefully extracting birth records and a sample of almost everything else except unsavory medical details or anything tainted with sex, he too found much of it "trivial and unimportant . . . being but a repetition of what has been recited many times." Curiously, a feminist history of midwifery published in the 1970s repeated the old dismissal: "Like many diaries of farm women, it is filled with trivia about domestic chores and pastimes."

Yet it is in the very dailiness, the exhaustive, repetitious dailiness, that the real power of Martha Ballard's book lies. To extract the river crossings without noting the cold days spent "footing" stockings, to abstract the births without recording the long autumns spent winding quills, pickling meat, and sorting cabbages, is to destroy the sinews of this earnest, steady, gentle, and courageous record. Martha sometimes slipped the folded half-sheets from which she constructed her diary into her bag when she crossed the river or waded through snow to sit out a tedious labor, and when she felt overwhelmed or enlivened by the very "trivia" the historians have dismissed, she said so, not in the soul-searching manner of a Puritan nor with the literary self-consciousness of a sentimentalist, but in a plain, matter-of-fact, and in the end unforgettable voice. For more than twenty-seven years, 9,965 days to be exact, she faithfully kept her record. Martha was not an introspective diarist, yet in this conscientious recording as much as in her occasional confessions, she revealed herself. "And now this year is come to a close," she wrote on December 31, 1800, "and happy is it if we have made a wise improvement of the time." For her, living was to be measured in doing. Nothing was trivial.

Because so few New England women of her generation left writing in any form, one searches for an explanation for the diary. Though her grandmother, Hannah Learned, was able to muster a clear but labored signature on the one surviving document bearing her name, her mother, Dorothy Moore, signed with a mark. On the male side of the family, however, there is a record of education. Martha's uncle Abijah Moore, who graduated from Yale in 1726, was the first college graduate from the town of Oxford. Martha's younger brother, Jonathan Moore, was the second. Jonathan graduated from Harvard College in 1761, serving for a time as librarian of the college before accepting a call as pastor of the First Congregational Church in Rochester, Massachusetts. Throughout her life Martha Ballard corresponded with "Brother Jonathan."

Although her handwriting is crude in comparison with her brother's and less certain than that of her husband, who was a surveyor and mapmaker as well as a miller, her ability to write cursive in any form is itself evidence that someone in Oxford in the 1740s was interested in educating girls. Judging from the diary, that education was quite conventional. Although Martha occasionally "perrused" newspapers, she mentioned only one book other than the Bible. One June 25, 1786, a Sunday, she wrote, "I have Red in Mr Marshalls gospel Mystery of Sanctification." The book was Walter Marshall's *Gospel-Mystery of Sanctification,* a work of popular piety first published in London in 1692, though reprinted many times

in the eighteenth century. Her concern with the spelling of the title is intriguing; normally, she showed little interest in such matters. Obviously having the book in her hand elevated her consciousness, though it had little effect on the rest of the passage. *Read* remained *Red*.

Martha's choice of reading material was conservative, at least on that Sunday in 1786. She was aware of more modern forms of English literature, however. Her younger sister, Dorothy Barton, had two daughters named after characters in the novels of Samuel Richardson. *Pamela* and *Clarissa Harlowe* Barton were frequent visitors to and sometime inhabitants of the Ballard house, as was their sister *Parthenia*. Classical or pseudo-classical names were still rare in New England in the 1760s, though they became more popular after the Revolution. The Ballards succumbed to the same impulse and displayed an uncharacteristic bit of whimsy when they named their third daughter *Triphene*.

By Oxford standards, the Moores were well educated and ambitious. The family also seems to have had a medical bent. Martha's uncle Abijah Moore was a physician, as were two of her brothers-in-law, including Stephen Barton, the father of Pamela, Parthenia, and Clarissa. The one hint that Martha herself was involved in caring for the sick in Oxford comes from a Barton family story recorded many years later. It survives in two versions.

One explains that during the pre-Revolutionary boycotts, when Stephen Barton was on a committee to see that no tea was bought in the town, he "was wont to put on his hat and go without while his sympathetic wife and her sister, Martha Moore Ballard, made a cup of tea in the cellar for some sick mother in the neighborhood whose sufferings patriotism and loyalty failed to heal." The other version comes from Dorothy and Stephen's granddaughter, a woman christened Clarissa Harlowe Barton, but known to millions of Americans by her nickname, Clara. Clara Barton, the founder of the American Red Cross, later recalled being entertained by her "interesting, precise and intelligent grandmother Barton, telling us of the tea parties she and her sister Aunt Ballard held in the cellar when grandfather was out or *up* and didn't know what was going on in his own disloyal and rebellious home." Although the neighborly ministrations of the first story become "tea parties" in this one, both emphasize Dorothy Barton's independence. According to Clara, the two sisters "hung blankets inside the cellar door to prevent the savory fumes of the tea from reaching the loyal and official olfactories of 'Pater familias.'" Martha's rebellion may have been less serious than her sister's. As we shall see, Ephraim Ballard was himself a reluctant supporter, at best, of the Revolution.

The best evidence of the practical side of Martha's education comes from the diary itself. When it opened in 1785, she knew how to manufacture salves, syrups, pills, teas, and ointments, how to prepare an oil emulsion (she called it an "oil a mulge"), how to poultice wounds, dress burns, treat dysentery, sore throat, frostbite, measles, colic, "hooping Cough," "Chin cough," "St. Vitas dance," "flying pains," "the salt rhume," and "the itch," how to cut an infant's tongue, administer a "clister" (enema), lance an abscessed breast, apply a "blister" or a "back plaster," induce vomiting, assuage bleeding, reduce swelling, and relieve a toothache, as well as deliver babies.

She later wrote that she delivered her first baby in July of 1778, less than a year after her arrival in Maine. This statement should not be taken entirely at face value. She no doubt officiated as a midwife for the first time in 1778, but she had probably assisted in dozens of births in Oxford. This was the era of "social childbirth," when female relatives and neighbors, as well as midwives, attended births. Most midwives began as observers, gradually assuming a more active role, until one day, when the old midwife was delayed or willing, they "performed." For Martha, moving to Maine probably accelerated this process. In Oxford, even if she had the ability to practice she may have had little opportunity, since there were many older women in the town. Her own Grandmother

Learned was alive until 1777. In Hallowell, by contrast, she was one of the older women in a young and rapidly growing town.

Giving birth to nine babies was also a part of her preparation as a midwife. As one eighteenth-century midwifery manual expressed it, "There is a tender regard one woman bears to another, and a natural sympathy in those that have gone thro' the Pangs of Childbearing; which, doubtless, occasion a compassion for those that labour under these circumstances, which no man can be a judge of." Martha's "natural" sympathy had also been developed through death. Between 1767 and 1770, Oxford lost 12 percent of its population in one of the worst diphtheria epidemics in New England's history. One hundred forty-four persons died, mostly children ages two to fourteen. Martha's uncle and aunt, Richard and Mary Moore, buried eight of their eleven children. Martha and Ephraim lost three of their six children in less than ten days. A row of tiny headstones in the burying ground behind the Oxford Congregational Church commemorates the Moore deaths. There are no Ballard stones. Martha memorialized her little girls in the diary she kept along the Kennebec.

June 17, 1786: "this is 17 years since the Death of my Daughter Triphene who Deceast AE 4 years & 3 months."

July 1, 1788: "It is 19 years this Day since the Death of my Daughter Dorothy." (Dorothy had been two.)

July 5, 1789: "20 years since my daughter Martha's death." (Martha was "8 years & 2 months & 28 days" when she died.)

Both of the Ballard sons, Cyrus, twelve, and Jonathan, six, survived the throat distemper. Of the four daughters, only Lucy, age ten, remained. "It was a very hott day & Continued so thro the sumer," Martha recalled in one of the entries remembering Triphene's death. She had reason to feel the heat in that summer of sorrow. She was seven and a half months pregnant when the first of her daughters died.

On August 6, 1769, amidst death, she gave birth.

The baby was named Hannah, for Mother Ballard. Two years later another baby girl was born. She became Dorothy, or "Dolly," for Grandmother Moore, for her Aunt Dorothy Barton, and for the sister who had died of diptheria. Perhaps there would have been another Triphene or Martha in 1773, but in that year Ephraim Ballard was in Maine searching out a new home. As a consequence, the last Ballard baby, named Ephraim for his father, was born in Hallowell in 1779.

When Ephraim Ballard ascended the Kennebec in 1775 in search of new land, he was doing what his great-grandfather had done more than a century before when he left Lynn, Massachusetts, to build mills in the new town of Andover and what his own father had done when he left Andover for Billerica and then Oxford. The Ballards had been millers for four generations in New England, and in three of those four they helped to settle new towns.

The French and Indian wars first led Oxford men to Maine. Martha's cousin Nathan Moore, a veteran of the invasion of Canada, was settled in Vassalboro on the Kennebec by 1768. Another cousin, Ebenezer Learned, also a veteran, became a proprietor of the new township of Livermore on the Androscoggin River, though he continued to live in Oxford. Ephraim went to Maine for the first time as a surveyor and agent for Cousin Ebenezer, though his interest soon turned from the Androscoggin to the Kennebec. By 1775 his brother Jonathan, his brother-in-law Thomas Towne, Martha's brother Ebenezer Moore, and her brother-in-law Stephen Barton had all settled on lands laid out by the Kennebec Proprietors. Removing to Maine became another way of remaining in Oxford.

In 1775, there were six incorporated townships along the Kennebec above Long Reach — Pownalboro, Gardinerstown, Hallowell, Winthrop, Vassalboro, and Winslow — the town names reflecting the family connections and political power of the Kennebec Proprietors, also known as the Plymouth Company because they traced their land claims to

seventeenth-century Pilgrim grants. Unlike the pioneer settlements of early Massachusetts, these Maine towns were laid out by merchant speculators, who, having no intention of migrating themselves, gave away some of the land to early settlers, looking for a return on their investment from later land sales and rents and from the proceeds of mills, ships, and stores run by hired agents, who were themselves often paid in land. In 1775 the Kennebec Proprietors owned more than 600,000 acres of wild land, though the exact boundaries of their grants were in dispute. Here indeed was work for a good surveyor, and opportunity perhaps to acquire land and mills.

On April 6, 1775, Ephraim secured a lease from Silvester Gardiner of Boston, one of the wealthiest of the Kennebec Proprietors, to "Fort Hallifax and all the land adjoining." The Fort, originally built by the Massachusetts government, stood on a peninsula between the Kennebec and Sebasticook rivers. Surrounded by 400 acres of timber, it was described by one contemporary as "a great Salmon fishery in the summer and a bass fishery in the Winter."

It was an impressive site, but the timing was bad. In April of 1775, as Ephraim was sailing up the Kennebec toward the Fort, Martha was in Oxford watching her cousin Ebenezer Learned muster troops to meet the Lexington and Concord alarm. In June, when Ephraim applied to the Lincoln County Court for a tavern license, the Oxford Minutemen were at Bunker Hill. When an advance party of Benedict Arnold's army reached Fort Halifax in September of 1775, they disdained the accommodations of the Fort, not only because it was in a "ruinous state" but because the proprietor (who was without question Ephraim Ballard) was reputed a "rank tory." Still, they were pleased with the man's willingness to exchange "a barrel of smoke-dried salmon for a barrel of pork, upon honest terms."

A year later, relations between Ephraim and the patriots were less cordial. In a petition to the General Court, the Winslow Committee of Safety complained that "Mr Ballard with a Number of People (supposed to be unfriendly to the grand American Cause) from the next Town were cutting and haling Mill Logs" on Fort lands. (The "next Town" was Vassalboro, where Ephraim's brother and a bevy of Moore relatives lived.) The General Court empowered the committee to take the Gardiner property "under their care."

Having lost one Tory property, Ephraim went downriver to Hallowell and acquired another, taking up the management of land and mills owned by John Jones, a longtime resident of the Kennebec and a Plymouth Company agent. Jones was a loyalist who had already been declared "inimical to the liberties and privileges of the United States" by a Hallowell town meeting, but he was foresighted enough to deed his property to his wife's relatives before fleeing to Canada. Ephraim's lease was secure. His own sympathies may have been with his landlord, but he knew how to make peace with a revolution. When he too was accused of "Treasonable & Enimical Conduct Against the United States of America," he not only managed to get the charges dropped but soon after was elected moderator of the Hallowell town meeting. According to a treasurer's account, he contributed 200 pounds (a standard assessment in this period of inflation) toward the support of a soldier at Fort Halifax.

Martha had joined her husband in Hallowell in October of 1777. "I first set my feet on the Kenebeck shore . . . at Mr John Jones' landing below the Hook," she later recalled, adding, "I spent 1 year and 17 days, then removed to his mill at Boman's brook." Jones's landing and his mills at Bowman's Brook were in opposite corners of the town. The landing was on the east side of the river in the southern half of the settlement, the section usually referred to as "the Hook," for Bumberhook Point, its most prominent feature. The mills were on the west side of the river in the northern half of the town (the part that separated in 1797 to become the town of Augusta). This area was called "the Fort," after old Fort Western, built by the Plymouth Company in 1754 as part of its line of defense on the Kennebec. Since 1769, the Fort

had been owned by James Howard, who used it as a dwelling house and store. (The restored Fort is now a museum owned and maintained by the city of Augusta.)

In 1777 there were 100 families in Hallowell, spread out along ten miles of river. Most people still lived in their first log houses, though a few, perhaps including John Jones, had managed to build frame houses and barns. The settlers had come from more than thirty different towns, some from Rhode Island and Nantucket, a few from New Hampshire, several from the British Isles, most from Massachusetts and Maine. They had come in small clusters of kin. There were two Howard brothers with their progeny, three Sewall cousins, two generations of Conys, strings of Savages and Clarks, and so on. Although most of the Ballard and Moore relatives were in other Kennebec towns, Ephraim's nephew and namesake, Ephraim Towne, was also a tenant of John Jones in Hallowell. In 1778, Towne married his cousin Lucy Ballard, Martha and Ephraim's oldest daughter.

Letters from John Jones to Towne provide the only glimpse we have of these years. "I have had an acompt of what you have met with or had your House serched for me," Jones wrote in the autumn of 1778. "I am very sorry that they should trouble themselves concerning me. I hant dun them no ronge. I sincear wish Everybody would miend their own business." When Kennebec patriots continued to mind Jones's business, he joined the British resistance at Fort George. His military forays into the region gave new point to his old nickname, "Black Jones." In one exploit he kidnapped Colonel Charles Cushing of Pownalboro, dragging him from his house barefoot in the night. His letters to Towne say less about politics, however, than about their common interest in the farm. "I am afraid there will be a famin for bread if the war continues," he wrote in February of 1779. He urged his tenant to "buy sum oxen or furrow cows" while he could, to set out apple trees on the hill behind the barn, and to "git a Salmon net maide, for Provisions is intolerable Dear." When shearing time came he hoped Towne would take care of his wool, though "if you need of it before I come you or your father Ballard may use what you stand in need of.

Ten years later, Jones had not yet come. He made an attempt in 1785, the first year Martha kept her diary, but was soon spirited out of town. "A gang went to Samuel Duttuns & took John Jones, brought him to Pollards, tarried till morn when they Set out with him for Wiscasset," Martha wrote. Characteristically, she offered no judgment on the behavior either of Jones or of his attackers. Nor does her diary open in time to record what may have been a last vigilante action against her own family. In 1784 Lucy and Ephraim Towne moved from Hallowell to Winslow, the place where Ephraim Ballard had had his first encounter with the Revolution. According to an oral tradition preserved in the Towne family, the young couple transported their household goods upriver on a flatboat, leaving their furniture on the wharf overnight. "Somebody tied one of the chairs to the top of a birch tree," their great-granddaughter recalled, "and when they went to get the furniture in the morning, here was a chair in the top of a tree." In her mouth the incident is an amusing but inexplicable event. Was tying furniture in trees some species of frontier humor, a folk form of welcome? The political context suggests otherwise. Apparently somebody in Winslow resented Ephraim Towne's association with John Jones, and perhaps, too, with that "rank tory" who had once cut timber at Fort Halifax.

When the diary opened, there were seven Ballards living in John Jones's house on Bowman's Brook — Martha and Ephraim and five unmarried children — Cyrus, Jonathan, Hannah, Dolly, and Ephraim. There were usually one or two hired helpers as well. All these people crowded into an unfinished house that had two rooms on the main floor (Martha called them simply the "east room" and the "west room") and two unfinished chambers above, which were unusable in winter. In addition there were a "seller," a barn, and various "yards," some fenced, some defined only by their proximity to a significant structure or

natural barrier, as in "I sowd parsnip & Carrot seed *in the gardin by the Barn.*" Or "I howd the Beans & Cucumbers *in the yard by the Brook.*" Or "Houghed the plants *before the door.*" Or "Cutt Aulders and maid a sort of a fence part round *the yard By the mill Pond.*"

Housework extended from the west room to the yards. Martha Ballard and her daughters bleached newly spun thread on the grass and hung laundry on such fences as they had, though there were risks in such a practice. "Hannah washt Daniels Blankett & our swine tore it into strips," Martha wrote on one fateful day. (No matter, the girls cut up the remnants and made a warm petticoat for one of Lucy's children.) There were no sheep yet, but Ephraim owned a horse and a pair of oxen and Martha milked both a red and a "speckled" cow. Chickens pecked in a dooryard cluttered with wood chips and animal droppings, giving a comforting domesticity to a setting that was still wilderness beyond the clearings for hay and corn. "There was a moose by our gardin this afternoon," Martha wrote into the margin of her diary on one April day. In November of 1787, she noted, "Hannah & Dolly were fritened by a Baire between here & Neighbor Savages." In such a setting an errant calf — or a neighbor's child — might wander "up the crik" and disappear.

Yet for all its wildness there was a motion, a life, in Hallowell that had been missing in Oxford. There were ships on the river and a continuous movement of settlers through the town and into the back country. Ephraim's mill was a ram against the wilderness, an engine for transforming woods into towns. On good days the saw kept a steady rhythm, the vertical blade moving up and down 120 times a minute, striking a rapid trochee ("Faaa-sher, Faaa-sher") that echoed through the trees as log after log inched along the wooden track. Weather and the changing seasons, as much as the availability of timber, regulated the operation, too much water being as much of a problem as too little. "Our saw mills go Briskly," Martha wrote on one day after a heavy rain, but on another, "The mills have been stopt from going by the freshet."

157

Ephraim and his sons operated a gristmill as well as a sawmill, both perhaps housed in the same building, the saw or saws in the story above, the grinding mechanism below. There is a fitting symbolism in the division of responsibility for the two. Cyrus, the quiet older son who into his forties moved in and out of his father's household, never marrying, never achieving full independence, was assigned the grinding. Jonathan, the flamboyant and rebellious younger brother, did the rafting and ripping. One wonders if Cyrus was impaired in some way, though his mother never wrote of it in her diary. His shoulders, at least, were powerful, since it was his job to "pick mill," that is, to work with a mallet and chisel to restore and maintain grooves on the granite millstones. "Son Town" too had a role in the family operation. Having carried away the eldest daughter to Winslow, he returned every week or so, rafting logs to the mill.

When conditions were right the mills went day and night, though mechanical and human failure as well as the weather could bring silence. "The cornmill ceast grinding till finisht repairing," Martha would write, or "Thee sweap of one of the mills got off thee Crank so neither of them were tended this night." Still the sounds of sawing were as much a part of spring on Bowman's Brook as the songs of birds, such an omnipresent part of Martha's world that she usually did not notice them unless they were gone, as one May evening, after the hired hand had gone to bed ill and Jonathan had returned late from two days on the river searching for logs that had gone adrift, when she noted quietly, "The mill Lies still."

Perhaps it was a sense of history or a craving for stability, perhaps only a practical need to keep birth records, that first motivated Martha to keep a diary. "Thee number of childn I have Extracted since I came to Kennebeck I find by written account & other Calculations to be 405," she wrote on December 31, 1791. The demands of a practice that averaged almost forty births a year even in the prediary period may eventually have made a "written account" essential. The diary opens on January 1, 1785, with short, choppy entries nineteen to the page. Gradually the entries become fuller and more regular. (The diary's overall average is six entries per page.) From the beginning she ruled a margin at the left of her page where she entered the day of the month. Soon she added a second column for the day of the week. By the end of 1787 she had added a right-hand margin where she summarized each day's events. A year or two later she began keeping a running head at the top of each page. Such changes suggest that she too could get lost in a stream of days. One delivery, one April day, could so easily fuse with another.

April 24, 1785: "I was Calld at 2 O Clock in the Morn to go to thee hook to Mrs Blake in travil."

April 18, 1786: "A rainy day. I was calld to Mr Gillmans at the hook to see his wife in Travil."

April 22, 1787: "I Was calld to Mr Welmans at 9 this morn. His wife Safe Delivd at 7 Evn of a son . . . it rained this Evinng."

April 28, 1788: "Rain, Snow & Haill & Cold [but this time no deliveries!]"

And then on April 24, 1789, the dramatic encounter with the spring freshet. "A sever Storm of rain. I was Calld at 1 h pm from Mrs Husseys by Ebenzer Hewin. . . ."

Both the difficulty and the value of the diary lie in its astonishing steadiness. Consider again that sequence of entries for April 23 through 26, 1789. The central story — Martha's crossing and recrossing of the Kennebec — is clear enough, but on first reading the reader is unlikely to notice a subplot being played out at the Hussey house while Martha was traveling through the April storm to the Hewins delivery. In fact, it is not even apparent at first that she has left one pregnant woman to attend another. Recall that she initially crossed the river on April 23 "to go to Mr Bullins," that a few hours later as she was about to return home after stopping in at "Capt Coxes & Mr Goodins," she was "Calld in at Mrs Husseys." She

"Tarried all night" at the Husseys', leaving about one the next afternoon when Ebenezer Hewins came through the storm to fetch her to his wife's delivery. She did not, however, return home after leaving the Hewins house, which was on the same side of the river as her own, but crossed the Kennebec once again to the Husseys.

In the entry for November 25 we find out why: "Mr Hewins attended me to Mrs Husseys. We arivd at 11 h morn. Mrs Norcross was in Travill. Her women were immediately Calld & Shee was Safe Delivrd at 5 hours 30 minutes Evening of a fine son." Then she added as a kind of aside: "Her Husband & Mrs Delino & her Childn went on board bound for Nantucket Early this morn." With some attention to context (and a quick search of family records), the characters in this little drama can be straightened out — Mrs. Norcross and Mrs. Delano were Mrs. Hussey's daughters.

Now look at the sequence of events so casually described in the entry. The ship bound for Nantucket left "Early" in the morning; the midwife arrived at eleven; the baby was born at 5:30 that afternoon. What we don't know is whether Mrs. Norcross was already in labor when her husband and sister sailed down the river, having risen early to catch the northwest wind that would make for easy sailing to Long Reach. Probably not. Earlier entries for the month suggest that Mr. Norcross had been waiting in port for almost two weeks anticipating the birth of his child. Martha first went to the Hussey house on April 9 and was still there two days later when "Captain Norcross came home" with the first ships of the season. She left on the eleventh, returned on the thirteenth, left again on the eighteenth, and was back the next day, remaining until April 20. When she was finally "called in" at the Hussey house on April 23, she had already spent a total of nine days waiting for a baby that would not arrive. It is doubtful she would have left Mrs. Norcross again for the Hewins delivery if there had been any sign of labor. That flat entry,

"Her Husband & Mrs Delino & her Childn went on board bound for Nantucket Early this morn" was an ironic commentary on a month's frustration. The watched pot would not boil.

Here the more interesting point may not be the departure of the seafaring father (for men the conflict between work and family is an old and continuing one) but the presence of the distant sister. Betsy Delano, whose husband was also a mariner, lived in Nantucket. Did she sail up the river with Philip Norcross on April 11 hoping to attend her sister's delivery? Or had she spent the winter months in Hallowell with her mother while her own husband was at sea?

A second subplot is suggested by a clue so subtle that without long acquaintance with Martha Ballard's habits of deference, it is easily missed. She wrote of going to *Mrs* rather than to *Mr* Hussey's house, though in the same section she spoke of going to *Mr* Bullins, *Capt* Coxes, and *Mr* Goodins. In Martha Ballard's world, houses belonged to men. That in April of 1789 the Hussey house seemed to belong to a wife is significant. Obed Hussey was in Wiscasset jail, imprisoned for debt. She alluded to his situation on April 18, during one of her many visits to Mrs. Norcross. "Mrs Hussey Gone to see her Husband," she wrote, though with typical restraint she said nothing more. Obed Hussey was eighty years old that year. He never again saw his warehouses and fishing seines along the Kennebec. "Esquire Hussey expired in prison," Martha noted on June 17, 1790.

A different kind of adversity is suggested in the dramatic journey across swollen streams and deep gullies to the Hewinses' delivery. That Ebenezer Hewins was trying to carve out a farm in the second mile of settlement suggests something about his own status. Earlier arrivals, like the Husseys and the Ballards, lived near the river. There is a kind of disorder as well as excitement suggested by Ebenezer Hewins's precipitous fetching of the midwife, a feeling compounded later by the entry regarding the burning of the cloak, and by the knowledge that Martha Ballard had delivered the Hewinses' first baby in 1787 just two months after the couple were married.

The problem is not that the diary is trivial but that it introduces more stories than can easily be recovered and absorbed. It is one thing to describe Martha's journey across the Kennebec, another to assess the historical significance of Nancy Norcross's lingering labor, Obed Hussey's sojourn in jail, or Zilpha and Ebenezer Hewins's hasty marriage. Taken alone, such stories tell us too much and not enough, teasing us with glimpses of intimate life, repelling us with a reticence we cannot decode. Yet, read in the broader context of the diary and in relation to larger themes in eighteenth-century history, they can be extraordinarily revealing.

Each of the subplots in the April 1789 passage relates to a larger question in social history. Nancy Norcross suffered lingering labor in an era when old childbirth practices were being challenged in both England and America by a new "scientific" obstetrics promoted by male physicians. Obed Hussey languished in debtor's prison in an age when debtor petitions and even debtor insurrections were convulsing the nation and when some men were taking to the streets or the woods to preserve their property. Ebenezer and Zilpha Hewins married at a time of high premarital pregnancy rates in America, a period when political essayists as well as novelists were obsessed with the theme of seduction. The late eighteenth century was not only an era of political revolution but of medical, economic, and sexual transformation. Not surprisingly, it was also a time when a new ideology of womanhood self-consciously connected domestic virtue to the survival of the state. The nature of these phenomena is still being debated in the literature, yet few scholars would disagree that the period of Martha's diary, 1785–1812, was an era of profound change, or that in some still dimly understood way, the nation's political revolution and the social revolutions that accompanied it were related. It is not as easy as it once was to dismiss domestic concerns as "trivia."

Martha Ballard's diary connects to several prominent themes in the social history of the early Republic, yet it does more than reflect an era. By restoring a lost substructure of eighteenth-century life, it transforms the nature of the evidence upon which much of the history of the period has been written. The point can be illustrated by comparing evidence from her book with three documents left by prominent Hallowell men, Daniel Cony, William Howard, and Henry Sewall.

Daniel Cony was the Kennebec's best-known physician. He was studying medicine with his brother-in-law, Dr. Samuel Curtis of Marlborough, Massachusetts, at the time of the Lexington alarm. He marched with the Minutemen, served as adjutant of the regiment of infantry with General Horatio Gates at Saratoga, and according to the town historian "was at the surrender of Burgoyne, but not in any of the battles which preceded that event." He arrived in Hallowell in 1778, the same year as Martha, and became, in the words of a contemporary, a "faithful labourer in the medical field," and, we might add, an earnest promoter of medical organization. Though he practiced 150 miles into the hinterland, Cony was an early member of the Massachusetts Medical Society centered in Boston, and he continued that membership even after he became president of a new Kennebec Medical Society founded in 1797.

Cony was one of a handful of Maine physicians mentioned in James Thacher's *American Medical Biography,* published in Boston in 1828. He was, by all accounts, a leader in his profession, an associate if not a peer of New England's most progressive physicians, the very group of men who were promoting the new scientific obstetrics. Significantly, his only contribution to the literature of the Massachusetts Medical Society was an obstetrical paper, a one-page account of "a circumstance which I had never before met with" in a delivery he performed in August of 1787. Since this brief paper makes no mention of a midwife, or of any woman other than the patient, it might seem that the obstetrical revolution was complete in

Hallowell by that date, that doctors had supplanted midwives.

Martha's diary confirms that Cony delivered at least one woman in August 1787 — his own wife — but it reduces his obstetrical career to its proper place in the medical history of the town. Several doctors, including some from neighboring towns, occasionally attended births in Hallowell, but their work was supplementary to that of the midwives. Martha herself attended 60 percent of the births in Hallowell in the year Cony presented his paper to the Massachusetts Medical Society, and she was not the only female practitioner active at the time. Martha and her peers were not only handling most of the deliveries, they were providing much of the medical care as well. In Martha's diary, it is doctors, not midwives, who seem marginal.

William Howard, the man who helped Martha Ballard across the river on April 26 when she was returning from the Hussey house, was the wealthiest man in the town. The son and son-in-law of Hallowell's earliest settlers, he lived and traded at Fort Western in partnership with his brother Samuel, a mariner. A surviving account book listed under the names of William and Samuel Howard provides rich material for assessing the external economy of the Kennebec in the last decade of the eighteenth century. A standard merchant's ledger with debit and credit entries for each customer listed on opposite pages, it begins in 1788, though it carries some balances forward "from another Book," now lost. Most entries date from 1788 through 1792, though a few go to 1800 or beyond. Almost all, including those for the Ballards, are listed under the name of a male head of household. Male products — lumber, fish, and furs — dominate the credit side of the ledger.

One might conclude from such a record that Kennebec women had no role in economic life beyond their own households. An intriguing page at the very end of the account book lists flaxseed sold by the Kennebec Agricultural Society, yet there is little evidence in the account book itself of any sort of textile production in the town. Martha's diary tells us what happened to the seed. It not only records when Ephraim Ballard planted the flax, but when she and her daughters weeded and harvested it. It not only identifies the male helpers who turned and broke it, but the many female neighbors who assisted her and her daughters with the combing, spinning, reeling, boiling, spooling, warping, quilling, weaving, bucking, and bleaching that transformed the ripe plant into finished cloth. Martha's diary fills in the missing work — and trade — of women.

It also provides additional detail on the day-to-day operation of the male economy. Like most merchants, Howard served as a kind of banker, settling third-party debts with store goods or cash. Ephraim Ballard's accounts are typical, listing salt, rum, molasses, and nails on the debit side, several thousand feet of "clear" and "merchantable" boards among the credits, and on both sides of the ledger "notes" or "orders" on other men. On May 3, 1790, for example, the Howards debited Ephraim's account for "Willard Spoldings order dated 9 of June 1786" and "John Spoldings order dated 1 of July 1786." The diary shows where those orders came from. Early in April of 1786, Martha had noted, "Mr Ballard Been out to purchase Loggs." Twice in the next few weeks she wrote that "the Spolldings" had brought timber into the "Crik." She made no mention of the Spoldings on June 9 or on July 1, the dates given on the orders brought to William Howard, but she did note that Ephraim had gone to Pownalboro court on one of those days and to Vassalboro to "assist Brother Moore Rais his hous" on the other. Together the account book and the diary tell us how Ephraim Ballard "purchaced" logs for his sawmill. Contracting with men like the Spoldings, he paid in credit at the local stores, settling debts at court days and house-raisings, eventually balancing his own accounts with sawn boards.

Martha had a part in all this, as she noted on April 25: "Thee Spolldings brot Loggs. We had 9 men dind beside our own famely." But she did far more than support Ephraim's efforts. During that same week, she noted that a hired hand had performed an errand for her at one of the stores at the Hook, bringing home "6 galn of Rhum, 2 lb Coffee, 5 lb sugar, & some Tobacco & 1 bushl ¼ of salt from Joseph Williams for me for assisting his wife in travil with her Last Child." A few days later, she reported sending twenty-one skeins of tow yarn to Mrs. Chamberlain to weave. The Howard account book tells us a great deal about the male economy of eighteenth-century Hallowell. Martha's diary shows how women and men worked together to sustain this eighteenth-century town.

The comparisons with Henry Sewall are more direct, since he, too, kept a diary. Like Cony, Sewall was a veteran of the Continental Army. He had come to Hallowell from York, Maine, in 1784, shortly after experiencing an intense religious conversion. Appointed clerk of the U.S. District Court in 1789, he was also for thirty-two years the town clerk of Hallowell and Augusta and for seventeen years the registrar of deeds for Kennebec County. His clear, almost mechanically even handwriting fills the pages of town and county records. The diary he kept from 1776 to 1842 is as remarkable in its own way as Martha's (though less steady).

In April of 1789, while she was fighting the spring freshet in Hallowell, he was far away in New York City attempting to establish himself in business. His diary entry for April 23, the day she sank in the mire while stepping out of her canoe, marks the distance between her world and his. He wrote:

About 2 o'clock P.M. Genl Washington, the illustrious President of the United States, arrived in this city. He approached in a barge which was built here for his use. On his passing the Battery, a federal salute was fired, which was followed by an instantaneous display of colors from all the shipping in the harbour. On his landing, the federal salute was repeated and all the bells in the city rang peals of joy upon the glad occasion.

For Sewall this was an especially joyous moment, for he had served under Washington. "I took a stand on the roof of Mr. Rob. Hunter's house," he continued, "where I had the satisfaction of seeing once more my quondam General; now advanced to the chief magistracy of the empire, which his valour & magnanimity (under providence) protected and established under the most trying circumstances."

It is not easy to bring together the heroism of Sewall's "quondam General" with the heroism of Martha Ballard as she journeyed back and forth across the Kennebec that same week. The Revolution, the ratification of the Constitution, and the election of Washington certainly affected her life (if only in providing her with grandsons named George, Samuel Adams, and DeLafayette), but the political events that inhabit so much of the foreground in Sewall's diary are only a hazy background, if that, in hers. Yet the converse is also true. In fact, we can learn far more about the world of war and politics from Martha's diary than we can about domestic life from Henry's. Eight times Martha Ballard crossed the river to deliver Tabitha Sewall. Not until the fourth delivery did Henry note her presence, and then only twice after that. Nor did he once mention the fees he paid her, nor the names of the other women present, nor the complications (social and medical) that attended the births. Sewall had little to say about the women of Hallowell, including his own wife. It is Martha's diary, not his, that tells us Tabitha was a bonnet-maker.

Yet it is his diary rather than Martha's that describes the symbolic importance of women in the new republic. On February 22, 1800, he helped organize a parade to commemorate the death of his former commander, General Washington. At the head, following a military escort, were "16 Misses, clad in white, with black hats & cloaks, & white scarfs," representatives of the then sixteen states in the Union. (According to a later account, based on oral tradition, the white scarfs were "fastened on the right shoulder with a black and white rosette; tied under the left arm, with long ends falling to the bottom of the dress.") Led by the young women, the memorial procession passed into the meeting house, the militia companies followed by judges, lawyers, physicians, members of the fire society, and other dignitaries, "the music playing a dead march, & a detachment from Captain Bowman's artillery firing minute guns during the whole." For the young Daughters of Columbia it must have been an impressive occasion, a ritual identification of their own lives with the survival of the new nation.

Martha attended the service at the meeting house "to commemorate the Death of General George Washington." Significantly, she said nothing at all about the parade of young women, though she noted the presence of "the Lodg of Hallowell, Captain Casts Company of militia, and a larg concoarce of people." Her life had been altered by the Revolution, but her identity was unrelated to the rituals of republicanism. In 1800, she was far more concerned with the death of Nabby Andros, a neighbor's daughter, than with the demise of General Washington. Her values had been formed in an older world, in which a woman's worth was measured by her service to God and her neighbors rather than to a nebulous and distant state. For Martha, politics was what men did at town meetings — necessary perhaps, but often troublesome and divisive. Though she lived through a Revolution, she was more a colonial goodwife than a Republican Mother. Her story allows us to see what was lost, as well as what was gained, in the political, economic, and social transformations of the eighteenth and early nineteenth centuries.

To understand Martha's world we must approach it on its own terms, neither as a golden age of household productivity nor as a political void from which a later feminist consciousness emerged. Martha's diary reaches to the marrow of eighteenth-century life. The trivia that so annoyed earlier readers provide a consistent, daily record of the operation of a female-managed economy. The scandals excised by local historians provide insight into sexual behavior, marital and extramarital, in a time of tumult and change. The remarkable birth records, 814 deliveries in all, allow the first full accounting of delivery practices and of obstetrical mortality in any early American town. The family squabbles that earlier readers (and abridgers) of the diary found almost as embarrassing as the sexual references show how closely related Martha's occupation was to the life cycle of her own family, and reveal the private politics behind public issues like imprisonment for debt. The somber record of her last years provides rare evidence on the nature of aging in the preindustrial world, and shows the pull of traditional values in an era of economic and social turmoil.

The heroism is there, too. In the last decade of her life, when the world seemed to be falling apart around her — armed settlers attacking surveyors in the woods, husbands and fathers killing themselves, and, in the case of her neighbor Captain Purrinton, his wife and children as well — Martha found the courage to continue her work. On April 4, 1812, she rode "on horsback without a pillion" to a delivery. On April 26, 1812, just a month before her death, she attended her last birth.

The structure of the diary forces us to consider midwifery in the broadest possible context, as one specialty in a larger neighborhood economy, as the most visible feature of a comprehensive and little-known system of early health care, as a mechanism of social control, a strategy for family support, and a deeply personal calling. One might wish for more detail, for more open expressions of opinion, fuller accounts of medical remedies or obstetrical complications, more candor in describing physicians or judges, and less circumspection in recording scandal, yet for all its reticence, Martha's diary is an unparalleled document in early American history. It is powerful in part because it is so difficult to use, so unyielding in its dailiness.

QUESTIONS TO CONSIDER

1. Ulrich says that earlier historians thought Martha Ballard's diary too trivial to be of real interest. Why did they think so? Has she shown it to be more rewarding? If so, how has she done so?

2. What important role did Martha Ballard, her daughters, and other women play in Hallowell's economic life beyond the home?

3. What can you learn from Ulrich's comparison of the ordinary records left by men and those left by women?

4. Ulrich describes Martha Ballard as being from an older world, one already disappearing in revolutionary America. What does she mean by this and how was the world in which Ballard moved different from the one growing up around her?

5. What role did a midwife play in eighteenth-century America and how important was it? Was the midwife's status already being challenged?

12

The Personal Side of a Developing People

JACK LARKIN

The previous selection found profound significance in the life of one woman in a single community; the essay that follows focuses on broad patterns of social behavior in the young Republic as a whole. The differences between that America and ours can be astounding but so can the similarities, and you will want to note those as you read. In his narrative, Jack Larkin, chief historian of Old Sturbridge Village in Massachusetts, relies on contemporary observers of the young nation to answer several fascinating questions: What were people then really like? What did they eat and drink? What did they wear? What did they do for amusement? How did they occupy their leisure time? How did they deal with tension and stress? How did they make love?

The picture that emerges is of a vibrant, busy, contentious people who grew taller than the average Europeans, who spat tobacco, wore dour expressions, slept in bug-ridden beds, dumped their sewage in the streets, pursued the pleasures of the flesh more than we might have imagined, and drank too much liquor. Indeed, as Larkin reports, their per capita annual consumption is estimated "at the equivalent of three and one-half gallons of pure two-hundred-proof alcohol," which prompted one historian to term it the era of "the alcoholic Republic."

Larkin also discusses customs of courtship and marriage, sexual attitudes, and instances of premarital intercourse in the era of the young Republic. As Larkin points out, Americans of the early nineteenth century "were remarkably straitlaced about sexual matters in public and eager to insist upon the 'purity' of their manners." But their actual practices were a different matter. "Bundling," the custom of allowing a premarital couple to sleep together (they were supposed to keep their clothes on), was still being practiced. Moreover, pregnancy was a frequent "prelude to marriage." In the early colonial period, 20 percent of the native-born brides were with child. In rural New England in the last decades of the eighteenth century, the figure had risen to 30 percent. As Larkin points out, "the frequency of sexual intercourse before marriage was surely higher, since some couples would have escaped early pregnancy." For "reining in the passions," health specialists such as Sylvester Graham preached sexual restraint and prescribed a strict regimen of diet and exercise to control "animal lusts." What was more, there appeared in the 1830s a new theory of female sexuality, which held that "carnal passion" was not natural in a woman. In her role as mother and "guardian of the home," the theory went, she had no interest in sex beyond bearing children. Although Larkin does not say so, this new theory of female sexuality was linked to the concomitant doctrine of "sexual spheres," which arose to justify and perpetuate the practice of segregating women in the sphere of the home and men in politics and wage-earning (this is discussed in detail in selection 22, "Women and Their Families on the Overland Trails"). Why do you suppose such theories emerged? As you study "the personal side of a developing people," note the significance of patterns of regional, ethnic, and class distinctiveness in the young Republic.

GLOSSARY

BUNDLING   The custom of allowing a premarital couple to sleep "on the same bed without undressing."

CHAMBER POTS   Saved early Americans a trip to the outhouse on cold, dark nights.

CHAMBER SETS   "Matching basin and ewer [a pitcher with a wide spout] for private bathing."

CLAPP, SUMNER G.   Minister who led a temperance campaign in Enfield, Massachusetts.

DRAMMING   Ritual of downing a glass of hard cider twice a day.

GRAHAM, SYLVESTER   Author and lecturer who preached sexual restraint and a strict regimen of diet and exercise to control physical passions; his call for dietary reform, for eating bread and water in place of animal flesh, coffee, and tea, spawned a dietary movement the adherents to which called themselves *Grahamites*. The graham cracker is named after him.

HALL, MARGARET   Prominent Scottish visitor to America whose letters home complained about the bugs and filth she saw there.

MILLER-WEAVER FEUD   Protracted quarrel between two bellicose families in York, Pennsylvania.

☆

DOUR VISAGES

Contemporary observers of early-nine-teenth-century America left a fragmentary but nonetheless fascinating and revealing picture of the manner in which rich and poor, South-erner and Northerner, farmer and city dweller, free-man and slave presented themselves to the world. To begin with, a wide variety of characteristic facial ex-pressions, gestures, and ways of carrying the body re-flected the extraordinary regional and social diversity of the young republic.

When two farmers met in early-nineteenth-cen-tury New England, wrote Francis Underwood, of En-field, Massachusetts, the author of a pioneering 1893 study of small-town life, "their greeting might seem to a stranger gruff or surly, since the facial muscles were so inexpressive, while, in fact, they were on excellent terms." In courtship and marriage, countrymen and women were equally constrained, with couples "wear-ing all unconsciously the masks which custom had pre-scribed; and the onlookers who did not know the secret would think them cold and indifferent."

Underwood noted a pervasive physical as well as emotional constraint among the people of Enfield; it was rooted, he thought, not only in the self-denying ethic of their Calvinist tradition but in the nature of their work. The great physical demands of un-mechanized agriculture gave New England men, like other rural Americans, a distinctively ponderous gait and posture. Despite their strength and endurance, farmers were "heavy, awkward and slouching in

movement" and walked with a "slow inclination from side to side."

Yankee visages were captured by itinerant New England portraitists during the early nineteenth cen-tury, as rural storekeepers, physicians, and master craftsmen became the first more or less ordinary Americans to have their portraits done. The portraits caught their caution and immobility of expression as well as recording their angular, long-jawed features, thus creating good collective likenesses of whole communities.

The Yankees, however, were not the stiffest Americans. Even by their own impassive standards, New Englanders found New York Dutchmen and Pennsylvania German farmers "clumsy and chill" or "dull and stolid." But the "wild Irish" stood out in America for precisely the opposite reason. They were not "chill" or "stolid" enough, but loud and expan-sive. Their expressiveness made Anglo-Americans uncomfortable.

The seemingly uncontrolled physical energy of American blacks left many whites ill at ease. Of the slaves celebrating at a plantation ball, it was "impossi-ble to describe the things these people did with their bodies," Frances Kemble Butler, an English-born ac-tress who married a Georgia slave owner, observed, "and above all with their faces. . . ." Blacks' expres-sions and gestures, their preference for rhythmic rather than rigid bodily motion, their alternations of energy and rest made no cultural sense to observers who saw only "antics and frolics," "laziness," or "sav-agery." Sometimes perceived as obsequious, childlike, and dependent, or sullen and inexpressive, slaves also wore masks — not "all unconsciously" as Northern farm folk did, but as part of their self-protective strat-egies for controlling what masters, mistresses, and other whites could know about their feelings and motivations.

American city dwellers, whose daily routines were driven by the quicker pace of commerce, were easy to distinguish from "heavy and slouching" farmers at-

Excerpt from *The Reshaping of Everyday Life in the United States 1790–1840* by Jack Larkin. Copyright © 1988 by Jack Larkin. Re-printed by permission of HarperCollins Publishers, Inc.

Country revelers at a quilting "frolic" in the days of the early Republic. This 1813 painting, by German-born John Lewis Krimmel, is conspicuous for its fine detail and racial contrasts. Notice how well dressed the newly arrived whites are in comparison with the fiddler. Krimmel's comic portrayal marked the start of an almost *constant popular association of blacks with music and music making. It also contributed to the development of degrading racial stereotypes: note that both the fiddler and the serving girl have toothy grins and oversized red lips. (Courtesy The Henry Francis duPont Winterthur Museum)*

tuned to slow seasonal rhythms. New Yorkers, in particular, had already acquired their own characteristic body language. The clerks and commercial men who crowded Broadway, intent on their business, had a universal "contraction of the brow, knitting of the eyebrows, and compression of the lips . . . and a hurried walk." It was a popular American saying in the 1830s, reported Frederick Marryat, an Englishman who traveled extensively in the period, that "a New York merchant always walks as if he had a good dinner before him, and a bailiff behind him."

Northern and Southern farmers and city merchants alike, to say nothing of Irishmen and blacks, fell well short of the standard of genteel "bodily carriage" enshrined in both English and American etiquette books and the instructions of dancing masters: "flexibility in the arms . . . erectness in the spinal column . . . easy carriage of the head." It was the ideal of the British aristocracy, and Southern planters came closest to it, expressing the power of their class in the way they stood and moved. Slave owners accustomed to command, imbued with an ethic of honor and pride, at ease in the saddle, carried themselves more gracefully than men hardened by toil or preoccupied with commerce. Visiting Washington in 1835, the Englishwoman Harriet Martineau contrasted not the politics but the postures of Northern and Southern congressmen. She marked the confident bearing, the "ease and frank courtesy . . . with an occasional touch of arrogance" of the slaveholders alongside the "cautious . . . and too deferential air of the members of the North." She could recognize a New Englander "in the open air," she claimed, "by his deprecatory walk."

Local inhabitants' faces became more open, travelers observed, as one went west. Nathaniel Hawthorne found a dramatic contrast in public appearances only a few days' travel west of Boston. "The people out here," in New York State just west of the Berkshires, he confided to his notebook in 1839, "show out their character much more strongly than they do with us," in his native eastern Massachusetts. He compared the "quiet, silent, dull decency . . . in our public assemblages" with Westerners' wider gamut of expressiveness, "mirth, anger, eccentricity, all showing themselves freely." Westerners in general, the clergyman and publicist Henry Ward Beecher observed, had "far more freedom of manners, and more frankness and spontaneous geniality" than did the city or country people of the New England and Middle Atlantic states, as did the "odd mortals that wander in from the western border," that Martineau observed in Washington's political population.

☆

A PUNGENT FOLK

Early-nineteenth-century Americans lived in a world of dirt, insects, and pungent smells. Farmyards were strewn with animal wastes, and farmers wore manure-spattered boots and trousers everywhere. Men's and women's working clothes alike were often stiff with dirt and dried sweat, and men's shirts were often stained with "yellow rivulets" of tobacco juice. The locations of privies were all too obvious on warm or windy days. Unemptied chamber pots advertised their presence. Wet baby "napkins," today's diapers, were not immediately washed but simply put by the fire to dry. Vats of "chamber lye" — highly concentrated urine used for cleaning type or degreasing wool — perfumed all printing offices and many households. "The breath of that fiery bar-room," as Underwood described a country tavern, "was overpowering. The odors of the hostlers' boots, redolent of fish-oil and tallow, and of buffalo-robes and horse-blankets, the latter reminiscent of equine ammonia, almost got the better of the all-pervading fumes of spirits and tobacco."

Densely populated, but poorly cleaned and drained, America's cities were often far more noisome than its farmyards. Horse manure thickly covered city streets, and few neighborhoods were free from the spreading stench of tanneries and slaughterhouses. New York City accumulated so much refuse that it was generally believed the actual surfaces of the streets had not been seen for decades. During her stay in Cincinnati, the English writer Frances Trollope followed the practice of the vast majority of American city housewives when she threw her household "slops" — refuse food and dirty dishwater — out into the street. An irate neighbor soon informed her that municipal ordinances forbade "throwing such things at the sides of the streets" as she had done; "they must just all be cast right into the middle and the pigs soon takes them off." In most cities hundreds, sometimes thousands, of free-roaming pigs scavenged the garbage; one exception was Charleston, South Carolina, where buzzards patrolled the streets. By converting garbage into pork, pigs kept city streets cleaner than they would otherwise have been, but the pigs themselves befouled the streets and those who ate their meat — primarily poor families — ran greater than usual risks of infection.

☆

PRIVY MATTERS

The most visible symbols of early American sanitation were privies or "necessary houses." But Americans did not always use them; many rural householders simply took to the closest available patch of woods or brush. However, in more densely settled communities and in regions with cold winters, privies were in widespread use. They were not usually put in out-of-the-way locations. The fashion of some Northern farm families, according to Robert B. Thomas's *Farmer's Almanack* in 1826, had long been to have their "necessary planted in a garden or other conspicuous place." Other countryfolk went even further in turning human wastes to agricultural account and built their outhouses "within the territory of a hog yard, that the swine may root and ruminate and devour the nastiness thereof." Thomas was a long-standing critic of primitive manners in the countryside and roundly condemned these traditional sanitary arrangements as demonstrating a "want of taste, decency, and propriety." The better arranged necessaries of the prosperous emptied into vaults that could be opened and cleaned out. The dripping horse-drawn carts of the "nocturnal goldfinders," who emptied the vaults and took their loads out for burial or water disposal — "night soil" was almost never used as manure — were a familiar part of nighttime traffic on city streets.

The humblest pieces of American household furniture were the chamber pots that allowed people to avoid dark and often cold nighttime journeys outdoors. Kept under beds or in corners of rooms, "chambers" were used primarily upon retiring and arising. Collecting, emptying, and cleaning them remained an unspoken, daily part of every housewife's routine.

Nineteenth-century inventory takers became considerably more reticent about naming chamber pots than their predecessors, usually lumping them with miscellaneous "crockery," but most households probably had a couple of chamber pots; genteel families reached the optimum of one for each bedchamber. English-made ceramic pots had become cheap enough by 1820 that few American families within the reach of commerce needed to go without one. "Without a pot to piss in" was a vulgar tag of long standing for extreme poverty; those poorest households without one, perhaps more common in the warm South, used the outdoors at all times and seasons.

The most decorous way for householders to deal with chamber-pot wastes accumulated during the night was to throw them down the privy hole. But more casual and unsavory methods of disposal were still in wide use. Farm families often dumped their chamber pots out the most convenient door or window. In densely settled communities like York, Pennsylvania, the results could be more serious. In 1801, the York diarist Lewis Miller drew and then described an event in North George Street when "Mr. Day an English man [as the German-American Miller was quick to point out] had a bad practice by pouring out of the upper window his filthiness . . . one day came the discharge . . . on a man and wife going to a wedding, her silk dress was fouled."

☆

LETTING THE BEDBUGS BITE

Sleeping accommodations in American country taverns were often dirty and insect-ridden. The eighteenth-century observer of American life Isaac Weld saw "filthy beds swarming with bugs" in 1794; in 1840 [English novelist] Charles Dickens noted "a sort of game not on the bill of fare." Complaints increased in intensity as travelers went south or west. Tavern beds were uniquely vulnerable to infestation by whatever insect guests travelers brought with them. The bedding of most American households was surely less foul. Yet it was dirty enough. New England farmers were still too often "tormented all night by bed bugs," complained *The Farmer's Almanack* in 1837, and books of domestic advice contained extensive instructions on removing them from feather beds and straw ticks.

Journeying between Washington and New Orleans in 1828, Margaret Hall, a well-to-do and cultivated Scottish woman, became far more familiar with intimate insect life than she had ever been in the genteel houses of London or Edinburgh. Her letters home, never intended for publication, gave a graphic and unsparing account of American sanitary conditions. After sleeping in a succession of beds with the "usual complement of fleas and bugs," she and her party had themselves become infested: "We bring them along with us in our clothes and when I undress I find them crawling on my skin, nasty wretches." New and distasteful to her, such discoveries were commonplace among the ordinary folk with whom she lodged. The American children she saw on her Southern journey were "kept in such a state of filth," with clothes "dirty and slovenly to a degree," but this was "nothing in comparison with their heads . . . [which] are absolutely crawling!" In New Orleans she observed women picking through children's heads for lice, "catching them according to the method depicted in an engraving of a similar proceeding in the streets of Naples."

☆

BIRTH OF THE BATH

Americans were not "clean and decent" by today's standards, and it was virtually impossible that they should be. The furnishings and use of rooms in most American houses made more than the most elementary washing difficult. In a New England farmer's household, wrote Underwood, each household member would "go down to the 'sink' in the lean-to,

next to the kitchen, fortunate if he had not to break ice in order to wash his face and hands, or more fortunate if a little warm water was poured into his basin from the kettle swung over the kitchen fire." Even in the comfortable household of the prominent minister Lyman Beecher in Litchfield, Connecticut, around 1815, all family members washed in the kitchen, using a stone sink and "a couple of basins."

Southerners washing in their detached kitchens or, like Westerners in warm weather, washed outside, "at the doors . . . or at the wells" of their houses. Using basins and sinks outdoors or in full view of others, most Americans found anything more than "washing the face and hands once a-day," usually in cold water, difficult, even unthinkable. Most men and women also washed without soap, reserving it for laundering clothes; instead they used a brisk rubbing with a coarse towel to scrub the dirt off their skins.

Gradually the practice of complete bathing spread beyond the topmost levels of American society and into smaller towns and villages. This became possible as families moved washing equipment out of kitchens and into bedchambers, from shared space to space that could be made private. As more prosperous households furnished one or two of their chambers with washing equipment — a washstand, a basin, and a ewer, or large-mouthed pitcher — family members could shut the chamber door, undress, and wash themselves completely. The daughters of the Larcom family, living in Lowell, Massachusetts, in the late 1830s, began to bathe in a bedchamber in this way; Lucy Larcom described how her oldest sister started to take "a full cold bath every morning before she went to her work . . . in a room without a fire," and the other young Larcoms "did the same whenever we could be resolute enough." By the 1830s better city hotels and even some country taverns were providing individual basins and pitchers in their rooms.

At a far remove from "primitive manners" and "bad practices" was the genteel ideal of domestic sanitation embodied in the "chamber sets" — matching basin and ewer for private bathing, a cup for brushing the teeth, and a chamber pot with cover to minimize odor and spillage — that American stores were beginning to stock. By 1840 a significant minority of American households owned chamber sets and washstands to hold them in their bedchambers. For a handful there was the very faint dawning of an entirely new age of sanitary arrangements. In 1829 the new Tremont House hotel in Boston offered its patrons indoor plumbing: eight chambers with bathtubs and eight "water closets." In New York City and Philadelphia, which had developed rudimentary public water systems, a few wealthy households had water taps and, more rarely, water closets by the 1830s. For all others flush toilets and bathtubs remained far in the future.

The American people moved very slowly toward cleanliness. In "the backcountry at the present day," commented the fastidious author of the *Lady's Book* in 1836, custom still "requires that everyone should wash at the pump in the yard, or at the sink in the kitchen." Writing in 1846, the physician and health reformer William Alcott rejoiced that to "wash the surface of the whole body in water daily" had now been accepted as a genteel standard of personal cleanliness. But, he added, there were "multitudes who pass for models of neatness and cleanliness, who do not perform this work for themselves half a dozen times — nay once — a year." As the better-off became cleaner than ever before, the poor stayed dirty.

☆

BESOTTED ERA

In the early part of the century America was a bawdy, hard-edged, and violent land. We drank more than we ever had before or ever would again. We smoked and chewed tobacco like addicts and fought and quarreled on the flimsiest pretexts. The tavern was the most important gateway to the primarily male world of drink and disorder: in sight of the village church in most American communities, observed Daniel Drake, a Cincinnati physician who wrote a reminiscence of his Kentucky boyhood, stood the village tavern, and the two structures "did in fact represent two great opposing principles."

The great majority of American men in every region were taverngoers. The printed street directories of American cities listed tavernkeepers in staggering numbers, and even the best-churched parts of New England could show more "licensed houses" than meetinghouses. In 1827 the fast-growing city of Rochester, New York, with a population of approximately eight thousand, had nearly one hundred establishments licensed to sell liquor, or one for every eighty inhabitants.

America's most important centers of male sociability, taverns were often the scene of excited gaming and vicious fights and always of hard drinking, heavy smoking, and an enormous amount of alcohol-stimulated talk. City men came to their neighborhood taverns daily, and "tavern haunting, tippling, and gaming," as Samuel Goodrich, a New England historian and publisher, remembered, "were the chief resources of men in the dead and dreary winter months" in the countryside.

City taverns catered to clienteles of different classes: sordid sailors' grog-shops near the waterfront were rife with brawling and prostitution; neighborhood taverns and liquor-selling groceries were visited by craftsmen and clerks; well-appointed and relatively decorous places were favored by substantial merchants. Taverns on busy highways often specialized in teamsters or stage passengers, while country inns took their patrons as they came.

Taverns accommodated women as travelers, but their barroom clienteles were almost exclusively male. Apart from the dockside dives frequented by prostitutes, or the liquor-selling groceries of poor city neighborhoods, women rarely drank in public.

Gambling was a substantial preoccupation for many male citizens of the early republic. Men played billiards at tavern tables for money stakes. They threw dice in "hazard," slamming the dice boxes down so hard and so often that tavern tables wore the characteristic scars of their play. Even more often Americans sat down to cards, playing brag, similar to modern-day poker, or an elaborate table game called faro. Outdoors they wagered with each other on horse races or bet on cockfights and wrestling matches.

Drink permeated and propelled the social world of early-nineteenth-century America — first as an unquestioned presence and later as a serious and divisive problem. "Liquor at that time," recalled the builder and architect Elbridge Boyden, "was used as commonly as the food we ate." Before 1820 the vast majority of Americans considered alcohol an essential stimulant to exertion as well as a symbol of hospitality and fellowship. Like the Kentuckians with whom Daniel Drake grew up, they "regarded it as a duty to their families and visitors . . . to keep the bottle well replenished." Weddings, funerals, frolics, even a casual "gathering of two or three neighbors for an evening's social chat" required the obligatory "spirituous liquor" — rum, whiskey, or gin — "at all seasons and on all occasions."

Northern householders drank hard cider as their common table beverage, and all ages drank it freely. Dramming — taking a fortifying glass in the forenoon and again in the afternoon — was part of the daily regimen of many men. Clergymen took sustaining libations between services, lawyers before going to court, and physicians at their patients' bedsides. To raise a barn or get through a long day's haying without fortifying drink seemed a virtual impossibility. Slaves enjoyed hard drinking at festival times and at Saturday-night barbecues as much as any of their countrymen. But of all Americans they probably drank the least on a daily basis because their masters could usually control their access to liquor.

In Parma, Ohio, in the mid–1820s, Lyndon Free-

LIFE IN AN AMERICAN HOTEL?

*This British cartoon suggests the American propensity to violence in a hard-edged, hard-drinking era, when people fought often and with relish. Perhaps the irritable fellow with the gun spent a sleepless night battling the hotel's bed bugs. (*Punch, *June 28, 1856)*

man, a farmer, and his brothers were used to seeing men "in their cups" and passed them by without comment. But one dark and rainy night they discovered something far more shocking, "nothing less than a *woman beastly drunk* . . . with a flask of whiskey by her side." American women drank as well as men, but usually much less heavily. They were more likely to make themselves "tipsy" with hard cider and alcohol-containing patent medicines than to become inebriated with rum or whiskey. Temperance advocates in the late 1820s estimated that men consumed fifteen times the volume of distilled spirits that women did; this may have been a considerable exaggeration, but there was a great difference in drinking habits between the sexes. Americans traditionally found drunkenness tolerable and forgivable in men but deeply shameful in women.

By almost any standard, Americans drank not only nearly universally but in large quantities. Their yearly consumption at the time of the Revolution has been estimated at the equivalent of three and one-half gallons of pure two-hundred-proof alcohol for each person. After 1790 American men began to drink even more. By the late 1820s their imbibing had risen to an all-time high of almost four gallons per capita.

Along with drinking went fighting. Americans fought often and with great relish. York, Pennsylvania, for example, was a peaceable place as American communities went, but the Miller and Weaver families had a long-running quarrel. It had begun in 1800 when the Millers found young George Weaver stealing apples in their yard and punished him by "throwing him over the fence," injuring him painfully. Over the years hostilities broke out periodically. Lewis Miller remembered walking down the street as a teenaged boy and meeting Mrs. Weaver, who drenched him with the bucket of water she was carrying. He retaliated by "turning about and giving her a kick, laughing at her, this is for your politeness." Other York households had their quarrels too; in "a general fight on Beaver Street," Mistress Hess and Mistress Forsch tore each other's caps from their heads. Their husbands and then the neighbors interfered, and "all of them had a knock down."

When Peter Lung's wife, Abigail, refused "to get up and dig some potatoes" for supper from the yard of their small house, the Hartford, Connecticut, laborer recalled in his confession, he "kicked her on the side . . . then gave her a violent push" and went out to dig the potatoes himself. He returned and "again kicked her against the shoulder and neck." Both had been drinking, and loud arguments and blows within the Lung household, as in many others, were routine. But this time the outcome was not. Alice Lung was dead the next day, and Peter Lung was arrested, tried, and hanged for murder in 1815.

In the most isolated, least literate and commercialized parts of the United States, it was "by no means uncommon," wrote Isaac Weld, "to meet with those who have lost an eye in a combat, and there are men who pride themselves upon the dexterity with which they can scoop one out. This is called *gouging*."

☆

PUBLIC PUNISHMENT

The penal codes of the American states were far less bloodthirsty than those of England. Capital punishment was not often imposed on whites for crimes other than murder. Yet at the beginning of the nineteenth century many criminal offenses were punished by the public infliction of pain and suffering. "The whipping post and stocks stood on the green near the meetinghouse" in most of the towns of New England and near courthouses everywhere. In Massachusetts before 1805 a counterfeiter was liable to have an ear cut off, and a forger to have one cropped or partially amputated, after spending an hour in the pillory. A criminal convicted of manslaughter was set up on the gallows to have his forehead branded with a letter M. In most jurisdictions town officials flogged petty thieves as punishment for their crime. In New Haven, Connecticut, around 1810, Charles Fowler, a local historian, recalled seeing the "admiring students of [Yale] college" gathered around to watch petty criminals receive "five or ten lashes . . . with a rawhide whip."

Throughout the United States public hangings brought enormous crowds to the seats of justice and sometimes seemed like brutal festivals. Thousands of spectators arrived to pack the streets of courthouse towns. On the day of a hanging near Mount Holly, New Jersey, in the 1820s, the scene was that of a holiday: "around the place in every direction were the assembled multitudes — some in tents, and by-wagons, engaged in gambling and other vices of the sort, in open day." In order to accommodate the throngs, hangings were usually held not in the public square but on the outskirts of town. The gallows erected on a hill or set up at the bottom of a natural amphitheater allowed onlookers an unobstructed view. A reprieve or stay of execution might disappoint a crowd intent on witnessing the deadly drama and provoke a riot, as it did in Pembroke, New Hampshire, in 1834.

☆

RISE OF RESPECTABILITY

At a drunkard's funeral in Enfield, Massachusetts, in the 1830s — the man had strayed out of the road while walking home and fallen over a cliff, "his stiffened fingers still grasping the handle of the jug" — Rev. Sumner G. Clapp, the Congregationalist minister of Enfield, mounted a log by the woodpile and preached the town's first temperance sermon before a crowd full of hardened drinkers. In this way Clapp began a campaign to "civilize" the manners of his parishioners, and "before many years there was a great change in the town; the incorrigible were removed by death, and others took warning." Drinking declined sharply, and along with it went "a general reform in conduct."

Although it remained a powerful force in many parts of the United States, the American way of drunkenness began to lose ground as early as the mid–1820s. The powerful upsurge in liquor consumption had provoked a powerful reaction, an unprecedented attack on all forms of drink that gathered momentum in the Northeast. Some New England clergymen had been campaigning in their own communities as early as 1810, but their concerns took on organized impetus with the founding of the American Temperance Society in 1826. Energized in part by a concern for social order, in part by evangelical piety, temperance reformers popularized a radically new way of looking at alcohol. The "good creature" became "demon rum"; prominent physicians and writers on physiology, like Benjamin Rush, told Americans that alcohol, traditionally considered healthy and fortifying, was actually a physical and moral poison. National and state societies distributed anti-liquor tracts, at first calling for moderation in drink but increasingly demanding total abstinence from alcohol.

To a surprising degree these aggressive temperance campaigns worked. By 1840 the consumption of alcohol had declined by more than two-thirds, from close to four gallons per person each year to less than one and one-half. Country storekeepers gave up the sale of spirits, local authorities limited the number of tavern licenses, and farmers even abandoned hard cider and cut down their apple orchards. The shift to temperance was a striking transformation in the everyday habits of an enormous number of Americans. "A great, though silent change," in Horace Greeley's words, had been "wrought in public sentiment." . . .

Closely linked as they were to drink, such diversions as gambling, racing, and blood sports also fell to the same forces of change. In the central Massachusetts region that George Davis, a lawyer in Sturbridge, knew well, until 1820 or so gaming had "continued to prevail, more and more extensively." After that "a blessed change had succeeded," overturning the scenes of high-stakes dice and card games that he knew in his young manhood. Impelled by a new perception of its "pernicious effects," local leaders gave it up and placed "men of respectable standing" firmly in opposition. Racecourses were abandoned and "planted to corn." Likewise, "bear-baiting, cock-fighting, and other cruel amusements" began to dwindle in the Northern countryside. Elsewhere the rude life of the tavern and "cruel amusements" remained widespread, but some of their excesses of "sin and shame" did diminish gradually.

Over the first four decades of the nineteenth century the American people increasingly made churchgoing an obligatory ritual. The proportion of families affiliated with a local church or Methodist circuit rose dramatically, particularly after 1820, and there were fewer stretches of the wholly pagan, unchurched territory that travelers had noted around 1800. "Since 1830," maintained Emerson Davis in his retrospect of America, *The Half Century*, ". . . the friends of the Sabbath have been gaining ground. . . . In 1800, good men slumbered over the desecration of the Sabbath. They have since awoke. . . ." The number of Sunday mails declined, and the campaign to eliminate the delivery of mail on the Sabbath entirely grew stronger. "In the smaller cities and towns," wrote Mrs. Trollope in 1832, worship and "prayer meetings" had come to "take the place of almost all other amusements." There were still communities near the edge of settlement where a traveler would "rarely find either churches or chapels, prayer or preacher," but it was the working-class neighborhoods of America's larger cities that were increasingly the chief strongholds of "Sunday dissipation" and "Sabbath-breaking."

Whipping and the pillory, with their attentive audiences, began to disappear from the statute book, to be replaced by terms of imprisonment in another new American institution, the state penitentiary. Beginning with Pennsylvania's abolition of flogging in 1790 and Massachusetts's elimination of mutilating punishments in 1805, several American states gradually accepted John Hancock's view of 1796 that "mutilating or lacerating the body" was less an effective punishment than "an indignity to human nature." Connecticut's town constables whipped petty criminals for the last time in 1828.

Slaveholding states were far slower to change their provisions for public punishment. The whipping and mutilation of blacks may have become a little less ferocious over the decades, but the whip remained the essential instrument of punishment and discipline. "The secret of our success," thought a slave owner, looking back after emancipation, had been "the great motive power contained in that little instrument." Delaware achieved notoriety by keeping flogging on the books for whites and blacks alike through most of the twentieth century.

Although there were important stirrings of sentiment against capital punishment, all American states continued to execute convicted murderers before the mid–1840s. Public hangings never lost their drawing power. But a number of American public officials began to abandon the long-standing view of executions as instructive communal rituals. They saw the crowd's holiday mood and eager participation as sharing too much in the condemned killer's own brutality. Starting with Pennsylvania, New York, and Massachusetts in the mid-1830s, several state legislatures voted to take executions away from the crowd, out of the public realm. Sheriffs began to carry out death sentences behind the walls of the jailyard, before a small assembly of representative onlookers. Other states clung much longer to tradition and continued public executions into the twentieth century.

☆

SEX LIFE
OF THE NATIVES

Early-nineteenth-century Americans were more licentious than we ordinarily imagine them to be.

"On the 20th day of July" in 1830, Harriet Winter, a young woman working as a domestic in Joseph Dunham's household in Brimfield, Massachusetts, "was gathering raspberries" in a field west of the house. "Near the close of day," Charles Phelps, a farm laborer then living in the town, "came to the field where she was," and in the gathering dusk they made love — and, Justice of the Peace Asa Lincoln added in his account, "it was the Sabbath." American communities did not usually document their inhabitants' amorous rendezvous, and Harriet's tryst with Charles was a commonplace event in early-nineteenth-century America. It escaped historical oblivion because she was unlucky, less in becoming pregnant than in Charles's refusal to marry her. Asa Lincoln did not approve of Sabbath evening indiscretions, but he was not pursuing Harriet for immorality. He was concerned instead with economic responsibility for the child. Thus he interrogated Harriet about the baby's father — while she was in labor, as was the long-customary practice — in order to force Charles to contribute to the maintenance of the child, who was going to be "born a bastard and chargeable to the town."

Some foreign travelers found that the Americans they met were reluctant to admit that such things happened in the United States. They were remarkably straitlaced about sexual matters in public and eager to insist upon the "purity" of their manners. But to take such protestations at face value, the unusually candid Englishman Frederick Marryat thought, would be "to suppose that human nature is not the same everywhere."

The well-organized birth and marriage records of a number of American communities reveal that in late-eighteenth-century America pregnancy was frequently the prelude to marriage. The proportion of brides who were pregnant at the time of their weddings had been rising since the late seventeenth century and peaked in the turbulent decades during and after the Revolution. In the 1780s and 1790s nearly one-third of rural New England's brides were already with child. The frequency of sexual intercourse before marriage was surely higher, since some couples would have escaped early pregnancy. For many couples sexual relations were part of serious courtship. Premarital pregnancies in late-eighteenth century Dedham, Massachusetts, observed the local historian Erastus Worthington in 1828, were occasioned by "the custom then prevalent of females admitting young men to their beds, who sought their company in marriage."

Pregnancies usually simply accelerated a marriage that would have taken place in any case, but community and parental pressure worked strongly to assure it. Most rural communities simply accepted the "early" pregnancies that marked so many marriages, although in Hingham, Massachusetts, tax records suggest that the families of well-to-do brides were considerably less generous to couples who had had "early babies" than to those who had avoided pregnancy.

"Bundling very much abounds," wrote the anonymous author of "A New Bundling Song," still circulating in Boston in 1812, "in many parts in country towns." Noah Webster's first *Dictionary of the American Language* defined it as the custom that allowed couples "to sleep on the same bed without undressing" — with, a later commentator added, "the shared understanding that innocent endearments should not be exceeded." Folklore and local tradition, from Maine south to New York, had American mothers tucking bundling couples into bed with special chastity-protecting garments for the young woman or a "bundling board" to separate them.

In actuality, if bundling had been intended to allow courting couples privacy and emotional intimacy but not sexual contact, it clearly failed. Couples may have begun with bundling, but as courtship advanced, they clearly pushed beyond its restraints, like the "bundling maid" in "A New Bundling Song" who would "sometimes say when she lies down/She can't be cumbered with a gown."

Young black men and women shared American whites' freedom in courtship and sexuality and sometimes exceeded it. Echoing the cultural traditions of West Africa, and reflecting the fact that their marriages were not given legal status and security, slave communities were somewhat more tolerant and accepting of sex before marriage.

Gradations of color and facial features among the slaves were testimony that "thousands," as the abolitionist and former slave Frederick Douglass wrote, were "ushered into the world annually, who, like myself, owe the existence to white fathers, and those fathers most frequently their own masters." Sex crossed the boundaries of race and servitude more often than slavery's defenders wanted to admit, if less frequently than the most outspoken abolitionists claimed. Slave women had little protection from whatever sexual demands masters or overseers might make, so that rapes, short liaisons, and long-term "concubinage" all were part of plantation life.

As Nathaniel Hawthorne stood talking with a group of men on the porch of a tavern in Augusta, Maine, in 1836, a young man "in a laborer's dress" came up and asked if anyone knew the whereabouts of Mary Ann Russell. "Do you want to use her?" asked one of the bystanders. Mary Ann was, in fact, the young laborer's wife, but she had left him and their child in Portland to become "one of a knot of whores." A few years earlier the young men of York, Pennsylvania, made up a party for "overturning and pulling to the ground" Eve Geese's "shameful house" of prostitution in Queen Street. The frightened women fled out the back door as the chimney collapsed around them; the apprentices and young journeymen — many of whom had surely been previous customers — were treated by local officials "to wine, for the good work."

From medium-sized towns like Augusta and York to great cities, poor American women were sometimes pulled into a darker, harsher sexual world, one of vulnerability, exploitation, and commerce. Many prostitutes took up their trade out of poverty and domestic disaster. A young widow or a country girl arrived in the city and, thrown on her own resources, often faced desperate economic choices because most women's work paid too poorly to provide decent food, clothing, and shelter, while other women sought excitement and independence from their families.

As cities grew, and changes in transportation involved more men in long-distance travel, prostitution became more visible. Men of all ages, married and unmarried, from city lawyers to visiting country storekeepers to sailors on the docks, turned to brothels for sexual release, but most of the customers were young men, living away from home and unlikely to marry until their late twenties. Sexual commerce in New York City was elaborately graded by price and the economic status of clients, from the "parlor houses" situated not far from the city's best hotels on Broadway to the more numerous and moderately priced houses that drew artisans and clerks, and finally to the broken and dissipated women who haunted dockside grogshops in the Five Points neighborhood.

From New Orleans to Boston, city theaters were important sexual marketplaces. Men often bought tickets less to see the performance than to make assignations with the prostitutes, who sat by custom in the topmost gallery of seats. The women usually received free admission from theater managers, who claimed that they could not stay in business without the male theatergoers drawn by the "guilty third tier."

Most Americans — and the American common law — still did not regard abortion as a crime until the fetus had "quickened" or began to move perceptibly in the womb. Books of medical advice actually contained prescriptions for bringing on delayed menstrual periods, which would also produce an abortion if the woman happened to be pregnant. They suggested heavy doses of purgatives that created violent cramps, powerful douches, or extreme kinds of physical activity, like the "violent exercise, raising great weights . . . strokes on the belly . . . [and] falls" noted in William Buchan's *Domestic Medicine,* a manual read widely through the 1820s. Women's folklore echoed most of these prescriptions and added others, particularly the use of two American herbal preparations — savin, or the extract of juniper berries, and Seneca snakeroot — as abortion-producing drugs. They were dangerous procedures but sometimes effective.

☆

REINING IN
THE PASSIONS

Starting at the turn of the nineteenth century, the sexual lives of many Americans began to change, shaped by a growing insistence on control: reining in the passions in courtship, limiting family size, and even redefining male and female sexual desire.

Bundling was already on the wane in rural America before 1800; by the 1820s it was written about as a rare and antique custom. It had ceased, thought an elderly man from East Haddam, Connecticut, "as a consequence of education and refinement." Decade by decade the proportion of young women who had conceived a child before marriage declined. In most of the towns of New England the rate had dropped from nearly one pregnant bride in three to one in five or six by 1840; in some places prenuptial pregnancy dropped to 5 percent. For many young Americans this marked the acceptance of new limits on sexual behavior, imposed not by their parents or other authorities in their communities but by themselves.

These young men and women were not more closely supervised by their parents than earlier generations had been; in fact, they had more mobility and greater freedom. The couples that courted in the new style put a far greater emphasis on control of the passions. For some of them — young Northern merchants and professional men and their intended brides — revealing love letters have survived for the years after 1820. Their intimate correspondence reveals that they did not give up sexual expression but gave it new boundaries, reserving sexual intercourse for marriage. Many of them were marrying later than their parents, often living through long engagements while the husband-to-be strove to establish his place in the world. They chose not to risk a pregnancy that would precipitate them into an early marriage.

Many American husbands and wives were also breaking with tradition as they began to limit the size of their families. Clearly, married couples were renegotiating the terms of their sexual lives together, but they remained resolutely silent about how they did it. In the first two decades of the nineteenth century, they almost certainly set about avoiding childbirth through abstinence, coitus interruptus, or male withdrawal, and perhaps sometimes abortion. These contraceptive techniques had long been traditional in preindustrial Europe, although previously little used in America.

As they entered the 1830s, Americans had their first opportunity to learn, at least in print, about more effective or less self-denying forms of birth control.

They could read reasonably inexpensive editions of the first works on contraception published in the United States: Robert Dale Owen's *Moral Physiology* of 1831 and Dr. Charles Knowlton's *The Fruits of Philosophy* of 1832. Both authors frankly described the full range of contraceptive techniques, although they solemnly rejected physical intervention in the sexual act and recommended only douching after intercourse and coitus interruptus. Official opinion, legal and religious, was deeply hostile. Knowlton, who had trained as a physician in rural Massachusetts, was prosecuted in three different counties for obscenity, convicted once, and imprisoned for three months.

But both works found substantial numbers of Americans eager to read them. By 1839 each book had gone through nine editions, putting a combined total of twenty to thirty thousand copies in circulation. An American physician could write in 1850 that contraception had "been of late years so much talked of." Greater knowledge about contraception surely played a part in the continuing decline of the American birthrate after 1830.

New ways of thinking about sexuality emerged that stressed control and channeling of the passions. Into the 1820s almost all Americans would have subscribed to the commonplace notion that sex, within proper social confines, was enjoyable and healthy and that prolonged sexual abstinence could be injurious to health. They also would have assumed that women had powerful sexual drives.

Starting with his "Lecture to Young Men on Chastity" in 1832, Sylvester Graham articulated very different counsels about health and sex. Sexual indulgence, he argued, was not only morally suspect but psychologically and physiologically risky. The sexual overstimulation involved in young men's lives produced anxiety and nervous disorders, "a shocking state of debility and excessive irritability." The remedy was diet, exercise, and a regular routine that pulled the mind away from animal lusts. Medical writings that discussed the evils of masturbation, or "solitary vice," began to appear. Popular books of advice, like William Alcott's *Young Man's Guide,* gave similar warnings. They tried to persuade young men that their health could be ruined, and their prospects for success darkened, by consorting with prostitutes or becoming sexually entangled before marriage.

A new belief about women's sexual nature appeared, one that elevated them above "carnal passion." Many American men and women came to believe during the nineteenth century that in their true and proper nature as mothers and guardians of the home, women were far less interested in sex than men were. Women who defined themselves as passionless were in a strong position to control or deny men's sexual demands either during courtship or in limiting their childbearing within marriage.

Graham went considerably farther than this, advising restraint not only in early life and courtship but in marriage itself. It was far healthier, he maintained, for couples to have sexual relations "very seldom."

Neither contraception nor the new style of courtship had become anything like universal by 1840. Prenuptial pregnancy rates had fallen, but they remained high enough to indicate that many couples simply continued in familiar ways. American husbands and wives in the cities and the Northern countryside were limiting the number of their children, but it was clear that those living on the farms of the West or in the slave quarters had not yet begun to. There is strong evidence that many American women felt far from passionless, although others restrained or renounced their sexuality. For many people in the United States, there had been a profound change. Reining in the passions had become part of everyday life.

☆

SMOKING AND SPITTING

"Everyone smokes and some chew in America," wrote Isaac Weld in 1795. Americans turned tobacco, a new and controversial stimulant at the time of colonial settlement, into a crucially important staple crop and made its heavy use a commonplace—and a never-ending source of surprise and indignation to visitors. Tobacco use spread in the United States because it was comparatively cheap, a homegrown product free from the heavy import duties levied on it by European governments. A number of slave rations described in plantation documents included "one hand of tobacco per month." Through the eighteenth century most American smokers used clay pipes, which are abundant in colonial archeological sites, although some men and women dipped snuff or inhaled powdered tobacco.

Where the smokers of early colonial America "drank" or gulped smoke through the short, thick stems of their seventeenth-century pipes, those of 1800 inhaled it more slowly and gradually; from the early seventeenth to the late eighteenth century, pipe stems became steadily longer and narrower, increasingly distancing smokers from their burning tobacco.

In the 1790s cigars, or "segars," were introduced from the Caribbean. Prosperous men widely took them up; they were the most expensive way to consume tobacco, and it was a sign of financial security to puff away on "long-nines" or "principe cigars at three cents each" while the poor used clay pipes and much cheaper "cut plug" tobacco. After 1800 in American streets, barrooms, stores, public conveyances, and even private homes it became nearly impossible to avoid tobacco chewers. Chewing extended tobacco use, particularly into workplaces; men who smoked pipes at home or in the tavern barroom could chew while working in barns or workshops where smoking carried the danger of fire.

"In all the public places of America," wrote Charles Dickens, multitudes of men engaged in "the odious practice of chewing and expectorating," a recreation practiced by all ranks of American society. Chewing stimulated salivation and gave rise to a public environment of frequent and copious spitting, where men every few minutes were "squirting a mouthful of saliva through the room."

Spittoons were provided in the more meticulous establishments, but men often ignored them. The floors of American public buildings were not pleasant to contemplate. A courtroom in New York City in 1833 was decorated by a "mass of abomination" contributed to by "judges, counsel, jury, witnesses, officers, and audience." The floor of the Virginia House of Burgesses in 1827 was "actually flooded with their horrible spitting," and even the aisle of a Connecticut meetinghouse was black with the "ejection after ejection, incessant from twenty mouths," of the men singing in the choir. In order to drink, an American man might remove his quid, put it in a pocket or hold it in his hand, take his glassful, and then restore it to his mouth. Women's dresses might even be in danger at fashionable balls. "One night as I was walking upstairs to valse," reported Margaret Hall of a dance in Washington in 1828, "my partner began clearing his throat. This I thought ominous. However, I said to myself, 'surely he will turn his head to the other side.' The gentleman, however, had no such thought but deliberately shot across me. I had not courage enough to examine whether the result landed in the flounce of my dress."

The segar and the quid were almost entirely male appurtenances, but as the nineteenth century began, many rural and lower-class urban women were smoking pipes or dipping snuff. During his boyhood in New Hampshire, Horace Greeley remembered, "it was often my filial duty to fill and light my mother's pipe."

After 1820 or so tobacco use among women in the North began to decline. Northern women remembered or depicted with pipe or snuffbox were almost all elderly. More and more Americans adopted a genteel standard that saw tobacco use and womanliness — delicate and nurturing — as antithetical, and young women avoided it as a pollutant. For them, tobacco use marked off male from female territory with increasing sharpness.

In the households of small Southern and Western farmers, however, smoking and snuff taking remained common. When women visited "among the country people" of North Carolina, Frances Kemble Butler reported in 1837, the "proffer of the snuffbox, and its passing from hand to hand, is the usual civility." By the late 1830s visiting New Englanders were profoundly shocked when they saw the women of Methodist congregations in Illinois, including nursing mothers, taking out their pipes for a smoke between worship services.

☆

FROM DEFERENCE TO EQUALITY

The Americans of 1820 would have been more recognizable to us in the informal and egalitarian way they treated one another. The traditional signs of deference before social superiors — the deep bow, the "courtesy," the doffed cap, lowered head, and averted eyes — had been a part of social relationships in colonial America. In the 1780s, wrote the American poetess Lydia Huntley Sigourney in 1824, there were still "individuals . . . in every grade of society" who had grown up "when a bow was not an offense to fashion nor . . . a relic of monarchy." But in the early nineteenth century such signals of subordination rapidly fell away. It was a natural consequence of the Revolution, she maintained, which, "in giving us liberty, obliterated almost every vestige of politeness of the 'old school.'" Shaking hands became the accustomed American greeting between men, a gesture whose symmetry and mutuality signified equality. Frederick Marryat found in 1835 that it was "invariably the custom to shake hands" when he was introduced to Americans and that he could not carefully grade the acknowledgment he would give to new acquaintances according to their signs of wealth and breeding.

He found instead that he had to "go on shaking hands here, there and everywhere, and with everybody." Americans were not blind to inequalities of economic and social power, but they less and less gave them overt physical expression. Bred in a society where such distinctions were far more clearly spelled out, Marryat was somewhat disoriented in the United States; "it is impossible to know who is who," he claimed, "in this land of equality."

Well-born British travelers encountered not just confusion but conflict when they failed to receive the signs of respect they expected. Margaret Hall's letters home during her Southern travels outlined a true comedy of manners. At every stage stop in the Carolinas, Georgia, and Alabama, she demanded that country tavernkeepers and their households give her deferential service and well-prepared meals; she received instead rancid bacon and "such an absence of all kindness of feeling, such unbending frigid heartlessness." But she and her family had a far greater share than they realized in creating this chilly reception. Squeezed between the pride and poise of the great planters and the social debasement of the slaves, small Southern farmers often displayed a prickly insolence, a considered lack of response, to those who too obviously considered themselves their betters. Greatly to their discomfort and incomprehension, the Halls were experiencing what a British traveler more sympathetic to American ways, Patrick Shirreff, called "the democratic rudeness which assumed or presumptuous superiority seldom fails to experience."

☆

LAND OF ABUNDANCE

In the seventeenth century white American colonials were no taller than their European counterparts, but by the time of the Revolution they were close to their late-twentieth-century average height for men of slightly over five feet eight inches. The citizens of the early republic towered over most Europeans.

Americans' early achievement of modern stature — by a full century and more — was a striking consequence of American abundance. Americans were taller because they were better nourished than the great majority of the world's peoples.

Yet not all Americans participated equally in the nation's abundance. Differences in stature between whites and blacks, and between city and country dwellers, echoed those between Europeans and Americans. Enslaved blacks were a full inch shorter than whites. But they remained a full inch taller than European peasants and laborers and were taller still than their fellow slaves eating the scanty diets afforded by the more savagely oppressive plantation system of the West Indies. And by 1820 those who lived in the expanding cities of the United States — even excluding immigrants, whose heights would have reflected European, not American, conditions — were noticeably shorter than the people of the countryside, suggesting an increasing concentration of poverty and poorer diets in urban places.

Across the United States almost all country households ate the two great American staples: corn and "the eternal pork," as one surfeited traveler called it, "which makes its appearance on every American table, high and low, rich and poor." Families in the cattle-raising, dairying country of New England, New York, and northern Ohio ate butter, cheese, and salted beef as well as pork and made their bread from wheat flour or rye and Indian corn. In Pennsylvania, as well as Maryland, Delaware, and Virginia, Americans ate the same breadstuffs as their Northern neighbors, but their consumption of cheese and beef declined every mile southward in favor of pork.

Farther to the south, and in the West, corn and corn-fed pork were truly "eternal"; where reliance on them reached its peak in the Southern uplands, they were still the only crops many small farmers raised. Most Southern and Western families built their diets around smoked and salted bacon, rather than the Northerners' salt pork, and, instead of wheat or rye bread, made cornpone or hoecake, a coarse, strong bread, and hominy, pounded Indian corn boiled together with milk.

Before 1800, a game — venison, possum, raccoon, and wild fowl — was for many American households "a substantial portion of the supply of food at certain seasons of the year," although only on the frontier was it a regular part of the diet. In the West and South this continued to be true, but in the Northeast game became increasingly rare as forests gave way to open farmland, where wild animals could not live.

Through the first half of the eighteenth century, Americans had been primarily concerned with obtaining a sufficiency of meat and bread for their families; they paid relatively little attention to foodstuffs other than these two "staffs of life," but since that time the daily fare of many households had grown substantially more diverse. . . .

Important patterns of regional, class, and ethnic distinctiveness remain in American everyday life. But they are far less powerful, and less central to understanding American experience, than they once were. Through the rest of the nineteenth century and into the twentieth, the United States became ever more diverse, with new waves of Eastern and Southern European immigrants joining the older Americans of Northern European stock. Yet the new arrivals — and even more, their descendants — have experienced the attractiveness and reshaping power of a national culture formed by department stores, newspapers, radios, movies, and universal public education. America, the developing nation, developed into us. And perhaps our manners and morals, to some future observer, will seem as idiosyncratic and astonishing as this portrait of our earlier self.

QUESTIONS TO CONSIDER

1. Compare Larkin's description of American urban conditions, crime, disorder, and drunkenness with the conditions Page Smith found in seventeenth-century London (selection 2). Were these Americans worse or better off than their English forbears? How did the American legal response to crime and disorder compare with the earlier British model?

2. Bacterial pollution from animal and human wastes, offal, open drains, and contaminated water were major threats to American health in the early nineteenth century. Are we more fortunate nearly two centuries later, or have we found new ways to poison our environment? Which era do you think is the more deadly?

3. Larkin is a social and cultural historian. What sources has he used to compile his vivid account of everyday life among ordinary Americans in the early nineteenth century? What are the advantages of using these sources? potential disadvantages?

4. Larkin points out that American women drank less than a third as much as American men at the turn of the nineteenth century and that alcohol consumption by slaves was also limited. A few decades later, women spearheaded the temperance movement in communities all over the country. What issues of social control do you suppose were in operation throughout this period?

5. In what personal ways are these ordinary nineteenth-century Americans different from us today? How are they the same? What distinctively American traits does Larkin suggest were born in this era?

VII

To Have and Have Not

13

The Louisiana Purchase:
A Dangerous Precedent

WALTER LaFEBER

Students of the past have long debated what determines the course of history. There are those who maintain that great "forces" shape the direction and composition of human societies; some even argue that people, individuals, are not important. There are others, however, who focus on the human side of the past, examining how the interaction of people and events dictates the course of subsequent events. From this view, human beings are not mere cogs in the engines of history; they can and do make a difference. Portrait of America stresses the latter view of history. In the next two selections, the authors describe in human terms some major political and judicial developments in the young Republic, from the dawn of the nineteenth century to the turbulent 1820s. The third selection describes "the river of black struggle" for liberty in the same period.

Let us pick up political events where Edmund S. Morgan leaves off in his assessment of George Washington in selection 10. When John Adams replaced Washington as president in 1796, Federalist leaders were extremely apprehensive about the French Revolution and the anarchy and violence that seemed to characterize it. Might the French virus spread to America as it appeared to be spreading across Europe? Might a conspiracy already be under way in the United States to fan the flames of revolution, to unleash the American mob on Federalist leaders, to destroy the order and stability they had worked so hard to establish? Since 1793, when a Frenchman, Citizen Genêt, had tried to enlist American men and privateers for the French cause, the Federalists had feared revolution in their midst. Champions of a strong government to maintain order, apostles of elitist rule and the sanctity of private property, the Federalists soon equated the Republicans under Madison and Jefferson with revolution, chaos, and destruction. After all, did the Republicans not support the French? Did they not defend the mob here at home? Did they not call for more democracy in government (although many of their leaders paradoxically were southern slave owners)?

The harried Federalists barely fought off a Republican attempt to seize the government in 1796, when Adams defeated Jefferson by only three votes in the electoral college. Then, as though the Republican threat were not bad enough, trouble broke out with revolutionary France. In the notorious XYZ affair, French agents tried to extract a bribe from American representatives sent to negotiate about deteriorating Franco-American relations. Many Americans thought the nation's honor had been besmirched and demanded a war of revenge. In response, the Federalists undertook an undeclared sea war against France that lasted from 1798 to 1800. Using the war as a pretext to consolidate their power, bridle the Republicans, and prevent revolution in the United States, the Federalists passed the Alien and Sedition Acts. These, they declared, were necessary for the nation's security in the war with France.

The Alien Act severely restricted the rights and political influence of immigrants, who usually joined the Republicans after they were naturalized and who might be carrying the French virus. The Sedition Act made hostile criticism of Federalist policies punishable by fine and imprisonment. The Republicans, decrying such government censorship, launched a counterattack against Federalist "despotism." The Federalists were so discredited by the Alien and Sedition laws, and so divided by an irreconcilable feud between Adams and Hamilton, that the Republicans were able to win the government in 1801. Their victory marked the decline and eventually the end of the Federalist party as a national political organization.

Jefferson liked to describe his rise to power as "the revolution of 1800." But was it really a revolution? True, the Republicans allowed the hated Alien and Sedition Acts to expire in 1801, reduced the residence requirement for naturalized citizenship from fourteen years to five so that America could again function as an "asylum" for "oppressed humanity," inaugurated a new fiscal policy of government frugality and efficiency, and strove to retire the national debt of $83 million in sixteen years. Jefferson also repudiated the idea of government by and for a political elite. Yet he and his top administrators were as educated, talented, and upper class as their Federalist predecessors. Moreover, while Jefferson embraced the laissez-faire principle that that government is best which governs least, he found that reversing all Federalist commitments could cause confusion and consternation across the land. Therefore, he and his followers permitted the United States Bank to continue operating (it closed in 1811 when its charter ran out), and they maintained Federalist measures for refunding the national debt, stimulating American shipping, and assuming the states' Revolutionary War debts. Nor did Jefferson's "revolution of

1800" change the condition of America's enslaved blacks. As president, the author of the Declaration of Independence carefully avoided the subject of bondage.

"What is practicable," Jefferson said, "must often control what is pure theory." As Washington's secretary of state, Jefferson had demanded a strict construction of the Constitution, arguing that what was not specifically delegated to the federal government was reserved to the states. By that argument, he had opposed Secretary of the Treasury Alexander Hamilton's sweeping economic schemes. But when he became president and saw a chance to double the size of the United States by purchasing the Louisiana Territory, Jefferson abandoned strict construction and embraced the Federalist doctrine of "loose construction," for that was the only way he could justify the annexation of territory. In the next selection, distinguished historian Walter LaFeber discusses the intriguing case of Jefferson and the Louisiana Purchase, pointing out how the Federalists and the Jeffersonian Republicans switched roles when it came to interpreting the president's constitutional authority. As LaFeber sees it, Jefferson and his supporters set "a dangerous precedent" in the Louisiana Purchase: they transformed the Constitution into "an instrument for imperial expansion," he argues, and made it possible for the president and Congress to stretch and even violate the Constitution if they considered it to be in the national interest. As Jefferson proved, any president could stretch the Constitution in order to pursue an expansionist foreign policy — especially if his party controlled Congress. Indeed, as LaFeber says, later presidents did exactly that.

In selection 8, we saw Jefferson in a different light, as reluctant slaveholder, philosopher of liberty, and author of the Declaration of Independence. In this selection, we see a pragmatic politician who abandoned his own political philosophy and party doctrine in order to gain a practical objective — to annex Louisiana and thereby enlarge "the empire of liberty." How do you reconcile the Jefferson who wrote the Declaration of Independence and who demanded a strict construction of the Constitution with the Jefferson who used party politics to force through Congress a measure of questionable constitutional legality? What does this tell you about the nature of American politics? about Jefferson himself? In selection 8, Douglas Wilson argued that Jefferson intended to include blacks in the proposition that all men were created equal and entitled to the unalienable rights of life, liberty, and the pursuit of happiness. Yet in the debates over Louisiana, Jefferson opposed a proposed ban on slavery in the new territory, arguing that Creoles — Louisianans of French ancestry — were incapable of self-government, and permitting only white men of his own choosing to govern there. How do you account for this apparent inconsistency?

GLOSSARY

ADAMS, JOHN QUINCY   Newly elected member of Congress from Massachusetts who favored the Louisiana treaty but was appalled that Jefferson interpreted the Constitution so broadly as to let him rule in the Louisiana Territory.

BRECKINRIDGE, JOHN   Kentucky senator who had helped Jefferson write the Kentucky resolutions and who longed to control the Mississippi River.

GALLATIN, ALBERT   Jefferson's secretary of the treasury who advised the president that the United States, as an "aspect of its sovereignty," had the right to annex territory.

HILLHOUSE, JAMES   Senator from Connecticut who proposed that slavery be banned in the Louisiana Territory, thus precipitating a debate that anticipated arguments that would later threaten to disrupt the Union.

LINCOLN, LEVI   Jefferson's attorney general who tried to get around constitutional objections to the Louisiana Purchase by saying that the French defined the territory as an extension of the state of Georgia or of the Mississippi Territory.

LIVINGSTON, ROBERT R.   United States minister to France who, with James Monroe, negotiated the treaty that purchased Louisiana for the United States.

RANDOLPH, JOHN   Virginia member of Congress who broke with Jefferson when the president violated his own constitutional doctrine.

VIRGINIA AND KENTUCKY RESOLUTIONS   Jefferson and Madison helped draft these state resolutions, which denounced the Federalists for expanding federal power beyond constitutional limits and argued that the states should have the authority to decide the constitutionality of federal acts.

Thomas Jefferson was one of the greatest expansionists in an American history full of ardent expansionists. But then, he believed the success of America's great experiment in democracy demanded an expanding territory. In the Virginian's mind, the republic must be controlled by ambitious, independent, property-holding farmers, who would form the incorruptible bedrock of democracy. As he wrote in 1785 in his Notes on the State of Virginia, "Those who labour in the earth are the chosen people. . . . Corruption of [their] morals . . . is a phenomenon of which no age nor nation has furnished an example." Americans who worked the land would never become dependent on factory wages. "Dependence begets subservience and venality," Jefferson warned in *Notes,* "and prepares fit tools for the designs of ambition."

But Jefferson's virtuous farmers needed land, and their population was growing at an astonishing rate. Jefferson and his close friend and Virginia neighbor, James Madison, had studied the birthrate carefully. The two men rightly perceived that Americans were nearly doubling their population every 25 to 27 years. Moreover, the number of immigrants seemed to be increasing so quickly that as early as 1785 Jefferson had actually suggested restricting their numbers. Virginia provided a striking example of how fast land was being peopled. The region on the state's western frontier had filled with settlers so quickly that in 1792 it became the state of Kentucky. Unless something was done, Jefferson declared, Virginia would within the next century be burdened with "nearly the state of population in the British islands." Given Jefferson's convictions about the corruption to be found in Britain's cities, the analogy was damning.

During his first term as President (1801–1805), Jefferson had the chance to obtain that "extension of territory which the rapid increase of our numbers will

Walter LaFeber, "The Louisiana Purchase: A Dangerous Precedent," *Constitution* (vol. 5, no. 3) (Fall 1993), 4–7, 74–80. Reprinted by permission of the author.

call for" by purchasing Louisiana, an area larger than Western Europe. In a single step he could double the size of the United States and open the possibility of an "empire for liberty," as he later described it, of mind-boggling proportions.

The President was playing for large stakes. Louisiana stretched from the Mississippi westward to the Rocky Mountains, and from Canada's Lake of the Woods southward to the Gulf of Mexico. If annexed, these 825,000 square miles would give the new nation access to one of the world's potentially richest trading areas. The Missouri, Kansas, Arkansas and Red rivers and their tributaries could act as giant funnels carrying goods into the Mississippi and then down to New Orleans. Even in the 1790s, with access to the Mississippi only from the east, the hundreds of thousands of Americans settled along the river depended on it and on the port of New Orleans for access to both world markets and imported staples for everyday living. "The Mississippi is to them everything," Secretary of State James Madison observed privately in November 1802. "It is the Hudson, the Delaware, the Potomac, and all the navigable rivers of the Atlantic formed into one stream."

Louisiana had long been a focus for imperial ambitions. The French had largely controlled the region until 1763 when, after losing the so-called Seven Years War, they were forced to cede it to Spain. But in 1799 Napoleon Bonaparte became head of the French government, and the next year he seized the opportunity to retake the territory. In exchange for his promise to make the Spanish royal family rulers of Tuscany, Spain handed over Louisiana. Though Bonaparte never bothered to carry out his end of the bargain, he set in motion plans for a New World colonial empire that would make Louisiana the food source for the rich French sugar island of Saint Domingue (Haiti) in the Caribbean.

Jefferson and Madison reacted with alarm. A decaying Spanish empire along the western American border was little threat. But Napoleon was something else. He would dam up American expansionism and perhaps attract settlements east of the Mississippi away from the United States. In 1801, after hearing rumors of Napoleon's bargain with Spain, Jefferson ordered Robert R. Livingston to Paris as the new U.S. minister. He instructed Livingston to talk Napoleon out of occupying Louisiana or, if that was impossible, to buy New Orleans. By 1802 both Jefferson and Livingston began to mention the possibility of acquiring not just the port, but also its vast interior.

Jefferson told Livingston that if France insisted on occupying New Orleans, he would consider an Anglo-American alliance against France. That threat was probably empty. But others were not. In February the Senate authorized Jefferson to create an 80,000-man army to defend the Mississippi. Although the House adjourned before acting on the measure, the President had already begun strengthening forts along the river. He sent three artillery and four infantry companies into position north of New Orleans. The commander of these forces, William C.C. Claiborne, assured him that these troops could seize New Orleans if they attacked before French forces arrived to strengthen the Spanish garrison.

But just as war with Napoleon loomed in the early months of 1803, Jefferson faced a crisis of quite another kind. He knew that the Constitution had no provision giving him the power to take New Orleans — let alone an area such as Louisiana that would double the nation's size — and he believed he could take no action not explicitly authorized by the Constitution.

This conviction was no mere infatuation with theory. As George Washington's secretary of state from 1790 until 1793, Jefferson had fought Secretary of the Treasury Alexander Hamilton's attempt to interpret the Constitution's phrases in broad terms. Beaten by Hamilton over such critical issues as whether the Constitution permitted the United States to create a national bank, or the federal government to assume state debts, Jefferson resigned from the cabinet. He retired to Monticello and — even as Vice-President under the Federalist President John Adams — organized the Republican Party to take power and, as he saw it, restore the Constitution's true meaning. "The powers not delegated to the United States," he wrote in a debate with Hamilton in 1790 and 1791, "are reserved to the States respectively, or to the people." He warned, in words that were later to cause him anguish, that "to take a single step beyond the boundaries thus specially drawn around the powers of Congress is to take possession of a boundless field of power, no longer susceptible of any definition."

In 1798 Jefferson's fears seemed to come true. Enmeshed in undeclared war with France on the high seas, the Federalists tried to force Americans to cooperate with Adams's war plans by passing the Alien and Sedition Acts. These measures gave President John Adams the power to arrest and imprison his critics. Jeffersonians believed the acts were aimed at them — and with good reason: the 14 indictments and 10 convictions that occurred under the act were against members of the Republican Party. In secret, Jefferson and Madison helped the Virginia and Kentucky legislatures draft resolutions that condemned the Federalists for enlarging central government — especially presidential — powers beyond the limits set by the Constitution. The resolutions argued that a state should have the power to decide whether federal governmental acts were constitutional or not. Demanding that Congress support a strict construction of the 1787 document, Jefferson won what he called "the revolution of 1800," which threw Adams and the Hamiltonians out of office. The "sum of good government," he observed in his 1801 inaugural address, was small and limited government.

Thus Jefferson's dilemma in January and February 1803. As he and his closest advisers agreed, nothing in the Constitution explicitly permitted the government to annex and govern new territory — let alone a territory so immense that it would transform the nation's political balance. Reading that power into the Constitution's general wording, Jefferson warned, could so twist and distort the document that American liberty would be threatened. "Our peculiar security is in possession of a written Constitution," he

wrote privately to a close friend. "Let us not make it a blank paper by construction." By no means, however, was he willing to turn away Louisiana.

In January 1803, Jefferson discussed these difficulties with Attorney General Levi Lincoln and the brilliant young secretary of the treasury, Albert Gallatin. Lincoln suggested that Jefferson have the French, if they sold any part of the territory, designate it as an extension of the Mississippi Territory or the state of Georgia. Gallatin retorted that if the central government lacked the constitutional power to annex new territory, then so did the states. By mid-January he had given Jefferson his rather Hamiltonian view of the matter: "1st. That the United States as a nation have an inherent right to acquire territory. 2nd. That whenever that acquisition is by treaty, the same constituted authorities in whom the treaty-making power is vested [that is, in the President and the Senate] have a constitutional right to sanction the acquisition. 3rd. That whenever the territory has been acquired, Congress have the power either of admitting into the Union as a new State, or of annexing to a State with the consent of that State, or of making regulations for the government of such territory."

In acquiring a territorial empire over the next century, Americans were to follow precisely these principles. But Gallatin's views did little to quell Jefferson's uneasiness, which reached a climax on July 3 when he learned that the two U.S. diplomats in Paris, Robert R. Livingston and James Monroe, had signed a treaty in which Napoleon sold Louisiana to the United States for $11,250,000. A separate agreement stipulated that the United States would assume $3,750,000 more for claims of U.S. citizens against France. The two diplomats also agreed that for 12 years French and Spanish ships would receive special tariff rates over other foreign ships and merchandise in New Orleans. The inhabitants of the vast territory, moreover, were to receive full constitutional rights as soon as possible.

These last provisions were to bedevil Jefferson. Giving French and Spanish traders preferences in New Orleans violated the Constitution's provisions that duties be levied uniformly throughout the nation. Granting full constitutional rights to the many non-Americans, especially nonwhites, in this vast area went against Jefferson's better judgment — not to mention the devout wishes of conservative and increasingly agitated New Englanders.

On July 16, Jefferson placed the agreements before his cabinet (or "executive council" as it was then known) and suggested that Congress "be obliged to ask from the people an amendment to the Constitution authorizing their receiving the province into the Union, and providing for its government." Gallatin, Madison, Lincoln, Secretary of War Henry Dearborn and Secretary of the Navy Robert Smith vigorously disagreed. They did not share the President's constitutional sensitivities.

The council pointed out a more immediate danger: the treaty provided for an exchange of ratifications within six months of the signing on April 30, 1803. No constitutional amendment could be passed by the necessary two-thirds vote in both houses of Congress and the three fourths of the states in the time remaining. But if there were any delay, Napoleon could renounce the agreement and recommence his empire building along the Mississippi. The advisers urged that Jefferson call a special session of Congress in October and rush the treaty and conventions through without mentioning the amendment.

Jefferson's friends warned him that if he so much as hinted at the need for an amendment, the treaty's enemies — most notably, New England Federalists whose fear of a vast western empire beyond their control was matched only by their hatred of Jefferson — would delay and probably kill the agreements. The President realized this. Nevertheless, that summer he tried to write at least two drafts of an amendment. He admitted to his close friend, Senator John Breckinridge of Kentucky, that in agreeing to the purchase he had gone far beyond what the Constitution permitted. Breckinridge, who had written the Kentucky Resolutions with Jefferson just four years earlier, disagreed. He had long nurtured the ambition to control

New Orleans and the trans-Mississippi — an ambition that in the 1790s had led him to plot secretly (and in some Easterners' eyes, treasonously) with a French agent to gain control of the river without the knowledge or approval of the Washington administration. In any case, the President's desire for empire was becoming overwhelming. "I infer," he wrote Madison later in August, "that the less we say about constitutional difficulties respecting Louisiana the better, and that what is necessary for surmounting them must be done sub silentio."

Jefferson found these "constitutional difficulties" distinctly less important after he received two letters. In the first, which arrived from Paris on August 17, Livingston warned that Napoleon now regretted having signed the treaty. The French leader was searching for any excuse ("the slightest alteration" made by the United States, in the envoy's words) to avoid carrying it out. If Congress did not act within the six-month limit, the First Consul would renounce the deal. The second letter carried a long-expected message from the Spanish minister in Washington, Marquis de Casa Yrujo. It reached Jefferson on September 12. The king of Spain, Yrujo wrote, was shocked that Napoleon had sold Louisiana. The French leader had no right to do so. The President now had to fear that either his majesty or Napoleon might use this message as an excuse to reclaim New Orleans and the interior.

Livingston's note decided Jefferson, and Yrujo's protest reinforced his determination. The President concluded that although it would be advisable to push for an amendment, it could be done only after Congress had acted on the agreements and the territory was safely in hand. In the meantime, he told Gallatin, Congress should approve the documents "without talking."

Jefferson needed two thirds of the Senate to ratify his treaty and a simple majority of the House to carry the agreements into effect. In the Senate, where his forces were led by the loyal Breckinridge, his party held 25 seats to the Federalists' nine; in the House the numbers were also overwhelming — 103 to 39. Jef-

This painting shows Americans James Monroe and Robert Livingston and the French Finance Minister signing the Louisiana Purchase treaty in 1803. As one historian noted, the transaction enlarged the size of the United States by "about 140 per cent," adding 50,000 new citizens and some 150,000 Native Americans to the national realm. (The Granger Collection, New York)

delicately put it, exchange information for the sake of the "public interest."

Many New England Federalists feared the idea of annexing a vast territory whose people would over time develop immense political power — and, no doubt, be forever grateful to Jeffersonians. A Boston Federalist newspaper sniffed that Louisiana was nothing more than "a great waste, a wilderness unpeopled with any beings except wolves and wandering Indians. . . . We are to give money of which we have too little for land of which we already have too much." Senator William Plumer, a Federalist from New Hampshire, warned that New England would not "tamely shrink into a state of insignificance."

On October 17, 1803, Jefferson told the Congress he had summoned into session that he was sending it the treaty and the accompanying agreements. Nothing was said about a constitutional amendment. The measures were being whipped through after only three days of debate when a crisis developed. Senate Federalists demanded that Jefferson send the documents proving that Napoleon had rightfully obtained Louisiana from Spain and so had the power to sell the territory. This demand presented a problem: the documents did not exist. Republicans nevertheless closed ranks and "with unblushing front" (as Plumer sarcastically commented) voted down the resolution on the grounds that such information was not needed. The agreements were then rammed through, 24 to 7. "The Senate," Plumer complained, "have taken less time to deliberate on this most important treaty than they allowed themselves on the most trivial Indian contract."

Next the papers went to the House for legislation that would authorize monetary payments to carry out the agreements. Again the Federalists demanded documents, particularly a deed of cession from Spain to France. The request touched a nerve. Seven years earlier, Madison, then the Jeffersonian leader in a Federalist-dominated House of Representatives, had tried to kill the Jay treaty with Great Britain by demanding all appropriate documents. President Washington had

ferson, however, left nothing to chance. Regularly working 10 to 13 hours a day to ensure that his wishes were carried out, he became the most powerful party leader in the republic's short history. Such a regimen left, according to this remarkably organized man, "an interval of 4 hours for riding, dining, and a little unbending." Even then he used the dinner hour several times a week to invite congressional members, stoke them with excellent food and wine and, as Jefferson refused on the grounds that the House was obliged to carry out treaties that, under the Constitution, only the Senate had to ratify. Madison protested, but he was beaten in a showdown vote that had large implications for the constitutional role the House was to play in future U.S. foreign policy. Now, in 1803, the roles were reversed. As the Federalists demanded the deed, Samuel Mitchill of New York rose to reply on behalf of the Jeffersonians that if the President had thought the House needed to see any more papers, he certainly would have sent them. After that disingenuous response, the House voted down the Federalist demand by two votes.

In his pioneering analysis of how rapidly presidential power grew during the Jeffersonian years, Abraham Sofaer argues that the Virginian set a precedent in refusing to acknowledge the Federalists' call for the documents. President Washington had taken the position that, yes, papers that Congress had requested did exist, but, no, he did not have to send certain confidential papers to Congress. The Jeffersonians had responded vigorously that such official information could be demanded and used by the people's representatives in the legislature. In 1803, however, (and again during the treason trial of former Vice-President Aaron Burr in 1807) Jefferson took the position that it was unnecessary to tell the Congress (or the court) that such papers even existed. Instead, he labeled the documents "private" or "confidential" and kept them out of sight. The people's representatives in Congress apparently had a limited right to know, and the limits were determined by the President.

This embarrassment eased in December 1803 when Jefferson learned that Napoleon had finally pressured Spain into giving him official possession of Louisiana. In January 1804, the forces Jefferson had dispatched under Claiborne's command a year earlier controlled the region. The Stars and Stripes replaced the French Tricolor over New Orleans.

One major obstacle remained, however. Jefferson had to create, and Congress approve, a government for this vast territory. The region held fewer than 100,000 inhabitants, and Jefferson believed, rightly as it turned out, that only half of those were white and that the remainder were largely Indian and African-American. The President indicated from the start of the debate that he thought only whites could govern the territory. But even some of them were suspect. New Orleans had attracted renegades and runaways, like former New York district attorney, Edward Livingston, who had moved to New Orleans after he was suspected of having illegally siphoned money from his office. Roman Catholic groups, long protected by Spain, were fearful and suspicious of Jefferson's intentions. As for the large population of Creoles (those with French ancestry born in Louisiana), the President believed they were "as yet as incapable of self-government as children." When a Creole delegation traveled to Washington to demonstrate its ability to lobby, it was turned away.

Congress divided the region into two districts: Orleans (the future state of Louisiana) and Louisiana. Late in 1803 the President sent Congress a bill for governing the area during the next year. This measure gave the inhabitants guarantees for their "liberty, property, and religion," which the treaty had obligated him to grant. There was, however, no self-government, no indication that, to repeat one of Jefferson's earlier principles, governments derived "their just powers from the consent of the governed." Military officers, chosen by the President, were to rule in the iron-handed manner of the former Spanish governor. They were responsible to no local authorities, but only to the President in the faraway city of Washington. Senator John Quincy Adams, who had just won election from Massachusetts, supported the annexation, but he was appalled that the Constitution was being interpreted as giving the President authority to rule the territory as a colony. When Adams moved that a constitutional amendment be considered to make such rule legitimate, no senator seconded his proposal. Jefferson's governing bill passed the Senate 26 to 6.

The House's view of Jefferson's constitutional

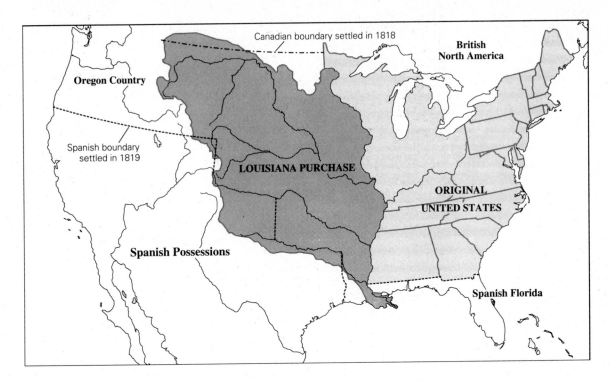

Map of the Louisiana Purchase

powers was revealed when angry Federalists attacked the treaty provision that gave French and Spanish merchants trade preferences in New Orleans. Joseph H. Nicholson of Maryland replied for the Jeffersonians that the whole of Louisiana "is in the nature of a colony whose commerce may be regulated without any reference to the Constitution" and its provision that duties be uniformly imposed throughout the Union. Madison, with his sensitivity to such issues, excused the Jeffersonians' tough approach by granting that while "Republican theory" would not immediately govern the newly annexed people, "it may fairly be expected that every blessing of liberty will be extended to them as fast as they shall be prepared and disposed to receive it." The secretary of state was known for choosing his words carefully.

From January through March 1804, Congress discussed Jefferson's plans for a more permanent government, which would last until both sections of Louisi-

ana had enough white settlers to be entrusted with regular territorial government. Few problems arose in the debates until Senator James Hillhouse of Connecticut proposed that slavery be prohibited from both parts of the purchase. A struggle erupted in the Senate that previewed some of the arguments that later threatened to splinter the Union. When one slave-state senator tried to stop the uproar by saying, "I am unwilling to think let alone speak on this subject," another grimly warned that "if we leave it, it will follow us." Jefferson notably refused to support Hillhouse, and Senator James Jackson of Georgia led the opposition to the Connecticut senator by declaring that Louisiana could "not be cultivated" without slavery. He urged that the people on the scene (many of whom owned slaves) be allowed to decide. "You cannot prevent slavery. . . . Men will be governed by their interest not the law." In the end, though, Congress again broadly construed its power by recogniz-

195

ing slavery where it existed in the purchase, while allowing a previous act to stand that stringently limited the slave trade. Provisions were added to prevent Orleans, a center of the foreign slave trade, from becoming a state until after the 1810 census. This delay not only appeased New England Federalists but also prevented Orleans' entry as a state until after 1808 when, as the Constitution provided, the foreign trade in slaves was to end.

The final bill gave the President the power to appoint governors over Orleans and Louisiana who, with a small legislative body they were to choose, would rule autocratically. The rights of the inhabitants were not "self-evident," as Jefferson had once described them, but were granted by the will of the central government. The law became effective October 1, 1804.

In less than one year Jefferson had enlarged the central government's constitutional powers more broadly than had Washington and Adams in 12 years. He had set a dangerous precedent, moreover, by arguing that when time was of the essence, the President and Congress could ignore, perhaps violate, the Constitution if they considered it to be in the national interest. Critics called Jefferson's government in Louisiana "about as despotic as that of Turkey in Asia." The President and his supporters responded that such a government was, unfortunately, necessary to ensure that the vast territory would remain orderly until enough white Americans could populate the region. The new states would then prosper as a part of the Union with rights equal to those of the older parts.

Critics were not reassured. "We rush like a comet into infinite space," Fisher Ames of Massachusetts warned. "In our wild career we may jostle some other world out of its orbit, but we shall, in every event, quench the light of our own." John Randolph of Virginia had a less apocalyptic response to Jefferson's actions. He had helped the President push the Louisiana legislation through the House. But by 1806 he had turned against his fellow Virginian for having overthrown Republican constitutional doctrine. There

were only "two parties in all States," Randolph concluded, "the *ins* and the *outs*." The ins construed governmental power broadly for the gain of their own "patronage and wealth," while the outs tried to limit such power. "But let the *outs* get in . . . and you will find their Constitutional scruples and arguments vanish like dew before the morning sun."

As the ins, Jefferson and his supporters realized larger objectives than "patronage and wealth." They succeeded in transforming the Constitution into an instrument for imperial expansion, which made it possible for Jefferson to resolve the crisis in his great democratic experiment.

But the transformation of the Constitution for the sake of "enlarging the empire of liberty" had a price. The President, as Jefferson had demonstrated, could find in the Constitution virtually any power he needed to carry out the most expansive foreign policy, especially if his party commanded a majority in Congress. Loose construction was given the seal of bipartisanship as the Republicans, now the ins, out-Hamiltoned Hamilton in construing the 1787 document broadly. Such loose construction would be used by others, among them President James K. Polk from 1845 to '46 as he maneuvered Mexico into a war in order to annex California, President William McKinley between 1898 and 1901 when he expanded U.S. power into the Philippines and landed troops in China, and President Harry S Truman when he claimed the authority to wage war in Korea. Jefferson's experiment in democracy cast long shadows.

QUESTIONS TO CONSIDER

1. Why was Louisiana such an attractive prize to so many? Why was Jefferson in particular tempted by it? Who was generally opposed to the acquisition of the Louisiana Territory and why?

2. Describe the constitutional questions raised by the acquisition of Louisiana. What was Jefferson's decision, and how did it compare with the position he

took during his constitutional debates with Alexander Hamilton and the Federalists in the 1790s? How do you reconcile this portrait of the political Jefferson with the one drawn by Douglas Wilson in selection 8? How do you think Jefferson compares with the President Washington of selection 10?

3.   What kind of government did Jefferson recommend for the Louisiana Territory and why? What social and political ironies are there in this choice?

4.   What position did Jefferson take on slavery in the new territory, and how does it jibe with his feelings on slavery as portrayed by Douglas Wilson in selection 8? How did Congress deal with this issue?

5.   In what ways does LaFeber find the Louisiana Purchase "a dangerous precedent"? Do you agree? What might have happened if we had not bought Louisiana?

14

The Great Chief Justice

BRIAN MCGINTY

As the court of last appeal in all matters involving the Constitution, the United States Supreme Court may be the most powerful branch of the federal government. It has the authority to uphold or strike down federal and state legislation, overturn decisions by lower courts, and determine the rights of individuals. Consequently, as in the modern struggle over abortion, the Court often stands at the center of national controversy.

You may be surprised to read in this selection that the Court was not always supreme, that in the first decade of its existence it was a maligned junior branch of the federal government, ignored by lawyers and scorned by politicians. How did it change into the powerful national tribunal we know today? As Brian McGinty points out, Chief Justice John Marshall made the nation's high tribunal a court that is supreme in fact as well as in name. During his thirty-four years on the bench (from 1801 to 1835), Marshall, a dedicated Federalist, also read the basic tenets of federalism into American constitutional law: the supremacy of the nation over the states, the sanctity of contracts, the protection of property rights, and the superiority of business over agriculture.

If you fear you are about to read a dull and dreary essay on constitutional law, don't despair. McGinty's warm portrait of the chief justice personalizes the major currents of the period and captures Marshall the human being in vivid scenes. We see him doing his own shopping for groceries, frequenting taverns and grog shops (he loves wine so much that a colleague quips, "the Chief was brought up on Federalism and Madeira"), and carrying a turkey for a young jurist who is too embarrassed to do so in public. Marshall clashes repeatedly with Jefferson over fundamental political and constitutional issues; later, Mar-

shall tangles with Andrew Jackson in defending the treaty rights of the Cherokee Indians, a subject to be treated in more detail in selection 21.

It was Marshall's Court decisions, however, that had the biggest influence on his country. As McGinty says, Marshall's ruling in Marbury v. Madison, which established the principle of judicial review, was perhaps the most important decision ever to come from the United States Supreme Court. Judicial review empowered the Supreme Court to interpret the meaning of the Constitution and so to define the authority of the national government and the states. The system of judicial review helped ensure the flexibility of the Constitution — so much so that a document originally designed for a small, scattered, largely agrarian population on the East Coast could endure for two centuries, during which the United States became a transcontinental, then a transpacific urban and industrial nation. That the Constitution has been able to grow and change with the country owes much to John Marshall.

GLOSSARY

BURR, AARON   First United States citizen to be tried for treason; Marshall helped acquit him in his trial before the Supreme Court.

FEDERALISTS   Those such as Washington, Hamilton, and Marshall who favored a strong federal government and a stable, well-ordered society run by the great landowners and merchants.

GIBBONS V. OGDEN (1824)   Case in which Marshall upheld federal jurisdiction over interstate commerce.

McCULLOCH V. MARYLAND (1819)   Case in which Marshall ruled that the first United States Bank was constitutional and that the state of Maryland could not tax it.

MARBURY V. MADISON (1803) Case in which Marshall established the principle of judicial review, which empowered the Supreme Court to interpret the Constitution and thus to define the authority of the national government and the states.

STORY, JOSEPH   Associate justice on the Marshall Court and the chief justice's personal friend.

WYTHE, GEORGE   Professor at the College of William and Mary in Virginia who was a mentor to Marshall, Jefferson, and Henry Clay (to be treated in a later selection); he was the first law professor in the United States.

WORCESTER V. GEORGIA (1832)   Marshall decision forbidding the state of Georgia to violate the treaty rights of the Cherokee.

He was a tall man with long legs, gangling arms, and a round, friendly face. He had a thick head of dark hair and strong, black eyes — "penetrating eyes," a friend called them, "beaming with intelligence and good nature." He was born in a log cabin in western Virginia and never wholly lost his rough frontier manners. Yet John Marshall became a lawyer, a member of Congress, a diplomat, an advisor to presidents, and the most influential and respected judge in the history of the United States. "If American law were to be represented by a single figure," Supreme Court Justice Oliver Wendell Holmes, Jr., once said, "sceptic and worshipper alike would agree without dispute that the figure could be but one alone, and that one John Marshall."

To understand Marshall's preeminence in American legal history it is necessary to understand the marvelous rebirth the United States Supreme Court experienced after he became its chief justice in 1801. During all of the previous eleven years of its existence, the highest judicial court in the federal system had been weak and ineffectual — ignored by most of the nation's lawyers and judges and scorned by its principal politicians. Under Marshall's leadership, the court became a strong and vital participant in national affairs. During his more than thirty-four years as chief justice of the United States, Marshall welded the Supreme Court into an effective and cohesive whole. With the support of his colleagues on the high bench, he declared acts of Congress and of the president unconstitutional, struck down laws that infringed on federal prerogatives, and gave force and dignity to basic guarantees of life and liberty and property. Without John Marshall, the Supreme Court might never have been anything but an inconsequential junior partner of the executive and legislative branches

of the national government. Under his guidance and inspiration, it became what the Constitution intended it to be — a court system in fact as well as in name.

Born on September 4, 1755, in Fauquier County, Virginia, John Marshall was the oldest of fifteen children born to Thomas Marshall and Mary Randolph Keith. On his mother's side, the young Virginian was distantly related to Thomas Jefferson, the gentlemanly squire of Monticello and author of the Declaration of Independence. Aside from this kinship, there was little similarity between Marshall and Jefferson. A son of the frontier, Marshall was a backwoodsman at heart, more comfortable in the company of farmers than intellectuals or scholars. Jefferson was a polished aristocrat who liked to relax in the library of his mansion near Charlottesville and meditate on the subtleties of philosophy and political theory.

The contrast between the two men was most clearly drawn in their opposing political beliefs. An advocate of limiting the powers of central government, Thomas Jefferson thought of himself first and foremost as a Virginian (his epitaph did not even mention the fact that he had once been president of the United States). Marshall, in contrast, had, even as a young man, come to transcend his state roots, to look to Congress rather than the Virginia legislature as his government, to think of himself first, last, and always as an American. Throughout their careers, their contrasting philosophies would place the two men at odds.

Marshall's national outlook was furthered by his father's close association with George Washington and his own unflinching admiration for the nation's first president. Thomas Marshall had been a schoolmate of Washington and, as a young man, helped him survey the Fairfax estates in northern Virginia. John Marshall served under Washington during the bitter winter at Valley Forge and later became one of the planter-turned-statesman's most loyal supporters.

Years after the Revolution was over, Marshall attributed his political views to his experiences as a foot soldier in the great conflict, recalling that he grew up

From "The Great Chief Justice" by Brian McGinty, *American History Illustrated* (September 1988), pp. 8–14, 46–47. Reprinted by permission of Cowles Magazines, publisher of *American History Illustrated*.

Chester Harding's 1829 portrait of John Marshall. The chief justice, writes Brian McGinty, "was a tall man with long legs, gangling arms, and a round, friendly face. He had a thick head of dark hair and strong, black eyes — 'penetrating eyes,' a friend called them, 'beaming with intelligence and good nature.'" (Washington and Lee University, Virginia)

"at a time when a love of union and resistance to the claims of Great Britain were the inseparable inmates of the same bosom — when patriotism and a strong fellow feeling with our suffering fellow citizens of Boston were identical; — when the maxim 'united we stand, divided we fall' was the maxim of every orthodox American . . ." "I had imbibed these sentiments so thoughroughly (sic) that they constituted a part of my being," wrote Marshall. "I carried them with me into the army where I found myself associated with brave men from different states who were risking life and everything valuable in a common cause believed by all to be most precious; and where

I was confirmed in the habit of considering America as my country, and Congress as my government."

After Washington's death, Marshall became the great man's biographer, penning a long and admiring account of Washington's life as a farmer, soldier, and statesman, expounding the Federalist philosophy represented by Washington and attacking those who stood in opposition to it. Jefferson, who detested Federalism as much as he disliked Marshall, was incensed by the biography, which he branded a "five-volume libel."

Frontiersman though he was, Marshall was no bumpkin. His father had personally attended to his earliest schooling, teaching him to read and write and giving him a taste for history and poetry (by the age of twelve he had already transcribed the whole of Alexander Pope's *Essay on Man*). When he was fourteen, Marshall was sent to a school a hundred miles from home, where future president James Monroe was one of his classmates. After a year, he returned home to be tutored by a Scottish pastor who had come to live in the Marshall house. The future lawyer read Horace and Livy, pored through the English dictionary, and scraped at least a passing acquaintance with the "Bible of the Common Law," William Blackstone's celebrated *Commentaries on the Laws of England*.

In 1779, during a lull in the Revolution, young Marshall attended lectures at the College of William and Mary in Williamsburg. He remained at the college only a few weeks, but the impression made on him by his professor there, George Wythe, was lasting. A lawyer, judge, and signer of the Declaration of Independence, Wythe is best remembered today as the first professor of law at any institution of higher learning in the United States. As a teacher, he was a seminal influence in the development of American law, counting among his many distinguished students Thomas Jefferson, John Breckinridge, and Henry Clay.

Marshall did not remain long at William and Mary. It was the nearly universal custom then for budding lawyers to "read law" in the office of an older lawyer or judge or, failing that, to appeal to the greatest teacher of all — experience — for instruction. In August 1780, a few weeks before his twenty-fifth birthday, Marshall appeared at the Fauquier County Courthouse where, armed with a license signed by Governor Thomas Jefferson of Virginia, he was promptly admitted to the bar.

His first cases were not important, but he handled them well and made a favorable impression on his neighbors; so favorable that they sent him to Richmond in 1782 as a member of the Virginia House of Delegates. Though he retained a farm in Fauquier County all his life, Richmond became Marshall's home after his election to the legislature. The general courts of Virginia held their sessions in the new capital, and the commonwealth's most distinguished lawyers crowded its bar. When Marshall's fortunes improved, he built a comfortable brick house on the outskirts of the city, in which he and his beloved wife Polly raised five sons and one daughter (four other offspring died during childhood).

Marshall's skill as a lawyer earned him an enthusiastic coterie of admirers and his honest country manners an even warmer circle of friends. He liked to frequent the city's taverns and grog shops, more for conviviality than for refreshment, and he was an enthusiastic member of the Barbecue Club, which met each Saturday to eat, drink, "josh," and play quoits.

Marshall liked to do his own shopping for groceries. Each morning he marched through the streets with a basket under his arm, collecting fresh fruits, vegetables, and poultry for the Marshall family larder. Years after his death, Richmonders were fond of recalling the day when a stranger came into the city in search of a lawyer and found Marshall in front of the Eagle Hotel, holding a hat filled with cherries and speaking casually with the hotel proprietor. After Marshall went on his way, the stranger approached the proprietor and asked if he could direct him to the best lawyer in Richmond. The proprietor replied quite readily that the best lawyer was John Marshall,

the tall man with the hat full of cherries who had just walked down the street.

But the stranger could not believe that a man who walked through town so casually could be a really "proper barrister" and chose instead to hire a lawyer who wore a black suit and powdered wig. On the day set for the stranger's trial, several cases were scheduled to be argued. In the first that was called, the visitor was surprised to see that John Marshall and his own lawyer were to speak on opposite sides. As he listened to the arguments, he quickly realized that he had made a serious mistake. At the first recess, he approached Marshall and confessed that he had come to Richmond with a hundred dollars to hire the best lawyer in the city, but he had chosen the wrong one and now had only five dollars left. Would Marshall agree to represent him for such a small fee? Smiling good-naturedly, Marshall accepted the five dollars, then proceeded to make a brilliant legal argument that quickly won the stranger's case.

Marshall was not an eloquent man; not eloquent, that is, in the sense that his great contemporary, Patrick Henry, a spellbinding courtroom orator, was eloquent. Marshall was an effective enough speaker; but, more importantly, he was a rigorously logical thinker. He had the ability to reduce complex issues to bare essentials and easily and effortlessly apply abstract principles to resolve them.

Thomas Jefferson (himself a brilliant lawyer) was awed, even intimidated, by Marshall's powers of persuasion. "When conversing with Marshall," Jefferson once said, "I never admit anything. So sure as you admit any position to be good, no matter how remote from the conclusion he seeks to establish, you are gone. . . . Why, if he were to ask me if it were daylight or not, I'd reply, 'Sir, I don't know, I can't tell.'"

Though Marshall's legal prowess and genial manner won him many friends in Richmond, his political views did little to endear him to the Old Dominion's political establishment. While Jefferson and his followers preached the virtues of agrarian democracy, viewing with alarm every step by which the fledgling national government extended its powers through the young nation, Marshall clearly allied himself with Washington, Alexander Hamilton, and John Adams and the Federalist policies they espoused.

Marshall was not a delegate to the convention that met in Philadelphia in 1787 to draft a constitution for the United States, but he took a prominent part in efforts to secure ratification of the Constitution, thereby winning the special admiration of George Washington. After taking office as president, Washington offered Marshall the post of attorney general. Marshall declined the appointment, as he did a later offer of the prestigious post of American minister to France, explaining that he preferred to stay in Richmond with his family and law practice.

He did agree, however, to go to Paris in 1798 as one of three envoys from President John Adams to the government of revolutionary France. He did this, in part, because he was assured that his duties in Paris would be temporary only, in part because he believed he could perform a real service for his country, helping to preserve peaceful relations between it and France during a time of unusual diplomatic tension.

After Marshall joined his colleagues Elbridge Gerry and Charles Pinckney in Paris, he was outraged to learn that the French government expected to be paid before it would receive the American emissaries. Marshall recognized the French request as a solicitation for a bribe (the recipients of the payments were mysteriously identified as "X," "Y," and "Z"), and he refused to consider it.

Thomas Jefferson, who was smitten with the ardor and ideals of the French Revolution, suspected that Marshall and his Federalist "cronies" were planning war with France to promote the interests of their friends in England. But the American people believed otherwise. When they received news of the "XYZ Affair," they were outraged. "Millions for defense," the newspapers thundered, "but not one cent for trib-

ute!" When Marshall returned home in the summer of 1798, he was welcomed as a hero. In the elections of the following fall, he was sent to Congress as a Federalist representative from Richmond.

Jefferson was not pleased. He declined to attend a dinner honoring Marshall in Philadelphia and wrote worried letters to his friends. Though he deprecated his fellow Virginian's popularity, alternatively attributing it to his "lax, lounging manners" and his "profound hypocrisy," Jefferson knew that Marshall was a potentially dangerous adversary. A half-dozen years before the Richmonder's triumphal return from Paris, Jefferson had written James Madison a cutting letter about Marshall that included words he would one day rue: "I think nothing better could be done than to make him a judge."

In Congress, Marshall vigorously supported the Federalist policies of President John Adams. Adams took note of the Virginian's ability in 1800 when he appointed him to the important post of secretary of state, a position that not only charged him with conduct of the country's foreign affairs but also left him in effective charge of the government during Adam's frequent absences in Massachusetts.

John Marshall's future in government seemed rosy and secure in 1800. But the elections in November of that year changed all that, sweeping Adams and the Federalists from power and replacing them with Jefferson and the Democratic Republicans.

After the election, but before Adam's term as president expired, ailing Supreme Court Chief Justice Oliver Ellsworth submitted his resignation. Casting about for a successor to Ellsworth, Adams sent John Jay's name to the Senate, only to have Jay demand that it be withdrawn. The thought of leaving the appointment of a new chief justice to Jefferson was abhorrent to Adams, and the president was growing anxious. He summoned Marshall to his office to confer about the problem.

"Who shall I nominate now?" Adams asked dejectedly. Marshall answered that he did not know. He had previously suggested that Associate Justice William Paterson be elevated to the chief justiceship, but Adams had opposed Paterson then and Marshall supposed that he still did. The president pondered for a moment, then turned to Marshall and announced: "I believe I shall nominate you!"

Adams's statement astounded Marshall. Only two years before, Marshall had declined the president's offer of an associate justiceship, explaining that he still hoped to return to his law practice in Richmond. "I had never before heard myself named for the office," Marshall recalled later, "and had not even thought of it. I was pleased as well as surprized (sic), and bowed my head in silence."

Marshall's nomination was sent to the Senate and promptly confirmed, and on February 4, 1801, he took his seat as the nation's fourth Chief Justice. As subsequent events would prove, it was one of the most important dates in American history.

With Thomas Jefferson in the Executive Mansion and John Marshall in the Chief Justice's chair, it was inevitable that the Supreme Court and the executive branch of the government should come into conflict. Marshall believed firmly in a strong national government and was willing to do all he could to strengthen federal institutions. Jefferson believed as firmly in state sovereignty and the necessity for maintaining constant vigilance against federal "usurpations." In legal matters, Jefferson believed that the Constitution should be interpreted strictly, so as to reduce rather than expand federal power.

Marshall, in contrast, believed that the Constitution should be construed fairly so as to carry out the intentions of its framers. Any law or executive act that violated the terms of the Constitution was, in Marshall's view, a nullity, of no force or effect; and it was the peculiar prerogative of the courts, as custodians of the laws of the land, to strike down any law that offended the Supreme Law of the Land.

Jefferson did not question the authority of the courts to decide whether a law or executive act violated the Constitution, but he believed that the other branches of the government also had a duty and a right to decide constitutional questions. In a controversy between the Supreme Court and the president, for example, the Supreme Court could order the president to do whatever the Court thought the Constitution required him to do; but the president could decide for himself whether the Supreme Court's order was proper and whether or not it should be obeyed.

As he took up the duties of the chief justiceship, Marshall contemplated his role with uncertainty. The Supreme Court in 1801 was certainly not the kind of strong, vital institution that might have been expected to provide direction in national affairs. There were six justices when Marshall joined the Court, but none (save the Chief Justice himself) was particularly distinguished. One or two men of national prominence had accepted appointment to the Court in the first eleven years of its existence, but none had remained there long. John Jay, the first Chief Justice, had resigned his seat in 1795 to become governor of New York. During the two years that John Rutledge was an associate justice, he had regarded the Court's business as so trifling that he did not bother to attend a single session, and he finally resigned to become chief justice of South Carolina. The Court itself had counted for so little when the new capitol at Washington was being planned that the architects had made no provision for either a courtroom or judges' chambers, and the justices (to everyone's embarrassment) found that they had to meet in a dingy basement room originally designed for the clerk of the Senate.

How could Chief Justice Marshall use his new office to further the legal principles in which he believed so strongly? How could he strengthen the weak and undeveloped federal judiciary when most of the nation's lawyers and judges regarded that judiciary as superfluous and unnecessary? How could he implement his view of the Supreme Court as the final arbiter of constitutional questions when the President of the United States — his old nemesis, Thomas Jefferson — disagreed with that view so sharply? It was not an easy task, but John Marshall was a resourceful man, and he found a way to accomplish it.

His opportunity came in 1803 in the case of *Marbury* v. *Madison*. William Marbury was one of several minor federal judges who had been appointed during the closing days of John Adams's administration. When Jefferson's secretary of state, James Madison, refused to deliver the commissions of their offices, the judges sued Madison to compel delivery. In 1789, Congress had passed a law granting the Supreme Court authority to issue writs of mandamus, that is, legally enforceable orders compelling public officials to do their legal duties. Following the mandate of Congress, Marbury and the other appointees filed a petition for writ of mandamus in the Supreme Court.

Marshall pondered the possibilities of the case. He was sure that Marbury and his colleagues were entitled to their commissions, and he was just as sure that Jefferson and Madison had no intention of letting them have them. He could order Madison to deliver the commissions, but the secretary of state would certainly defy the order; and, as a practical matter, the Court could not compel obedience to any order that the president refused to acknowledge. Such an impasse would weaken, not strengthen, the federal union, and it would engender unprecedented controversy. No, there must be a better way. . . .

All eyes and ears in the capitol were trained on the lanky Chief Justice as he took his seat at the head of the high bench on February 24, 1803, and began to read the Supreme Court's opinion in *Marbury* v. *Madison*.

The evidence, Marshall said, clearly showed that Marbury and the other judges were entitled to their commissions. The commissions had been signed and sealed before John Adams left office and were, for all legal purposes, complete and effective. To withhold them, as Jefferson and Madison insisted on doing, was an illegal act. But the Supreme Court would not order the secretary of state to deliver the commissions

because the law authorizing it to issue writs of mandamus was unconstitutional: the Constitution does not authorize the Supreme Court to issue writs of mandamus; in fact, it prohibits it from doing so. And any law that violates the Constitution is void. Since the law purporting to authorize the Supreme Court to act was unconstitutional, the Court would not — indeed, it could not — order Madison to do his legal duty.

If historians and constitutional lawyers were asked to name the single most important case ever decided in the United States Supreme Court, there is little doubt that the case would be *Marbury* v. *Madison*. Though the dispute that gave rise to the decision was in itself insignificant, John Marshall used it as a springboard to a great constitutional pronouncement. The rule of the case — that the courts of the United States have the right to declare laws unconstitutional — was immediately recognized as the cornerstone of American constitutional law, and it has remained so ever since.

More than a half-century would pass before the Supreme Court would again declare an act of Congress unconstitutional, but its authority to do so would never again be seriously doubted. Marshall had made a bold stroke, and he had done so in such a way that neither Congress, nor the president, nor any other public official had any power to resist it. By denying relief to Marbury, he had made the Supreme Court's order marvelously self-enforcing!

Predictably, Thomas Jefferson was angry. If the Supreme Court could not issue writs of mandamus, Jefferson asked, why did Marshall spend so much time discussing Marbury's entitlement to a commission? And why did the Chief Justice lecture Madison that withholding the commission was an illegal act?

The president thought for a time that he might have the Chief Justice and his allies on the bench impeached. After a mentally unstable federal judge in New Hampshire was removed from office, Jefferson's supporters in the House of Representatives brought a bill of impeachment against Marshall's colleague on the Supreme Court, Associate Justice Samuel Chase. Chase was a Federalist who had occasionally badgered witnesses and made intemperate speeches, but no one seriously contended that he had committed an impeachable offense (which the Constitution defines as "treason, bribery, or other high crimes and misdemeanors"). So the Senate, three quarters of whose members were Jeffersonians, refused to remove Chase from office. Marshall breathed a deep sigh of relief. Had the associate justice been impeached, the chief had no doubt that he himself would have been Jefferson's next target.

Though he never again had occasion to strike down an act of Congress, Marshall delivered opinions in many cases of national significance; and, in his capacity as circuit judge (all Supreme Court justices "rode circuit" in the early years of the nineteenth century), he presided over important, sometimes controversial, trials. He was the presiding judge when Jefferson's political arch rival, Aaron Burr, was charged with treason in 1807. Interpreting the constitutional provision defining treason against the United States, Marshall helped to acquit Burr, though he did so with obvious distaste. The Burr prosecution, Marshall said, was "the most unpleasant case which has been brought before a judge in this or perhaps any other country which affected to be governed by law."

On the high bench, Marshall presided over scores of precedent-setting cases. In *Fletcher* v. *Peck* (1810) and *Dartmouth College* v. *Woodward* (1819), he construed the contracts clause of the Constitution so as to afford important protection for the country's growing business community. In *McCulloch* v. *Maryland* (1819), he upheld the constitutionality of the first Bank of the United States and struck down the Maryland law that purported to tax it. In *Gibbons* v. *Ogden* (1824), he upheld federal jurisdiction over interstate commerce and lectured those (mainly Jeffersonians) who persistently sought to enlarge state powers at the expense of legitimate federal authority.

Though Marshall's opinions always commanded respect, they were frequently unpopular. When, in

Worcester v. *Georgia* (1832), he upheld the treaty rights of the Cherokee Indians against encroachments by the State of Georgia, he incurred the wrath of President Andrew Jackson. "John Marshall has made his decision," "Old Hickory" snapped contemptuously. "Now let him enforce it!" Marshall knew, of course, that he could not enforce the decision; that he could not enforce any decision that did not have the moral respect and acquiescence of the public and the officials they elected. And so he bowed his head in sadness and hoped that officials other than Andrew Jackson would one day show greater respect for the nation's legal principles and institutions.

Despite the controversy that some of his decisions inspired, the Chief Justice remained personally popular; and, during the whole of his more than thirty-four years as head of the federal judiciary, the Court grew steadily in authority and respect.

Well into his seventies, Marshall continued to ride circuit in Virginia and North Carolina, to travel each year to his farm in Fauquier County, to attend to his shopping duties in Richmond, and to preside over the high court each winter and spring in Washington. On one of his visits to a neighborhood market in Richmond, the Chief Justice happened on a young man who had been sent to fetch a turkey for his mother. The youth wanted to comply with his mother's request, but thought it was undignified to carry a turkey in the streets "like a servant." Marshall offered to carry it for him. When the jurist got as far as his own home, he turned to the young man and said, "This is where I live. Your house is not far off; can't you carry the turkey the balance of the way?" The young man's face turned crimson as he suddenly realized that his benefactor was none other than the Chief Justice of the United States.

Joseph Story, who served as an associate justice of the Supreme Court for more than twenty years of Marshall's term as chief justice, spent many hours with the Virginian in and out of Washington. Wherever Story observed Marshall, he was impressed by his modesty and geniality. "Meet him in a stagecoach, as a stranger, and travel with him a whole day," Story said, "and you would only be struck with his readiness to administer to the accommodations of others, and his anxiety to appropriate the least to himself. Be with him, the unknown guest at an inn, and he seemed adjusted to the very scene, partaking of the warm welcome of its comforts, wherever found; and if not found, resigning himself without complaint to its meanest arrangements. You would never suspect, in either case, that he was a great man; far less that he was the Chief Justice of the United States."

In his youth, Marshall had been fond of corn whiskey. As he grew older, he lost his appetite for spirits but not for wine. He formulated a "rule" under which the Supreme Court judges abstained from wine except in wet weather, but Story said he was liberal in allowing "exceptions." "It does sometimes happen," Story once said, "the Chief Justice will say to me, when the cloth is removed, 'Brother Story, step to the window and see if it does not look like rain.' And if I tell him that the sun is shining brightly, Judge Marshall will sometimes reply, 'All the better; for our jurisdiction extends over so large a territory that it must be raining somewhere.'" "You know," Story added, "that the Chief was brought up upon Federalism and Madeira, and he is not the man to outgrow his early prejudices."

In Richmond, Marshall held regular dinners for local lawyers, swapped stories with old friends, and tossed quoits with his neighbors in the Barbecue Club. An artist named Chester Harding remembered seeing the chief justice at a session of the Barbecue Club in 1829. Harding said Marshall was "the best pitcher of the party, and could throw heavier quoits than any other member of the club." "There were several ties," he added, "and, before long, I saw the great Chief Justice of the United States, down on his knees, measuring the contested distance with a straw, with as much earnestness as if it had been a point of law; and if he proved to be in the right, the woods would ring with his triumphant shout."

In 1830, a young Pennsylvania congressman and future president of the United States commented on Marshall's enduring popularity among his neighbors. "His decisions upon constitutional questions have ever been hostile to the opinions of a vast majority of the people in his own State," James Buchanan said, "and yet with what respect and veneration has he been viewed by Virginia? Is there a Virginian whose heart does not beat with honest pride when the just fame of the Chief Justice is the subject of conversation? They consider him, as he truly is, one of the great and best men which this country has ever produced."

Marshall was nearly eighty years old when he died in Philadelphia on July 6, 1835. His body was brought back to Virginia for burial, where it was met by the longest procession the city of Richmond had ever seen.

In the contrast between proponents of strong and weak national government, Marshall had been one of the foremost and clearest advocates of strength. The struggle — between union and disunion, between federation and confederation, between the belief that the Constitution created a nation and the theory that it aligned the states in a loose league — was not finally resolved until 1865. But the struggle *was* resolved. "Time has been on Marshall's side," Oliver Wendell Holmes, Jr., said in 1901. "The theory for which Hamilton argued, and he decided, and Webster spoke, and Grant fought, is now our cornerstone."

Justice Story thought that Marshall's appointment to the Supreme Court contributed more "to the preservation of the true principles of the Constitution than any other circumstances in our domestic history." "He was a great man," Story said. "I go farther; and insist, that he would have been deemed a great man in any age, and of all ages. He was one of those, to whom centuries alone give birth."

John Adams and Thomas Jefferson both lived long and distinguished lives, but neither ever gave an inch in their differences of opinion over Marshall. Jefferson went to his grave bemoaning the "cunning and sophistry" of his fellow Virginian. Adams died secure in the belief that his decision to make Marshall chief justice had been both wise and provident. Years later, Adams called Marshall's appointment "the pride of my life." Time has accorded Thomas Jefferson a great place in the affections of the American people, but, in the controversy over John Marshall, the judgment of history has come down with quiet strength on the side of John Adams.

QUESTIONS TO CONSIDER

1. John Marshall and Thomas Jefferson were both Virginians; they were also distant relatives. How did they turn out to be so different? How has McGinty's article altered or expanded your view of the Thomas Jefferson you met in selections 8 and 13?

2. *Marbury* v. *Madison* was a case of small immediate significance in 1803, a legal squabble over a few petty government appointments. How did it turn out to have such enormous consequences for America's governmental structure? What implications did Marshall's legal actions have for the Supreme Court's future, particularly when the Court was pitted against a popular president?

3. In *Marbury* v. *Madison* and in a few other cases, Chief Justice Marshall, a staunch Federalist, wrote decisions unfavorable to his party's interests. What elements in his character caused him to ignore party politics? Discuss the precedents that may have been set by his actions.

4. McGinty's biography alternates episodes from Marshall's famous legal career with anecdotes from his private life. Do you find this technique distracting, or does it help you to understand Marshall more fully? What sort of man do the personal anecdotes reveal? Are these traits evident in Marshall's long career as chief justice?

5. We live today under a strong central government that owes much to legal decisions written by Chief Justice Marshall more than 150 years ago. Discuss the ways in which the United States today is a "Federalist" rather than a "Republican" nation.

15

The River of Black Struggle 1800–1823

Vincent Harding

While John Marshall was sitting on the bench, handing down judicial rulings aimed at stabilizing the Republic, there was another America, a black America, struggling on the underside of society to gain its freedom, its wholeness and humanity. Let us pick up the story of that struggle with the outbreak of the Revolution. The labor of slaves, as we have seen, was indispensable to the American cause. Hoping to disrupt the American war effort, the British invited the slaves to desert their American masters and join the British side, ultimately promising freedom if they did so. This promise horrified the American patriots. "Hell itself," one cried, "could not have vomited anything more black than this design of emancipating our slaves."

The Americans had reason to be worried, for their slaves went over to the British in ever increasing numbers. That blacks fought against the Revolution turns received notions of freedom and oppression on their heads. From the view of fleeing slaves, the redcoats were the liberators, the American patriots the oppressors. To forestall mass slave defections, the Americans started recruiting blacks as soldiers too; some states even offered freedom in exchange for military service (South Carolina, however, offered white volunteers a bounty in slaves, in the form of one adult black to each private, three adult blacks and a child to each colonel). Altogether some five thousand blacks served the American cause. But approximately 100,000 blacks, a fifth of the slave population in revolutionary America, were "loyalists," who sided with the British. When the war ended, General Washington, angry because some of his own slaves had fled, demanded that the defeated British return the black loyalists to their American masters. The British, however, asserted that the blacks had been emancipated in accordance with royal policy. In the end, the British did give up blacks who had been seized by royal forces and refugees who had come to British lines after the war had ended. Other black loyalists wound up in slavery in the British West Indies; three thousand more were colonized in Nova Scotia, where they braved discrimination and established a community that still exists.

The black patriots, by contrast, gained a measure of freedom when the northern states abolished slavery. New Jersey even allowed them to vote — for a while. But most "free" blacks in the North languished in a twilight zone between bondage and full liberty. As Leon Litwack observes in North of Slavery (1961), "Until the post-Civil War era, in fact, most northern whites would maintain a careful distinction between granting Negroes legal protection — a theoretical right to life, liberty, and property — and political and social equality. No statute or court decision could immediately erase from the public mind, North or South, that long and firmly held conviction that the African race was inferior and therefore incapable of being assimilated politically, socially, and most certainly physically with the dominant and superior white society." As a contemporary said of northern blacks, "Chains of a stronger kind still manacled their limbs, from which no legislative act could free them; a mental and moral subordination and inferiority, to which . . . custom has here subjected all the sons and daughters of Africa."

There were northern blacks, of course, who overcame the obstacles against them and managed to lead prominent and influential lives. Phillis Wheatley of Boston was an internationally known poet, whose Poems on Various Subjects, Religious and Moral, was the first book published by a black woman in America and only the second by an American woman. Prince Hall, one of several thousand blacks who fought for America in the Revolution, formed the first black Masonic lodge. And Benjamin Banneker, born a free black in slave-holding Maryland, became a well-known astronomer and the most famous African American in the young Republic.

In the South, meanwhile, slavery took even deeper root with the invention of the cotton gin in 1793, and blacks on the booming plantations sank into bleak despair. Here "the human cattle moved," recalled Frederick Douglass, a former slave, "hurried on by no hope of reward, no sense of gratitude . . . no prospect of bettering their condition; nothing, save the dread and terror of the slave-driver's lash. So goes one day, and so comes and goes another." Yet, as Vincent Harding observes, the slaves were anything but passive drones, submitting to their lot without complaint. They resisted bondage every way they could: they ran away, faked illness, broke hoes, and resorted to other forms of sabotage. Inspired by the charismatic Toussaint L'Ouverture and the great slave rebellion he led on Santo Domingo in the Caribbean, southern blacks also plotted insurrection, something their masters most feared from them. In the selection that follows, Harding, a scholar and civil rights activist who once wrote speeches for Martin Luther King, Jr., describes the African American resistance to slavery and racial discrimination in the first decades of the new century. His riveting narrative will introduce you to such insurrectionists as Gabriel Pros-

ser, Denmark Vesey, and "Gullah Jack" Pritchard, and to a number of nameless individuals, men and women alike, who left their mark on the wall of slave resistance. In recounting their story, as one critic put it, Harding "has invented a new genre" of historical narrative, "combining the skills of the scholarly historian with the voice of soul." He also employs an imaginative metaphor, calling the struggle for freedom a "long, continuous river, sometimes powerful, tumultuous, and roiling with life; at other times meandering and turgid" and "all too often steaked and running with blood." That river of protest was a self-liberating struggle in which the blacks themselves defined their freedom, fought, and died for it. "At its best," Harding writes, "the river of our struggle has moved consistently toward the ocean of humankind's most courageous hopes for freedom and integrity, forever seeking what black people in South Carolina said they sought in 1865: 'the right to develop our whole being.'"

GLOSSARY

BROWN, FATHER MORRIS   A leader of "the Charleston movement for religious freedom" and first bishop of the independent African Church of Charleston, South Carolina.

FEREBEE, BOB   A free man and reputed leader of a "self-determining band of fugitive slaves" who defied white authority; he was executed in 1823.

L'OUVERTURE, TOUSSAINT   Leader of the slave rebellion on the French island of Santo Domingo in the 1790s; the rebellion resulted in the black Republic of Haiti.

POYAS, PETER, AND NED POYAS Conspirators in the 1822 insurrection plot in Charleston, South Carolina.

PRITCHARD, "GULLAH JACK"   One of the Charleston conspirators and an African conjurer who practiced magic and summoned the spirits of the homeland.

PROSSER, GABRIEL   The leader of the insurrection plot in Richmond in 1800.

VESEY, DENMARK   A free black man who organized the Charleston rebellion plot of 1822.

I have nothing more to offer than what George Washington would have had to offer had he been taken by the British and put to trial by them. I have adventured my life in endeavoring to obtain the liberty of my countrymen, and am a willing sacrifice to their cause.

Courtroom Testimony,
Anonymous Black Insurrectionist, 1804

*I*t was a new century and we were a long way from home.

In America we were still largely people of the coasts and the rivers, people of the verdant fields, forests, and mountainsides, but this was not the land, these were not the waters, not the hills which had been the dwelling places of our fathers and mothers from the beginning of human time. Instead we were here as unwilling accomplices in the intrusion upon the spirits of other men's forebears, prisoner companions to the desecration of the mounds of the natives of these lands, worker captives in a place which was itself being taken captive.

We were a long way from home. Yet all of America had become our home. In the cities and settlements of the Atlantic coast, from Boston to Savannah, we were the dark and dangerous presence. In New York and Norfolk, in Philadelphia and Charleston we were on the wharves unloading the ships, watching — with what mixed feelings in our hearts? — the new bewildered children of Africa arrive. We were the carpenters and the cooks, the ironworkers and the porters, the chimney sweeps and the coopers, the butchers, sailors, and blacksmiths.

Back in the limitless rural area where the vast majority of Americans lived, we also lived and worked. In the darkness

"Rebels, Resistants, and Outlyers: Building the River's Power" from *There Is a River,* copyright © 1981 by Vincent Harding, reprinted by permission of Harcourt Brace & Company.

of the mornings we walked out from our cabins into the vast expanse of cotton, fields of tobacco, rows of corn; waded in the paddies where the endless acres of rice plants awaited our coming. Often the crops and the earth reminded us of our homeland, but we were a long way from home.

We were by the rivers again, but not the Gambia and the Sierra Leone, not the Congo and the Niger. Instead we worked the crops and built the houses and guided the boats along rivers whose very names evoked the unquiet spirits of the land: Roanoke and Potomac, Chattahooche and Allegheny, Mississippi and Tennessee. And we followed the rivers and the paths, and helped slash new roads into the countless acres of land being wrested from the natives of this place.

We moved with the nation across the Appalachians and found new homes in places like Cincinnati and Pittsburgh, and out in the Indiana Territory and down in the flatlands of the Mississippi Territory. (Soon after, when the victorious revolution of Africa's children in San Domingo helped to convince Napoleon to sell the Indian land the French had claimed as their own, we moved there with the white slaveholding settlers and found children of Africa already in the territory called Louisiana.) We were everywhere, but in some places there were only lonely scatterings of blackness, for our locus was the South, and the South had now extended westward beyond the Mississippi River.

We were far from home, yet some of us were not sure if we were near or far. For some had been in North America, living and enduring here with the people from England and Ireland and Scotland and Europe, for five and six generations. At the same time, with every movement of a slave ship into the Eastern harbors, new African captives arrived, bearing word and proof of a homeland, lending credence to the stories passed on through the generations, affirming the songs sung in the brush arbors of the night. Where was our home?

The new century cast into painful relief all the strange complexities and profound dilemmas which time and the increasingly long exile had brought to our situation and our struggle. By 1800 there were somewhat more than one million children of Africa living in the new nation, comprising approximately twenty percent of the population. Most of us — some 900,000 — were held in legal slavery. The rest occupied that limbo assigned to men and women who live as "free" in a society committed to their slavery.

The situation was crowded with hard choices, with brutal tensions that bore directly on the nature and status of black struggle. As a people they had been in America for generations, but there seemed no end to slavery. Indeed, the cotton mills of England had now found new life in the use of steam, and the cotton fields of America promised fantastic new yields with the coming of the cotton gin. Neither of these developments carried any hope of relief for Africa's children at the outset of the new century. Neither seemed to clarify the direction black struggle should take. Meanwhile the voluminous laws which supported black bondage were constantly being reproduced, reshaped, and redefined. The purchase of Louisiana in 1803 soon provided new lands for slavery, new impetus for the slave trade, new justifications for the nation's commitment to our bondage.

Indeed, in these turn-of-the-century years tens of thousands of new Africans were poured into the cauldron of American slavery. Even in the North, where some sixty percent of the small black minority lived as "free" people, and where slavery was on its way to legal death, the dilemmas were similarly harsh. For in 1800 there was no state in which black people could educate their children, earn a living, find proper housing, exercise voting rights — in short, exist in dignity — without constant, often brutal struggle against the white majority and its laws and customs. And when the beleaguered Northern blacks tried to raise their voices on behalf of their kinsmen in the South, they encountered even more evidence of the depths of white racism.

Thus in 1800 the outspoken black community of Philadelphia, under the leadership of Absolem Jones, sent a petition to Congress calling for legislative action against the African slave trade as well as for laws which would gradually abolish slavery. It was put forward in a respectful tone, a quiet call for justice. In

Philadelphia's proud African-American community not only established its own churches, such as the African Methodist Church shown here, but petitioned Congress to abolish the African slave trade and end slavery by gradual means. (Courtesy of the Historical Commission of Mother Bethel AME Church, Philadelphia)

Congress the usual treatment for all antislavery petitions from white constituents was to refer them to a committee and kill them. However, in response to this black petition Harrison Gray Otis, a Massachusetts congressman, opposed even that negative form of recognition. To acknowledge this word from black people, he said, "would have an irritating tendency, and must be mischievous to America very soon. It would teach them the art of assembling together, debating and the like, and would soon . . . extend from one end of the Union to the other." After a two-day debate, devoted largely to the promulgation of views like those of Otis, the House voted 85–1 to offer "no encouragement or countenance" to such messages from the children of Africa in America.

As the new century began, it often appeared as if the future lay wholly, securely, with white men like these, deniers of black rights, opponents to the development of black humanity. On the surface, the new age seemed only to have reinforced the old bondage now spreading across the land. But white surfaces concealed many things, especially the insistent black river, steadily moving, beating against and beneath the walls of slavery. In 1800, rising from under the surface, black people made it clear again that men and women born into slavery were not necessarily born to be slaves. That was the testimony from Henrico County, Virginia, where a group of Africans had been born into bondage but had grown to love freedom. The three brothers had been given names which perhaps revealed the quiet, radical hope of their family: Solomon, Martin, and Gabriel — Biblical monarch, religious leader, angel of God. According to the law of Virginia and America, they were slaves, property of a tavern keeper named Thomas Prosser. Still, by the time they reached their twenties, these tall, sturdy young men knew they were meant to be free, and they were prepared to wage hard and decisive struggle for that costly freedom, not only for themselves but for others as well.

In the spring of 1800, as the sharp, sometimes fiercely divisive sounds of the white Federalist and Republican debates echoed through the states, the Virginia brothers and their comrades began to organize among their people, and the leadership passed finally into Gabriel's hands. At twenty-four he was the youngest — and the tallest, standing well over six feet. With his dark complexion, prominent scars, and Ethiopian features, he was a striking figure. Later he was described by the Virginia authorities as possessing "courage and intellect above his rank in life." White authorities did not know Gabriel's rank in life, but his fellow Africans evidently did, for by the summer he and his two brothers had gathered an impressive cadre of comrades for the proposed struggle. Under the cover of funerals and other black religious gatherings, and in the hours after sundown when the exiled African community reaffirmed its integrity through singing and praying and loving and planning and escaping —

in those times and hours, Gabriel presented his plan. It was strategically simple and seemed sound. Several hundred men would make a surprise midnight attack on Richmond to capture arms, burn warehouses, and perhaps take the governor as hostage, thereby inspiring a general uprising among thousands of Africans.

In addition to their own fierce determination to be free, Gabriel and his two brothers had been spurred on by two rather different models, and they systematically shared this inspiration with all potential recruits. Wherever they gathered, the three young men spoke of the brilliant example of the Africans of San Domingo, and of God's assistance to the children of Israel. Martin was a preacher, and he backed up Gabriel's love of Toussaint [L'Ouverture] with his own encouragement from the Scriptures. When doubts were raised, it was Martin who told the people that "their cause was similar to [the] Israelites," and he read the Bible to them: "God says, if we worship him . . . five of you shall conquer an hundred and a hundred a thousand of your enemies." For his own personal statement, Martin simply said, "I can no longer bear what I have borne."

The men they recruited realized that they were being called to make a fundamental break with their own past, to offer a radical challenge to white society, and therefore to risk their lives and the lives of their families. In the course of organizing, one of the group's lieutenants (who later testified against the others) told a potential recruit named King, "The negroes are about to rise, and fight the white people for our freedom." King's response was chilling and direct: "I was never so glad to hear anything in my life. . . . I could slay white people like sheep." At the same time some sensed the need for their struggle to maintain an essential continuity with the African past. So a key recruiter named George proposed that the conspirators make full use of the peculiar gifts of those native-born Africans who had remained close to the cultic practices of the homeland, suggesting that "he hire his own time, travel down country to what he called the "pipeing tree,' and enlist the 'Outlandish people,' for they were supposed to deal with Witches and Wizards and this would be useful in Armies to tell when any calamity was about to befall them."

The fate of this proposal is not known, but there is evidence that Gabriel did not take the traditions of Africa as seriously as did others in his group. Indeed, in black lore there is a suggestion that such a move as George proposed would have saved the plot from its untoward ending. But Gabriel had his mind set: they would move at midnight on August 30, 1800, carrying a flag with the motto "Death or Liberty" — the battle cry of San Domingo. Although it was later said that Gabriel had planned "to subdue the whole of the country where slavery was permitted, but no further," we are not certain how well the bold leader understood the nature of the forces which could ultimately be brought to bear against his insurrection, including the troops of the national government.

By the end of August widespread organizing had evidently gone on among the black community of Henrico County and the surrounding areas. Many of the rebels held regular transport jobs as boatmen and as carriage and wagon drivers, and so enjoyed a mobility that was of great importance to their organizing work. When the time for the attack came, accounts of what finally happened vary, but certain matters are sure: at noontime on the appointed day it began to rain, and soon the worst storm in living memory broke over the area. The invasion of the city was called off by Gabriel when it was clear that several rivers and creeks on the way to Richmond would not be fordable, and that the planned operations would be impossible in the storm.

No one knows how many men and women were gathering when the word of delay was given; estimates range from dozens to more than a thousand. However, before the rain had stopped, the mission was betrayed by informers, and white search parties were soon scouring the countryside. Although his two brothers were captured early in the search, Ga-

briel managed to escape for a time. Finally, near the end of September, he was apprehended at Norfolk, while hiding on board a coastal schooner, the *Mary*. By this time most of his fellow leaders had been captured and executed, along with many persons whose involvement was at best peripheral. Nevertheless, Gabriel refused to confess or to discuss the planned insurrection, even when confronted by Gov. James Monroe. One morning in October, he went to his death without flinching.

Even in his failure, the Virginian had deeply stirred the black river of struggle. His name was on the lips of his people in many parts of the state and elsewhere. That was why Monroe could write from Richmond, "It was distinctly seen that [the plot] embraced most of the slaves in this city and neighborhood," and that "there was good cause to believe that the knowledge of such a project pervaded other parts, if not the whole state."

Did it reach Southhampton County, not far away, where a child named Nat was born on Benjamin Turner's plantation? And what of Charleston? Did Denmark Vesey, just purchasing his freedom, hear of Gabriel and the price he had paid?

Although the fear of widespread black rebellion was akin to an occupational disease among Southern white officials, Monroe did not speak from idle anxiety. Not only did he recognize seething radical power and possibilities when he faced a man like Gabriel, but he must have known of other disquieting events. In the weeks following the trials there was word of "a series of small, insurrectionary actions" throughout Virginia. For example, it was reported that in Hanover County black people had been "very riotous and ungovernable" following the discovery of Gabriel's conspiracy. Some black men had gone so far as to break into a jail "and set free two insurrectionists who were handcuffed and chained to the floor." After they had been set free, the prisoners themselves attacked the guard, knocked him down, stamped on him, then escaped. It was against such a background that Mon-

Slaves picking cotton on a Southern plantation. "We were a long way from home," Harding says of enslaved African Americans. "In the darkness of the mornings we walked out from our cabins into the vast expanse of cotton, fields of tobacco, rows of corn; waded in the paddies where the endless acres of rice plants awaited our coming. Often the crops and the earth reminded us of our homeland, but we were a long way from home." (Reproduced form Ballou's Pictorial 14:49, Courtesy of the Trustees of the Boston Public Library)

roe concluded his letter: "Unhappily, while this class of people exists among us we can never count with certainty on its tranquil submission." His opinion was widely shared throughout Virginia, while as far away as the territory of Mississippi, Gov. Winthrop Sergeant informed his fellow slaveholders of Gabriel's attempt, "warning them to be watchful of a similar uprising in the vicinity."

Actions like those attempted by Gabriel caught most attention and fired the imaginations of blacks and whites alike, but always, behind and beneath those larger, organized attempts were the subterranean acts of individual defiance, resistance, creative rebellion, sabotage, and flight. This anonymous, pul-

sating movement persisted wherever there was slavery in America. It rose out of the broad base of all the men, women, and children who offered their personal, rudimentary challenges to the system. One time it was manifested in the decision of a solitary person to kill his master on a dark road as they traveled home at night. Another time it came when a group of black men determined that white patrolmen had broken up their social gatherings once too often and chose to resist to the death.

Most often the efforts at resistance were on a small scale; only by accident did they leap into wider significance. Such an incident occurred in York, Pennsylvania, where in the spring of 1803 a black woman was convicted of attempting to poison two white persons. But after her conviction, other blacks in the town made several attempts to burn major sections of York to the ground; within three weeks eleven buildings were destroyed. Only after the militia and special patrols were called out, and a curfew was enforced against the black population, did the black fire cease in York.

In the minds of the keepers of America's law and order, all such fires had to be watched carefully. This was no time to take lightly rebellious black action anywhere, for the revolution in San Domingo was still erupting, and everywhere in white America it was a source of conversation and fear. The African revolutionaries on the island were successfully resisting all Napoleon's efforts to break their will. Indeed, by the spring of 1803 their implacable resistance had utterly destroyed some of France's finest — and most cruel — military forces, and driven them from San Domingo. This totally unexpected turn of events helped convince the French ruler that his vision of an American empire must be abandoned. (As a result, he was willing to sell the entire Louisiana Territory to the United States, doubling the nation's area in one stroke.) But few whites anywhere seemed able to hear the indomitable General Dessalines when he and his comrades in leadership on San Domingo declared in 1803: "Towards those men who do us justice, we will act as brothers." Neither the white Americans, who had no special desire for African brothers, nor the French, who still hoped desperately to find a way to reassert their domination over these black revolutionaries, were able to absorb such words. Instead, most whites could only tremble when on January 1, 1804, the revolutionaries declared the creation of Haiti, a new independent African nation, and Dessalines put forth its motto: "Independence or Death! Let these sacred words serve to rally us . . . let them be signals of battle and of our reunion."

Then, after a year of military, diplomatic, and political threats and maneuvers, extending beyond San Domingo to the rivalries of the European and North American worlds, after several attempts by Napoleon to use the local French settlers to help undermine the revolution — after all that and more, the time for threats and maneuvers was up. Now, the overwhelming thirst for revenge against French treachery and brutality which had been building up within some of the Haitian revolutionaries finally won the day. Before March 1805 was over Dessalines "the liberator" became Dessalines "the avenger." His order for the death of all French settlers who had refused the hand of brotherhood was mercilessly carried out by Haitian soldiers and civilians. The terrible burdens of a land already engorged with blood were multiplied, and the cries of thousands of white men, women, and children became a bitter counterpoint to the agonizing, echoing calls of the tens of thousands of the island's people who for years had fallen under the fire, guns, and swords of the armies of the motherland.

There was no way to contain these cries of anguish, rage, and victory, and when news of the latest developments in Haiti reached America, new tremors of excitement ran deep within the black community there. For years afterward, memories of this time when neighboring Africans seized their own freedom, created a nation, and repelled elements of Europe's greatest military force would live and grow in black tradition. As for American whites, they were understandably stunned and fearful. Although they held an overwhelming numerical advantage in the nation, there were many localities in Virginia and South Carolina, for instance, where slaveholders and their white neighbors were far outnumbered. And in spite of their denials, whites had every reason to believe that the Africans around them also loved liberty and craved independence. So the developments in Haiti stimulated a renewed campaign in America to erect every possible legal barrier against that revolutionary incubus.

But some men were not content with laws and regulations. In 1804, shortly after Dessalines's cry of "Death to the whites" resounded throughout Europe and its colonies, William Claiborne, the new governor of the Louisiana Territory, reported on the special precautions he had taken: "All vessels with slaves on board are stopped at Plaquemine, and are not permitted to pass without my consent. This is done to prevent the bringing of Slaves that have been concerned in the insurrections of St. Domingo; but while any importations are admitted, many bad characters will be introduced." It was, of course, too late: the "bad characters" had been coming by ship for decades and so were already there, waiting for the day. Indeed, such characters were everywhere. In the year of Governor Claiborne's searches, a black insurrectionist in Virginia declared in the course of his trial: "I have nothing more to offer than what George Washington would have had to offer had he been taken by the British and put to trial by them. I have adventured my life in endeavoring to obtain the liberty of my countrymen, and am a willing sacrifice to their cause." This was indeed bad: black men were comparing themselves to the heroes of the white "revolution," claiming a legitimacy which was dangerous in slaves.

Meanwhile, after several years of intermittent debates in Congress, the white heirs of the American revolutionary tradition were finally developing a new version of their own response to black slavery — one which avoided the central issues and affirmed the deepest contradictions. In the late winter of 1806–07, when they finally kept a promise of their Revolution and legislated an official end to American participation in the African slave trade, the bill was intentionally so weak that its provisions proved easy to circumvent. More ironic yet, the law proposed that any Africans found on interdicted slaving ships, instead of being hastened toward freedom, should be sold into bondage in the South. The law was to go into effect in January 1808. Not long before that, two boatlands of Africans brought to Charleston for sale had offered their own response to the slave trade: while awaiting sale in the slave pens, a number of them starved themselves to death.

In the North, the options for struggle were usually not so harshly limited, especially for those free blacks who had been in the country for some time, learned its language, and studied its contradictions. Though their resistance was generally less stark and less costly than that in Charleston's slave pens, their continuing uses of white American political and religious assumptions contributed an important element to the developing protest traditions of black struggle. In 1808, a member of Boston's African Society spoke to that organization on the topic, "The Sons of Africa: An Essay on Freedom." In the course of his lecture he put forward words which held significant portent, saying, "Men have exercised authority over our nation as if we were their property, by depriving us of our freedom as though they had a command from heaven thus to do. But, we ask, if freedom is the right of one nation; why not the right of all nations of the earth?"

Quietly, forcefully, certain questions were being raised by the blacks in America. Didn't black people have the same right and responsibility to fight for their liberty as white America had to fight for its independence? And were Africans in America not a nation? In the decades ahead these basic, radical questions would moil the river, thrusting black struggle onward with their force.

The seemingly confident surface of America's Natural Rights philosophy was not the only white theory and practice under constant attack from the underground black struggle. The religion of white America, which in most situations was meant to assure the tranquil submission of its captives, was insistently, continually wrested from the white mediators by black hands and minds, and transformed into an instrument of struggle. The Scriptures, the theology, the doctrine, the very places of worship were repeatedly transmuted in the alchemy of the black movement. This was seen in Gabriel's use of the preaching meetings, and explains the laws against independent black gatherings for worship, and the anger of Richard Byrd of Virginia in 1810, who "felt that slave preachers used their religious meetings as veils for revolutionary schemes." He was right — not only about one General Peter, a religious revolutionary operating from Virginia's Isle of Wight, but about others as well, such as those who in that same year sent messages of rebellion from nearby North Carolina, saying, "Freedom we want and will have, for we have served this cruel land enuff." Such men, like their ancestors on the slave ships, would hammer any object, any doctrine, into a weapon for the struggle toward freedom. Indeed, to love freedom so fully in the midst of slavery *was* religion, *was* radical.

Nor were such radicals difficult to find, even after slave ships had been searched to weed them out, and laws passed to guarantee their death. They appeared in the Pointe Coupée section of Louisiana in January 1811, even though some twenty-five men and women had been executed less than two decades earlier in the same area for the same kind of thrust toward freedom. This time several hundred black men organized, secured some guns, flags, and drums, and on the night of January 8 began "marching from plantation to plantation, slaves everywhere joining them." It was a familiar scene, though in their march the group managed to kill only one white person (or so the records say). Nevertheless, their marching presence was so threatening that wagons and cartloads of white refugees were soon pouring into New Orleans seeking safety. However, before long a group of well-armed planters, assisted by militiamen of the territory and almost three hundred troops of the U.S. Army, met the poorly armed black forces, broke the uprising, and killed scores of other black persons in the days that followed. Thus the forces of the American government moved again to guarantee black bondage, presenting a harsh challenge to the radical black movement toward freedom.

By then it had become strikingly apparent that the military power of the democratic American state would be used insistently to tighten the chains of slavery. Nevertheless, the movements of the river went forward, often buoyed by the desperate hope that some countervailing, supporting forces might be brought to bear on their behalf against the over-whelming weight of white America's national power. That hope was sometimes based in magic powers brought from the homeland, sometimes in the mysterious arrival of African forces from Santo Domingo or elsewhere. Often, hope was focused on America's white national enemies, chief among whom was still Great Britain.

Thus during the War of 1812 thousands of fugitives broke loose from slavery, and in some places tried to organize insurrections, expecting help from the English. In 1813, along the South Carolina coast there was much excited talk of a British invasion, and an insurrection was planned to coincide with it. In the course of the almost nightly planning meetings, black people on one of the Sea Islands apparently developed a song expressing their commitment to the struggle, a song lacking any of the ambiguity that usually attached to black songs of struggle and faith. At the beginning and close of each meeting, they are said to have sung:

Hail! all hail! ye Afric clan
Hail! ye oppressed, ye Afric band,
Who toil and sweat in Slavery bound;
And when your health & strength are gone
Are left to hunger & to mourn,
Let *Independence* be your aim,
Ever mindful what 'tis worth.
Pledge your bodies for the prize
Pile them even to the skies!

Firm, united let us be,
Resolved on death or liberty
As a band of Patriots joined
Peace and Plenty we shall find.

After stanzas of similar sentiments, the song ended with these lines:

Arise! Arise! Shake off your chains
Your cause is just so heaven ordains
To you shall Freedom be proclaimed
Raise your arms & bare your breasts,

Almighty God will do the rest.
Blow the clarion! a warlike blast!
Call every Negro from his task!
Wrest the scourge from Buckra's hand,
And drive each tyrant from the land.

Current knowledge of the origins of this song is third-hand. If it was indeed created by the children of Africa out of the river of their struggle, it testified to a deep wrestling with the white American world. It called for independence for black people. It saw the liberating possibilities of the religion of Jesus and the Israelites. It demanded that all who loved tyranny be driven from the land — a demand which could be made only by those who now believed that they had some firm right to the land themselves. At every level, this was a radical statement for black bondspeople, and the call to arms was only the most obvious level of its radical thrust.

Africans in America were a long way from home, separated in some cases by several generations, and yet, if such things as presence, work, and blood counted, there were few places in the young nation which black people could not rightfully call home. But the claims of black work and blood, and the undeniable, troubling reality of black presence, were insistently denied by whites; and among black people themselves, America was often considered only a second home. Therefore Africa's children had only begun to make those just claims which flow out of a people's right to the territory they have helped develop and create. In its talk of driving tyrants from the land, the Sea Island battle hymn implied a contrast between prison ships and prison states, recognizing that while the ocean-going ships might be taken over only to be abandoned on Africa's coasts, this new land might have to be taken over to be transformed into a new home.

Of course, at profound and difficult levels, the claim to the American land as a home was complicated by the relationship of black struggle to the dark natives of North America, and to the fight they were waging in various parts of the continent. In fact, throughout the American sojourn Africans found themselves in a special and often cruelly difficult relationship to those beleaguered people who had invested their spirits in this land for thousands of years. That relationship between Africans and Native Americans affected the black struggle, from the earliest days of flight right down to the Seminole wars.

For the black people of the Southern states, Florida was a focal point for this intertwined struggle. For three hundred years — from the initial Spanish settlements through the brief period of British domination, to the time when the United States forced its rights to the area — the territory had been a crucial sanctuary for black outlyers and other runaways, who made it a base for their attacks in various Southern states and a beacon of freedom for other captives. In doing this, they were often assisted by the Native Americans who shared the area with them. Then, during the War of 1812, hundreds of militant Creek Indians fled to Florida following their defeat by the white Americans in the Creek War of 1813–14, while thousands of additional black fugitives made their way into the area as well. During the war the British sought to recruit these disaffected groups, both of whom responded; by the end of 1814 at least four hundred black fugitives had enlisted, and were armed and uniformed as part of the British forces. In exchange for this service, the black men were promised their hard-earned freedom, as well as land in either Florida or the British West Indies.

At the war's end, when the British finally withdrew and Spain resumed nominal control, both blacks and Indians were once more on their own in the grueling struggle for freedom against the American forces. Although some black people departed on the British transports, most remained to carry on the fight. They were aided in this when, just before they pulled out in the spring of 1815, British officers turned over to a group of the black soldiers and their families, plus a few of their Indian allies, one of their newest and best forts on the southwest coast of Florida. The fort at Prospect Bluff on the Apalachicola River was renamed "the Negro Fort" and occupied by more than three hundred men, women, and children, mostly black, commanded by a fugitive slave named Garson and a Choctaw chief. In addition, approximately a thousand men, women and children lived in settlements along the river under the fort's protection. Immediately the group began both to symbolize and to demonstrate possibilities of such a sanctuary in the heart of the South, by using the fort as a base for marauding expeditions against slaveholders and as a haven for other fugitives. Men, women, and children came there from Georgia, the Mississippi Territory, and as far away as Tennessee. Thus not only were black people defying white law and order and creating new visions of their own possibilities, but valuable white property was roaming free, and even more of it was being daily endangered — all with the co-operation of those perennial "bad characters," the Indians.

Obviously, this situation presented fundamental dangers to the keepers of the society. On June 26, 1816, the *Savannah Journal* said of the black fort: "It was not to have been expected, that an establishment so pernicious to the Southern States, holding out to a part of their population temptations to insubordination, would have been suffered to exist after the close of the war. . . . How long shall this evil requiring immediate remedy be permitted to exist?" Within a month the question had been answered, not simply by "the Southern States," but once again by the military forces of the federal government. Gen. Andrew Jackson — whose fame had recently been made, with a certain black assistance, in the battle of New Orleans — was the commander of the Southwestern Military District of the United States. In July 1816 he sent a unit of federal troops, backed by naval gunboats, to destroy the fort "and restore the stolen negroes and property to their rightful owners."

After an initial encounter in which the waiting blacks and Indians captured a small vessel on reconnaissance and killed several crew members, the United States forces sent a delegation to call for the fort's surrender. Garson and his Choctaw comrade refused the demand, and the delegation reported that the black fugitive leader had "heaped much abuse on the Americans." Indeed, it was said that Garson declared he would "sink any American vessels that should attempt to pass" the fort. Learning of this defiant spirit, one of the American officers commented: "We were pleased with their spirited opposition . . . though they were Indians, negroes, and our enemies. Many circumstances convinced us that most of them were determined never to be taken alive."

Most of them were not. Early in the morning of July 27, 1816, after four days of negotiations, skirmishes, and waiting, the American gunboats moved into position near the fort. The inexperienced gunners of the fortress fired first and missed. The first shot fired in return found its way into a powder magazine which had been left open. The terrifying explosion which followed was so powerful that it was reportedly heard and felt in Pensacola, some sixty miles away. Fewer than fifty of the fort's inhabitants survived the disaster, many of them so burned and mutilated that there was little hope for their survival.

In a sense, the battle at the Negro fort was a prelude to the First Seminole War, and announced the crucial role of black people in it. But for the long run the blinding explosion signaled something even more important: the fact that black men and women who broke away toward freedom had always to estimate the range of the cannon of the American government. In essence, then, the chilling sounds of the guns at Apalachicola were meant to deny the captive children of Africa — and the native peoples of America — any sanctuary from white domination, exploitation, and destruction, any right to claim the land as their own. Apalachicola meant that all such claims were guaranteed to drive endless streams of blood into the river of struggle; and the harrowing cries of the dying were harsh reminders of the realities which surrounded every black fortress in the midst of a hostile white society.

Faced with these bitter truths, some Africans were again exploring return to the homeland as a path toward that new life which seemed so hard to find on the bloody American ground. Indeed, under the leadership of stalwart men like Paul Cuffee, some Afro-Americans had already returned home: surely there was something tempting in letters they sent to friends here. One said: "Be not fearful to come to Africa, which is your country by right. . . . Though you are free, that is not your country. Africa, not America, is your country and your home." The letter was obviously addressed to the black "free" minority. Did it have any meaning for those who had to defend their "illegal" freedom in the forts of Florida, the swamps of North Carolina, the bayous of Louisiana?

Some answers came slowly. But Denmark Vesey, one of the "free" minority in Charleston, South Carolina, had clearly answered the question of African repatriation for himself. In 1800 Vesey, then in his thirties, had bought his freedom from the ship's captain who held legal possession of him, and with whom he had already spent many years on voyages. In the course of those trips Vesey had traveled through the Caribbean, where in his adolescence he spent three months in San Domingo. He had apparently spent some time in Africa also. Since the beginning of the century, Vesey had lived in the ambiguous world of a free black in Charleston, working as a skilled and much-respected carpenter, while serving as a leader in the powerful African church there. His tall, spare figure was well known on the streets of the city and in the country districts surrounding it. By 1817 he had amassed savings of several thousand dollars, probably making him one of the wealthiest black men in the city. On at least one occasion he had been offered a chance to return to Africa as a free man. For it was a time when white, usually Southern-dominated organizations like the American Colonization Society were developing programs and raising funds to encourage the voluntary emigration of free blacks — those thorns in the side of slavery — from the United States to West Africa and other locations. But Vesey clearly shared the sentiments of the free black persons in Philadelphia who responded directly to the Colonization Society in 1817 by declaring: "We will never separate ourselves voluntarily from the slave population of this country; they are our brethren by the ties of consanguinity, of suffering and of wrong; and we feel that there is more virtue in suffering privations with them, than fancied advantages for a season."

By that time Denmark Vesey was intimately familiar with many aspects of "the ties of consanguinity, of suffering and of wrong." At least one of his wives and some of his children were in slavery. He had seen the oppression and injustice meted out by the white community all around him, and he stood firm as a symbol of defiant resistance in the black community. However, it was not mere sentiment or ties of blood and oppression which kept him in Charleston when he could have begun a new life elsewhere. By 1817 Vesey had evidently decided that the only new life he desired was a struggle for the freedom of his people. One of his companions said that Vesey often rebuked any of his friends who offered the customary black gesture of bowing to a white person on the street. Vesey claimed that "all men were born equal, and that he was surprised that anyone would degrade himself by such conduct; that he would never cringe to whites, nor ought any who had the feelings of a man." Such feelings were not uncommon in the black community, and were often expressed within its confines. It was not common, however, to act on them publicly or urge others to do the same. Denmark Vesey did both, and plunged forthrightly into the stream of black radicalism.

He acted because he believed that, both in Charleston and outside of it, history was evolving in ways which could be bent for the purposes of black freedom. Within the port city those historical developments were focused in the church, the heartland of institutional black concern. By the end of the War of 1812 the black Methodists in Charleston — the single largest black denomination — outnumbered the white membership ten to one. They had developed a quarterly conference of their own, and had custody of their own collections and control over the church trials of their own members. This independence was intolerable for the supervising white Methodists (and probably their non-Methodist friends as well). In 1815 they had acted against this black freedom, taking away privileges that they claimed were theirs to give, asserting that the African people had abused their freedom.

This was the decisive signal for a secession movement which had been stirring within the African churches. In 1816 Father Morris Brown and other black Charleston church leaders had gone to Philadelphia to confer with Richard Allen and other founders of the newly formed African Methodist Episcopal Church. Later in that year Brown and another elder were ordained for pastorates in Charleston. By 1817 an independent African Association was organized in the city. Then in 1818, on the occasion of a dispute over a burial ground, more than three-fourths of the six thousand black Methodists of Charleston withdrew from the white-dominated churches. Morris Brown was appointed bishop, and the independent African Church of Charleston was established.

The Charleston movement for religious independence was a crucial form of mass black struggle which would be revived in and through the black churches more than a century later. Following the Philadelphia example, it challenged white domination, white control, white definitions of religious life and church polity. It participated in the growing movement among African people in America to establish relatively autonomous religious institutions where black life could be shaped and affirmed under black control. In the context of American slavery, the secession was a budding radicalism, and if the religious authorities of Charleston did not recognize it, the white secular authorities certainly did. (In many cases, of course, they were the same.) That was why the city consistently harassed and broke up the meetings of the newly established independent black congregations. That was

why there were periodic arrests — sometimes of the leaders alone, and sometimes of large numbers of members — and why some were kept in jail, some banished, and others publicly whipped and otherwise punished. Finally, in 1821, the city of Charleston closed the Hamstead church, which had provided key leadership in the movement.

The spirit of resistance and struggle had been lodged deeply in the black community's religious life, and the white authorities were not the only ones who recognized its larger potential. Denmark Vesey and certain special companions of his had known it long before; indeed they had helped to nurture it. But the closing of the church was the stimulus for organizing black discontent and resistance into something more effective than anger. Vesey had been a member of the Hamstead church, as had his friends Rolla Bennett, "Gullah Jack" Pritchard, Monday Gell, and Ned and Peter Poyas. They began meeting with some of the discontented members of the black community, often in Vesey's own house, sometimes in the areas for religious gatherings on plantations, at other times in the brush arbors outside the rural cabins. Vesey and his comrades believed that the suppression of the church had provided the issue around which they could rally the Charleston-area black community in a full-scale rebellion against white power. Within Charleston itself history had moved, and Vesey interpreted its movement to the black community. As one participant remembered it, the black leader said again and again that "we were deprived of our rights and privileges by the white people and that our Church was shut up so that we could not use it, and that it was high time for us to seek for our rights, and that we were fully able to conquer the whites if we were only unanimous and courageous, as the Santo Domingo people were."

The San Domingo revolution was the second movement in history to which Vesey turned the minds of the people. He had been to the island as a boy. There is evidence as well that one of Vesey's comrades, the brilliant Monday Gell, had corresponded with the president of the troubled black republic. So as an insurrection was organized, Africa's children in and around Charleston were told that "Santo Domingo and Africa will assist us to get our liberty, if we will only make the motion first." That recurring pan-African element of black struggle, which had originated in the slave castles and on the ships, was now revived again in a fierce hope of help from elsewhere in the African diaspora. Of course, in Gullah Jack the Charleston conspirators already had Africa and its spirits with them in a peculiar way: he was a conjurer from among the Gullah people who lived on the coasts of the homeland, and his comrades in the conspiracy believed that he would call upon the fathers in their behalf, and would develop potions and powders to protect them.

But neither Haiti nor Africa was the center of their hope. Rather it was another movement in history, another diaspora, which was used more effectively in rallying the insurrectionary forces. At almost every meeting, it was said, Vesey or one of his comrades "read to us from the Bible, how the children of Israel were delivered out of Egypt from bondage." That theme was struck insistently: the deliverance from Egypt, the movement of God among his captive people. (No wonder, then, that in some black traditions it is said that Vesey or his fellows were the inspiration for the ageless black song of faith and struggle, "Go Down, Moses." Was it out there in the fields, late in the Carolina nighttime, that a voice first lifted the slow and halting melody?)

But Vesey went further. He did not merely speak of the mysterious action of God in plagues upon an Egyptian people, for that might have been misunderstood as a call to wait passively for divine intervention. Indeed, he constantly read to the people: "Behold the day of the Lord cometh, and thy spoil shall be divided in the midst of thee. For I shall gather all nations against Jerusalem to battle; and the city shall be taken. . . . And they utterly destroyed all that was in the city, both man and woman, young and old, and

ox and sheep, and ass, with the edge of the sword." That message was unambiguous. And assurance for the faint of heart was there, too: "Then shall the Lord go forth, and fight against those nations, as when he fought in the day of battle." Even one of the noncanonical books of the Old Testament Apocrapha, *Tobit,* was brought to bear, to strengthen, to urge the children of Africa into battle for justice, for freedom.

They needed every available encouragement, for even though blacks outnumbered whites in the city of Charleston, and held nearly a ten-to-one advantage in the surrounding areas, they lacked arms. The plans, similar to those of Gabriel, were to sweep into the city from seven different points, capture arms from the arsenal, set fire to the whole area, kill all whites who came into their path, and if necessary make good an escape to the Caribbean or Africa.

As with many of the attempted insurrections in this phase of black struggle — as is the case, indeed, with insurrections everywhere — there was considerable vagueness concerning ultimate objectives. Part of that ambiguity lay in the dilemma of their basic situation: assuming immediate victory, how would thousands of black people make their way in safety to Haiti or Africa, as the armed forces of the white American national government bore down upon them? Could there really be any mass abandonment of the Southern prison-state at this stage of history? And if it could not be abandoned, how could it be held and sustained as a free territory in the midst of a white-dominated country?

The existing records do not provide any real sense of how Vesey and his comrades answered such questions. However, there is a possibility that the resolute leader believed history to be moving so decisively in favor of black freedom that such desperate flight or beleaguered military action might not be necessary after their victory in Charleston. He had read accounts of the recent bitter debates in Congress over the Missouri Compromise, and there is some evidence that Vesey had either himself come to believe, or at least had convinced others, that the federal government was abandoning its protection of slavery. If that were true, it might not be necessary to face any forces other than those of South Carolina.

Whatever their ultimate objective, Vesey and his companions apparently did an outstanding job of organizing. This was evident from the first comrades in arms whom the black leader had chosen. One white official wrote:

In the selection of his leaders Vesey showed great penetration and sound judgement. Rolla was plausible and possessed uncommon self-determination; bold and ardent, he was not to be deterred from his purpose by danger. Ned's appearance indicated that he was a man of firm nerves, and desperate courage. Peter was intrepid and resolute, true to his engagements, and cautious in observing secrecy where it was necessary; he was not to be daunted nor impeded by difficulties. . . . Gullah Jack was regarded as a sorcerer, and as such feared by the natives of Africa, who believe in witchcraft. He was not only considered invulnerable, but that he could make others so by his charms. . . . His influence among the Africans was inconceivable. Monday was firm, resolute, discreet, and intelligent.

Such were Vesey's lieutenants. Together they prepared for a deadline in the second week of July 1822. Blacksmiths were making bayonets and spikes. Others were to obtain daggers, swords, fuses, and powder. Disguises, wigs, and false mustaches were to be contrived. The draymen, carters, and butchers were to supply the horses. Plantation people were recruited from the surrounding areas, some from as far away as eighty miles outside of the city. They were to bring whatever weapons they could obtain. However, most of the active participants were from the urban black artisan population, both enslaved and free. Within the limitations of the time, Denmark Vesey and his comrades had built an all-class black movement.

Of course, a rebellion which meant to capture an important city needed quantity as well as quality and breadth, and the leaders seemed to have made hundreds of contacts over the months of patient organizing. But that success carried within it the elements of defeat; for as knowledge of at least the general plans spread among an ever-widening circle of black people, so did the likelihood of betrayal become more an imminent danger. At the end of May 1822, the possibility became a reality when a slave who had been contacted as a likely recruit reported the contact to his master. From that point on, the carefully constructed plan began to break down as the white authorities initiated a series of probing arrests, questionings, and releases, followed by new arrests. Though their initial information was fragmentary and did not immediately include Vesey's role, they were clearly on the trail.

Near the beginning of June, before the whites had worked their way through to the heart of the insurrectionary plans, Vesey attempted to recoup the situation by moving up the time of the attack to June 16. But by then not only was it impossible to reestablish contact with his far-flung network of recruits in time, but the authorities were sufficiently alerted to stymie the move before it could take on any real life. By June 22, Vesey and the rest of his comrades had been rounded up for a long, involved trial that was held under a law enacted "for the better ordering and governing of Negroes and other slaves in this state." Even during the trial it was not easy to order and govern the African people of the Charleston area. They knew what the planned insurrection might have meant to them, and attempted to get close enough to the courtroom to receive news of its action. But black people were not allowed within several hundred yards of the building; indeed, federal troops "guarded the prison and court day and night to prevent blacks from freeing prisoners and continuing the conspiracy."

Within the courthouse, most of the leaders of the insurrection remained faithful to their commitments and refused to identify their comrades. Then, before the trial was over, the deepest meaning of black radical struggle was set in relief by the words of the oppressors. When Denmark Vesey was being sentenced, the presiding magistrate said to him: "It is difficult to imagine what *infatuation* could have prompted you to attempt an enterprise so wild and visionary. You were a free man; were comparatively wealthy; and enjoyed every comfort, compatible with your situation. You had therefore, much to risk and little to gain. From your age and experience you *ought* to have known, that success was impracticable."

If one forgot the slavery of Vesey's own children and wives for the moment, then it was possible to say that he was especially fortunate — an unusual and even well-to-do Negro, since assets of eight thousand dollars would have been impressive for any Charleston white man at the time. But Denmark Vesey had chosen to identify himself as an integral part of the black river, of Tomba's river, of Gabriel's river, of Temba's river, of the river that was created by the countless thousands before him. Neither his freedman's status, his wealth, his age, nor his relative security could cut him off from the oppression and injustice his people suffered. He had rejected the precarious security of his "class" to join the struggle to overcome the entire system of white supremacy and slavery, and to smash all the false distinctions it had created, even among the children of Africa. At the age of fifty-five, Denmark Vesey had chosen to die.

The white rulers could not, or would not, understand such things. The magistrate concluded: "Your professed design was to trample on all laws, human and divine; to riot in blood, outrage, rapine, and conflagration, and to introduce anarchy and confusion in their most horrid forms. Your life has become, therefore, a just and necessary sacrifice, at the shrine of indignant justice." According to the record, Denmark Vesey and his men "mutually supported each other, and died obedient to the stern and emphatic injunction of their comrade, Peter Poyas: 'Do not open your lips! Die silent, as you shall see me do.'" In Peter's trunk a letter was found with these words: "Fear not, the Lord God that delivered Daniel is able to deliver us." Perhaps he believed it.

Didn't my Lord
Deliver Daniel,
Then why not ev'ry man?

Nor was Peter the only one. There is evidence that on July 2, 1822, the day of their execution, another attempt at insurrection was made by the persistent, committed black people who had joined the struggle in Charleston. State militia held back the demonstration, but "so determined, however, were they to strike a blow for liberty that it was found necessary for the federal government to send soldiers to maintain order." The basic testimony of the slave ships remained: almost any serious black movement toward liberty confronted white law, white firearms, and the quest for white order.

While major plots like Vesey's presented the most obvious challenges, they were constantly sustained by thousands of nameless black people like those in Charleston who attended the execution of their leaders, who were arrested and beaten for wearing black to mourn the death of Vesey and Poyas, of Gullah Jack and Ned, and more than thirty others. At the same time the poisoning, the arson, the flight from slavery still fed the subterranean streams.

Throughout this period the fugitive outlyers who stayed in the South continued to be a persistent judgment and challenge. In the spring following Vesey's death, the profound effect that a company of outlyers might have on the workings of slavery was seen in the southern portion of Virginia's Norfolk County. In May 1823 it was reported that the white residents of the area "have for some time been kept in a state of mind peculiarly harassing and painful, from the too apparent fact that their lives are at the mercy of a band of lurking assassins, against whose fell designs neither the power of the law, or vigilance, or personal strength and intrepidity, can avail."

This group of what Governor Claiborne of Louisiana would have called "bad characters" were in fact former slaves of the area. "These desperadoes are runaway negroes (commonly called outlyers). . . . Their first object is to obtain a gun and ammunition, as well as to procure game for subsistence as to defend themselves from attack, or accomplish objects of vengeance." In the course of their struggle to remain free, and as part of their warfare on slaveowners and patrollers, the self-determining black band had killed several white men. One slaveholder in the area received a note from the group, "suggesting it would be healthier for him to remain indoors at night." He took the suggestion.

Finally the state militia was dispatched. In June they captured the reputed leader, Bob Ferebee, a black who had lived independently as a free man and fugitive for six years. In July 1823 — just one year after the execution of Denmark Vesey and his comrades — Bob Ferebee met the logical results of white justice, became another strange fruit, witnessing in the wind of Virginia.

As usual, the executions were not deterrents. Ferebee and his band had already offered their contribution to the struggle, and their existence had made a point to both blacks and whites. They were "bad niggers" — "desperadoes" elevated to an organizational level. They had inspired deep, open fear in the white community, and for a time had been the hunters rather than the hunted. Their leader had remained free for six years; others had most likely been outlyers for even longer, for the Dismal Swamp offered protection for many children of Africa for long periods of time. (Some persons were said to have been born and died in such refuges.) This band and others like it provided an essential and unambiguous challenge to the system of slavery and its law and order. . . .

. . . The early nineteenth-century black community in slavery — the community that knew names like Gabriel, Vesey, and Ferebee — lived close to the active, radical depths of the river of black struggle. Occasionally they were swept in by its force; most often, they operated at less costly levels, but knew of the radical movements. Engaged in day-to-day survival to maintain integrity, identity, and life, the vast majority who formed the mainstream were constantly in touch with the runaways, outlyers, and arsonists, and with those men and women who sneaked back into their cabins before dawn after attending secret planning meetings. In addition, the fugitive, exciting word from white political sources, telling of arguments and debates over the operation of the institution of slavery, continued to seep into the life of the Southern black community, hinting, suggesting, revealing the basic tensions which lurked deep in the larger white society. Always, too, there was word from farther away (and nearer), from San Domingo and other parts of the African diaspora in the Caribbean — word of struggle and victory, even of emancipation. Then, beyond and above all these, was the word from the Lord, word from the Word, word of delivering Daniel, word that "Jesus do most anything/Oh, no man can hinder me." There were words not only to hear, but to eat and drink, words to ponder, words to surrender to.

The river of black struggle held all these speaking, acting, and enlivening words, all these bold, challenging heroic lives, and it was always moving, rising in the midst of the slave community. Therefore this was not a community caught in the flatness of despair. It was not a community without hope. It lived with brutality, but did not become brutish. Often it was treated inhumanely, but it clung to its humanity. There was too much in the river which suggested other possibilities, announced new comings, and hurled restless movements against the dam of white oppression. Always, under the surface of slavery, the river of black struggle flowed with, and was created by, a black community that moved actively in search of freedom, integrity, and home — a community that could not be dehumanized.

In 1831, the river of black struggle produced the bloodiest slave rebellion in southern history. In the sleepy backwater of Southhampton County, Virginia, a band of slave insurgents, led by a preacher and mystic named Nat Turner, went on a gruesome rampage: they hacked some sixty whites to death, including women and children, in a trail of destruction that led to the very outskirts of Jerusalem, the county seat. At last, the militia crushed the rebellion and white authorities sent Nat Turner to the hanging tree, but not before vengeful whites had slaughtered more than 120 innocent blacks, decapitating some and leaving their heads on signposts as a warning to potential insurrectionists. Rocked to their foundations by the Nat Turner rebellion, Virginia and other southern states revised and strengthened their slave codes, restricting blacks so severely that they would never again be able to mount an insurrection. Yet, as Harding writes, the river of black struggle flowed on in other ways, "forcing the issue of the nation's future, never allowing any of our God-driven, freedom-seeking, Jerusalem-marching fathers to have died in vain, pointing the way."

QUESTIONS TO CONSIDER

1. Santo Domingo is a leitmotif of this selection. What happened there and with what result? What significance did it commonly hold for American blacks in the nineteenth century? What did the example of Santo Domingo Southerners mean for a white?

2. What was the role of religion and the Bible in black resistance to slavery? What was their role in the Gabriel Prosser and Denmark Vesey revolts? Under what circumstances was the African Methodist Episcopal church formed?

3. How does Harding judge the federal government's ban on the slave trade in 1808? How do American and British treatments of the slaves compare during the Revolution and the War of 1812? What irony has often been remarked in this?

4. Describe the revolts organized by Gabriel Prosser and Denmark Vesey. What similarities and differences do you see in the leadership, organization, inspiration, and consequences? Why does Harding stress the classlessness of the Vesey revolt? How did the black and white populations react to these revolts?

5. Large-scale revolts such as Denmark Vesey's were not the only form of black resistance to slavery. What other examples does Harding discuss? What conclusions about the slaves does Harding draw from this history of resistance?

VIII

FREEDOM'S FERMENT:
THE AGE OF JACKSON

16

The Jacksonian Revolution

ROBERT V. REMINI

The age of Jackson was a turbulent era — a period of boom and bust, of great population shifts into the cities and out to the frontier, of institutionalized violence and racial antagonisms, of utopian communities, reform movements, the abolitionist crusade, and the "great southern reaction" in defense of slavery. It was also a time of graft and corruption, of machine politics and ruthless political bosses. But above all, it was an age of the self-made man, a time when privilege and elitist rule gave way to the vestiges of popular democracy — at least for white males. Between the 1820s and the 1840s, America witnessed the rise of universal manhood suffrage for whites, long ballots, national nominating conventions, and grassroots political parties.

The man who gave the age its name was a self-made planter and slaveholder of considerable wealth. Like most aristocrats from the Tennessee country of his day, Andrew Jackson could not spell, he lacked education and culture, but he did aspire to wealth and military glory, both of which he won. Despite his harsh, gaunt features, he looked like a gentleman and a soldier, and in calm moods he could be gentle, even grave.

In politics, however, Jackson was an "aggressive, dynamic, charismatic, and intimidating individual," as Robert V. Remini describes him. He became a symbol of "the common man," Remini says, because he was devoted to liberty and democracy and had a powerful faith in "the people." In Remini's view, Jackson's ascension to the presidency in 1828 launched a genuine revolution against the "gentry republic" founded by the signers in which the rich and powerful ruled. The Jacksonian revolution, Remini argues, moved America toward a more democratic system in which the government was responsive to the popular will. In Remini's view, Jackson himself played a major role in the shift toward democracy — that is, toward a system of true majority rule, not just rule by a propertied elite. He set out to make the president and every other federal official answerable to the people. Thus, he favored abolishing the electoral college and rotating every elected office. He even challenged the role of the Supreme Court as the final arbiter in interpreting the Constitution, a subject covered in selection 14. In Remini's view, Jackson also inaugurated the history of powerful executive leadership in this country. He used his veto power more than all his predecessors combined and asserted the right of the chief executive to initiate legislation, which altered the president's relationship with Congress and made the president the head of state. Surprisingly enough, Remini does not mention Jackson's crucial role in solving the nullification crisis of 1832, which Remini heralds elsewhere as the single most important achievement of Jackson's presidency. That event is discussed in the portrait of Henry Clay (selection 18).

As Remini explains in an afterword, his view of Jackson is a revival of a once popular interpretation that had fallen into disfavor. The author of a recent three-volume biography of Jackson and perhaps the country's leading Jackson scholar, Remini disputes those who have dismissed Jackson as an opportunist and a fraud masquerading as a man of the people. Remini even defends Jackson's Indian removal policy, which so offends many modern Americans. That policy is discussed in selection 21.

Remini's interpretation is provocative. Do you agree that a slave owner could really be a man of the people? As you ponder that question, remember Professor Wilson's warning about presentism. Jackson himself would have answered the question with a resounding yes on two counts. First, the Jacksonian revolution ushered in universal white manhood suffrage in most states and created a true mass electorate. Second, the people in Jackson's day was a political concept that included all those who could vote. That meant white men almost exclusively. Women, slaves, and free blacks outside New England were all denied the electoral franchise and were excluded from the idea of the people. They had no will to which Jackson or any other government official could be responsive.

Because Remini makes much of the transition from Washington's generation to Jackson's, you may want to compare the records and outlooks of the two presidents (for an analysis of Washington, see selection 10). But Remini's essay is best studied and discussed in conjunction with the next two selections, which feature abolitionist William Lloyd Garrison and Whig leader Henry Clay, respectively. The three readings afford dramatically different perspectives on the search for liberty in Jacksonian America.

GLOSSARY

BENSON, LEE   Quantifying historian who dismissed as "clap trap" Jacksonian rhetoric about "the people" and democracy.

CALHOUN, JOHN C.   South Carolina planter and Jackson's first vice president, he later broke with Jackson and helped form the rival Whig party.

CLAY, HENRY   Kentucky planter and one of the great leaders of the rival Whig party (see selection 18).

DEMOCRATIC PARTY   New political organization, formed around the Jackson presidency, that opposed a strong central government and a broad interpretation of the Constitution; Jackson himself and many Democrats were against government-financed internal improvements.

DUANE, WILLIAM   Jackson's secretary of the treasury; Old Hickory fired him when he refused to transfer federal deposits from the National Bank.

HOFSTADTER, RICHARD   Historian whose book *The American Political Tradition* (1948) argues that the typical Jacksonian was "an expectant capitalist," a "man on the make."

INTERNAL IMPROVEMENTS   Roads, railroads, and canals financed by the federal government or the states.

NATIONAL BANK (SECOND BANK OF THE UNITED STATES)   Founded in 1816 by congressional charter to run twenty years, the bank was supposed to stabilize the national economy by issuing sound paper money, serving as a depository for federal funds, and establishing branches across the country; Jackson vetoed the bank recharter bill.

OLIGARCHY   System of government in which a dominant class rules.

PROGRESSIVE HISTORIANS   Those in the early part of the twentieth century who "dubbed the Jacksonian revolution an age of egalitarianism that produced the rise of the common man," first in the western states, then in the older ones in the East.

SCHLESINGER, ARTHUR M., JR.   Historian who argued in 1945 that the Jacksonian revolution was an effort on the part of the "less fortunate," urban working classes and yeoman farmers, to challenge the power of the wealthy business community.

SPOILS SYSTEM   Pejorative term for Jackson's principle of rotation in office.

"TIPPECANOE AND TYLER TOO"   Campaign slogan for Whig candidates William Henry ("Tippecanoe") Harrison and John Tyler in the "log cabin" presidential campaign of 1840.

TOCQUEVILLE, ALEXIS DE   French aristocrat who visited the United States in 1831 and wrote the classic *Democracy in America* on the basis of his observations; he praised "the general equality of condition among the people" in America but feared that industrialization would create a new class of dependent workers and a new ruling aristocracy.

VAN BUREN, MARTIN ("LITTLE VAN")   New Yorker who advocated the two-party system, served as Jackson's second vice president, and succeeded him in the White House in 1837.

WEBSTER, DANIEL   Great Whig leader who represented Massachusetts in the Senate.

WHIG PARTY   Coalition of Jackson haters that favored a strong central government and federally financed international improvements (treated in detail in selection 18).

A NEW GENERATION
OF POLITICAL LEADERS

"What?" cried the outraged North Carolina lady when she heard the dreadful news. "Jackson up for president? Jackson? Andrew Jackson? The Jackson that used to live in Salisbury? Why, when he was here, he was such a rake that my husband would not bring him into the house! It is true, he might have taken him out to the stable to weigh horses for a race, and might drink a glass of whiskey with him there. Well, if Andrew Jackson can be president, anybody can!"

Indeed. After forty years of constitutional government headed by presidents George Washington, John Adams, Thomas Jefferson, James Madison, James Monroe, and John Quincy Adams, the thought of Gen. Andrew Jackson of Tennessee — "Old Hickory" to his devoted soldiers — succeeding such distinguished statesmen came as a shock to some Americans in 1828. And little did they know at the time that Old Hickory would be followed in succession by the little Magician, Tippecanoe and Tyler, too, Young Hickory, and then Old Rough and Ready.

What had happened to the American political process? How could it come about that the Washingtons, Jeffersons, and Madisons of the world could be replaced by the Van Burens, Harrisons, Tylers, and Taylors? What a mockery of the political system bequeathed by the Founding Fathers!

The years from roughly 1828 to 1848 are known today as the Age of Jackson or the Jacksonian era. To many contemporaries, they initiated a "revolution," a shocking overthrow of the noble republican standards

of the founders by the "common people," who in 1828 preferred as president a crude frontiersman like Andrew Jackson to a statesman of proven ability with a record of outstanding public service like John Quincy Adams.

Over the forty years following the establishment of the American nation under the Constitution, the United States had experienced many profound changes in virtually all phases of life. Following the War of 1812, the industrial revolution took hold and within thirty years all the essential elements for the creation of an industrial society in American were solidly in place. At the same time, a transportation revolution got underway with the building of canals, bridges, and turnpikes, reaching a climax of sorts in the 1820s with the coming of the railroads. The standard of living was also improved by numerous new inventions. Finally, many of the older eastern states began to imitate newer western states by democratizing their institutions, for example, amending their constitutions to eliminate property qualifications for voting and holding office, thereby establishing universal white manhood suffrage.

The arrival of many thousands of new voters at the polls in the early nineteenth century radically changed American politics. In the past, only the wealthy and better educated were actively involved in government. Moreover, political parties were frowned upon by many of the Founding Fathers. Parties stood for factions or cliques by which greedy and ambitious men, who had no interest in serving the public good, could advance their private and selfish purposes. John Adams spoke for many when he declared that the "division of the republic into two great parties . . . is to be dreaded as the greatest political evil under our Constitution."

But times had changed. An entirely new generation of politicians appeared at the outbreak of the War of 1812, men like Henry Clay, John C. Calhoun, Martin Van Buren, and Daniel Webster, who regarded political parties more favorably. Indeed, the party structure that had emerged before the end of President

This article appeared in the January 1988 issue and is reprinted with permission from *The World & I,* a publication of The Washington Times Corporation, copyright © 1988.

Washington's administration had been their corridor to power, since none of them could offer to their constituents a public record to match what the founders had achieved.

None had fought in the revolution. None had signed the Declaration or participated in the debates leading to the writing and adoption of the Constitution. Some of them — Martin Van Buren is probably the best example — actually considered parties to be beneficial to the body politic, indeed essential to the proper working of a democratic society. Through the party system, Van Buren argued, the American people could more effectively express their will and take measures to ensure that that will was implemented by their representatives. "We must always have party distinctions," he wrote, "and the old ones are the best. . . . Political combinations between the inhabitants of the different states are unavoidable and the most natural and beneficial to the country is that between the planters of the South and the plain Republicans of the North."

In supporting Andrew Jackson for the presidency in 1828 and trying to win support from both planters and plain Republicans, Van Buren affirmed his belief in the American need for a two-party system. Jackson's election, he told Thomas Ritchie, editor of the Richmond *Enquirer,* "as the result of his military services without reference to party, and, as far as he alone is concerned, scarcely to principle, would be one thing. His election as the result of combined and concerted effort of a political party, holding in the main, to certain tenets and opposed to certain prevailing principles, might be another and far different thing."

Van Buren eventually formed an alliance with John C. Calhoun and a number of other southern politicians, and led the way in structuring a political organization around the presidential candidacy of Andrew Jackson. That organization ultimately came to be called the Democratic Party. Its leaders, including Jackson, Van Buren, Calhoun, and Thomas Hart

Benton, claimed to follow the republican doctrines of Thomas Jefferson. Thus they opposed both a strong central government and a broad interpretation of the Constitution, and they regarded the states, whose rights must be defended by all who cared about preserving individual liberty, as a wholesome counterweight to the national government. Many of them opposed the idea of the federal government sponsoring public works, arguing that internal improvements dangerously inflated the power of the central government and jeopardized liberty. As president, Andrew Jackson vetoed the Maysville road bill and contended that the national government should avoid internal improvements as a general practice, except for those essential to the national defense.

The political philosophy these Democrats espoused was fundamentally conservative. It advocated economy in operating the government because a tight budget limited government activity, and Jackson swore that if ever elected president he would liquidate the national debt. True to his word, he labored throughout his administration to cut expenditures by vetoing several appropriations bills he tagged as exorbitant, and he finally succeeded in obliterating the national debt altogether in January 1835 — a short-lived accomplishment.

The organization of the Democratic Party in its initial stages included a central committee, state committees, and a national newspaper located in Washington, D.C., the *United States Telegraph,* which could speak authoritatively to the party faithful. In time it was said that the Democratic organization included "a chain of newspaper posts, from the New England States to Louisiana, and branching off through Lexington to the Western States." The supporters of Jackson's election were accused by their opponents of attempting to regulate "the popular election by means of organized clubs in the States, and organized presses everywhere."

Democrats took particular delight in celebrating the candidacy of Andrew Jackson. They found that Old Hickory's personality and military accomplish-

When Jackson set out for his inauguration in Washington, D.C., large crowds turned out to see "the man of the people." This prompted an old Federalist to cry, "The reign of KING MOB seemed triumphant." But a westerner thought it "a proud day for the people. General Jackson is their own President." (New York Historical Society)

ments made him an attractive and viable candidate for the ordinary voter. Indeed his career and personality stirred the imagination of Democratic leaders around the country and they devised new methods, or improved old ones, to get across the message that Andrew Jackson was a "man of the people." "The Constitution and liberty of the country were in imminent peril, and he has preserved them both!" his supporters boasted. "We can sustain our republican principles . . . by calling to the presidential chair . . . ANDREW JACKSON."

Jackson became a symbol of the best in American life — a self-made man, among other things — and party leaders adopted the hickory leaf as their symbol. Hickory brooms, hickory canes, hickory sticks shot up everywhere — on steeples, poles, steamboats, and stage coaches, and in the hands of all who could wave them to salute the Old Hero of New Orleans. "In every village, as well as upon the corners of many city streets," hickory poles were erected. "Many of these poles were standing as late as 1845," recorded one contemporary, "rotten mementoes [*sic*] of the delirium of 1828." The opponents of the Democratic Party were outraged by this crude lowering of the political process. "Planting hickory trees!" snorted the Washington *National Journal* on May 24, 1828. "Odds nuts and drumsticks! What have hickory trees to do with republicanism and the great contest?"

The Democrats devised other gimmicks to generate excitement for their ticket. "Jackson meetings" were held in every county where a Democratic organization existed. Such meetings were not new, of course. What was new was their audience. "If we go into one of these meetings," declared one newspaper, "of whom do we find them composed? Do we see there the solid, substantial, moral and reflecting yeomanry of the country? No. . . . They comprise a large portion of the dissolute, the noisy, the discontented, and designing of society." The Democratic press retorted with the claim that these so-called dissolute were actually the "bone and muscle of American society. They are the People. The real People who understand that Gen. Jackson is one of them and will defend their interests and rights."

The Jacksonians were also very fond of parades and barbecues. In Baltimore a grand barbecue was scheduled to commemorate the successful defense of the city when the British attacked during the War of 1812. But the Democrats expropriated the occasion and converted it into a Jackson rally. One parade started with dozens of Democrats marching to the beat of a fife and drum corps and wearing no other insignia save "a twig of the sacred [hickory] tree in their hats." Trailing these faithful Jacksonians came "gigantic hickory poles," still live and crowned with green foliage, being carted in "on eight wheels for the purpose of being planted by the democracy on the eve of the election." These poles were drawn by eight horses, all decorated with "ribbons and mottoes." Perched in the branches of each tree were a dozen Democrats, waving flags and shouting, "Hurrah for Jackson!"

"Van Buren has learned you know that the *Hurra Boys* were for Jackson," commented one critic, "and to my regret they constitute a powerful host." Indeed they did. The number of voters in the election of 1828 rose to 1,155,340, a jump of more than 800,000 over the previous presidential election of 1824.

The Hurra Boys brought out the voters in 1828, but at considerable cost. The election set a low mark for vulgarity, gimmickry, and nonsensical hijinks. Jackson's mother was accused of being a prostitute brought to America to service British soldiers, and his wife was denounced as an "adulteress" and bigamist. "Ought a convicted adulteress and her paramour husband to be placed in the highest offices of this free and Christian land?" asked one editor. But the Democrats were no better, accusing John Quincy Adams of pimping for the czar of Russia.

The tone and style of this election outraged many voters who feared for the future of American politics. With so many fresh faces crowding to the polls, the old republican system was yielding to a new democratic style and that evolution seemed fraught with all the dangers warned against by the Founding Fathers. Jackson's subsequent victory at the polls gave some Americans nightmares of worse things to come.

At his inauguration people came from five hundred miles away to see General Jackson, wrote Daniel Webster, "and they really seem to think that the country is rescued from some dreadful danger!" They nearly wrecked the White House in their exuberance. Their behavior shocked Joseph Story, an associate justice of the Supreme Court, and sent him scurrying home. "The reign of KING MOB seemed triumphant," he wailed. But a western newspaper disagreed. "It was a proud day for the people," reported the *Argus of Western America*. "General Jackson is *their own* President."

Jackson himself was fiercely committed to democracy. And by democracy he meant majoritarian rule. "The people are the government," he wrote, "administering it by their agents; they are the Government, the sovereign power." In his first message to Congress as president, written in December 1829, Jackson announced: "The majority is to govern." To the people belonged the right of "electing their Chief Executive." He therefore asked Congress to adopt an amendment that would abolish the College of Electors. He wanted all "intermediary" agencies standing between the people and their government swept away, whether erected by the Founding Fathers or not. "The people are sovereign," he reiterated. "Their will is absolute."

So committed was Jackson to the principle of popular self-rule that he told historian-politician George Bancroft that "every officer should in his turn pass before the people, for their approval or rejection." And he included federal judges in this sweeping generalization, even justices of the Supreme Court. Accordingly, he introduced the principle of rotation, which limited government appointments to four years. Officeholders should be regularly rotated back home and replaced by new men, he said. "The duties of all public officers are . . . so plain and simple that men of intelligence may readily qualify themselves for their performance." Otherwise abuse may occur. Anyone who has held office "a few years, believes he has a life estate in it, a vested right, & if it has been held 20 years or upwards, not only a vested right, but that it ought to descend to his children, & if no children than the next of kin — This is not the principles of our government. It is rotation in office that will perpetuate our liberty." Unfortunately, hack politicians equated rotation with patronage and Jackson's enemies quickly dubbed his principle "the spoils system."

But it was never meant to be a spoils system. Jackson wanted *every* office of government, from the highest to the lowest, within the reach of the electorate, arguing that "where the people are everything . . . there and there only is liberty." Perhaps his position was best articulated by Alexis de Tocqueville, the French visitor in the 1830s whose *Democracy in America* remains one of the most profound observations about American life in print. "The people reign in the American political world," declared Tocqueville, "as the Deity does in the universe. They are the cause and aim of all things; everything comes from them, and everything is absorbed in them." The "constant celebration" of the people, therefore, is what Jackson and the Democratic Party provided the nation during his eight years in office. It is what Jacksonian Democracy was all about.

As president, Jackson inaugurated a number of important changes in the operation of government. For example, he vetoed congressional legislation more

According to Professor Remini, Jackson "was fiercely committed to democracy. And by democracy he meant majoritarian rule." Jackson himself wrote, "The people are the government, administering it by their agents; they are the Government, the sovereign power." Oil on Canvas by Ralph E.W. Earl, circa 1834. (Courtesy, Tennessee State Museum, Tennessee Historical Society Collection)

times than all his predecessors combined, and for reasons other than a bill's presumed lack of constitutionality. More importantly, by the creative use of his veto power be successfully claimed for the chief executive the right to participate in the legislative process. He put Congress on notice that they must consider his views on all issues *before* enacting them into law or run the risk of a veto. In effect he assumed the right to initiate legislation, and this essentially altered the relationship between the executive and the Congress. Instead of a separate and equal branch of the government, the president, according to Jackson, was the head of state, the first among equals.

Jackson also took a dim view of the claim that the

Supreme Court exercised the final and absolute right to determine the meaning of the Constitution. When the court decided in *McCulloch vs. Maryland* that the law establishing a national bank was constitutional, Jackson disagreed. In his veto of a bill to recharter the Second National Bank in 1832, he claimed among other things that the bill lacked authority under the Constitution, despite what the high court had decided. Both the House and Senate, as well as the president, he continued, must decide for themselves what is and what is not constitutional before taking action on any bill. The representatives of Congress ought not to vote for a bill, and the president ought not to sign it, if they, in their own good judgment, believe it unconstitutional. "It is as much the duty of the House of Representatives, of the Senate, and of the President to decide upon the constitutionality of any bill or resolution which may be presented to them for passage or approval as it is of the supreme judges when it may be brought before them for judicial decision." Jackson did not deny the right of the Supreme Court to judge the constitutionality of a bill. What he denied was the presumption that the Court was the final or exclusive interpreter of the Constitution. All three branches should rule on the question of constitutionality, Jackson argued. In this way the equality and independence of each branch of government is maintained. "The authority of the Supreme Court," he declared, "must not, therefore, be permitted to control the Congress, or the Executive when acting in their legislative capacities, but to have only such influence as the force of their reasoning may deserve." What bothered Jackson was the presumption that four men could dictate what 15 million people may or may not do under their constitutional form. To Jackson's mind that was not democratic but oligarchic. But that was precisely the intention of the Founding Fathers: to provide a balanced mix of democratic, oligarchic, and monarchical forms in the Constitution.

Of course Jackson was merely expressing his own opinion about the right of all three branches to pass on the constitutionality of all legislation, an opinion the American people ultimately rejected. The great fear in a democratic system — one the Founding Fathers knew perfectly well — was the danger of the majority tyrannizing the minority. Jackson would take his chances. He believed the American people were virtuous and would always act appropriately. "I for one do not despair of the republic," he wrote. "I have great confidence in the virtue of a great majority of the people, and I cannot fear the result. The republic is safe, the main pillars [of] virtue, religion and morality will be fostered by a majority of the people." But not everyone shared Jackson's optimism about the goodness of the electorate. And in time — particularly with the passage of the Fourteenth Amendment — it fell to the courts to guard and maintain the rights of the minority.

Jackson summed up his assertion of presidential rights by declaring that he alone — not Congress, as was usually assumed — was the sole representative of the American people and responsible to them. After defeating Henry Clay in the 1832 election, he decided to kill the Second National Bank by removing federal deposits because, as he said, he had received a "mandate" from the people to do so. The Senate objected and formally censured him, but Jackson, in response, merely issued another statement on presidential rights and the democratic system that had evolved over the last few years.

By law, only the secretary of the treasury was authorized to remove the deposits, so Jackson informed his secretary, William Duane, to carry out his order. Duane refused pointblank. And he also refused to resign as he had promised if he and the president could not agree upon a common course of action with respect to the deposits. Thereupon, Jackson sacked him. This was the first time a cabinet officer had been fired, and there was some question whether the president had this authority. After all, the cabinet positions were created by Congress and appointment required the consent of the Senate. Did that not imply that removal also required senatorial consent — particularly the treasury secretary, since he handled public funds that were controlled by Congress? The law creating the Treasury Department never called in an "executive" department, and it required its secretary to report to the Congress, not the president. None of this made a particle of difference to Andrew Jackson. All department heads were *his* appointees and they would obey *him* or pack their bags. The summary dismissal of Duane was seen by Jackson's opponents as a presidential grab for the purse strings of the nation. And in fact presidential control over all executive functions gave the chief executive increased authority over the collection and distribution of public funds.

☆

THE JACKSONIAN REVOLUTION

By the close of 1833 many feared that Andrew Jackson was leading the country to disaster. Henry Clay regularly pilloried the president on the Senate floor. On one occasion he accused Jackson of "open, palpable and daring usurpation" of all the powers of government. "We are in the midst of a revolution," Clay thundered, "hitherto bloodless, but rapidly tending towards a total change of the pure republican character of the Government."

A "revolution" — that was how the opposition Whig Party characterized Jackson's presidency. The nation was moving steadily away from its "pure republican character" into something approaching despotism. What the nation was witnessing, cried Clay, was "the concentration of all power in the hands of one man." Thereafter Whig newspapers reprinted a cartoon showing Jackson as "King Andrew the First." Clad in robes befitting an emperor, he was shown wearing a crown and holding a scepter in one hand and a scroll in the other on which was written the word "veto."

Democrats, naturally, read the "revolution" differently. They saw it as the steady progress of the country from the gentry republic originally established by the Founding Fathers to a more democratic system that mandated broader representation in government and a greater responsiveness to popular will.

Andrew Jackson did not take kindly to Clay's verbal mauling. "Oh, if I live to get these robes of office off me," he snorted at one point, "I will bring the rascal to a dear account." He later likened the senator to "a drunken man in a brothel," reckless, destructive, and "full of fury."

Other senators expressed their opposition to this "imperial" president and seconded Clay's complaints. John C. Calhoun, who by this time had deserted to the enemy camp, adopted the Kentuckian's "leading ideas of revolution" and charged that "a great effort is now making to choke and stifle the voice of American liberty." And he condemned Jackson's insistence on taking refuge in democratic claims. The president "tells us again and again with the greatest emphasis," he continued, "that he is the immediate representative of the American people! What effrontery! What boldness of assertion! Why, he never received a vote from the American people. He was elected by electors . . . who are elected by Legislatures chosen by the people."

Sen. Daniel Webster and other Whigs chimed in. "Again and again we hear it said," rumbled Webster, "that the President is responsible to the American people! . . . And this is thought enough for a limited, restrained, republican government! . . . I hold this, Sir, to be a mere assumption, and dangerous assumption." And connected with this "airy and unreal responsibility to the people," he continued, "is another sentiment . . . and that is, that the President is the direct representative of the American people." The sweep of his language electrified the Senate. And "if he may be allowed to consider himself as the sole representative of all the American people," Webster concluded, "then I say, Sir, that the government . . . has already a master. I deny the sentiment, and therefore protest against the language; neither the sentiment nor the language is to be found in the Constitution of this Country."

Jackson's novel concept that the president served as the people's tribune found immediate acceptance by the electorate, despite the warnings of the Whigs. In effect, he altered the essential character of the presidency. He had become the head of government, the one person who would formulate national policy and direct public affairs. Sighed Senator Benjamin W. Leigh of Virginia: "Until the President developed the faculties of the Executive power, all men thought it inferior to the legislature — he manifestly thinks it superior: and in his hands [it] . . . has proved far stronger than the representatives of the States."

☆

JACKSON INTERPRETED

From Jackson's own time to the present, disagreement and controversy over the significance of his presidency has prevailed. In the twentieth century the disagreements intensified among historians. Confusion over the meaning of Jacksonian Democracy, varying regional support for democratic change, and the social and economic status of the Democrats and Whigs have clouded the efforts of scholars to reach reliable conclusions about the Old Hero and the era that bears his name.

Andrew Jackson himself will always remain a controversial figure among historians. That he can still generate such intense partisan feeling is evidence of his remarkable personality. He was an aggressive, dynamic, charismatic, and intimidating individual. And although modern scholars and students of history either admire or dislike him intensely, his rating as president in polls conducted among historians over the past thirty years varies from great to near great. He carries an enormous burden in winning any popularity contest because of his insistence on removing the

eastern Indians west of the Mississippi River and on waging a long and vicious war against the Second National Bank of the United States.

His first biographer, James Parton, wrote a three-volume *Life of Andrew Jackson* (1859, 1860), and came away with mixed feelings about the man and his democracy. At times Parton railed against the mindless mob "who could be wheedled, and flattered, and drilled," but at other times he extolled democracy as the mark of an enlightened society. What troubled Parton particularly was the spoils system. Rotation, he wrote, is "an evil so great and so difficult to remedy, that if all his other public acts had been perfectly wise and right, this single feature of his administration would suffice to render it deplorable rather than amiable."

William Graham Sumner's *Andrew Jackson* (1882) was relentlessly critical of his subject, deploring in particular Jackson's flawed moral charter and emotional excesses. Sumner and other early historians, such as Herman von Holst and James Schouler, constituted what one student of the Jacksonian age called a "liberal patrician" or "Whig" school of history. These individuals came from European middle- or upper middle-class families with excellent backgrounds of education and public service. Because their class had been ousted from political power, these historians were biased against Jacksonian Democracy, and their books reflect their prejudice.

The interpretation of Old Hickory and his adherents took a sharp about-face with the appearance in 1893 of the vastly influential article by Frederick Jackson Turner, "The Significance of the Frontier in American History." Turner argued that American democracy emerged from the wilderness, noting that universal white manhood suffrage guaranteed by the new western states became something of a model for the older, eastern states. Naturally Jackson and his followers were seen as the personification of this frontier democracy. The thesis was advanced and sometimes amplified by Charles A. Beard, Vernon L. Parrington, and other western and southern historians of the early twentieth century who were caught up in the reform movement of the Progressive era. They dubbed the Jacksonian revolution an age of egalitarianism that produced the rise of the common man. Jackson himself was applauded as a man of the people. Thus the liberal patrician school of historiography gave way to the Progressive school.

This interpretation dovetailed rather well with the views of Tocqueville. During his visit, Tocqueville encountered a widespread belief in egalitarianism but worried that majoritarian rule could endanger minority rights. There are so many sharp and accurate insights into American society and institutions in *Democracy in America* that it ought to be the first book anyone reads in attempting to understand the antebellum period of American history. Among other things, he catches the American just as he is emerging from his European and colonial past and acquiring many of the characteristics of what are generally regarded as typically American today.

Tocqueville's democratic liberalism, augmented by the works of the Progressive historians — especially Turner, Beard and Parrington — dominated historical thought about the American past for the next fifty years or more. Almost all the Progressive historians stressed the role of geographic sections in the nation, and Turner at one point even denied any class influence in the formation of frontier democracy. The only important negative voice concerning Jackson during this period came from Thomas P. Abernethy, whose *From Frontier to Plantation in Tennessee: A Study in Frontier Democracy* (1932) insisted that Jackson himself was a frontier aristocrat, an opportunist, and a land speculator who strongly opposed the democratic forces in his own state of Tennessee.

The virtual shattering of the Progressive school's interpretation of Jacksonian Democracy came with the publication of one of the most important historical monographs ever written concerning American history: *The Age of Jackson* (1945), by Arthur M. Schlesinger, Jr. The classic work virtually rivals in importance the frontier thesis of Frederick Jackson Turner. It is a landmark study and represents the beginning of modern scholarship on Jackson and his era.

Schlesinger argued that class distinctions rather than sectional differences best explain the phenomenon of Jacksonian Democracy. He interpreted Jackson's actions and those of his followers as an effort of the less fortunate in American society to combat the power and influence of the business community. The working classes in urban centers as well as the yeoman farmers, he argued, were the true wellsprings of the Jacksonian movement. Jacksonian Democracy evolved from the conflict between classes and best expressed its goals and purposes in the problems and needs facing urban laborers. Schlesinger singled out the bank war as the most telling example of the conflict and as the fundamental key to a fuller understanding of the meaning of Jacksonian Democracy. What attracted many historians to this pathbreaking study, besides its graceful and majestic style, was Schlesinger's perceptive definition of Jacksonian Democracy and a precise explanation of its origins.

The reaction to Schlesinger's work was immediate and dramatic. It swept the historical profession like a tornado, eliciting both prodigious praise and, within a relatively short time, fierce denunciations. Bray Hammond, in a series of articles as well as his *Banks and Politics in America from the Revolution to the Civil War* (1957), and Richard Hofstadter, in his *The American Political Tradition and the Men Who Made It* (1948), contended that the Jacksonians were not the champions of urban workers or small farmers but rather ambitious and ruthless entrepreneurs principally concerned with advancing their own economic and political advantage. They were "men on the make" and frequently captains of great wealth. According to Hofstadter, the Jacksonians were not so much hostile to business as they were hostile to being excluded from entering the confined arena of capitalists. Where Schlesinger had emphasized conflict in explaining the Jacksonian era, Hofstadter insisted that consensus best characterized the period. The entrepreneurial thesis, as it was called, found strong support among many young scholars who constituted the Columbia University school of historians. In a series of articles and books produced by these critics, Jackson himself was described as an inconsistent opportunist, a strikebreaker, a shady land speculator, and a political fraud. Marvin Meyers, in his *The Jackson Persuasion* (1957), provides a slight variation on the entrepreneurial thesis by arguing that Jacksonians did indeed keep their eyes on the main chance but yearned for the virtues of a past agrarian republic. They hungered after the rewards of capitalism but looked back reverentially on the blessings of a simpler agrarian society.

A major redirection of Jacksonian scholarship came with the publication of Lee Benson's *The Concept of Jacksonian Democracy: New York as a Test Case* (1961). This work suggested a whole new approach to the investigation of the Jacksonian age by employing the techniques of quantification to uncover solid, factual data upon which to base an analysis. Moreover, Benson emphasized social questions and found that such things as ethnicity and religion were far more important than economics in determining how a person voted or which party won his allegiance. He dismissed Jacksonian rhetoric about democracy and the rights of the people as "claptrap" and contended that local issues in elections meant more to the voters than national issues. Andrew Jackson himself was dismissed as unimportant in understanding the structure and meaning of politics in this period. In time, some college textbooks virtually eliminated Jackson from any discussion of this period except to mention that he opposed social reforms and that his removal of the Indians was one of the most heinous acts in American history. . . .

[In more recent years] Jackson has been somewhat restored to his former importance, if not his former heroic stature. My own three-volume life of Old Hickory, *Andrew Jackson and the Course of American Empire, 1767–1821; Andrew Jackson and the Course of American Freedom, 1822–1832; Andrew Jackson and the Course of American Democracy, 1833–1845* (1977, 1981, 1984) highlights Schlesinger's findings and Jackson's faith and commitment to liberty and democracy. I contend that Jackson was in fact a man of the people, just as the Progressive historians had argued, and that he actively attempted to advance democracy by insisting that all branches of government, including the courts, reflect the popular will. I also tried to show that, for a number of reasons, the president's policy of Indian removal was initiated to spare the Indian from certain extinction. And Francis Paul Prucha has argued persuasively that Indian removal was probably the only policy possible under the circumstances.

The study of the Jacksonian era is essential for any serious examination of the evolution of the American presidency. This has been widely recognized since the avalanche of articles and books triggered by the appearance of Schlesinger's monumental work. Jackson himself has never lost his ability to excite the most intense passions and interest among students of American history. No doubt scholars and popular writers will continue to debate his role as a national hero and as an architect of American political institutions.

QUESTIONS TO CONSIDER

1. The first decades of the nineteenth century were a dynamic period for the young Republic. What kinds of changes were occurring in American life?

2. Americans today often express pride at the thought that any American can become president, but in 1828 many Americans were worried by precisely the same notion. Why? How had the founders conceived of republicanism, and what were their fears of majority rule? Were those fears entirely unjustified?

3. What were the basic tenets of the new Democratic party and its leader, Andrew Jackson? What did

Jackson give as the principles behind his most important policies? How did his opponents view those policies, their purposes and consequences?

4.   Robert Remini says that Jackson "altered the essential character of the presidency." What had been its character, according to Remini, and how and why did Jackson transform it?

5.   Andrew Jackson has been interpreted in very different, even conflicting, ways by different historians at different times. What are some of the most influential interpretations and their authors? What is it in Jackson that has elicited such varying responses? What can these varying interpretations tell you about the historians and the periods that shaped those historians?

17

"Woe If It Comes with Storm and Blood and Fire": William Lloyd Garrison and the Abolitionist Crusade

RALPH KORNGOLD

In the Jacksonian era, the existence of slavery in a society dedicated to freedom remained America's central paradox. While white men enjoyed greater opportunity and more political rights, while the nation attempted to mold itself into a popular democracy, two-and-a-half million southern blacks remained in chains. Moreover, most northern states either retained or now enacted black codes that discriminated against free blacks, denying them the right to vote, hold political office, work at skilled jobs, live in white neighborhoods, or attend public schools (although they had to pay school taxes). Only in Massachusetts and a few other New England states did African American citizens enjoy more or less the same rights as white people. But white racial hostility often flared up in New England, too. In fact, hundreds of race riots broke out all over the North during the age of Jackson; in many of the riots, angry whites — including leaders of the community — burned black ghettos and beat up and killed black people.

It was inevitable that some whites would become upset about such injustice, would become distressed and then angered about the contradiction of slavery and racial discrimination in a self-proclaimed free and just society. Some Americans — southern and northern Quakers particularly — had, in fact, opposed slavery since the colonial period. But in the 1820s — a decade of religious and political ferment, a decade when the struggle began for universal manhood suffrage — the antislavery movement truly took shape. Groups of Quakers and free blacks collected antislavery petitions and sent them to Congress, where intimidated southerners had them tabled, and Benjamin Lundy, a Baltimore Quaker, not only started publishing The Genius of Universal Emancipation but organized antislavery societies in the South itself. At this time, most antislavery whites (a distinct minority of the population) were both gradualists and colonizationists such as Henry Clay. But by the 1830s, some had emphatically changed their minds. They renounced colonization, demanded immediate emancipation, organized a national antislavery society, and started an abolitionist crusade that would haunt the American conscience and arouse latent racism everywhere in the land.

The best-known leader of the crusade was William Lloyd Garrison. A shy, intense, bespectacled young man who came from a broken home (his father had run away), he was raised by his mother as an ardent Baptist; later, he became a radical Christian perfectionist. Initially, Garrison too was a gradualist and a colonizer. But in 1829, after he went to work for Lundy's paper, Garrison renounced colonization and came out for immediate emancipation. Ralph Korngold speculates that Garrison was influenced by the abolitionist writings of James Duncan and the Reverend George Bourne, who denounced slavery as a sin and demanded that blacks be freed at once.

At any rate, in the columns of Lundy's paper, Garrison conducted a stunning moral attack against slavery and anybody who condoned or perpetuated it. For example, when he learned that a ship belonging to Francis Todd of Newburyport, Massachusetts (Garrison's hometown), was taking a cargo of slaves from Baltimore to New Orleans, Garrison castigated him as a highway robber and a murderer. The man, a highly respected citizen and a church deacon, slapped Garrison with a $5,000 libel suit. The court decided against Garrison and fined him $50, but he couldn't pay and had to go to jail. Korngold's narrative opens with Garrison in prison. It follows his career as he founded his antislavery newspaper, the Liberator, and launched his moral crusade against slavery, that "sum of villanies."

Garrison's method, as Korngold explains, was to overcome slavery by nonviolent "moral suasion" — that is, by arousing the conscience of the nation in favor of immediate emancipation. Korngold says it would be more accurate to call Garrison's method "moral pressure." By immediate emancipation, however, Garrison did not mean that slaves should be "let loose to roam as vagrants" or that they should be "instantly invested with all political rights and privileges." What he wanted was to break the chains on African Americans, guarantee them the protection of the law, preserve their families, and place them under "benevolent supervision" until they learned religion and became "economically secure," whereupon they were to be assimilated into American society.

While Garrison doubted that slavery could ever be abolished by peaceful means,

Korngold argues, he nevertheless thought the effort should be made. And that effort had an enormous influence on the country (see selection 18 for Henry Clay's response to the abolitionist movement). As you read Korngold's portrait, note how the South reacted to Garrison's attack and to Walker's Appeal, a pamphlet by Boston free black David Walker. Note, too, that Garrison also championed the rights of free blacks. And yet he refused to speak out against the exploitation of northern workers as a class and thus lost an important potential ally.

GLOSSARY

ALCOTT, A. BRONSON   Samuel May's brother-in-law, "mystic," teacher, and abolitionist.

ALCOTT, LOUISA MAY   Bronson Alcott's daughter, popular novelist *(Little Women),* and author of the famous Civil War song, "Battle Hymn of the Republic."

BEECHER, LYMAN   Well-known Calvinist minister who was preaching in Litchfield, Connecticut, in 1831; the next year, he became president of Lane Theological Seminary in Cincinnati, Ohio; his daughter, Harriet Beecher Stowe, wrote *Uncle Tom's Cabin* (1852).

BIRNEY, JAMES G.   Kentucky slave owner and Alabama solicitor general who freed his slaves, relocated in the North, joined the abolitionist movement, and became the presidential candidate of the Liberty party in 1840 and 1844 (see selection 18).

CLAY, CASSIUS M.   Kentucky slave owner who was converted to abolition by William Lloyd Garrison; Clay established an antislavery paper in Lexington called the *True American,* which urged gradual emancipation; a mob suppressed it in 1845.

KNAPP, ISAAC   Garrison's partner at the *Liberator.*

LIBERATOR   Garrison's abolitionist newspaper, first published on January 1, 1831, in Boston; although it never had a circulation of more than three thousand, the *Liberator* was nevertheless the most famous abolitionist newspaper of the antebellum era.

MAY, SAMUEL J.   Unitarian minister who, like Garrison, had first been a colonizationist; Garrison converted him to immediate abolitionism.

OTIS, HARRISON   Boston mayor in 1831; southern governors demanded that he shut down Garrison's "incendiary" paper.

SEWALL, SAMUEL E.   May's cousin and a Boston lawyer who actually importuned Garrison to tone down his violent language; nevertheless, he became a Garrison disciple.

TURNER, NAT   Slave mystic and preacher who led the 1831 slave rebellion in Virginia, the bloodiest insurrection in southern history.

WALKER, DAVID   Boston free black whose pamphlet, *Walker's Appeal* (1829), urged the slaves to revolt.

☆ 1 ☆

While in prison Garrison had prepared three lectures. The first contrasted the program of the Colonization Society with his own; the second gave a vivid description of the slavery system; the third showed the extent to which the North shared responsibility for the "peculiar institution." After his release he left Baltimore for the North, intending to make a lecture tour of several months' duration and then launch an antislavery weekly in Washington. If he later chose Boston, it was because Lundy moved the *Genius* to the National Capital. Garrison had become convinced the North needed enlightenment even more than the South. In the first issue of his new paper he was to write:

"During my recent tour for the purpose of exciting the minds of the people by a series of discourses on the subject of slavery, every place that I visited gave fresh evidence of the fact, that a greater revolution in public sentiment was to be effected in the free States — *and particularly in New England* — than at the South. I found contempt more bitter, opposition more active, detraction more relentless, prejudice more stubborn, and apathy more frozen, than among slaveowners themselves."

He delivered his lectures in Philadelphia, where he was the guest of James and Lucretia Mott, whose influence was to be largely responsible for his abandonment of religious orthodoxy. "If my mind has since become liberalized in any degree (and I think it has burst every sectarian trammel)," he wrote, "if theological dogmas which I once regarded as essential to Christianity, I now repudiate as absurd and pernicious, — I am largely indebted to them for the changes." When he reached Massachusetts he decided that his native Newburyport should be the first to

hear his message. But he had reckoned without Mr. [Francis] Todd, whose influence was sufficiently great to have the trustees of the Presbyterian Church intervene when the minister offered Garrison the use of the church auditorium. The pastor of the Second Congregational Church came to the rescue and he was able to deliver his first lecture. Then again Todd intervened. Garrison made no further attempt to enlighten his native town, and left for Boston.

☆ 2 ☆

In Boston Garrison took lodgings as usual at Parson Collier's, and then called on the Reverend Lyman Beecher, hoping to enlist his moral support. Dr. Beecher, however, was not the man to identify himself with an unpopular cause. ("True wisdom," he said in one of his Seminary lectures, "consists in advocating a cause only so far as the community will sustain the reformer.") He now excused himself, saying: "I have too many irons in the fire already."

"Then," replied the young zealot, "you had better let them all burn than to neglect your duty to the slave."

Dr. Beecher did not think so. "Your zeal," he said, "is commendable, but you are misguided. If you will give up your fanatical notions and be guided by us [the clergy] we will make you the Wilberforce of America."

When not looking for a hall in which to deliver his message Garrison wrote letters to public men imploring them to declare themselves for immediate emancipation. He wrote to [William Ellery] Channing, to [Daniel] Webster and to several others, but received no reply. His search for a meeting place likewise remained unrewarded. Finally he inserted the following advertisement in the Boston *Courier:*

WANTED — For three evenings, a Hall or meetinghouse (the latter would be preferred), in which to vindicate the rights of TWO MILLIONS of American citizens who are

---

From pages 42–64 in *Two Friends of Man* by Ralph Korngold, published by Little, Brown & Co., 1950. Reprinted by special permission of Mrs. Ralph Korngold.

now groaning in servile chains in this boasted land of liberty; and also to propose just, benevolent, and constitutional measures for their relief. As the addresses will be gratuitous, and as the cause is of public benefit, I cannot consent to remunerate any society for the use of its building. If this application fails, I propose to address the citizens of Boston in the open air, on the Common.

Wm. Lloyd Garrison

No. 30, Federal Street, Oct. 11, 1830

The advertisement attracted the attention of sexagenarian Abner Kneeland, founder of the First Society of Free Enquirers. Kneeland was an atheist, and his society made war on religion. A few years later he was to be indicted for having published in his paper, the Boston *Enquirer*, a "scandalous, injurious, obscene, blasphemous and profane libel of and concerning God." His society was the lessee of Julian Hall, on the northwest corner of Milk and Congress Streets. He had no sooner read Garrison's advertisement than he offered him the use of the hall.

It was only a couple of years since Garrison had written about "the depravity and wickedness of those . . . who reject the gospel of Jesus Christ," but he now saw no reason why he should "reject the co-operation of those who . . . make no pretense to evangelical piety" when "the religious portion of the community are indifferent to the cries of suffering humanity."

William Lloyd Garrison, *celebrated abolitionist and editor of the* controversial Liberator. *"I will be as harsh as truth, and as uncompromising as justice," wrote Garrison in his manifesto in the first issue of the* Liberator. *On the subject of slavery, "I do not wish to think, or speak, or write, with moderation. . . . I am in earnest — I will not equivocate — I will not excuse — I will not retreat a single inch — AND I WILL BE HEARD." (Department of Special Collections, Wichita State University Library)*

☆ 3 ☆

The hall was filled. Dr. Beecher and other notables were present. Three men were there who were destined to become Garrison's staunch friends and supporters. They had come together and were seated side by side. The eldest was Samuel J. May, a Unitarian minister from Brooklyn, Connecticut, who was visiting his father, Colonel Joseph May, a prosperous Bos-

ton merchant. His friends called him "God's chore boy," for while far less combative than Garrison, he was just as ready to rush to the succor of anyone in need of assistance. Sitting beside him was his brother-in-law, Bronson Alcott, whose daughter Louisa May Alcott was to become a popular novelist. He was a philosopher and a mystic who combined great profundity with great extravagance of thought. The Sage of Concord has called him "the most refined and the most advanced soul we have ever had in New England," and "the most remarkable and the highest genius of his time." Along with gems of thought worthy of Aristotle, Alcott propounded such absurdities as that the atmosphere surrounding the earth was the accumulated exhalation of mankind, and that the weather was fair or foul depending on whether good or evil thought predominated! He would say in all seriousness to a friend: "Men must have behaved well today to have such fine sunshine." The third man was May's cousin, Samuel E. Sewall, a Boston attorney and a direct descendant of the judge of that name who a hundred and thirty years before had written the first antislavery pamphlet in America.

When the speaker had finished, May turned to his two companions and said: "That is a providential man; he is a prophet; he will shake our nation to its center, but he will shake slavery out of it. We ought to know him, we ought to help him. Come, let us go and give him our hands." When they had done so, May said to the young lecturer: "Mr. Garrison, I am not sure that I can endorse all you have said this evening. Much of it requires careful consideration. But I am prepared to embrace you. I am sure you are called to a great work, and I mean to help you."

Alcott suggested that all come home with him. They accepted and remained in animated conversation until after midnight. Garrison told his new friends of his plan to launch an antislavery paper in Boston, which he intended to call the *Liberator*. Sewall thought the name too provoking and suggested the *Safety Lamp*. Garrison would not hear of it. "Provoking!" That was exactly what he meant it to be. Slavery in the United States had now lasted over two hundred years. During nearly three quarters of that time the Quakers had agitated against it in their inoffensive, conciliatory fashion. What had been accomplished? There were now more than four times as many slaves as when they began their propaganda. New Slave States had been added to the Union. The slave laws were more oppressive than ever. He meant to agitate. He meant to call hard names. He meant to make it

impossible for any man to confess without shame that he was the owner of slaves. He was prepared for any sacrifice: "A few white victims must be sacrificed to open the eyes of this nation and show the tyranny of our laws. I expect and am willing to be persecuted, imprisoned and bound for advocating African rights; and I should deserve to be a slave myself if I shrunk from that duty or danger."

May was so fascinated by the young man's enthusiasm that the following morning, immediately after breakfast, he called on him at his boardinghouse and remained until two in the afternoon. Before the week was over he and Sewall had made arrangements for Garrison to repeat his lectures at Athenaeum Hall.

The Sunday following, May occupied the pulpit at "Church Green," in Summer Street. So filled was he with Garrison's message that he interpolated his sermon with frequent references to slavery and finished with an appeal to the congregation to help abolish the institution before it destroyed the Republic. He was aware of the mounting uneasiness among his listeners, and having pronounced the benediction, said: "Every one present must be conscious that the closing remarks of my sermon have caused an unusual emotion throughout the church. I am glad. . . . I have been prompted to speak thus by the words I have heard during the past week from a young man hitherto unknown, but who is, I believe, called of God to do a greater work for the good of our country than has been done by any one since the Revolution. I mean William Lloyd Garrison. He is going to repeat his lectures the coming week. I advise, I exhort, I entreat — would that I could compel! — you to go and hear him."

The following day May's father, Colonel Joseph May, was walking down State Street when a friend rushed up to him and impulsively grasped his hand.

"Colonel," he said, "you have my sympathy. I cannot tell you how much I pity you."

The old man looked at him astounded. "Sympathy? Pity? For what?"

The other appeared embarrassed. "Well," he said,

"I hear your son went mad at 'Church Green' yesterday."

☆ 4 ☆

In a small chamber, friendless and unseen,
    Toiled o'er his types one poor, unlearned young
      man;
The place was dark, unfurnitured and mean,
    Yet there the freedom of a race began.

Help came but slowly; surely, no man yet
    Put lever to the heavy world with less;
What need of help? He knew how types were set,
    He had a dauntless spirit and a press.

James Russell Lowell, the author of these lines, has availed himself of the usual poetic license. The room on the third floor of Merchants' Hall, in Boston, where on January 1, 1831, Garrison launched the *Liberator,* was not particularly small, being eighteen feet square, and not one, but two unlearned young men "toiled over the types," for he and Isaac Knapp of Newburyport had joined forces. Later they were aided by a Negro apprentice. The windows were grimy and spattered with printer's ink, as were the dingy walls. There was a press, picked up at a bargain, a couple of composing stands with worn secondhand type, a few chairs and a long table covered with exchanges, at which the editor attended to his correspondence. In a corner of the room was a mattress on which the two friends slept, for they could not afford the luxury of a boardinghouse. They lived on bread, milk and a little fruit, sharing the first two with a cat who, when Garrison sat down to write, would jump on the table and rub her fur caressingly against his bald forehead. Although the paper advocated temperance as well as abolition, Knapp found it impossible to wean himself from his craving for strong drink, a weakness which eventually led to his undoing.

In the literature of social protest few lines are more stirring than the following paragraph from Garrison's salutatory to the public in the first number of the *Liberator:*

"I am aware that many object to the severity of my language; but is there not cause for severity? I *will* be as harsh as truth, and as uncompromising as justice. On this subject, I do not wish to think, or speak, or write, with moderation. No! No! Tell a man whose house is on fire to give a moderate alarm; tell him to moderately rescue his wife from the hands of the ravisher; tell the mother to gradually extricate her babe from the fire into which it has fallen — but urge me not to use moderation in a cause like the present. I am in earnest — I will not equivocate — I will not excuse — I will not retreat a single inch — AND I WILL BE HEARD."

The last statement proved prophetic. The *Liberator* never paid expenses, never had over three thousand subscribers, but its message became known from coast to coast and across the Atlantic. The paper had a fertilizing influence that caused the sprouting of various forms of opposition to slavery, of most of which Garrison disapproved, but for all of which he was directly or indirectly responsible. There were to be Abolitionists who formed political parties and others who abstained from voting; those who were orthodox churchmen and those who set out to destroy organized religion; those who believed in nonresistance and those who advocated armed intervention; those who wished to arouse the slaves to revolt and those who opposed this; those determined to remain within constitutional limits and those who scoffed at the Constitution. The Liberty Party, the Free-Soil Movement, the Republican Party — all, to a greater extent than their leaders cared to acknowledge, owed their existence to Garrison. He was the sower who went forth to sow and whose seed fell onto fertile ground, blossoming forth in a variety of shapes. He was the spiritual father of innumerable children, most of whom disowned him. He shamed a reluctant nation into doing what it did not wish to do, and the nation has never forgiven him. In 1853, [abolitionist] Wendell Phillips said:

"The community has come to hate its reproving Nathan so bitterly, that even those whom the relenting part of it is beginning to regard as standard-bearers of the antislavery host think it unwise to avow any connection or sympathy with him. I refer to some of the leaders of the political movement against slavery. . . . They are willing to confess privately, that our movement produced theirs, and that its continued existence is the very breath of their life. But, at the same time, they would fain walk on the road without being soiled by too close contact with the rough pioneers who threw it up. . . . If you tell me that they cherished all these principles in their own breasts before Mr. Garrison appeared, I can only say, if the antislavery movement did not give them their ideas, it surely gave them the courage to utter them."

☆ 5 ☆

"Why so hot my little man?" wrote Ralph Waldo Emerson; and at another time: "There is a sublime prudence which, believing in a vast future, sure of more to come than is yet seen, postpones always the present hour to the whole life." But now see Emerson, returning from Boston in 1850, a copy of the [new] Fugitive Slave Law in his pocket, writing in his Journal: "This filthy enactment was made in the nineteenth century — I will not obey it — by God!" What has become of the "sublime prudence"? To refuse to obey the Fugitive Slave Law meant to incur a thousand dollar fine and be liable to pay another thousand to the claimant of the fugitive, not to speak of a possible six months in jail. Was it that Emerson had come to agree with Whittier that a civilized man could no more obey the Fugitive Slave Law, even when a Lincoln set out to enforce it, than he could become a cannibal?

Garrison never worried about keeping cool. He

agreed with Burke that "To speak of atrocious crimes in mild language is treason to virtue," with Luther that "Those things that are softly dealt with, in a corrupt age, give people but little concern, and are presently forgotten." Samuel J. May once said to him: "O, my friend, do try to moderate your indignation, and keep more cool; why, you are all on fire." His friend replied: "Brother May, I have need to be *all on fire,* for I have mountains of ice about me to melt."

Was the method effective? That it made it well-nigh impossible to spread the gospel of emancipation in the South admits of no doubt. But except among Southern Quakers such propaganda had borne no fruit. Indeed, while at one time the slaveholders had been willing to concede that slavery was an evil and a curse, foisted upon the South by the mother country, after years of propaganda by Quakers and others they had arrived at the conclusion that it was the best of all possible labor systems, far superior to that prevailing in the North. This change of outlook was clearly perceptible at the time of the Missouri Compromise, long before the appearance of the *Liberator.* It was due to the fact that the invention of the cotton gin had made slavery far more profitable.

When Garrison began publication of his paper nearly all opposition to slavery had disappeared, North as well as South. Albert Bushnell Hart, in a profound study of the subject, wrote: "When Jackson became President in 1829, anti-slavery seemed, after fifty years of effort, to have spent its force. The voice of the churches was no longer heard in protest; the abolitionist societies were dying out; there was hardly an abolitionist militant in the field. . . . In Congress there was only one antislavery man and his efforts were without avail." But in 1839 the managers of the Massachusetts Anti-Slavery Society were able to declare: "Ten years ago a solitary individual stood up as the advocate of immediate and unconditional emancipation. Now, that individual sees about him hundreds of thousands of persons, of both sexes, members of every sect and party, from the most elevated to the humblest rank of life. In 1829 not an Anti-Slavery Society of a genuine stamp was in existence. In 1839 there are nearly two thousand such societies swarming and multiplying in all parts of the free States. In 1829 there was but one Anti-Slavery periodical in the land. In 1839 there are fourteen. In 1829 there was scarcely a newspaper of any religious or political party which was willing to disturb the 'delicate' question of slavery. In 1839 there are multitudes of journals that either openly advocate the doctrine of immediate and unconditional emancipation, or permit its free discussion in their columns. Then scarcely a church made slaveholding a bar to communion. Now, multitudes refuse to hear a slaveholder preach, or to recognize one as a brother. Then, no one petitioned Congress to abolish slavery in the District of Columbia. Now, in one day, a single member of the House of Representatives (John Quincy Adams) has presented one hundred and seventy-six such petitions in detail; while no less than seven hundred thousand persons have memorialized Congress on that and kindred subjects."

Garrison was to say: "In seizing the trump of God, I had indeed to blow a 'jarring blast' — but it was necessary to wake up a nation then slumbering in the lap of moral death. . . . What else but the *Liberator* primarily, (and of course instrumentally,) has effected this change? Greater success than I have had, no man could reasonably desire, or humbly expect."

When in 1837 Dr. William Ellery Channing complimented James G. Birney on the reasonableness and moderation of his antislavery paper, in contrast with the *Liberator,* which he accused of being "blemished by a spirit of intolerance, sweeping censure and rash, injurious judgment," the former Kentucky slaveholder and Solicitor General of Alabama replied: "Our country was asleep, whilst slavery was preparing to pour its 'leprous distilment' into her ears. So deep was becoming her sleep that nothing but a rude and almost ruffian-like shake could rouse her to a contemplation of her danger. If she is saved, it is because she has been thus treated." He left no

doubt about whom he had in mind when he said on another occasion: "My anti-slavery trumpet would never have roused the country — Garrison alone could do it."

Another former Kentucky slaveholder, the famous Cassius Marcellus Clay, who while a student at Yale heard Garrison speak and became a convert, wrote: "There is one saying of his [Garrison's] traducers, and the traducers of those who act with him, . . . that 'they have set back the cause of emancipation by agitation'! Nothing is more false. The cause of emancipation advances only with agitation: let that cease and despotism is complete."

☆ 6 ☆

Garrison did not expect to convert the slaveholders. He considered such an attempt a waste of time. In 1837 he wrote to Elizabeth Pease: "I have relinquished the expectation that they [the slaveholders] will ever, by mere moral suasion, consent to emancipate their victims." In 1840 he wrote to Elizabeth's brother Joseph: "There is not any instance recorded either in sacred or profane history, in which the oppressors and enslavers of mankind, except in individual cases, have been induced, by mere moral suasion, to surrender their despotic power, and let the oppressed go free; but in nearly every instance, from the time that Pharaoh and his hosts were drowned in the Red Sea, down to the present day, they have persisted in their evil course until sudden destruction came upon them, or they were compelled to surrender their ill-gotten power in some other manner."

Others were of the same opinion. Cassius M. Clay wrote: "The slaveholders have just as much intention of yielding up their slaves as the sum of the kings of the earth have of laying down, for the benefit of the people, their sceptres." In August, 1855, Abraham Lincoln was to write to George Robertson of Kentucky that the Tsar of Russia would abdicate and free his serfs sooner than American slaveholders would voluntarily give up their slaves. "Experience has demonstrated, I think, that there is no peaceful extinction of slavery in prospect for us."

Garrison feared, like Lincoln, that slavery would never be abolished except by force of arms, but he believed there was one other method worth trying. When Jesus of Nazareth called the Pharisees "fools," "hypocrites," "devourers of widows' houses," "serpents," "generation of vipers" — and asked, "How can ye escape the damnation of hell?" — he was obviously not using moral *suasion,* but moral *pressure.* This was the method Garrison had decided to adopt. Shortly after he founded the *Liberator,* he told Samuel J. May: "Until the term 'slaveholder' sends as deep a feeling of horror to the hearts of those who hear it applied to any one as the term, 'robber,' 'pirate,' 'murderer' do, we must use and multiply epithets when condemning the sins of him who is guilty of 'the sum of all villainies.'" He hoped to arouse such a feeling of abhorrence and storm of disapproval in the North (and in fact throughout the civilized world) that the South would be forced to yield. That the method offered some hope of success was acknowledged by General Duff Green, who wrote: "We believe that we have most to fear from the organized action upon the conscience and fears of the slaveholders themselves. . . . It is only by alarming the consciences of the weak and feeble, and diffusing among our own people a morbid sensibility on the question of slavery, that the abolitionists can accomplish their object."

The method did not succeed any more than it had succeeded in Christ's time; but who will say that it was not worth trying? Nor can it be said that it produced no results. If Garrison failed to shame and intimidate the South, he yet succeeded in arousing such an aversion to, and fear of, slavery in the North that war seemed preferable to allowing it to spread. Archibald H. Grimké has well said: "The public sentiment which Lincoln obeyed, [Garrison and] Phillips created."

☆ 7 ☆

About a year before the appearance of the *Liberator,* David Walker, a Boston Negro who made a living as an old-clothes man, published a pamphlet entitled *Walker's Appeal.* He boldly called upon the slaves to revolt. "If you commence," he wrote, "make sure work — do not trifle, for they will not trifle with you — they want us for their slaves, and think nothing of murdering us in order to subject us to that wretched condition — therefore, if there is an attempt made by us, kill or be killed." There were three editions of the pamphlet, copies of which found their way into the Slave States. The consternation these produced in the South bordered on the ridiculous and was eloquent testimony of the fear that lurked under the South's brave exterior. Governors sent special messages to Legislatures. Repressive laws were hastily passed. Incoming ships and trains were searched. Colored seamen were taken from Northern ships entering Southern ports and imprisoned. "How much is it to be regretted," declared *Niles' Weekly Register,* "that a negro dealer in old clothes, should thus excite two states to legislative action." Walker, however, died in June, 1830, and the South breathed a sigh of relief.

Then, in January, 1831, again in the city of Boston, appeared the *Liberator,* and in an early issue of the paper a poem from the editor's pen warning of the danger of a slave uprising if emancipation were delayed. One stanza read:

> Woe if it come with storm, and blood, and fire,
> When midnight darkness veils the earth and sky!
> Woe to the innocent babe — the guilty sire —
> Mother and daughter — friends of kindred tie!
> *Stranger and citizen alike shall die!*
> Red-handed slaughter his revenge shall feed,
> And Havoc yell his ominous death-cry;
> And wild Despair in vain for mercy plead —
> While Hell itself shall shrink, and sicken at the
> deed!

The slave uprising in the French colony of San Domingo towards the close of the eighteenth century proved there were reasons for the warning. Garrison, however, did not advise the slaves to revolt. He had condemned *Walker's Appeal* in the *Genius,* and the last stanza of his poem read:

Not by the sword shall your deliverance be;
  Not by the shedding of your masters' blood,
Not by rebellion — or foul treachery,
  Upspringing suddenly, like swelling flood:
Revenge and rapine ne'er did bring forth good.
  God's *time is best!* — nor will it long delay:
Even now your barren cause begins to bud,
  And glorious shall the fruit be! — Watch and
    pray,
For, lo! the kindling dawn, that ushers in the day!

Shortly after the appearance of this poem, on August 22, 1831, there took place in Southampton County, Virginia, the most sanguinary slave uprising in the annals of American slavery. A Negro mystic named Nat Turner, a slave belonging to a small planter, gathered a band of followers variously estimated at from forty to two hundred, and after killing his master and the latter's family, moved from plantation to plantation, slaughtering between fifty and sixty persons, men, women and children. Bands of white men and the state militia finally subdued the rebels, but not without committing outrages upon innocent Negroes surpassing in cruelty anything of which Turner had been guilty. Finally, the Negro leader and nineteen of his followers were hanged. The uprising was responsible for a sensational debate in the Virginia Legislature during which slavery was condemned in language as violent as any Garrison had ever used. For a while indeed it seemed that what years of propaganda by the Quakers had failed to accomplish would come as a result of Turner's bloodletting. Governor John Floyd of Virginia noted in his diary: "Before I leave this Government I will have contrived to have a law passed gradually abolishing slavery in this state."

But the people and the authorities eventually got over their fright and began looking about for a scapegoat. Walker was read, but there was Garrison and his paper. Turner and his confederates had denied that they had read either *Walker's Appeal* or the *Liberator,* and no evidence to the contrary was introduced; but Governor Floyd wrote to Governor James Hamilton of South Carolina that black preachers had read from the pulpit the inflammatory writings of Walker and Garrison, which may or may not have been true. Anyway, Harrison Gray Otis, Mayor of Boston, received letters from the Governors of Virginia and Georgia "severally remonstrating against an incendiary newspaper published in Boston, and, as they alleged, thrown broadcast among their plantations, inciting to insurrection and its horrid results."

Mayor Otis was puzzled. Although the *Liberator* had now been published in Boston for nearly a year, he had never seen a copy or even heard of the paper's existence. "It appeared on enquiry," he wrote, "that no member of the city government, nor any person of my acquaintance, had ever heard of the publication. Some time afterward, it was reported to me by the city officers that they had ferreted out the paper and its editor; that his office was an obscure hole, his only visible auxiliary a negro boy, and his supporters a very few insignificant persons of all colors. This information, with the consent of the aldermen, I communicated to the above-named governors, with an assurance of my belief that the new fanaticism had not made, nor was likely to make, proselytes among the respectable classes of our people. In this, however, I was mistaken."

Neither the Mayor of Boston nor the Governor of Massachusetts felt he possessed the power to stop publication of the *Liberator,* though both regretted that shortcoming in the law. The South was indignant. The Columbia (South Carolina) *Telescope* believed the matter called for armed intervention. "They [the people of Massachusetts] permit a battery to be erected upon their territory, which fires upon us, and we should be justified in invading that territory to silence their guns," the editor declared. A Vigilance Committee in Columbia offered a reward of fifteen hundred dollars for the arrest and conviction of any person "distributing or circulating the *Liberator* or any other publication of a seditious nature." Georgetown, District of Columbia, passed a law forbidding any colored person to take the *Liberator* from the post-office on pain of twenty dollars' fine and thirty days' imprisonment. In Raleigh, North Carolina, the grand jury found a true bill against Garrison and Knapp in the hope of extraditing them. A correspondent in the *Washington National Intelligence* proposed that the President of the United States or the Governor of Virginia demand Garrison's extradition, and in case of refusal by the Governor of Massachusetts "the people of the South offer an adequate reward to any person who will deliver him dead or alive, into the hands of the authorities of any State South of the Potomac." He did not have long to wait. On November 30, 1831, the Senate and the House of Representatives of Georgia appropriated five thousand dollars to be paid by the Governor "to any person or persons who shall arrest, bring to trial and prosecute to conviction, under the laws of the State, the editor or publisher of a certain paper called the *Liberator,* published in the town of Boston and State of Massachusetts."

Garrison was not in the least intimidated and wrote defiantly: "A price upon the head of a citizen of Massachusetts — for what? For daring to give his opinion of the moral aspect of slavery! . . . Know this, ye Senatorial Patrons of kidnappers! that we despise your threats as much as we deplore your infatuation; nay, more — know that a hundred men stand ready to fill our place as soon as it is made vacant by violence."

☆ 8 ☆

On his last visit to the United States, General Lafayette expressed his astonishment at the increase in racial prejudice. He recalled that in Washington's army, white and black had fought side by side and had messed together in harmony. Now, however, in the Free as well as in the Slave States, free Negroes were despised, persecuted, deprived of most of the prerogatives of the free man, permitted to earn a living only at the most menial and ill-paid employments.

A glance at some of the laws governing the free people of color leaves no doubt concerning the tenuous nature of the freedom they enjoyed. In Maryland a Justice of the Peace could order a free Negro's ears cropped for striking a white man even in self-defense. A free Negro entering that State incurred a penalty of fifty dollars for every week spent within its borders, and if unable to pay was sold into slavery. In Georgia the penalty for teaching a free Negro to read or write was five hundred dollars if the offender was white, if colored he was fined and flogged at the discretion of the court. In Virginia and South Carolina any Justice of the Peace could disband a school where free Negroes or their offspring were taught to read or write, fine the teacher five hundred dollars and have twenty lashes administered to each pupil. In Louisiana a fine of like amount awaited the zealous Christian who taught a free Negro in Sunday School. In Mississippi and the District of Columbia a Negro unable to prove his legal right to freedom could be sold into slavery. In South Carolina a Negro who "entertained" a runaway slave by giving him as much as a crust of bread was fined fifty dollars, and if unable to pay was sold. In several Slave States free Negroes were not permitted to assemble for religious purposes unless white people were present, and they were forbidden to preach. In Ohio a white man who hired a Negro or mulatto even for a day made himself liable for his future support. In the Free States, Negro children could not attend public school and little or no provision was made for their instruction. In several Free and of course in all the Slave States, free people of color were denied the right of suffrage.

Custom solidified this edifice of injustice. It made it well-nigh impossible for an artisan, mechanic or shopkeeper to employ a colored apprentice. In the North as well as in the South, Negroes were required to travel in the steerage of a boat or on the outside of a stagecoach, when they were not barred altogether. When a convention of colored people in Philadelphia made a brave attempt to establish a manual labor school for Negroes in New Haven, Connecticut, the Mayor called a mass meeting of the citizens, and such a hue and cry arose that the plan had to be abandoned. When Noyes Academy, in Canaan, New Hampshire, admitted a few colored students, three hundred citizens with a hundred yoke of oxen dragged the building from its foundation and deposited it outside the town. In church, Negroes had to sit in separate pews — which in the Baptist Church at Hartford, Connecticut, were boarded up and provided with peepholes. When in Houghton, Massachusetts, a colored man acquired a white man's pew, the church authorities had the floor removed in that part of the edifice. . . .

☆ 9 ☆

Garrison championed the free people of color as fervently as the slaves. "This then is my consolation," he wrote on one occasion: "if I cannot do much in this quarter towards abolishing slavery, I may be able to elevate our free colored population in the scale of society." Speaking before a colored convention in Philadelphia he said with feeling: "I never rise to address a colored audience without feeling ashamed of my color; ashamed of being identified with a race of men who have done you so much injustice and yet retain so large a portion of your brethren in servitude."

No matter how pressing his work, he would lay it aside when invited to address a colored audience. He did not flatter his listeners, but urged them to be worthy of liberty, to be temperate, industrious and to surpass the white man in virtue, which, he assured them,

was no difficult task. They must not resort to violence, but should incessantly petition to be permitted to vote, to send their children to public school and to exercise every other right of the freeman. "If your petition is denied seven times, send it seven times seven."

His influence was great among them. Once in Boston, when he had addressed them on temperance, they immediately formed a temperance society, which within a few days counted one hundred and fifty members. "Such acts as these, brethren, give me strength and boldness in your cause," he assured them. Henry E. Benson, in a letter to Isaac Knapp, described a scene that took place in Providence, Rhode Island, after Garrison had addressed a colored audience. "After the meeting," he wrote, "the poor creatures wept and sobbed like children — they gathered round him anxious to express their gratitude for what he had done for them, and tell him how well they loved him."

So persistent was he in their defense that some believed him to be colored, and when he advocated the repeal of the Massachusetts law against intermarriage, the rumor spread that he meant to marry a Negress. No resentment at the rumor is noticeable in this mild denial he published in the *Liberator:* "We declare that our heart is neither affected *by,* nor pledged *to,* any lady, black or white, bond or free."

☆ 10 ☆

If "the style is the man," then one might have expected Garrison in his maturity to have been a scowling, brusque, bitter, opinionated individual. Such in fact was the mental image formed by many. The reality confounded Buffon's maxim. Josiah Copley, editor of a religious paper in Pittsburgh, Pennsylvania, happening to be in Boston in 1832, called on Garrison after some hesitation. "I never was more astonished," he wrote. "All my preconceptions were at fault. My ideal of the man was that of a stout, rugged, dark-visaged desperado — something like we picture a pirate. He was a quiet, gentle and I might say handsome man — a gentleman indeed, in every sense of the word."

William H. Herndon, Lincoln's law partner, who visited Garrison in the latter's old age, wrote: "I had imagined him a shriveled, cold, selfish, haughty man, one who was weak and fanatically blind to the charities and equities of life, at once whining and insulting, mean and miserable, but I was pleasantly disappointed. I found him warm, generous, approachable, communicative; he has some mirth, some wit, and a deep abiding faith in coming universal charity. I was better and more warmly received by him than by any man in Boston."

Harriet Martineau, famous British authoress, who met Garrison in 1835, declared: "His aspect put to flight in an instant what prejudices his slanderers had raised in me. I was wholly taken by surprise. It was a countenance glowing with health and wholly expressive of purity, animation and gentleness. I did not now wonder at the citizen who, seeing a print of Garrison at a shop window without a name to it, went in and bought it and framed it as the most saintlike of countenances. The end of the story is, that when the citizen found whose portrait he had been hanging in his parlor, he took the print out of the frame and huddled it away."

The preponderance of opinion is that his conversation was the very opposite of his writing — mild, tolerant, disarming. Miss Martineau wrote: "Garrison had a good deal of a Quaker air; and his speech is deliberate like a Quaker's but gentle as a woman's. . . . Every conversation I had with him confirmed my opinion that sagacity is the most striking attribute of his conversation. It has none of the severity, the harshness, the bad taste of his writing; it is as gladsome as his countenance, and as gentle as his voice."

Harriet Beecher Stowe, who had confided to one of Garrison's sons that she was "dreadfully afraid" of his father, having made the editor's acquaint-ance, wrote to him: "You have a remarkable tact at conversation."

Ralph Waldo Emerson, who for a long time had been prejudiced against him, in 1844 wrote in his Journal: "The haters of Garrison have lived to rejoice in that grand world movement which, every age or two, casts out so masterly an agent for good. I cannot speak of the gentleman without respect."

☆ 11 ☆

In the first number of the *Liberator,* where appeared Garrison's immortal challenge to the slaveholders, one may read these lines from the editor's pen:

"An attempt has been made — it is still making — we regret to say, with considerable success — to inflame the minds of our working classes against the more opulent, and to persuade them that they are contemned and oppressed by a wealthy aristocracy. That public grievances exist, is unquestionably true; but they are not confined to any one class of society. Every profession is interested in their removal — the rich as well as the poor. It is in the highest degree criminal, therefore, to exasperate our mechanics to deeds of violence, or to array them under a party banner; for it is not true, that, at any time, they have been the objects of reproach. . . . We are the friends of reform; but that is not reform, which, in curing one evil, threatens to inflict a thousand others."

The reason for this outburst was an attempt by Seth Luther and others to organize a Working Men's Party and to form labor unions.

In the fifth number of the paper a correspondent pointed out to Garrison that he was wrong in trying to discourage labor's attempts to organize:

"Although you do not appear to have perceived it, I think there is a very intimate connexion between the interests of the working men's party and your own. . . . In the history of the origin of slavery is to be found the explanation of the evils we deplore and

Helen Eliza Benson Garrison not only shared her husband's commitment to reform but provided him with the refuge of a stable personal life. "By her unwearied attentions to my want, her sympathetic regards, her perfect equanimity of mind," Garrison said, "she is no trifling support to abolitionism, inasmuch as she lightens my labors, and enables me to find exquisite delight in the family circle, as an off-set to public adversity." (The Bettmann Archive)

seek to remove, as well as those you have attacked. . . . We seek to enlighten our brethren in the knowledge of their rights and duties. . . . It is a duty owed by working men to themselves and the world to exert their power through the ballot-box."

Garrison replied: "There is a prevalent opinion that . . . the poor and vulgar are taught to consider the opulent as their natural enemies. Where is the evidence that our wealthy citizens, as a body, are hostile to the interests of the laboring classes? It is not in their commercial enterprises, which whiten the ocean with canvas and give employment to a useful and numerous class of men. It is not found in the manufacturing establishments, which multiply labor and cheapen the necessities of the poor. It is not found in the luxuries of their tables, or the adornments of their dwellings, for which they must pay in proportion to their extravagance. . . . Perhaps it would be the truth to affirm, that mechanics are more inimical to the success of each other, more unjust toward each other, than the rich are toward them."

Yet in 1831, and for a long time thereafter, the hours of labor in New England factories were from five in the morning until seven-thirty in the evening — the working day being thirteen and one half hours. The two half hours allowed for breakfast and midday dinner were as tiring as any, since the workers had to hurry home, bolt their food and hasten back to the factory to escape a fine. In 1849 a report submitted to the American Medical Association by one of its members contained the statement that "there is not a State's prison, or house of correction in New England, where the hours of labor are so long, the hours for meals so short, or the ventilation so much neglected, as in all the cotton mills with which I am acquainted." In Boston Irish workmen were forced to labor fifteen hours a day, including Sunday. The death rate among them was so appalling that it was claimed the Irish lived on an average only fourteen years after reaching Boston. The Cochee Manufacturing Company required its workers to sign an agreement to "conform in all respects to the regulations which are now, or may be hereafter adopted . . . and to work for such wages as the company may see fit to pay." Workers were commonly required to buy at the company store and were usually in debt to their employers. If they attempted to leave their employment without paying what they owed they were imprisoned. In 1831 there were over fifteen hundred people imprisoned for debt in Boston alone, more than half of whom owed less than twenty dollars. It may therefore be said that a system of veritable peonage prevailed.

Strikes were frequent, but prior to 1860 not a single strike was won in Massachusetts, and not until

1874 did that State have any legal restriction on the number of hours adult wageworkers could be required to work. Employers in other parts of the country often gave working conditions in New England as an excuse for not improving labor's lot.

In view of all this, how could a man ready for almost any sacrifice for the sake of the Negro have remained indifferent to the lot of white wageworkers?

Garrison was an individualist. In his opinion, if a man was not a chattel, he was master of his own fate. If he was poor the fault was his. In the days of handicraft, poverty had indeed usually been the result of shiftlessness; but the poverty of the factory worker was more often due to the greed of the employer. The handicraftsman, having finished his apprenticeship, looked forward to being his own master. If he worked long hours he was buoyed up by the hope of getting ahead in the world. But later, only the exceptional man could hope to become a factory owner or even a foreman. Garrison, grown to maturity in a transition period, failed to grasp that the average wageworker's only hope of improving his lot was to unite with his fellows.

When Garrison wrote "Mechanics are more inimical to the success of each other, more unjust toward each other than the rich are towards them," he failed to comprehend that fear was at the bottom of this. Yankee workmen feared the competition of Irish immigrants and sometimes rioted against them. White workmen were hostile to Negroes for the same reason and opposed emancipation fearing it would result in hordes of Negroes from the South invading the North and lowering their standard of living, already sufficiently low. Southern leaders shrewdly exploited this fear. In 1843, Henry Clay wrote to the Reverend Calvin Colton, urging him to prepare a popular tract whose "great aim and object . . . should be to arouse the laboring classes of the free States against abolition. The slaves, being free, would be dispersed throughout the Union; they would enter into competition with the free laborer; with the American, the Irish, the German; reduce his wages; be confounded with him,

and affect his moral and social standing. And as the ultras go for both abolition and amalgamation, show that their object is to unite in marriage the laboring white man and the laboring black man, and to reduce the white laboring man to the despised and degraded condition of the black man."

The situation required shrewd and careful handling. Most of all it required a thorough understanding of the problem. Garrison lacked that understanding, and antagonized his natural allies. As a result American wageworkers remained indifferent, if not hostile, to Abolition. Some regarded it as a plot of the employers to lower wages. Others saw it as a scheme of professional philanthropists. The editor of the *Chronicle,* a Massachusetts weekly devoted to the interests of labor, wrote: "Philanthropists may speak of negro slavery, but it would be well first to emancipate the slaves at home. Let us not stretch our ears to catch the sound of the lash on the flesh of our oppressed black, while the oppressed in our midst are crying in thunder tones, and calling upon us for assistance."

QUESTIONS TO CONSIDER

1. Garrison always insisted that he was a Christian pacifist who expected to abolish slavery through nonviolent methods. How, then, can you explain his words in 1850 that in order to achieve black emancipation "a few white victims must be sacrificed to open the eyes of this nation and show the tyranny of our laws"?

2. When Samuel May spoke from the pulpit at "Church Green" in Boston in 1830, condemning slavery and exhorting the congregation to help destroy the institution before the institution destroyed the nation, his amazed audience thought he had lost his mind. What conclusions can you draw from this incident about the attitudes of northern whites toward African Americans, slavery, and abolitionists?

3. Analyze the effectiveness of Garrison's method of achieving the abolition of slavery. Would a cooler,

more moderate approach than his have made more headway, especially in the South? In what national context did Garrison propose his radical objective of immediate emancipation? How did that context affect his choice of tactics?

4. Compare the treatment of free blacks in the North and in the South. Was racial prejudice, like the institution of slavery, confined below the Mason-Dixon Line?

5. Southern proslavery apologists frequently pointed to the evils of what they called "wage slavery" among the northern working classes. They accused abolitionists of hypocrisy in ignoring the harsh "slavery" in their own backyards while condemning the South's more "benevolent" institution of black slavery. How valid were these accusations when leveled at Garrison?

18

Henry Clay, the American System, and the Sectional Controversy

STEPHEN B. OATES

This selection presents a third view of the Jacksonian era, from the perspective of a man who fought against both Andrew Jackson and the abolitionists, particularly the political wing of the movement. Indeed, Henry Clay was Jackson's arch rival on the political battleground of the 1830s, which saw a major new party, the Whigs, organize under the leadership of Clay, John C. Calhoun, and Daniel Webster. A coalition of Jackson haters, the Whigs favored an active federal role in stimulating economic and industrial growth (the Jacksonians, by contrast, preferred a policy of laissez faire, or minimal government interference in economic affairs). On the platform, Whig campaigners such as young Abraham Lincoln of Illinois championed the Whig principles of national order and unity and called for a strong federal government with responsibility to provide a prosperous, stable economy that allowed everyone an opportunity to get ahead. Unlike Jackson, the Whigs favored internal improvements — roads, railroads, and canals — financed by the federal government, federal subsidies to help the states build their own canals and turnpikes, and state banks to ensure financial growth and stability. Lincoln summed up the Whig creed when he said, "The legitimate object of government is 'to do for the people what needs to be done, but which they can not, by individual effort, do at all, or do so well, for themselves.'"

Henry Clay, whom Lincoln idolized, was the most glamorous of the three Whig leaders, all of whom served in the Senate. His nickname, "Prince Hal," fit him to the dot. Charming, debonair, arrogant, and exceedingly ambitious, Clay considered himself the best politician in the land and viewed the presidency as his almost by divine right. He tried five times to reach the White House but never made it, to his bafflement and despair. As historian Holman Hamilton has said, Clay was "one of the most spectacular victims of what became an American tradition." Hamilton explains: "From Clay's day well into the 20th century, only one sitting senator was elected president of the United States, and not a single chief executive was chosen wholly because of an outstanding congressional career." Had Clay had an outstanding military career, or any military career at all, he would probably have won the White House.

Henry Clay's was a household name in his day, yet few Americans in the 1990s would be able to state with precision who he was or what he did beyond negotiating certain compromises over slavery. In point of fact, Clay's illustrious political career spanned the entire first half of the nineteenth century, and he left an indelible mark on the America of those years. He coined the term self-made man to describe an ambitious individual such as himself — the ultimate go-ahead American. And his rise to national prominence was meteoric. He became a United States senator at age twenty-nine, speaker of the House of Representatives at thirty-three. Within a few years, "Harry of the West," another of his nicknames, was one of the most powerful men in Washington, a nationalist with a sweeping vision of a powerful, productive, and unified America. He helped lead America into the ill-starred War of 1812 with England and went on to serve for twenty years in the Senate. At a time when political debates were major theater, Clay was one of America's greatest orators — people flocked to Washington just to watch him perform.

As the selection that follows shows, Clay did indeed help forge several significant compromises to save the Union. But his great plan for national growth and unity — the celebrated American System — never became a reality in his day because of the inflammable slavery issue. An antislavery slaveholder like Jefferson, his hero, Clay genuinely hated the institution and searched desperately and in vain for some way to solve the slavery problem. His solution, gradual emancipation and the voluntary repatriation of free blacks to Africa, resurrected Jefferson's old scheme and brought Clay into a dramatic collision with the abolitionists, black and white alike. As we shall see, Clay's solution proved unworkable. At one point, gazing into the future, he saw the country in flames, torn apart by civil war, and he begged his countrymen to find some way to avert such a disaster.

Reading the life of Henry Clay will introduce you to some of the most important themes, events, and historical figures in the first fifty years of the new century. This portrait attempts to personalize the historical record, to thrust a face and a personality into the vortex of events. It focuses on the human side of the past, showing how the interaction of individuals and events dictates the course of history.

GLOSSARY

ALABAMA LETTERS   Clay's public statements during the 1844 presidential canvass favoring Texas annexation so long as it did not provoke a war with Mexico.

AMERICAN COLONIZATION SOCIETY   Private philanthropic organization, cofounded by Clay, that sought financial aid from governments and citizens alike for the voluntary repatriation of free blacks to the African colony of Liberia.

AMERICAN SYSTEM   Economic program championed by Clay that called for a protective tariff, a national bank, and internal improvements.

ASHLAND   Clay's Kentucky plantation and his proudest possession.

COMPROMISE OF 1850   Warded off a powerful disunion movement over the issue of slavery in the territories. The compromise, the work of Clay and Stephen A. Douglas of Illinois, among others, admitted California as a free state, organized the territories of New Mexico and Utah without congressional conditions on slavery, outlawed the slave trade in the national capital, and created a stringent new fugitive slave law.

DOUGLASS, FREDERICK   A former slave and editor of a black newspaper in Rochester, New York, Douglass was one of the great leaders and orators of the abolitionist movement.

GREAT SOUTHERN REACTION   To counteract the abolitionist argument that slavery was a sin, southerners defended slavery as "a positive good."

LIBERTY PARTY   Antislavery third party that ran James G. Birney for the presidency in 1840 and again in 1844. The party advocated that the federal government abolish slavery in all areas under its jurisdiction — namely, Washington, D.C., and the territories — and that it outlaw the interstate slave trade.

MISSOURI COMPROMISE (FIRST)   Admitted Missouri as a slave state and Maine as a free state and drew an imaginary line that divided the rest of the Louisiana Purchase into slave and free territory.

MISSOURI COMPROMISE (SECOND)   Engineered by Clay, this "sleight-of-hand solution" allowed Missouri to retain a Negro exclusion clause in its constitution so long as the legislature pledged never to restrict persons who were or might become United States citizens.

NULLIFICATION   Doctrine formulated by John C. Calhoun that the states were supreme in the American confederation and that each state had the power to nullify within its borders any federal measure it disliked.

POLK, JAMES K.   Expansionist Democrat who became president in 1844 and led the country to war with Mexico in 1846.

SLAVE TRADE (INTERNATIONAL)   Outlawed by Congress in 1808.

WARHAWKS   Hotspurs such as Clay, mainly from the South and West, who advocated a second war with England. They got their wish in the War of 1812.

Had we attended one of his speeches in the United States Senate in the 1830s, we would have found the galleries crowded with people who had come out to enjoy the show. In his day, political oratory was a form of theater, and he excelled at it. Always elegantly dressed, he spoke with impeccable elocution and theatrical gestures, his gray-blue eyes glittering with amused contempt for the inferior mortals sitting around him. He was tall and slender, with a receding hairline, a long nose, and a mouth so wide that he could never learn to spit. Nicknamed "Prince Hal," he exuded a charm and physical magnetism that few could resist. In the galleries women would smile, bewitched, when he made a point with a graceful sweep of his arm, his head held high, his whole body moving to the rhythms of his voice. He was a master of the bon mot and the satiric jest, and he even used his snuff box to dramatic effect. As ambitious as he was arrogant, he was certain that his destiny was to become president of the United States and to forge the nation into a great world power.

When he spoke of his early years, Henry Clay spun a myth of himself as a poor, orphaned, uneducated "mill boy from the Slashes." Thus he wove his story into his mythic vision of America as a land of limitless opportunity where even the lowest-born had the right to rise, to go as far as his talent and toil would take him. In reality, Clay was the scion of tobacco planters of Tidewater Virginia. At the time he was born, on April 12, 1777, his preacher father owned twenty-one slaves and a four-hundred-acre homestead in an area in Hanover County called The Slashes. Henry's father died when he was four, leaving his mother to raise him and his four brothers and three sisters. The boy loved his mother deeply, would

An earlier version of this essay, entitled "Harry of the West," appeared in the October–November 1991 issue of *Timeline,* a publication of the Ohio Historical Society.

always think of her with warmth in his heart. His formal education was about average for children of his time, consisting of three years before the master of the neighborhood log school. Inspired by Patrick Henry, he developed a passion for public speaking and practiced it wherever he could, haranguing livestock in the barn or assemblies of trees in the forest.

In 1791 his mother married a kindly man named Henry Watkins, who moved the family to his home in Richmond. Taking a particular interest in young Henry, Watkins found him employment in a retail store and then in the clerk's office in the High Court Chancery. When the family migrated to Kentucky, Clay remained in Richmond, where he had fallen under the spell of the chancellor, a bald, erudite gentleman of the Enlightenment named George Wythe.

As it happened, Wythe had been Thomas Jefferson's mentor, had taught him law, the classics, and an adamant hatred of slavery. Like Wythe, Jefferson had denounced human bondage as a "blot" on Virginia, a "great political and moral evil" that should be gradually abolished. Now Clay too became Wythe's protégé; he too damned slavery as "the greatest of human evils" and embraced the "sacred cause" of gradual emancipation, turning to Jefferson's own *Notes on Virginia,* published in 1785, for a plan to bring that about. Jefferson called for the state of Virginia to free all its slaves who were born after the scheme was adopted; first they were to live with their parents as charges of the state, which was to provide for their education in the arts, the sciences, and the practical aspects of farming; they were to be freed at a prescribed age — eighteen for females, twenty-one for males — and then colonized outside Virginia so as to avoid race-mixing, a prospect that filled Jefferson with loathing. Jefferson hoped that the other slave states would follow Virginia's example and that bondage would ultimately disappear in America, thus consummating the promise of the Revolution.

It was a vain hope. In 1796 the Virginia legislature emphatically rejected a variation of Jefferson's plan; it did so because slavery was the cornerstone of

Henry Clay coined the term "self-made man" to describe ambitious gentlemen like himself. He created his own nirvana at Ashland, his plantation near Lexington. It featured immaculate grounds, tree-lined paths, and rolling bluegrass meadows where blooded cattle and horses grazed. Ashland was hardly nirvana for Clay's slaves, who resided in rude cabins not shown here and whose labor made it possible for him to pursue a political career. (Ohio Historical Society)

Virginia's entire way of life: it was a potent status symbol, a valuable labor system, and an indispensable means of race control in a white man's country. Even so, Wythe still hoped that somehow, someday, slavery could be removed from the commonwealth, and he passed that hope on to Clay, who echoed his mentor's impassioned rhetoric about the Rights of Man.

Under Wythe's influence, Clay had decided to become a lawyer. He studied one year with the attorney general of the commonwealth and at age twenty was admitted to the Virginia bar. By then he stood well over six feet, with a slender, loose-jointed frame, prematurely white hair, and a wide and winning smile. He could have remained in Richmond, where he had friends and connections. But he decided that the new state of Kentucky offered better opportunities for a

young lawyer on the rise. In late 1797 Clay turned up in Lexington, "the Athens of the West," owning only his clothes, the horse he was riding, and an ambition to get ahead that burned in him like a furnace.

No sooner had he arrived in Kentucky, a slave state, than he plunged into an abolition movement, aligning himself with a group of reformers who called for a new state constitution that would allow for general, gradual emancipation similar to Jefferson's plan. Just turned twenty-one, a member of the Lexington bar for only one month, Clay published in the *Kentucky Gazette* a ringing appeal to Kentuckians to rid themselves of the curse of slavery. "Can any humane man be happy and contented when he sees near thirty thousand of his fellow beings around him, deprived of all rights which make life desirable, transferred like cattle from the possession of one to another?" Borrowing an argument from Jefferson, Clay pointed out that blacks were not the only victims of bondage. "All America acknowledges the existence of slavery to be an evil, which while it deprives the slave of the best gift of heaven, in the end injures the master too, by laying waste his lands, enabling him to live indolently, and thus contracting all the vices generated by a state of idleness. If it be this enormous evil," said Clay, "the sooner we attempt its destruction the better."

But the vast majority of white Kentuckians, from wealthy planters to nonslaveholding farmers, objected to emancipation in any form, lest it result in racial violence and amalgamation, that bugaboo of white supremacists everywhere in the Republic. In 1799 Kentucky voters sent an overwhelming number of anti-emancipation delegates to a state constitutional convention, which went on to draft a new charter that incorporated the proslavery provisions of the old, thus smashing the hopes of Clay and the other reformers that Kentucky might lead the way in removing slavery from America.

Clay always insisted that this was one of his bitterest disappointments. Yet he considered himself a realist.

There was no point, he decided, in crusading for an unpopular cause, so he accepted the will of the majority and proceeded to blend into his Kentucky environment. In 1799, the same year Kentucky turned back the gradual-emancipation movement, Clay bought a slave, married the eighteen-year-old daughter of Lexington's most prosperous businessman and speculator, and started building what became a lucrative law practice.

Clay was living in the age of the go-ahead man, a time when an entire generation of white American males reached out and seized the future as if by divine right. Clay came to personify the acquisitive spirit of the era and even coined the term "self-made man" to describe an individual like himself — the ultimate go-ahead American. His rise to wealth and power was so meteoric that it earned him another of his nicknames: he was the Star of the West, a man who reflected perfectly the heady optimism of his young section.

By age twenty-eight, Clay had risen to the top of the legal profession in Kentucky and was serving in the state legislature as a Jeffersonian and a spokesman for the lawyer aristocracy centered in Lexington. Suave as he was, he could be touchy about his honor. When a Federalist adversary called him a liar, Clay challenged him to a duel with pistols at ten paces; both were wounded in the ensuing faceoff, which got them censured by the Kentucky legislature. The episode, however, scarcely hurt Clay in his spectacular rise to power. At age twenty-nine, he became a United States senator when the Kentucky legislature chose him to fill out the term of John Adair, who had resigned. One of Clay's first speeches was an impassioned denunciation of the international slave trade, whose atrocities appalled him. Later he called it "the most abominable traffic that ever disgraced the annals of the human race." No politician was happier than he when Congress, following President Jefferson's lead, outlawed the "infamous commerce" in 1808.

Back in Kentucky, Clay acquired a plantation near Lexington, named it Ashland, built a brick mansion on it, and bought additional slaves to work his fields

— all before he turned thirty. He could be seen at Olympian Springs, a fashionable resort near Lexington, where wealthy members of the master class met for mint juleps, billiards, and cards as well as medicinal baths. He soon ruled over an impressive personal empire comprising six hundred acres on the home plantation, a second farm, a house in Lexington, and additional land in Missouri.

Ashland was his proudest possession. Here he created his own nirvana, with immaculate grounds and tree-lined paths, flourishing fields of corn, hemp, and rye, and rolling bluegrass meadows, landscaped with clusters of trees like a park, where his blooded cattle and horses grazed. He kept buying slaves, too, rooting himself ever deeper into the very system he abhorred. Eventually he owned sixty of his "fellow human beings," a number that ranked him in the middle of the planter class, considerably behind Jefferson, who held some two hundred slaves when he left the presidency, and Washington, who owned more than three hundred when he died.

To justify being a slaveowner, Clay resorted to the Jeffersonian rationalization that slave labor was "a necessary evil" and that he was at least a "kind" master. There was, of course, no such thing as a kind slavemaster — the ownership of another human being was in itself a cruel act, a violent act. Over the years Clay did manumit several of his slaves who gave him faithful service. But like every other master, he knew that the whip made the slave system work, and his overseer used it to keep Clay's "people" in line. Perhaps that is why Kentucky slaves sang a work song about him:

> Heave away! Heave away!
> I'd rather co't a yeller gal,
> Dan work for Henry Clay
> Heave away, yaller gal, I want to go.

Actually, several of his slaves did leave, demonstrating with their feet what they thought of their treatment under Clay. At least one of his slaves, a woman named Black Lottie, sued for her freedom while the Clays were living in Washington, D.C. To forestall further defections, Clay dealt harshly with Black Lottie: he had her jailed while successfully contesting the suit, then dragged her back into a life she hated. When another house servant, a mulatto boy, took flight from Clay's wife, Clay offered a $50 reward for his capture and made a remark that betrayed his true feelings about kindness to slaves. "We have spoiled him," Clay said, "by good treatment."

At least one of Clay's slaves, a man who escaped to Canada, accused him in the abolitionist press of being heartless and cruel. The man claimed that Clay had once had him stripped and whipped with 150 lashes on his naked back for a trifling offense. Clay's overseer testified that the slave in question had been insolent and violent, which presumably, at least in the overseer's eyes, justified such brutal punishment.

Claiming to be a kind participant in a brutal system was not Clay's only contradiction when it came to slavery. While he damned the international slave trade in some of his most memorable utterances, he no longer condemned the *domestic* slave trade in Kentucky, despite its cruel breakup of families, its brutal coffles, rancid jails, and demeaning auctions. In private conversation Clay said that internal slave traders performed a service for Kentucky: they acted "as scavengers for the public" by "carrying off the vicious and incorrigible [slaves] to another country where new characters may be formed with better habit and propensities."

Meanwhile, Clay continued to prosper politically. Deciding to forego the Senate so that he could be "an immediate representative of the people," he ran for the national House of Representatives in 1811 and won easily. On his first day there, he was elected Speaker of the House, a remarkable achievement for a man of only thirty-three. He was now Harry of the West, the spokesman for his entire section, which, in addition to Kentucky, included the new free state of Ohio and the free territories of the Old Northwest. In

Congress, Clay articulated the West's militant nationalism. He led the Warhawks in clamoring for another war against England, boasting that the Kentucky militia alone could seize Upper Canada; he helped push President Madison into the War of 1812 and stood resolutely by him throughout the vicissitudes of that unpopular conflict.

By now, Clay had earned a reputation as a bon vivant with a love for his glass and a singular passion for cards. His love for gambling became legendary. In Washington he won $1,500 in a single night, only to lose $600 in another. In one marathon match, he won $40,000 from a friend, but because Clay was a gentleman, he settled for the man's $500 note. A few nights later, Clay lost $60,000 to the same friend, who returned the favor by asking only that Clay hand back the $500 note.

In 1814 Clay was one of three U.S. commissioners sent to Ghent, Belgium, to negotiate a peace treaty with Britain. He saved the Mississippi River for the United States when he blocked a move by fellow commissioner John Quincy Adams to give England free access to the Mississippi in exchange for fisheries in Newfoundland. Working by day and gambling and drinking by night, Clay seemed never to sleep. Such debauchery shocked Adams, a prudish man who always rose early and read five chapters of his Bible before breakfast. When Adams awoke in his room, he noted with disgust, the company in Clay's quarters was often just departing. There was gossip that Clay sought the pleasures of women, too, in Ghent as well as in America. But such stories were unsubstantiated. From all appearances, he remained loyal to his wife, Lucretia, throughout their married life.

As postwar Speaker of the House, Clay became one of the most powerful men in Washington, a brilliant parliamentarian and mesmerizing orator who helped raise legislative leadership to supremacy in national affairs. In a day of rampant localism, Clay had an international vision, a dream of the United States as the world's foremost power. His vision, fueled by his ambition, made him aspire to the presidency with palpable self-confidence. Certain that he had never met his superior, he thought himself the best man to lead America into a golden new age of prosperity and world prominence.

With fellow congressman John C. Calhoun, who was then in his nationalist phase, Clay devised the celebrated American System to implement his vision. It called for a tariff to protect America's infant industries, a national bank to stimulate and stabilize the country financially, and internal improvements to promote the general welfare. In the long run, Clay and his supporters hoped to unify the country by establishing a mutually supporting and balanced economy of manufacturing, commerce, and agriculture. In this scheme of things, each of the three great sections was to produce what suited it best: the South was to concentrate on staples like cotton and rice, the West on livestock and grain, and the Northeast on manufactures. Clay conceded that the system was founded on sectional interests, yet he believed that the whole — national interest — would exceed the sum of its parts.

On paper it was a brilliant idea. In reality it was doomed by the combustible slavery issue, which split Clay's own section, bitterly divided the country into slave and free states, and eventually blew them apart. Clay was aware of the danger: the Missouri crisis of 1819–21 revealed to him and his generation the grim possibility of sectional war over slavery. The crisis came about when Missouri sought to enter the Union as a slave state. At that time the free states had a majority in the House of Representatives and a margin of one state in the Senate. The admission of Alabama, due to take place in December 1819, would tie the score. If Missouri entered the Union as a slave state, it would not only give the South a one-state margin in the Senate but open a gateway for proslavery expansion into the West.

To prevent that, Senator James Tallmadge, Jr., of New York proposed an amendment to the Missouri enabling bill that prohibited white settlers from taking any more slaves into Missouri and decreed that all henceforth born there would be freed at age twenty-five, which was a variation on Jefferson's plan. The Tallmadge Amendment provoked riotous debates in Congress, with both sides threatening war. "If you persist, the Union will be dissolved," a Georgia senator told Tallmadge. "You have kindled a fire which seas of blood can only extinguish." Retorted Tallmadge, "If a dissolution of the Union must take place, let it be so! If civil war . . . must come, I can only say, let it come!"

Contrary to legend, Clay did not put forth the compromise that averted a blowup in 1820. In fact, he sided with the South, contending that slavery was a state institution and that Congress had no constitutional authority to prohibit bondage in Missouri after it had become a state. With the fate of his American System hanging in the balance, he complained that "it is a most unhappy question, awakening sectional feelings, and exasperating them to the highest degree. The words, civil war, and disunion, are uttered almost without emotion." When a compromise package finally emerged, Clay threw his enormous influence behind it, thus ensuring its passage. The Compromise of 1820 admitted Maine as a free state and Missouri as a slave state, thus maintaining an equilibrium of power between North and South in the Senate. It also divided the rest of the Louisiana Purchase Territory at the latitude of 36° 30′ north, excluding slavery above that line and endorsing the principle of congressional nonintervention south of it. In practice, this meant that slavery could and did expand there.

It was the second Missouri Compromise for which Clay was responsible and for which he became famous. When Missouri adopted a constitution that excluded free blacks from entering the state, antislavery northerners leaped on the offending passage as a violation of the privileges and immunities clause of the federal Constitution and demanded that Missouri delete the restriction or be kept out of the Union. This in turn only provoked southerners into renewed threats of secession and war. "Unhappy subject!" Clay exclaimed. Yet his sympathies again were Southern.

Indeed, it seemed to him that free-state forces were ganging up on Missouri and the South since few places in the country allowed free blacks equal privileges and immunities with whites. To make matters worse, he had resigned as speaker, leaving the House rudderless in the currents of the controversy. When nobody else would do so, the go-ahead man himself took charge and promoted compromise with all his powers of persuasion: "he begs, instructs, adjures, supplicates, & beseeches us to have mercy on the people of Missouri," reported one northern congressman. Clay wanted mercy for the *white* people of Missouri; he had no interest whatever in the rights of black Americans there. In the end, Congress approved his compromise, which allowed Missouri to retain its exclusion clause as long as the legislature pledged never to restrict persons who were or might become U.S. citizens. It was, as one writer has pointed out, "a sleight-of-hand solution, upholding the supremacy of the federal Constitution in the face of the Missouri provision that flagrantly violated it." Yet it avoided apparent catastrophe and won Clay kudos throughout the country as a man for whom Union was his motto, conciliation his maxim.

Clay hoped that the slavery issue was now "happily settled" and that "mutual forbearance and mutual toleration" would restore "concord and harmony" to the country. But in truth he worried about the future of the Union, worried that slavery and its concomitant problem — the presence of blacks in a white man's country — would continue to inflame and divide white Americans. To Clay, it seemed clear that both slaves and free blacks had to be removed if the nation was ever to be united under the banners of his American System.

The slavery issue haunted him. Despite his own status as a slaveowner, Clay hated the peculiar institution, consistently calling it the "greatest of human evils" and a "great stain upon the American name," and he hoped that all the southern states would one day eradicate it by schemes of gradual emancipation. The problem, of course, was how to persuade them

to do so, especially in view of what had happened to gradual emancipation in Kentucky. The more he thought about that, the more Clay believed that emancipation had failed there for want of a program of colonization that would ease white racial fears by resettling the liberated blacks outside the country. Had not Jefferson warned that emancipation without colonization was unacceptable to whites? For Clay the key to emancipation was to establish a successful colonization scheme first, as an inducement to the states to act. They might be willing to rid themselves of slavery, he reasoned, if they could count on a flourishing colonization operation to siphon off liberated blacks.

Throughout the next three decades, Clay held up the American Colonization Society, a private, "philanthropic" organization he had co-founded in 1816, as the instrument for the nation's salvation. It became his panacea, a cure-all that would save the nation from the horrors of sectional war over slavery. Sponsored at its inception by such prominent figures as James Madison, John Marshall, Daniel Webster, Andrew Jackson, and Francis Scott Key, the society sought financial aid from governments and citizens alike for the voluntary repatriation of free blacks in Liberia. The society's leading spokesman and its third president, Clay rehearsed again and again what he deemed to be the manifold benefits of deporting "free persons of color."

First, colonization would remove "the most vicious," "degraded," and "contaminated" class in America, whose wretched condition was the inevitable consequence of liberating members of an inferior race and allowing them to remain among the superior white race, with its "unconquerable prejudices."

Second, there was "a peculiar, moral fitness in restoring blacks to the land of their fathers," Clay argued. If through such black "missionaries" Americans could give heathen Africa "the blessings of our arts, our civilization and our religion, may we not hope that America will extinguish a great portion of that moral debt which she has contracted to that unfortunate continent?" Clay seemed blissfully unaware of the contradiction involved in this point, never explaining how a "vicious," "degraded" people were supposed to civilize a "pagan" continent. Nor was his disparaging description of free blacks likely to draw many of them to his voluntary program. He was directing his arguments exclusively at white Americans, especially skeptical slaveholders, who tended to view colonization as abolitionism in disguise.

Clay assured them that the society entertained "no purpose, on its own authority or by its own means, to attempt emancipation partial or general." Nor did it desire that the national government remove slavery, for the society acknowledged that only the states where it existed had the power to do that. The goal of the society, Clay explained, was to point the way, to demonstrate to the slave states that colonization was practicable, in hopes that they would incorporate the society's plan into their own schemes of gradual emancipation. Clay contended that if the southern states freed and transported only the annual increase of blacks within their borders, the value of slave labor would one day diminish to the point where it would succumb to superior white labor, and the states would thus "rid themselves of a universally acknowledged curse."

For all the zeal and sincerity Clay brought to his arguments, they seemed to have been devised in never-never land. In the end, they failed to win over a single slave state, not even Kentucky. In truth, many slaveowners called Clay a traitor to his region for even suggesting gradual emancipation by the states. The society also offended genuine abolitionists like William Lloyd Garrison. Calling it "malignant," "sinful," and "inhumane," "the foulest conspiracy in the history of the world," Garrison led the New England Antislavery Society in a successful campaign against it in his region. But the main reason the colonization society failed was because the vast majority of free blacks opposed it and refused to participate in its voluntary program. No matter how badly America

treated them, as black spokesman Frederick Douglass said, it was their country too: they had roots here, families here, and most had no intention of leaving. In the thirty-six years Clay was associated with the society, it persuaded only 6,792 black volunteers to relocate in Liberia. Thus the society never had a viable operation to offer the slave states as an enticement to emancipation. Instead of dying out, as Clay hoped, slavery became more entrenched in the South than ever.

Frustrated in his efforts to remove slavery, Clay also suffered a string of personal and political defeats that scarred him deeply. His wife bore him eleven children, five sons and six daughters, but all his daughters died, the last in 1835. Clay was inconsolable. "Alas! my dear wife, the great Destroyer has come and taken away from us our dear, dear, only daughter!" Lucretia said he never recovered from the loss. His sons were a source of sorrow, too. His eldest, Theodore, suffered brain damage in an accident, became mentally deranged, and had to be institutionalized. Another son, Thomas, almost cost Clay his cherished plantation. When Thomas's Lexington manufacturing firm collapsed, Clay had to sell off his additional property and mortgage Ashland itself to pay his son's debts. Later, thanks to the generosity of friends throughout the country, Clay was able to repurchase the mortgage.

Meanwhile, Clay found himself on a political roller coaster. In 1824 he made his first bid for the presidency, but ran last in a controversial, four-man race that put pious John Quincy Adams in the White House. It was a galling setback for a man of Clay's enormous ambitions. He spent four miserable years as Adams's secretary of state, the dullest position he ever held, and then had to sit on the sidelines while Andrew Jackson, a military man Clay despised, beat Adams for the presidency in 1828. Three years later, to put Clay into a more advantageous position for seeking the presidency, the Kentucky legislature again sent him to the United States Senate, where he served on and off for the next twenty years, always with his eye on the other end of Pennsylvania Avenue.

Clay stood in the center of the impassioned debates in the Senate over the Compromise of 1850. In his major speech, Clay begged his colleagues to pause "at the edge of the precipice" of civil war. Too sick to continue, he had to escape to the seashore, leaving others to negotiate the final compromise. (Ohio Historical Society)

As senator, Clay employed all his prodigious skills to get his American System established, only to see Jackson destroy the second Bank of the United States, which Clay had sought to recharter, and South Carolina almost detonate a civil war by nullifying Clay's protective tariff of 1832 as well as the tariff of 1828. The slavery issue was involved, too, since the nullifiers, led by eagle-eyed John C. Calhoun, hoped to legitimize nullification as a shield against federal tampering with the peculiar institution in the southern states. Clay saw slavery involved in another way, since

he considered it a wasteful labor system that retarded economic development, and blamed it for the economic ills then plaguing South Carolina.

Once again, slavery and sectionalism were playing havoc with Clay's dream of a united American empire. Thundering defiance, South Carolina raised twenty-five thousand volunteers and prepared for war. When Jackson threatened to hang Calhoun and vowed to hurl a federal army into South Carolina to uphold national authority, Clay was appalled. Once again he stepped in to mediate, forging a compromise tariff acceptable to South Carolina. The nation had another reprieve, and Clay had a new nickname: the Great Pacificator. The nullification crisis, however, had shaken him profoundly: he had peered into the future and grimaced at what he saw. "We want no war," he pleaded with his countrymen, "above all no civil war, no family strife. We want no sacked cities, no desolated fields, no smoking ruins, no streams of American blood shed by American arms!"

By 1832 Clay was trapped in a monstrous contradiction: he was promoting a program of nationalism based on sectional interests at a time when sectionalism threatened the nation's very existence. Yet he fought doggedly on. From the Senate, he dueled and harassed Jackson, calling King Andrew a menace to the country. Supremely confident, Clay ran against Jackson in the 1832 presidential election, but he was no match for the popular president and suffered a disastrous defeat. Clay plunged into gloom. What was wrong with the country that it would not, could not, see that he was its president of destiny? He helped found the Whig party, a coalition of Jackson haters, and employed it to promote his programs and his ambitions. But the Jacksonians remained so powerful that Clay did not even offer himself as candidate in the presidential canvass of 1838, which put Jackson's successor, Martin Van Buren, in the White House.

Enduring four years of Little Van was almost more than Clay could bear. In his eyes the country desperately needed him as president, needed Harry of the West to heal its divisions and restore its prosperity after the disastrous 1837 panic. To make matters worse, the abolitionists had launched a crusade that further polarized the country. Demanding that the slaves be emancipated "immediately" and assimilated into America's social order, they held rallies across the North, bombarded the South with abolitionist literature, and inundated Congress with petitions. Soon they invaded politics, too, organizing the Liberty party and promoting antislavery men for state and national office.

Clay was horrified. He thought the abolitionists "rash and impolitic," not to say dangerous. Yet the stridency of the Great Southern Reaction distressed him, too. To counter the abolitionist attack, southern spokesmen argued that slavery was a "positive good" ordained by God from the beginning of time. Gone was the Jeffersonian argument that slavery was "a necessary evil." Now proslavery apologists proclaimed it "the greatest of all blessings" and the *sine qua non* of southern patriotism. In 1837, on the floor of the Senate, speaking in his rapid-fire fashion, John C. Calhoun warned that overturning slavery in the South would result in a war of extermination between the races, and he insisted that the abolitionists be silenced.

In the ensuing war of words over slavery, Clay tried to stand in the middle. In the Senate he expressed "the strongest disapprobation of the course of the northern abolitionists, who were intermeddling with a subject that no way concerned them." Yet he emphatically disagreed with Calhoun, too. *"I consider slavery as a curse,"* Clay told the Senate, "a curse to the master, a wrong, a grievous wrong to the slave. In the abstract it is ALL WRONG; and no possible contingency can make it right."

Clay succeeded only in provoking both sides, as proslavery men damned him as an abolitionist, and the abolitionists castigated him as a canting hypocrite. How, they demanded, could a man who held slaves, represented a slave state, and advocated colonization be a true friend of liberty? In his newspaper, *The North Star,* Frederick Douglass declared Clay's "the most helpless, illogical, and cowardly apologies" for the wrong of slavery Douglass had ever heard. "You are at this moment," Douglass told Clay, "the robber of nearly fifty human beings, of their liberty, compelling them to live in ignorance." If the senator meant what he said about the crime of bondage, Douglass said, then he should emancipate his human property and enlist in the abolitionist cause. "Let me ask if you think that God will hold you guiltless in the great day of account, if you die with the blood of these fifty slaves clinging to your garments[?]"

Stung by such criticism, Clay struck back in self-defense. He told one abolitionist, "Excuse me, Mr. Mendenhall, for saying that my slaves are as well fed and clad, look as sleek and hearty, and are quite as civil and respectful in their demeanor, and as little disposed to wound the feelings of any one, as you are." Yet, Clay perceived what the controversy cost him politically. "The Abolitionists are denouncing me as a slaveholder," he wrote in 1838, "and slaveholders as an Abolitionist, whilst they both unite on Mr. Van Buren."

Convinced that he had to make a choice, Clay sided with his fellow slaveholders. In an 1839 speech in the Senate, he not only defended slavery but accused the abolitionists of promoting amalgamation ("revolting admixture, alike offensive to God and man") and trying to foment civil war. The speech so excited Calhoun that he leaped to his feet and happily proclaimed it "the finishing stroke" to the abolitionists in American politics. It was a premature benediction, since the Liberty party ran James G. Birney for president in the election of 1840. Alas for Clay, he lost the Whig party nomination to war hero William Henry Harrison, who went on to win the presidency that year. Clay could hardly believe that the Whigs preferred a political tyro like Harrison to himself. When Harrison died, Clay felt even more cheated since Vice-President John Tyler of Virginia, a cranky, old-school Democrat, now succeeded to the presidency. After Tyler vetoed Clay's attempts to recharter the national bank and raise the tariff, the go-ahead man was so disillusioned that he resigned from the Senate, said he was "retiring" from politics, and went home to his stock farming, his family, and his slaves.

He soon came out of retirement, thanks to a ground swell of popular support for him as president. The fact was, Harry of the West towered over his lackluster rivals, so much so that by 1843 more than two hundred Whig newspapers and seventeen Whig conventions or Whig-dominated legislatures had announced for him. When he spoke at a barbecue in Dayton, Ohio, more than 100,000 people turned out for the event, in what was perhaps the largest political

gathering the Republic had witnessed thus far. It was clear to party bigwigs that, lacking another military man to run in the 1844 presidential contest, Clay was the only potential winner they had. When the Whig national convention nominated him by acclamation, Clay had never seemed so close to the White House and the consummation of his dreams.

His victory seemed assured when the Democrats nominated James K. Polk, the first dark-horse candidate in American presidential history. The Democrats thereupon endorsed the annexation of slaveholding Texas, an explosive issue that Clay's forces had hoped to keep out of the campaign. Clay had gone on record as opposing annexation, on the grounds that "annexation and war with Mexico are identical." What America needed, he said, was "union, peace, and patience." Now the Democrats shrewdly linked Texas annexation to Oregon and the popular notion that America had a God-given right to rule the continent. Sensing that they had Clay on the run, the Democrats grew malicious. They attacked him as a duelist, a rake, and an abolitionist who opposed Texas annexation because he wanted to free the blacks. This in turn aroused zealots of the Liberty party. Fearful that antislavery voters would go for Clay, they pummelled him as a "man-stealer" under the sway of the Slave Power.

The Texas question proved Clay's downfall. Convinced that his southern support was slipping away, he resorted to a desperate ploy, asserting in a series of labored public statements — "the Alabama letters" — that he had no personal objection to annexation, indeed that he would like to have Texas, slavery and all, if it could be done "without dishonor" and "without war." The Alabama letters may have won Clay some support in the South, but they cost him pivotal New York State, where antislavery Whigs went for Birney and threw the state and the election itself to Polk. Clay lost by only 38,000 popular votes out of a total of 2,700,000 cast. It was the most painful setback of his political life. Blaming it on fraud, slander, and abolitionism, he declared himself "forever off the public stage."

The annexation of Texas led to exactly what Clay had feared — war with Mexico. That war hurt him personally, for it took his favorite son, Henry Clay, Jr., who fell at Buena Vista. It also made a military hero of Zachary Taylor, who won the Whig nomination and the presidency in 1848. Clay was thoroughly disgusted that the party had again passed over him in favor of a man utterly devoid of political experience. Clay was certain that had he been the nominee, *he* would have been sitting in the White House in Taylor's place. This overlooked a crucial fact. Clay lacked the one thing — military glory — that had ensured the victory of the Whig party's only two elected presidents. Had he possessed a military record, he would doubtless have won the presidency long before.

In 1849 the Kentucky legislature again elected Clay to the Senate. Seventy-two now, he was tired and in poor health; the bons mots and repartee no longer came so quickly as they once had. What was more, he had a haunting fear that he had failed in politics, having been unable to win the presidency, the pinnacle of his ambition, or to unite the country behind his American System. What he had was a reputation as the Great Compromiser — "I go for honorable compromise whenever it can be made," he said. "Life itself is but a compromise." And now, in the winter of 1849–50, the country needed him again as sectional mediator, for the Mexican War had thrust the slavery question back into the center of American politics, precipitating a desperate power struggle between free and slave states for control of the territories and ultimately of the nation itself.

At issue now was the status of slavery in the newly acquired territories of the Southwest. If northern free-soilers demanded that Congress ban slavery there, southern militants like Calhoun argued that Congress had a constitutional obligation to safeguard slave property in all federal territories. To make matters worse that fateful winter, California had drawn up a constitution prohibiting slavery and was ready for admission as a free state, with New Mexico not far behind. The California and New Mexico questions rocked Congress to its foundations. Two new free states would alter the balance of power against the South, perhaps forever, and southerners swore they would sunder the Union before they would let that happen. "Slavery here is the all-engrossing theme," Clay wrote a friend; "and my hopes and my fears alternately prevail as to any settlement of the vexed question."

Frail and weak, racked by a persistent cough, Clay labored once again to avert catastrophe. In January 1850 he introduced in the Senate eight separate measures designed to settle all current disputes in the vexed slavery question. Among other things, his measures called for California to enter the Union as a free state, for New Mexico and Utah territories to be organized without congressional conditions on slavery (Clay assumed that Mexican law, which had abolished it, would continue in both territories), for the slave trade to be outlawed in the District of Columbia, and for a stringent new fugitive slave law to be enacted as a sop to southerners. At one point in his speech, Clay mentioned a "precious relic" he had recently received — it was a fragment that had been taken from the coffin of George Washington. Holding it aloft, Clay said that the "venerated" father of the country was warning Congress from Mount Vernon not to destroy his handiwork. In his major speech in February, Clay beseeched his colleagues to pause "at the edge of the precipice, before the fearful and disastrous leap is taken into the yawning abyss below." If the Union were dissolved, he fervently prayed that he might not live "to behold the sad and heart-rending spectacle."

But his separate compromise measures ran into seemingly insurmountable opposition from both sides. Frustrated in his initial efforts, Clay tried a new tack. In May he offered all of his proposals in a single omnibus bill, only to see it sink in a vortex of acrimonious speeches, amendments, and shouts to adjourn.

It was too much for him. Lacking the strength or the will to continue, he left for Rhode Island, to rest and recuperate on the seashore before returning to Washington. It remained for Senator Stephen A. Douglas of Illinois, in a remarkable display of legislative skill, to guide Clay's measures one by one into law. In Washington crowds shouted "The Union is saved!" and drank toasts of champagne and whiskey. President Millard Fillmore went so far as to pronounce the Compromise of 1850 "a final settlement" of all sectional disputes. But events were to prove how wrong he was. The compromise contained a fatal measure, the draconian fugitive slave law, which inflamed sectional passions anew and took the country another step toward the very precipice Clay had hoped to avoid.

In late 1851, back in Washington after a long stay at Ashland, Clay tried to resume his duties, but he was suffering from insomnia and coughing worse than ever. When a friend urged him not to be despondent, Clay showed a flash of his old go-ahead spirit. "Sir," he said with eyes blazing, "there is no such word in my vocabulary." By June 1852, too sick to go home, he lay dying in a bed in the National Hotel, his son Thomas at his side. At one point he called out, "My mother, mother, mother!" On June 29 he murmured, "I believe, my son, I am going," and asked Thomas to button his shirt collar. He caught Thomas's hand, held it tight, and then let go.

Clay's will provided for the gradual liberation and colonization of all children born after January 1, 1850, to the thirty-five slaves he held when he died. In the end, the act was all Clay accomplished in removing slavery from his troubled country, which continued its headlong rush toward its own destruction. Ironically, the Union disintegrated over the election of a Republican president who deeply admired Clay, who hated slavery as Clay had hated it, and who found only in "the sad spectacle" of civil war a means of vanquishing it.

QUESTIONS TO CONSIDER

1. Describe the development over time of Henry Clay's feelings about slavery. What was his youthful judgment on the South's peculiar institution and under what influences did it form? How and why did his early position change? Can these early tensions be seen throughout his life?

2. What solution to the slavery problem did Henry Clay eventually put forward? To whom was he most indebted for his plan? What were the methods and purpose of the American Colonization Society? It was supported by many prominent Americans, so why did it fail?

3. What were the basic tenets and purpose of Henry Clay's American System? How did the particular political climate of the country at that time doom its fulfillment during Clay's life?

4. Describe the basic issues and outcomes of the Missouri Compromise and the Compromise of 1850. Why were these crises so explosive? What role did Henry Clay play in them and what did he hope to accomplish? Did he succeed?

5. Although Henry Clay was an enormously popular and widely admired figure, he was forever disappointed in his highest political ambitions. What reasons for this can you find in the political climate of the time? How did Clay contribute to his own disappointment with the particular positions he took? In his role as "the Great Compromiser" how effective was he in easing sectional tensions and averting disunion?

IX

THE GROWTH
OF TECHNOLOGY

19

The Lords and the Mill Girls

MAURY KLEIN

One group of Massachusetts businessmen tried to avoid the ugly factory towns and horrible working conditions that Korngold describes in his profile of Garrison (selection 17). They formed the Boston Associates, an organization of financiers who built a model mill town in Massachusetts called Lowell. The story of Lowell — America's first planned industrial community — tells us a great deal about the dreams and realities of a nation already undergoing considerable industrial and urban growth. Maury Klein relates that story with a vivid pen — the landscaped town on the banks of the Concord and Merrimack rivers that commanded worldwide attention, the healthy farm girls who worked its looms. In 1833, President Andrew Jackson and Vice President Martin Van Buren visited Lowell and watched transfixed as 2,500 mill girls, clad in blue sashes and white dresses, with parasols above their heads, marched by two abreast. "Very pretty women, by the Eternal!" exclaimed the president. Although they loathed Jackson, the members of the Boston Associates were pleased with his observation, for they were proud of their working girls — the showpieces of what they believed was the model of enlightened industrial management.

To their delight, Lowell became a famous international attraction. English visitors were especially impressed, because female workers in England's coal mines toiled in incredible misery: naked, covered with filth, they had to pull carts of coal on their hands and knees through dark, narrow tunnels. By contrast, as one historian has said, Lowell seemed a "female paradise." Equally impressive was the remarkable productivity of Lowell's

278

"power-driven machinery." Before long, Lowell became (in Linda Evans's words) "the heart of the American textile industry and of the industrial revolution itself."

Lowell's relatively well-disciplined and well-treated work force seemed to demonstrate that industrial capitalism need not be exploitive. Even so, the Lowell system was paternalistic and strict. Sensitive to criticism that it was immoral for women to work, the mill bosses maintained close supervision over their female operatives, imposing curfews and compulsory church attendance. Nevertheless, the mill girls, as they were called, were transformed by their work experience. As Linda Evans says, "Most of these workers saw their mill work as a way to reestablish their value to the family," because they were no longer a burden to their parents (indeed, they could send money home now) and because they could save for their own dowries. "Soon," writes Evans, "it was hard to separate their sense of duty from their sense of independence." They felt a group solidarity, too, and in their boardinghouses created "a working-class female culture." They also became aware of themselves as a working class with special problems, for they were powerless and had few options. They could not find other jobs, as could their male counterparts, could not become sailors or dockhands or work on construction gangs. For most of the women, mill work was their only option.

As others have said, their very powerlessness led to the eventual demise of the "paternalistic factory system." As more and more textile firms moved to Lowell and other towns, the pressure of competition led to overproduction, to the same cycles of boom and bust that plagued the entire national economy. Thanks to overproduction, many mills fell into decline; wages dropped and working conditions deteriorated. In a display of solidarity, the mill girls organized a union and went on strikes to protest wage cuts and rising rents. In 1844, organized as the Lowell Female Labor Reform Association, they campaigned for a ten-hour work day and even took their grievances to the state legislature. As Maury Klein points out in the selection that follows, "their efforts were dogged, impressive, and ultimately futile," because they lacked political leverage. The union failed, and the textile bosses eventually replaced most of their once-prized mill girls with another labor force — desperate immigrants, most from Ireland, who worked for lower wages and were far less demanding. By 1860, Lowell had become another grim and crowded mill town, another "squalid slum." As you ponder Lowell's story, consider what it suggests about the nature of American industrialization and about the special problems of women and labor in an industrializing society. Do you agree with Klein, that what happened in Lowell reveals some harsh truths about the incompatibility of democratic ideals and the profit motive?

GLOSSARY

APPLETON, NATHAN One of the largest stockholders in the Merrimack Manufacturing Company.

BAGLEY, SARAH One of several women leaders of the Lowell Female Labor Reform Association and the ten-hour workday movement.

BOOTT, KIRK Planned and supervised the building of the Lowell mill village, which Klein calls, "the nation's first planned industrial community."

BOSTON ASSOCIATES Founders of Lowell and the Merrimack Manufacturing Co., their textile empire eventually comprised 8 major firms, 20 mills, and more than 6,000 employees.

LOWELL, FRANCIS CABOT "Farsighted merchant" who formed the Boston Associates and pioneered a unique textile mill at Waltham; after his death, the associates established another mill village on the Merrimack River and named it *Lowell*.

LOWELL FEMALE LABOR REFORM ASSOCIATION Formed by the mill girls in 1844 to protest falling wages, this women's labor union campaigned for a ten-hour day and other reforms during its short existence.

LOWELL OFFERING Monthly magazine edited and published by the Lowell mill girls.

MERRIMACK MANUFACTURING COMPANY The new corporation that ran the Lowell mill and turned it into "the largest and most unique mill town in the nation."

WALTHAM SYSTEM Unique production methods at Francis Lowell's mill.

☆

THE ASSOCIATES

They flocked to the village of Lowell, these visitors from abroad, as if it were a compulsory stop on the grand tour, eager to verify rumors of a utopian system of manufacturers. Their skepticism was natural, based as it was on the European experience where industry had degraded workers and blighted the landscape. In English manufacturing centers such as Manchester, observers had stared into the pits of hell and shrank in horror from the sight. Charles Dickens used this gloomy, putrid cesspool of misery as a model in *Hard Times,* while Alexis de Tocqueville wrinkled his nose at the "heaps of dung, rubble from buildings, putrid, stagnant pools" amid the "huge palaces of industry" that kept "air and light out of the human habitations which they dominate. . . . A sort of black smoke covers the city. . . . Under this half daylight 300,000 human beings are ceaselessly at work. A thousand noises disturb this damp, dark labyrinth, but they are not at all the ordinary sounds one hears in great cities."

Was it possible that America could produce an alternative to this hideous scene? It seemed so to the visitors who gaped in wonderment at the village above the confluence of the Concord and Merrimack rivers. What they saw was a planned community with mills five to seven stories high flanked by dormitories for the workers, not jammed together but surrounded by open space filled with trees and flower gardens set against a backdrop of the river and hills beyond. Dwelling houses, shops, hotels, churches, banks, even a library lined the streets in orderly, uncrowded rows.

Maury Klein, "The Lords and the Mill Girls," from "From Utopia to Mill Town" by Maury Klein in *American History Illustrated,* October and November 1981. Reprinted by permission of Cowles Magazines, publisher of *American History Illustrated.*

Lowell, Massachusetts, was a model mill town located on the banks of the Concord and Merrimack rivers. The community attracted worldwide attention because it presented a sharp contrast to the squalor of manufacturing centers in England and Europe. The buildings stood in groups separated by trees, shrubs, and strips of lawn that were attractively landscaped and reminiscent of a college campus. (Worcester Art Museum, Worcester, Massachusetts)

Taken whole, the scene bore a flavor of meticulous composition, as if a painting had sprung to life.

The contrast between so pristine a vision and the nightmare of Manchester startled the most jaded of foreigners. "It was new and fresh, like a setting at the opera," proclaimed Michel Chevalier, a Frenchman who visited Lowell in 1834. The Reverend William Scoresby, an Englishman, marveled at how the buildings seemed "as fresh-looking as if built within a year." The indefatigable Harriet Martineau agreed, as did J. S. Buckingham, who pronounced Lowell to be "one of the most remarkable places under the sun." Even Dickens, whose tour of America rendered him immune to most of its charms, was moved to lavish praise on the town. "One would swear," he added "that every 'Bakery,' 'Grocery' and 'Bookbindery'

and every other kind of store, took its shutters down for the first time, and started in business yesterday."

If Lowell and its social engineering impressed visitors, the mill workers dazzled them. Here was nothing resembling Europe's *Untermenschen,* that doomed proletariat whose brief, wretched lives were squeezed between child labor and a pauper's grave. These were not men or children or even families as found in the Rhode Island mills. Instead Lowell employed young women, most of them fresh off New England farms, paid them higher wages than females earned anywhere else (but still only half of what men earned), and installed them in dormitories under strict supervision. They were young and industrious, intelligent, and entirely respectable. Like model citizens of a burgeoning republic they saved their money, went

281

to church, and spent their leisure hours in self-improvement.

More than one visitor hurried home to announce the arrival of a new industrial order, one capable of producing goods in abundance without breaking its working class on the rack of poverty. Time proved them wrong, or at best premature. The Lowell experiment lasted barely a generation before sliding back into the grinding bleakness of a conventional mill town. It had survived long enough to tantalize admirers with its unfulfilled promise and to reveal some harsh truths about the incompatibility of certain democratic ideals and the profit motive.

The founding fathers of Lowell were a group known as the Boston Associates, all of whom belonged to that tight knit elite whose dominance of Boston society was exceeded only by their stranglehold on its financial institutions. The seed had been planted by Francis Cabot Lowell, a shrewd, far-sighted merchant who took up the manufacture of cotton cloth late in life. A trip abroad in 1810 introduced him to the cotton mills of Lancashire and to a fellow Boston merchant named Nathan Appleton. Blessed with a superb memory and trained in mathematics, Lowell packed his mind with details about the machinery shown him by unsuspecting mill owners. The Manchester owners jealously hoarded their secrets and patents, but none regarded the wealthy American living abroad for his health as a rival.

Once back in America, Lowell recruited a mechanical genius named Paul Moody to help replicate the machines he had seen in Manchester. After much tinkering they designed a power loom, cottonspinning frame, and some other machines that in fact improved upon the English versions. As a hedge against inexperience Lowell decided to produce only cheap, unbleached cotton sheeting. The choice also enabled him to use unskilled labor, but where was he to find even that? Manchester drew its workers from the poorhouses, a source lacking in America. Both the family system and use of apprentices had been tried in Rhode Island with little success. Most men preferred farming their own land to working in a factory for someone else.

But what about women? They were familiar with spinning and weaving, and would make obedient workers. Rural New England had a surplus of daughters who were considered little more than drains on the family larder. To obtain their services Lowell need only pay decent wages and overcome parental reservations about permitting girls to live away from home. This could be done by providing boarding houses where the girls would be subject to the strict supervision of older women acting as chaperones. There would be religious and moral instruction enough to satisfy the most scrupulous of parents. It was an ingenious concept, one that cloaked economic necessity in the appealing garb of republican ideals.

Lowell added yet another wrinkle. Instead of forming a partnership like most larger businesses, he obtained a charter for a corporation named the Boston Manufacturing Company. Capitalized at $300,000 the firm started with $100,000 subscribed by Lowell and a circle of his caste and kin: Patrick Tracy Jackson and his two brothers, Nathan Appleton, Israel Thorndike and his son, two brothers-in-law, and two other merchants. Jackson agreed to manage the new company, which chose a site at the falls on the Charles River at Waltham. By late 1814 the first large integrated cotton factory in America stood complete, along with its machine shop where Lowell and Moody reinvented the power loom and spinner.

Production began in 1815, just as the war with England drew to a close. The mill not only survived the return of British competition but prospered in spectacular fashion: during the years 1817–1824 dividends averaged more than nineteen percent. Moody's fertile mind devised one new invention after another, including a warp-yarn dresser and double speeder. His innovations made the firm's production methods so unique that they soon became known as the "Waltham system." As Gilman Ostrander observed, "The Waltham method was characterized by an overriding emphasis upon standardization, integration, and mechanization." The shop began to build machinery for sale to other mills. Even more, the company's management techniques became the prototype on which virtually the entire textile industry of New England would later model itself.

Lowell did not live to witness this triumph. He died in 1817 at the age of forty-two, having provided his associates with the ingredients of success. During the next three years they showed their gratitude by constructing two more mills and a bleachery, which exhausted the available water power at Waltham. Eager to expand, the Associates scoured the rivers of New England for new sites. In 1821 Moody found a spot on the Merrimack River at East Chelmsford that seemed ideal. The river fell thirty-two feet in a series of rapids and there were two canals, one belonging to the Pawtucket Canal Company and another connecting to Boston. For about $70,000 the Associates purchased control of the Canal Company and much of the farmland along the banks.

From that transaction arose the largest and most unique mill town in the nation. In this novel enterprise the Associates seemed to depart from all precedent, but in reality they borrowed much from Waltham. A new corporation, the Merrimack Manufacturing Company, was formed with Nathan Appleton and Jackson as its largest stockholders. The circle of inventors was widened to include other members of the Boston elite such as Daniel Webster and the Boott brothers, Kirk and John. Moody took some shares but his ambitions went no further; he was content to remain a mechanic for the rest of his life. The memory of Francis Cabot Lowell was honored by giving the new village his name.

The task of planning and overseeing construction was entrusted to Kirk Boott. The son of a wealthy Boston Anglophile, Boott's disposition and education straddled the Atlantic. He obtained a commission in the British army and fought under Wellington until the War of 1812 forced his resignation. For several years he studied engineering before returning home in 1817 to take up his father's business. A brilliant, energetic, imperious martinet, Boott leaped at the opportunity to take charge of the new enterprise. As Hannah Josephson observed, he became "its town planner, its architect, its engineer, its agent in charge of production, and the leading citizen of the new community."

The immensity of the challenge appealed to Boott's ordered mind. He recruited an army of 500 Irish laborers, installed them in a tent city, and began transforming a pastoral landscape into a mill town. A dam was put across the river, the old canal was widened, new locks were added, and two more canals were started. The mills bordered the river but not with the monotony of a wall. Three buildings stood parallel to the water and three at right angles in a grouping that reminded some of Harvard College. Trees and shrubs filled the space between them. The boarding houses, semi-detached dwellings two-and-a-half stories high separated by strips of lawn, were set on nearby streets along with the superintendents' houses and long brick tenements for male mechanics and their families. It was a standard of housing unknown to working people anywhere in the country or in Europe. For himself Boott designed a Georgian mansion ornamented with a formidable Ionic portico.

Lowell emerged as the nation's first planned industrial community largely because of Boott's care in realizing the overall concept. At Waltham the boarding houses had evolved piecemeal rather than as an integral part of the design. The Associates took care to avoid competition between the sites by confining Lowell's production to printed calicoes for the higher priced market. While Waltham remained profitable, it quickly took a back seat to the new works. The machine shop provided a true barometer of change. It not only produced machinery and water wheels for Lowell but also oversaw the construction of mills and housing. Shortly before Lowell began production in 1823, the Associates, in Nathan Appleton's words, "arranged to equalize the interest of all the stockholders in both companies" by formally purchasing

Waltham's patterns and patent rights and securing Moody's transfer to Lowell. A year later the entire machine shop was moved to Lowell, leaving Waltham with only a maintenance facility.

The success of the Lowell plant prompted the Associates to unfold ambitious new plans. East Chelmsford offered abundant water power for an expanding industry; the sites were themselves a priceless asset. To use them profitably the Associates revived the old Canal Company under a new name, the Locks and Canals Company, and transferred to it all the land and water rights owned by the Merrimack Company. The latter then bought back its own mill sites and leased the water power it required. Thereafter the Locks and Canals Company sold land to other mill companies, leased water power to them at fixed rates per spindle, and built machinery, mills, and housing for them.

This organizational arrangement was as far advanced for the times as the rest of the Lowell concept. It brought the Associates handsome returns from the mills and enormous profits from the Locks and Canals Company, which averaged twenty-four percent in dividends between 1825 and 1845. As new companies like the Hamilton, Appleton, and Lowell corporations were formed, the Associates dispersed part of their stock among a widening network of fellow Brahmins. New partners entered their exclusive circle, including the Lawrence brothers, Abbott and Amos. Directories of the companies were so interlocked as to avoid any competition between them. In effect the Associates had created industrial harmony of the sort J. P. Morgan would later promote under the rubric "community of interest."

By 1836 the Associates had invested $6.2 million in eight major firms controlling twenty five-story mills with more than 6,000 employees. Lowell had grown into a town of 18,000 and acquired a city charter. It boasted ten churches, several banks to accommodate the virtue of thrift on the part of the workers, long rows of shops, a brewery, taverns, schools, and other appurtenances of progress. Worldwide attention had transformed it into a showcase. Apart from the influx of foreigners and other dignitaries, it had already been visited by a president the Associates despised (Andrew Jackson), and by a man who would try three times to become president (Henry Clay).

The Associates basked in this attention because they viewed themselves as benevolent, far-seeing men whose sense of duty extended far beyond wealth. To be sure the life blood of the New England economy flowed through their counting houses from their domination of banks, insurance companies, railroads, shipping, and mills elsewhere in New England. Yet such were the rigors of their stern Puritan consciences that for them acquisition was all consuming without being all fulfilling. Duty taught that no fortune was so ample that more was not required. Economist Thorstein Veblen later marveled at the "steadfast cupidity" that drove these men "under pain of moral turpitude, to acquire a 'competence,' and then unremittingly to augment any competence acquired."

Not content with being an economic and social aristocracy, the Associates extended their influence to politics, religion, education, and morality. Lowell fit their *raison d'être* so ideally because it filled their coffers while at the same time reflecting their notion of an orderly, paternal community imbued with the proper values. The operatives knew their place, deferred to the leadership of the Associates, shared their values. . . .

☆

THE MILL GIRLS

In promoting their mills as an industrial utopia [the Associates] were quick to realize that the girls were the prime attraction, the trump card in their game of benevolent paternalism. As early as 1827 Captain Basil Hall, an Englishman, marveled at the girls on their way to work at six in the morning, "nicely dressed, and glittering with bright shawls and showy-colored gowns and gay bonnets . . . with an air of lightness, and an elasticity of step, implying an obvious desire to get to their work."

Observers who went home to rhapsodize about Lowell and its operatives as a model for what the factory system should become trapped themselves in an unwitting irony. While there was much about the Lowell corporations that served later firms as model, the same did not hold true for their labor force. The young women who filled the mills, regarded by many as the heart of the Lowell system, were in fact its most unique element and ultimately its most transient feature. They were of the same stock and shared much the same culture as the men who employed them. This relative homogeneity gave them a kinship of values absent in later generations of workers. Benita Eisler has called them "the last WASP labor force in America."

The women who flocked to Lowell's mills came mostly from New England farms. Some came to augment the incomes of poor families, others to earn money for gowns and finery, to escape the bleak monotony of rural life, or sample the adventure of a fresh start in a new village. Although their motives were mixed, they chose the mills over such alternatives as teaching or domestic service because the pay was better and the work gave them a sense of independence. Lucy Larcom, one of the most talented and articulate of the mill girls, observed that:

Country girls were naturally independent, and the feeling that at this new work the few hours they had of everyday leisure were entirely their own [and] was a satisfaction to them. They preferred it to going out as "hired help." It was like a young man's pleasure in entering upon business for himself.

Leisure hours were a scarce commodity. The mill tower bells tolled the girls to work before the light of day and released them at dusk six days a week, with the Sabbath reserved for solemn observance. The work day averaged twelve-and-a-half hours, depending on the season, and there were only three holidays

a year, all unpaid: Fast Day, the Fourth of July, and Thanksgiving. Wages ranged between $2 and $4 a week, about half what men earned. Of this amount $1.25 was deducted for board, to which the company contributed another twenty-five cents. Meager as these sums appear, they exceeded the pay offered by most other mills.

The work rooms were clean and bright for a factory, the walls whitewashed and windows often garnished with potted flowers. But the air was clogged with lint and fumes from the whale-oil lamps hung above every loom. Since threads would snap unless the humidity was kept high, windows were nailed shut even in the summer's heat, and the air was sprayed with water. Delicate lungs were vulnerable to the ravages of tuberculosis and other respiratory ailments. More than one critic attributed the high turnover rate to the number of girls "going home to die."

The machines terrified newcomers with their thunderous clatter that shook the floor. Belts and wheels, pulleys and rollers, spindles and flyers, twisted and whirled, hissing and buzzing, always in motion, a cacophonous jungle alien to rural ears. At first the machines looked too formidable to master. One girl, in the story recalling her first days at Lowell, noted that:

she felt afraid to touch the loom, and she was almost sure she could never learn to weave; the harness puzzled and the reed perplexed her; the shuttle flew out and made a new bump on her head; and the first time she tried to spring the lathe she broke a quarter of the threads. It seemed as if the girls all stared at her, and the overseers watched every motion, and the day appeared as long as a month had at home. . . . At last it was night. . . . There was a dull pain in her head, and a sharp pain in her ankles; every bone was aching, and there was in her ears a strange noise, as of crickets, frogs and jews-harps, all mingling together.

Once the novelty wore off, the strangeness of it all gave way to a more serious menace: monotony.

The boarding houses provided welcome havens from such trials. These were dwellings of different sizes, leased to respectable high-toned widows who served as housemothers for fifteen to thirty girls. They kept the place clean and enforced the company rules, which were as strict as any parent might want. Among other things they regulated conduct, imposed a ten o'clock curfew, and required church attendance. The girls were packed six to a bedroom, with three beds. One visitor described the small rooms as "absolutely choked with beds, trunks, band-boxes, clothes, umbrellas and people," with little space for other furniture. The dining room doubled as sitting room, but in early evening it was often besieged by peddlers of all sorts.

This cramped arrangement suited the Associates nicely because it was economical and reinforced a sense of group standards and conformity. Lack of privacy was old hat to most rural girls, though a few complained. Most housemothers set a good table and did not cater to dainty appetites. One girl reported dinner as consisting of "meat and potatoes, with vegetables, tomatoes and pickles, pudding or pie, with bread, butter, coffee or tea." English novelist Anthony Trollope was both impressed and repulsed by the discovery that meat was served twice a day, declaring that for Americans "to live a day without meat would be as great a privation as to pass a night without a bed."

The corporations usually painted each house once a year, an act attributed by some to benevolence and others to a shrewd eye for public relations and property values. Their zeal for cleanliness did not extend to bathing facilities, which were minimal at best. More than one visitor spread tales of dirt and vermin in the boarding houses, but these too were no strangers to rural homes. Like the mills, later boarding houses were built as long dormitory rows unleavened by strips of lawn or shrubbery, but the earlier versions retained a quaint charm for visitors and inhabitants.

Above all the boarding houses were, as Hannah Josephson stressed, "a woman's world." In these cluttered cloisters the operatives chatted, read, sewed, wrote letters, or dreamed about the day when marriage or some better opportunity would take them from the mills. They stayed in Lowell about four years on the average, and most married after leaving. The mill experience was, in Thomas Dublin's phrase, simply "a stage in a woman's life cycle before marriage." For many girls the strangeness of it all was mitigated by the presence of sisters, cousins, or friends who had undertaken the same adventure.

Outside the boarding house the girls strolled and picnicked in the nearby countryside, attended church socials, paid calls, and shopped for the things they had never had. Dozens of shops vied with the savings banks for their hard-earned dollars and won more than their share of them. Those eager to improve their minds, and there were many, patronized the library and the Lyceum, which for fifty cents offered a season ticket for twenty-five lectures by such luminaries as Ralph Waldo Emerson, Horace Mann, John Quincy Adams, Horace Greeley, Robert Owen, and Edward Everett. Some were ambitious enough to attend evening classes or form study groups of their own in everything from art to German.

Above all the girls read. Their appetite for literature was voracious and often indiscriminate. So strong was this ardor that many slipped their books into the mills, where such distractions were strictly forbidden. It must have pained overseers to confiscate even Bibles from transgressors, but the large number that filled their drawers revealed clearly the Associates' determination to preserve the sharp distinction between the Lord's business and their own.

No one knows how many of the girls were avid readers, but the number probably exceeded the norm for any comparable group. Where so many read, it was inevitable that some would try their hand at writing. By the early 1840s Lowell boasted seven Mutual Self-Improvement Clubs. These were the first women's literary clubs in America, and the members consisted entirely of operatives. From two of these groups emerged a monthly magazine known as the

Lowell Offering which in its brief life span (1841–1845) achieved a notoriety and reputation far in excess of its literary merits. The banner on its cover described the contents as *A Repository of Original Articles, Written Exclusively by Females Actively Employed in the Mills.*

No other aspect of Lowell rivaled the *Offering* as a symbol for the heights to which an industrial utopia might aspire. Observers at home and abroad were astounded at the spectacle of factory workers — women no less — capable of producing a literary magazine. Even Charles Dickens, that harsh critic of both English industrialism and American foibles, hurried this revelation to his readers:

I am now going to state three facts, which will startle a large class of readers on this side of the Atlantic very much. First, there is a joint-stock piano in a great many of the boarding-houses. Secondly, nearly all these young ladies subscribe to circulating libraries. Thirdly, they have got up among themselves a periodical ... which is duly printed, published, and sold; and whereof I brought away from Lowell four hundred good solid pages, which I have read from beginning to end.

As the *Offering's* fame grew, the Associates were not slow to appreciate its value. Nothing did more to elevate their esteem on both sides of the Atlantic. Contrary to the belief of some, the magazine never became a house organ. Both editors, Harriet Farley and Harriott Curtis, were veterans of the mills who opened their columns to critics and reformers while keeping their own editorial views within more discreet and refined bounds. For their part the Associates were too shrewd not to recognize that the *Offering's* appeal, its effectiveness as a symbol of republican virtues, lay in its independence. To serve them best it must not smack of self-serving, and it did not.

Although the magazine's prose and poetry seldom rose above mediocre, the material offered revealing insights into every aspect of factory life. Inevitably it attracted authors eager to voice grievances or promote

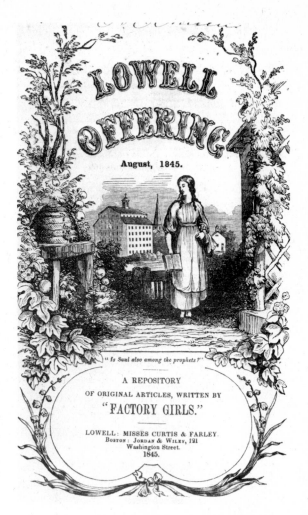

Woman factory workers at the Lowell mills were avid readers. They also formed self-improvement clubs and published their own monthly magazine, the Lowell Offering, The *Offering became a symbol for the heights to which an industrial utopia might aspire. As Maury Klein comments, "Observers at home and abroad were astounded at the spectacle of factory workers — women no less — capable of producing a literary magazine." (Lowell Historical Society)*

remedies. The editors trod a difficult path between the genteel pretensions of a literary organ and a growing militancy among operatives concerned with gut issues. Few of the girls subscribed to the *Offering* anyway; most of the copies went to patrons in other states or overseas. Small wonder that critics charged the magazine had lost touch with actual conditions in the mills or the real concerns of their operatives.

The *Offering* folded in part because it reflected a system hurrying toward extinction. By the 1840s, when Lowell's reputation as an industrial utopia was still at its peak, significant changes had already taken place. Hard times and swollen ranks of stockholders clamoring for dividends had dulled the Associates' interest in benevolent paternalism. It had always been less a goal than a by-product and not likely to survive a direct conflict with the profit motive. The result was a period of several years during which Lowell coasted on its earlier image while the Associates dismantled utopia in favor of a more cost-efficient system.

The self-esteem of the Associates did not permit them to view their actions in this light, but the operatives felt the change in obvious ways. Their work week increased to seventy-five hours with four annual holidays compared to sixty-nine hours and six holidays for the much maligned British textile workers. To reduce unit costs, girls tended faster machines and were paid lower wages for piecework. That was called speedup; in another practice known as stretch-out, girls were given three or four looms where earlier they had tended one or two. Overseers and second hands were offered bonuses for wringing more productivity out of the workers.

At heart the utopian image of Lowell, indeed the system itself, rested on the assumption that grateful, obedient workers would not bite the hand of their masters. When operatives declined to accept this role, factory agents countered with dismissals and blacklists. The result was a growing sense of militancy among the girls and the first stirrings of a labor movement. In 1834 and 1836 there occurred spontaneous "turnouts" or strikes in Lowell, the first protesting wage cuts and the second an increase in the board charge. Neither achieved much, although a large number of girls (800 and 2,500) took part. The Associates showed their mettle in one instance by turning a widow with four children out of her boarding house because her eleven-year-old daughter, a bobbin girl, had followed the others out. "Mrs. Hanson, you could not prevent the older girls from turning out," the corporate agent explained sternly, "but your daughter is a child, and her you could control."

Between 1837 and 1842 a national depression drove wages down and quieted labor unrest at Lowell. When conditions improved and wages still fell, the disturbances began anew. In December 1844 five mill girls met to form the Lowell Female Labor Reform Association; within a year the organization had grown to 600 members in Lowell and had branches elsewhere in New England. Since unions had no legal status or power to bargain directly, LFLRA could only appeal to public opinion and petition the General Court (state legislature) for redress.

For three years the organization dispatched petitions and testified before legislative commissions on behalf of one issue in particular; the ten-hour workday. Led by Sarah Bagley and other women of remarkable energy and intelligence, LFLRA joined hands with workingmen's groups in the push for shorter hours. Their efforts were dogged, impressive, and ultimately futile. As their ranks swelled, they suffered the usual problems of divided aims and disagreement over tactics. More than that, the LFLRA failed in the end simply because it had determination but no leverage. Legislators and other officials did not take them seriously because they were women who had no business being involved in such matters and could not vote anyway. By 1847 LFLRA was little more than a memory. The ten-hour movement lived on, but did not succeed until 1874.

During its brief life LFLRA did much to shatter the image of Lowell as an industrial utopia. The Associates held aloof from controversy and allowed editors, ministers, and distinguished visitors to make their case. There were those who preserved Lowell as a symbol because they wanted to believe, needed to believe in what it represented. After several years of constant labor strife, however, few could overlook the problems pointed up by LFLRA: more work for less pay, deteriorating conditions in the mills and boarding houses, blacklists, and more repressive regulations. Lowell had lost much of what had made it special and was on the verge of becoming another bleak and stifling mill town.

Gradually the river and countryside disappeared behind unbroken walls of factory or dormitory. Nature approached extinction in Lowell, and so did the girls who had always been the core of its system. In 1845 about ninety percent of the operatives were native Americans, mostly farm girls; by 1850 half the mill workers were Irish, part of the flood that migrated after the famine years of 1845–46. The Irish girls were illiterate, docile, and desperate enough to work for low wages. They preferred tenements with their friends and family to boarding houses, which relieved the Associates of that burden. It did not take the Associates long to appreciate the virtues of so helpless and undemanding a work force. In these immigrants they saw great promise for cheap labor comparable to that found in English mill towns like Manchester.

The Associates had lost their bloom as models of propriety and benevolence. Some called them "lords of the loom" and consigned them to the same terrace of Inferno as the South's "lords of the lash." How ironic it was for Nathan Appleton, the most beloved of souls with an unmatched reputation for philanthropy and civic virtue, that his mills were the first to be called "soulless corporations."

So it was that Lowell's utopian vision ended where industrialism began. In time the Irish would rise up in protest as their predecessors had done, but behind them came waves of Dutch, Greek, and French Canadian immigrants to take their places in the mills. The native New England girls continued to flee the mills or shy away from them in droves, until by 1860 they were but a small minority. Their departure marked the emergence of Lowell as a mill town no different than any other mill town. One of the girls, peering from her boarding house window, watched the growing stories of a new mill snuff out her view of the scenery beyond and caught the significance of her loss. In her lament could be found an epitaph for Lowell itself:

Then I began to measure . . . and to calculate how long I would retain this or that beauty. I hoped that the brow of the hill would remain when the structure was complete. But no! I had not calculated wisely. It began to recede from me . . . for the building rose still higher and higher. One hope after another is gone . . . one image after another, that has been beautiful to our eye, and dear to our heart has forever disappeared. How has the scene changed! How is our window darkened!

QUESTIONS TO CONSIDER

1. Thomas Jefferson, an agrarian idealist, hated the idea of America's becoming an industrial nation, basing his feelings on the evils of European cities. How did the city of Lowell, at least in its early years, escape the evils Jefferson believed inherent in urban industrial life?

2. Klein says that what happened at Lowell reveals that the profit motive and certain democratic ideals are incompatible. Do you agree? Was the Lowell experiment doomed from its inception because of conflicting goals?

3. Why did the Boston Associates choose young women from rural parts of New England to be operatives in their Lowell textile mills? What were the advantages of a female labor force?

4. Examine boardinghouse life at Lowell from the perspective of the female mill workers. What were the advantages and drawbacks to living in the boardinghouses? In what way, if any, was boardinghouse life conducive to the development of a positive female subculture?

5. By the 1840s, changes taking place in the Lowell boarding houses and in the factories indicated the breakdown of that model factory town. Describe these changes and the reasons for growing labor militancy among the once "docile" female work force.

20

"Hell in Harness":
The Iron Horse and the Go-Ahead Age

PAGE SMITH

The development of steam power was one of the great technological accomplishments of the late eighteenth and nineteenth centuries. In an age of giant rockets, space shuttles, and satellite probes of other planets, we tend to forget that the "advanced" steam engine, patented by England's James Watts in 1769, fostered myriad technological innovations that came to characterize industrial society.

A significant improvement over an earlier "atmospheric" engine, Watts's machine transformed the textile industry in Europe as well as in America. The steam engine had an equally profound effect on the history of transportation. As train historian David Plowden said in the August/September, 1989 issue of Timeline *magazine, "The railroad builder and the locomotive shattered a fixed distance-time equation for overland travel" that had existed for centuries. Until the advent of the steam engine, people had relied on nature for locomotion — on wind, water, and animals. In the "turnpike and canal eras," which lasted from around 1790 to the 1830s, Americans tried to alter nature by creating roads and waterways, but nature still furnished the power for the boats and barges, wagons and stages. The emergence of the steam-powered locomotive in the 1820s and 1830s was a quantum leap forward. In Plowden's words, "It was a symbol of man's will to rise above nature." Soon a locomotive driven by the steam engine could pull a train of cars at thirty miles per hour, doing so with a chugging roar and puffs of black smoke that would thrill generations of Americans.*

The early railroad promoters, however, found themselves in a bitter struggle with canal and steamboat interests for transportation supremacy. But with the advantages of speed, year-round operation, and location almost anywhere, the railroads were the way of the future. By the 1850s, the age of the iron horse had arrived: thousands of miles of railroad track, shining beneath iron wheels that transported the cargo of a nation, lay across a bustling land. The railroads tied the East to the Middle West; they caused astonishing growth in existing cities such as Chicago that lay along their routes; they spawned foundries, machine shops, new tools, and "a dizzying proliferation of inventions and improvements," as Page Smith says in this selection. Railroads also inspired the American imagination, as poets and storytellers heard America singing in the music of the trains, in the clang of their bells, in the hum of their wheels, and in the throb of their engines. The train even attracted a new breed of artist — the photographer. Railroads were to become America's principal form of transportation, remaining so until the interstate highway system replaced them in the middle of the next century.

Yet, as Smith notes, there was a down side to the railroad boom: along with it came an insatiable American need to "go ahead," to travel faster and make more money regardless of the consequences to human life. In truth, the locomotives smoking up the sky presaged an industrial society with pollutants and destructive forces that would eventually imperil humankind itself. But all that lay in the future. For Americans of the mid-nineteenth century, the train was the supreme example of the illimitable aspiration and resourcefulness of the human spirit.

GLOSSARY

BALTIMORE & OHIO RAILROAD
Established in 1828 by Baltimore merchants to capitalize on the western trade; by 1830, a horse-drawn "train" was operating on thirteen miles of track heading west; the company later switched to the newfangled steam-powered locomotives, designed the passenger car, and went on to become one of the country's leading railroads, with lines that reached clear to St. Louis, Missouri.

DEWITT CLINTON Built by the Mohawk and Hudson Railroad, this improved steam locomotive made a historic run in 1832, pulling three cars at thirty miles per hour.

COOPER, PETER Glue maker and inventor who built America's first steam-powered locomotive, a crude little machine that performed erratically; George Johnson and James Milholland produced an improved version called the *Tom Thumb.*

DAVIS, PHINEAS A watchmaker who built the steam locomotive, the *York,* which won an award from the Baltimore & Ohio Railroad for being "the most improved engine."

GO-AHEAD AGE "The age of technology wherein any ambitious and dexterous farm boy might dream of becoming as rich as [fur-dealing mogul] John Jacob Astor or Peter Cooper"; the age produced "the disposition to see the world in terms of practical problems to be solved." Americans in the go-ahead age became preeminent problem solvers.

PENNSYLVANIA RAILROAD   Led other railroads in building "a 'through line' with a uniform gauge" and "in dressing its train 'captain' or conductor in a uniform."

STEPHENSON, GEORGE   British engineer who developed the first passenger railroad locomotive.

TOM THUMB   America's first steam-powered locomotive, built by Peter Cooper and improved by George Johnson, a skilled mechanic, and his apprentice, James Milholland; on its maiden run in 1830, the little one-horse engine raced a real horse, attaining a speed of 18 miles per hour; alas, the locomotive blew its safety valve and lost the race. Nevertheless it inspired confidence in the steam locomotive and dreams of building railroads "with immense stretches of very rough country to pass."

Tracks preceded trains. Enterprising entrepreneurs began laying crude tracks in the 1820s to carry horse-drawn carriages. The advantages were that a horse could pull a much heavier load faster and passengers much more comfortably on tracks than on the commonly rutted and unpaved roads of the time. Rails were usually made of wood with bands of iron on top. In Maryland experiments were conducted with stone "rails" covered with iron. The iron-covered wooden rails proved unsatisfactory as soon as the first steam engines were introduced; they had a tendency to tear loose and curl up, especially at the high rates of speed that the steam engines were soon capable of attaining — as much as fifteen miles an hour.

In England, steam engines at first seemed most promising in carrying passengers over ordinary roads and turnpikes. The Duke of Wellington's barouche was drawn by a steam engine and attained a speed of more than twenty-five miles an hour. English experiments in the use of rails were confined primarily to the hauling of heavy loads by horse or mule and, more and more frequently, by the use of some kind of steam engine.

In America, Peter Cooper, a successful businessman, saw the possibilities of combining rails and steam engines. While Cooper was neither an engineer nor an artisan, he did not hesitate to involve himself in the design of a locomotive, buying up unmounted gun barrels to use as tubes in the engine's boiler. When the locomotive failed to perform satisfactorily, Cooper turned the job of making a better one over to George Johnson, the owner of a machine shop and a skilled mechanic, who set to work with his young apprentice, James Milholland. While Johnson and Milholland were working on an improved version of Cooper's train, the *Stourbridge Lion,* imported from

Extracts from *A People's History of the American Revolution,* Vol. IV, *The Nation Comes of Age,* pages 262–282, copyright McGraw-Hill Publishing Company. Used by permission of the author.

This is an oil painting of the first railway on the Mohawk and Hudson Road, completed in 1831. Because boilers on the early trains were wood fired, they had to stop frequently for fresh supplies of wood. (Detail of painting by Edward Lamson Henry, Collection of Albany Institute of History and Art, Albany, New York. Gift of Catherine Gensevoort Lansing)

England, arrived in New York, followed by several other engines which were eagerly studied; the best features were quickly incorporated into the American machine.

Fourteen miles of railroad had meanwhile been laid between Baltimore and Ellicott's Mills, allowing horse-drawn carriages to make the trip in record time. The run to Ellicott's Mills was made by the horse carriage three times a day at a charge of twenty-five cents.

By May 30, 1830, Cooper's steam engine was ready to be tested. Cooper himself took the throttle of the *Tom Thumb,* with the president and the treasurer of the Baltimore & Ohio Company beside him. The *Tom Thumb* had a fourteen-inch piston stroke, weighed barely a ton, and developed slightly more than one horsepower, but it drew a weight of more than four tons at the rate of fifteen miles an hour. To draw attention to this new machine, Cooper adver-

tised "a race between a Gray Horse and *Tom Thumb.*" The race took place on August 28, 1830, and a passenger on the coach drawn by the locomotive wrote: "The trip was most interesting. The curves were passed without difficulty, at a speed of fifteen miles an hour. . . . The day was fine, the company in the highest spirits, and some excited gentlemen of the party pulled out memorandum books, and when at the highest speed, which was eighteen miles an hour, wrote their names and some connected sentences, to prove that even at that great velocity it was possible to do so." It was on the way back to Baltimore that the famous race occurred. At first the horse, with quicker acceleration, raced out ahead but as the engine got up steam it overtook and passed the gray. Just at that moment the safety valve on the engine blew open and the train lost pressure and fell behind, despite Peter Cooper's frantic efforts to repair the damage.

George Stephenson, the great British engineer, had

been working for almost a decade to perfect a practical engine. He had, in the process, built a dozen locomotives of various types in the well-equipped workshops of the Liverpool and Manchester Railroad and he had the stimulus of half a dozen active competitors. The United States had entered the field late and with far more modest resources, but within two years Cooper had produced the first practical passenger railroad locomotive. Engines designed by Stephenson soon outstripped the *Tom Thumb,* but American railroad building was on its way. When the Baltimore and Ohio offered a four-thousand-dollar reward for the most improved engine, Johnson and Milholland had one waiting. Its most serious rival was one designed and built by Phineas Davis, a watchmaker. Three other engines were also entered, each with important original features and all differing greatly in design. The *York,* built by Davis, won the first prize and Davis became an employee of the Baltimore and Ohio Railroad. It soon seemed as though every ambitious young engineer in the United States who could round up a few financial backers was making a locomotive. A year after the *Tom Thumb* made its historic run, the Mohawk and Hudson Railroad was completed and an engine named the *DeWitt Clinton* drew three cars at speeds that at times reached thirty miles an hour.

The Baltimore and Ohio Railroad Company had been formed on July 4, 1828, and the cornerstone laid by ninety-year-old Charles Carroll of Carrollton. But the course of the railroads, as they were soon called, proved far from smooth. They were opposed by the farmers, through whose lands their right-of-ways must run, in an alliance with the officers and stockholders of canal and highway companies (who rightly saw the railroads as dangerous competition), and by the teamsters (whose jobs were threatened). The engines themselves were so unpredictable that teams of horses had to be kept at way stations to pull broken-down trains to their destination. . . .

By 1832 — two years after *Tom Thumb's* famous trip — Pennsylvania alone had sixty-seven railroad tracks from a few hundred yards to twenty-two miles in length, many of them constructed of wood. When the Baltimore and Ohio built a passenger carriage with seats on either side of a center aisle, there were strong objections that such an aisle would simply become an extended spittoon, but this seating arrangement soon became standard on most lines. (Davy Crockett was widely reported to have exclaimed at his first sight of a train: "Hell in harness, by the 'tarnal!")

Locomotives proved easier to build and to improve in efficiency than rails. Many rails were imported from England at an exorbitant cost. The six miles of railroad between Philadelphia and Germantown, for example, cost some thirty thousand dollars per mile and the rails, weighing thirty-nine pounds to the yard, were English-made.

On his way from Quincy to Washington in the fall of 1833 to take his seat in Congress, John Quincy Adams rode on the Amboy railroad from Amboy to Philadelphia. The train consisted of two locomotives, "each drawing an accommodation car, a sort of moving stage, in a square, with open railing, a platform and a row of benches holding forty or fifty persons; then four or five cars in the form of large stage coaches, each in three compartments, with doors of entrance on both sides." Each train ended with a high-piled baggage car, in which the passengers' luggage was covered with an oilcloth. The train sped along at almost thirty miles an hour, but after ten miles it had to stop to allow the wheels to be oiled. Despite this precaution, in another five miles a wheel on one of the cars caught fire and slipped off, killing one passenger and badly maiming another. Of the sixteen passengers in the coach only one escaped injury.

Boilers on the early trains were wood-fired and, like steamboats, trains had to stop frequently to take on fresh supplies of wood. The remarkable thing is that in spite of all these difficulties — the constraints imposed by state legislatures under the control of the canal and highway interests, the scarcity of money, the inadequacy of the rails themselves, the constant litigation, the restrictive municipal ordinances that for a time forbade the building of railroad stations in cities, the disastrous accidents that plagued every line, the barns and fields set afire by sparks that showered from primitive smokestacks — the building of engines and railway tracks went inexorably on.

Boston, which had seen the greater part of the vast commerce with the Mississippi Valley West go to New York with the construction of the Erie Canal, took the lead in developing railroad links with the West, thereby regaining much of its lost financial eminence. New York, anxious to protect the investment of the state and its citizens in the canal, did all it could to impede the development of competing railroads.

By 1850 there were some three thousand miles of track running from Boston to the principal cities of New England and westward to Ohio, representing an investment of seventy million dollars. Of even greater significance was the fact that most of the lines made money. . . .

The railroad mania exceeded, if possible, the earlier canal mania. Canals still continued to be built, of course, and fierce competition developed between canals and railroads, but an extraordinary amount of technical skill and ingenuity was channeled into the development of railroads and the locomotives and the cars that passed over them. Hardly a month passed without some important innovation which, as soon as it had proved itself (and often before), was adopted by other designers and builders. It was as though a particular quality in the American character, until now more or less dormant, had been activated. For forty years — from 1789 to 1830 — the canal, the steamboat, and the bridge had been the primary fields of engineering development. Now, with the "discovery" of the railroad, the machine shop claimed equal importance with the farm or factory and Americans revealed more dramatically than ever before their astonishing facility for marshaling human energies and material resources to meet a particular challenge. Barns became foundries, warehouses were converted into machine shops. New tools were built and old

tools improved. Moreover, the primary activity of building locomotives spawned a host of subsidiary and only indirectly related undertakings. Farmers with a bent for mechanics began working on an improved plow. Longer and stronger bridges had to be built to carry heavier and heavier trains, and there were tunnels to be built through mountains that blocked the way. It was clear that principles developed in making locomotives — such elements as pistons and valves — were adaptable to other processes. So there was a dizzying proliferation of inventions and improvements. Dedicated from the first moment to finding labor-saving methods and building labor-saving tools, thereby improving the ratio between work and its monetary return, a new breed of Americans — men like Peter Cooper and Mathias Baldwin and thousands of their less well-known compatriots — ushered in the "go-ahead age," the age of technology wherein any ambitious and dexterous farm boy might dream of becoming as rich as John Jacob Astor or Peter Cooper. A disposition to see the world in terms of practical problems to be solved was both the condition and the consequence of such a habit of mind, and it certainly contributed directly to the optimistic strain in American character. Wherever one looked he or she could see signs of "progress" and improvement in man's long war against nature. Everywhere "nature" was in retreat and civilization in advance. The Indian was nature, the natural man, and he was giving way to the determination of the American to cultivate the land and obey the biblical injunction to make it fruitful and to be fruitful himself, the determination to organize space and apply ideas to landscape with such single-minded zeal and unwearying industry that the landscape must succumb. Philip Hone noted proudly in his diary: "There was never a nation on the face of the earth which equalled this in rapid locomotion." A message had been carried from President Tyler in Washington to New York, a distance of some 225 miles, in twenty-four hours.

In the face of every obstacle the promoters of the railroads pushed ahead, raising their capital primarily by public subscription. A train of seventeen cars ran from Baltimore to Washington in 1835 in two hours and fifteen minutes, carrying relatives of Washington, Adams, Jefferson, and Madison. But antirailroad teamsters still waylaid trains and shot at crews from ambush, and two years later the Depression of 1837 brought railroad building to a virtual halt. It was eleven years before stockholders in the Baltimore and Ohio got any return on their investment and then it was a mere 2 percent. Construction had gone on during that period to connect Baltimore with the Ohio River commerce at the cost of $7,500,000, and only the intervention of the famous British banking house of Alexander Baring made it possible to avoid bankruptcy.

The biggest impediments to the railroads were laws designed to protect the investors in canals. The Chesapeake and Ohio canal, for example, cost $60,000 a mile to build and took twenty-two years to complete, by which time many of the original investors had died. The most notable feature of the canal was a tunnel 3,118 feet long which required the use of headlamps on barges through it, and despite the fact that the Baltimore and Ohio Railroad ran its tracks parallel to the river, the transportation of Cumberland coal down the canal brought in substantial revenues for years, although not enough to pay its enormous costs. Protracted and expensive as its construction was, the canal was by any standard one of the great engineering feats of the century, second only to the Erie Canal. Legislators were under enormous pressure to protect such a huge investment.

A number of states passed laws requiring the railroads, after they had recouped the cost of their construction, to pay all profits above 10 percent to rival canal companies. Other laws prohibited trains from entering into or passing through the incorporated areas of cities and towns. Some states included in railroad franchises the requirement that railroads sell their tracks and stock to the state after twenty years — at the state's evaluation. Other provisions limited the carrying of freight by train to those times of the year when the canals were frozen. Freight and passenger rates of trains were frequently tied to those of canal transportation to keep the trains from drawing off business. A more practical obstacle was the fact that virtually every railroad company, many of which ran no more than fifty to a hundred miles, had a different gauge, so that freight and passengers had to be unloaded and loaded again at the boundary of every company. Everything in America was bound to have a moral dimension; the railroads must be seen as not merely having a remarkable effect on commerce but as improving morals. In this spirit the Western Railroad Company of Massachusetts sent a circular to all the clergy of the state pointing out "the moral effects of rail-roads" and urging them "to take an early opportunity to deliver a discourse before your congregation, on the moral effect of rail-roads on our wide extended country" — thereby, presumably, encouraging investment.

Since nature and morality (and, indeed, religion) were intertwined, the railroad train must be somehow reconciled with nature. [Ralph Waldo] Emerson, who believed that everything worked for the best, had no trouble in effecting the reconciliation. He was entranced by the technological revolution ushered in by the train. In 1834 he wrote in his journal: "One has dim foresight of the hitherto uncomputed mechanical advantages who rides on the rail-road and moreover a practical confirmation of the ideal philosophy that Matter is phenomenal whilst men & trees & barns whiz by you as fast as the leaves of a dictionary. As our teakettle hissed along through a field of mayflowers, we could judge of the sensations of a swallow who skims by trees & bushes with about the same speed. The very permanence of matter seems compromised & oaks, fields, hills, hitherto esteemed symbols of stability do absolutely dance by you." The railroads had introduced a "multitude of picturesque traits into our pastoral scenery," Emerson wrote, "the tunneling of the mountains, the bridging of streams . . . the encounter at short distances along the track of gangs of laborers . . . the character of the work itself which so violates and revolutionizes the primal and immemorial forms of nature; the villages of shanties at the edge of the beautiful lakes . . . the blowing of rocks, explosions all day, with the occasional alarm of a frightful accident." These all served to "keep the senses and the imagination active."

The train, Emerson believed, would complete the conquest of the continent, carrying Americans to every corner and making the United States "Nature's nation." The ambivalence of Emerson's own view of nature is suggested by his remark that "Nature is the noblest engineer, yet uses a grinding economy, working up all that is wasted to-day into to-morrow's creation. . . ." Thus nature was a good Puritan after all, a hard worker who wasted nothing.

In fairness to Emerson it must be said that, visiting the industrial midlands of England, he had second thoughts about the happy union of nature and technology. "A terrible machine has possessed itself of the ground, the air, the men and women, and hardly even thought is free," he wrote. Everything was centered in and conditioned by the omnipresent factory. In 1853, no longer rhapsodic about railroads, he wrote: "The Railroad has proved too strong for all our farmers & has corrupted them like a war, or the incursion of another race — has made them all amateurs, given the young men an air their fathers never had; they look as if they might be railroad agents any day."

By the early 1840s the railroads had an irresistible momentum. Small lines constantly consolidated in an effort to increase their access to capital and improve their service. New lines were established and as soon as they proved themselves (or went bankrupt) they were taken up by larger lines and incorporated into a "system." This process of consolidation was noted by Sidney George Fisher in 1839. "The whole route from Washington to N. York," he wrote, "is now owned by gigantic corporations, who of course manage the lines solely with a view to profit, without reference to the convenience or accommodation of passengers. Heretofore the line on the Chesapeake has been unrivalled for speed, cleanliness, civility of offi-

cers & servants, and admirable accommodations of every kind. Secure now from any competition, & sure that all persons must travel by their conveyance, they charge what they please, and the fare & accommodations will I doubt not be as wretched as that of the line to N. York." British capital and the labor of Irish immigrants were two essential ingredients in the extraordinary expansion of the railroads in the decade of the 1840s. The prize was the produce of the Mississippi Valley, the great bulk of which had to be carried down the Mississippi and its tributaries to New Orleans. To carry it by rail to New York and the large East Coast cities and ports would generate enormous profits. The Pennsylvania Railroad took the lead in building a "through line" of uniform gauge (this meant a shift from primarily passenger service to freight and passenger) and in dressing its train "captain" or conductor in a uniform with blue coat and brass buttons. Coal was the principal freight on short hauls within states. Wheat and lumber were common loads on long hauls. Perhaps most important were the changes in the patterns of urban and rural life that the building of innumerable feeder lines brought about. Farmers within a radius of a hundred miles or more of a city could now ship fresh produce — milk, eggs, fruit and vegetables — to city markets. The farmer was thus disposed to specialize, to raise cash crops in sufficient quantity to make it practical to ship them to city markets. Dairy farms and one-crop farms thus began to replace general farming. As the farmer came to depend on distant city markets, he also became vulnerable to the operations of middlemen or wholesalers, who offered the lowest possible price for his produce, and from fluctuations in demand resulting from economic cycles. The farmer thus lost a measure of his cherished independence in return for more hard money. In turn the city, guaranteed a supply of essential foods, was able to grow at an unprecedented rate.

Much of the capital required to build railroads and develop coal mines as ancillary to them came from England. An English family named Morrison started the Hazelton Coal Company at Hazelton, Pennsylvania. Sidney George Fisher's brother Henry was the American representative for the coal company and for the Reading Railroad, which the Morrison family also owned. "The railroad," Sidney wrote, "is excellent, you roll along with great speed and great smoothness, and there is very little jar or noise, the cars are very comfortable, and there is but one source of annoyance, the cinders & smoke from the engine." The mining town of Tamaqua, not far from the Hazelton mine, was "a miserable village, wretched houses & population, produced by and dependent on the Little Schuylkill mines which are all around the town & make the whole place black with coal dust." Hazelton was a pleasant "new town" located in a pine forest under which lay "immense and rich veins of coal." The ground was undermined for miles around with diggings and the Morrisons, Fisher reported, owned "1800 acres of the finest coal land in the state, the buildings, mines, railroad & machinery."

In time the legal impediments to railroad building were struck down by courts or repealed by state legislatures. The emphasis now shifted to providing incentives for building railroads, especially in the Mississippi Valley region, where vast expanses of lands were unsold and unsettled because of their distance from markets. Most settlement took place along rivers and waterways that provided access to markets. Illinois set aside eleven million dollars in 1837, the year of the depression, to build a railroad that would run through the center of the state down to the Ohio River, but the state was in such desperate financial circumstances that it was fourteen years before any substantial progress was made in building the Central Illinois Railroad to link the Great Lakes with the Ohio and the Mississippi, making Chicago the terminus for the proposed route. Irishmen again provided the workers, and the death toll from disease was a heavy one. Cholera was especially deadly in the crowded and unsanitary work camps. "Our laborers," an engineer wrote, "numbered from 5,000 to 8,000 men. We had to recruit in New York and New Orleans paying transportation to Illinois . . . but the men

would desert when the cholera epidemics broke out and scatter like frightened sheep. Men at work one day, were in their graves the next. . . . It was dangerous during the summer months to eat beef, butter, or drink milk. Our difficulties were increased by the groggeries and whisky that got in our camps. Drunken frolics ended in riots, when a contractor was murdered and state troops called out. One hundred and fifty laborers left in a body after the riot." . . .

The Central Illinois cost ten million dollars more to build than its projectors had estimated. The state gave the company 2,595,000 acres of land along its right-of-way. Abraham Lincoln was an attorney for the railroad; when he submitted a bill for $2,000 for his services and the railroad protested that that was more than Daniel Webster would have charged, Lincoln raised his fee to $5,000, took the railroad to court, and won his claim. Land through which the railroad passed rose in value from sixteen cents an acre to ten dollars an acre in a five-year period and a decade later to thirty dollars an acre.

The South now lagged behind the North and West in railroad building. All told, the feverish decade of building in the forties resulted in quadrupling the number of miles of railroad. This was all accomplished at enormous cost (the better part of it never recovered) and great loss of life (primarily Irish). When Alexander Mackay visited the United States in 1846 he found "an unbroken line of railway communication extending from Boston . . . to beyond Macon in Georgia, a distance of upwards of 1,200 miles." Lines reached out from Philadelphia to Pittsburgh, and the Baltimore and Ohio was pushing through the Cumberland Gap into the Mississippi Valley. Over 5,700 miles of railway had been completed, 2,000 of it within New England and New York state, and more than 4,000 miles of additional railway were under construction. In the 1850s the railroad mileage of the nation quadrupled once more.

Of all those who profited from the incredible expansion of the railroads none rose as dizzily as the city of Chicago. As Gustaf Unonius wrote in 1860, "The web of railroads which Chicago has spun around itself during the last ten years is the thing that more than anything else has contributed to its wealth and progress." The first locomotive reached the city in 1851. Seven years later it was the terminus of more than a dozen trunk lines. Three lines ran from Chicago to New York in less than thirty six-hours (it once had taken ten days to make the trip). Daily 120 trains, some of them hauling as many as forty freight cars, arrived and departed from the stations in various parts of the city. "It should be mentioned," Unonius wrote, "that all these railroads, altogether measuring five thousand miles in length, which radiate from Chicago as a central point in that immense iron web, the threads of which cross each other everywhere in the extensive Mississippi valley, are private undertakings." Private undertakings, as we have noted, with considerable public encouragement.

The passion to "go ahead," the endless emphasis on speed, exacted a heavy price in lives and serious injuries. In 1838 alone 496 persons died and many more were seriously injured in boiler explosions, not to mention those killed or injured in wrecks. Sidney George Fisher noted in his diary that there had been an accident on the North Pennsylvania Railroad in which thirty-nine persons had been killed and seventy-two wounded. One of the cars had caught fire and seventeen people had been burned to death. "These horrible scenes," he added, "are constantly recurring, and there seems no remedy." And Philip Hone wrote: "I never open a newspaper that does not contain some account of disasters and loss of life on railroads. They do a retail business in human slaughter, whilst the wholesale trade is carried on (especially on Western waters) by the steamboats. This world is going on too fast. Improvements, Politics, Reform, Religion — all fly. Railroads, steamers, packets, race against time and beat it hollow. Flying is dangerous. By and by we shall have balloons and pass over to Europe between sun and sun. Oh, for the good old days of heavy post-coaches and speed at the rate of six miles an hour!"

Captain Marryat ascribed such American "recklessness" to "the insatiate pursuit of gain among a people who consider that time is money, and who are blinded by their eagerness in the race for it. . . . At present, it certainly is more dangerous to travel one week in America than to cross the Atlantic a dozen times. The number of lives lost in one year by accidents in steamboats, railroads, and coaches was estimated . . . at *one thousand seven hundred and fifty!*" To Hone such disasters were "a stigma on our country; for these accidents (as they are called) seldom occur in Europe. . . . But we have become the most careless, reckless, headlong people on the face of the earth. 'Go ahead' is our maxim and password; and we do go ahead with a vengeance, regardless of the consequences and indifferent about the value of human life." His reflections were prompted by a report of the burning of the *Ben Sherrod*. The boat's crew, according to newspaper reports, was drunk and the wood took fire. "Out of 235 persons, 175 were drowned or burned to death." By the end of the year fifty-five steamboats had blown up, burned, or run aground and sunk on the Mississippi River alone; thirteen sunk on the Ohio and two on the Missouri.

When Marryat ventured by rail around the United States in the 1830s he wrote: "At every fifteen miles of the railroads there are refreshment rooms; the cars stop, all the doors are thrown open, and out rush the passengers, like boys out of school, and crowd around the tables to solace themselves with pies, patties, cakes, hard-boiled eggs, ham, custards, and a variety of railroad luxuries, too numerous to mention. The bell rings for departure, in they all hurry with their hands and mouths full, and off they go again, until the next stopping place induces them to relieve the monotony of the journey by masticating without being hungry." By the time Isabella Bird traveled west twenty years later there were numerous conveniences not available to Marryat. Bird reported that "water-carriers, book, bon-bon, and peach vendors" were "forever passing backwards and forewards." Baggage could be checked with metal checks, which was a novelty and a great convenience. Bird also discovered "through tickets," a single long ticket bought at the station of origin, for an entire trip of fifteen hundred miles on a dozen different lines.

Since Americans traveled so perpetually, travelers' accommodations were generally excellent, clean, and comfortable and virtually interchangeable. Marryat observed that "the wayside inns are remarkable for their uniformity; the furniture of the bar-room is invariably the same: a wooden clock, map of the United States, a map of the state, the Declaration of Independence, a looking-glass, with a hair-brush and comb hanging on it, *pro bono publico;* sometimes with the extra embellishment of one or two miserable pictures, such as General Jackson scrambling upon a horse, with fire and steam coming out of his nostrils, going to the battle of New Orleans, etc. etc." . . .

The feverish railroad building of the 1840s and 1850s opened up a large part of the still undeveloped land of the Mississippi Valley and provided a tremendous stimulus to business activity, although it did not prevent the devastating Depression of 1857. Perhaps most important of all, it had tied the Old West or the Near West to the Northeast and thereby laid the foundation for preserving the Union.

One can only attempt to convey the nature of the railroad boom by such phrases as "reckless enthusiasm" and "extravagant passion." The American public, which had so recently fallen in love with canals, now made trains the objects of its collective affection. Canals suddenly seemed hopelessly pokey and out of date although they continued to be an important part of the transportation network. The loss of money and loss of life attendant upon the marvelous new invention seemed to most people an in-no-way unacceptable price to pay for the intoxicating sense of *speed,* of being drawn along as fast as the wind. So began a hundred-year-long love affair between Americans and railroads. If any one invention or device can be said to have had a determining effect on the history of a people, it was certainly the railroad train on the his-

tory of the people of the United States. In the beginning everything was [by water]. Water was the element on which Americans moved — lakes, rivers, and canals provided the initial circulatory system of American travel and American commerce. Now it was iron and soon it would be steel. The canal was an adaption of nature to human needs. The train, with its relentless disposition to go straight and level to its destination, was the subjugation of nature, man's greatest triumph over a world of curves and declivities.

QUESTIONS TO CONSIDER

1. Even more than the factory, the railroad is a symbol of mid-nineteenth-century America, for it was the railroad that linked the agricultural heartland to the industrial cities. How did the growth of the railroad change the way farmers farmed? How did it influence changes in industry?

2. What effect do you think fast travel to practically everywhere may have had on family life? What effect would increased mobility via railroad have had on westward expansion? on immigration?

3. Where does the railroad fit into nineteenth-century America's long philosophic love affair with nature? What did people dislike about the railroad?

4. Which technologies in our own day do you think have expanded with the rapidity of railroads in the mid-nineteenth century and with similar effect?

5. It seems ironic that in present-day America trains evoke nostalgia for a way of life that was slower, safer, and more gracious than our own, for safety and graciousness were the very qualities that nineteenth-century people thought the railroads had destroyed. What do you see as the future of railroads in the United States? What advantages do trains have over airplanes and automobiles? what disadvantages? In a world clouded by pollution and threatened with a scarcity of fossil fuels, what role might the railroads play?

X

BEYOND THE
MISSISSIPPI

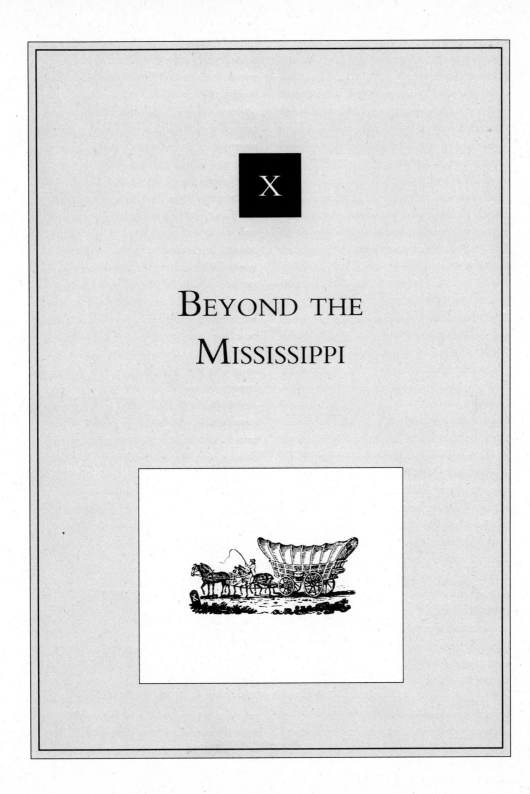

21

The Trail of Tears

DEE BROWN

One of the most unhappy chapters in American history is the way whites treated Indians. American Indian policy, however, must be seen in the context of the entire European conquest of the New World. That conquest began with Columbus, who gave the people the name Indios *and kidnapped ten San Salvador Indians, taking them back to Spain to learn the white man's ways. In the ensuing four centuries, as Dee Brown writes in* Bury My Heart at Wounded Knee, *"several million Europeans and their descendants undertook to enforce their ways upon the people of the New World," and when these people would not accept European ways, they were fought, enslaved, or exterminated.*

Whites in North America joined the conquest in the colonial period, when they drove most of the eastern tribes into the interior. This pattern of "Indian removal" continued through the eighteenth and nineteenth centuries. When Jefferson came to power, his administration began an official United States policy of Indian removal either by treaty or by outright warfare. During the next three decades, most tribes of the Old Northwest were "removed" in that manner to west of the Mississippi. When a thousand hungry Sac and Fox Indians recrossed the river into Illinois in 1832, militia and federal troops repelled the "invasion" in what became known as the Black Hawk War, in which young Abraham Lincoln commanded a militia company. The Sac and Fox retreated across the Mississippi into Wisconsin, but white soldiers pursued and needlessly slaughtered most of them.

The most forceful champion of removal was Andrew Jackson, whom the Indians called Sharp Knife. In their view, Jackson was an incorrigible Indian hater. In his frontier years he had waged war against the tribes in the South — the Cherokee, Choctaw, Chicasaw, Creek, and Seminole, known as the Five Civilized Tribes, because most had well-

developed agricultural societies. These tribes were still clinging to their tribal lands when Jackson took office. At once, he announced that the tribes must be sent away to "an ample district west of the Mississippi," and Congress responded with the Indian Removal Act, which embodied his recommendations. Under Jackson's orders, federal officials set about "negotiating" treaties with the southern tribes, with the implication that military force would be used if they did not consent to expulsion. In a subsequent act, passed in 1830, Congress guaranteed that all of the United States west of the Mississippi "and not within the states of Missouri and Louisiana or the Territory of Arkansas" would constitute "a permanent Indian frontier."

But settlers moved into Indian country before Washington could put the law into effect. So United States policymakers were obliged to shift the "permanent Indian frontier" from the Mississippi to the 95th meridian, again promising that everything west of this imaginary line would belong to the Indians "for as long as trees grow and water flows." In the late 1830s, United States soldiers rounded up the Cherokees in Georgia and herded them west into Indian country in what ranks among the saddest episodes in the sordid story of white-Indian relations in this country. Nor were the Cherokees the only Indians who were expelled. The other "civilized tribes" also suffered on the Trails of Tears to the new Indian Territory. What happened to the Cherokee is the subject of the next selection, written with sensitivity and insight by Dee Brown, a prolific historian of the West and of Native Americans.

In selection 16, Robert Remini defends Jackson's Indian policy, contending that the Five Civilized Tribes would have been exterminated had he not removed them. Remini is probably right. By this time, as Brown has said elsewhere, the Wampanoag of Massasoit "had vanished, along with the Chesapeakes, the Chicahominys, and the Potomacs of the great Powhatan confederacy. (Only Pocahontas was remembered.) Scattered or reduced to remnants were the Pequots, Montauks, Nanticokes, Madchapungas, Catawbas, Cheraws, Miamis, Hurons, Eries, Mohawks, Senecas, and Mohegans. . . . Their musical names have remained forever fixed on the American land, but their bones are forgotten in a thousand burned villages or lost in forests fast disappearing before the axes of twenty million invaders."

GLOSSARY

BOUDINOT, ELIAS Coleader of a Cherokee delegation that agreed to resettlement in the West, he had established the Cherokee's first tribal newspaper, the *Cherokee Phoenix*.

CROCKETT, DAVY Member of Congress from Tennessee who sympathized with the Cherokee's plight and damned the "cruel, unjust" way they were treated.

RIDGE, MAJOR Coleader of a Cherokee delegation that agreed to resettlement in the West.

ROSS, JOHN Cherokee leader who tried to save the Cherokee nation in Georgia; he protested to the federal government when the state of Georgia annexed all Cherokee lands within its borders.

SCOTT, WINFIELD Commander of the army forces that rounded up the Cherokee and herded them to present-day Oklahoma.

TSALI Aging Smoky Mountain Cherokee who resisted removal by force; Scott had him, his brother, and two of his sons executed by a firing squad.

UTSALA Chief of the Cherokee who avoided removal by hiding in the Smoky Mountains.

In the spring of 1838, Brigadier General Winfield Scott with a regiment of artillery, a regiment of infantry, and six companies of dragoons marched unopposed into the Cherokee country of northern Georgia. On May 10 at New Echota, the capital of what had been one of the greatest Indian nations in eastern America, Scott issued a proclamation:

The President of the United States sent me with a powerful army to cause you, in obedience to the treaty of 1835, to join that part of your people who are already established in prosperity on the other side of the Mississippi. . . . The emigration must be commenced in haste. . . . The full moon of May is already on the wane, and before another shall have passed away every Cherokee man, woman and child . . . must be in motion to join their brethren in the west. . . . My troops already occupy many positions . . . and thousands and thousands are approaching from every quarter to render resistance and escape alike hopeless. . . . Will you then by resistance compel us to resort to arms? Or will you by flight seek to hide yourselves in mountains and forests and thus oblige us to hunt you down? Remember that in pursuit it may be impossible to avoid conflicts. The blood of the white man or the blood of the red man may be spilt, and if spilt, however accidentally, it may be impossible for the discreet and humane among you, or among us, to prevent a general war and carnage.

For more than a century the Cherokees had been ceding their land, thousands of acres by thousands of acres. They had lost all of Kentucky and much of Tennessee, but after the last treaty of 1819 they still had remaining about 35,000 square miles of forested mountains, clean, swift-running rivers, and fine meadows. In this country which lay across parts of Georgia, North Carolina, and Tennessee they culti-

From "The Trail of Tears" by Dee Brown in *American History Illustrated*, June 1972. Reprinted by permission of Cowles Magazines, publisher of *American History Illustrated*.

vated fields, planted orchards, fenced pastures, and built roads, houses, and towns. Sequoya had invented a syllabary for the Cherokee language so that thousands of his tribesmen quickly learned to read and write. The Cherokees had adopted the white man's way — his clothing, his constitutional form of government, even his religion. But it had all been for nothing. Now these men who had come across the great ocean many years ago wanted all of the Cherokees' land. In exchange for their 35,000 square miles the tribe was to receive five million dollars and another tract of land somewhere in the wilderness beyond the Mississippi River.

This was a crushing blow to a proud people. "They are extremely proud, despising the lower class of Europeans," said Henry Timberlake, who visited them before the Revolutionary War. William Bartram, the botanist, said the Cherokees were not only a handsome people, tall, graceful, and olive-skinned, but "their countenance and actions exhibit an air of magnanimity, superiority and independence."

Ever since the signing of the treaties of 1819, Major General Andrew Jackson, a man they once believed to be their friend, had been urging Cherokees to move beyond the Mississippi. Indians and white settlers, Jackson told them, could never get along together. Even if the government wanted to protect the Cherokees from harassment, he added, it would be unable to do so. "If you cannot protect us in Georgia," a chief retorted, "how can you protect us from similar evils in the West?"

During the period of polite urging, a few hundred Cherokee families did move west, but the tribe remained united and refused to give up any more territory. In fact, the council leaders passed a law forbidding any chief to sell or trade a single acre of Cherokee land on penalty of death.

In 1828, when Andrew Jackson was running for President, he knew that in order to win he must sweep the frontier states. Free land for the land-hungry settlers became Jackson's major policy. He ham-

mered away at this theme especially hard in Georgia, where waves of settlers from the coastal low-lands were pushing into the highly desirable Cherokee country. He promised the Georgians that if they would help elect him President, he would lend his support to opening up the Cherokee lands for settlement. The Cherokees, of course, were not citizens and could not vote in opposition. To the Cherokees and their friends who protested this promise, Jackson justified his position by saying that the Cherokees had fought on the side of the British during the Revolutionary War. He conveniently forgot that the Cherokees had been his allies during the desperate War of 1812, and had saved the day for him in his decisive victory over the British-backed Creeks at Horseshoe Bend. (One of the Cherokee chiefs who aided Jackson was Junaluska. Said he afterward: "If I had known that Jackson would drive us from our homes I would have killed him that day at the Horseshoe.")

Three weeks after Jackson was elected President, the Georgia legislature passed a law annexing all the Cherokee country within that state's borders. As most of the Cherokee land was in Georgia and three-fourths of the tribe lived there, this meant an end to their independence as a nation. The Georgia legislature also abolished all Cherokee laws and customs and sent surveyors to map out land lots of 160 acres each. The 160-acre lots were to be distributed to white citizens of Georgia through public lotteries.

To add to the pressures on the Cherokees, gold was discovered near Dahlonega in the heart of their country. For many years the Cherokees had concealed the gold deposits, but now the secret was out and a rabble of gold-hungry prospectors descended upon them.

John Ross, the Cherokees' leader, hurried to Washington to protest the Georgia legislature's actions and to plead for justice. In that year Ross was 38 years old; he was well-educated and had been active in Cherokee government matters since he was 19. He was adjutant of the Cherokee regiment that served with Jackson at Horseshoe Bend. His father had been one of a group of Scottish emigrants who settled near the Cherokees and married into the tribe.

In Washington, Ross found sympathizers in Congress, but most of them were anti-Jackson men and the Cherokee case was thus drawn into the whirlpool of politics. When Ross called upon Andrew Jackson to request his aid, the President bluntly told him that "no protection could be afforded the Cherokees" unless they were willing to move west of the Mississippi.

While Ross was vainly seeking help in Washington, alarming messages reached him from Georgia. White citizens of that state were claiming the homes of Cherokees through the land lottery, seizing some of them by force. Joseph Vann, a hard-working half-breed, had carved out an 800-acre plantation at Spring Place and built a fine brick house for his residence. Two men arrived to claim it, dueled for it, and the winner drove Vann and his family into the hills. When John Ross rushed home he found that the same thing had happened to his family. A lottery claimant was living in his beautiful home on the Coosa River, and Ross had to turn north toward Tennessee to find his fleeing wife and children.

During all this turmoil, President Jackson and the governor of Georgia pressed the Cherokee leaders hard in attempts to persuade them to cede all their territory and move to the West. But the chiefs stood firm. Somehow they managed to hold the tribe together, and helped dispossessed families find new homes back in the wilderness areas. John Ross and his family lived in a one-room log cabin across the Tennessee line.

In 1834, the chiefs appealed to Congress with a memorial in which they stated that they would never voluntarily abandon their homeland, but proposed a compromise in which they agreed to cede the state of Georgia a part of their territory provided that they would be protected from invasion in the remainder. Furthermore, at the end of a definite period of years to be fixed by the United States they would be willing to become citizens of the various states in which they resided.

"Cupidity has fastened its eye upon our lands and our homes," they said, "and is seeking by force and by every variety of oppression and wrong to expel us from our lands and our homes and to tear from us all that has become endeared to us. In our distress we have appealed to the judiciary of the United States, where our rights have been solemnly established. We have appealed to the Executive of the United States to protect those rights according to the obligation of treaties and the injunctions of the laws. But this appeal to the Executive has been made in vain."

This new petition to Congress was no more effectual than their appeals to President Jackson. Again they were told that their difficulties could be remedied only by their removal to the west of the Mississippi.

For the first time now, a serious split occurred among the Cherokees. A small group of subchiefs decided that further resistance to the demands of the Georgia and United States governments was futile. It would be better, they believed, to exchange their land and go west rather than risk bloodshed and the possible loss of everything. Leaders of this group were Major Ridge and Elias Boudinot. Ridge had adopted his first name after Andrew Jackson gave him that rank during the War of 1812. Boudinot was Ridge's nephew. Originally known as Buck Watie, he had taken the name of a New England philanthropist who sent him through a mission school in Connecticut. Stand Watie, who later became a Confederate general, was his brother. Upon Boudinot's return from school to Georgia he founded the first tribal newspaper, the *Cherokee Phoenix,* in 1827, but during the turbulence following the Georgia land lotteries he was forced to suspend publication.

And so in February 1835 when John Ross journeyed to Washington to resume his campaign to save the Cherokee nation, a rival delegation headed by

Ridge and Boudinot arrived there to seek terms for removal to the West. The pro-removal forces in the government leaped at this opportunity to bypass Ross's authority, and within a few days drafted a preliminary treaty for the Ridge delegation. It was then announced that a council would be held later in the year at New Echota, Georgia, for the purpose of negotiating and agreeing upon final terms.

During the months that followed, bitterness increased between the two Cherokee factions. Ridge's group was a very small minority, but they had the full weight of the United States government behind them, and threats and inducements were used to force a full attendance at the council which was set for December 22, 1835. Handbills were printed in Cherokee and distributed throughout the nation, informing the Indians that those who did not attend would be counted as assenting to any treaty that might be made.

During the seven days which followed the opening of the treaty council, fewer than five hundred Cherokees, or about 2 percent of the tribe, came to New Echota to participate in the discussions. Most of the other Cherokees were busy endorsing a petition to be sent to Congress stating their opposition to the treaty. But on December 29, Ridge, Boudinot and their followers signed away all the lands of the great Cherokee nation. Ironically, thirty years earlier Major Ridge had personally executed a Cherokee chief named Doublehead for committing one of the few capital crimes of the tribe. That crime was the signing of a treaty which gave away Cherokee lands.

Charges of bribery by the Ross forces were denied by government officials, but some years afterward it was discovered that the Secretary of War had sent secret agents into the Cherokee country with authority to expend money to bribe chiefs to support the treaty of cession and removal. And certainly the treaty signers were handsomely rewarded. In an era when a dollar would buy many times its worth today, Major Ridge was paid $30,000 and his followers received several thousand dollars each. Ostensibly they were being paid for their improved farmlands, but the amounts were far in excess of contemporary land values.

John Ross meanwhile completed gathering signatures of Cherokees who were opposed to the treaty. Early in the following spring, 1836, he took the petition to Washington. More than three-fourths of the tribe, 15,964, had signed in protest against the treaty.

When the governor of Georgia was informed of the overwhelming vote against the treaty, he replied: "Nineteen-twentieths of the Cherokees are too ignorant and depraved to entitle their opinions to any weight or consideration in such matters."

The Cherokees, however, did have friends in Congress. Representative Davy Crockett of Tennessee denounced the treatment of the Cherokees as unjust, dishonest, and cruel. He admitted that he represented a body of frontier constituents who would like to have the Cherokee lands opened for settlement, and he doubted if a single one of them would second what he was saying. Even though his support of the Cherokees might remove him from public life, he added, he could not do otherwise except at the expense of his honor and conscience. Daniel Webster, Henry Clay, Edward Everett, and other great orators of the Congress also spoke for the Cherokees.

When the treaty came to a final decision in the Senate, it passed by only one vote. On May 23, 1836, President Jackson signed the document. According to its terms, the Cherokees were allowed two years from that day in which to leave their homeland forever.

The few Cherokees who had favored the treaty now began making their final preparations for departure. About three hundred left during that year and then early in 1837 Major Ridge and 465 followers departed by boats for the new land in the West. About 17,000 others, ignoring the treaty, remained steadfast in their homeland with John Ross.

For a while it seemed that Ross might win his long

fight, that perhaps the treaty might be declared void. After the Secretary of War, acting under instructions from President Jackson, sent Major William M. Davis to the Cherokee country to expedite removal to the West, Davis submitted a frank report: "That paper called a treaty is no treaty at all," he wrote, "because it is not sanctioned by the great body of the Cherokees and was made without their participation or assent. . . . The Cherokees are a peaceable, harmless people, but you may drive them to desperation, and this treaty cannot be carried into effect except by the strong arm of force."

In September 1836, Brigadier General Dunlap, who had been sent with a brigade of Tennessee volunteers to force the removal, indignantly disbanded his troops after making a strong speech in favor of the Indians: "I would never dishonor the Tennessee arms in a servile service by aiding to carry into execution at the point of the bayonet a treaty made by a lean minority against the will and authority of the Cherokee people."

Even Inspector General John E. Wool, commanding United States troops in the area, was impressed by the united Cherokee resistance, and warned the Secretary of War not to send any civilians who had any part in the making of the treaty back into the Cherokee country. During the summer of 1837, the Secretary of War sent a confidential agent, John Mason, Jr., to observe and report. "Opposition to the treaty is unanimous and irreconcilable," Mason wrote. "They say it cannot bind them because they did not make it; that it was made by a few unauthorized individuals; that the nation is not party to it."

The inexorable machinery of government was already in motion, however, and when the expiration date of the waiting period, May 23, 1838, came near, Winfield Scott was ordered in with his army to force compliance. As already stated, Scott issued his proclamation on May 10. His soldiers were already building thirteen stockaded forts — six in North Carolina, five in Georgia, one in Tennessee, and one in Alabama. At these points the Cherokees would be concentrated to await transportation to the West. Scott then ordered the roundup started, instructing his officers not to fire on the Cherokees except in case of resistance. "If we get possession of the women and children first," he said, "or first capture the men, the other members of the same family will readily come in."

James Mooney, an ethnologist who afterwards talked with Cherokees who endured this ordeal, said that squads of troops moved into the forested mountains to search out every small cabin and make prisoners of all the occupants however or wherever they might be found. "Families at dinner were startled by the sudden gleam of bayonets in the doorway and rose up to be driven with blows and oaths along the weary miles of trail that led to the stockades. Men were seized in their fields or going along the road, women were taken from their spinning wheels and children from their play. In many cases, on turning for one last look as they crossed a ridge, they saw their homes in flames, fired by the lawless rabble that followed on the heels of the soldiers to loot and pillage. So keen were these outlaws on the scent that in some instances they were driving off the cattle and other stock of the Indians almost before the soldiers had fairly started their owners in the other direction."

Long afterward one of the Georgia militiamen who participated in the roundup said: "I fought through the Civil War and have seen men shot to pieces and slaughtered by thousands, but the Cherokee removal was the cruelest work I ever knew."

Knowing that resistance was futile, most of the Cherokees surrendered quietly. Within a month, thousands were enclosed in the stockades. On June 6 at Ross's Landing near the site of present-day Chattanooga, the first of many departures began. Eight hundred Cherokees were forcibly crowded onto a flotilla of six flatboats lashed to the side of a steamboat. After surviving a passage over rough rapids which smashed the sides of the flatboats, they landed at Decatur, Alabama, boarded a railroad train (which was a new and terrifying experience for most of them), and after reaching Tuscumbia were crowded upon a Tennessee River steamboat again.

Throughout June and July similar shipments of several hundred Cherokees were transported by this long water route — north on the Tennessee River to the Ohio and then down the Mississippi and up the Arkansas to their new homeland. A few managed to escape and make their way back to the Cherokee country, but most of them were eventually recaptured. Along the route of travel of this forced migration, the summer was hot and dry. Drinking water and food were often contaminated. First the young children would die, then the older people, and sometimes as many as half the adults were stricken with dysentery and other ailments. On each boat deaths ran as high as five per day. On one of the first boats to reach Little Rock, Arkansas, at least a hundred had died. A compassionate lieutenant who was with the military escort recorded in his diary for August 1: "My blood chills as I write at the remembrance of the scenes I have gone through."

When John Ross and other Cherokee leaders back in the concentration camps learned of the high mortality among those who had gone ahead, they petitioned General Scott to postpone further departures until autumn. Although only three thousand Cherokees had been removed, Scott agreed to wait until the summer drought was broken, or no later than October. The Cherokees in turn agreed to organize and manage the migration themselves. After a lengthy council, they asked and received permission to travel overland in wagons, hoping that by camping along the way they would not suffer as many deaths as occurred among those who had gone on the river boats.

During this waiting period, Scott's soldiers continued their searches for more than a thousand Cherokees known to be still hiding out in the deep wilderness of the Great Smoky Mountains. These Cherokees had organized themselves under the leadership of a chief named Utsala, and had developed warning systems to prevent captures by the bands of soldiers. Occasionally, however, some of the fugitives were caught and herded back to the nearest stockade.

One of the fugitive families was that of Tsali, an aging Cherokee. With his wife, his brother, three sons and their families, Tsali had built a hideout somewhere on the border between North Carolina and Tennessee. Soldiers surrounded their shelters one day, and the Cherokees surrendered without resistance. As they were being taken back toward Fort Cass (Calhoun, Tennessee) a soldier prodded Tsali's wife sharply with a bayonet, ordering her to walk faster. Angered by the brutality, Tsali grappled with the soldier, tore away his rifle, and bayoneted him to the ground. At the same time, Tsali's brother leaped upon another soldier and bayoneted him. Before the remainder of the military detachment could act, the Cherokees fled, vanishing back into the Smokies where they sought refuge with Chief Utsala. Both bayoneted soldiers died.

Upon learning of the incident, Scott immediately ordered that Tsali must be brought in and punished. Because some of his regiments were being transferred elsewhere for other duties, however, the general realized that his reduced force might be occupied for months in hunting down and capturing the escaped Cherokee. He would have to use guile to accomplish the capture of Tsali.

Scott therefore dispatched a messenger — a white man who had been adopted as a child by the Cherokees — to find Chief Utsala. The messenger was instructed to inform Utsala that if he would surrender Tsali to General Scott, the Army would withdraw from the Smokies and leave the remaining fugitives alone.

When Chief Utsala received the message, he was suspicious of Scott's sincerity, but he considered the general's offer as an opportunity to gain time. Perhaps with the passage of time, the few Cherokees remaining in the Smokies might be forgotten and left alone forever. Utsala put the proposition to Tsali: If he went in and surrendered, he would probably be put to

Trail of Tears, *an oil painting by Robert Lindneux. The first group of Cherokee started on their journey west on October 1, 1838. When all the groups had reached the new Indian Territory, as Dee Brown indicates, "the Cherokees had lost about four thousand by* deaths — *or one out of every four members of the tribe — most of the deaths brought about as the direct result of the enforced removal." (Woolaroc Museum, Bartlesville, Oklahoma)*

death, but his death might insure the freedom of a thousand fugitive Cherokees.

Tsali did not hesitate. He announced that he would go and surrender to General Scott. To make certain that he was treated well, several members of Tsali's band went with him.

When the Cherokees reached Scott's headquarters, the general ordered Tsali, his brother, and three sons arrested, and then condemned them all to be shot to death. To impress upon the tribe their utter helplessness before the might of the government, Scott selected the firing squad from Cherokee prisoners in one of the stockades. At the last moment, the general spared Tsali's youngest son because he was only a child.

(By this sacrifice, however, Tsali and his family gave the Smoky Mountain Cherokees a chance at survival in their homeland. Time was on their side, as Chief Utsala had hoped, and that is why today there is a small Cherokee reservation on the North Carolina slope of the Great Smoky Mountains.)

With the ending of the drought of 1838, John Ross and the 13,000 stockaded Cherokees began preparing for their long overland journey to the West. They assembled several hundred wagons, filled them with blankets, cooking pots, their old people and small children, and moved out in separate contingents along a trail that followed the Hiwassee River. The first party of 1,103 started on October 1.

"At noon all was in readiness for moving," said an observer of the departure. "The teams were stretched out in a line along the road through a heavy forest, groups of persons formed about each wagon. The day was bright and beautiful, but a gloomy thoughtfulness was depicted in the lineaments of every face. In all the bustle of preparation there was a silence and stillness of the voice that betrayed the sadness of the heart. At length the word was given to move on. Going Snake, an aged and respected chief whose head eighty summers had whitened, mounted on his favorite pony and led the way in silence, followed by a number of younger men on horseback. At this very moment a low sound of distant thunder fell upon my ear . . . a voice of divine indignation for the wrong of my poor and unhappy countrymen, driven by brutal power from all they loved and cherished in the land of their fathers to gratify the cravings of avarice. The sun was unclouded — no rain fell — the thunder rolled away and seemed hushed in the distance."

Throughout October, eleven wagon trains departed and then on November 4, the last Cherokee exiles moved out for the West. The overland route for these endless lines of wagons, horsemen, and people on foot ran from the mouth of the Hiwassee in Tennessee across the Cumberland plateau to McMinnville and then north to Nashville where they crossed the Cumberland River. From there they followed an old trail to Hopkinsville, Kentucky, and continued northwestward to the Ohio River, crossing into southern Illinois near the mouth of the Cumberland. Moving straight westward they passed through Jonesboro and crossed the Mississippi at Cape Girardeau, Missouri. Some of the first parties turned southward through Arkansas; the later ones continued westward through Springfield, Missouri, and on to Indian Territory.

A New Englander traveling eastward across Kentucky in November and December met several contingents, each a day apart from the others. "Many of the aged Indians were suffering extremely from the fatigue of the journey," he said, "and several were quite ill. Even aged females, apparently nearly ready to drop into the grave, were traveling with heavy burdens attached to their backs — on the sometimes frozen ground and sometimes muddy streets, with no covering for the feet except what nature had given them. . . . We learned from the inhabitants on the road where the Indians passed, that they buried fourteen or fifteen at every stopping place, and they make a journey of ten miles per day only on an average. They will not travel on the Sabbath . . . they must stop, and not merely stop — they must worship the Great Spirit, too; for they had divine service on the Sabbath — a camp meeting in truth."

Autumn rains softened the roads, and the hundreds of wagons and horses cut them into molasses, slowing movement to a crawl. To add to their difficulties, tollgate operators overcharged them for passage. Their horses were stolen or seized on pretext of unpaid debts, and they had no recourse to the law. With the coming of cold damp weather, measles and whooping cough became epidemic. Supplies had to be dumped to make room for the sick in the jolting wagons.

By the time the last detachments reached the Mississippi at Cape Girardeau it was January, with the river running full of ice so that several thousand had to wait on the east bank almost a month before the channel cleared. James Mooney, who later heard the story from survivors, said that "the lapse of over half a century had not sufficed to wipe out the memory of the miseries of that halt beside the frozen river, with hundreds of sick and dying penned up in wagons or stretched upon the ground, with only a blanket overhead to keep out the January blast."

Meanwhile the parties that had left early in October were beginning to reach Indian Territory. (The first arrived on January 4, 1839.) Each group had lost from thirty to forty members by death. The later detachments suffered much heavier losses, especially toward the end of their journey. Among the victims was the wife of John Ross.

Not until March 1839 did the last of the Cherokees reach their new home in the West. Counts were made of the survivors and balanced against the counts made at the beginning of the removal. As well as could be estimated, the Cherokees had lost about four thousand by deaths — or one out of every four members of the tribe — most of the deaths brought about as the direct result of the enforced removal. From that day to this the Cherokees remember it as "the trail where they cried," or the Trail of Tears.

QUESTIONS TO CONSIDER

1. Discuss Andrew Jackson's position on the Cherokees. Did he accurately reflect white attitudes toward and assumptions about the Indians?

2. How did factionalism within the Cherokee nation help the state of Georgia and the federal government to carry out their policy of Indian removal?

3. On December 29, 1835, a Cherokee treaty council signed away the Cherokee's tribal lands and agreed to the tribe's being moved west of the Mississippi. What methods did the United States government use to obtain this treaty? Discuss the paradox of how a nation such as the United States, founded on democratic principles of government, could justify signing such a fraudulent treaty.

4. The framers of the Constitution were men of property who also held republican ideals (see selection 9). The Boston Associates, who founded Lowell, Massachusetts, were also wealthy men who tried and ultimately failed to combine benevolent and material ideas (see selection 19). How does the experience of Indian removal also illustrate America's conflict between benevolence and greed, idealism and pragmatism?

22

Women and Their Families
on the
Overland Trails

Johnny Faragher
and Christine Stansell

After the War of 1812, America turned away from Old World entanglements and sought to extend its "natural sphere of influence" westward. Pioneers moved in sporadic waves out to the Mississippi River and beyond. Jefferson had made this westward movement possible by purchasing the vast Louisiana Territory from France in 1803. He had also begun American dreams of a transcontinental empire when he sent Lewis and Clark out to the Pacific and back. In the next two decades, Americans occupied the fertile Mississippi Valley, creating the new states of Louisiana, Indiana, Mississippi, Illinois, Alabama, and Missouri. At the same time, army explorers and scientists undertook expeditions up the Arkansas and Missouri rivers, finding that the complex river systems offered tremendous possibilities for commerce and trade. In the Adams-Onís Treaty of 1819, Spain gave the United States its claims to the Oregon country, an expansive region lying north of the Red and Arkansas rivers and the 42nd parallel. After Mexico revolted against Spain in 1822, the Mexican Republic also ratified the Adams-Onís Treaty, thus clearing the way for an American march to the Pacific.

American fur companies, operating out of St. Louis and Independence, Missouri, had already sent trappers and traders out into the awesome Rocky Mountains. These fabled mountain men blazed trails and explored rich mountain valleys across the Oregon country, reporting back that the region was excellent for settlement. In the 1830s and 1840s, Americans from the fringes of the South and the old northwestern states headed across the trails the mountain men had blazed, establishing American outposts in Oregon and California. Meanwhile, other settlers — most of them from the Border South — migrated into Mexican-held Texas, where they eventually revolted and set up an independent republic.

In the 1840s — an era of unprecedented westward expansion — the United States virtually doubled its territory. It annexed the Republic of Texas, drove the British out of Oregon with threats of violence, and acquired California and the rest of the Southwest in a highly controversial war with Mexico.

The "glacial inexorability" of this westward sweep, as historian T. H. Watkins phrased it, gave birth to a faith called Manifest Destiny, a belief that Americans had a natural, God-given right to expand their superior institutions and way of life across the continent. And woe indeed to anybody — British, Mexican, or Indian — who stood in the way. To clear the way for Anglo-American settlement, the government rescinded the "permanent" frontier it had granted the Indians west of the 95th meridian and in the 1850s adopted a policy of concentration, which forced them into specified areas in various parts of the West. To justify their broken promises and treaties, white Americans contended that they were the dominant race and so were responsible for the Indians — "along with their lands, their forests, and their mineral wealth." God wished the white men to have all the lands of the West, because they knew how to use the soil and the pagan Indians did not.

Still, as historian Bernard De Voto has reminded us, other energies besides Manifest Destiny thrust America westward. Some southerners, for example, desired the empty lands for southern expansion, in order to maintain an equilibrium of power in Washington between slave and free states. Both southern and northern interests sought to control the Middle West for political and economic gain; and American industrial interests exhibited a "blind drive" to establish ports on the West Coast, thereby opening the Pacific Ocean and distant Asia to United States commercial expansion. There was another story in America's inexorable westward march — the story of the people who made the grueling trek across the overland trails to start new lives. The pioneers — men and women alike — are stock figures in frontier mythology. What were they really like? In their discussion of the conditions of life for women and their families on the Oregon and California trails, Johnny Faragher and Christine Stansell draw on contemporary diaries and letters to take us beyond the stereotypes. In the process, they raise some provocative questions. Did members of a westering family share the same attitudes? Was the women's experience different from the men's? Did the overland emigration alter eastern conventions about family structure and "proper" women's roles? In answering such questions, the authors paint a vivid and realistic portrait of daily life, family roles, work tasks, cultural expectations, and women's ties with one another, as the wagons headed toward the Pacific.

GLOSSARY

BEECHER, CATHARINE A leading advocate of separate spheres of responsibility for men and women.

"CULT OF TRUE WOMANHOOD" Argued that the true place for the American woman was her home, where she enjoyed "real economy and control" in child-rearing, household economy, and the moral and religious life of the family."

SEXUAL SPHERES The doctrine in Jacksonian America that justified segregating women in the home and men in politics and wage earning.

From 1841 until 1867, the year in which the transcontinental railroad was completed, nearly 350,000 North Americans emigrated to the Pacific coast along the western wagon road known variously as the Oregon, the California, or simply the Overland Trail. This migration was essentially a family phenomenon. Although single men constituted the majority of the party which pioneered large-scale emigration on the Overland Trail in 1841, significant numbers of women and children were already present in the wagon trains of the next season. Families made up the preponderant proportion of the migrations throughout the 1840s. In 1849, during the overwhelmingly male Gold Rush, the number dropped precipitously, but after 1851 families once again assumed dominance in the overland migration. The contention that "the family was the one substantial social institution" on the frontier is too sweeping, yet it is undeniable that the white family largely mediated the incorporation of the western territories into the American nation.

The emigrating families were a heterogeneous lot. Some came from farms in the midwest and upper South, many from small midwestern towns, and others from northeastern and midwestern cities. Clerks and shopkeepers as well as farmers outfitted their wagons in Independence, St. Louis, or Westport Landing on the Missouri. Since costs for supplies, travel, and settlement were not negligible, few of the very poor were present, nor were the exceptionally prosperous. The dreams of fortune which lured the wagon trains into new lands were those of modest men whose hopes were pinned to small farms or larger dry-goods stores, more fertile soil or more customers, better market prospects and a steadily expanding economy.

This article is reprinted from *Feminist Studies,* Volume 2, Number 2/3 (1975): 150–166 by permission of the publisher, Feminist Studies, Inc., c/o Women's Studies Program, University of Maryland, College Park, MD 20742.

For every member of the family, the trip West was exhausting, toilsome, and often grueling. Each year in late spring, westbound emigrants gathered for the journey at spots along the Missouri River and moved out in parties of ten to several hundred wagons. Aggregates of nuclear families, loosely attached by kinship or friendship, traveled together or joined an even larger caravan. Coast-bound families traveled by ox-drawn wagons at the frustratingly slow pace of fifteen to twenty miles per day. They worked their way up the Platte River valley through what is now Kansas and Nebraska, crossing the Rockies at South Pass in southwestern Wyoming by mid-summer. The Platte route was relatively easy going, but from present-day Idaho, where the roads to California and Oregon diverged, to their final destinations, the pioneers faced disastrous conditions: scorching deserts, boggy salt flats, and rugged mountains. By this time, families had been on the road some three months and were only at the midpoint of the journey; the environment, along with the wear of the road, made the last months difficult almost beyond endurance. Finally, in late fall or early winter the pioneers struggled into their promised lands, after six months and over two thousand miles of hardship.

As this journey progressed, bare necessity became the determinant of most of each day's activities. The primary task of surviving and getting to the coast gradually suspended accustomed patterns of dividing work between women and men. All able-bodied adults worked all day in one way or another to keep the family moving. Women's work was no less indispensable than men's; indeed, as the summer wore on, the boundaries dividing the work of the sexes were threatened, blurred, and transgressed.

The vicissitudes of the trail opened new possibilities for expanded work roles for women, and in the cooperative work of the family there existed a basis for a vigorous struggle for female-male equality. But most women did not see the experience in this way. They viewed it as a male enterprise from its very inception. Women experienced the breakdown of the sexual division of labor as a dissolution of their own autonomous "sphere." Bereft of the footing which this independent base gave them, they lacked a cultural rationale for the work they did, and remained estranged from the possibilities of the enlarged scope and power of family life on the trail. Instead, women fought *against* the forces of necessity to hold together the few fragments of female subculture left to them. We have been bequeathed a remarkable record of this struggle in the diaries, journals, and memoirs of emigrating women. In this study, we will examine a particular habit of living, or culture, in conflict with the new material circumstances of the Trail, and the efforts of women to maintain a place, a sphere of their own.

The overland family was not a homogeneous unit, its members imbued with identical aspirations and desires. On the contrary, the period of westward movement was also one of multiplying schisms within those families whose location and social status placed them in the mainstream of national culture. Child-rearing tracts, housekeeping manuals, and etiquette books by the hundreds prescribed and rationalized to these Americans a radical separation of the work responsibilities and social duties of mothers and fathers; popular thought assigned unique personality traits, spiritual capacities, and forms of experience to the respective categories of man, woman, and child. In many families, the tensions inherent in this separatist ideology, often repressed in the everyday routines of the East, erupted under the strain of the overland crossing. The difficulties of the emigrants, while inextricably linked to the duress of the journey itself, also revealed family dynamics which had been submerged in the less eventful life "back home."

A full-blown ideology of "woman's place" was absent in preindustrial America. On farms, in artisan shops, and in town market-places, women and children made essential contributions to family income and subsistence; it was the family which functioned as the basic unit of production in the colony and the young nation. As commercial exchanges displaced the local markets where women had sold surplus dairy products and textiles, and the workplace drifted away from the household, women and children lost their bread-winning prerogatives.

In Jacksonian America, a doctrine of "sexual spheres" arose to facilitate and justify the segregation of women into the home and men into productive work. While the latter attended to politics, economics, and wage-earning, popular thought assigned women the refurbished and newly professionalized tasks of child-rearing and housekeeping. A host of corollaries followed on the heels of these shifts. Men were physically strong, women naturally delicate; men were skilled in practical matters, women in moral and emotional concerns; men were prone to corruption, women to virtue; men belonged in the world, women in the home. For women, the system of sexual spheres represented a decline in social status and isolation from political and economic power. Yet it also provided them with a psychological power base of undeniable importance. The "cult of true womanhood" was more than simply a retreat. Catharine Beecher, one of the chief theorists of "woman's influence," proudly quoted Tocqueville's observation that "in no country has such constant care been taken, as in America, to trace two clearly distinct lines of action for the two sexes, and to make them keep pace with the other, but in two pathways which are always different." Neither Beecher nor her sisters were simply dupes of a masculine imperialism. The supervision of child-rearing, household economy, and the moral and religious life of the family granted women a certain degree of real autonomy and control over their lives as well as those of their husbands and children....

At its very inception, the western emigration sent tremors through the foundations of this carefully compartmentalized family structure. The rationale behind pulling up stakes was nearly always economic advancement; since breadwinning was a masculine concern, the husband and father introduced the idea of going West and made the final decision. Family

participation in the intervening time ran the gamut from enthusiastic support to stolid resistance. Many women cooperated with their ambitious spouses: "The motive that induced us to part with pleasant associations and the dear friends of our childhood days, was to obtain from the government of the United States a grant of land that 'Uncle Sam' had promised to give to the head of each family who settled in this new country." Others, however, only acquiesced. "Poor Ma said only this morning, 'Oh, I wish we never had started,'" Lucy Cooke wrote her first day on the trail, "and she looks so sorrowful and dejected. I think if Pa had not passengers to take through she would urge him to return; not that he should be so inclined." Huddled with her children in a cold, damp wagon, trying to calm them despite the ominous chanting of visiting Indians, another woman wondered "what had possessed my husband, anyway, that he should have thought of bringing us away out through this God forsaken country." Similar alienation from the "pioneer spirit" haunted Lavinia Porter's leave-taking:

I never recall that sad parting from my dear sister on the plains of Kansas without the tears flowing fast and free.... We were the eldest of a large family, and the bond of affection and love that existed between us was strong indeed ... as she with the other friends turned to leave me for the ferry which was to take them back to home and civilization, I stood alone on that wild prairie. Looking westward I saw my husband driving slowly over the plain; turning my face once more to the east, my dear sister's footsteps were fast widening the distance between us. For the time I knew not which way to go, nor whom to follow. But in a few moments I rallied my forces ... and soon overtook the slowly moving oxen who were bearing my husband and child over the green prairie ... the unbidden tears would flow in spite of my brave resolve to be the courageous and valiant frontierswoman.

Her dazed vacillation soon gave way to a private conviction that the family had made a dire mistake: "I would make a brave effort to be cheerful and patient until the camp work was done. Then starting out ahead of the team and my men folks, when I thought I had gone beyond hearing distance, I would throw myself down on the unfriendly desert and give way like a child to sobs and tears, wishing myself back home with my friends and chiding myself for consenting to take this wild goose chase." Men viewed drudgery, calamity, and privation as trials along the road to prosperity, unfortunate but inevitable corollaries of the rational decision they had made. But to those women who were unable to appropriate the vision of the upwardly mobile pilgrimage, hardship and the loss only testified to the inherent folly of the emigration, "this wild goose chase."

If women were reluctant to accompany their men, however, they were often equally unwilling to let them go alone. In the late 1840s, the conflict between wives and their gold-crazed husbands reveals the determination with which women enforced the cohesion of the nuclear family. In the name of family unity, some obdurate wives simply chose to blockbust the sexually segregated Gold Rush: "My husband grew enthusiastic and wanted to start immediately," one woman recalled, "but I would not be left behind. I thought where he could go I could and where I went I could take my two little toddling babies." Her family departed intact. Other women used their moral authority to smash the enterprise in its planning stages. "We were married to live together," a wife acidly reminded her spouse when he informed her of his intention to join the Rush: "I am willing to go with you to any part of *God's Foot Stool* where you think you can do best, and under these circumstances you have no right to go where I cannot, and if you do you need never return for I shall look upon you as dead." Roundly chastised, the man postponed his journey until the next season, when his family could leave with him. When included in the plans, women seldom wrote of their husbands' decisions to emigrate in their diaries or memoirs. A breadwinner who tried to leave alone, however, threatened the family unity

A frontier woman and her children stand at the Grand Canyon in Arizona. Drudgery and deprivation, the fragility of children, and the hostile environment were not the only problems facing women on the westward journey. Many bitterly regretted the loss of the homes, companionship, and responsibilities that had been theirs in the East. Surely, as Stansell and Faragher tell us, "Harriet Ward's cry — 'Oh, shall we ever live like civilized beings again?' — reverberated through the thoughts of many of her sisters." (Keystone-Mast Collection, California Museum of Photography, University of California, Riverside)

upon which his authority was based; only then did a wife challenge his dominance in worldly affairs.

There was an economic reason for the preponderance of families on the Trail. Women and children, but especially women, formed an essential supplementary work force in the settlements. The ideal wife in the West resembled a hired hand more than a nurturant Christian housekeeper. Narcissa Whitman wrote frankly to aspiring settlers of the functional necessity of women on the new farms: "Let every young man bring a wife, for he will want one after he gets here, if he never did before." In a letter from California, another seasoned woman warned a friend in Missouri that in the West women became "hewers of wood and drawers of water everywhere." Mrs. Whitman's fellow missionary Elkanah Walker was unabashedly practical in beseeching his wife to join him: "I am tired of keeping an old bachelor's hall. I want someone to get me a good supper and let me take my ease and when I am very tired in the morning I want someone to get up and get breakfast and let me lay in bed and take my rest." It would be both simplistic and harsh to argue that men brought their families West or married because of the labor power of women and children; there is no doubt, however, that the new Westerners appreciated the advantages of familial labor. Women were not superfluous; they were workers. The migration of women helped to solve the problem of labor scarcity, not only in the early years of the American settlement on the coast, but throughout the history of the continental frontier.

In the first days of the overland trip, new work requirements were not yet pressing and the division of labor among family members still replicated familiar patterns. Esther Hanna reported in one of her first diary entries that "our men have gone to build a bridge across the stream, which is impassable," while she baked her first bread on the prairie. Elizabeth Smith similarly described her party's day: "rainy . . . Men making rafts. Women cooking and washing. Children crying." When travel was suspended, "the men were generally busy mending wagons, harnesses, yokes, shoeing the animals etc., and the women washed clothes, boiled a big mess of beans, to warm over for several meals, or perhaps mended clothes." At first, even in emergencies, women and men hardly considered integrating their work. "None but those who have cooked for a family of eight, crossing the plains, have any idea of what it takes," a disgruntled

woman recalled: "My sister-in-law was sick, my niece was much younger than I, and consequently I had the management of all the cooking and planning on my young shoulders." To ask a man to help was a possibility she was unable even to consider.

The relegation of women to purely domestic duties, however, soon broke down under the vicissitudes of the Trail. Within the first few weeks, the unladylike task of gathering buffalo dung for fuel (little firewood was available *en route*) became women's work. As one traveler astutely noted, "force of surroundings was a great leveler"; miles of grass, dust, glare, and mud erased some of the most rudimentary distinctions between female and male responsibilities. By summer, women often helped drive the wagons and the livestock. At one Platte crossing, "the men drawed the wagons over by hand and the women all crossed in safety"; but at the next, calamity struck when the bridge collapsed, "and then commenced the hurry and bustle of repairing; all were at work, even the women and children." Such crises, which compounded daily as the wagons moved past the Platte up the long stretches of desert and coastal mountains, generated equity in work; at times of Indian threats, for example, both women and men made bullets and stood guard. When mountain fever struck the Pengra family as they crossed the Rockies, Charlotte relieved her incapacitated husband of the driving while he took care of the youngest child. Only such severe afflictions forced men to take on traditionally female chores. While women did men's work, there is little evidence that men reciprocated.

Following a few days in the life of an overland woman discloses the magnitude of her work. During the hours her party traveled, Charlotte Pengra walked beside the wagons, driving the cattle and gathering buffalo chips. At night she cooked, baked bread for the next noon meal, and washed clothes. Three successive summer days illustrate how trying these small chores could be. Her train pulled out early on a Monday morning, only to be halted by rain and a flash flood; Mrs. Pengra washed and dried her family's wet clothes in the afternoon while doing her daily baking. On Tuesday the wagons pushed hard to make up for lost time, forcing her to trot all day to keep up. In camp that night there was no time to rest. Before going to bed, she wrote, "Kept busy in preparing tea and doing other things preparatory for the morrow. I baked a cracker pudding, warm biscuits and made tea, and after supper stewed two pans of dried apples, and made two loaves of bread, got my work done up, beds made, and child asleep, and have written in my journal. Pretty tired of course." The same routine devoured the next day and evening: "I have done a washing. Stewed apples, made pies and baked a rice pudding, and mended our wagon cover. Rather tired." And the next: "baked biscuits, stewed berries, fried meat, boiled and mashed potatoes, and made tea for supper, afterward baked bread. Thus you see I have not much rest." Children also burdened women's work and leisure. During one quiet time, Helen Stewart retreated in mild defiance from her small charges to a tent in order to salvage some private time: "It is exceeding hot . . . some of the men is out hunting and some of them sleeping. The children is grumbling and crying and laughing and howling and playing all around." Although children are notably absent in women's journals, they do appear, frightened and imploring, during an Indian scare or a storm, or intrude into a rare and precious moment of relaxation, "grumbling and crying."

Because the rhythm of their chores was out of phase with that of the men, the division of labor could be especially taxing to women. Men's days were toilsome but broken up at regular intervals with periods of rest. Men hitched the teams, drove or walked until noon, relaxed at dinner, traveled until the evening camp, unhitched the oxen, ate supper, and in the evening sat at the campfire, mended equipment, or stood guard. They also provided most of the labor in emergencies, pulling the wagons through mires, across treacherous river crossings, up long grades, and down precipitous slopes. In the pandemonium of a steep descent,

you would see the women and children in advance seeking the best way, some of them slipping down, or holding on to the rocks, now taking an "otter slide," and then a run til some natural obstacle presented itself to stop their accelerated progress and those who get down safely without a hurt or a bruise, are fortunate indeed. Looking back to the train, you would see some of the men holding on to the wagons, others slipping under the oxen's feet, some throwing articles out of the way that had fallen out, and all have enough to do to keep them busily occupied.

Women were responsible for staying out of the way and getting themselves and the children to safety, men for getting the wagons down. Women's work, far less demanding of brute strength and endurance, was nevertheless distributed without significant respite over all waking hours: mealtimes offered no leisure to the cooks. "The plain fact of the matter is," a young woman complained,

we *have no time for sociability*. From the time we get up in the morning, until we are on the road, it is hurry scurry to get breakfast and put away the things that necessarily had to be pulled out last night — while under way there is no room in the wagon for a visitor, nooning is barely long enough to eat a cold bite — and at night all the cooking utensils and provisions are to be gotten about the camp fire, and cooking enough to last until the next night.

After supper, the men gathered together, "lolling and smoking their pipes and guessing, or maybe betting, how many miles we had covered during the day," while the women baked, washed, and put the children to bed before they finally sat down. Charlotte Pengra found "as I was told before I started that there is no rest in such a journey."

Unaccustomed tasks beset the travelers, who were equipped with only the familiar expectation that work was divided along gender lines. The solutions which sexual "spheres" offered were usually irrelevant to the new problems facing families. Women, for example, could not afford to be delicate: their new duties demanded far greater stamina and hardiness than their traditional domestic tasks. With no tradition to deal with the new exigencies of fuel-gathering, cattle-driving, and cooking, families found that "the division of labor in a party . . . was a prolific cause of quarrel." Within the Vincent party, "assignments to duty were not accomplished without grumbling and objection . . . there were occasional angry debates while the various burdens were being adjusted," while in "the camps of others who sometimes jogged along the trail in our company . . . we saw not a little fighting . . . and these bloody fisticuffs were invariably the outcome of disputes over division of labor." At home, these assignments were familiar and accepted, not subject to questioning. New work opened the division of labor to debate and conflict.

By midjourney, most women worked at male tasks. The men still retained dominance within their "sphere," despite the fact that it was no longer exclusively masculine. Like most women, Lavinia Porter was responsible for gathering buffalo chips for fuel. One afternoon, spying a grove of cottonwoods half a mile away, she asked her husband to branch off the trail so that the party could fell trees for firewood, thus easing her work. "But men on the plains I had found were not so accommodating, nor so ready to wait upon women as they were in more civilized communities." Her husband refused and Porter fought back: "I was feeling somewhat under the weather and unusually tired, and crawling into the wagon told them if they wanted fuel for the evening meal they could get it themselves and cook the meal also, and laying my head down on a pillow, I cried myself to sleep." Later that evening her husband awakened her with a belated dinner he had prepared himself, but despite his conciliatory spirit their relations were strained for weeks: "James and I had gradually grown silent and taciturn and had unwittingly partaken of the gloom and somberness of the dreary landscape." No longer a housewife or a domestic ornament, but a laborer in a male arena, Porter was still subordinate to her husband in practical matters.

Lydia Waters recorded another clash between new work and old consciousness: "I had learned to drive an ox team on the Platte and my driving was admired by an officer and his wife who were going with the mail to Salt Lake City." Pleased with the compliment, she later overheard them "laughing at the thought of a woman driving oxen." By no means did censure come only from men. The officer's wife as well as the officer derided Lydia Waters, while her own mother indirectly reprimanded teenaged Mary Ellen Todd. "All along our journey, I had tried to crack that big whip," Mary Ellen remembered years later:

Now while out at the wagon we kept trying until I was fairly successful. How my heart bounded a few days later when I chanced to hear father say to mother, "Do you know that Mary Ellen is beginning to crack the whip." Then how it fell again when mother replied, "I am afraid it isn't a very lady-like thing for a girl to do." After this, while I felt a secret joy in being able to have a power that set things going, there was also a sense of shame over this new accomplishment.

To understand Mrs. Todd's primness, so incongruous in the rugged setting of the Trail, we must see it in the context of a broader struggle on the part of women to preserve the home in transit. Against the leveling forces of the Plains, women tried to maintain the standards of cleanliness and order that had prevailed in their homes back East.

Our caravan had a good many women and children and although we were probably longer on the journey owing to their presence — they exerted a good influence, as the men did not take such risks with Indians . . . were more alert about the care of teams and seldom had accidents; more attention was paid to cleanliness and sanitation and, lastly, but not of less importance, meals were more regular and better cooked thus preventing much sickness and there was less waste of food.

Sarah Royce remembered that family wagons "were

easily distinguished by the greater number of conveniences, and household articles they carried." In the evenings, or when the trains stopped for a day, women had a chance to create with few props a flimsy facsimile of the home.

Even in camp women had little leisure time, but within the "hurry scurry" of work they managed to re-create the routine of the home. Indeed, a female subculture, central to the communities women had left behind, reemerged in these settings. At night, women often clustered together, chatting, working, or commiserating, instead of joining the men: "High teas were not popular, but tatting, knitting, crochetting, exchanging recipes for cooking beans or dried apples or swopping food for the sake of variety kept us in practice of feminine occupations and diversions." Besides using the domestic concerns of the Trail to reconstruct a female sphere, women also consciously invoked fantasy: "Mrs. Fox and her daughter are with us and everything is so still and quiet we can almost imagine ourselves at home again. We took out our Daguerreotypes [photographs] and tried to live over again some of the happy days of 'Auld Lang Syne.'" Sisterly contact kept "feminine occupations" from withering away from disuse: "In the evening the young ladies came over to our house and we had a concert with both guitars. Indeed it seemed almost like a pleasant evening at home. We could none of us realize that we were almost at the summit of the Rocky Mountains." The hostess added with somewhat strained sanguinity that her young daughter seemed "just as happy sitting on the ground playing her guitar as she was at home, although she does not love it as much as her piano." Although a guitar was no substitute for the more refined instrument, it at least kept the girl "in practice with feminine occupations and diversions": unlike Mary Ellen Todd, no big whip would tempt her to unwomanly pleasure in the power to "set things going."

But books, furniture, knick-knacks, china, the daguerreotypes that Mrs. Fox shared, or the guitars of young musicians — the "various articles of ornament and convenience" — were among the first things discarded on the epic trash heap which trailed over the mountains. On long uphill grades and over sandy deserts, the wagons had to be lightened; any materials not essential to survival were fair game for disposal. Such commodities of woman's sphere, although functionally useless, provided women with a psychological lifeline to their abandoned homes and communities, as well as to elements of their identities which the westward journey threatened to mutilate or entirely extinguish. Losing homely treasures and memorabilia was yet another defeat within an accelerating process of dispossession.

The male-directed venture likewise encroached upon the Sabbath, another female preserve. Through the influence of women's magazines, by mid-century Sunday had become a veritable ladies' day; women zealously exercised their religious influence and moral skill on the day of their families' retirement from the world. Although parties on the Trail often suspended travel on Sundays, the time only provided the opportunity to unload and dry the precious cargo of the wagons — seeds, food, and clothing — which otherwise would rot from dampness. For women whose creed forbade any worldly activity on the Sabbath, the work was not only irksome and tedious but profane.

This is Sabath it is a beautiful day indeed we do not use it as such for we have not traveled far when we stop in a most lovely place oh it is such a beautiful spot and take everything out of our wagon to air them and it is well we done it as the flower was damp and there was some of the other ones flower was rotten . . . and we baked and boiled and washed oh dear me I did not think we would have abused the sabeth in such a manner. I do not see how we can expect to get along but we did not intend to do so before we started.

Denied a voice in the male sphere that surrounded them, women were also unable to partake of the limited yet meaningful power of women with homes. On almost every Sunday, Helen Stewart lamented the disruption of a familiar and sustaining order of life, symbolized by the household goods strewn about the ground to dry: "We took everything out the wagons and the side of the hill is covered with flower biscuit meat rice oat meal clothes and such a quantity of articles of all discertions to many to mention and childre[n] included in the number. And hobos that is neather men nor yet boys being in and out hang about."

The disintegration of the physical base of domesticity was symptomatic of an even more serious disruption in the female subculture. Because the wagon trains so often broke into smaller units, many women were stranded in parties without other women. Since there were usually two or more men in the same family party, some male friendships and bonds remained intact for the duration of the journey. But by midway in the trip, female companionship, so valued by nineteenth-century women, was unavailable to the solitary wife in a party of hired men, husband, and children that had broken away from a larger train. Emergencies and quarrels, usually between men, broke up the parties. Dr. Powers, a particularly ill-tempered man, decided after many disagreements with others in his train to make the crossing alone with his family. His wife shared neither his misanthropy nor his grim independence. On the day they separated from the others, she wrote in her journal: "The women came over to bid me goodbye, for we were to go alone, all alone. They said there was no color in my face. I felt as if there was none." She perceived the separation as a banishment, almost a death sentence: "There is something peculiar in such a parting on the Plains, one there realizes what a goodbye is. Miss Turner and Mrs. Hendricks were the last to leave, and they bade me adieu the tears running down their sun-burnt cheeks. I felt as though my last friends were leaving me, for what — as I thought then — was a Maniac." Charlotte Pengra likewise left Missouri with her family in a large train. Several weeks out, mechanical problems detained some of the wagons, including those of the other three women. During the month they were separated, Pengra became increasingly dispirited and anxious: "The roads have been good today — I feel lonely and almost disheartened. . . . Can hear the wolves howl very distinctly. Rather ominis, perhaps you think . . . Feel very tired and lonely — our folks not having come — I fear some of them ar sick." Having waited as long as possible for the others, the advance group made a major river crossing. "Then I felt that indeed I had left all my friends," Pengra wrote, "save my husband and his brother, to journey over the dreaded Plains, without one female acquaintance even for a companion — of course I wept and grieved about it but to no purpose."

Others echoed her mourning. "The whipporwills are chirping," Helen Stewart wrote, "they bring me in mind of our old farm in pensillvania the home of my childhood where I have spent the happiest days I will ever see again. . . . I feel rather lonesome today oh solitude solitude how I love it if I had about a dozen of my companions to enjoy it with me." Uprootedness took its toll in debilitation and numbness. After a hard week, men "lolled around in the tents and on their blankets seeming to realize that the 'Sabbath was made for man,'" resting on the palpable achievements of miles covered and rivers crossed. In contrast, the women "could not fully appreciate physical rest, and were rendered more uneasy by the continual passing of emigrant trains all day long. . . . To me, much of the day was spent in meditating over the past and in forebodings for the future."

The ultimate expression of this alienation was the pressure to turn back, to retrace steps to the old life. Occasionally anxiety or bewilderment erupted into open revolt against going on.

This morning our company moved on, except one family. The woman got mad and wouldn't budge or let the children go. He had the cattle hitched on for three hours and coaxed her to go, but she wouldn't stir. I told my husband the circumstances and he and Adam Polk and Mr. Kimball went and each one took a young one and crammed them in the wagon, and the husband drove off and left her sitting. . . . She cut across and overtook her husband. Meantime he sent his boy back to camp after a horse he had left, and when she came up her husband said, "Did you meet John?" "Yes," was the reply, "and I picked up a stone and knocked out his brains." Her husband went back to ascertain the truth and while he was gone she set fire to one of the wagons. . . . He saw the flames and came running and put it out, and then mustered spunk enough to give her a good flogging.

Short of violent resistance, it was always possible that circumstances would force a family to reconsider and turn back. During a cholera scare in 1852, "women cried, begging their men to take them back." When the men reluctantly relented, the writer observed that "they did the hooking up of their oxen in a spiritless sort of way," while "some of the girls and women were laughing." There was little lost and much regained for women in a decision to abandon the migration.

Both sexes worked, and both sexes suffered. Yet women lacked a sense of inclusion and a cultural rationale to give meaning to the suffering and the work; no augmented sense of self or role emerged from augmented privation. Both women and men also complained, but women expanded their caviling to a generalized critique of the whole enterprise. Margaret Chambers felt "as if we had left all civilization behind us" after crossing the Missouri, and Harriet Ward's cry from South Pass — "Oh, shall we ever live like civilized beings again?" — reverberated through the thoughts of many of her sisters. Civilization was far more to these women than law, books, and municipal government; it was pianos, church societies, daguerreotypes, mirrors — in short, their homes. At their most hopeful, the exiles perceived the Trail as a hellish but necessary transition to a land where they could renew their domestic mission: "Each advanced step of the slow, plodding cattle carried us farther and farther from civilization into a desolate, barbarous country. . . . But our new home lay beyond all this

and was a shining beacon that beckoned us on, inspiring our hearts with hope and courage." At worst, temporary exigencies became in the minds of the dispossessed the omens of an irrevocable exile: "We have been travelling with 25–18–14–129–64–3 wagons — now all alone — how dreary it seems. Can it be that I have left my quiet little home and taken this dreary land of solitude in exchange?"

Only a minority of the women who emigrated over the Overland Trail were from the northeastern middle classes where the cult of true womanhood reached its fullest bloom. Yet their responses to the labor demands of the Trail indicate that "womanliness" had penetrated the values, expectations, and personalities of midwestern farm women as well as New England "ladies." "Women's sphere" provided them with companionship, a sense of selfworth, and most important, independence from men in a patriarchal world. The Trail, in breaking down sexual segregation, offered women the opportunities of socially essential work. Yet this work was performed in a male arena, and many women saw themselves as draftees rather than partners. . . .

Nonetheless, the journals of overland women are irrefutable testimony to the importance of a separate female province. Such theorists as Catharine Beecher were acutely aware of the advantages in keeping life divvied up, in maintaining "two pathways which are always different" for women and men. The women who traveled on the Overland Trail experienced firsthand the tribulations of integration which Beecher and her colleagues could predict in theory.

QUESTIONS TO CONSIDER

1. How did necessity on the Overland Trail open up new work roles for women? Did women tend to regard these new "opportunities" to share in men's work as a gain or as a loss in status?

2. How does the sphere theory, which emerges in

Jacksonian America, lead to a decline in woman's social, political, and economic status but a gain in her psychological and emotional status? Was the so-called cult of true womanhood simply a sexist ideology forced on oppressed American females?

3. Contrast the goals of men and women on the Trail. Why did women feel particularly alienated by the migration experience?

4. How were women on the trail able to create a positive female subculture? What difficulties did they encounter?

5. Faragher and Stansell remind us that historians have often associated positive work roles for women with the absence of narrow definitions of woman's place. Why is this association inaccurate in describing women's experiences on the Overland Trail?

XI

LIFE
IN THE
MILITANT SOUTH

23

This Cargo of Human Flesh

WILLIAM WELLS BROWN

Thanks to the influence of the 1939 motion picture Gone with the Wind, *many white Americans still think of the Old South as a romantic land of magnolias and landscaped manors, of cavalier gentlemen and happy darkies, of elegant ladies and breathless belles in crinoline — an ordered, leisurely world in which men and women, blacks and whites, all had their destined place. This view of Dixie is one of America's most enduring myths (*Gone with the Wind *still commands huge audiences when it runs on television). The real world of the Old South was far more complex and cruel.*

Modern historical studies have demonstrated that antebellum Dixie was a rigidly patriarchal, slave-based social order that might have lasted indefinitely had not the Civil War broken out. At no time was slavery on the verge of dying out naturally. Tobacco cultivation may have become unprofitable by the Revolutionary period, but the invention of the cotton gin in 1793 stimulated cotton production immeasurably and created a tremendous demand for slave labor. Thanks to the cotton gin, slavery spread beyond the fertile black belt of Alabama and Mississippi, out to the Kansas-Missouri border, to the fringes of western Arkansas, and to south and east Texas. Although Congress outlawed the foreign slave trade in 1808 (it simply continued as illicit traffic), the number of slaves rose dramatically so that by 1860 there were nearly 4 million in fifteen slave states, including Delaware and Maryland. Slavery remained profitable, too, as evidenced by the fact that in 1860 a prime field hand sold for $1,250 in Virginia and $1,800 on the auction blocks in New Orleans. A "fancy girl" went for as high as $2,500. Still, from the southern white's viewpoint, the profitability of slavery was not the crucial issue. Had slavery proved too costly in its plantation setting, southerners would have found other ways to use slave labor and keep blacks in chains, to maintain white male supremacy in the region.

The two selections that follow portray life in the Old South from the point of view of two of its most significant figures: the slave and the planter's wife. The patriarchal South depended for its very existence on black slaves and white women, both of whom had strictly defined roles. We begin with a contemporary account of slavery written by William Wells Brown. The son of a white slaveholder and a black mother, Brown ran away from his master and escaped to the North, where he befriended William Lloyd Garrison and lectured widely on slavery for the Western New York Anti-Slavery Society and the Massachusetts Anti-Slavery Society. Brown became a successful author, writing the first novel, the first play, and the first black history by an African American, in addition to his autobiography.

In his account of life under the lash, excerpted here, we gain melancholy insight into what it was like to be a slave in antebellum Dixie. We see how vulnerable African Americans were, how easily they were whipped and sold and otherwise abused, the victims of white people's every caprice, every whim. We meet a kind, decent white man named Elijah Lovejoy, who "hired" Brown's service for a time (later, Lovejoy would publish an antislavery newspaper in Illinois, just across the river from St. Louis, and a Missouri mob would murder him). We also meet a slave trader, a man who bought and sold blacks for a profit; we visit the wretched slave pens of New Orleans and witness a slave auction. And we see how slavery (in Brown's words) could make its victims "lying and mean." Brown's story underscores what was said in the protrait of Henry Clay (selection 18): there was no such thing as a kind slaveholder, for the ownership of another human being in itself was a cruel act, a violent act.

GLOSSARY

COLBURN, JOHN   Missouri hotel owner and an "inveterate hater of the negro" who readily beat the slaves hired out to him.

COOK, MR.   The overseer on the Missouri plantation where Brown was held a slave.

CYNTHIA   Mr. Walker made her his housekeeper and forced her to be his mistress and the mother of his children.

FREELAND, MAJOR   St. Louis proprietor to whom Brown was hired out; when Brown ran away from him, the major had him chased down with dogs and flogged.

HIRING OUT   Practice by which a master hired out the service of a slave for wages; the master got the wages.

OVERSEER   A hired supervisor, usually white, of slaves and their work.

RANDALL   A "valuable" and "able-bodied" slave who stood up to Mr. Cook and was brutally whipped for it.

SOUL DRIVER   Blacks' term for a slave trader or "speculator."

WALKER, MR.   Slave trader who bought slaves in Missouri and sold them down the Mississippi, at Natchez and New Orleans; he hired Brown out and put him in charge of the slaves to be sold down river.

☆ 1 ☆

My master owned about forty slaves, twenty-five of whom were field hands. He removed from Kentucky to Missouri, when I was quite young, and settled thirty or forty miles above St. Charles, on the Missouri, where, in addition to his practice as a physician, he carried on milling, merchandizing and farming. He had a large farm, the principal productions of which were tobacco and hemp. The slave cabins were situated on the back part of the farm, with the house of the overseer, whose name was Grove Cook, in their midst. He had the entire charge of the farm, and having no family, was allowed a woman to keep house for him, whose business it was to deal out the provisions for the hands.

A woman also kept at the quarters to do the cooking for the field hands, who were summoned to their unrequited toil every morning at four o'clock, by the ringing of a bell, hung on a post near the house of the overseer. They were allowed half an hour to eat their breakfast, and get to the field. At half past four, a horn was blown by the overseer, which was the signal to commence work; and every one that was not on the spot at the time, had to receive ten lashes from the negro-whip, with which the overseer always went armed. The handle was about three feet long, with the butt-end filled with lead, and the lash six or seven feet in length, made of cowhide, with platted wire on the end of it. This whip was put in requisition very frequently and freely, and a small offence on the part of a slave furnished an occasion for its use. During the time that Mr. Cook was overseer, I was a house servant — a situation preferable to that of a field hand, as I was better fed, better clothed, and not obliged to rise at the ringing of the bell, but about half an hour after.

From *Narrative of William W. Brown, A Fugitive Slave,* second edition, enlarged, by William Wells Brown. Boston: Published at the Anti-Slavery Office, 1848.

I have often laid and heard the crack of the whip, and the screams of the slave. My mother was a field hand, and one morning was ten or fifteen minutes behind the others in getting into the field. As soon as she reached the spot where they were at work, the overseer commenced whipping her. She cried, "Oh! pray — Oh! pray — Oh! pray" — these are generally the words of slaves when imploring mercy at the hands of their oppressors. I heard her voice, and knew it, and jumped out of my bunk, and went to the door. Though the field was some distance from the house, I could hear every crack of the whip, and every groan and cry of my poor mother. I remained at the door, not daring to venture any farther. The cold chills ran over me, and I wept aloud. After giving her ten lashes, the sound of the whip ceased, and I returned to my bed, and found no consolation but in my tears. It was not yet daylight.

☆ 2 ☆

My master being a political demagogue, soon found those who were ready to put him into office, for the favors he could render them; and a few years after his arrival in Missouri, he was elected to a seat in the Legislature. In his absence from home, everything was left in charge of Mr. Cook, the overseer, and he soon became more tyrannical and cruel. Among the slaves on the plantation, was one by the name of Randall. He was a man about six feet high, and well-proportioned, and known as a man of great strength and power. He was considered the most valuable and able-bodied slave on the plantation; but no matter how good or useful a slave may be, he seldom escapes the lash. But it was not so with Randall. He had been on the plantation since my earliest recollection, and I had never known of his being flogged. No thanks were due to the master or overseer for this. I have often heard him declare, that no white man should ever whip him — that he would die first.

Cook, from the time that he came upon the plantation, had frequently declared, that he could and would flog any nigger that was put into the field to work under him. My master had repeatedly told him not to attempt to whip Randall, but he was determined to try it. As soon as he was left sole dictator, he thought the time had come to put his threats into execution. He soon began to find fault with Randall, and threatened to whip him, if he did not do better. One day he gave him a very hard task, — more than he could possibly do; and at night, the task not being performed, he told Randall that he should remember him the next morning. On the following morning, after the hands had taken breakfast, Cook called out to Randall, and told him that he intended to whip him, and ordered him to cross his hands and be tied. Randall asked why he wished to whip him. He answered, because he had not finished his task the day before. Randall said that the task was too great, or he should have done it. Cook said it made no difference, — he should whip him. Randall stood silent for a moment, and then said, "Mr. Cook, I have always tried to please you since you have been on the plantation, and I find you are determined not to be satisfied with my work, let me do as well as I may. No man has laid hands on me, to whip me, for the last ten years, and I have long since come to the conclusion not to be whipped by any man living." Cook, finding by Randall's determined look and gestures, that he would resist, called three of the hands from their work, and commanded them to seize Randall, and tie him. The hands stood still — they knew Randall — and they also knew him to be a powerful man, and were afraid to grapple with him. As soon as Cook had ordered the men to seize him, Randall turned to them, and said — "Boys, you all know me; you know that I can handle any three of you, and the man that lays hands on me shall die. This white man can't whip me himself, and therefore he has called you to help him." The overseer was unable to prevail upon them to seize and secure Randall, and finally ordered them all to go to their work together.

Nothing was said to Randall by the overseer, for more than a week. One morning, however, while the hands were at work in the field, he came into it, accompanied by three friends of his, Thompson, Woodbridge and Jones. They came up to where Randall was at work, and Cook ordered him to leave his work, and go with them to the barn. He refused to go; whereupon he was attacked by the overseer and his companions, when he turned upon them, and laid them, one after another, prostrate on the ground. Woodbridge drew out his pistol, and fired at him, and brought him to the ground by a pistol ball. The others rushed upon him with their clubs, and beat him over the head and face, until they succeeded in tying him. He was then taken to the barn, and tied to a beam. Cook gave him over one hundred lashes with a heavy cowhide, had him washed with salt and water, and left him tied during the day. The next day he was untied, and taken to a blacksmith's shop, and had a ball and chain attached to his leg. He was compelled to labor in the field, and perform the same amount of work that the other hands did. When his master returned home, he was much pleased to find that Randall had been subdued in his absence.

☆ 3 ☆

Soon afterwards, my master removed to the city of St. Louis, and purchased a farm four miles from there, which he placed under the charge of an overseer by the name of Friend Haskell. He was a regular Yankee from New England. The Yankees are noted for making the most cruel overseers.

My mother was hired out in the city, and I was also hired out there to Major Freeland, who kept a public house. He was formerly from Virginia, and was a horse-racer, cock-fighter, gambler, and withal an inveterate drunkard. There were ten or twelve servants in the house, and when he was present, it was cut and slash — knock down and drag out. In his fits of anger,

The scars on the back of this Louisiana bondsman testify to the violence inherent in the slave system. Overseers and slave traders meted out punishment with a sinister weapon called the negro whip. The handle was some three feet long, with the butt end filled with lead; the lash was six or seven feet long and made of cowhide, with platted wire on the end of it. According to William Wells Brown, "This whip was put in requisition very frequently and freely, and a small offence on the part of a slave furnished an occasion for its use." (Photograph by Chandler Seever, circa 1860, Massachusetts Historical Society)

he would take up a chair, and throw it at a servant; and in his more rational moments, when he wished to chastise one, he would tie them up in the smokehouse, and whip them; after which, he would cause a fire to be made of tobacco stems, and smoke them. This he called "*Virginia play.*"

I complained to my master of the treatment which I received from Major Freeland; but it made no difference. He cared nothing about it, so long as he received the money for my labor. After living with Major Freeland five or six months, I ran away, and went into the woods back of the city; and when night came on, I made my way to my master's farm, but was afraid to be seen, knowing that if Mr. Haskell, the overseer, should discover me, I should be again carried back to Major Freeland; so I kept in the woods. One day, while in the woods, I heard the barking and howling of dogs, and in a short time they came so near, that I knew them to be the bloodhounds of Major Benjamin O'Fallon. He kept five or six, to hunt runaway slaves with.

As soon as I was convinced that it was them, I knew there was no chance of escape. I took refuge in the top of a tree, and the hounds were soon at its base, and there remained until the hunters came up in a half or three quarters of an hour afterwards. There were two men with the dogs, who, as soon as they came up, ordered me to descend. I came down, was tied, and taken to [the] St. Louis jail. Major Freeland soon made his appearance, and took me out, and ordered me to follow him, which I did. After we returned home, I was tied up in the smokehouse, and was very severely whipped. After the Major had flogged me to his satisfaction, he sent out his son Robert, a young man eighteen or twenty years of age, to see that I was well smoked. He made a fire of tobacco stems, which soon set me to coughing and sneezing. This, Robert told me, was the way his father used to do to his slaves in Virginia. After giving me what they conceived to be a decent smoking, I was untied and again set to work.

Robert Freeland was a "chip off the old block." Though quite young, it was not unfrequently that he came home in a state of intoxication. He is now, I believe, a popular commander of a steamboat on the Mississippi River. Major Freeland soon after failed in business, and I was put on board the steamboat Missouri, which plied between St. Louis and Galena. The commander of the boat was William B. Culver. I remained on her during the sailing season, which was the most pleasant time for me that I had ever experienced. At the close of navigation, I was hired to Mr. John Colburn, keeper of the Missouri Hotel. He was from one of the Free States; but a more inveterate hater of the negro, I do not believe ever walked on God's green earth. This hotel was at that time one of the largest in the city, and there were employed in it twenty or thirty servants, mostly slaves.

Mr. Colburn was very abusive, not only to the servants, but to his wife also, who was an excellent woman, and one from whom I never knew a servant to receive a harsh word; but never did I know a kind one to a servant from her husband. Among the slaves employed in the hotel, was one by the name of Aaron, who belonged to Mr. John F. Darby, a lawyer. Aaron was the knife-cleaner. One day, one of the knives was put on the table, not as clean as it might have been. Mr. Colburn, for this offence, tied Aaron up in the woodhouse, and gave him over fifty lashes on the bare back with a cowhide, after which, he made me wash him down with rum. This seemed to put him into more agony than the whipping. After being untied, he went home to his master, and complained of the treatment which he had received. Mr. Darby would give no heed to anything he had to say, but sent him directly back. Colburn, learning that he had been to his master with complaints, tied him up again, and gave him a more severe whipping than before. The poor fellow's back was literally cut to pieces; so much so, that he was not able to work for ten or twelve days.

There was also, among the servants, a girl whose master resided in the country. Her name was Patsey. Mr. Colburn tied her up one evening, and whipped her until several of the boarders came out and begged him to desist. The reason for whipping her was this. She was engaged to be married to a man belonging to Major William Christy, who resided four or five miles north of the city. Mr. Colburn had forbid her to see John Christy. The reason of this was said to be the regard which he himself had for Patsey. She went to meeting that evening, and John returned home with her. Mr. Colburn had intended to flog John, if he came within the inclosure; but John knew too well the temper of his rival, and kept at a safe distance — so he took vengeance on the poor girl. If all the slave-drivers had been called together, I do not think a more cruel man than John Colburn, — and he too a northern man, — could have been found among them.

While living at the Missouri Hotel, a circumstance occurred which caused me great unhappiness. My master sold my mother, and all her children, except myself. They were sold to different persons in the city of St. Louis.

☆ 4 ☆

I was soon after taken from Mr. Colburn's, and hired to Elijah P. Lovejoy, who was at that time publisher and editor of the "St. Louis Times." My work, while with him, was mainly in the printing office, waiting on the hands, working the press, &c. Mr. Lovejoy was a very good man, and decidedly the best master that I had ever had. I am chiefly indebted to him, and to my employment in the printing office, for what little learning I obtained while in slavery.

Though slavery is thought, by some, to be mild in Missouri, when compared with the cotton, sugar and rice growing States, yet no part of our slaveholding country, is more noted for the barbarity of its inhabitants, than St. Louis. It was here that Col. Harney, a United States officer, whipped a slave woman to death. It was here that Francis McIntosh, a free colored man from Pittsburgh, was taken from the steamboat Flora, and burned at the stake. During a residence of eight years in this city, numerous cases of extreme cruelty came under my own observation —

to record them all, would occupy more space than could possibly be allowed in this little volume. I shall, therefore, give but a few more, in addition to what I have already related.

Capt. J. B. Brunt, who resided near my master, had a slave named John. He was his body servant, carriage driver, &c. On one occasion, while driving his master through the city, — the streets being very muddy, and the horses going at a rapid rate, — some mud splattered upon a gentleman by the name of Robert More. More was determined to be revenged. Some three or four months after this occurrence, he purchased John, for the express purpose, as he said, "to tame the d —— d nigger." After the purchase, he took him to a blacksmith's shop, and had a ball and chain fastened to his leg, and then put him to driving a yoke of oxen, and kept him at hard labor, until the iron around his leg was so worn into the flesh, that it was thought mortification would ensue. In addition to this, John told me that his master whipped him regularly three times a week for the first two months: — and all this to "*tame him.*" A more noble looking man than he, was not to be found in all St. Louis, before he fell into the hands of More; and a more degraded and spirit-crushed looking being was never seen on a southern plantation, after he had been subjected to this "*taming*" process for three months. The last time that I saw him, he had nearly lost the entire use of his limbs.

While living with Mr. Lovejoy, I was often sent on errands to the office of the "Missouri Republican," published by Mr. Edward Charles. Once, while returning to the office with type, I was attacked by several large boys, sons of slaveholders, who pelted me with snow-balls. Having the heavy form of type in my hands, I could not make my escape by running; so I laid down the type and gave them a battle. They gathered around me, pelting me with stones and sticks, until they overpowered me, and would have captured me, if I had not resorted to my heels. Upon my retreat, they took possession of the type; and what to do to regain it I could not devise. Knowing Mr. Lovejoy to be a very humane man, I went to the office, and laid the case before him. He told me to remain in the office. He took one of the apprentices with him, and went after the type, and soon returned with it; but on his return informed me that Samuel McKinney had told him that he would whip me, because I had hurt his boy. Soon after, McKinney was seen making his way to the office by one of the printers, who informed me to the fact, and I made my escape through the back door.

McKinney not being able to find me on his arrival, left the office in a great rage, swearing that he would whip me to death. A few days after, as I was walking along Main Street, he seized me by the collar, and struck me over the head five or six times with a large cane, which caused the blood to gush from my nose and ears in such a manner that my clothes were completely saturated with blood. After beating me to his satisfaction, he let me go, and I returned to the office so weak from the loss of blood, that Mr. Lovejoy sent me home to my master. It was five weeks before I was able to walk again. During this time, it was necessary to have some one to supply my place at the office, and I lost the situation.

After my recovery, I was hired to Capt. Otis Reynolds, as a waiter on board the steamboat Enterprize, owned by Messrs. John and Edward Walsh, commission merchants at St. Louis. This boat was then running on the upper Mississippi. My employment on board was to wait on gentlemen, and the captain being a good man, the situation was a pleasant one to me — but in passing from place to place, and seeing new faces every day, and knowing that they could go where they pleased, I soon became unhappy, and several times thought of leaving the boat at some landing place, and trying to make my escape to Canada, which I had heard much about as a place where the slave might live, be free, and be protected.

But whenever such thoughts would come into my mind, my resolution would soon be shaken by the remembrance that my dear mother was a slave in St. Louis, and I could not bear the idea of leaving her in that condition. She had often taken me upon her knee, and told me how she had carried me upon her back to the field when I was an infant — how often she had been whipped for leaving her work to nurse me — and how happy I would appear when she would take me into her arms. When these thoughts came over me, I would resolve never to leave the land of slavery without my mother. I thought that to leave her in slavery, after she had undergone and suffered so much for me, would be proving recreant to the duty which I owed to her. Besides this, I had three brothers and a sister there, — two of my brothers having died. . . .

A few weeks after, on our downward passage, the boat took on board, at Hannibal, a drove of slaves, bound for the New Orleans market. They numbered from fifty to sixty, consisting of men and women from eighteen to forty years of age. A drove of slaves on a southern steamboat, bound for the cotton or sugar regions, is an occurrence so common, that no one, not even the passengers, appear to notice it, though they clank their chains at every step. There was, however, one in this gang that attracted the attention of the passengers and crew. It was a beautiful girl, apparently about twenty years of age, perfectly white, with straight light hair and blue eyes. But it was not the whiteness of her skin that created such a sensation among those who gazed upon her — it was her almost unparalleled beauty. She had been on the boat but a short time, before the attention of all the passengers, including the ladies, had been called to her, and the common topic of conversation was about the beautiful slave-girl. She was not in chains. The man who claimed this article of human merchandise was a Mr. Walker, — a well known slave-trader, residing in St. Louis. There was a general anxiety among the passengers and crew to learn the history of the girl. Her master kept close by her side, and it would have been considered impudent for any of the passengers to have spoken to her, and the crew were not allowed to have any conversation with them. When we reached St. Louis, the slaves were removed to a boat bound for New Orleans, and the history of the beautiful slave-girl remained a mystery.

I remained on the boat during the season, and it was not an unfrequent occurrence to have on board gangs of slaves on their way to the cotton, sugar and rice plantations of the South.

Toward the latter part of the summer, Captain Reynolds left the boat, and I was sent home. I was then placed on the farm under Mr. Haskell, the overseer. As I had been some time out of the field, and not accustomed to work in the burning sun, it was very hard; but I was compelled to keep up with the best of the hands.

I found a great difference between the work in a steamboat cabin and that in a corn-field.

My master, who was then living in the city, soon after removed to the farm, when I was taken out of the field to work in the house as a waiter. Though his wife was very peevish, and hard to please, I much preferred to be under her control than the overseer's. They brought with them Mr. Sloane, a Presbyterian minister; Miss Martha Tulley, a niece of theirs from Kentucky; and their nephew William. The latter had been in the family a number of years, but the others were all newcomers.

Mr. Sloane was a young minister, who had been [in] the South but a short time, and it seemed as if his whole aim was to please the slaveholders, especially my master and mistress. He was intending to make a visit during the winter, and he not only tried to please them, but I think he succeeded admirably. When they wanted singing, he sung; when they wanted praying, he prayed; when they wanted a story told, he told a story. Instead of his teaching my master theology, my master taught theology to him. While I was with captain Reynolds, my master "got religion," and new laws were made on the plantation. Formerly, we had the privilege of hunting, fishing, making splint brooms, baskets, &c. on Sunday; but this was all stopped. Every Sunday, we were all compelled to at-

336

tend meeting. Master was so religious, that he induced some others to join him in hiring a preacher to preach to the slaves.

☆ 5 ☆

My master had family worship, night and morning. At night, the slaves were called in to attend; but in the mornings, they had to be at their work, and master did all the praying. My master and mistress were great lovers of mint julep, and every morning, a pitcher-full was made, of which they all partook freely, not excepting little master William. After drinking freely all around, they would have family worship, and then breakfast. I cannot say but I loved the julep as well as any of them, and during prayer was always careful to seat myself close to the table where it stood, so as to help myself when they were all busily engaged in their devotions. By the time prayer was over, I was about as happy as any of them. A sad accident happened one morning. In helping myself, and at the same time keeping an eye on my old mistress, I accidentally let the pitcher fall upon the floor, breaking it in pieces, and spilling the contents. This was a bad affair for me; for as soon as prayer was over, I was taken and severely chastised.

My master's family consisted of himself, his wife, and their nephew, William Moore. He was taken into the family, when only a few weeks of age. His name being that of my own, mine was changed, for the purpose of giving precedence to his, though I was his senior by ten or twelve years. The plantation being four miles from the city, I had to drive the family to church. I always dreaded the approach of the Sabbath; for, during service, I was obliged to stand by the horses in the hot broiling sun, or in the rain, just as it happened.

One Sabbath, as we were driving past the house of D. D. Page, a gentleman who owned a large baking establishment, as I was sitting upon the box of the carriage, which was very much elevated, I saw Mr. Page pursuing a slave around the yard, with a long whip, cutting him at every jump. The man soon escaped from the yard, and was followed by Mr. Page. They came running past us, and the slave perceiving that he would be overtaken, stopped suddenly, and Page stumbled over him, and falling on the stone pavement, fractured one of his legs, which crippled him for life. The same gentleman, but a short time previous, tied up a woman of his, by the name of Delphia, and whipped her nearly to death; yet he was a deacon in the Baptist church, in good and regular standing. Poor Delphia! I was well acquainted with her, and called to see her while upon her sick bed; and I shall never forget her appearance. She was a member of the same church with her master.

Soon after this, I was hired out to Mr. Walker; the same man whom I have mentioned as having carried a gang of slaves down the river, on the steamboat Enterprize. Seeing me in the capacity of steward on the boat, and thinking that I would make a good hand to take care of slaves, he determined to have me for that purpose; and finding that my master would not sell me, he hired me for the term of one year.

When I learned the fact of my having been hired to a negro speculator, or a "soul-driver" as they are generally called among slaves, no one can tell my emotions. Mr. Walker had offered a high price for me, as I afterwards learned, but I suppose my master was restrained from selling me by the fact that I was a near relative of his. On entering the service of Mr. Walker, I found that my opportunity of getting to a land of liberty was gone, at least for the time being. He had a gang of slaves in readiness to start for New Orleans, and in a few days we were on our journey. I am at a loss of language to express my feelings on that occasion. Although my master had told me that he had not sold me, and Mr. Walker had told me that he had not purchased me, I did not believe them; and not until I had been to New Orleans, and was on my return, did I believe that I was not sold.

There was on the boat a large room on the lower deck, in which the slaves were kept, men and women, promiscuously — all chained two and two, and a strict watch kept that they did not get loose; for cases have occurred in which slaves have got off their chains, and made their escape at landing-places, while the boats were taking in wood — and with all our care, we lost one woman who had been taken from her husband and children, and having no desire to live without them, in the agony of her soul jumped overboard, and drowned herself. She was not chained.

It was almost impossible to keep that part of the boat clean.

On landing at Natchez, the slaves were all carried to the slave-pen, and there kept one week, during which time, several of them were sold. Mr. Walker fed his slaves well. We took on board, at St. Louis, several hundred pounds of bacon (smoked meat) and cornmeal, and his slaves were better fed than slaves generally were in Natchez, so far as my observation extended.

At the end of a week, we left for New Orleans, the place of our final destination, which we reached in two days. Here the slaves were placed in a negro-pen, where those who wished to purchase could call and examine them. The negro-pen is a small yard, surrounded by buildings, from fifteen to twenty feet wide, with the exception of a large gate with iron bars. The slaves are kept in the buildings during the night, and turned out into the yard during the day. After the best of the stock was sold at private sale at the pen, the balance were taken to the Exchange Coffee House Auctions Rooms, kept by Isaac L. McCoy, and sold at public auctions. After the sale of this lot of slaves, we left New Orleans for St. Louis.

☆ 6 ☆

On our arrival at St. Louis, I went to Dr. Young, and told him that I did not wish to live with Mr. Walker any longer. I was heart-sick at seeing my fellow-creatures bought and sold. But the Dr. had hired me for the year, and stay I must. Mr. Walker again commenced purchasing another gang of slaves. He bought a man of Colonel John O'Fallon, who resided in the suburbs of the city. This man had a wife and three children. As soon as the purchase was made, he was put in jail for safe keeping, until we should be ready to start for New Orleans. His wife visited him while there, several times, and several times when she went for that purpose was refused admittance.

In the course of eight or nine weeks Mr. Walker had his cargo of human flesh made up. There was in this lot a number of old men and women, some of them with gray locks. We left St. Louis in the steamboat Carlton, Captain Swan, bound for New Orleans. On our way down, and before we reached Rodney,[1] the place where we made our first stop, I had to prepare the old slaves for market. I was ordered to have the old men's whiskers shaved off, and the gray hairs plucked out where they were not too numerous, in which case he had a preparation of blacking to color it, and with a blacking-brush we would put it on. This was new business to me, and was performed in a room where the passengers could not see us. These slaves were also taught how old they were by Mr. Walker, and after going through the blacking process, they looked ten or fifteen years younger; and I am sure that some of those who purchased slaves of Mr. Walker, were dreadfully cheated, especially in the ages of the slaves which they bought.

We landed at Rodney, and the slaves were driven to the pen in the back part of the village. Several were sold at this place, during our stay of four or five days, when we proceeded to Natchez. There we landed at night, and the gang were put in the warehouse until morning, when they were driven to the pen. As soon as the slaves are put in these pens, swarms of planters may be seen in and about them. They knew when Walker was expected, as he always had the time advertised beforehand when he would be in Rodney,

---

[1]Mississippi.

Natchez, and New Orleans. These were the principal places where he offered his slaves for sale. . . .

The next day we proceeded to New Orleans, and put the gang in the same negro-pen which we occupied before. In a short time, the planters came flocking to the pen to purchase slaves. Before the slaves were exhibited for sale, they were dressed and driven out into the yard. Some were set to dancing, some to jumping, some to singing, and some to playing cards. This was done to make them appear cheerful and happy. My business was to see that they were placed in those situations before the arrival of the purchasers, and I have often set them to dancing when their cheeks were wet with tears. As slaves were in good demand at that time, they were all soon disposed of, and we again set out for St. Louis.

On our arrival, Mr. Walker purchased a farm five or six miles from the city. He had no family, but made a housekeeper of one of his female slaves. Poor Cynthia! I knew her well. She was a quadroon, and one of the most beautiful women I ever saw. She was a native of St. Louis, and bore an irreproachable character for virtue and propriety of conduct. Mr. Walker bought her for the New Orleans market, and took her down with him on one of the trips that I made with him. Never shall I forget the circumstances of that voyage! On the first night that we were on board the steamboat, he directed me to put her into a stateroom he had provided for her, apart from the other slaves. I had seen too much of the workings of slavery, not to know what this meant. I accordingly watched him into the stateroom, and listened to hear what passed between them. I heard him make his base offers, and her reject them. He told her that if she would accept his vile proposals, he would take her back with him to St. Louis, and establish her as his housekeeper at his farm. But if she persisted in rejecting them, he would sell her as a field hand on the worst plantation on the river. Neither threats nor bribes prevailed, however, and he retired, disappointed of his prey.

The next morning, poor Cynthia told me what had past, and bewailed her sad fate with floods of tears. I

comforted and encouraged her all I could; but I fore-saw but too well what the result must be. Without entering into any farther particulars, suffice it to say that Walker performed his part of the contract, at that time. He took her back to St. Louis, established her as his mistress and housekeeper at his farm, and before I left, he had two children by her. But, mark the end! Since I have been at the North, I have been credibly informed that Walker has been married, and, as a pre-vious measure, sold poor Cynthia and her four chil-dren (she having had two more since I came away) into hopeless bondage!

He soon commenced purchasing to take up the third gang. We took steamboat, and went to Jefferson City, a town on the Missouri river. Here we landed, and took stage for the interior of the State. He bought a number of slaves as he passed the different farms and villages. After getting twenty-two or twenty-three men and women, we arrived at St. Charles, a village on the banks of the Missouri. Here he purchased a woman who had a child in her arms, appearing to be four or five weeks old.

We had been travelling by land for some days, and were in hopes to have found a boat at this place for St. Louis, but were disappointed. As no boat was ex-pected for some days, we started for St. Louis by land. Mr. Walker had purchased two horses. He rode one, and I the other. The slaves were chained together, and we took up our line of march, Mr. Walker taking the lead, and I bringing up the rear. Though the dis-tance was not more than twenty miles, we did not reach it the first day. The road was worse than any that I have ever travelled.

Soon after we left St. Charles, the young child grew very cross, and kept up a noise during the greater part of the day. Mr. Walker complained of its crying several times, and told the mother to stop the child's d —— d noise, or he would. The woman tried to keep the child from crying, but could not. We put up at night with an acquaintance of Mr. Walker, and in the morning, just as we were about to start, the child again commenced crying. Walker

stepped up to her, and told her to give the child to him. The mother tremblingly obeyed. He took the child by one arm, as you would a cat by the leg, walked into the house, and said to the lady,

"Madam, I will make you a present of this little nigger; it keeps such a noise that I can't bear it."

"Thank you, sir," said the lady.

The mother, as soon as she saw that her child was to be left, ran up to Mr. Walker, and falling upon her knees begged him to let her have her child; she clung around his legs, and cried, "Oh, my child! my child! master, do let me have my child! oh, do, do, do. I will stop its crying, if you will only let me have it again." . . .

Mr. Walker commanded her to return into the ranks with the other slaves. Women who had children were not chained, but those that had none were. As soon as her child was disposed of, she was chained in the gang. . . .

We finally arrived at Mr. Walker's farm. He had a house built during our absence to put slaves in. It was a kind of domestic jail. The slaves were put in the jail at night, and worked on the farm during the day. They were kept here until the gang was completed, when we again started for New Orleans, on board the steamboat North America, Capt. Alexander Scott. We had a large number of slaves in this gang. One, by the name of Joe, Mr. Walker was training up to take my place, as my time was nearly out, and glad was I. We made our first stop at Vicksburg, where we re-mained one week and sold several slaves.

Mr. Walker, though not a good master, had not flogged a slave since I had been with him, though he had threatened me. The slaves were kept in the pen, and he always put up at the best hotel, and kept his wines in his room, for the accommodation of those who called to negotiate with him for the purchase of slaves. One day while we were at Vicksburg, several gentlemen came to see him for this purpose, and as usual the wine was called for. I took the tray and started around with it, and having accidentally filled some of the glasses too full, the gentlemen spilled the wine on their clothes as they went to drink. Mr. Walker apologized to them for my carelessness, but looked at me as though he would see me again on this subject.

After the gentlemen had left the room, he asked me what I meant by my carelessness, and said that he would attend to me. The next morning, he gave me a note to carry to the jailer, and a dollar in money to give to him. I suspected that all was not right, so I went down near the landing were I met with a sailor, and walking up to him, asked him if he would be so kind as to read the note for me. He read it over, and then looked at me. I asked him to tell me what was in it. Said he,

"They are going to give you hell."

"Why?" said I.

He said, "This is a note to have you whipped, and says that you have a dollar to pay for it."

He handed me back the note, and off I started. I knew not what to do, but was determined not to be whipped. I went up to the jail — took a look at it, and walked off again. As Mr. Walker was acquainted with the jailer, I feared that I should be found out if I did not go, and be treated in consequence of it still worse.

While I was meditating on the subject, I saw a colored man about my size walk up, and the thought struck me in a moment to send him with my note. I walked up to him, and asked him who he belonged to. He said he was a free man, and had been in the city but a short time. I told him I had a note to go into the jail, and get a trunk to carry to one of the steamboats; but was so busily engaged that I could not do it, although I had a dollar to pay for it. He asked me if I would not give him the job. I handed him the note and the dollar, and off he started for the jail.

I watched to see that he went in, and as soon as I saw the door close behind him, I walked around the corner, and took my station, intending to see how my friend looked when he came out. I had been there but a short time, when a colored man came around the corner, and said to another colored man with whom he was acquainted —

"They are giving a nigger scissors in the jail."

"What for?" said the other. The man continued,

"A nigger came into the jail, and asked for the jailer. The jailer came out, and he handed him a note, and said he wanted to get a trunk. The jailer told him to go with him, and he would give him the trunk. So he took him into the room, and told the nigger to give up the dollar. He said a man had given him the dollar to pay for getting the trunk. But that lie would not answer. So they made him strip himself, and then they tied him down, and are now whipping him."

I stood by all the while listening to their talk, and soon found out that the person alluded to was my customer. I went into the street opposite the jail, and concealed myself in such a manner that I could not be seen by any one coming out. I had been there but a short time, when the young man made his appearance, and looked around for me. I, unobserved, came forth from my hiding-place, behind a pile of brick, and he pretty soon saw me and came up to me complaining bitterly, saying that I had played a trick upon him. I denied any knowledge of what the note contained and asked him what they had done to him. He told me in substance what I heard the man tell who had come out of the jail.

"Yes," said he, "they whipped me and took my dollar, and gave me this note."

He showed me the note which the jailer had given him, telling him to give it to his master. I told him I would give him fifty cents for it, — that being all the money I had. He gave it to me, and took his money. He had received twenty lashes on his bare back, with the negro-whip.

I took the note and started for the hotel where I had left Mr. Walker. Upon reaching the hotel, I handed it to a stranger whom I had not seen before, and requested him to read it to me. As near as I can recollect, it was as follows: —

Dear Sir: — By your direction, I have given your boy twenty lashes. He is a very saucy boy, and tried to make me believe that he did not belong to you, and I put it on to him well for lying to me. I remain,

Your obedient servant.

It is true that in most of the slave-holding cities, when a gentleman wishes his servants whipped, he can send him to the jail and have it done. Before I went in where Mr. Walker was, I wet my cheeks a little, as though I had been crying. He looked at me, and inquired what was the matter. I told him that I have never had such a whipping in my life, and handed him the note. He looked at it and laughed — "and so you told him that you did not belong to me." "Yes, sir," said I. "I did not know that there was any harm in that." He told me I must behave myself, if I did not want to be whipped again.

This incident shows how it is that slavery makes its victims lying and mean; for which vices it afterwards reproaches them, and uses them as arguments to prove that they deserve no better fate. I have often, since my escape, deeply regretted the deception I practised upon this poor fellow; and I heartily desire that it may be, at some time or other, in my power to make him amends for his vicarious sufferings in my behalf.

☆ 7 ☆

In a few days we reached New Orleans, and arriving there in the night, remained on board until morning. While at New Orleans this time, I saw a slave killed; an account of which had been published by Theodore D. Weld, in his book entitled, "Slavery as it is." The circumstances were as follows. In the evening, between seven and eight o'clock, a slave came running down the levee, followed by several men and boys.

The whites were crying out, "Stop that nigger, stop that nigger"; while the poor panting slave, in almost breathless accents, was repeating, "I did not steal the meat — I did not steal the meat." The poor man at last took refuge in the river. The whites who were in pursuit of him, ran on board of one of the boats to see if they could discover him. They finally espied him under the bow of the steamboat Trenton. They got a pike-pole, and tried to drive him from his hiding place. When they would strike at him, he would dive under the water. The water was so cold, that it soon became evident that he must come out or be drowned.

While they were trying to drive him from under the bow of the boat or drown him, he would in broken and imploring accents say, "I did not steal the meat; I did not steal the meat. My master lives up the river. I want to see my master. I did not steal the meat. Do let me go home to master." After punching him, and striking him over the head for some time, he at last sank in the water, to rise no more alive.

On the end of the pike-pole with which they were striking him was a hook which caught in his clothing, and they hauled him on the bow of the boat. Some said he was dead, others said he was *"playing possum,"* while others kicked him to make him get up, but it was no use — he was dead.

As soon as they became satisfied of this, they commenced leaving, one after another. One of the hands on the boat informed the captain that they had killed the man, and that the dead body was lying on the deck. The captain came on deck, and said to those who were remaining, "You have killed this nigger; now take him off my boat." The captain's name was Hart. The dead body was dragged on shore and left there. I went on board of the boat where our gang of slaves were, and during the whole night my mind was occupied with what I had seen. Early in the morning, I went on shore to see if the dead body remained there. I found it in the same position that it was left the night before. I watched to see what they would

341

do with it. It was left there until between eight and nine o'clock, when a cart, which takes up the trash out of the streets, came along, and the body was thrown in, and in a few minutes more was covered over with dirt which they were removing from the streets. During the whole time, I did not see more than six or seven persons around it, who, from their manner, evidently regarded it as no uncommon occurrence.

During our stay in the city, I met with a young white man with whom I was well acquainted in St. Louis. He had been sold into slavery, under the following circumstances. His father was a drunkard, and very poor, with a family of five or six children. The father died, and left the mother to take care of and provide for the children as best she might. The eldest was a boy, named Burrill, about thirteen years of age, who did chores in a store kept by Mr. Riley, to assist his mother in procuring a living for the family. After working with him two years, Mr. Riley took him to New Orleans to wait on him while in that city on a visit, and when he returned to St. Louis, he told the mother of the boy that he had died with the yellow fever. Nothing more was heard from him, no one supposing him to be alive. I was much astonished when Burrill told me his story. Though I sympathized with him, I could not assist him. We were both slaves. He was poor, uneducated, and without friends; and if living, is, I presume, still held as a slave.

After selling out this cargo of human flesh, we returned to St. Louis, and my time was up with Mr. Walker. I had served him one year, and it was the longest year I ever lived.

QUESTIONS TO CONSIDER

1.   When abolitionists such as William Lloyd Garrison charged that slavery was a brutal institution, southern whites responded that slaves represented too large a financial investment for their owners to treat them cruelly (see selection 17). How would William Wells Brown have responded to this argument?

2.   Southern whites insisted that under the benevolent institution of slavery, blacks were too contented, too loyal, and too cowardly to resist their bondage. How did the actual slave behavior that Brown witnessed compare with this image? Why do you think southern whites insisted on this picture of the slave's personality?

3.   Contrast the image slaveholders projected about themselves — refined, cultured gentlemen and their ladies — with the reality that Brown encountered in his own life under the lash.

4.   Brown's master was a religious man who considered himself a good Christian. What role did religion play in supporting slavery? How were ministers and slaveholders able to reconcile their Christianity with the owning of human beings?

5.   Abolitionists accused slaveholders of licentious behavior and called the South "a giant brothel." Southern whites denied these accusations and defended the "purity" of southern civilization. How would Brown have responded?

24

The Myth of the
Southern Lady

ANNE FIROR SCOTT

The man of antebellum America was an enterprising builder of farms and plantations, factories and railroads, hard at work making his fortune in a bustling, materialistic society. For most white men of the period, the opportunities for individual advancement and self-fulfillment became increasingly plentiful. But it was not so for women. They were barred from polls and politics, most professions and occupations; if they were married, their earnings legally belonged to their husbands. As we saw in "The Lords and the Mill Girls" (selection 19), farm and immigrant women might secure low-paying, low-skill jobs in mills and factories, but the only place for the "true woman" was the home — or at least so said the nineteenth-century women's magazines and religious journals, which reflected the pervasive attitudes of a male-dominated world. Most men — and a great many women — firmly held that the ideal woman was pious, pure, submissive, and domesticated, caring for her husband and rearing her children with a fragile, unquestioning sweetness. As historian Barbara Welter has wryly observed, "It was a fearful obligation, a solemn responsibility, which the nineteenth-century American woman had — to uphold the pillars of the temple with her frail white hand." Those who nurtured the cult of true womanhood thundered at those who questioned the old virtues, branding them all as enemies of God, of the Republic, of civilization itself.

This viewpoint especially prevailed in antebellum Dixie, where preachers, planters, novelists, and other molders of opinion were fanatical in idealizing and idolizing southern women. The southern belle, in fact, became an exaggeration of the ideal woman so cher-

ished in antebellum (or pre–Civil War) America. In the spirited essay that follows, historian Anne Firor Scott examines the myth of the southern lady as it flourished in the patriarchal South and explains that the need to preserve the slave system contributed in large part to the insistence on perfect yet submissive women. As Scott points out, southern writers also created "the myth of the southern gentleman" — he was honorable, firm, and authoritative, "a perfect patriarch" — which complemented the image of the ideal southern lady as devoted, domesticated, and submissive. Readers may want to compare the idealized role of the southern lady with the role of the pioneer women discussed in selection 22.

GLOSSARY

FITZHUGH, GEORGE Virginia proslavery theorist who held that women and children must "recognize their proper and subordinate place" and must be utterly obedient to "lord and master," the male head of the family.

HUNDLEY, DANIEL Alabama lawyer and social analyst who insisted that southern women "content themselves with their humble household duties"; Hundley also mythologized the southern gentleman as the ideal patriarch.

LONGSTREET, AUGUSTUS BALDWIN Southern minister, educator, lawyer, and author of "realistic" stories about life in middle Georgia.

TUCKER, BEVERLY Antebellum southern novelist who supported the image of the southern lady.

PAGE, THOMAS NELSON Summed up the image of the ideal southern lady: "her life was one long act of devotion. . . ."

If talking could make it so antebellum southern women of the upper class would have been the most perfect examples of womankind yet seen on earth. If praise could satisfy all of woman's needs, they would also have been the happiest. Literary journals, sermons, novels, commencement addresses — wherever men spoke there was praise of Woman, and exhortation to further perfection.

This marvelous creation was described as a submissive wife whose reason for being was to love, honor, obey, and occasionally amuse her husband, to bring up his children and manage his household. Physically weak, and "formed for the less laborious occupations," she depended upon male protection. To secure this protection she was endowed with the capacity to "create a magic spell" over any man in her vicinity. She was timid and modest, beautiful and graceful, "the most fascinating being in creation . . . the delight and charm of every circle she moves in."

Part of her charm lay in her innocence. The less a woman knew of life, Ellen Glasgow once remarked bitterly, the better she was supposed to be able to deal

Selection from Anne Firor Scott, *The Southern Lady, from Pedestal to Politics,* pages 4–21, copyright © 1970 by The University of Chicago. Reprinted by permission of the publisher.

with it. Her mind was not logical, but in the absence of reasoning capacity her sensibility and intuition were highly developed. It was, indeed, to her advantage that "the play of instincts and of the feelings is not cramped by the controlling influence of logic and reason." She was capable of acute perceptions about human relationships, and was a creature of tact, discernment, sympathy, and compassion. It was her nature to be self-denying, and she was given to suffering in silence, a characteristic said to endear her to men. Less endearing, perhaps, but no less natural, was her piety and her tendency to "restrain man's natural vice and immorality." She was thought to be "most deeply interested in the success of every scheme which curbs the passions and enforces a true morality." She was a natural teacher, and a wise counselor to her husband and children.

Thomas Nelson Page, writing many years after the Civil War, summed up the image:

Her life was one long act of devotion, — devotion to God, devotion to her husband, devotion to her children, devotion to her servants, to the poor, to humanity. Nothing happened within the range of her knowledge that her sympathy did not reach and her charity and wisdom did not ameliorate. She was the head and font of the church. . . . The training of her children was her work. She watched over them, inspired them, led them, governed them; her will impelled them; her word to them, as to her servants, was law. She reaped the reward . . . their sympathy and tenderness were hers always, and they worshipped her.

Even a realist like Augustus Baldwin Longstreet was obviously influenced by the image when he came to describe a southern matron in one of his stories:

. . . pious but not austere, cheerful, but not light; generous but not prodigal; economical, but not close; hospitable but not extravagant. . . . To have heard her converse you would have supposed she did nothing but read, to have looked through the departments of her household you would have

Painting by Alice Ravenal Huger Smith of a southern lady and her daughter in the "stack-yard" of the plantation. In patriarchal Dixie, the perfect lady was regal in bearing but submissive in all things to her husband; she was the mistress of her household, her slaves, and her children but not of herself. Living up to the idealized image of southern womanhood required intense inner struggle and self-repression, yet few women questioned the reality of the image or the need to maintain it. (The Gibbes Museum of Art/Carolina Art Association)

supposed she never read. . . . Everything under her care went on with perfect system.

Oddly enough this paragon of virtue was thought to need the direction and control of some man. A person identified only as "president of the oldest college in Virginia" published a letter to his newly married daughter in an early issue of the *Southern Literary Messenger*. The wife's conduct alone, he asserted, determined the happiness or misery of a marriage. She must resolve at the outset never to oppose her husband, never to show displeasure, no matter what he might do. A man had a right to expect his wife to place perfect confidence in his judgment and to believe that he always knew best. "A difference with your husband ought to be considered the greatest calamity," wrote the father, adding that a woman who permitted differences to occur could expect to lose her husband's love and all hope of happiness. He concluded with the usual injunctions that she should be amiable, sweet, prudent, and devoted, that she should regulate her servants with a kind but firm hand, cultivate her mind by reading history and not corrupt it with novels, and manage her domestic concerns with neatness, order, economy, and judgment.

A novelist echoed the opinions of the college president. "In the heart of woman, uncorrupted by a false philosophy which would unfit her for her proper sphere, the proudest feeling is that of admiration for her husband. . . . this is as God meant it should be. To this state the natural feelings of a woman's heart will tend, let quacks in education do what they will."

From earliest childhood girls were trained to the ideals of perfection and submission. A magazine for children published in Charleston, recording the death of a seven-year-old, spoke of her as "peculiarly amiable and engaging; her behaviour marked with a delicate sense of propriety, happily mingled with an artless innocence." She was praised for being kind and considerate to her servants. The fiction in the same magazine was filled with pious, obedient little girls. Boarding schools for young ladies, to which more and more girls were sent as the century wore on, emphasized correct female behavior more than intellectual development. In at least one school the girls wrote their English compositions on such subjects as modesty, benevolence, and the evils of reading novels.

By the time they arrived at their teens most girls had absorbed the injunctions of the myth. One young woman wrote in her diary that she longed to die because she had not found a husband, adding, "I know I would make a faithful, obedient wife, loving with all my heart, yielding entire trust in my husband."

The image of the submissive woman was reinforced by evangelical theology. Daniel R. Hundley, a young Alabama lawyer who wrote a sociological analysis of the antebellum South, relied on Saint Paul's authority for asserting that women should "content themselves with their humble household duties." Southern pulpits repeated the apostle's injunction that women should keep silent in the churches. One minister argued that women needed "the hope and prospects of religion more . . . than the other sex" to soften the pains of living and help women bear with patience and submission the inevitable trials of life, among which he suggested might be "a husband of acid temper." A North Carolina doctor wrote that "God in his inscrutable wisdom has appointed a place and duty for females *out of which* they can neither accomplish their destiny nor secure their happiness!!"

Southern women sought diligently to live up to the prescriptions, to attain the perfection and the submissiveness demanded of them by God and man. John Donald Wade, whose researches into the life of Augustus Baldwin Longstreet reinforced his understanding of the social history of middle Georgia, concluded that "men found intelligence in woman a quality that in general distressed more than it pleased. When they did not openly condemn they treated it with insulting condescension. *The women proved themselves marvelously adaptable.*" A woman novelist suggested something about the ongoing struggle to live up to the expectations of men:

To repress a harsh answer, to confess a fault, and to stop (right or wrong) in the midst of self-defence, in gentle submission, sometimes requires a struggle like life and death; but these *three* efforts are the golden threads with which domestic happiness is woven; once begin the fabric with this woof, and trials shall not break or sorrow tarnish it.

Men are not often unreasonable; their difficulties lie in not understanding the moral and physical structure of our sex. . . . How clear it is, then, that woman loses by petulance and recrimination! Her first study must be self-control, almost to hypocrisy. A good wife must smile amid a thousand perplexities, and clear her voice to tones of cheerfulness when her frame is drooping with disease or else languish alone.

Women made heroic efforts to live up to what was expected of them. One, who could hardly bear the sound of her husband tuning his violin, bit her lip and said nothing, murmuring about self-abnegation. There was no rest for the conscience. "We owe it to our husbands, children and friends," wrote a Louisiana housewife, "to represent as nearly as possible the ideal which they hold so dear." "'Tis man's to act, 'tis woman's to endure," reflected an Alabama novelist in the midst of trials with a husband she did not much respect, and financial problems beyond her power to solve. Women were made, indeed, the long-suffering wife of the violinist concluded, "to suffer and be strong." "Give me a double portion of the grace of thy Spirit that I may learn meekness," wrote the self-flagellating wife of a minister.

Even more effort, if possible, went into the struggle to live up to what God was presumed to expect of women. A young bride laid down a program for herself:

1.　To read the Bible and pray after rising in the morning and sometime after breakfast.

2.　To pray again before dinner and read the Bible in the evening and pray before bed.

3.　To obey my husband in all things reasonable.

4.　"I will endeavor to use patience and forebearance towards my son [her husband's son by an earlier marriage] and correct him in a spirit of mildness for every offense of which he may be guilty.

5.　"I will endeavor to offend not with the tongue, but hold it in with bit and bridle and speak charitably of all persons."

6.　"I will endeavor to do good unto all as far as it is in my power, especially unto the household of faith."

7.　"I will endeavor to subdue every evil propensity by the assistance of Divine Grace, and by practicing

that degree of fasting and abstinence which my health will admit of."

This same woman kept a religious diary devoted entirely to daily meditations and painful examination of her progress in the endless struggle for religious perfection. Shortly after her marriage she begged God to cleanse her of secret faults, to save her from impatience and hastiness of temper, and to give her "perfect resignation to Thy Holy Will concerning me." In succeeding entries she deplored her own hardness of heart and expressed guilt when she did not bear severe pain with Christian fortitude.

This was not just one aberrant perfectionist. There are numerous similar letters and diaries. "I feel this day heavy and sad and I would ask myself why and the answer is I feel cold in religious matters oh why am I thus?" "I feel that I am worthless and through the merits of Christ's all-atoning blood alone can I be saved." "Mr. B. [her husband] says we must try to live holier. Oh that I could. Spent some time today reading, weeping and praying." "Help me O Lord for I am poor and weak, help me for I am desolate, in Thee alone have I hope." "As for myself I find my heart so full of sinful feelings that I am ready to say 'I am chief of sinners.'" "Lord I feel that my heart is a cage of unclean beasts." "I see so much of sin, so many things to correct, that I almost despair of being a perfect christian." "Oh! for an increased degree of peace to know and do my redeemers will, to live more as I should."

The biblical verse most frequently quoted in southern women's diaries was from Jeremiah: "The heart is deceitful above all things and desperately wicked: who can know it?" There are references to sins too awful even to be recorded in a private journal, accompanied by allusions to cold hearts.

Many women assumed that if they were unhappy or discontented in the "sphere to which God had appointed them" it must be their own fault and that by renewed effort they could do better. "My besetting sins are a roving mind and an impetuous spirit," wrote one woman whose diary is filled with admonitions to herself to be systematic, diligent, prudent, economical, and patient with her servants. Josephine Clay Habersham was a gentle and gifted woman who presided with skill and dignity over a large plantation in eastern Georgia. A devoted mother who could write, "I wish always to have a sweet babe to mind, care for and love," she still felt it necessary to make a constant effort to cultivate a cheerful spirit, to ask God for help with her "dull and wayward heart," and to ask forgiveness for not being a more faithful servant. A girl of eighteen prayed to be useful and bemoaned the "vain desires that every now and then trouble this prevailing one [to love God] and my flesh is so weak, I am always failing."

Women whose families and friends thought them "spotless" were themselves convinced that their souls were in danger. One prayed to God to be delivered from the "serpent whose folds are around my limbs; his sting in my heart." A Mississippi woman found her mind "sunk in a state of apathy from which I can with difficulty arouse myself" and was sure that this was because she had neglected her duty and transgressed God's holy laws. She was constantly concerned lest "the world and its cares have too large a share of my time and affections."

For many of these women the brief span of earthly life was chiefly important as preparation for eternity, and much of their self-exhortation centered on being ready to die. They prayed for the will to "overcome every evil propensity . . . to be calm and collected at all times," so as to be ready to depart from the world at a moment's notice in a state of grace, or for the power to bring other sinners to the "throne of peace." Such women were cast into deep depression when they gave way to temper, slapped a child, or admonished a slave. One woman scolded herself, "I am not as much engaged in religion as I should be . . . too worldly." An unattainable perfection was the only standard.

There is little doubt that religious faith served an important function at a time when many children and adults died for no apparent reason. A firm belief that death was a manifestation of God's will made it easier to bear what otherwise would have been an intolerable burden. It is also clear that the requirements for salvation dovetailed neatly with the secular image of women. Religious women were persuaded that the very qualities which made any human being a rich, interesting, assertive personality — a roving mind, spirit, ambition — were propensities to be curbed. No matter what secret thoughts a woman might have about her own abilities, religion confirmed what society told her — namely, that she was inferior to men.

The language of piety and the desire for salvation, the belief in an eternal life, were not, of course, confined to women. The same phrases abound in the letters, diaries, and sermons of many men. The significant difference was that for men submission to God's will in spiritual matters was considered to be perfectly compatible with aggressive behavior and a commanding position in life. Men expected to be obeyed by women, children, and slaves, to be the decision makers and the ultimate source of secular authority.

Daniel Hundley's myth of the southern gentleman complements the image of the southern lady. The gentleman, Hundley insisted, in addition to being finely formed and highly educated, was firm, commanding, and a perfect patriarch. "The natural dignity of manner peculiar to the southern gentleman is doubtless owing to his habitual use of authority from his earliest years." The weakness and dependence of women was thrown into bold relief by his virility and mastery of his environment. Husbands were frequently referred to in the words used for God: Lord and Master.

The rigid definition of the proper role and behavior of southern women requires explanation. It is not that the constellation of ideas which constituted the image of the southern lady was peculiar to the American South; men in Victorian England conjured up a similar myth in poems like Coventry Patmore's "The Angel in the House." Harriet Martineau was speaking of all American women, not just those of the South, when she described them as lying down at night "full of self-reproach for the want of piety which they do not know how to attain." But, as William R. Taylor has noted, southern plantation novelists were "fanatical" in idolizing and idealizing southern women. The evidence adduced in this chapter bears out his observation with respect to southern men in general.

Such men continued an old tradition in Western history. The myth of the lady was associated with medieval chivalry. Books of advice on proper behavior for both men and women dated back to the invention of printing. Castiglione's *The Courtier,* a sixteenth-century book of etiquette, set the style for such books, and by the eighteenth century books specifically directed to women were widely read in England and in America. Usually written by men, they emphasized the softness, purity, and spirituality of women while denying them intellectual capacity. Women were instructed to please their husbands, attend to their physical needs, cover up their indiscretions, and give them no cause for worry. All such descriptions and injunctions were included in the southern creed.

But the fact that such ideas had been around for a long time does not explain why they were so enthusiastically embraced by antebellum southerners. Other models were available for a sparsely settled rural society. The good woman of Proverbs, for example, who worked willingly with her hands, got up early and set all in her household to work, bought and sold land, and didn't worry about her appearance might have been an excellent ideal. Why was she not chosen?

We know very little about the relationship of ideology to social structures and understand very little about the social consequences of unconscious needs.

Even so, it is possible to speculate that, as with so much else in the antebellum South, slavery had a good deal to do with the ideal of the southern lady. Because they owned slaves and thus maintained a traditional landowning aristocracy, southerners tenaciously held on to the patriarchal family structure. The patriarchy had been the norm in seventeenth-century England. Transported to Virginia and adopted as a social pattern by the planters there, it lived on into the nineteenth century in the whole South. A future officer of the Confederacy explained the theory of the family common among his contemporaries, and related it directly to the institution of slavery:

The Slave Institution of the South increases the tendency to dignify the family. Each planter is in fact a Patriarch — his position compels him to be a ruler in his household. From early youth, his children and servants look up to him as the head, and obedience and subordination become important elements of education. . . . Domestic relations become those which are most prized.

Women, along with children and slaves, were expected to recognize their proper and subordinate place and to be obedient to the head of the family. Any tendency on the part of any of the members of the system to assert themselves against the master threatened the whole, and therefore slavery itself. It was no accident that the most articulate spokesmen for slavery were also eloquent exponents of the subordinate role of women. George Fitzhugh, perhaps the most noted and certainly among the most able of these spokesmen, wrote, for example:

So long as she is nervous, fickle, capricious, delicate, diffident and dependent, man will worship and adore her. Her weakness is her strength, and her true art is to cultivate and improve that weakness. Woman naturally shrinks from public gaze, and from the struggle and competition of life . . . in truth, woman, like children, has but one right and that is the right to protection. The right to protection involves the obligation to obey. A husband, a lord and master, whom she should love, honor and obey, nature designed for every woman. . . . If she be obedient she stands little danger of maltreatment.

If the need to maintain the slave system contributed to the insistence upon perfect, though submissive, women, so did the simple fact that a male-dominated society was good for men. Some of the characteristics demanded of the southern lady were also expected of women in other parts of the United States and require no more complex explanation than that any ruling group can find a theory to justify its position. Like aristocrats, Communists, and bourgeois businessmen, southern men had no trouble finding theoretical support for a way of life that was decidedly to their advantage. Obedient, faithful, submissive women strengthened the image of men who thought themselves vigorous, intelligent, commanding leaders.

Such women also contributed considerably to manly creature comforts. Ellen Glasgow put it this way in one of her novels:

The cares she met with such serenity had been too heavy for her strength; they had driven the bloom from her cheeks and the lustre from her eyes; and, though she had not faltered at her task, she had drooped daily and grown older than her years. The master might live with lavish disregard of the morrow, not the master's wife. For him were the open house, the shining table, the well-stocked wine cellar and the morning rides over the dewey fields; for her the care of her home and children, and of the souls and bodies of the black people that had been given into her hands.

Despite the vigor of their statements, there is some evidence that southern men did not feel altogether secure in their self-proclaimed position of lord and master of the whole patriarchy. Fear lay beneath the surface of the flowery praise of woman and the insistence that God had made her the way men wanted

her to be. Otherwise it is hard to see why men spent so much time and energy stating their position. One of Beverly Tucker's leading characters discussed the way he proposed to educate his daughter. She must be raised, he said, to take for granted her husband's superiority, to rely on his wisdom, to take pride in his distinction. "Even should her faculties be superior to his, he cannot raise her so high but that she will still feel herself a creature of his hands."

What were they afraid of, these would-be patriarchs who threatened to withdraw their love from women who disagreed with them or aspired to any forbidden activity? Partly, perhaps, that the women to whom they had granted the custody of conscience and morality might apply that conscience to male behavior — to sharp trading in the market place, to inordinate addiction to alcohol, to nocturnal visits to the slave quarters. Men were aware, too, that the woman who had been so firmly put in her place, the home, often showed unusual power within that restricted domain. She raised the children; she set the standards for behavior. In 1802 a visiting Englishman commented that in North Carolina "the legislative and executive powers of the house belong to the mistress, the master has nothing to do with administration; he is a monument of uxoriousness and passive endurance." Two decades later a North Carolinian wrote to a friend contemplating matrimony that he must be "prepared to have his nose occasionally ground . . . and that he must not drink or play cards." If women could exert so much power even in their restricted position who could tell what they might do with more freedom?

The omens were there to see. Southern men often identified the work of the hated abolitionists with the work of "strong-minded" northern women. A Virginian wrote to a friend in 1853:

You have doubtless seen in the newspapers the struggle we had with the strong-minded women as they call themselves in the World Temperance Convention. If you have seen a true account of the matter you will see that we gained·a perfect triumph, and I believe have given a rebuke to this most impudent clique of unsexed females and rampant abolitionists which must put down the petticoats — at least as far as their claim to take the platforms of public debate and enter into all the rough and tumble of the war of words.

His college professor correspondent replied: "I most heartily rejoice with you in the defeat of those shameless amazons." It was a paradox that men who asserted that God made woman as they wished her to be, or that the feminine qualities they admired were given by nature, were afraid that women would break out of the God-given and natural mode of behavior.

If these speculations ring true, one pressing question still remains. Since the ideal of perfection placed a great strain upon women, why did they tolerate their role? One reason is suggested by the early indoctrination already mentioned: the institutions and mores of the society all pointed in the same direction. Churches, schools, parents, books, magazines, all promulgated the same message: be a lady and you will be loved and respected and supported. If you defy the pattern and behave in ways considered unladylike you will be unsexed, rejected, unloved, and you will probably starve.

The persistence of the complementary images of the soft, submissive, perfect woman and of the strong, commanding, intelligent, and dominant man in the face of an exigent reality that often called for quite different qualities suggests that these images had deep significance for the men and women who believed in them. A society increasingly threatened from the outside had every reason to try to diminish internal threats to its stability. George Fitzhugh made this quite explicit when he equated any change in the role of women *or* in the institution of slavery with the downfall of the family and the consequent demise of society. If the distance between the myth and reality became so great that it could not be overlooked, then the situation might be threatening indeed.

Though many southern women were worried about slavery, few had any vision of a society different from the one they knew. Perhaps they, too, sensed a threat of social disorganization inherent in any challenge to male dominance. For whatever reasons, most of them tried to live up to the Sisyphean task expected of them.

QUESTIONS TO CONSIDER

1. Compare the role of the southern lady with that of the mill girl (selection 19) and the pioneer woman (selection 22). How does the reality of each female's life square with the image of the "true woman"?

2. Examine the role of evangelical Protestantism in reinforcing the passive image of women. What similarities do you see with Christianity's role in supporting black slavery?

3. The cult of true womanhood was an ideal of female behavior. What evidence does Scott present that real southern women took this ideal seriously and attempted to live up to its exacting standards? What were the costs and gains of these attempts?

4. Examine the words of southern writers such as George Fitzhugh and Beverly Tucker on the subject of women. What fears and threats lurk behind their glorified praise of southern womanhood?

5. Why did southern whites, male and female, regard the maintenance of the feminine domestic ideal as crucial for the present and future stability of their slave-based society?

The Death of Slavery

25

Why the War Came: The Sectional Struggle over Slavery in the Territories

David Herbert Donald

Modern scholarship has thoroughly documented the central role of slavery in the sectional controversy and the outbreak of the civil war. As James McPherson says in Battle Cry of Freedom: The Civil War Era *(1988), "the greatest danger to American survival at midcentury . . . was sectional conflict between North and South over the future of slavery." Indeed, from the 1840s on, every major sectional conflict involved the complex slavery problem, especially the expansion of slavery into the western territories and any future territories the United States might acquire. By 1848, in the words of Richard H. Sewell, slavery had become "the issue in American politics."*

As we saw in the portrait of Henry Clay (selection 18), the Union almost dissolved over the status of slavery in the territory acquired from Mexico. The Compromise of 1850 averted disaster at that juncture, and many Americans regarded it as "a final settlement" of all sectional hostilities, particularly over slavery in the national lands. That divisive issue did indeed appear to be settled. The new southwestern territories, Utah and New Mexico, had been organized without congressional conditions on slavery, which meant that the two territories could decide the issue as they wished. Utah went on to legalize the institution in 1852, and New Mexico did likewise seven years later (in 1860, however, Utah had only twenty-nine slaves and New Mexico had none). Oregon Territory, on the other hand, had outlawed slavery, and it remained prohibited by the Missouri Compromise line in the vast northern section of the old Louisiana Purchase territory, which included Minnesota Territory and an immense unorganized section.

In 1854, Congress organized that section by creating the new territories of Kansas and Nebraska. Had the Missouri Compromise line remained in effect, slavery would have been prohibited in both territories. But the Kansas-Nebraska Act overturned the Missouri Compromise and decreed that the people of each territory would decide whether to legalize or outlaw slavery. This formula was called popular sovereignty. Until the settlers of the two territories voted on the issue, southerners were free to take their slaves into a vast domain once preserved for freedom. What had caused Congress to enact such a disastrous measure? David Donald argues that southerners on Capitol Hill maneuvered Stephen A. Douglas, chief architect of the measure, into the explicit repeal of the Missouri Compromise line, because they believed that slavery would die out if it could not expand into new territory.

As it turned out, the Kansas-Nebraska Act was a monumental fiasco that reopened the divisive issue of slavery in the territories and inflamed sectional hostilities worse than ever. The measure led to the disintegration of the Whig party, to the emergence of the new all-northern Republican party, dedicated to stopping the spread of slavery, and to civil war on the Kansas prairies. Because slavery was a national problem that affected both sections of the country, armed pioneers from North and South alike poured into Kansas, establishing rival settlements and rival constitutions and governments. Lying in the nation's heartland, Kansas became the battleground for the sectional struggle over the territories and future states, a struggle that would determine whether the free states or the slave states would control the Union. Abraham Lincoln captured the sectional polarization perfectly when he wrote a southerner: "You think slavery is right and ought to be extended; while we think it is wrong and ought to be restricted. That I suppose is the rub." It was the rub indeed. And no event better illustrates that rub than the struggle over Bleeding Kansas. When Americans started killing Americans there over the future of slavery, it was a dress rehearsal for the national cataclysm a few years later.

In the selection that follows, Pulitzer prize-winning historian David Donald discusses how the combustible issue of slavery in the territories, revived by the Kansas-Nebraska Act, divided the nation into hostile sections. He places special emphasis upon how peoples' perception of reality dictated the course of the North and South over the territorial issue. The successive clashes set in motion by the Kansas-Nebraska Act, Donald writes, eroded "the traditional bonds of Union" — national political parties, a faith in the Constitution, and nationalistic oratory — and sent the country hurtling toward civil war.

Donald's account is best read with the first half of the next selection on Lincoln. As you reflect on the two readings, consider a couple of crucial questions. Why did the process of compromise break down after 1854? Was the breakup of the Union inevitable?

GLOSSARY

AMERICAN PARTY (OR KNOW NOTHINGS)   An anti–Catholic, anti-foreign party that appeared briefly on the national stage in the mid-1850s.

"APPEAL OF THE INDEPENDENT DEMOCRATS IN CONGRESS"   Issued by Salmon P. Chase, Joshua R. Giddings, and other antislavery leaders, the appeal denounced the Kansas-Nebraska Act as part of a sinister plot to spread slavery into the territories.

BORDER RUFFIANS   Proslavery Missourians who invaded neighboring Kansas, terrorizing free-state communities and voting illegally in Kansas elections; in 1855, they helped elect a proslavery territorial legislature.

BROOKS, PRESTON S.   South Carolina member of Congress who in 1856 assaulted Republican senator Charles Sumner in the Senate chamber, beating him brutally with a cane; in a recent speech, Sumner had impugned the honor of Brooks's relative, Senator Andrew Pickens Butler of South Carolina. Brooks then resigned his seat and returned home in triumph. South Carolina gave him a new cane and defiantly sent him back to Congress.

BROWN, JOHN   Northern abolitionist who in May 1856 directed the massacre of five proslavery men on Pottawatomie Creek in eastern Kansas. He did so in retaliation for the atrocities of proslavery forces: they had murdered six free-state men in cold blood and had sacked the free-state settlement of Lawrence, killing several others. The Pottawatomie massacre ignited a civil war in Kansas that left two hundred people dead and cost some $2 million in destroyed property.

BUCHANAN, JAMES   Democratic president, 1857–1861, who tried to force Congress to admit Kansas as a slave state, a move that further split the national Democratic party.

BUFORD, JEFFERSON   Alabamian who led 350 southerners to Kansas to save it for slavery.

DAVIS, JEFFERSON   United States senator from Mississippi who demanded a federal slave code that would protect slavery in all the territories.

DOUGLAS, STEPHEN A.   United States senator from Illinois and architect of the Kansas-Nebraska Act, who for the rest of the 1850s would defend popular sovereignty as *the* solution to the slavery question in the territories; known as the Little Giant.

DRED SCOTT DECISION (1857)   Handed down by a prosouthern Supreme Court, it held that neither Congress nor the territories (as creatures of Congress) could outlaw slavery, on the ground that this would violate the property rights clause of the United States Constitution. The decision also ruled that blacks could not be United States citizens.

FRÉMONT, JOHN CHARLES   The Republican party's first nominee for president, he ran against Democrat James Buchanan in 1856; Frémont lost.

NEW ENGLAND EMIGRANT AID COMPANY   Under its auspices, bands of armed northerners went to Kansas to make it a free territory and ultimately a free state.

PIERCE, FRANKLIN   Democratic president, 1853–1857, who signed the disastrous Kansas-Nebraska Bill into law.

POPULAR SOVEREIGNTY   The doctrine, incorporated in the Kansas-Nebraska Act, that the settlers of a territory would determine the status of slavery there by voting it in or out.

POTTAWATOMIE MASSACRE   See *Brown, John.*

SECESSIONISTS   Southerners who believed that only by seceding from the Union and forming an independent confederacy could the South preserve its slave-based way of life.

SUMNER, CHARLES   Prominent Republican senator from Massachusetts, he was brutally beaten by Preston S. Brooks after delivering a speech on the "crime against Kansas" committed by proslavery forces.

TANEY, ROGER BROOKE   A Maryland Democrat and a former slaveholder, Chief Justice Taney wrote the majority opinion in the *Dred Scott* decision, handed down by the Supreme Court in 1857.

WILMOT PROVISO   Introduced in Congress by David Wilmot of Pennsylvania, the proviso called for the prohibition of slavery in the territory acquired from Mexico in the Mexican-American War (1846–1848); the proviso was adopted in the House, but failed in the Senate.

YANCEY, WILLIAM L.   Best-known of the southern secessionist orators, this Alabama hotspur hated the North and warned that slave insurrections would result if abolitionists there got their way.

[W hat] led to the breakdown of the Compromise of 1850 . . . was . . . the further agitation of the question of slavery in the national territories. This had been a central issue in the crisis of 1849–1850, until the compromise brought about what President [Millard] Fillmore praised as a settlement "in its character final and irrevocable." Finality and irrevocability lasted just long enough to see that amiable mediocrity, Franklin Pierce, installed in the White House in 1853, when the territorial question erupted again. The Kansas-Nebraska Act of 1854, the rise of the Republican party, the Dred Scott decision of 1857, the Lincoln-Douglas debates of 1858, the split between the Northern and Southern wings of the Democratic party, the election of Abraham Lincoln in 1860, and the secession of the Southern states — all directly stemmed from the renewed dispute over the status of slavery in the territories.

☆   I   ☆

In order to understand why this issue was, and remained, such a central one, it is necessary to recognize that, to a considerable extent, it was a surrogate. Under the Constitution there was nothing that the federal government could do about matters that most deeply troubled Southerners. Washington could not keep their section from falling behind the free states in wealth and in numbers. The South lost control of the House of Representatives in the 1840s; with the admission of Wisconsin (1848) and California as free states, it no longer had a majority in the Senate; and, after the death of Zachary Taylor, no Southern man could realistically aspire to become President. But the Constitution gave the federal government no author-

From David Herbert Donald, *Liberty and Union* (D.C. Heath 1978). Reprinted by permission of the author.

ity over these matters. The one field of legislation affecting the sectional balance in which the government clearly had power to act was the regulation of the national territories. Similarly Northerners, many of whom were deeply troubled by the moral, economic, and political consequences of slavery, recognized that the Constitution gave the federal government no power over the peculiar institution within the states where it existed. The national territory constituted one of the few areas where the federal government unquestionably did have authority to act adversely toward slavery.

But even this perspective on the territorial question is too narrow. When Northern spokesmen vowed to resist at all costs the further extension of slavery into the national territories, they were not merely expressing their general aversion to slavery; they were voicing a condemnation of the whole Southern way of life as being fundamentally un-American. Increasingly, many Northerners viewed the South, which they considered monolithic, as a barrier to the achievement of the American ideal of democratic equality. While the rest of the United States was making great economic progress, the South exhibited the symptoms of "premature and consumptive decline." In contrast to the thrift, industry, and prosperity of the free states stood the "worn out soil, dilapidated fences and tenements, and air of general desolation" of the South. Northerners were sturdy, equal, free men; Southern whites belonged either to a so-called aristocracy or they were "poor, shiftless, lazy, uninstructed, cowed non-slaveholders."

In this Northern view, slavery was responsible for the backwardness of the South. Condemnation of the peculiar institution did not derive primarily from the abolitionists' moral abhorrence of slavery. Indeed, David Wilmot explained that he and his fellow free-soilers had "no squeamish sensitiveness upon the subject of slavery, no morbid sympathy for the slave." Northern hostility toward the South and slavery stemmed, instead, from a sense that a distinctive culture was rising in that region, one that rejected the

basic and hitherto shared American values of individualism and democracy.

Simultaneously, Southerners were developing a set of stereotypes concerning the North. They found it hard to distinguish between abolitionists and free-soilers and viewed all Northerners, with the exception of a few political allies, as enemies of the South, bent upon the total destruction of its society. In Southern minds it was the free, not the slave, states that were losing sight of the basic, cherished American values. The growth of Northern manufacturing and commerce, the rise in the North of cities as large and as pestilent as those of Europe, and the influx of vast numbers of Irish and German immigrants changed the character of Americans in the free states. "The high-toned New England spirit has degenerated into a clannish feeling of profound Yankeeism," lamented a Tennessee historian. "The masses of the North are venal, corrupt, covetous, mean, and selfish." The "Yankee-Union," agreed another Southerner, had become "vile, rotten, infidelic, puritanic, and negro-worshipping." Considering themselves as a permanent, self-conscious minority in the United States, Southerners felt they were daily threatened by an alien and fundamentally hostile Northern majority.

It is, on the whole, beside the point that neither of these opposing stereotypes bore much relationship to reality. Political democracy was about as prevalent in one section as in another. Most Southern whites were sober, hard-working yeoman farmers who had little or nothing to do with slavery; they were, in most respects, comparable to the small farmers of the North and West. There were very few large slaveholders in the South, just as there were very few wealthy Northern manufacturers; and the great Southern planters were, like their Northern counterparts, hard-driving, tight-fisted, and usually prosperous businessmen. But, as so often is the case, facts have less to do with determining the course of history than [peoples'] perceptions of them.

Even so, the existence of these obverse stereotypes of North and South did not necessarily lead to conflict except for the fact that, ironically, both value systems shared one fundamental belief: that slave society had to expand or perish. The origin of this idea is obscure. Perhaps it stemmed from the American experience that as the fertility of Eastern lands was depleted the center of agricultural production moved steadily West. The accuracy of this belief is debatable. Some historians argue that Southern lands were becoming exhausted, that the best tracts were being engrossed by large planters, and that small farmers had no choice but to emigrate to new territories where, perhaps, they might become great slaveowners. If there were no further slave territories into which they could move, they would be obliged to remain at home, where they would form a discontented element ultimately subversive of the slave-plantation system. Moreover, these historians add, the slave population in the United States was rapidly increasing; by 1890, it was predicted, the South would have ten million slaves. Since these could not all be profitably employed, their value would drastically drop unless they could be taken to new territory.

Other historians question this internal dynamic of slavery expansion. They point to the modern quantitative studies showing that the Southern economy during the 1850s was in very good condition, not merely in the recently opened lands of the lower Mississippi Valley but also in the older seaboard slave states. The rate of economic growth in the South, taken as a whole, was greater during the 1850s than the national average, and that section suffered far less than did the North from the panic of 1857. The per capita income of Southern white farmers (which is, of course, very different from the per capita income of all whites and blacks in the region) was not significantly lower than it was in the North. On the whole, they conclude, slavery was a very profitable institution where it already existed, and there was no special reason why — apart from the generally expansive temper of all Americans — for economic reasons it had to be extended into additional territory. But, once again, in history fact is often less important than belief.

Certain it is that virtually every Southern spokesman believed that slavery must expand or die. The same arguments for expansion appeared so frequently in the political rhetoric of the period that they became standard fare. Jefferson Davis perhaps best expressed two of the major doctrines. "We of the South," he explained, "are an agricultural people, and we require an extended territory. Slave labor is a wasteful labor, and it therefore requires a still more extended territory than would the same pursuits if they could be prosecuted by the more economical labor of white men." Restriction of slave territory, Davis noted in a secondary argument, would "crowd upon our soil an overgrown black population, until there will not be room in the country for the whites and blacks to subsist in, and in this way [it would] destroy the institution [of slavery] and reduce the whites to the degraded position of the African race."

Acting on such imperatives, Southern leaders had constantly to seek new areas into which slavery might be extended. Southerners were behind the numerous filibustering expeditions in the Caribbean during the 1850s. . . . [Their failure] made Southern leaders the more insistent that slavery must be given a chance in all the territory already part of the United States, since the peculiar institution must expand or die.

Northern free-soilers accepted this premise of slavery expansion but drew from it a conclusion exactly opposite from the Southerners'. If the extension of slavery could be prevented, they concluded, the whole slave system must collapse. Charles Sumner, the Massachusetts antislavery spokesman who succeeded in 1851 to [Daniel] Webster's place in the Senate, was confident that if slavery was restricted to the states where it presently existed it would soon die, "as a poisoned rat dies of rage in its hole." Then, Sumner predicted, the slaveholding oligarchy that now ruled the South would sink into impotence, and nonslaveholding whites would come to realize that just as a "blade of grass would not grow where the horse of Attila had trod," so could no "true prosperity spring up in the foot-prints of the slave." They would ultimately force "open the gates of Emancipation in the Slave States." Containment, in short, really meant abolition.

☆ II ☆

These rival sectional stereotypes, with their shared conclusion about the importance of the expansion of slavery, are what made the political controversies of the 1850s such intense struggles over what appears to be a very narrow issue. In every instance the pattern was the same: a powerful and growing majority based in the North opposed an entrenched and increasingly unified minority in the South. The consequence of the successive clashes was to weaken, one after another, the traditional bonds of Union.

After the enactment of the Compromise of 1850, the first great territorial question to come before Congress concerned Kansas — a vast area including not merely the present states of Kansas and Nebraska but most of the rest of the Louisiana Purchase west of Iowa. There were pressing reasons for creating a territorial government for this area. Settlers were already pushing into Kansas from Missouri and Iowa, but they could secure no valid titles to their farms until the federal government extinguished the Indian claims and made a land survey. Territorial organization was also necessary before a transcontinental railroad could be built through the region. Ever since the acquisition of California, the need for direct rail connection with the Pacific coast had been obvious. Some preferred a Southern route, and in order to facilitate its construction the Pierce administration in 1853 purchased an additional tract of land, known as the Gadsden Purchase, from Mexico. Others looked for a railroad connecting Lake Superior with the Oregon country. Stephen A. Douglas, the chairman of the powerful Senate Committee on Territories, was not opposed to either of these plans, but he also wanted a middle route, connecting San Francisco with St. Louis and

Chicago. But before Congress could authorize such a road, it had to provide a government for the territory through which it would run.

By the 1850s any proposal to organize a new territory immediately raised the question of the status of slavery in that territory. In the case of Kansas, the answer at first seemed simple and obvious: the Missouri Compromise had excluded slavery from this region. But by this time Southerners, convinced that slavery must expand or die and unable to acquire further foreign soil, were unwilling to abide by that restriction. Perhaps few Southern congressmen, who were better informed than most of their constituents, ever thought Kansas would become a slave state, but they knew that if they accepted a prohibition on slavery they would be assailed at home. In Mississippi, John A. Quitman thundered that the expansion of slavery was a question of conscience, on which no compromise was ever possible. . . . The South Carolina fire-eater, Robert Barnwell Rhett, declared that Southern rights had to be maintained even if not a single Southern planter ever set foot in the territory. "But the right is important," Rhett insisted, "because it applies to future acquisitions of territory; and by refusing to acknowledge the obligations of the Missouri compromise, you force open the whole question of power." With such war drums beating in the background, Southern votes in 1853 defeated a proposal to organize Kansas as a free territory.

Douglas cared little about slavery one way or the other, but he cared a great deal about the organization of Western territories and the construction of a transcontinental railroad. In 1854, hoping to create a territorial government in Kansas, he sponsored a bill that discreetly failed to mention either slavery or the Missouri Compromise. When Southern senators, whose votes were needed to pass the bill, pointed out that his measure would, because of its silence, leave the Missouri Compromise restriction against slavery in effect, the "Little Giant" discovered that, through "clerical error," an essential section of his bill had been omitted, one that gave the inhabitants of the Kansas terri-

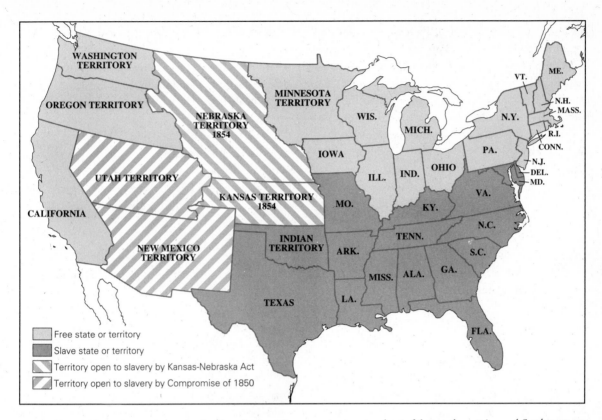

The Kansas-Nebraska Act, 1854, exacerbated sectional tension over slavery in the territories. The measure nullified the Missouri Compromise line, which had prohibited slavery in the old Louisiana Purchase above the latitude of 36° 30'. Two new territories were now carved out of that northern region, and Southerners were free to extend slavery there until such time as the residents voted to outlaw it.

tory the power to deal with slavery. Southern congressmen claimed that not even this resort to popular sovereignty was enough, and Douglas further amended his proposal to declare explicitly that the Missouri Compromise was "inoperative" and "void." At the same time he agreed to divide the huge region into two territories, Kansas and Nebraska.

Charged by critics with caving in to proslavery interests, Douglas was, in actuality, attempting to repeat in 1854 the coup he had brought off in the Compromise of 1850. He was willing to add to his bill almost any amendments concerning slavery because he thought them irrelevant and inconsequential. Since, as he believed, "the laws of climate, and of produc-

tion, and of physical geography have excluded slavery from that country," the wording of the legislation was a "matter of no practical importance." Douglas would, therefore, give the South the language it wanted and the North the substance. To make this compromise palatable, Douglas sought to sweeten it for all parties — just as he had done in 1850 — by sponsoring not one but at least three transcontinental railroad projects, which would give speculators, builders, and politicians in all sections urgent practical reasons for backing his measure.

But the strategy that had succeeded in 1850 failed in 1854. To be sure, Southerners, after an initial period of indifference, came out in support of Douglas's bill and they bullied President Pierce into endorsing it. Following one of the bitterest debates ever to occur in Congress, during which Douglas demonstrated again his superb gifts as a parliamentary tactician, both the Senate and the House passed the bill, and it received the President's signature on May 30. But this time there was no hurrahing that Douglas had saved the Union, no vast public celebration of the new compromise. Instead, when Douglas returned to Illinois at the end of the hard-fought session, he found his way from Washington to Chicago lighted by bonfires where he was being burned in effigy.

Three things had gone wrong with Douglas's calculations. First, the congressional debates on the Kansas-Nebraska bill were so protracted and intricate, so demanding on his time, that he was unable to give sufficient attention to his railroad proposals, which were bottled up in committee, where they died. In 1854, therefore, he could not rally behind his new compromise the powerful influence of America's first big business, the railroad. Second, by permitting Southerners to maneuver him into outright repeal of the Missouri Compromise, Douglas, as many Northerners believed, came close to tampering with the Constitution. Of course, the Missouri Compromise was not part of the written Constitution, but it was an agreement that had almost constitutional status, having been observed loyally for more than three decades and having acquired, as Douglas himself declared in 1849, respect as "a sacred thing which no ruthless hand would ever be reckless enough to disturb." Third, the congressional maneuvering on the Kansas-Nebraska bill suggested to many Northerners that the great national political parties, which had hitherto served as agents of national unity and sectional conciliation, could instead be exploited to ensure minority rule rather than majority rights. Given a free choice, virtually all Northerners in Congress would have opposed the Kansas-Nebraska bill, but the Pierce administration, using every appeal, from party loyalty to political patronage, applied pressure so

intense that a majority of the free-state Democrats voted for it.

To many, this unprecedented misuse of a national party to promote a sectional interest served as a signal that a general political realignment in the United States was long overdue. As early as 1848, early moves in this direction had been made when young Northern Whigs opposed to slavery, disaffected Democratic followers of Martin Van Buren, and former Liberty party men coalesced to form the Free-Soil party. The Compromise of 1850 had weakened traditional parties in the South. . . .

. . . In the years after the passage of the Kansas-Nebraska Act, increasing numbers of Southern Whigs, whose state parties were already in disarray, slipped . . . into the Democratic party. As a consequence, all but one of the slave states voted for James Buchanan, the successful Democratic candidate for President, in 1856. But what the Democratic party gained in the South it lost in the North. Of the 86 Northern Democrats in the House of Representatives, 42 voted, despite all the pressure Pierce could bring to bear, against the Kansas-Nebraska Act. Though many of these remained in the Democratic party, others defected. As a result of these shifts, the center of gravity in the Democratic party shifted sharply to the South after 1854. The party that had once served as a strong bond of national unity now became an equally powerful force for divisive sectionalism.

Meanwhile a major new party opposed to the Democracy was emerging in the North. Early in the debates on Douglas's Kansas bill, antislavery leaders in Congress, including Salmon P. Chase and Joshua R. Giddings of Ohio and Sumner of Massachusetts, issued a widely circulated "Appeal of the Independent Democrats in Congress to the People of the United States," which denounced Douglas's measure "as a gross violation of a sacred pledge; as a criminal betrayal of precious rights; as part and parcel of an atrocious plot to exclude from a vast unoccupied region immigrants from the Old World and free laborers from our own States, and convert it into a dreary region of despotism, inhabited by masters and slaves." Skillfully incorporating two basic free-soil beliefs — that free labor and slave labor could not coexist within the same territory and that slavery blighted the economy wherever it was introduced — the Appeal served as a rallying point, during the protracted debates, for a protest movement throughout the North, in which antislavery Whigs, former members of the Liberty party, and free-soil Democrats joined. Initially given the awkward designation of the "anti-Nebraska" party, the coalition soon accepted the name "Republican." . . .

. . . The 1856 presidential election revealed even more decisively the shift in Northern voting patterns. Though Buchanan was elected, he carried only five of the free states and received fewer votes than the combined totals of the American party candidate, Fillmore, and the Republican nominee, the explorer and adventurer John C. Frémont. When voting returns are analyzed on a county-by-county basis, it becomes evident that in most of the free states the Republicans were neither simply former Whigs nor former Democrats masquerading under a new guise; the Republican party was a genuine fusion of free-soil elements from all the earlier parties. The new party was even more strongly sectional than the Democracy, for it had virtually no strength in any slave state. Thus in the North as in the South the party system, once a strong unifying bond for the nation, became a powerful divisive force.

☆ III ☆

Equally ominous was the weakening of the American faith in the Constitution that resulted, though less promptly, from the Kansas-Nebraska Act. Almost immediately it became apparent that Douglas's measure, designed to settle the problems of Kansas, aggravated them. Many of the difficulties in that territory were those of other frontier regions: disputes over land titles, controversies over lucrative governmental contracts for trading with the Indians and carrying the mails, rivalries over the location of county seats, and struggles for the multiplying number of public offices paying generous salaries and profitable fees. But in Kansas these questions took on added significance, because the vehement congressional debates had singled out this territory as the battleground of slavery and freedom. (Everybody conceded that Nebraska would become a free state. Significantly the usual frontier difficulties in that territory received little general attention and were readily settled.)

Since everybody agreed that slavery had to expand or die, and since Kansas was the only national territory into which it could conceivably expand, proslavery and antislavery forces girded up for Armageddon. Throughout the North, organizations such as the New England Emigrant Aid Company recruited quasi-military bands of settlers and sent them to Kansas to help make it a free state. In the South, Jefferson Buford of Alabama sold forty of his slaves to help finance a 350-man expedition designed to save Kansas for slavery. Buford's followers carried Bibles provided by citizens of Montgomery and raised aloft banners that read "The Supremacy of the White Race" and "Kansas, the Outpost." Most of these systematic efforts to colonize Kansas were not successful, and most immigrants to the territory drifted in independently, looking for land and fortune. The Southern contingent of settlers had a ready reserve force in the proslavery inhabitants of Missouri, who were prepared whenever called to pour over the border to cast ballots in territorial elections or to harass free-soilers.

Something close to a state of civil war in Kansas resulted from the frequent conflicts between the free-state settlers and the Southern immigrants reinforced by these Missouri "border ruffians." Both proslavery and free-soil groups held elections for constitutional conventions, and each faction boycotted the election sponsored by its rival. Rival conventions met and drew up constitutions, one guaranteeing slavery in Kansas, the other excluding it; and contending delegations sent to Washington sought congressional approval. A series of territorial governors sent by the federal government could do nothing to bring the opposing sides together.

The danger grew that the usual frontier lawlessness in Kansas might turn into organized blood-letting. On the night of May 24–25, 1856, John Brown, a dedicated, single-minded abolitionist who had emigrated to Kansas after an unsuccessful career in the East as a tanner, sheep raiser, and land speculator, opened hostilities. Without warning, he led a small party, consisting mostly of his own sons, in an attack on the cabins of two Southern families who lived on Pottawatomie Creek and murdered five men, leaving their gashed and mutilated bodies as a warning for other proslavery families to leave Kansas.* In revenge, Southern immigrants organized and attacked Brown at Osawatomie, where Brown's son Frederick was killed. Only Brown's departure for the East prevented further slaughter.

At this unpropitious moment, the Supreme Court of the United States decided to risk its prestige and the enormous respect that Americans gave to its exposition of the revered Constitution, in an effort to resolve the snarled question of the status of slavery in the national territories. The events leading up to the Dred Scott decision of 1857 were enormously complex, and no purpose is served by reviewing here the legal intricacies of the case before the Court. At issue was the legal status of Dred Scott, a Missouri slave, who had been taken in the 1830s by his owner, an army surgeon, first to Rock Island, Illinois, a state where slavery was prohibited by the Northwest Ordi-

Dred Scott in 1858, a year after the Supreme Court decision that bore his name. Originally called "Sam," Dred Scott, a slave, sought his freedom on the grounds that he had lived for a time in a free state and a free territory. His case led to one of the most infamous Supreme Court decisions in American judicial history. Bought and freed by a white benefactor in 1857, Scott became a porter at a St. Louis Hotel and died in 1858. (Missouri Historical Society)

nance and its own constitution, and subsequently to Fort Snelling in what is now Minnesota, part of the Louisiana Purchase from which slavery had been excluded by the Missouri Compromise. Scott returned with his owner to Missouri, but later he sued for his freedom on the ground that he had been resident first of a free state and then of a free territory. After complex and contradictory rulings in the lower courts, his case came before the Supreme Court for the definitive determination of two broad questions: (1) Was a Negro like Scott a citizen of the United States, who was, therefore, entitled to initiate a suit in the federal courts? (2) Was the congressional prohibi-

---

*Brown instigated the Pottawatomie massacre in retaliation for atrocities committed by proslavery forces in Kansas. See the *John Brown* entry in the glossary. — Ed.

tion of slavery in federal territories, whether in the Missouri Compromise or in subsequent legislation, constitutional?

Initially the justices of the high court planned to avoid these sweeping issues and to deliver a limited opinion, following numerous precedents, declaring that the status of Scott, who continued to be a resident of Missouri, was determined by Missouri state law. Such a decision would have left Scott a slave, but it would have avoided initiating broader controversy. . . .

. . . [But] the aged, high-minded Chief Justice, Roger B. Taney, believed that the American public wished it to settle, once and for all, the critically divisive question of slavery in the territories. In the years since the introduction of the Wilmot Proviso, there had been numerous proposals that the Supreme Court be asked to decide the whole territorial issue. . . .

Consequently, in March 1857, the Court gave such a decision. To be more accurate, it issued nine separate opinions, for each justice made a separate statement. Since these did not all address the same problems, it was not altogether easy to determine just what the Court had decided, but the chief justice seemed to speak for the majority of his brethren on the two essential issues. First he ruled that Scott, as a Negro, was not a citizen of the United States. Neither the Declaration of Independence nor the Constitution, he alleged, was intended to include blacks. The Founding Fathers, claimed Taney with a cheerful disregard of much historical evidence, lived at a period when Negroes were "regarded as beings of an inferior order, and altogether unfit to associate with the white race, . . . and so far inferior that they had no rights which the white man was bound to respect." As a noncitizen, Scott had no right to bring suit in United States courts. Addressing the second major issue, the chief justice announced that when Congress made regulations for governing the territories, its power was restrained by the Fifth Amendment to the Constitution, which prohibits the taking of property without "due process of law." All citizens had an equal right to

enter any of the national territories with their property, and slaves were a variety of property. It followed that any congressional enactment — and specifically the Missouri Compromise — that excluded slavery from any national territory was "not warranted by the Constitution" and was "therefore void."

With the advantage of hindsight, it is easy to argue that the Dred Scott decision was of no great practical consequence. Four months after the Court's ruling, Scott's owner manumitted him and his family. The Missouri Compromise, which the Court struck down, had already been repealed in the Kansas-Nebraska Act. The Dred Scott decision did not open vast new areas for the extension of slavery, simply because since 1854 slavery was already permitted in all the territories into which it might conceivably go.

If the practical results of the Dred Scott decision were negligible, its consequences for the American faith in constitutionalism, hitherto one of the strongest bonds of Union, were fateful. As was to be expected, Southerners generally welcomed the decision as a vindication of their rights, and a good many agreed with Jefferson Davis that it meant Congress must enact a slave code that gave positive protection to slavery in all the territories. Southern enthusiasm was tempered, however, by a recognition that most Northerners would not accept the Court's ruling as definitive.

In truth, there was virtually universal condemnation of the decision in the North. Douglas and his Northern Democratic following were hard hit, because the Court appeared to have announced that popular sovereignty was unconstitutional. If Congress could not exclude slavery from a territory, a handful of settlers clearly could not do so either. Attempting to respect the Court, to preserve his doctrine of popular sovereignty, and to keep the Democratic party intact, Douglas devised an elaborate straddle. He conceded the abstract right of the slaveowner to take his chattels into the national territory but pragmatically noted that it was "a barren and worthless right, unless sustained, protected and enforced by appropriate police regulations and local legislation. . . ." Republicans, who had no Southern constituency, did not suffer from the same constraints as Douglas and angrily denounced the Court's "false and wicked judgment," which, as the New York *Tribune* claimed, was "entitled to just as much moral weight as would be the judgment of a majority of those congregated in any Washington bar-room."

☆   IV   ☆

At just the time that the great unifying belief in constitutionalism was being eroded, the third great bond of Union, nationalistic oratory, was losing its force. In the South the death of Calhoun removed the last great orator for Union. Though Calhoun was a proponent of nullification and an advocate of Southern sectionalism, he always spoke of the Union with veneration. Even in his final address, explaining why he thought it too late in 1850 for meaningful compromise, he lamented the breaking of national ties.

Calhoun's successors had no such regrets. The most notable of the Southern sectionalist orators was William L. Yancey of Alabama, who was as unswerving in his hatred for the North as he was in his devotion to slavery. With spell-binding rhetoric, Yancey alerted his Southern audiences to the dangers that would result from the success of Northern abolitionism. The South, he predicted, would see a repetition of scenes from the Santo Domingo slave rebellion of the 1790s, "where wives were violated upon the bodies of their slaughtered husbands, and the banner of the inhuman fiends was the dead body of an infant, impaled upon a spear, its golden locks dabbled in gore, and its little limbs stiffened by the last agony of suffering nature." Openly an advocate of secession, Yancey explained the purpose of his orations: "All my aims and objects are to cast before the people of the South as great a mass of wrongs committed on them,

injuries and insults that have been done, as I possibly can. . . . All united may yet produce spirit enough to lead us forward, to call forth a Lexington, to fight a Bunker's Hill, to drive the [Northern] foe from the city of our rights."

Equally ominous was the disappearance of the oratory of national conciliation in the North. Charles Sumner was not merely Webster's successor in the Senate; he was the new voice of Massachusetts. Drawing upon his Harvard education, his broad reading, and his first-hand knowledge of European developments, Sumner deliberately set about preparing orations that would unite the North in opposition to the South. The very titles of his major addresses indicated his purpose: "Freedom National, Slavery Sectional," "The Barbarism of Slavery," and so on. Because of its consequences, Sumner's most famous oration was "The Crime Against Kansas," delivered in the Senate on May 19–20, 1856, as a commentary on the continuing violence in the Kansas territory. Taking as axiomatic the argument that slavery must expand or die, Sumner claimed that the disturbances in Kansas following the passage of the Kansas-Nebraska Act were evidence of the desperate attempt of Southerners to rape that "virgin territory, compelling it to the hateful embrace of slavery."

In his carefully prepared speech, Sumner attacked Douglas and made offensive personal references to the elderly South Carolina senator, Andrew Pickens Butler, whom he characterized as the Don Quixote of slavery, having "chosen a mistress to whom he has made his vows, and who, though ugly to others, is always lovely to him, though polluted in the sight of the world, is chaste in his sight . . . the harlot, Slavery." Butler was absent from the Senate during Sumner's speech, but his cousin, Representative Preston S. Brooks of South Carolina, seethed over the insult to his family and state. On May 22, before the Senate was called to order, Brooks entered the Senate chamber, approached Sumner, who was seated at his desk writing, and proceeded to punish him by beating him on the head and shoulders with a stout cane. He left Sumner bleeding and insensible in the aisle. It was nearly three years before Sumner recovered from his wounds. During that period, the Massachusetts legislature reelected him to the Senate, where his vacant chair spoke as powerfully for sectionalism as ever Webster had done for Union.

During these years of Sumner's silence, there sounded in the West an even more eloquent voice of sectionalism. [It was the voice of] Abraham Lincoln of Illinois. . . . In a series of nationally publicized debates with Douglas in the 1858 campaign [for the Little Giant's Senate seat, Lincoln] eloquently voiced both the aspirations and the fears of the free-soilers. If, to the present-day reader, the Lincoln-Douglas debates seem to revolve repetitiously around the one limited issue of slavery in the territories, it must be remembered that virtually every political leader in the North and the South agreed that that point was of the utmost importance, since slavery had to grow or it would wither away. After a strenuous campaign, Douglas was reelected to the Senate, but Lincoln emerged as the real victor. Throughout the North, antislavery men now perceived the issues in terms of the stark contrasts Lincoln had presented in the opening address of his campaign:

"A house divided against itself cannot stand."
I believe this government cannot endure, permanently half *slave* and half *free*.
I do not expect the Union to be *dissolved* — I do not expect the house to *fall* — but I *do* expect it will cease to be divided.
It will become *all* one thing, or *all* the other.

With the issue thus baldly stated, the outcome was simply a matter of time. The great forces that had once helped cement American unity — the Constitution, the political parties, the public oratory — now served to divide the people. The United States, it now appeared, was not, and never really had been, a na-

tion; it was merely a loose assemblage of diverse and conflicting groups, interests, and peoples. By the late 1850s these had polarized into two groups, a majority in the North, and a minority in the South. Neither majority nor minority was willing to yield on what both regarded as the vital issue of the expansion of slavery. And the war came.

Donald concedes that this "sketch" is oversimplified. For clarity, he had to "gloss over the fact that neither North nor South was monolithic" and that important groups in both sections dissented from the dominant attitudes. "When a historian speaks of 'the North' or 'the South,'" Donald writes, "he is using a convenient shorthand to refer to the articulate groups who gained control of the political machinery in those sections."

QUESTIONS TO CONSIDER

1.   What were the emerging visions that northerners and southerners had of each other in the 1850s? What basic belief about slavery did they share? Why does Donald say that the issue of slavery in the territories was in great part a "surrogate"? Do you agree with the implication that slavery itself was not the major issue dividing North and South? What do you think was the major cause of the Civil War?

2.   When Stephen A. Douglas put forth the Kansas-Nebraska Bill in 1854, what was his position on slavery and how did he hope to solve the problem? Why was the Kansas-Nebraska Bill a failure, and how did the failure affect the major political parties? What was its effect on the political process in Kansas?

3.   What were the major questions involved in the *Dred Scott* case, and how did the Supreme Court rule on them? What were the consequences of this decision? If Americans were losing their faith in the Constitution as Donald says, why do you think the *Dred Scott* decision caused such a furor?

4. According to Donald, how did the role of oratory change during the 1850s? What do you think is the significance of Brooks's attack against Sumner? If men such as Sumner and Lincoln were upholding sectionalism versus union, why do you think they would soon devote all their energies to prosecuting the Civil War?

5. As the bonds of union snapped, Donald says that the coming of civil war became "simply a matter of time." Do you agree that the Civil War was inevitable and, if you do, when do you think it became so and why?

26

Lincoln's Journey
to Emancipation

Stephen B. Oates

Nobody was more upset about the troubles in Kansas than Abraham Lincoln. For him and his Republican colleagues, the Kansas-Nebraska Act, the Kansas Civil War, and the Dred Scott decision were all part of an insidious design to spread slavery across the West and ultimately to nationalize that hated institution. From 1854 on, Lincoln was in the thick of the struggle to block slavery expansion, to keep the peculiar institution out of the territories by the force of national law. The first half of the next essay describes Lincoln's battles against both Stephen A. Douglas and proslavery southerners and discusses Lincoln's own solution to slavery before the Civil War, which was a modification of Jefferson's and Clay's plans. You will not only meet an eloquent public Lincoln with a vision of America's historic mission in the world but a private Lincoln troubled by doubts and insecurities, romantic difficulties, and an obsession with death. That same Lincoln, however, was as ambitious as he was deeply principled. He built up a remarkably success-ful law career, fought Douglas for his seat in the United States Senate, and carried the banner of slave containment all the way to the White House.

The second half of the essay traces Lincoln's evolving emancipation policy during the Civil War. Throughout the first year and a half of the conflict, Lincoln insisted that the North was fighting strictly to save the Union, not to free the slaves. But a combination of problems and pressures caused him to change his mind, and in September 1862, he issued the preliminary Emancipation Proclamation, to take effect on January 1, 1863. The proclamation announced that, after that date, Union military forces would liberate the slaves in the rebellious states.

How Lincoln approached the problem of slavery — and what he did about it — is one of the most written about and least understood facets of his presidency. Indeed, the subject has made Lincoln far more controversial than Andrew Jackson. Ever since he issued his proclamation, legends have flourished about Lincoln as the Great Emancipator — a man who dedicated himself to liberty and equality for all. On the other hand, counterlegends of Lincoln as a Great Racist eventually emerged among white segregationists and among many modern African Americans as well. Which view is correct? Should Lincoln be applauded as a great humanitarian, or was he just another white bigot, as one black historian recently contended? Or, as some of his contemporaries charged, was he an unscrupulous opportunist who sought to eradicate slavery merely for political and military expediency?

Drawing on modern scholarship about Lincoln's life and the times in which he lived, the author of this essay tries to answer the enduring questions about Lincoln and emancipation and to present a realistic portrait of one of the most mythologized human beings in American history. The author concludes that Lincoln truly hated slavery — "If slavery is not wrong," Lincoln thundered "nothing is wrong" — and that he attacked the peculiar institution in part because of deeply held moral principles. In the end, it was this tall and melancholy man who found in a terrible civil war the means of removing the paradox of slavery in "the land of the free."

GLOSSARY

CHANDLER, ZACHARIAH   One of three Republican senators who pressed Lincoln to free the slaves.

CONFISCATION ACT (SECOND)   Provided for the seizure and liberation of all slaves of people who supported or participated in the rebellion; the measure exempted slaveholders in the Confederacy who were loyal to the Union; most slaves would be freed only after case-by-case litigation in the federal courts.

DOUGLASS, FREDERICK   Eminent black abolitionist and editor who pressured Lincoln to free the slaves and enlist black soldiers.

EMANCIPATION PROCLAMATION (JANUARY 1, 1863)   Freed the slaves in the rebel states save for occupied Tennessee and certain areas in Virginia and Louisiana behind Union lines; announced that henceforth Lincoln's military forces would accept black men.

GEORGIA PEN   Slave-trading pen in Washington, D.C., that offended Lincoln.

LINCOLN, MARY TODD   Lincoln's wife and mother of four Lincoln boys, one of whom died in childhood and a second of whom (Willie) died during the Civil War.

REFUGEE SYSTEM   Installed by Lincoln's adjutant general in the Mississippi Valley in 1863; the adjutant enrolled all able-bodied black men in the army and put others to work as laborers in the military or on confiscated farms and plantations for wages.

SPEED, JOSHUA   Lincoln's intimate friend in whom he confided his romantic fears in the 1840s.

SUMNER, CHARLES   A personal friend of Lincoln's and a major Lincoln adviser on foreign affairs; one of three Republican senators who pressed Lincoln to free the slaves.

THIRTEENTH AMENDMENT   Ratified in December 1865, it guaranteed the permanency of Lincoln's Emancipation Proclamation by abolishing slavery everywhere in the country.

He comes to us in the mists of legend as a kind of homespun Socrates, brimming with prairie wit and folk wisdom. He is as honest, upright, God-fearing, generous, and patriotic an American as the Almighty ever created. Impervious to material rewards and social station, the Lincoln of mythology is the Great Commoner, a saintly Rail Splitter who spoke in a deep, fatherly voice about the genius of the plain folk. He comes to us, too, as the Great Emancipator who led the North off to Civil War to free the slaves and afterward offered his fellow Southerners a tender and forgiving hand.

There is a counterlegend of Lincoln — one shared ironically enough by many white Southerners and certain black Americans of our time. This is the legend of Lincoln as bigot, as a white racist who championed segregation, opposed civil and political rights for black people, wanted them all thrown out of the country. This Lincoln is the great ancestor of racist James K. Vardaman of Mississippi, of "Bull" Connor of Birmingham, of the white citizens' councils, of the Knights of the Ku Klux Klan.

Neither of these views, of course, reveals much about the man who really lived — legends and politicized interpretations seldom do. The real Lincoln was not a saintly emancipator, and he was not an unswerving racist either. To understand him and the liberation of the slaves, one must eschew artificial, arbitrary categories and focus on the man as he lived, on the flesh-and-blood Lincoln, on that flawed and fatalistic individual who struggled with himself and his countrymen over the profound moral paradox of slavery in a nation based on the Declaration of Independence. Only by viewing Lincoln scrupulously in the context of his own time can one understand the pain-

Reprinted from *Our Fiery Trial: Abraham Lincoln, John Brown, and the Civil War Era*, by Stephen B. Oates, copyright © 1978 by the University of Massachusetts press.

ful, ironic, and troubled journey that led him to the Emancipation Proclamation and to the Thirteenth Amendment that made it permanent.

☆ 2 ☆

As a man, Lincoln was complex, many-sided, and richly human. He was almost entirely self-educated, with a talent for expression that in another time and place might have led him into a literary career. He wrote poetry himself and studied Shakespeare, Byron, and Oliver Wendell Holmes, attracted especially to writings with tragic and melancholy themes. He examined the way celebrated orators turned a phrase or employed a figure of speech, admiring great truths greatly told. Though never much at impromptu oratory, he could hold an audience of 15,000 spellbound when reading from a written speech, singing out in a shrill, high-pitched voice that became his trademark.

He was an intense, brooding person, plagued with chronic depression most of his life. "I am now the most miserable man living," he said on one occasion in 1841. "If what I feel were equally distributed to the whole human family, there would not be one cheerful face on the earth." He added, "To remain as I am is impossible; I must die or be better."

At the time he said this, Lincoln had fears of sexual inadequacy, doubting his ability to please or even care for a wife. In 1842 he confided in his closest friend, Joshua Speed, about his troubles, and both confessed that they had fears of "nervous debility" with women. Speed went ahead and married anyway and then wrote Lincoln that their anxieties were groundless. Lincoln rejoiced, "I tell you, Speed, our forebodings, for which you and I are rather peculiar, are all the worst sort of nonsense." Encouraged by Speed's success, Lincoln finally wedded Mary Todd; and she obviously helped him overcome his doubts, for they developed a strong and lasting physical love for one another.

Still, Lincoln remained a moody, melancholy man, given to long introspections about things like death and mortality. In truth, death was a lifelong obsession with him. His poetry, speeches, and letters are studded with allusions to it. He spoke of the transitory nature of human life, spoke of how all people in this world are fated to die in the end—all are fated to die. He saw himself as only a passing moment in a rushing river of time.

Preoccupied with death, he was also afraid of insanity, afraid (as he phrased it) of "the pangs that kill the mind." In his late thirties, he wrote and rewrote a poem about a boyhood friend, one Matthew Gentry, who became deranged and was locked "in mental night," condemned to a living death, spinning out of control in some inner void. Lincoln retained a morbid fascination with Gentry's condition, writing about how Gentry was more an object of dread than death itself: "A human form with reason fled, while wretched life remains." Yet, Lincoln was fascinated with madness, troubled by it, afraid that what had happened to Gentry could also happen to him — his own reason destroyed, Lincoln spinning in mindless night without the power to know.

Lincoln was a teetotaler because liquor left him "flabby and undone," blurring his mind and threatening his self-control. And he dreaded and avoided anything which threatened that. In one memorable speech, he heralded some great and distant day when all passions would be subdued, when reason would triumph and "*mind, all conquering mind*," would rule the earth.

One side of Lincoln was always supremely logical and analytical. He was intrigued with the clarity of mathematics; and as an attorney he could command a mass of technical data. Yet he was also extremely superstitious, believed in signs and visions, contended that dreams were auguries of approaching triumph or calamity. He was skeptical of organized religion and never joined a church; yet he argued that all human destinies were controlled by an omnipotent God.

It is true that Lincoln told folksy anecdotes to illustrate a point. But humor was also tremendous therapy for his depressions — a device "to whistle down sadness," as a friend put it. Lincoln liked all kinds of jokes, from bawdy tales to pungent rib-ticklers like "Bass-Ackwards," a story he wrote down and handed a bailiff one day. Filled with hilarious spoonerisms, "Bass-Ackwards" is about a fellow who gets thrown from his horse and lands in "a great *tow-curd,*" which gives him a "*sick of fitness.*" About "*bray dake,*" he comes to and dashes home to find "the *door* sick abed, and his *wife* standing open. But thank goodness," the punch line goes, "she is getting right *hat* and *farty* again."

Contrary to legend, Lincoln was anything but a common man. In point of fact, he was one of the most ambitious human beings his friends had ever seen, with an aspiration for high station in life that burned in him like a furnace. Instead of reading with an accomplished attorney, as was customary in those days, he taught himself the law entirely on his own. He was literally a self-made lawyer. Moreover, he entered the Illinois legislature at the age of twenty-five and became a leader of the state Whig party, a tireless party campaigner, and a regular candidate for public office.

As a self-made man, Lincoln felt embarrassed about his log-cabin origins and never liked to talk about them. He seldom discussed his parents either and became permanently estranged from his father, who was all but illiterate. In truth, Lincoln had considerable hostility for his father's intellectual limitations, once remarking that Thomas "never did more in the way of writing than to bunglingly sign his own name." When his father died in a nearby Illinois county in 1851, Lincoln did not attend the funeral.

By the 1850s, Lincoln was one of the most sought-after attorneys in Illinois, with a reputation as a lawyer's lawyer — a knowledgeable jurist who argued appeal cases for other attorneys. He did his most influential legal work in the Supreme Court of Illinois, where he participated in 243 cases and won most of them. He commanded the respect of his colleagues,

all of whom called him "Mr. Lincoln" or just "Lincoln." Nobody called him Abe — at least not to his face — because he loathed the nickname. It did not befit a respected professional who'd struggled hard to overcome the limitations of his frontier background. Frankly, Lincoln enjoyed his status as a lawyer and politician, and he liked money, too, and used it to measure his worth. By the mid–1850s, thanks to a combination of talent and sheer hard work, Lincoln was a man of substantial wealth. He had an annual income of around $5,000 — the equivalent of many times that today — and large financial and real-estate investments.

Though a man of status and influence, Lincoln was as honest in real life as in the legend. Even his enemies conceded that he was incorruptible. Moreover, he possessed broad humanitarian views, some of them in advance of his time. Even though he was a teetotaler, he was extremely tolerant of alcoholics, regarding them not as criminals — the way most temperance people did — but as unfortunates who deserved understanding, not vilification. He noted that some of the world's most gifted artists had succumbed to alcoholism, because they were too sensitive to cope with their insights into the human condition. He believed that women, like men, should vote so long as they all paid taxes. And he had no ethnic prejudices. His law partner William Herndon, who cursed the Irish with a flourish, reported that Lincoln was not at all prejudiced against "the foreign element, tolerating — as I never could — even the Irish."

Politically, Lincoln was always a nationalist in outlook, an outlook that began when he was an Indiana farm boy tilling his father's mundane wheat field. While the plow horse was getting its breath at the end of a furrow, Lincoln would study Parson Weems's eulogistic biography of George Washington, and he would daydream about the Revolution and the origins of the Republic, daydream about Washington and Jefferson as great national statesmen who shaped the course of history. By the time he became a politician, Lincoln idolized the Founding Fathers as apostles of liberty (never mind for now that many of these apostles were also Southern slaveowners). Young Lincoln extolled the founders for beginning an experiment in popular government on this continent, to show a doubting Europe that people could govern themselves without hereditary monarchs and aristocracies. And the foundation of the American experiment was the Declaration of Independence, which in Lincoln's view contained the highest political truths in history: that all men are created equal and are entitled to freedom and the pursuit of happiness. Which for Lincoln meant that men like him were not chained to the condition of their births, that they could better their station in life and harvest the fruits of their own talents and industry. Thus he had a deep, personal reverence for the Declaration and insisted that all his political sentiment flowed from that document.

☆ 3 ☆

Which brings us to the problem and paradox of slavery in America. Lincoln maintained that he had always hated human bondage, as much as any abolitionist. His family had opposed the peculiar institution, and Lincoln had grown up and entered Illinois politics thinking it wrong. But before 1854 (and the significance of that date will become clear) Lincoln generally kept his own counsel about slavery and abolition. After all, slavery was the most inflammable issue of his generation, and Lincoln observed early on what violent passions Negro bondage — and the question of race that underlay it — could arouse in white Americans. In his day, as I have said, slavery was a tried and tested means of race control in a South absolutely dedicated to white supremacy. Moreover, the North was also a white supremacist region, where the vast majority of whites opposed emancipation lest it result in a flood of Southern blacks into the free states. And Illinois was no exception, as most whites

there were against abolition and were anti-Negro to the core. Lincoln, who had elected to work within the system, was not going to ruin his career by espousing an extremely unpopular cause. To be branded as an abolitionist in central Illinois — his constituency as a legislator and a U.S. congressman — would have been certain political suicide. At the same time, attorney Lincoln conceded that Southern slavery had become a thoroughly entrenched institution, that bondage where it already existed was protected by the Constitution and could not be molested by the national government.

Still, slavery distressed him. He realized how wrong it was that slavery should exist at all in a self-proclaimed free and enlightened Republic. He who cherished the Declaration of Independence understood only too well how bondage mocked and contradicted that noble document. Too, he thought slavery a blight on the American experiment in popular government. It was, he believed, the one retrograde institution that robbed the Republic of its just example in the world, robbed the United States of the hope it should hold out to oppressed people everywhere.

He opposed slavery, too, because he had witnessed some of its evils firsthand. In 1841, on a steamboat journey down the Ohio River, he saw a group of manacled slaves on their way to the cruel cotton plantations of the Deep South. Lincoln was appalled at the sight of those chained Negroes. Fourteen years later he wrote that the spectacle "was a continual torment to me" and that he saw something like it every time he touched a slave border. Slavery, he said, "had the power of making me miserable."

Again, while serving in Congress from 1847 to 1849, he passed slave auction blocks in Washington, D.C. In fact, from the windows of the Capitol, he could observe the infamous "Georgia pen" — "a sort of Negro livery stable," as he described it, "where droves of negroes were collected, temporarily kept, and finally taken to Southern markets, precisely like droves of horses." The spectacle offended him. He agreed with a Whig colleague that the buying and selling of human beings in the United States capital was a national disgrace. Accordingly Lincoln drafted a gradual abolition bill for the District of Columbia. But powerful Southern politicians howled in protest, and his own Whig support fell away. At that, Lincoln dropped his bill and sat in glum silence as Congress rocked with debates—with drunken fights and rumbles of disunion—over the status of slavery out in the territories. Shocked at the behavior of his colleagues, Lincoln confessed that slavery was the one issue that threatened the stability of the Union.

What could be done? Slavery as an institution could not be removed, and yet it should not remain either. Trapped in what seemed an impossible dilemma, Lincoln persuaded himself that if slavery were confined to the South and left alone there, time would somehow solve the problem and slavery would ultimately die out. And he told himself that the Founding Fathers had felt the same way, that they too had expected slavery to perish some day. In Lincoln's interpretation, they had tolerated slavery as a necessary evil, agreeing that it could not be eradicated where it already flourished without causing widescale wreckage. But in his view they had taken steps to restrict its growth (had excluded slavery from the old Northwest territories, had outlawed the international slave trade) and so had placed the institution on the road to extinction.

So went Lincoln's argument before 1854. The solution was to bide one's time, trust the future to get rid of slavery and square America with her own ideals. And he convinced himself that when slavery was no longer workable, Southern whites would gradually liberate the blacks on their own. They would do so voluntarily.

To solve the ensuing problem of racial adjustment, Lincoln insisted that the federal government should colonize all blacks in Africa, an idea he got from his political idol, Whig national leader Henry Clay. Said Lincoln in 1852: if the Republic could remove the danger of slavery and restore "a captive people to their long-lost fatherland," and do both so gradually

"that neither races nor individuals shall have suffered by the change," then "it will indeed be a glorious consummation."

☆　4　☆

Then came 1854 and the momentous Kansas-Nebraska Act, brainchild of Lincoln's archrival Stephen A. Douglas. The act overturned the old Missouri Compromise line, which excluded slavery from the vast northern area of the old Louisiana Purchase territory. The act then established a new formula for dealing with slavery in the national lands: now Congress would stay out of the matter, and the people of each territory would decide whether to retain or outlaw the institution. Until such time as the citizens of a territory voted on the issue, Southerners were free to take slavery into most western territories, including the new ones of Kansas and Nebraska. These were carved out of the northern section of the old Louisiana Purchase territory. Thanks to the Kansas-Nebraska Act, a northern domain once preserved for freedom now seemed open to proslavery invasion.

At once a storm of free-soil protest broke across the North, and scores of political leaders branded the Kansas-Nebraska Act as part of a sinister Southern plot to extend slave territory and augment Southern political power in Washington. There followed a series of political upheavals. A civil war blazed up in Kansas, as proslavery and free-soil pioneers came into bloody collisions on the prairie there — proof that slavery was far too volatile ever to be solved as a purely local matter. At the same time, the old Whig party disintegrated. In its place emerged the all-Northern Republican party, dedicated to blocking slavery extension and to saving the cherished frontier for free white labor. Then in 1857 came the infamous Dred Scott decision, handed down by the pro-Southern Supreme Court, which ruled that neither Congress nor a territorial government could outlaw slavery, because that would violate Southern property rights. As Lincoln and many others observed, the net effect of the decision was to legalize slavery in all federal territories from Canada to Mexico.

The train of ominous events from Kansas-Nebraska to Dred Scott shook Lincoln to his foundations. In his view, the Southern-controlled Democratic party — the party that dominated the Senate, the Supreme Court, and the presidency — had instituted a revolt against the Founding Fathers and the entire course of the Republic so far as slavery was concerned. Now human bondage was not going to die out. Now it was going to expand and grow and continue indefinitely, as Southerners dragged manacled Negroes across the West, adapting slave labor to whatever conditions they found there, putting the blacks to work in mines and on farms. Now Southerners would create new slave states in the West and make slavery powerful and permanent in America. Now the Republic would never remove the cancer that infected its political system, would never remove the one institution that marred its global image, would never remove a "cruel wrong" that mocked the Declaration of Independence.

Lincoln waded into the middle of the antiextension fight. He campaigned for the national Senate. He joined the Republican party. He thundered against the evil designs of the "Slave Power." He spoke with an urgent sense of mission that gave his speeches a searching eloquence — a mission to save the Republic's noblest ideals, turn back the tide of slavery expansion, restrict the peculiar institution once again to the South, and place it back on the road to extinction, as Lincoln believed the Founding Fathers had so placed it.

By 1858, Lincoln, like a lot of other Republicans, began to see a grim proslavery conspiracy at work in the United States. The first stage was to betray the founders and send slavery flooding all over the West. At the same time, proslavery theorists were out to undermine the Declaration of Independence, to discredit its equality doctrine as "a self-evident lie" (as many Southern spokesmen were actually saying), and to replace the Declaration with the principles of inequality and human servitude.

The next step in the conspiracy would be to nationalize slavery: the Taney Court, Lincoln feared, would hand down another decision, one declaring that states could not prohibit slavery either. Then the institution would sweep into Illinois, sweep into Indiana and Ohio, sweep into Pennsylvania and New York, sweep into Massachusetts and New England, sweep all over the Northern states, until at last slavery would be nationalized and America would end up a slave house. At that, as George Fitzhugh advocated, the conspirators would enslave all American workers regardless of color. The Northern free-labor system would be expunged, the Declaration of Independence overthrown, self-government abolished, and the conspirators would restore despotism with class rule and an entrenched aristocracy. All the work since the Revolution of 1776 would be obliterated. The world's best hope — America's experiment in popular government — would be destroyed, and mankind would spin backward into feudalism.

For Lincoln and his Republican colleagues, it was imperative that the conspiracy be blocked in its initial stage — the expansion of slavery into the West. In 1858 Lincoln set out after Douglas's Senate seat, inveighing against the Little Giant for his part in the proslavery plot and warning Illinois — and Northerners beyond — that only the Republicans could save their free-labor system and their free government. Now Lincoln openly and fiercely declaimed his antislavery sentiments. He hated the institution. He hated slavery because it degraded blacks and whites alike. Because it prevented the Negro from "eating the bread which his own hand earns." Because it not only contradicted the Declaration, but violated the principles of free labor, self help, social mobility, and economic independence, all of which lay at the center of Republican ideology, of Lincoln's ideology. Yet, while branding slavery as an evil and doing all they could to contain it in the South, Republicans would not, could not, molest the institution in those states where it already existed.

Douglas, fighting for his political life in free-soil Illinois, lashed back at Lincoln with unadulterated race-baiting. Throughout the Great Debates of 1858, Douglas smeared Lincoln and his party as Black Republicans, as a gang of radical abolitionists out to liberate all Southern slaves and bring them stampeding into Illinois and the rest of the North, where they would take away white jobs and copulate with white daughters. Again and again, Douglas accused Lincoln of desiring intermarriage and racial mongrelization.

Lincoln protested emphatically that race was not the issue between him and Douglas. The issue was whether slavery would ultimately triumph or ultimately perish in the United States. But Douglas understood the depth of anti-Negro feeling in Illinois, and he hoped to whip Lincoln by playing on white racial fears.

Forced to take a stand lest Douglas ruin him with his allegations, Lincoln conceded that he was not for Negro political or social equality. He was not for enfranchising Negroes, was not for intermarriage. There was, he said, "a physical difference" between blacks and whites that would "probably" always prevent them from living together in perfect equality. Having confessed his racial views, Lincoln then qualified them: if Negroes were not the equal of Lincoln and Douglas in moral or intellectual endowment, they *were* equal to Lincoln, Douglas, and "every living man" in their right to liberty, equality of opportunity, and the fruits of their own labor. (Later he insisted that it was bondage that had "clouded" the slaves' intellects and that Negroes were capable of thinking like whites.) Moreover, Lincoln rejected "the counterfeit argument" that just because he did not want a black woman for a slave, he necessarily wanted her for a wife. He could just let her alone. He could let her

alone so that she could also enjoy her freedom and "her natural right to eat the bread she earns with her own hands."

Exasperated with Douglas and white Negrophobia in general, Lincoln begged American whites "to discard all this quibbling about this man and the other man — this race and that race and the other race as being inferior," begged them to unite as one people and defend the ideals of the Declaration and its promise of liberty and opportunity for all.

Lincoln lost the 1858 Senate contest to Douglas. But in 1860 he won the Republican nomination for president and stood before the American electorate on the free-soil, free-labor principles of the Republican party. As the Republican standard bearer, Lincoln was uncompromising in his determination to prohibit slavery in the territories by national law and to save the Republic (as he put it) from returning to "class, caste, and despotism." He exhorted his fellow Republicans to stand firm in their duty: to brand slavery as an evil, contain it in the South, look to the future for slavery to die a gradual death, and promise colonization to solve the question of race. Some day, somehow, the American house must be free of slavery. That was the Republican vision, the distant horizon Lincoln saw.

Yet, for the benefit of Southerners, he repeated that he and his party would not harm slavery in the Southern states. The federal government had no constitutional authority in peace time to tamper with a state institution like slavery.

But Southerners refused to believe anything Lincoln said. In Dixie, orators and editors alike castigated him as a black-hearted radical, a "sooty and scoundrelly" abolitionist who wanted to free the slaves at once and mix the races. In Southern eyes, Lincoln was another John Brown, a mobocrat, a Southern hater, a chimpanzee, a lunatic, the "biggest ass in the United States," the evil chief of the North's "Black Republican, free love, free Nigger" party, whose victory would ring the bells of doom for the white man's

South. Even if Southerners had to drench the Union in blood, cried an Atlanta man, "the South, the loyal South, the Constitution South, would never submit to such humiliation and degradation as the inauguration of Abraham Lincoln."

After Lincoln's victory and the secession of the seven states of the Deep South, Lincoln beseeched Southerners to understand the Republican position on slavery. In his Inaugural Address of 1861, he assured them once again that the federal government would not free the slaves in the South, that it had no legal right to do so. He even gave his blessings to the original Thirteenth Amendment, just passed by Congress, that would have guaranteed slavery in the Southern states for as long as whites there wanted it. Lincoln endorsed the amendment because he thought it consistent with Republican ideology. Ironically, Southern secession and the outbreak of war prevented that amendment from ever being ratified.

When the rebels opened fire on Fort Sumter, the nation plunged into civil war, a conflict that began as a ninety-day skirmish for both sides, but that swelled instead into a vast and terrible carnage with consequences beyond calculation for those swept up in its flames. Lincoln, falling into a depression that would plague him through his embattled presidency, remarked that the war was the supreme irony of his life: that he who sickened at the sight of blood, who abhorred stridency and physical violence, was caught in a national holocaust, a tornado of blood and wreckage with Lincoln himself whirling in its center.

☆ 5 ☆

At the outset of the war, Lincoln strove to be consistent with all that he and his party had said about slavery: his purpose in the struggle was strictly to save the Union; it was not to free the slaves. He would crush the rebellion with his armies and restore the national authority in the South with slavery intact. Then Lin-

coln and his party would resume and implement their policy of slave containment.

There were other reasons for Lincoln's hands-off policy about slavery. Four slave states — Delaware, Maryland, Kentucky, and Missouri — remained in the Union. Should he try to free the slaves, Lincoln feared it would send the crucial border spiraling into the Confederacy, something that would be catastrophic for the Union. A Confederate Maryland would create an impossible situation for Washington, D.C. And a Confederate Missouri and Kentucky would give the rebels potential bases from which to invade Illinois, Indiana, and Ohio. So Lincoln rejected emancipation in part to appease the loyal border.

He was also waging a bipartisan war effort, with Northern Democrats and Republicans alike enlisting in his armies to save the Union. Lincoln encouraged this because he insisted that it would take a united North to win the war. An emancipation policy, he feared, would alienate Northern Democrats, ignite a racial powder keg in the Northern states, and possibly cause a civil war in the rear. Then the Union really would be lost.

But the pressures and problems of civil war caused Lincoln to change his mind, caused him to abandon his hands-off policy and hurl an executive fist at slavery in the rebel states, thus making emancipation a Union war objective. The pressures operating on Lincoln were complex and merit careful discussion.

First, from the summer of 1861 on, several Republican senators — chief among them, Charles Sumner of Massachusetts, Ben Wade of Ohio, and Zachariah Chandler of Michigan — sequestered themselves with Lincoln and implored and badgered him to free the slaves.[1] Sumner, as Lincoln's personal friend and

---

[1] These "more advanced Republicans," as the *Detroit Post and Tribune* referred to Sumner and his associates, belonged to a powerful minority faction of the party inaccurately categorized as "radicals," a misnomer that has persisted through the years. For a discussion of this point, see my article, "The Slaves Freed," *American Heritage* (December 1980), 74–83.

one of his chief foreign policy advisers, was especially persistent. Before secession, of course, Sumner and his colleagues had all adhered to the Republican position on slavery in the South. But civil war had now removed their constitutional scruples about the peculiar institution. After all, they told Lincoln, the Southern people were in rebellion against the national government; they could not resist that government and yet enjoy the protection of its laws. Now the senators argued that the national government could eradicate slavery by the War Power, and they wanted Lincoln to do it in his capacity as commander-in-chief. If he emancipated the slaves, it would maim and cripple the Confederacy and hasten an end to the rebellion.

Second, they pointed out that slavery had caused the war, was the reason why the Southern states had seceded, and was now the cornerstone of the confederacy. It was absurd, the senators contended, to fight a war without removing the thing that had brought it about. Should the South return to the Union with slavery intact, as Lincoln desired, Southerners would just start another war over slavery, whenever they thought it threatened again, so that the present struggle would have accomplished nothing, nothing at all. If Lincoln really wanted to save the Union, he must tear slavery out root and branch and smash the South's planter class — that mischievous class the senators thought had masterminded secession and fomented war.

Sumner, as a major Lincoln adviser on foreign affairs, also linked emancipation to foreign policy. On several occasions in 1861 and 1862, Britain seemed on the verge of recognizing the Confederacy as an independent nation — a move that would be calamitous for the Union. As a member of the family of nations, the Confederacy could form alliances and seek mediation and perhaps armed intervention in the American conflict. But, Sumner argued, if Lincoln made the obliteration of slavery a Union war aim, Britain would balk at recognition and intervention. Why so? Because she was proud of her antislavery tradition, Sumner contended, and would refrain from helping the South protect human bondage from Lincoln's armies. And whatever powerful Britain did, the rest of Europe was sure to follow.

Also, as Sumner kept reminding everyone, emancipation would break the chains of several million oppressed human beings and right America at last with her own ideals. Lincoln could no longer wait for the future to remove slavery. He must do it. The war, monstrous and terrible though it was, had given Lincoln the opportunity to do it.

Black and white abolitionists belabored that point too. They wrote Lincoln, petitioned him, and addressed him from the stump and in their newspapers. Foremost in that effort was Frederick Douglass, the most eminent African American of his generation, a handsome, eloquent man who had escaped from slavery in Maryland and become a self-made man like Lincoln, raising himself to prominence as an editor and reformer. From the outset, Douglass saw the end of slavery in this war, and he mounted a one-man crusade to win Lincoln to that idea. In his newspaper and on the platform, Douglass thundered at the man in the White House, playing on his personal feelings about slavery, rehearsing the same arguments that Sumner and his colleagues were giving Lincoln in person. You fight the rebels with only one hand, Douglass said. The mission of this war is the destruction of bondage as well as the salvation of the Union. "The very stomach of this rebellion is the negro in the condition of a slave. Arrest that hoe in the hands in the negro, and you smite rebellion in the very seat of its life," he said. "The Negro is the key of the situation — the pivot upon which the whole rebellion turns," he said. "Teach the rebels and traitors that the price they are to pay for the attempt to abolish this Government must be the abolition of slavery,"- he said. "Hence forth let the war cry be down with treason, and down with slavery, the cause of treason."

The pressure on Lincoln to strike at slavery was unrelenting. In between abolitionist delegations came Sumner and his stern colleagues again, with Vice-

President Hannibal Hamlin and Congressman Owen Lovejoy often with them. As the war progressed, they raised still another argument for emancipation, an argument Douglass and members of Lincoln's own Cabinet were also making. In 1862, his armies suffered from manpower shortages on every front. Thanks to repeated Union military failures and to a growing war weariness across the North, volunteering had fallen off sharply; and Union generals bombarded Washington with shrill complaints, insisting that they faced an overwhelming southern foe and must have reinforcements before they could win battles or even fight. While Union commanders often exaggerated rebel strength, Union forces did need reinforcements to carry out a successful offensive war. As Sumner reminded Lincoln, the slaves were an untapped reservoir of strength. "You need more men," Sumner said, "not only at the North, but at the South. You need the slaves." If Lincoln freed them, he could recruit black men into his armed forces, thus helping to solve his manpower woes.

On that score, the slaves themselves were contributing to the pressures on Lincoln to emancipate them. Far from being passive recipients of freedom, as Vincent Harding has rightly reminded us, the slaves *were* engaged in self-liberation, abandoning rebel farms and plantations and escaping to Union lines by the thousands. This in turn created a tangled legal problem that bedeviled the Lincoln administration. What was the status of such "contraband of war," as Union General Benjamin F. Butler designated them? Were they still slaves? Were they free? Were they somewhere in between? The administration tended to follow a look-the-other-way policy, allowing field commanders to solve the contraband problem any way they wished. Some officers sent the fugitives back to the Confederacy, others turned them over to refugee camps, where benevolent organizations attempted to care for them. But with more and more slaves streaming into Union lines, Sumner, several of Lincoln's Cabinet members, Douglass, and many others urged him to grant them freedom and enlist the able-bodied

men in the army. "Let the slaves and free colored people be called into service and formed into a liberating army," Douglass exhorted the President, "to march into the South and raise the banner of Emancipation among the slaves."

Lincoln, however, stubbornly rejected a presidential move against slavery. It was "too big a lick," he asserted. "I think Sumner and the rest of you would upset our applecart altogether if you had your way," he told some aggressive Republicans one day. "We didn't go into the war to put down slavery, but to put the flag back; and to act differently at this moment would, I have no doubt, not only weaken our cause, but smack of bad faith. . . . This thunderbolt will keep."

Nevertheless, Lincoln was sympathetic to the entire range of arguments Sumner and his associates rehearsed for him. Personally, Lincoln hated slavery as much as they did, and many of their points had already occurred to him. In fact, as early as November and December 1861, Lincoln began wavering in his hands-off policy about slavery, began searching about for some compromise — something short of a sweeping emancipation decree. Again he seemed caught in an impossible dilemma: how to remove the cause of the war, keep Britain out of the conflict, cripple the Confederacy and suppress the rebellion, and yet retain the allegiance of Northern Democrats and the critical border?

In March 1862, he proposed a plan to Congress he thought might work: a gradual, compensated emancipation program to commence in the loyal border states. According to Lincoln's plan, the border states would gradually abolish slavery themselves over the next thirty years, and the federal government would compensate slaveowners for their loss. The whole program was to be voluntary; the states would adopt their own emancipation laws without federal coercion.

At the same time, the federal government would sponsor a colonization program, which was also to be entirely voluntary. Without a promise of colonization, Lincoln understood only too well, most Northern whites would never accept emancipation, even if it were carried out by the states. From now on, every time he contemplated some new antislavery move, he made a great fuss about colonization: he embarked on a colonization project in central America and another in Haiti, and he held an interview about colonization with Washington's black leaders, an interview he published in the press. In part, the ritual of colonization was designed to calm white racial fears.

If his gradual, state-guided plan were adopted, Lincoln contended that a presidential decree — federally enforced emancipation — would never be necessary. Abolition would begin on the local level in the loyal border and then be extended into the rebel states as they were conquered. Thus by a slow and salubrious process would the cause of the rebellion be removed and the future of the Union guaranteed.

The plan failed. It failed because the border states refused to act. Lincoln couldn't even persuade Delaware, with its small and relatively harmless slave population, to adopt his program. In desperation, Lincoln on three different occasions — in the spring and summer of 1862 — pleaded with border-state congressmen to endorse his program. In their third meeting, held in the White House on July 12, Lincoln warned the border representatives that it was impossible now to restore the Union with slavery preserved. Slavery was doomed. They could not be blind to the signs, blind to the fact that his plan was the only alternative to a more drastic move against slavery, one that would cause tremendous destruction in the South. Please, he said, commend my gradual plan to your people.

But most of the border men turned him down. They thought his plan would cost too much, would only whip the flames of rebellion, would cause dangerous discontent in their own states. Their intransigence was a sober lesson to Lincoln. It was proof indeed that slaveowners — even loyal slaveowners — were too tied up in the slave system ever to free their own Negroes and voluntarily transform their way of life. If abolition must come, it must begin in the rebel South and then be extended into the loyal border later

on. Which meant that the president must eradicate slavery himself. He could no longer avoid the responsibility. By mid-July 1862, the pressures of the war had forced him to abandon his hands-off policy and lay a "strong hand on the colored element."

On July 13, the day after his last talk with the border men, Lincoln took a carriage ride with a couple of his cabinet secretaries. His conversation, when recounted in full, reveals a tougher Lincoln than the lenient and compromising president of the legend-building biographies. Lincoln said he was convinced that the war could no longer be won through forbearance toward Southern rebels, that it was "a duty on our part to liberate the slaves." The time had come to take a bold new path and hurl Union armies at "the heart of the rebellion," using the military to destroy the very institution that caused and now sustained the insurrection. Southerners could not throw off the Constitution and at the same time invoke it to protect slavery. They had started the war and must now face its consequences.

He had given this a lot of grave and painful thought, he said, and had concluded that a presidential declaration of emancipation was the last alternative, that it was "a military necessity absolutely essential to the preservation of the Union." Because the slaves were a tremendous source of strength for the rebellion, Lincoln must invite them to desert and "come to us and uniting with us they must be made free from rebel authority and rebel masters." His interview with the border men yesterday, he said, "had forced him slowly but he believed correctly to this conclusion."

On July 22, 1862, Lincoln summoned his cabinet members and read them a draft of a preliminary Emancipation Proclamation. Come January 1, 1863, in his capacity as commander-in-chief of the armed forces in time of war, Lincoln would free all the slaves everywhere in the rebel states. He would thus make it a Union objective to annihilate slavery as an institution in the Confederate South.

Contrary to what many historians have said,

Lincoln's projected Proclamation went further than anything Congress had done. True, Congress had just enacted (and Lincoln had just signed) the second confiscation act, which provided for the seizure and liberation of all slaves of people who supported or participated in the rebellion. Still, most slaves would be freed only after protracted case-by-case litigation in the federal courts. Another section of the act did liberate certain categories of slaves without court action, but the bill exempted loyal slaveowners in the rebel South, allowing them to keep their slaves and other property. Lincoln's Proclamation, on the other hand, was a sweeping blow against bondage as an institution in the rebel states, a blow that would free *all* the slaves there — those of secessionists and loyalists alike. Thus Lincoln would handle emancipation himself, avoid judicial red tape, and use the military to vanquish the cornerstone of the Confederacy. Again, he justified this as a military necessity to save the Union.

But Seward and other cabinet secretaries dissuaded Lincoln from issuing his Proclamation in July. Seward argued that the Union had won no clear military victories, particularly in the showcase Eastern theater. As a consequence, Europe would misconstrue the Proclamation as "our last shriek on the retreat," as a wild and reckless attempt to compensate for Union military ineptitude by provoking a slave insurrection behind rebel lines. If Lincoln must give an emancipation order, Seward warned, he must wait until the Union won a military victory.

Lincoln finally agreed to wait, but he was not happy about it: the way George B. McClellan and his other generals had been fighting in the Eastern theater, Lincoln had no idea when he would ever have a victory.

One of the great ironies of the war was that McClellan presented Lincoln with the triumph he needed. A Democrat who sympathized with Southern slavery and opposed wartime emancipation with a passion, McClellan outfought Robert E. Lee at Antietam Creek in September 1862, and forced the rebel army to withdraw. Thereupon Lincoln issued his pre-

liminary Proclamation, with its warning that if the rebellion did not cease by January 1, 1863, the executive branch, including the army and the navy, would destroy slavery in the rebel states.

As it turned out, the preliminary Proclamation ignited racial discontent in much of the lower North, especially the Midwest, and led to significant Democratic gains in the off-year elections of 1862. Many Northern Democrats were already upset with Lincoln's harsh war measures, especially his use of martial law and military arrests. But Negro emancipation was more than they could stand, and they stumped the Northern states that fall, beating the drums of Negrophobia, warning of massive influxes of Southern blacks into the North once emancipation came. When the 1862 ballots were counted, the Democrats had picked up thirty-four congressional seats, won two governorships, and gained control of three state legislatures. While the Republicans retained control of Congress, the future looked bleak indeed if the war ground on into 1864.

Republican analysts — and Lincoln himself — conceded that the preliminary Proclamation was a major factor in the Republican losses. But Lincoln told a delegation from Kentucky that he would rather die than retract a single word in his Proclamation.

As the New Year approached, conservative Republicans begged Lincoln to abandon his "reckless" emancipation scheme lest he shatter their demoralized party and wreck what remained of their country. But Lincoln stood firm. On New Year's day, 1863, he officially signed the final Emancipation Proclamation in the White House. His hand trembled badly, not because he was nervous, but because he had shaken hands all morning in a White House reception. He assured everyone present that he was never more certain of what he was doing. "If my name ever goes into history," he said, "it will be for this act." Then slowly and deliberately he wrote out his full name.

In the final Proclamation, Lincoln temporarily exempted occupied Tennessee and certain occupied places in Louisiana and Virginia. (Later, in reconstructing those states, he withdrew the exemptions and made emancipation a mandatory part of his reconstruction program.) He also excluded the loyal slave states because they were not in rebellion and he lacked the legal authority to uproot slavery there. He would, however, keep goading them to obliterate slavery themselves — and would later push a constitutional amendment that liberated their slaves as well. With the exception of the loyal border and certain occupied areas, the final Proclamation declared that as of this day, all slaves in the rebellious states were *forever free*." The document also asserted that black men — Southern and Northern alike — would now be enlisted in Union military forces.

Out the Proclamation went to an anxious and dissident nation. Later in the day an interracial crowd gathered on the White House lawn, and Lincoln greeted the people from an open window. The blacks cheered and sang, "Glory, Jubilee has come," and told Lincoln that if he would "come out of that palace, they would hug him to death." A black preacher named Henry M. Turner exclaimed that "it is indeed a time of times," that "nothing like it will ever be seen again in this life."

☆ 6 ☆

Lincoln's Proclamation was the most revolutionary measure ever to come from an American president up to that time. As Union armies punched into rebel territory, they would rip out slavery as an institution, automatically freeing all slaves in the areas and states they conquered. In this respect (as Lincoln said), the war brought on changes more vast, more fundamental and profound, than either side had expected when the struggle began. Now slavery would perish as the Confederacy perished, would die by degrees with every Union advance, every Union victory.

Moreover, word of the Proclamation hummed across the slave grapevine in the Confederacy; and as

Men of the Fifty-fourth Massachusetts (Colored) Infantry Regiment. Organized after the Emancipation Proclamation, the Fifty-fourth became the most famous black fighting unit in the Union Army. All the men in the regiment were volunteers, and nearly all were free blacks from the North. They enlisted for various reasons: to help free their brothers and sisters from bondage, prove that black men were not inferior, and help save the Union. The subject of the brilliant motion picture Glory *(1989), the Fifty-fourth led the federal assault on Fort Wagner in Charleston Harbor, losing its white officer and almost half its men. Although the attack was repulsed, the men of the Fifty-fourth proved that black soldiers could fight as well as white soldiers. All told, some 186,000 blacks served in the Union Army: they fought in 450 engagements and won 21 Congressional Medals of Honor. (Luis F. Emilio,* A Brave Black Regiment*)*

Union armies drew near, more slaves than ever abandoned rebel farms and plantations and (as one said)

"demonstrated with their feet" their desire for freedom.

The Proclamation also opened the army to black volunteers, and Northern free Negroes and Southern ex-slaves now enlisted as Union soldiers. As Lincoln said, "the colored population is the great *available* and yet unavailed of, force for restoring the Union." And he now availed himself of that force. In all, some 180,000 Negro fighting men — most of them emancipated slaves — served in Union forces on every major battlefront, helping to liberate their brothers and sisters in bondage and to save the Union. As Lincoln observed, the blacks added enormous and indispensable strength to the Union war machine.

Unhappily, the blacks fought in segregated units under white officers, and until late in the war received less pay than whites did. In 1864 Lincoln told Negro leader Frederick Douglass that he disliked the practice of unequal pay, but that the government had to make some concessions to white prejudices, noting that a great many Northern whites opposed the use of black soldiers altogether. But he promised that they would eventually get equal pay — and they did. Moreover, Lincoln was proud of the performance of his black soldiers: he publicly praised them for fighting "with clenched teeth, and steady eye, and well poised bayonet" to save the Union, while certain whites strove "with malignant heart" to hinder it.

After the Proclamation, Lincoln had to confront the problem of race adjustment, of what to do with all the blacks liberated in the South. By the spring of 1863, he had pretty well written off colonization as unworkable. His colonization schemes all floundered, in part because the white promoters were dishonest or incompetent. But the main reason colonization failed was because most blacks adamantly refused to participate in Lincoln's voluntary program. Across the North, free Negroes denounced Lincoln's colonization efforts — this was their country too! they cried — and they petitioned him to deport slaveholders instead.

As a consequence, Lincoln had just about concluded that whites and liberated blacks must somehow learn how to live together in this country. Still, he needed some device for now, some program that would pacify white Northerners and convince them that Southern freedmen would not flock into their communities, but would remain in the South instead. What Lincoln worked out was a refugee system, installed by his adjutant general in the occupied Mississippi Valley, which mobilized Southern blacks in the South, utilizing them in military and civilian pursuits there. According to the system, the adjutant general enrolled all able-bodied freedmen in the army, employed other ex-slaves as military laborers, and hired still others to work on farms and plantations for wages set by the government. While there were many faults with the system, it was predicated on sound Republican dogma; it kept Southern Negroes out of the North, and it got them jobs as wage earners, thus helping them to help themselves and preparing them for life in a free society.

Even so, emancipation remained the most explosive and unpopular act of Lincoln's presidency. By mid–1863, thousands of Democrats were in open revolt against his administration, denouncing Lincoln as an abolitionist dictator who had surrendered to radicalism. In the Midwest, dissident Democrats launched a peace movement to throw "the shrieking abolitionist faction" out of office and negotiate a peace with the Confederacy that would somehow restore the Union with slavery unharmed. There were large antiwar rallies against Lincoln's war for slave liberation. Race and draft riots flared in several Northern cities.

With all the public unrest behind the lines, conservative Republicans beseeched Lincoln to abandon emancipation and rescue his country "from the brink of ruin." But Lincoln seemed intractable. He had made up his mind to smash the slave society of the rebel South and eliminate "the cruel wrong" of Negro bondage, and no amount of public discontent, he indicated, was going to change his mind. "To use a coarse, but an expressive figure," he wrote one aggravated Democrat, "broken eggs cannot be mended.

I have issued the Proclamation, and I cannot retract it." Congressman Owen Lovejoy applauded Lincoln's stand. "His mind acts slowly," Lovejoy said, "but when he moves, it is *forward*."

He wavered once — in August 1864, a time of unrelenting gloom for Lincoln when his popularity had sunk to an all-time low and it seemed he could not be reelected. He confessed that maybe the country would no longer sustain a war for slave emancipation, that maybe he shouldn't pull the nation down a road it did not want to travel. On August 24 he decided to offer Confederate President Jefferson Davis peace terms that excluded emancipation as a condition, vaguely suggesting that slavery would be adjusted later "by peaceful means." But the next day Lincoln changed his mind. With awakened resolution, he vowed to fight the war through to unconditional surrender and to stick by emancipation come what may. He had made his promise of freedom to the slaves, and he meant to keep it so long as he was in office.

When he won the election of 1864, Lincoln interpreted it as a popular mandate for him and his emancipation policy. But in reality the election provided no clear referendum on slavery, since Republican campaigners had played down emancipation and concentrated on the peace plank in the Democratic platform. Nevertheless, Lincoln used his reelection to promote a constitutional amendment that would guarantee the freedom of all slaves, those in the loyal border as well as those in the rebel South. Since issuing his Proclamation, Lincoln had worried that it might be nullified in the courts or thrown out by a later Congress or a subsequent administration. Consequently he wanted a constitutional amendment that would safeguard his Proclamation and prevent emancipation from ever being overturned.

As it happened, the Senate in May of 1864 had already passed an emancipation amendment — the present Thirteenth Amendment — but the House had failed to approve it. After that Lincoln had insisted that the Republican platform endorse the measure. And now, over the winter of 1864 and 1865, he

put tremendous pressure on the House to endorse the amendment, using all his powers of persuasion and patronage to get it through. He buttonholed conservative Republicans and opposition Democrats and exhorted them to support the amendment. He singled out "sinners" among the Democrats who were "on praying ground," and informed them that they had a lot better chance for the federal jobs they desired if they voted for the measure. Soon two Democrats swung over in favor of it. With the outcome still in doubt, Lincoln participated in secret negotiations never made public — negotiations that allegedly involved the patronage, a New Jersey railroad monopoly, and the release of rebels related to Congressional Democrats — to bring wavering opponents into line. "The greatest measure of the nineteenth century," congressman Thaddeus Stevens claimed, "was passed by corruption aided and abetted by the purest man in America." On January 31, 1865, the House adopted the present Thirteenth Amendment by just three votes more than the required two-thirds majority. At once a storm of cheers broke over House Republicans, who danced around, embraced one another, and waved their hats and canes overhead. "It seemed to me I had been born with a new life," one Republican recalled, "and that the world was overflowing with beauty and joy."

Lincoln, too, pronounced the amendment "a great moral victory" and "a King's cure" for the evils of slavery. When ratified by the states, the amendment would end human bondage everywhere in America. Lincoln pointed across the Potomac. "If the people over the river had behaved themselves, I could not have done what I have."

☆ 7 ☆

Lincoln conceded, though, that he had not controlled the events of the war, but that events had controlled

The strain of war: at left, Abraham Lincoln in Springfield, Illinois, on June 3, 1860. At right, after four years of war, Lincoln posed for photographer Alexander Gardner in Washington, April 10, 1865.

(Photo on left: Chicago Historical Society, photo on right: Brown University, McClennan Lincoln Collection)

him instead, that God had controlled him. He thought about this a great deal, especially at night when he couldn't sleep, trying to understand the meaning of the war, to understand why it had begun and grown into such a massive revolutionary struggle, consuming hundreds of thousands of lives (the final casualties would come to 620,000 on both sides). By his second inaugural, he had reached an apocalyptic conclusion about the nature of the war — had come to see it as a divine punishment for the "great offense" of slavery, as a terrible retribution God had visited on a guilty people, in North as well as South. Lincoln's vision was close to that of old John Brown, who had prophesied on the day he was hanged, on that balmy December day back in 1859, that the crime of slavery could not be purged away from this guilty land except by blood. Now, in his second Inaugural Address, Lin-

coln too contended that God perhaps had willed this "mighty scourge of War" on the United States, "until all the wealth piled by the bondman's two hundred and fifty years of unrequited toil shall be sunk, and until every drop of blood drawn with the lash, shall be paid by another drawn with the sword."

In the last paragraph of his address, Lincoln said he would bind the nation's wounds "with malice toward none" and "charity for all." Yet that did not mean he would be so gentle and forgiving in reconstruction as most biographers have contended. He would be magnanimous in the sense that he wouldn't resort to mass executions or even mass imprisonment of Southern "traitors," as he repeatedly called them. He would not even have the leaders tried and jailed, though he said he would like to "frighten them out of the country." Nevertheless, still preoccupied with the war as a grim

386

purgation which would cleanse and regenerate his country, Lincoln endorsed a fairly tough policy toward the conquered South. After Lee surrendered in April 1865, Lincoln publicly endorsed limited suffrage for Southern blacks, announcing that the intelligent ex-slaves and especially those who had served in Union military forces should have the vote. This put him in advance of most Northern whites. And it put him ahead of most Republicans as well — including many of the so-called radicals — who in April 1865 shrank from Negro suffrage out of fear of their own white constituents. True, Sumner, Salmon Chase, and a few of their colleagues now demanded that all Southern black men be enfranchised in order to protect their freedom. But Lincoln was not far from their position. In a line in his last political speech, April 11, 1865, he granted that the Southern black man deserved the vote, though Lincoln was not quite ready to make that mandatory. But it seems clear in what direction he was heading.

Moreover, in a cabinet meeting on Good Friday, 1865, Lincoln and all his Secretaries endorsed the military approach to reconstruction and conceded that an army of occupation might be necessary to control the rebellious white majority in the conquered South. During the war, Lincoln had always thought the military indispensable in restoring civilian rule in the South. Without the army, he feared that the rebellious Southern majority would overwhelm the small Unionist minority there — and maybe even reenslave the blacks. And he was not about to let the latter happen. The army had liberated the blacks in the war, and the army might well have to safeguard their freedom in reconstruction.

☆ 8 ☆

He had come a long distance from the young Lincoln who entered politics, quiet on slavery lest he be branded an abolitionist, opposed to Negro political rights lest his political career be jeopardized, con-vinced that only the future could remove slavery in America. He had come a long way indeed. Frederick Douglass, who interviewed Lincoln in the White House in 1863, said he was "the first great man that I talked with in the United States freely who in no single instance reminded me of the difference between himself and myself, of the difference of color." Douglass, reflecting back on Lincoln's presidency, recalled how in the first year and a half of the war, Lincoln "was ready and willing" to sacrifice black people for the benefit and welfare of whites. But since the preliminary Emancipation Proclamation, Douglass said, American blacks had taken Lincoln's measure and had come to admire and some to love this enigmatic man. Though Lincoln had taxed Negroes to the limit, they had decided, in the roll and tumble of events, that "the how and the man of our redemption had somehow met in the person of Abraham Lincoln."

But perhaps it was Lincoln himself who best summed up his journey to emancipation — his own as well as that of the slaves. In December 1862, after the calamitous by-elections of that year, in the midst of rising racial protest against his emancipation policy, Lincoln asked Congress — and Northern whites beyond — for their support. "The dogmas of the quiet past," he reminded them, "are inadequate to the stormy present. The occasion is piled high with difficulty, and we must rise with the occasion. As our case is new, so we must think anew, and act anew. We must disenthrall our selves, and then we shall save our country.

"Fellow-citizens, *we* cannot escape history. . . . The fiery trial through which we pass, will light us down, in honor or dishonor, to the latest generation. . . . In *giving* freedom to the slave, we *assure* freedom to the *free* — honorable alike in what we give, and what we preserve. We shall nobly save, or meanly lose, the last best, hope of earth."

QUESTIONS TO CONSIDER

1. Most of us are familiar with the story of "Honest Abe" Lincoln, the unambitious rail-splitting man of

the people. How does Oates's biographical portrait of Lincoln reveal the complex human being behind this mythical image?

2. How was Lincoln able to reconcile his reverence for the founders and the Constitution with the moral paradox of slavery in a free society? How did Lincoln hope to solve the problems of slavery and racial adjustment in America?

3. What was the so-called slave power conspiracy that Lincoln and many other Republicans feared by the late 1850s? How had the events of that crucial decade seemed to confirm their fears?

4. Oates says that the pressures and problems of fighting a civil war finally caused Lincoln to hurl an executive fist at slavery. What were the forces that led Lincoln to issue his Emancipation Proclamation?

5. Many of Lincoln's contemporaries as well as later scholars accused Lincoln of having made an empty gesture with the Emancipation Proclamation. How does Oates answer these accusations?

THE MIGHTY SCOURGE
OF WAR

27

Clara Barton's Finest Hour

STEPHEN B. OATES

When Lincoln first called for troops to put down the rebellion, thousands of northern women felt a powerful urge to serve. "Oh that I may have a hand or a foot or an eye or a voice, an influence on the side of freedom and my country!" cried Mary Livermore when she saw troops marching out of Boston in April 1861. During the next four years, northern women exerted a powerful influence on the side of freedom and country. In the process, they expanded the limits of what was possible for women and found a new sense of confidence and worth.

At first, women did what they could within women's sphere: they flew flags, encouraged their men to enlist, cheered them as they left for the front. They also formed soldiers' aid societies and set about assiduously collecting and forwarding supplies to Washington. Women provided the impetus for the formation of the United States Sanitary Commission (USSC), which became the official civilian relief agency for Lincoln's armies, and the twelve thousand local women's aid societies affiliated with the USSC made it the huge success that it was. Holding "sanitary fairs" and canvassing neighborhoods for donations, these societies raised a total of $50 million in money and supplies for the Union war effort. What was more, women provided the USSC with some of its most effective and creative leadership. Mary Livermore, directing the USSC's regional branch in Chicago, converted it into "an immense shipping business run mainly by women," and she awed Chicago businessmen with her organizational acumen. She helped work out a system of supply involving twelve principal railroad centers, each run by a woman executive; she assigned a quota to each of the thousand local aid societies under her charge, detailing the amount of hospital stores each was to raise (the word stores covered everything from medicines and liquor to food, blankets, and articles of clothing). When each society had collected its quota of supplies, it shipped them to the nearest railroad center, where women workers unpacked the boxes, inspected and graded their contents, repackaged them, and stamped the boxes with the initials USSC. A sanitary agent then forwarded them to the army. Thanks in large part to such collective efforts, Union soldiers were far better fed and cared for than their rebel counterparts.

The women of the war also expanded the boundaries of the traditional women's sphere. As men went away to the front, women replaced them in the Union work force. They moved into government jobs, appeared increasingly in classrooms, even operated farms. When Mary Livermore crossed rural Wisconsin and Iowa in 1863, she was amazed to find women "in the field everywhere, binding and shocking, and loading grain, until then an unusual sight."

As the selection that follows shows, thousands of women also became military nurses and hospital workers, thus invading an all-male domain; they served either in Dorothea Dix's Department of Female Nurses, under the auspices of the Sanitary Commission, or as independent hospital volunteers. The outstanding example of the latter group was Clarissa ("Clara") Barton of Worcester County, Massachusetts. This fierce-willed, ambitious woman became an "independent sanitary commission of one" who raised supplies and took them directly to the battlefield herself. In 1862, she made the Union battlefield hospital in the eastern theater her special province, and she cleared the way for other eastern women to follow her to the field. Although her name is most often associated with the American Association of the Red Cross, which she founded, her Civil War achievements — the subject of this selection — were significant, too. As the author tries to show, Barton's great service to the Union cause was an act of momentous self-discovery and self-empowerment and the foundation of the rest of her life. Barton's war career, moreover, affords a glimpse into the brutal medical side of the conflict and the inferno of combat as seen from a woman's perspective. She is a witness to a larger, more universal story about war itself, which she ended up hating. "If I were to speak of war," she said after the Civil War, "it would not be to show you the glories of conquering armies but the mischief and misery they strew in their tracks; and how, while they march on with tread of iron and plumes proudly tossing in the breeze, some one must follow closely in their steps, crouching to the earth, toiling in the rain and darkness, shelterless like themselves, with no thought of pride or glory, fame or praise, or reward; hearts breaking with pity, faces bathed in tears and hands in blood. This is the side which history never shows." This is the side you are about to see, as we follow Barton through some of the fiercest campaigns of the Civil War.

GLOSSARY

ANDERSONVILLE   Confederate prison in southwest Georgia where almost thirteen thousand Union prisoners died for want of proper food, sanitation, and medical care; Barton proposed and accompanied a postwar military expedition sent to Andersonville to mark the soldiers' mass graves with identifying headboards.

ANTIETAM (MARYLAND)   During this battle, September 17, 1862, Barton worked as a nurse in a farmhouse hospital that was often under fire.

BATTERY WAGNER   Confederate sand fortress on Morris Island, unsuccessfully stormed by black and white Union troops; Barton tended to fallen troops on the beach while under fire; she should have been in the motion picture *Glory* (1989).

DIX, DOROTHEA   Head of the Union's Department of Female Nurses.

ELWELL, JOHN J.   Chief quartermaster of the Department of the South and Barton's lover on Hilton Head, South Carolina, in 1863.

FAIRFAX STATION, VIRGINIA   Site of a Union evacuation hospital after the Battle of Second Bull Run (August 30–31, 1862); in this desperate hospital, Barton got her first experience nursing in the field.

FIFTY-FOURTH MASSACHUSETTS (COLORED) REGIMENT   Elect black outfit, led by Colonel Robert Gould Shaw, that led the abortive assaults on Battery Wagner, July 18, 1863.

GAGE, FRANCES   Ohio feminist and abolitionist who converted Barton to both causes; she and Barton became close friends during Barton's stay on Hilton Head.

GILLMORE, QUINCY A.   Commander of the Department of the South, with headquarters at Hilton Head.

LACY HOUSE   Plantation manor converted to a Union hospital during the Battle of Fredericksburg (December 13, 1862); the horrible sights Barton witnessed here would haunt her the rest of her days.

MOORE, CAPTAIN JAMES M.   Commanded the grave-marking expedition to Andersonville; he objected to Barton's presence on the mission, treated her with studied disrespect, and claimed all the credit for the work at Andersonville.

WELLES, CORNELIUS   Barton's faithful male assistant at Antietam and Fredericksburg.

Clara Barton's Civil War career is a perfect subject for a motion picture. The story has a tragic national context, a sympathetic and original lead character, a wartime love affair, powerful friendships, a sometimes antagonistic medical bureaucracy, a female adversary in Dorothea Dix, plenty of battlefield action seen from a unique perspective, and a compelling plot: a passionate, driven woman who invades a man's domain and helps change it forever.

Clara's role in the Civil War, however, has never been the subject of a motion picture, or fully and accurately told in any form. She is hardly mentioned in Civil War textbooks and general histories; their focus is almost exclusively on the men, anyway. The biographies about her — even the brilliant recent life by Elizabeth Brown Pryor — concentrate on her postwar years with the Red Cross. Even the highly acclaimed PBS series, "The Civil War," overlooks her contribution, although it does quote her a few times.

This is all rather incredible, since Clara Barton was one of the great figures of the Civil War. Her achievements challenged received notions of courage, helped liberate American women from the shackles of strict domesticity, and won her the undying love and respect of thousands of soldiers with whom she served in the Union's Army of the Potomac. The Twenty-first Massachusetts, which came from Clara's home state, even elected her "a daughter of the Regiment" and praised her for being "a ministering angel to our sick." An army surgeon went so far as to call her "the true heroine of the age," whose battlefield exploits made those of the then-commanding general, George B. McClellan, sink into "insignificance."

As a wartime nurse, Clara Barton had to learn from experience. So did her female colleagues. For America had no nursing schools for women at that time; indeed, nursing did not exist as a professional field, as

The outstanding battlefield nurse of the Civil War, Clara Barton invaded a hitherto male domain, braving deadly bullets and whirling canister to tend to her "dear boys" who fell in combat. Her one-woman relief agency brought supplies to Union field units sent to her from a network of women's aid societies. (Library of Congress)

we know it today. There were female nurses in the antebellum years, but theirs was generally regarded as a menial service. Most nurses worked in the home as "the patient's servant," occupying an "ambiguous position," as historian Susan Reverby says, between the cook and the lowly domestic. Women were also hired as nurses on a daily basis in the country's rudimentary hospitals. Military nursing, however, was exclusively a male enterprise. When the war came and casualties began to mount, the army Medical Department found itself dangerously short of army nurses. With patriotic women pouring into Washington, D.C., and offering to serve, the War Department established the Department of Female Nurses and ap-

An earlier version of this essay, entitled, "Clara Barton's Finest Hour," appeared in the January–February 1993 issue of *Timeline,* a publication of the Ohio Historical Society.

pointed imperious Dorothea Dix as its superintendent. During the course of the war, Dix enlisted more than 3,000 women nurses at a monthly salary of $12 each. Later in the war, the United States Sanitary Commission, established by prominent New Yorkers and subsequently appointed the official civilian relief agency of Lincoln's government, also fielded women nurses. Jane E. Schultz has turned up the astonishing fact that some twenty thousand women served in Union hospitals as paid nurses, matrons (women who ran diet kitchens and supervised nursing staffs), cooks, and laundresses. Among the cooks and laundresses were some two thousand black women, many of them escaped slaves. Most northern hospital workers were stationed in the base or general hospitals in and around Washington, D.C., and in other cities near the battlefronts.

Never a joiner, Clara Barton shunned affiliation with Dix's Department of Female Nurses and the U.S. Sanitary Commission. She became the supreme example of another type of female nurse: the do-it-yourself independent, who served in federal battlefield hospitals, alongside male attendants, who were usually either convalescents or soldiers detailed from the line. From the outset, Clara had to overcome both government and societal restraints against the presence of a woman on the battlefield. To her critics, she always retorted, "If you think war is rough and unseemly for a woman, I can only reply that it is rough and unseemly for a man too."

A slender woman who stood exactly five feet tall, with a round face, luminous, dark brown eyes, and silky brown hair worn parted in the middle and pulled into a knot in back of her head, Clara was a dynamo of nervous energy and determination, and she was full of contradictions. If she could be brave and a loyal, loving friend, she was also vain enough in her later years to do what a lot of us do at that stage: she lied about how old she was and dyed her hair in order to disguise the gray. In addition, she suffered from low self-esteem, which stemmed in large measure from her family background: she felt that her mother had

neglected her and that her family, including four considerably older siblings, had subordinated her to its needs. Nevertheless, thanks to an implacable will and a strong physical constitution, Clara left her mark on the military annals of the United States, and she attained a popularity unmatched by any other woman in the Civil War.

I am referring to her in this portrait as Clara, because that is how she was known to her legion of wartime friends. Calling her Barton makes her seem cold and distant, when she was anything but that: among adversaries she was a blunt and fiery presence they were not likely to forget; among friends and relatives she exuded a special warmth, engaging them in conversation — a favorite pastime — with a solicitous smile, a merry sparkle in her eyes, and a relaxed informality about her. She was Clara.

Raised largely by her warrior father, whom she idolized, Clara could ride a horse and shoot a pistol as well as any man. Since she regarded marriage as a form of murder, something that would destroy her very selfhood, she remained unwed, a "spinster," in a world that celebrated marriage and motherhood as the female ideal. She waged a lifetime battle against restrictions on women because of their sex; yet she had her share of male suitors, who found her attractive, admired her intelligence and loyalty, and treasured her sensitivity. Even so, she turned down all marriage proposals. Her independence, her struggle against the mores of her time and place, cost her a great deal emotionally, for she was given to recurring depressions, even thoughts of suicide. Yet, Clara was a survivor; she prevailed over her inner demons as well as outer adversity. During the 1850s, she was one of only a handful of women who found employment in the United States Patent Office in Washington, D.C., where she endured the taunts of male coworkers and fought a male-dominated bureaucracy to retain her precarious position.

Clara was thirty-nine when the war broke out, but looked ten years younger than that. She really wanted to become a soldier and emulate her father. But she

A Union field hospital in Virginia, 1864. This is the side of the war usually omitted in histories of the campaigns and biographies of the generals. The soldier on the right has had his lower arm amputated; *the man on the stretcher has lost part of his leg. (U.S. Army Military History Institute)*

was apparently too inhibited to enlist in the army by impersonating a male, as some women did. To vent her frustrations, she marched out to a firing range in Washington, aimed her revolver at a target fifty feet away, and put "nine balls successively within the space of six inches." If she could not be a soldier, she told herself, at least she could *help* soldiers. By the summer of 1861, she was a one-woman relief agency, soliciting and receiving supplies from various New England women's aid societies and taking them to the army camps across the Potomac. In the second year of the war, she persuaded the Quartermaster Department to furnish her four supply wagons and army teamsters to drive the mules, and Washingtonians became accustomed to the sight of bonneted Clara Barton, perched high in a covered wagon loaded with supplies, leading her mule-drawn caravan toward the battlefront. Clara went there entirely on her own initiative, as independent as she had ever been, unaffiliated with any of the nursing organizations. "While our soldiers can stand and fight," she announced, "I can stand and feed and nurse them."

And feed and nurse them she did, in field hospitals right behind the front lines. Here a second war was going on that claimed more lives than the shooting war itself. Two-thirds of the 360,000 Union deaths occurred in the hospitals, where surgeons and nurses, relying on primitive medical practices and dubious medicines, fought a losing battle to save wounded or diseased soldiers. As historian George Washington Adams has said, the Civil War came at "the very end of the medical 'middle ages.'" Since nobody knew what caused infection, surgeons worked with unsanitary scalpels and saws in unsanitary conditions. Recalled one Union surgeon: "We operated in old blood-stained and often pus-stained coats . . . with undisinfected hands. We used undisinfected instruments . . . and marine sponges which had been used in prior pus cases and only washed in tap water." The luckless soldier with a bone-breaking wound in the leg or arm faced certain amputation. If he was in a well-stocked hospital, the surgeon would put him mercifully to sleep with chloroform or ether. If both were lacking (and they often were at battlefield hospitals), the poor victim might get a shot of whiskey, or simply a slab of leather placed between his teeth, before the surgeon applied the saw. Because of the horrid conditions in the hospitals and the lack of proper medical treatment, the mortality rate — especially in the early part of the war — was appalling. Nearly every soldier with an abdominal wound died; some 60 percent of those with other wounds also died.

The real Civil War killer, however, was infectious disease. Dysentery and diarrhea were the worst, killing some 44,500 Union soldiers during the course of the war. Doctors tried to combat diarrhea-dysentery with laxatives, opium, castor oil, or Epsom salts. Other killer diseases were malaria and typhoid, which the crude medicines of the day could do little to stop. Doing the best they could with the medical knowledge of the day, physicians treated abdominal pains with blisters and "hot fomentation," and intestinal ulcers with oral doses of turpentine. As various historians have said, a soldier's safety was more imperiled if he had to undergo treatment in an army hospital than if he had fought all three days at Gettysburg.

By the summer of 1862 the battlefield hospital had become Clara Barton's war. In an open-air hospital near Fairfax Station, Virginia, she tended to wounded men as they arrived in two-wheeled carts and wagons from the nearby battlefield of Second Bull Run, which was fought in late August. Some three thousand wounded men lay on the sun-scorched hills while surgeons worked with "their knives and up-rolled sleeves and blood-smeared aprons, and by their sides [lay] ghastly heaps of cut off legs and arms." It

was here that Clara first began functioning as a free-lance battlefield nurse. She was no stranger to disease — she had ministered to her father and other family members when they were ill. But nursing men with gunshot wounds, with faces disfigured, chests and abdomens blasted open, arms and legs smashed or blown away, had to be learned on the job. She offered food and spirits to the wounded, bound their injuries, and uttered a prayer for the dying. She labored three days and nights with only a couple of hours of sleep; on the last day she withstood musket fire from Rebel snipers and stayed on until she and her female assistant had loaded the last wounded soldier onto the last train for Washington. They leaped aboard just as the conductor set the station afire so that the enemy could not use it. As the train rounded a curve, Clara saw Rebel cavalry dashing up to the burning station. Had the train been delayed a few minutes, she would have fallen into Confederate hands.

During the Battle of Antietam, some two and a half weeks later, Clara and her wagon train reached a makeshift hospital in a farmhouse on the Union right flank, and Clara hurried inside to distribute her supplies and assist the harried surgeons. The battle marked the bloodiest single day of combat in American military history. Some of the most savage fighting took place on the Union right, in the Cornfield, the East and West Woods, just beyond the farmhouse where Clara was stationed. Union artillery stood massed just behind the farmhouse, and Union infantry charged forward or fell back all around it. Artillery shells burst overhead, crashed into nearby trees, exploded in the yard in a tornado of noise that made the ground shake; one barrage was so terrifying that all the male attendants ran for shelter in the rear, but not Clara. She remained at the surgeon's side, holding a soldier's mangled leg while the doctor sawed it off without administering ether or chloroform (he had none). She did not flinch even though the poor fellow was screaming. Outside, dozens of men too injured to move lay about the barn; Clara tended to them while shells and musketry shredded the trees around her. She gave water to the wounded, stroked their hair, closed their eyes after they had died. As she held one young man in her arms, a bullet ripped through her sleeve and killed him. She was so profoundly shaken that she never mended the hole in that dress. Another man, hardly more than a boy, was in such pain from a bullet lodged in his face that he begged Clara to cut it out herself. Even though she had never cut human flesh before, she removed the bullet with her pocket knife.

After working at Antietam for three straight days with almost no sleep, she collapsed from fever and had to be carried by wagon back to her room in Washington. "When I looked in a mirror," she said later, "my face was still the color of gunpowder."

Clara's courage on the battlefield challenged received notions of military heroism in that romantic, sentimental era. The popular notion of heroism conjured up an armed male leading a glorious charge or demonstrating uncommon valor in killing the enemy. Like the surgeons she assisted, Clara showed a different kind of courage, unarmed courage, while under fire: as armed men set about the business of killing and maiming one another, Clara tried to save lives, to help put smashed bodies back together, with no weapons but her utensils and a soothing voice.

By now, Clara had a devoted assistant named Cornelius "Cornie" Welles, a strong individual in his own right, who had no problem taking orders from a woman. Not so the army teamsters assigned to handle her wagons and mule teams. Indignant that they had been put in the charge of "a *lady*," they challenged her authority one day: they refused to obey her instructions, cracking their long whips indignantly. Clara shamed them into submission with kindness. She prepared coffee and supper for the entire team, which she laid out on a cloth on the ground; she sat down and politely ate with them as though nothing had happened. The men were stunned. Later, their leader, George, apologized in behalf of them all. "We never seen a train under charge of a *woman* afore," he said, "and we didn't like it, and we've been mean and

contrary all day, and said a good many hard things, and you've treated us like gentlemen. We hadn't no right to expect that supper from you; it makes us ashamed, and we've come to ask your forgiveness." She assured him that she harbored no hard feelings. When she was ready for sleep, George hung a lighted lantern from the top of her ambulance, arranged a few blankets inside for her bed, helped her up the steps, and buckled the canvas down on the outside.

Clara's caravan rejoined the Army of the Potomac in time for the disastrous Union defeat at Fredericksburg, Virginia, in December 1862. The battle resulted in almost 13,000 Northern casualties, including 9,600 wounded. Clara seemed a ubiquitous presence, mothering and ministering to her "boys," as she called the wounded soldiers, wherever she found them. Most of the time she labored in the Lacy mansion, situated just across from Fredericksburg on the banks of the Rappahannock River. It had been converted into a Union hospital, and, under a tree in front of the house, lay a heap of feet, arms, and legs that had been tossed out the door. Inside, the dead and the dying were packed together on floors slippery with blood. They were wedged under tables and crammed into porticos; five men even lay on the four shelves of a common cupboard. As Clara came and went in the Lacy House, a delirious officer, fatally wounded, confused her for his wife. She tried to soothe a young boy of the Seventh Michigan, shot through the lungs and apparently dying, who refused to let the stretcher bearers remove him and clung to his pitiful spot, "a mere little white bundle of skin and bones," as she put it later. When she found another soldier bleeding to death, she applied a tourniquet to his wound. Afterward, every time she passed him, he tugged at her skirt and said, "You saved my life." Rising from the side of another badly wounded soldier, as she said later, "I wrung the blood from the bottom of my clothing, before I could step, for the weight about my feet."

Clara remained in the Lacy House until her supplies were exhausted and most of the wounded had been transferred to base hospitals in Washington, D.C. Then she returned there, too, waded through the mud to her boarding house, and climbed the long flight of stairs to her room. There, "cheerless, in confusion, and alone," she fell to the floor and wept.

Later, as she sat in her room contending with a mass of accumulated correspondence, she heard a limping footstep in the hallway and then a rap at her door. When she opened it, she was surprised to see a young man leaning on his crutch. It was her "hero of the *four words*" who said again, "you saved my life."

By the beginning of 1863, Dix's Department of Female Nurses and the U.S. Sanitary Commission had largely taken over relief work and nursing in the Eastern theater. The days of the free-lance independent appeared to be over there, as Dix sought to exclude all unaffiliated female nurses like Clara from medical service. Clara therefore resolved to get as far away from Dix as she could. In the spring of 1863, Clara sailed down to Hilton Head Island, off the coast of South Carolina, which comprised part of the Union's Department of the South. Here army and naval forces were planning a joint campaign to capture Charleston, a great blockade-running Rebel port and the birthplace of secession.

In the tropical climate of Hilton Head, Clara worked in hospitals and helped feed and clothe blacks who had escaped from bondage on the mainland. Here she had an affair with a married man, Colonel John J. Elwell of Cleveland, Ohio. Six feet tall, with a mustache and gentle gray eyes, Elwell had been a professor of "medical jurisprudence" before the war, and Clara found his learned charm irresistible. She walked with him on the beach and accompanied him to dances; they went riding past plantations whose occupied mansions were symbols of a dying way of life. She and Elwell read together, laughed together, and worried about the war together. They wrote one another intimate notes, and eventually their passion expressed itself physically: she would spend the night in his rooms and leave at dawn. Later he admitted that he loved Clara "all the law allows (and a little more

perhaps)." As Elizabeth Brown Pryor points out, this was the great love of Clara's life; yet she made no effort to win Elwell from his wife, nor did he offer to leave his wife for Clara. When she gazed at the ocean, Clara thought the waves were whispering "thus far shall thou go and no farther!"

While stationed at Hilton Head, Clara befriended Frances "Fanny" Gage, an older woman who had left her husband and many children in order to help the blacks on the South Carolina Sea Islands. Clara and Fanny Gage came to love one another deeply — theirs was a friendship that would last "to the death," as Fanny Gage put it later. This loving, passionate, philanthropic woman had a great influence on Clara. An ardent feminist, she converted Clara to the cause of women's suffrage. Under Fanny's influence, Clara also advocated equal political and economic rights for blacks as well.

In part, Clara's growing sensitivity to the plight of black people derived from close association with black female nurses on Hilton Head, most of whom were former slaves. Clara became a friend of Susie Taylor, a slender, dark-skinned woman whose husband was a noncommissioned officer in a Union regiment made up of former slaves. The two nurses often made their hospital rounds together. As Clara moved from bed to bed, she showed a special concern for black patients. "I honored her for her devotion and care of these men," Mrs. Taylor said later.

In July 1863, when Union forces set out to capture Morris Island and Battery Wagner in Charleston harbor, Clara accompanied the expedition as a battlefield nurse. Though not officially a fort, Battery Wagner was a huge, formidable stronghold, with siege mortars and field artillery trained on the only infantry approach to the battery — the narrow beach to the south. Such a powerful stronghold could never be taken by foot soldiers, yet an infantry assault was precisely what the Union commanders ordered, on the grounds that Wagner had to fall before an attack could be launched against Charleston itself. The Union's showcase black regiment, the Fifty-fourth

Massachusetts Infantry, consisting of black volunteers from all over the North, was to lead the assault.

Posted at a field hospital only a few hundred yards from the Rebel battery, Clara saw Union warships hurl hundreds of shells at it, sending up "spectacular geysers of smoke and sand." Then came the legendary assault of the Fifty-fourth Massachusetts, vividly captured in the 1989 motion picture, *Glory*. Clara went up to Lookout Hill, with Rebel shells exploding nearby, in order to witness the charge as it unfolded at twilight. "The scene was grand beyond description," she wrote later. "A long line of phosphorescent light streamed and shot along the waves ever surging on our right." She could hear the thud of Rebel canister hitting the assaulting troops. Transfixed with horror, she watched as black men in blue uniforms ran toward the fort now, Colonel Robert Gould Shaw in front with his drawn sword whipping the air. He led them into a moat in front of the rampart connecting the two bastions of the fort, scrambled up the banks, and clawed his way up the side of the rampart while cannons flashed, casting the scene in an eerie pulsing light. Shaw was the first to reach the top of the rampart, and Clara could see him standing alone, his sword pointing at the sky, in a surreal maelstrom of whirling iron and lead so loud and brilliant it seemed as though the world were coming apart. Then he disappeared in a swirl of smoke.

As the black soldiers followed Shaw up the side of the rampart, Colonel Elwell, standing with Gillmore and his staff, became increasingly distraught. When white support troops went forward into that murderous fire, Elwell cried, "My God, our men are being slaughtered." Bareheaded, he climbed onto his horse and spurred it furiously toward the battery, with his "long hair streaming in the wind." Clara was horrified. When she saw the Colonel fall wounded from his horse, she ran through the sand and helped him crawl back to the field hospital. Thinking him in good hands now, she turned back up the beach to help the other wounded. A war correspondent reported seeing her on the battlefield. "There, with the shot and shell flying and whispering about her, we find this noble and heroic Worcester woman stooping over the wounded soldier, tenderly administering to our brave men wounded."

Meanwhile the noise of hand-to-hand combat sounded from inside the battery. Before long, survivors of the assault began making their way back from the thundering walls of Wagner, staggering into the field hospital where the medical team awaited them in tents lit with lanterns. Clara came there, too, and stayed with her "boys" all that cloudy night. She would never forget what she had witnessed at Battery Wagner. "I can see again the scarlet flow of blood as it rolled over the black limbs beneath my hands, and the great heave of the human heart before it grew still."

Clara remained on Morris Island through August, toiling day by day under a blazing sun while Gillmore's little army dug a series of parallel siege lines that took them ever closer to the battery. The Rebels blasted them with constant artillery barrages. One shell burst almost on top of a Connecticut officer named Robert Leggett; the explosion blew his leg off. Clara sprang to his side, tore off some of her clothing, fashioned it into a tourniquet, and used it to tie off "the bleeding fragments," which stanched the flow of blood. A surgeon who examined Leggett said he was too weak to endure an operation. "He's dying, past being helped," the surgeon said, and walked away. Clara, however, refused to give up on the colonel and took care of him herself, bathing his face in water and calling him her "poor sufferer" and beseeching him not to die. To everyone's astonishment, he regained consciousness — brought back from the edge of oblivion, it appeared, by Clara's ministering. Gazing at her face, Leggett whispered that he couldn't believe he was alive, that it was a miracle, and that it was all due to Clara and that he would never, never forget it and that she was an angel.

By mid-August, Clara was worn down by exhaustion and sick with a fever. To make matters worse, she ran afoul of certain medical authorities, who disliked her and objected to her presence on the battlefield, and she was forced to return to Hilton Head for a time. Meanwhile, the Rebels finally abandoned Battery Wagner and nearby Battery Gregg, leaving the island in Union hands. Clara wrote a friend, "We have captured one fort — Gregg — and one charnel house — Wagner — and we have built one cemetery, Morris Island. The thousand little sand-hills that glitter in the pale moonlight are a thousand head-stones, and the restless ocean waves that roll and break upon the whitened beach sing an eternal requiem to the toil-worn, gallant dead who sleep beside."

Clara went on to serve in the macabre field hospitals in Fredericksburg during Grant's great offensive against Lee in the spring of 1864. The rest of the year found her working as a volunteer matron (she never received any pay during the war) in a field hospital of the Army of the James, which held Union fortifications before Richmond during Grant's siege of Petersburg to the South. Clara was in charge of the cooks, laundresses, and nursing staff, including male soldiers detailed from the line. After one battle on the Richmond line, a general saw Clara tending to the badly injured and claimed that her "beautiful arms" were "red with human blood to the shoulders."

By 1864 Clara so identified with her "boys" that she was calling herself a United States soldier. She was also an enthusiastic supporter of Lincoln, whose moves against slavery she deeply admired. Like him, she had initially favored a limited war, whose sole object was to save the Union, not to free the slaves. But as the war dragged on with no end in sight, she changed as Lincoln had changed: she applauded the harsh war measures he adopted, especially emancipation, which turned the conflict into a remorseless, revolutionary struggle. In her own searching for the meaning of this terrible war, Clara anticipated Lincoln's ringing second inaugural. "What of the campaign," she wrote her friend Frances Gage in May 1864. "I am holding my breath in awe at the vastness of the shadow that floats like a pall above our heads. . . . *Can* God behold and smite not? Ay, but he is smiting, — and this is his terrible retribution! Is this

war never to end, till for every African slave that ever dragged his chain an Anglo Saxon shall have suffered?"

Lincoln was to draw the same conclusion, asserting that God perhaps had willed this "mighty scourge of War" on this guilty land, "until all the wealth piled by the bondman's two hundred and fifty years of unrequited toil shall be sunk, and until every drop of blood drawn with the lash, shall be paid by another drawn from the sword."

Clara admired Lincoln so much that she intended to support him for re-election in 1864. "Who am I going to vote for?" she asked Gage rhetorically. "Why I thought for president Lincoln, to be sure. I *have* been voting for him for the last three years. I thought him honest, and true, and I believe that he sought the right with all his power, and would do it as fast as he saw it clearly, and I still think so. . . . I *honor* Mr. Lincoln and have believed, and still do, that his election was ordained, that he was raised up to meet this crisis, but it may also be that *no one* man could be constituted who should be equal to both the beginning and ending of this vast, this mighty change, the same mind that could guide safely in the outset may be too slow now, for war has had its effects upon us, and our temper as a people, wiped out our conservativeness and touched us with the fire of the old nations. We have grown enthusiastic, and shout loud and long, where once we should have looked on in silence. I have said from the first that I believed this whole thing was directly in the hands of Providence, and that so it would continue, and that if we had *need* of our present ruler, whom I have always contended was *appointed* and not elected, that if we had further need of him we should have him." Should the Republicans nominate another man in his stead, she would of course support him. But she hoped the nominee would be Lincoln, whose "care worn face" had become "very dear" to her.

Courageous though Clara was, her constant association with mutilated young men, with death and destruction on the battlefield, often left her depressed, lonely, and frightened. "This was one of the most down-spirited days that ever came to me," she recorded in her diary in 1864. "All the world appeared selfish and treacherous. I can get no hold on a good nobel sentiment *anywhere* — I have scanned over and over the whole moral horizon and it is all dark, the night clouds seem to have shut down, so stagnant, so dead, so selfish, so calculating. Is there no right? How shall the world move on in all this weight of dead morbid meanness?" Yet she stayed at the hospitals near Petersburg, nursing her boys. War's end found her back in Washington, running a one-woman search agency for thousands of missing soldiers. After Appomattox, she accompanied an army expedition to Andersonville, Georgia, the terrible Confederate prison where nearly thirteen thousand of the forty-five thousand incarcerated Union men had perished for want of proper food, sanitation, and medical care. Clara and the soldiers came there to identify the Union dead, erect proper grave markers for them, and establish a national cemetery. Inspired by a former Andersonville inmate named Dorence Atwater, who had kept a secret death register, Clara had actually conceived the idea of the expedition and had proposed it to the War Department. Secretary of War Edwin M. Stanton had praised her lavishly for her "good, sensible, practical, *unselfish* idea" and insisted that she and Atwater go along to make sure the work was done properly. At Andersonville, however, the Union workmen were so rude to Clara that she never went to the cemetery while they were there; she contented herself with nursing those who came down with fevers in Georgia's searing heat. In that way, she exercised real power over the very men who had insulted her.

Blacks came from miles around to meet Clara and to ask if Lincoln really had been assassinated and if they really were free. She stood brooding inside the Andersonville stockade, and later penned a memorable description of the prison that served as a benediction to the war itself: "I have looked over its 25 acres of pitiless stockade, its burrows in the earth, its stinted stream, its turfless hillsides, shadeless in summer and shelterless in winter — its wells and tunnels and caves — its 7 forts of death — its ball and chains — its stocks for torture — its kennels for blood-hounds — its sentry boxes and its deadline — and my heart sickened and stood still — my brain whirled — and the light of my eyes went out. And I said, 'Surely this was not the gate of hell, but hell itself.' And for comfort I turned away to the acres of crowded graves and I said, 'here at last was rest, and this to them was the gate of heaven.'"

When the work at the cemetery was completed, Clara gazed over the silent formations of white lettered headboards and thought this truly "the city of the dead." Before the expedition departed, she had the honor of raising the flag over that sacred, melancholy ground. When the flag unfurled in the wind, a small crowd sang "The Star Spangled Banner," and Clara covered her face and cried.

The Andersonville expedition ended in bitter controversy when the officer who commanded it, Captain James M. Moore, officially took all the credit for its work. A rude, spit-and-polish assistant quartermaster, he had disliked Clara's presence from the outset, thought a real "lady" would never have gone to such a place, and treated her with studied disrespect throughout the trip, as did his men. Back in Washington, Clara drew on all her political connections and all her powers of persuasion to gain government recognition of her missing-soldier work and a $15,000 congressional appropriation as a reward. Clara, however, never forgave Captain Moore for his "jealous wicked heart" and wrote that he would one day get the "execration" he deserved.

And so the war years came to a close for Clara. By now her hospital work had made her famous — "I appear to be known by reputation by every person in every train I enter and everywhere," she wrote in her diary. Indeed, a great many of her contemporaries considered her the outstanding battlefield nurse and relief worker of either sex in the showcase Eastern theater, perhaps of the entire war. Her pioneering efforts, in fact, had opened the way for other women to serve in battlefield hospitals in the East. An efficient and effective "Sanitary Commission of one," Clara had raised impressive quantities of supplies through her network of women's groups and had personally taken those supplies to the army in the field. Nobody else had done as much as she in acting as an individual conduit between the home front and the needy soldier on the battlefield. If historian Reid Mitchell is right, if the war's outcome owed much to the perseverance of the Union's common soldiers, then credit Clara Barton and the other women of the war for reinforcing their resolve.

Haunted by her memories of the war, unable to let go of them, Clara took to the lecture circuit, describing again and again what she had witnessed. She proved to be a gifted lecturer, with an eloquent, musical voice and a poetic bent to her descriptions that enthralled her audiences. Lyceums, literary societies, and veterans' organizations affiliated with the Grand Army of the Republic all vied for her services. One GAR post even named itself after her, which pleased Clara enormously, since she regarded herself as a veteran. As a speaker, she was so effective that she was able to demand, and get, the same fees as male lecturers received. This ship, our nation, she said in one speech in 1866, "has floated four years, not only in mist, but darkness and blood with neither rudder nor compass and made land at last. And not only this, but she came in with her decks laden to the waters edge with the rent shackles and broken bonds of a whole race of slaves. Then from off her blood-stained slippery decks came limping crawling weeping for joy three millions of God's *poor neglected, long-abandoned, late-remembered, downtrodden* children of the dust, and stood shouting Hozannahs beneath the broad folds [of the flag] floating above them."

Clara argued that the war had liberated women, too. By war's end, she told a Boston audience, the American woman was at least "fifty years in advance of the normal position which continued peace and existing conditions would have assigned her." She meant that American women of 1861 to 1865 had left the home in unprecedented numbers: they had entered government service, secured retail jobs, and toiled in war-related industry; some four hundred women had enlisted in the army disguised as men; and thousands had worked as nurses or raised supplies as Clara had done. In the process, Clara and her female colleagues had brought about a profound change in the field of American nursing. Regarded as a menial service before the war, it became a trained, paid profession for women after the conflict. In no comparable previous period had the American woman demanded and won so many new opportunities. As a consequence, she was now in "a new bold active position," Clara said, to gain rapid advancements.

For Clara, more accomplishments lay in the future — among other things, she would found the American Association of the Red Cross and would serve in field hospitals in Cuba during the Spanish-American War. But it was the Civil War that fired her imagination, the Civil War to which she kept returning in her speeches and reminiscences. As with millions of others in her generation, the war remained the central event of her life. It had given her and her entire generation of women a new sense of worth. "Only an opportunity was wanting for woman to prove to man that she *could* be in earnest," Clara declared, "that she had character, and firmness of purpose — that she *was* good for something in an emergency." The women of the war had not only demonstrated their competence to men, Clara believed, they had also proved it to themselves. They had "dug grand and deep and laid firm and forever the cornerstone of future womanhood."

QUESTIONS TO CONSIDER

1. Stephen Oates quotes George Washington Adams as saying that the Civil War came at "the very end of the medical 'middle ages.'" What were conditions like in the Civil War hospitals? How did the

doctors do their work, and what were the effects on the soldiers?

2.   How did the Civil War and the contributions of women to the war effort change the status and practice of nursing in the United States?

3.   How did her Civil War experiences and contacts shape and change Clara Barton's political and social ideas?

4.   Think back over Barton's various experiences during the war, whether in Washington or on the battlefield. In what ways did different men — politicians, workers, soldiers — react to her and the work she was doing? How did she deal with those who disapproved?

5.   Barton believed that American women were at least "fifty years in advance of" where they would have been had there been no Civil War. How did she arrive at such a conclusion? How does this compare with the experience and feelings of the women on the overland trails about whom you read in selection 22?

28

Why the Confederacy Lost

JAMES M. MCPHERSON

James M. McPherson, one of America's foremost authorities on the Civil War, argues that the rebellious southern states left the Union and formed the Confederacy because they perceived the Black Republican party as a revolutionary threat to their slave-based way of life. For McPherson, secession was therefore "a pre-emptive counterrevolution to prevent the Black Republican revolution from engulfing the South." That the new Confederacy was dedicated to saving slavery, both as a multibillion dollar labor system and a means of race control, cannot be doubted. The Confederates wrote a constitution that closely resembled the United States Constitution save for one crucial difference: the Confederate document specifically guaranteed slavery and affirmed states' rights. In Savannah, Georgia, rebel vice president Alexander H. Stephens made it unmistakably clear what the Confederacy stood for. "Our new government is founded upon exactly the opposite idea [from that of equality in the Declaration of Independence]; its foundations are laid, its cornerstone rests, upon the great truth that the negro is not equal to the white man; that slavery — subordination to the superior race — is his natural and normal condition. This, our new government, is the first in the history of the world based upon this great physical, philosophical, and moral truth."

From the outset, this new government was beset with internal problems: it lacked sound money, guns, factories, food, railroads, and harmonious political leadership. Still, with its excellent generals and soldiers, the possibility of foreign intervention, and other advantages, the Confederacy faced better odds in its war for independence than had the American colonies. Why, then, did the Confederacy go down to defeat? In the next selection, McPherson examines earlier explanations — that the North had "the strongest battal-

ions," that the South died of internal dissent and loss of will — and finds them lacking. He puts forth a cogent and convincing argument for rebel defeat that reflects an important body of modern thinking about the war. That thinking stresses the overriding importance of military operations, contending that ultimately the war was won or lost on the battlefield. As Lincoln himself said, it was upon "the progress of our arms" that everything else depended — public and soldier morale and political, economic, and social stability. To explain why the Confederacy lost (the "South" didn't lose, because four southern states and one hundred thousand southern men fought for the Union), McPherson offers the theory of contingency — the idea that at certain crucial points in military operations, either side could have won. He discusses four such "moments of contingency," or turning points. The first occurred in the summer of 1862 when it seemed that the South would triumph on the field of arms. The second came in the fall of 1862 when military fortunes swung back in favor of the North. The third took place in July 1863 when the Union won simultaneous victories at Gettysburg and Vicksburg. And the fourth came in the summer of 1864 when the Union war machine bogged down, and northern morale plummeted as a consequence; for a time, it appeared that Lincoln would not be reelected and that a Democrat would become president and negotiate peace with the Confederacy. But Union military victories in Georgia and Virginia hardened northern will to fight on, which "clinched matters for the North."

McPherson goes on to describe the war's most important consequences — the death of slavery and secession, the transformation of the country from a loose confederation of states and regions into an indivisible nation, and the triumph of the northern vision of America and the corresponding loss of the southern vision. This is state-of-the-art analysis, excerpted from McPherson's Pulitzer prize-winning Battle Cry of Freedom: The Civil War Era (1988).

GLOSSARY

ANTIETAM (MARYLAND)   Robert E. Lee and George B. McClellan fought to a draw here, in the bloodiest single day in American military history; the battle ended Lee's first invasion of the North.

ARMY OF THE POTOMAC   The Union's principal fighting force in the eastern theater and its greatest army of the war.

GETTYSBURG (PENNSYLVANIA)   Lee's greatest reversal, in July 1863, ended his second

invasion of the North; best known for Pickett's calamitous charge on the third day; Lee suffered such losses that he could never again mount the offensive.

GÖTTERDÄMMERUNG   In German mythology, the destruction of all gods and all things in a final battle with the forces of evil.

PERRYVILLE (KENTUCKY)   A Confederate invasion force under Braxton Bragg lost this battle in October 1862; Bragg's columns and a second rebel invasion force under Kirby Smith fell back into Tennessee.

VICKSBURG (MISSISSIPPI)   Rebel garrison on the Mississippi River; surrendered to Ulysses S. Grant on July 4, 1863, the same day that Lee retreated from Gettysburg.

CONFEDERATE GENERALS:

BEAUREGARD, PIERRE GUSTAVE TOUTANT   Led Confederate forces to victory at First Bull Run (or First Manassas), July 1861.

BRAGG, BRAXTON   Quarrelsome commander of the Army of Tennessee, the Confederacy's main army in the western theater; lost the Battle of Perryville and the battles around Chattanooga, October–November 1863.

HOOD, JOHN BELL   Led the Army of Tennessee to annihilation in the Battle of Nashville, December 1864.

JACKSON, THOMAS J. "STONEWALL" Defeated three separate Union forces in the Shenandoah Valley, spring 1862; became Lee's most brilliant divisional and corps commander; famous for his flanking march and attack at Chancellorsville, where he was mortally wounded by his own pickets.

JOHNSTON, ALBERT SIDNEY   Many Confederates considered him the best general in the rebel army; commanded the western forces early in the war and was killed in the Battle of Shiloh, Tennessee, April 1862.

JOHNSTON, JOSEPH EGGLESTON   Preferred to fight on the defensive; commanded the main Confederate Army in Virginia in the first half of 1862; fought against McClellan in the Peninsula campaign; was later sent West to coordinate rebel efforts to defend Vicksburg against Grant; contested Sherman's advance against Atlanta in 1864 and in the Carolinas in 1865.

LEE, ROBERT E.   The best rebel commander; preferred to fight on the offensive; led the Army of Northern Virginia, the Confederacy's showcase army, from June 1862 to April 1865, when he surrendered to Grant; won the Seven Days Battles before Richmond, the Second Battle of Bull Run, Fredericksburg, and Chancellorsville against inferior Union generals; promoted to general in chief of all rebel military forces near the end of the war.

PEMBERTON, JOHN   Rebel commander who surrendered Vicksburg, July 1865.

UNION GENERALS:

BURNSIDE, AMBROSE E.   Inept commander of the Army of the Potomac, 1862–1863, who lost to Lee in the Battle of Fredericksburg, December 1862.

GRANT, ULYSSES S.   The North's best general; captured forts Henry and Donnelson in Tennessee in 1862 and the great river garrison of Vicksburg in 1863; won the battles around Chattanooga in December of that year; became general in chief of all Union forces in 1864, and led the Army of the Potomac against Lee in a series of ferocious engagements around Richmond, finally pinning Lee down in the siege of Petersburg.

HOOKER, JOSEPH   Inept commander of the Army of the Potomac who lost to Lee at Chancellorsville, Virginia, May 1863.

McCLELLAN, GEORGE B.   Commander of the Army of the Potomac, 1861–1862; orchestrated the glacial-paced Peninsula campaign against Richmond; was driven back by Lee in the Seven Days and recalled to Washington; led the Potomac Army against Lee at Antietam and might have won the battle had he not been overly cautious; finally sacked by Lincoln on the ground that the general had "the slows."

MEADE, GEORGE GORDON   Led the Army of the Potomac in the Battle of Gettysburg, July 1863, and remained titular head of that army during Grant's great offensive against Lee, 1864–1865.

POPE, JOHN   Blusterous, incompetent commander of the Union's Army of Virginia;

decisively beaten by Lee and Jackson at Second Bull Run (Second Manassas), August 1863.

SHERMAN, WILLIAM TECUMSEH   Grant's subordinate commander in the West, 1862–1863; became the Union's top general there when Grant was promoted to supreme command; led the Army of Georgia on its famous march through Georgia and the Carolinas, 1864–1865.

The weeks after [Lincoln was assassinated in April 1865] passed in a dizzying sequence of events. Jarring images dissolved and re-formed in kaleidoscopic patterns that left the senses traumatized or elated: Lincoln lying in state at the White House on April 19 as General Grant wept un-abashedly at his catafalque; Confederate armies sur-rendering one after another as [Confederate Presi-dent] Jefferson Davis fled southward hoping to re-establish his government in Texas and carry on the war to victory; Booth killed in a burning barn in Vir-ginia; seven million somber men, women, and chil-dren lining the tracks to view Lincoln's funeral train on its way back home to Springfield; the steamboat *Sultana* returning northward on the Mississippi with liberated Union prisoners of war blowing up on April 27 with a loss of life equal to that of the *Titanic* a half-century later; Jefferson Davis captured in Georgia on May 10, accused (falsely) of complicity in Lincoln's assassination, imprisoned and temporarily shackled at Fortress Monroe, Virginia, where he remained for two years until released without trial to live on until his eighty-first year and become part of the ex-Con-federate literary corps who wrote weighty tomes to justify their Cause; the Army of the Potomac and Sherman's Army of Georgia marching 200,000 strong in a Grand Review down Pennsylvania Avenue on May 23–24 in a pageantry of power and catharsis be-fore being demobilized from more than one million soldiers to fewer than 80,000 a year later and an even-tual peacetime total of 27,000; weary, ragged Confed-erate soldiers straggling homeward begging or stealing food from dispirited civilians who often did not know where their own next meal was coming from; joyous black people celebrating the jubilee of a freedom whose boundaries they did not yet discern; gangs of southern deserters, guerrillas, and outlaws ravaging a

Excerpted from *Battle Cry of Freedom: The Civil War Era* by James M. McPherson. Copyright © 1988 by Oxford University Press, Inc. Reprinted by permission.

region that would not know real peace for many years to come.

The terms of that peace and the dimensions of black freedom would preoccupy the country for a decade or more. Meanwhile the process of chronicling the war and reckoning its consequences began immediately and has never ceased. More than 620,000 soldiers lost their lives in four years of conflict — 360,000 Yankees and at least 260,000 rebels. The number of southern civilians who died as a direct or indirect result of the war cannot be known; what *can* be said is that the Civil War's cost in American lives was as great as in all of the nation's other wars combined through Vietnam. Was the liberation of four million slaves and the preservation of the Union worth the cost? That question too will probably never cease to be debated — but in 1865 few black people and not many northerners doubted the answer.

In time even a good many southerners came to agree with the sentiments of Woodrow Wilson (a native of Virginia who lived four years of his childhood in wartime Georgia) expressed in 1880 when he was a law student at the University of Virginia: "*Because* I love the South, I rejoice in the failure of the Confederacy. . . . Conceive of this Union divided into two separate and independent sovereignties! . . . Slavery was enervating our Southern society. . . . [Nevertheless] I recognize and pay loving tribute to the virtues of the leaders of secession . . . the righteousness of the cause which they thought they were promoting — and to the immortal courage of the soldiers of the Confederacy." Wilson's words embodied themes that would help reconcile generations of southerners to defeat: their glorious forebears had fought courageously for what they believed was right; perhaps they deserved to win; but in the long run it was a good thing they lost. This Lost Cause mentality took on the proportions of a heroic legend, a southern *Götterdämmerung* with Robert E. Lee as a latter-day Siegfried.★

But a persistent question has nagged historians and mythologists alike: if Marse Robert was such a genius and his legions so invincible, why did they lose? The answers, though almost as legion as Lee's soldiers, tend to group themselves into a few main categories. One popular answer has been phrased, from the northern perspective, by quoting Napoleon's aphorism that God was on the side of the heaviest battalions. For southerners this explanation usually took some such form as these words of a Virginian: "They never whipped us, Sir, unless they were four to one. If we had had anything like a fair chance, or less disparity of numbers, we should have won our cause and established our independence." The North had a potential manpower superiority of more than three to one (counting only white men) and Union armed forces had an actual superiority of two to one during most of the war. In economic resources and logistical capacity the northern advantage was even greater. Thus, in this explanation, the Confederacy fought against overwhelming odds; its defeat was inevitable.

But this explanation has not satisfied a good many analysts. History is replete with examples of peoples who have won or defended their independence against greater odds: the Netherlands against the Spain of Philip II; Switzerland against the Hapsburg Empire; the American rebels of 1776 against mighty Britain; North Vietnam against the United States of 1970. Given the advantages of fighting on the defensive in its own territory with interior lines in which stalemate would be victory against a foe who must invade, conquer, occupy, and destroy the capacity to resist, the odds faced by the South were not formidable. Rather, as another category of interpretations has it, internal divisions fatally weakened the Confederacy: the state-rights conflict between certain governors and the Richmond government; the disaffection of non-slaveholders from a rich man's war and poor man's fight; libertarian opposition to necessary measures such as conscription and the suspension of habeas cor-

---

★In medieval German mythology, Siegfried slays the dragon Fafnir and wins the hand of Kriemhild, only to be killed at the behest of Queen Brünnhilde, whom he had once promised to wed .— Ed.

The outcome of the Civil War, argues James McPherson, was determined on the battlefield. This photograph shows Confederate dead after the 1862 battle of Antietam, which repelled a rebel invasion of the North and forestalled European recognition of the Confederacy. (Chicago Historical Society)

pus; the lukewarm commitment to the Confederacy by quondam Whigs and unionists; the disloyalty of slaves who defected to the enemy whenever they had a chance; growing doubts among slaveowners themselves about the justice of their peculiar institution and their cause. "So the Confederacy succumbed to internal rather than external causes," according to numerous historians. The South suffered from a "weakness in morale," a "loss of the will to fight." The Confederacy did not lack "the means to continue the struggle," but "the will to do so."

To illustrate their argument that the South could have kept fighting for years longer if it had tried harder, four historians have cited the instructive exam-

ple of Paraguay. That tiny country carried on a war for six years (1865–71) against an alliance of Brazil, Argentina, and Uruguay whose combined population outnumbered Paraguay's by nearly thirty to one. Almost every male from twelve to sixty fought in the Paraguayan army; the country lost 56 percent of its total population and 80 percent of its men of military age in the war. Indeed, "the Confederate war effort seems feeble by comparison," for a mere 5 percent of the South's white people and 25 percent of the white males of military age were killed. To be sure, Paraguay lost the war, but its "tenacity . . . does exhibit how a people can fight when possessed of total conviction."

It is not quite clear whether these . . . historians

think the South should have emulated Paraguay's example. In any case the "internal division" and "lack of will" explanations for Confederate defeat, while not implausible, are not very convincing either. The problem is that the North experienced similar internal divisions, and if the war had come out differently the Yankees' lack of unity and will to win could be cited with equal plausibility to explain that outcome. The North had its large minority alienated by the rich man's war/poor man's fight theme; its outspoken opposition to conscription, taxation, suspension of habeas corpus, and other war measures; its state governors and legislatures and congressmen who tried to thwart administration policies. If important elements of the southern population, white as well as black, grew disaffected with a war to preserve slavery, equally significant groups in the North dissented from a war to abolish slavery. One critical distinction between Union and Confederacy was the institutionalization of obstruction in the Democratic party in the North, compelling the Republicans to close ranks in support of war policies to overcome and ultimately to discredit the opposition, while the South had no such institutionalized political structure to mobilize support and vanquish resistance.

Nevertheless, the existence of internal divisions on both sides seemed to neutralize this factor as an explanation for Union victory, so a number of historians have looked instead at the quality of leadership both military and civilian. There are several variants of an interpretation that emphasizes a gradual development of superior northern leadership. In [P.G.T.] Beauregard, Lee, the two Johnstons [Albert Sidney and Joseph Eggleston], and [Stonewall] Jackson the South enjoyed abler military commanders during the first year or two of the war, while Jefferson Davis was better qualified by training and experience than Lincoln to lead a nation at war. But Lee's strategic vision was limited to the Virginia theater, and the Confederate government neglected the West, where Union armies developed a strategic design and the generals to carry it out, while southern forces floundered under in-

competent commanders who lost the war in the West. By 1863, Lincoln's remarkable abilities gave him a wide edge over Davis as a war leader, while in [Ulysses S.] Grant and [William Tecumseh] Sherman the North acquired commanders with a concept of total war and the necessary determination to make it succeed. At the same time, in [Secretary of War] Edwin M. Stanton and [Quartermaster General] Montgomery Meigs, aided by the entrepreneurial talent of northern businessmen, the Union developed superior managerial talent to mobilize and organize the North's greater resources for victory in the modern industrialized conflict that the Civil War became.

This interpretation comes closer than others to credibility. Yet it also commits the fallacy of reversibility — that is, if the outcome had been reversed some of the same factors could be cited to explain Confederate victory. If the South had its bumblers like [Braxton] Bragg and [John C.] Pemberton and [John Bell] Hood who lost the West, and Joseph Johnston who fought too little and too late, the North had its [George B.] McClellan and [George Gordon] Meade who threw away chances in the East and its [John] Pope and [Ambrose E.] Burnside and [Joseph] Hooker who nearly lost the war in that theater where the genius of Lee and his lieutenants nearly won it, despite all the South's disadvantages. If the Union had its Stanton and Meigs, the Confederacy had its [Ordnance Chief] Josiah Gorgas and other unsung heroes who performed miracles of organization and improvisation. If Lincoln had been defeated for re-election in 1864, as he anticipated in August, history might record Davis as the great war leader and Lincoln as an also-ran.

Most attempts to explain southern defeat or northern victory lack the dimension of *contingency* — the recognition that at numerous critical points during the war things might have gone altogether differently. Four major turning points defined the eventual outcome. The first came in the summer of 1862, when the counter-offensives of Jackson and Lee in Virginia and Bragg and Kirby Smith in the West arrested the momentum of a seemingly imminent Union victory. This assured a prolongation and intensification of the conflict and created the potential for Confederate success, which appeared imminent before each of the next three turning points.

The first of these occurred in the fall of 1862, when battles at Antietam [Maryland] and Perryville [Kentucky] threw back Confederate invasions, forestalled European mediation and recognition of the Confederacy, perhaps prevented a Democratic victory in the northern elections of 1862 that might have inhibited the government's ability to carry on the war, and set the stage for the Emancipation Proclamation which enlarged the scope and purpose of the conflict. The third critical point came in the summer and fall of 1863 when [Union victories at] Gettysburg, Vicksburg, and Chattanooga turned the tide toward ultimate northern victory.

One more reversal of that tide seemed possible in the summer of 1864 when appalling Union casualties and apparent lack of progress especially in Virginia brought the North to the brink of peace negotiations and the election of a Democratic president. But [Sherman's] capture of Atlanta and [Philip] Sheridan's destruction of [Jubal] Early's [rebel] army in the Shenandoah Valley clinched matters for the North. Only then did it become possible to speak of the inevitability of Union victory. Only then did the South experience an irretrievable "loss of the will to fight."

Of all the explanations for Confederate defeat, the loss of will thesis suffers most from its own particular fallacy of reversibility — that of putting the cart before the horse. Defeat causes demoralization and loss of will; victory pumps up morale and the will to win. Nothing illustrates this better than the radical transformation of *northern* will from defeatism in August 1864 to a "depth of determination . . . to fight to the last" that "astonished" a British journalist a month later. The southern loss of will was a mirror image of this northern determination. These changes of mood were caused mainly by events on the battlefield. Northern victory and southern defeat in the war can-

not be understood apart from the contingency that hung over every campaign, every battle, every election, every decision during the war. . . .

Arguments about the causes and consequences of the Civil War, as well as the reasons for northern victory, will continue as long as there are historians to wield the pen — which is, perhaps even for this bloody conflict, mightier than the sword. But certain large consequences of the war seem clear. Secession and slavery were killed, never to be revived during the century and a quarter since Appomattox. These results signified a broader transformation of American society and polity punctuated if not alone achieved by the war. Before 1861 the two words "United States" were generally rendered as a plural noun: "the United States *are* a republic." The war marked a transition of the United States to a singular noun. The "Union" also became the nation, and Americans now rarely speak of their Union except in an historical sense. Lincoln's wartime speeches betokened this transition. In his first inaugural address he used the word "Union" twenty times and the word "nation" not once. In his first message to Congress, on July 4, 1861, he used "Union" thirty-two times and "nation" three times. In his letter to [*New York Tribune* editor] Horace Greeley of August 22, 1862, on the relationship of slavery to the war, Lincoln spoke of the Union eight times and of the nation not at all. Little more than a year later, in his address at Gettysburg, the president did not refer to the "Union" at all but used the word "nation" five times to invoke a new birth of freedom and nationalism for the United States. And in his second inaugural address, looking back over the events of the past four years, Lincoln spoke of one side seeking to dissolve the *Union* in 1861 and the other accepting the challenge of war to preserve the *nation.*

The old federal republic in which the national government had rarely touched the average citizen except through the post-office gave way to a more centralized polity that taxed the people directly and created an internal revenue bureau to collect these

A scene during the Battle of Gettysburg, July 1–3, 1863. The summer and fall of that year marked the war's third critical point, when Union victories at Gettysburg, Vicksburg, and Chattanooga *"turned the tide toward ultimate northern victory." (Courtesy of the Ann S. K. Brown Military Collection, Brown University Library)*

taxes, drafted men into the army, expanded the jurisdiction of federal courts, created a national currency and a national banking system, and established the first national agency for social welfare — the Freedmen's Bureau. [That bureau provided food and schools for the former slaves, helped them find jobs, and made certain they received fair wages.] Eleven of the first twelve amendments to the Constitution had limited the powers of the national government; six of the next seven, beginning with the Thirteenth Amend-

ment in 1865, vastly expanded those powers at the expense of the states.

This change in the federal balance paralleled a radical shift of political power from South to North. During the first seventy-two years of the republic down to 1861 a slaveholding resident of one of the states that joined the Confederacy had been President of the United States for forty-nine of those years — more than two-thirds of the time. In Congress, twenty-three of the thirty-six speakers of the House and twenty-four of the presidents pro tem of the Senate had been southerners. The Supreme Court always had a southern majority; twenty of the thirty-five justices to 1861 had been appointed from slave states. After the war a century passed before a resident of an ex-Confederate state was elected president. For half a century *none* of the speakers of the House or presidents pro tem of the Senate came from the South, and only five of the twenty-six Supreme Court justices appointed during that half-century were southerners.

These figures symbolize a sharp and permanent change in the direction of American development. Through most of American history the South has seemed different from the rest of the United States, with "a separate and unique identity . . . which appeared to be out of the mainstream of American experience." But when did the northern stream become the mainstream? From a broader perspective it may have been the *North* that was exceptional and unique before the Civil War. The South more closely resembled a majority of the societies in the world than did the rapidly changing North during the antebellum generation. Despite the abolition of legal slavery or serfdom throughout much of the western hemisphere and western Europe, most of the world — like the South — had an unfree or quasi-free labor force. Most societies in the world remained predominantly rural, agricultural, and labor-intensive; most, including even several European countries, had illiteracy rates as high or higher than the South's 45 percent; most like the South remained bound by traditional values and networks of family, kinship, hierarchy, and patriarchy. The North — along with a few countries of northwestern Europe — hurtled forward eagerly toward a future of industrial capitalism that many southerners found distasteful if not frightening; the South remained proudly and even defiantly rooted in the past before 1861.

Thus when secessionists protested that they were acting to preserve traditional rights and values, they were correct. They fought to protect their constitutional liberties against the perceived northern threat to overthrow them. The South's concept of republicanism had not changed in three-quarters of a century; the North's had. With complete sincerity the South fought to preserve its version of the republic of the founding fathers — a government of limited powers that protected the rights of property and whose constituency comprised an independent gentry and yeomanry of the white race undisturbed by large cities, heartless factories, restless free workers, and class conflict. The accession to power of the Republican party, with its ideology of competitive, egalitarian, free-labor capitalism, was a signal to the South that the northern majority had turned irrevocably toward this frightening, revolutionary future. Indeed, the Black Republican party appeared to the eyes of many southerners as "essentially a revolutionary party" composed of "a motley throng of Sans culottes . . . Infidels and freelovers, interspersed by Bloomer women, fugitive slaves, and amalgamationists." Therefore secession was a pre-emptive counterrevolution to prevent the Black Republican revolution from engulfing the South. "*We* are not revolutionists," insisted James B. D. DeBow and Jefferson Davis during the Civil War, "We are resisting revolution. . . . We are conservative."

Union victory in the war destroyed the southern vision of America and ensured that the northern vision would become the American vision. Until 1861, however, it was the North that was out of the mainstream, not the South. Of course the northern states, along with Britain and a few countries in northwestern Europe, were cutting a new channel in world history that would doubtless have become the mainstream even if the American Civil War had not happened. Russia had abolished serfdom in 1861 to complete the dissolution of this ancient institution of bound labor in Europe. But for Americans the Civil War marked the turning point. A Louisiana planter who returned home sadly after the war wrote in 1865: "Society has been completely changed by the war. The [French] revolution of '89 did not produce a greater change in the 'Ancien Régime' than this has

413

in our social life." And four years later George Ticknor, a retired Harvard professor, concluded that the Civil War had created a "great gulf between what happened before in our century and what has happened since, or what is likely to happen hereafter. It does not seem to me as if I were living in the country in which I was born." From the war sprang the great flood that caused the stream of American history to surge into a new channel and transferred the burden of exceptionalism from North to South.

QUESTIONS TO CONSIDER

1. McPherson discusses several traditional interpretations of why the Confederacy lost the Civil War. What were they, and which does he consider to be the strongest and the weakest? How does he refute them all?

2. McPherson bases his own explanation of the Confederacy's defeat on the idea of contingency. What does he mean by this, and what does he consider the critical turning points of the war? When does he think northern victory became inevitable?

3. How does McPherson defend his conviction that the most crucial element in all the developments and consequences of the Civil War, including the political and the social, was what happened on the battlefield? Do you agree? why?

4. Discuss McPherson's argument that the Civil War changed the United States from a union into a nation. What did this change entail and signify?

5. Explain McPherson's idea that, contrary to our usual notion, before the Civil War it was the North and not the South that was exceptional. Do you think this fits in with Douglas Wilson's discussion of presentism in selection 8?

A Troubled Peace

29

From Slavery to Freedom:
The Birth of the Modern Black Community

ERIC FONER

For African Americans in North and South alike, the Civil War had profound religious meaning from the beginning. Hundreds of thousands, writes Vincent Harding, "believed unwaveringly that their God moved in history to deliver his people, and they had been looking eagerly, praying hourly, waiting desperately for the glory of the coming of the Lord. For them, all the raucous, roaring guns of Charleston Harbor and Bull Run, of Antietam and Fort Pillow, of Shiloh and Murfreesboro and Richmond were the certain voice of God, announcing his judgment across the bloody stretches of the South, returning blood for blood to the black river." During the course of that war, African Americans believed, God did deliver them. He drove out the rebels and slaveholders, just as he had once driven out the Hittites and Canaanites. With the Confederacy's collapse, as one song went, "slavery chain done broke at last."

> Slavery chain done broke at last!
> Broke at last! Broke at last!
> Slavery chain done broke at last!
> Gonna praise God till I die!

Some reacted to their liberation with cautious elation. When a young Virginia woman heard her former masters weeping over the capture of Jefferson Davis, she went down to a spring alone and cried out, "Glory, glory, hallelujah to Jesus! I's free! I's free!" Suddenly afraid, she looked about. What if the white folks heard her? But seeing no one, she fell to the ground and kissed it, thanking "Master Jesus" over and over. For her, freedom meant hope — hope that she could find her husband and four children who had been sold to a slave trader.

Others celebrated their liberation in public. In Athens, Georgia, they danced around a liberty pole; in Charleston, they paraded through the streets. Many African Americans, however, were wary and uncertain. "You're joking me," one man said when the master told him he was free. He asked some neighbors if they were free also. "I couldn't believe we was all free alike," he said. Some African Americans, out of feelings of obligation or compassion, remained on the home place to help their former masters. But others were hostile. When a woman named Cady heard that the war was over, she decided to protest the cruel treatment she had suffered as a slave. She threw down her hoe, marched up to the big house, found the mistress, and flipped her dress up. She told the white woman, "Kiss my ass!"

For Cady, for the young black woman, for hosts of other African Americans, freedom meant an end to the manifold evils of slavery; it meant the right to say what they felt and go where they wanted. But what else did freedom mean? In this selection, Eric Foner, today's leading Reconstruction scholar, describes how the former slaves in the first critical year or so of Reconstruction defined and exercised freedom for themselves. Above all, they wanted independence from their former masters, wanted control of their families, churches, and schools. And they wanted their own land, too, and mules to work it. As they set about expanding, consolidating, and strengthening their traditional institutions and forging their own political culture, African Americans in Reconstruction formed the modern black community, one "whose roots lay deep in slavery but whose structure and values reflected the consequences of emancipation."

It is an inspiring story, and Foner relates it with great insight. Instead of being passive and undeserving recipients of freedom (as an earlier generation of histories portrayed them), the former slaves in Foner's telling reached out and seized control of their destinies. As they sought independence from white control, Foner says, the former slaves actively sought inclusion in the body politic. Across the South, they held political conventions in which they demanded their "equal rights as citizens." They would not gain the right to vote and to hold public office until 1867, when the Republican-controlled Congress assumed control of southern restoration, in what became known as Radical Reconstruction. But "the seeds that flowered then," as Foner notes, "were planted in the first years of freedom." What happened to African American dreams of economic independence and full citizenship after the Radicals took over is treated in the last selection, "Reconstruction: The Revolution That Failed."

GLOSSARY

FREEDMEN'S BUREAU Established by congressional statute in March 1865, the Bureau of Freedmen, Refugees, and Abandoned Lands was supposed to provide food and schools for the former slaves, help them secure jobs, and make certain they received fair wages.

LAND DISTRIBUTION Had the federal government seized the estates of ex–Confederates and distributed the land among the former slaves, it "would have had profound consequences for Southern society, weakening the land-based economic and political power of the old ruling class, offering blacks a measure of choice as to whether, when, and under what circumstances to enter the labor market, and affecting the former slaves' conception of themselves." In the next selection, you will see what happened to the idea of land distribution.

LYNCH, JAMES D. African American who served as Mississippi's secretary of state during Reconstruction.

PEARCE, REV. CHARLES H. "Preachers played a central role in Reconstruction black politics," Foner writes. The Reverend Pearce held "several Reconstruction offices in Florida."

RAPIER, JAMES T. African American member of Congress from Alabama during Reconstruction.

SHARECROPPING System of renting land by which a tenant farmer paid the land owner a share of the tenant's crop as rent.

Freedom came in different ways to different parts of the South. In large areas, slavery had disintegrated long before Lee's surrender, but elsewhere, far from the presence of federal troops, blacks did not learn of its irrevocable end until the spring of 1865. Despite the many disappointments that followed, this generation of blacks would always regard the moment when "de freedom sun shine out" as the great watershed of their lives. Houston H. Holloway, who had been sold three times before he reached the age of twenty in 1865, later recalled with vivid clarity the day emancipation came to his section of Georgia: "I felt like a bird out of a cage. Amen. Amen. Amen. I could hardly ask to feel any better than I did that day. . . . The week passed off in a blaze of glory."

"Freedom," said a black minister, "burned in the black heart long before freedom was born." But what did "freedom" mean? "It is necessary to define that word," Freedmen's Bureau Commissioner O. O. Howard told a black audience in 1865, "for it is most apt to be misunderstood." Howard assumed a straightforward definition existed. But "freedom" it-self became a terrain of conflict, its substance open to different and sometimes contradictory interpretations, its content changing for whites as well as blacks in the aftermath of the Civil War.

Blacks carried out of bondage an understanding of their new condition shaped both by their experience as slaves and by observation of the free society around them. What one planter called their "wild notions of rights and freedom" encompassed, first of all, an end to the myriad injustices associated with slavery. Some, like black minister Henry M. Turner, stressed that freedom meant the enjoyment of "our rights in com-mon with other men." "If I cannot do like a white man I am not free," Henry Adams told his former

---

"The Meaning of Freedom" from *A Short History of Reconstruction* by Eric Foner. Copyright © 1990 by Eric Foner. Reprinted by permission of HarperCollins Publishers, Inc.

Former slaves pose in front of the ruins of Richmond, Virginia, after the cruel war was over. African Americans like these, writes Eric Foner, formed the modern black community, by expanding, consoli- *dating, and strengthening their traditional institutions and forging their own political culture. (Library of Congress)*

master in 1865. "I see how the poor white people do. I ought to do so too, or else I am a slave."

But underpinning the specific aspirations lay a broader theme: a desire for independence from white control, for autonomy both as individuals and as members of a community being transformed by emancipation. Before the war, free blacks had created churches, schools, and mutual benefit societies, while slaves had forged a culture centered on the family and church. With freedom, these institutions were consolidated, expanded, and liberated from white supervision, and new ones — particularly political organizations — joined them as focal points of black life. In stabilizing their families, seizing control of their

churches, greatly expanding their schools and benevolent societies, staking a claim to economic independence, and forging a political culture, blacks during Reconstruction laid the foundation for the modern black community, whose roots lay deep in slavery but whose structure and values reflected the consequences of emancipation.

☆

FROM SLAVERY TO FREEDOM

Long after the end of the Civil War, the experience of bondage remained deeply etched in blacks' collective memory. The freedmen resented not only the brutal incidents of slavery but the fact of having been held as slaves at all. During a visit to Richmond, Scottish minister David Macrae was surprised to hear a former slave complain of past mistreatment, while acknowledging he had never been whipped. "How were you cruelly treated then?" asked Macrae. "I was cruelly treated," answered the freedman, "because I was kept in slavery."

In countless ways, the newly freed slaves sought to overturn the real and symbolic authority whites had exercised over every aspect of their lives. Blacks relished opportunities to flaunt their liberation from the innumerable regulations, significant and trivial, associated with slavery. Freedmen held mass meetings and religious services unrestrained by white surveillance, acquired previously forbidden dogs, guns, and liquor, and refused to yield the sidewalks to whites. They dressed as they pleased, black women sometimes wearing gaudy finery, carrying parasols, and replacing the slave kerchief with colorful hats and veils. Whites complained of "insolence" and "insubordination" among the freedmen, by which they meant any departure from the deference and obedience expected under slavery. On the Bradford plantation in Florida, one untoward incident followed another. First, the family cook told Mrs. Bradford "if she want any dinner she kin cook it herself." Then the former slaves went off to a meeting with Northern soldiers to discuss "our freedom." Told that she and her daughter could not attend, one woman replied "they were now free and if she saw fit to take her daughter into that crowd it was nobody's business." "Never before had I a word of impudence from any of our black folk," recorded nineteen-year-old Susan Bradford, "but they are not ours any longer."

Among the most resented of slavery's restrictions was the rule, enforced by patrols, than no black could travel without a pass. With emancipation, it seemed that half the South's black population took to the roads. Southern towns and cities experienced an especially large influx of freedmen during and immediately after the Civil War. In the cities, many blacks believed, "freedom was free-er." Here were schools, churches, and fraternal societies, as well as the army (including, in 1865, black soldiers) and the Freedmen's Bureau, offering protection from the violence so pervasive in much of the rural South. Between 1865 and 1870, the black population of the South's ten largest cities doubled, while the number of white residents rose by only ten percent. Smaller towns, from which blacks had often been excluded as slaves, experienced even more dramatic increases.

Black migrants who hoped to find urban employment often encountered severe disappointment. The influx from the countryside flooded the labor market, consigning most urban blacks to low-wage, menial employment. Unable to obtain decent housing, black migrants lived in squalid shantytowns on the outskirts of Southern cities, where the incidence of disease and death far exceeded that among white city dwellers. The result was a striking change in Southern urban living patterns. Before the war, blacks and whites had lived scattered throughout Southern cities. Reconstruction witnessed the rise of a new, segregated, urban geography.

No aspect of black mobility was more poignant than the effort to reunite families separated during slavery. "In their eyes," wrote a Freedmen's Bureau agent, "the work of emancipation was incomplete until the families which had been dispersed by slavery were reunited." One freedman, writing from Texas, asked the Bureau's aid in locating "my own dearest relatives," providing a long list of sisters, nieces, nephews, uncles, and in-laws, none of whom he had seen since his sale in Virginia twenty-four years before. A typical plea for help appeared in the Nashville *Colored Tennessean:*

During the year 1849, Thomas Sample carried away from this city, as his slaves, our daughter, Polly, and son. . . . We will give $100 each for them to any person who will assist them . . . to get to Nashville, or get word to us of their whereabouts.

Although vulnerable to disruption, strong family ties had existed under slavery. Emancipation allowed blacks to solidify their family connections, and most freedmen seized the opportunity. Many families, in addition, adopted the children of deceased relatives and friends rather than see them apprenticed to white masters or placed in Freedmen's Bureau orphanages. By 1870, a large majority of blacks lived in two-parent households.

But while emancipation strengthened the preexisting black family, it also transformed the roles of its members and relations among them. One common, significant change was that slave families, separated because their members belonged to different owners, could now live together. More widely noticed by white observers in early Reconstruction was the withdrawal of black women from field labor.

Beginning in 1865, and for years thereafter, Southern whites throughout the South complained of the difficulty of obtaining female field laborers. Planters, Freedmen's Bureau officials, and Northern visitors all ridiculed the black "female aristocracy" for "acting the *lady*" or mimicking the family patterns of middle-class whites. White employers also resented their inability to force black children to labor in the fields, especially after the spread of schools in rural areas. Contemporaries appeared uncertain whether black women, black men, or both were responsible for the withdrawal of females from agricultural labor. There is no question that many black men considered it manly to have their wives work at home and believed that, as head of the family, the male should decide how its labor was organized. But many black women desired to devote more time than under slavery to caring for their children and to domestic responsibilities like cooking, sewing, and laundering.

The shift of black female labor from the fields to the home proved a temporary phenomenon. The rise of renting and sharecropping, which made each family responsible for its own plot of land, placed a premium on the labor of all family members. The dire poverty of many black families, deepened by the de-pression of the 1870s, made it essential for both women and men to contribute to the family's income. Throughout this period, a far higher percentage of black than white women and children worked for wages outside their homes. Where women continued to concentrate on domestic tasks, and children attended school, they frequently engaged in seasonal field labor. Thus, emancipation did not eliminate labor outside the home by black women and children, but it fundamentally altered control over their labor. Now blacks themselves, rather than a white owner or overseer, decided where and when black women and children worked.

For blacks, liberating their families from the authority of whites was an indispensable element of freedom. But the family itself was in some ways transformed by emancipation. Although historians no longer view the slave family as matriarchal, it is true that slave men did not function as economic breadwinners and that their masters wielded authority within the household. In a sense, slavery had imposed on black men and women the rough "equality" of powerlessness. With freedom came developments that strengthened patriarchy within the black family and consigned men and women to separate spheres.

Outside events strongly influenced this development. Service in the Union Army enabled black men to participate more directly than women in the struggle for freedom. The Freedmen's Bureau designated the husband as head of the black household, insisting that men sign contracts for the labor of their entire families and establishing lower wage scales for women. After 1867 black men could serve on juries, vote, hold office, and rise to leadership in the Republican party, while black women, like their white counterparts, could not. And black preachers, editors, and politicians emphasized women's responsibility for making the home "a place of peace and comfort" for men and urged them to submit to their husbands' authority.

Not all black women placidly accepted the increasingly patriarchal quality of black family life. Indeed, many proved more than willing to bring family disputes before public authorities. The records of the Freedmen's Bureau contain hundreds of complaints by black women of beatings, infidelity, and lack of child support. Some black women objected to their husbands' signing labor contracts for them, demanded separate payment of their wages, and refused to be liable for their husbands' debts at country stores. Yet if emancipation not only institutionalized the black family but also spawned tensions within it, black men and women shared a passionate commitment to the stability of family life as the solid foundation upon which a new black community could flourish.

☆

BUILDING THE BLACK COMMUNITY

Second only to the family as a focal point of black life stood the church. And, as in the case of the family, Reconstruction was a time of consolidation and transformation for black religion. With the death of slavery, urban blacks seized control of their own churches, while the "invisible institution" of the rural slave church emerged into the light of day. The creation of an independent black religious life proved to be a momentous and irreversible consequence of emancipation.

In antebellum Southern Protestant congregations, slaves and free blacks had enjoyed a kind of associate membership. Subject to the same rules and discipline as whites, they were required to sit in the back of the church or in the gallery during services and were excluded from Sabbath schools and a role in church governance. In the larger cities, the number of black members often justified the organization of wholly black congregations and the construction of separate churches, although these were legally required to have white pastors. In the aftermath of emancipation, the wholesale withdrawal of blacks from biracial congregations redrew the religious map of the South. Two causes combined to produce the independent

black church: the refusal of whites to offer blacks an equal place within their congregations and the black quest for self-determination.

Throughout the South, blacks emerging from slavery pooled their resources to purchase land and erect their own churches. Before the buildings were completed, they held services in structures as diverse as a railroad boxcar, where Atlanta's First Baptist Church gathered, or an outdoor "bush arbor," where the First Baptist Church of Memphis congregated in 1865. The first new building to rise amid Charleston's ruins was a black church on Calhoun Street; by 1866 ten more had been constructed. In the countryside, a community would often build a single church, used in rotation by the various black denominations. By the end of Reconstruction in 1877, the vast majority of Southern blacks had withdrawn from churches dominated by whites. On the eve of the war, 42,000 black Methodists worshipped in biracial South Carolina churches; by the 1870s, only 600 remained.

The church was "the first social institution fully controlled by black men in America," and its multiple functions testified to its centrality in the black community. Churches housed schools, social events, and political gatherings. In rural areas, church picnics, festivals, and excursions often provided the only opportunity for fellowship and recreation. The church served as an "Ecclesiastical Court House," promoting moral values, adjudicating family disputes, and disciplining individuals for adultery and other illicit behavior. In every black community, ministers were among the most respected individuals, esteemed for their speaking ability, organizational talents, and good judgment on matters both public and private.

Inevitably, too, preachers played a central role in Reconstruction black politics. Many agreed with Rev. Charles H. Pearce, who held several Reconstruction offices in Florida, that it was "impossible" to separate religion and politics: "A man in this State cannot do his whole duty as a minister except he looks out for the political interests of his people." Even those preachers who lacked ambition for political position sometimes found it thrust upon them. Often among the few literate blacks in a community, they were called on to serve as election registrars and candidates for office. Over 100 black ministers, hailing from North and South, from free and slave backgrounds, and from every black denomination from African Methodist Episcopal to Primitive Baptist, would be elected to legislative seats during Reconstruction.

Throughout Reconstruction, religious convictions shaped blacks' understanding of the momentous events around them, the language in which they voiced aspirations for justice and autonomy. Blacks inherited from slavery a distinctive version of Christian faith, in which Jesus appeared as a personal redeemer offering solace in the face of misfortune, while the Old Testament suggested that they were a chosen people, analogous to the Jews in Egypt, whom God, in the fullness of time, would deliver from bondage. "There is no part of the Bible with which they are so familiar as the story of the deliverance of the Children of Israel," a white army chaplain reported in 1866.

Emancipation and the defeat of the Confederacy strongly reinforced this messianic vision of history. Even nonclerics used secular and religious vocabulary interchangeably, as in one 1867 speech recorded by a North Carolina justice of the peace:

He said it was not now like it used to be, that . . . the negro was about to get his equal rights. . . . That the negroes owed their freedom to the courage of the negro soldiers and to God. . . . He made frequent references to the II and IV chapters of Joshua for a full accomplishment of the principles and destiny of the race. It was concluded that the race have a destiny in view similar to the Children of Israel.

The rise of the independent black church was accompanied by the creation of a host of fraternal, benevolent, and mutual aid societies. In early Reconstruction, blacks created literally thousands of such organizations; a partial list includes burial societies, debating clubs, Masonic lodges, fire companies, drama societies, trade associations, temperance clubs, and equal rights leagues. Offering social fellowship, sickness and funeral benefits, and, most of all, a chance to manage their own affairs, these voluntary associations embodied a spirit of collective self-improvement. Robert G. Fitzgerald, who had been born free in Delaware, served in both the U.S. Army and Navy, and came to Virginia to teach in 1866, was delighted to see rural blacks establishing churches, lyceums, and schools. "They tell me," he recorded in his diary, "before Mr. Lincoln made them free they had nothing to work for, to look up to, now they have everything, and will, by God's help, make the best of it." Moreover, the spirit of mutual self-help extended outward from the societies to embrace destitute nonmembers. In 1865 and 1866, blacks in Nashville, Jackson, New Orleans, and Atlanta, as well as in many rural areas, raised money to establish orphanages, soup kitchens, employment agencies, and poor relief funds.

Perhaps the most striking illustration of the freedmen's quest for self-improvement was their seemingly unquenchable thirst for education. Before the war, every Southern state except Tennessee had prohibited the instruction of slaves, and although many free blacks had attended school and a number of slaves became literate through their own efforts or the aid of sympathetic masters, over ninety percent of the South's adult black population was illiterate in 1860. Access to education for themselves and their children was, for blacks, central to the meaning of freedom, and white contemporaries were astonished by their "avidity for learning." Adults as well as children thronged the schools. A Northern teacher in Florida reported how one sixty-year-old woman, "just beginning to spell, seems as if she could not think of any thing but her book, says she spells her lesson all the evening, then she dreams about it, and wakes up thinking about it."

Northern benevolent societies, the Freedmen's Bureau, and, after 1868, state governments provided most of the funding for black education during

A class at the Zion School for Colored Children in Charleston, South Carolina. During Reconstruction, the Freedmen's Bureau, a federal agency, established African-American schools like this one throughout the conquered South. (The Granger Collection, New York)

Reconstruction. But the initiative often lay with blacks themselves. Urban blacks took immediate steps to set up schools, sometimes holding classes temporarily in abandoned warehouses, billiards rooms, or, in New Orleans and Savannah, former slave markets. In rural areas, Freedmen's Bureau officials repeatedly expressed surprise at discovering classes organized by blacks already meeting in churches, basements, or private homes. And everywhere there were children teaching their parents the alphabet at home, laborers on lunch breaks "poring over the elementary pages," and the "wayside schools" described by a Bureau officer:

A negro riding on a loaded wagon, or sitting on a hack waiting for a train, or by the cabin door, is often seen, book in hand delving after the rudiments of knowledge. A group on the platform of a depot, after carefully conning an old spelling book, resolves itself into a class.

Throughout the South, blacks in 1865 and 1866 raised money to purchase land, build schoolhouses, and pay teachers' salaries. Some communities voluntarily taxed themselves; in others black schools charged tuition, while allowing a number of the poorest families to enroll their children free of charge. Black artisans donated their labor to construct schoolhouses, and black families offered room and board to teachers to supplement their salaries. By 1870, blacks had expended over $1 million on education, a fact that long remained a point of collective pride. "Whoever may hereafter lay claim to the honor of 'establishing' . . . schools," wrote a black resident of Selma in 1867, "I trust the fact will never be ignored that Miss Lucy Lee, one of the emancipated, was the pioneer teacher of the colored children, . . . without the aid of Northern societies."

Inevitably, the first black teachers appeared incompetent in Northern eyes, for a smattering of education might place an individual in front of a class. One poignantly explained, "I never had the chance of goen to school for I was a slave until freedom. . . . I am the only teacher because we can not doe better now." Yet even an imperfect literacy, coupled with the courage often required to establish a rural school in the face of local white opposition, marked these teachers as community leaders. Black teachers played numerous roles apart from education, assisting freedmen in contract disputes, engaging in church work, and drafting petitions to the Freedmen's Bureau, state officials, and Congress. Like the ministry, teaching frequently became a springboard to political office. At least seventy black teachers served in state legislatures during Reconstruction. And many black politicians were linked in other ways to the quest for learning, like Alabama Congressman Benjamin S. Turner, an ex-slave "destitute of education," who financed a Selma school.

Not surprisingly, the majority of black teachers who held political office during Reconstruction had been free before the Civil War. Indeed the schools, like the entire institutional structure established by blacks during Reconstruction, symbolized the emergence of a community that united the free and the freed, and Northern and Southern blacks. The process occurred most smoothly in the Upper South, where the cultural and economic gap between free blacks and slaves had always been less pronounced than in the urban Deep South. While generally lighter in color than slaves, most Upper South free blacks were poor urban workers or farm laborers, often tied to the slave community through marriage and church membership. In cities like New Orleans, Mobile, Savan-

nah, and Charleston, however, affluent mulatto elites responded with deep ambivalence to the new situation created by emancipation. Even in New Orleans, where politically conscious free blacks had already moved to make common cause with the freedmen, a sense of exclusivity survived the end of slavery. The Freedmen's Bureau found many free blacks reluctant to send their children to school with former slaves.

After New Orleans, the South's largest and wealthiest community of free blacks resided in Charleston, although the free elite there was neither as rich nor as culturally distinct as its Louisiana counterpart. Arriving in Charleston in November 1865, Northern journalist John R. Dennett found some members of the free elite cultivating their old exclusiveness. Others, however, took the lead in organizing assistance for destitute freedmen and in teaching the former slaves. Sons and daughters of prominent free families, mostly young people in their twenties, fanned out into the South Carolina countryside as teachers and missionaries. Several thereby acquired positions of local political leadership and later returned to Charleston as constitutional convention delegates and legislators. Thus the children of the Charleston elite cast their lot with the freedmen, bringing, as they saw it, modern culture to the former slaves. This encounter was not without its tensions. But in the long run it hastened the emergence of a black community stratified by class rather than color, in which the former free elite took its place as one element of a new black bourgeoisie, instead of existing as a separate caste as in the antebellum port cities.

In the severing of ties that had bound black and white families and churches to one another under slavery, the coming together of blacks in an explosion of institution building, and the political and cultural fusion of former free blacks and former slaves, Reconstruction witnessed the birth of the modern black community. All in all, the months following the end of the Civil War were a period of remarkable accomplishment for Southern blacks. Looking back in January 1866, the Philadelphia-born black missionary

Jonathan C. Gibbs could only exclaim: "we have progressed a century in a year."

☆

THE ECONOMICS OF FREEDOM

Nowhere were blacks' efforts to define their freedom more explosive for the entire society than in the economy. Freedmen brought out of slavery a conception of themselves as a "Working Class of People" who had been unjustly deprived of the fruits of their labor. To white predictions that they would not work, blacks responded that if any class could be characterized as lazy, it was the planters, who had "lived in idleness all their lives on stolen labor." It is certainly true that many blacks expected to labor less as free men and women than they had as slaves, an understandable aim considering the conditions they had previously known. "Whence comes the assertion that the 'nigger won't work'?" asked an Alabama freedman. "It comes from this fact: . . . the freedman refuses to be driven out into the field two hours before day, and work until 9 or 10 o'clock in the night, as was the case in the days of slavery."

Yet freedom meant more than shorter hours and payment of wages. Freedmen sought to control the conditions under which they labored, end their subordination to white authority, and carve out the greatest measure of economic autonomy. These aims led them to prefer tenancy to wage labor, and leasing land for a fixed rent to sharecropping. Above all, they inspired the quest for land. Owning land, the freedmen believed, would "complete their independence."

To those familiar with the experience of other postemancipation societies, blacks' "mania for owning a small piece of land" did not appear surprising. Freedmen in Haiti, the British and Spanish Caribbean, and Brazil all saw ownership of land as crucial to economic independence, and everywhere former slaves sought to avoid returning to plantation labor.

Unlike freedmen in other countries, however, American blacks emerged from slavery convinced that the federal government had committed itself to land distribution. Belief in an imminent division of land was most pervasive in the South Carolina and Georgia lowcountry, but the idea was shared in other parts of the South as well, including counties that had never been occupied by federal troops. Blacks insisted that their past labor entitled them to at least a portion of their owners' estates. As an Alabama black convention put it: "The property which they hold was nearly all earned by the sweat of *our* brows."

In some parts of the South, blacks in 1865 did more than argue the merits of their case. Hundreds of freedmen refused either to sign labor contracts or to leave the plantations, insisting that the land belonged to them. On the property of a Tennessee planter, former slaves not only claimed to be "joint heirs" to the estate but, the owner complained, abandoned the slave quarters and took up residence "in the rooms of my house." Few freedmen were able to maintain control of land seized in this manner. A small number did, however, obtain property through other means, squatting on unoccupied land in sparsely populated states like Florida and Texas, buying tiny city plots, or cooperatively purchasing farms and plantations. Most blacks, however, emerged from slavery unable to purchase land even at the depressed prices of early Reconstruction and confronted by a white community unwilling to advance credit or sell them property. Thus, they entered the world of free labor as wage or share workers on land owned by whites. The adjustment to a new social order in which their persons were removed from the market but their labor was bought and sold like any other commodity proved in many respects difficult. For it required them to adapt to the logic of the economic market, where the impersonal laws of supply and demand and the balance of power between employer and employee determine a laborer's material circumstances.

Most freedmen welcomed the demise of the paternalism and mutual obligations of slavery and embraced many aspects of the free market. They patron-ized the stores that sprang up throughout the rural South, purchasing "luxuries" ranging from sardines, cheese, and sugar to new clothing. They saved money to build and support churches and educate their chil-dren. And they quickly learned to use and influence the market for their own ends. The early years of Re-construction witnessed strikes or petitions for higher wages by black urban laborers, including Richmond factory workers, Jackson washerwomen, New Or-leans and Savannah stevedores, and mechanics in Columbus, Georgia. In rural areas, too, planta-tion freedmen sometimes bargained collectively over contract terms, organized strikes, and occasionally even attempted to establish wage schedules for an entire area. Blacks exploited competition between planters and nonagricultural employers, seeking work on railroad construction crews and at turpentine mills and other enterprises offering pay far higher than on the plantations.

Slavery, however, did not produce workers fully socialized to the virtues of economic accumulation. Despite the profits possible in early postwar cotton farming, many freedmen strongly resisted growing the "slave crop." "If ole massa want to grow cotton," said one Georgia freedman, "let him plant it himself." Many freedmen preferred to concentrate on food crops and only secondarily on cotton or other staples to obtain ready cash. Rather than choose irrevocably between self-sufficiency and market farming, they hoped to avoid a complete dependence on either while taking advantage of the opportunities each could offer. As A. Warren Kelsey, a representative of Northern cotton manufacturers, shrewdly observed:

The sole ambition of the freedman at the present time ap-pears to be to become the owner of a little piece of land, there to erect a humble home, and to dwell in peace and security at his own free will and pleasure. If he wishes, to cultivate the ground in cotton on his own account, to be able to do so without anyone to dictate to him hours or system of labor, if he wishes instead to plant corn or sweet

potatoes — to be able to do *that* free from any outside con-trol. . . . That is their idea, their desire and their hope.

Historical experience and modern scholarship sug-gest that acquiring small plots of land would hardly, by itself, have solved the economic plight of black families. Without control of credit and access to mar-kets, land reform can often be a hollow victory. And where political power rests in hostile hands, small landowners often find themselves subjected to op-pressive taxation and other state policies that severely limit their economic prospects. In such circumstances, the autonomy offered by land ownership tends to be defensive, rather than the springboard for sustained economic advancement. Yet while hardly an eco-nomic panacea, land redistribution would have had profound consequences for Southern society, weak-ening the land-based economic and political power of the old ruling class, offering blacks a measure of choice as to whether, when, and under what circum-stances to enter the labor market, and affecting the former slaves' conception of themselves.

Blacks' quest for economic independence not only threatened the foundations of the Southern political economy, it put the freedmen at odds with both for-mer owners seeking to restore plantation labor disci-pline and Northerners committed to reinvigorating staple crop production. But as part of the broad quest for individual and collective autonomy, it remained central to the black community's effort to define the meaning of freedom. Indeed, the fulfillment of other aspirations, from family autonomy to the creation of schools and churches, all greatly depended on success in winning control of their working lives and gaining access to the economic resources of the South.

☆

ORIGINS OF BLACK POLITICS

If the goal of autonomy inspired blacks to withdraw from religious and social institutions controlled by whites and to attempt to work out their economic destinies for themselves, in the polity, "freedom" meant inclusion rather than separation. Recognition of their equal rights as citizens quickly emerged as the animating impulse of Reconstruction black politics. In the spring and summer of 1865, blacks organized a seemingly unending series of mass meetings, parades, and petitions demanding civil equality and suffrage as indispensable corollaries of emancipation. By midsummer, "secret political Radical Associations" had been formed in Virginia's major cities. Richmond blacks first organized politically to protest the army's rounding up of "vagrants" for plantation labor, but soon expanded their demands to include the right to vote and the removal of the "Rebel-controlled" local government.

Statewide conventions held throughout the South in 1865 and early 1866 offered the most visible evidence of black political organization. Several hundred delegates attended these gatherings, some selected by local meetings, others by churches, fraternal societies, Union Leagues, and black army units, still others simply appointed by themselves. The delegates "ranged all colors and apparently all conditions," but urban free mulattoes took the most prominent roles, and former slaves were almost entirely absent from leadership positions. But other groups also came to the fore in 1865. In Mississippi, a state with few free blacks before the war, ex-slave army veterans and their relatives comprised the majority of the delegates. Alabama and Georgia had a heavy representation of black ministers, and all the conventions included numerous skilled artisans.

The prominence of free blacks, ministers, artisans, and former soldiers in these early conventions foreshadowed black politics for much of Reconstruction. From among these delegates emerged such prominent officeholders as Alabama Congressman James T. Rapier and Mississippi Secretary of State James D. Lynch. In general, however, what is striking is how few of these early leaders went on to positions of prominence. In most states, political mobilization had advanced far more rapidly in cities and in rural areas occupied by federal troops during the war than in the bulk of the plantation counties, where the majority of the former slaves lived. The free blacks of Louisiana and South Carolina who stepped to the fore in 1865 remained at the helm of black politics throughout Reconstruction; elsewhere, however, a new group of leaders, many of them freedmen from the black belt, soon superseded those who took the lead in 1865.

The debates at these conventions illuminated conflicting currents of black public life in the immediate aftermath of emancipation. Tensions within the black community occasionally rose to the surface. One delegate voiced resentment that a Northern black had been chosen president of North Carolina's convention. By and large, however, the proceedings proved harmonious, the delegates devoting most of their time to issues that united blacks rather than divided them. South Carolina's convention demanded access to all the opportunities and privileges enjoyed by whites, from education to the right to bear arms, serve on juries, establish newspapers, assemble peacefully, and "enter upon all the avenues of agriculture, commerce, [and] trade."

The delegates' central preoccupation, however, was equality before the law and the suffrage. In justifying their demand for the vote, the delegates invoked America's republican traditions, especially the Declaration of Independence — "the broadest, the deepest, the most comprehensive and truthful definition of human freedom that was ever given to the world." The North Carolina freedmen's convention portrayed the Civil War and emancipation as chapters in the onward march of "progressive civilization," embodiments of "the fundamental truths laid down in the great charter of Republican liberty, the Declaration of Independence." Such language was not confined to the convention delegates. Eleven Alabama blacks, who complained of contract frauds, injustice before the courts, and other abuses, concluded their

petition with a revealing masterpiece of understate-
ment: "This is not the pursuit of happiness."

Like their Northern counterparts during the Civil
War, Southern blacks proclaimed their identification
with the nation's history, destiny, and political system.
The abundance of letters and petitions addressed by
black gatherings and ordinary freedmen to military
officials, the Freedmen's Bureau, and state and federal
authorities, as well as the decision of a number of conventions to send representatives to Washington to
lobby for black rights, revealed a belief that the political order was at least partially open to their influence.
"We are Americans," declared a meeting of Norfolk
blacks, "we know no other country, we love the land
of our birth." Their address reminded white Virginians that in 1619, "our fathers as well as yours were
toiling in the plantations on James River" and that a
black man, Crispus Attucks, had shed "the first
blood" in the American Revolution. And, of course,
blacks had fought and died to save the Union. America, resolved one meeting, was "now *our* country —
made emphatically so by the blood of our brethren."

Despite the insistence on equal rights, the convention resolutions and public addresses generally
adopted a moderate tone, offering "the right hand of
fellowship" to Southern whites. Even the South Carolina convention, forthright in claiming civil and political equality and in identifying its demand with "the
cause of millions of oppressed men" throughout the
world, took pains to assure the state's white minority
of blacks' "spirit of meekness," their consciousness of
"your wealth and greatness, and our poverty and
weakness."

To some extent, this cautious tone reflected a realistic assessment of the political situation at a time
when Southern whites had been restored to local
power by President Johnson and Congress had not yet
launched its own Reconstruction policy. But the
blend of radicalism and conciliation also mirrored the
indecision of an emerging black political leadership
still finding its own voice in 1865 and 1866 and dom-

inated by urban free blacks, ministers, and others who
had in the past enjoyed harmonious relations with at
least some local whites and did not always feel the bitter resentments of rural freedmen.

Nor did a coherent economic program emerge
from these assemblies. Demands for land did surface at
local meetings that chose convention delegates. Yet
such views were rarely expressed among the
conventions' leadership. By and large, economic concerns figured only marginally in the proceedings, and
the addresses and resolutions offered no economic
program apart from stressing the "mutual interest" of
capital and labor and urging self-improvement as the
route to personal advancement. The ferment rippling
through the Southern countryside found little echo at
the state conventions of 1865, reflecting the paucity
of representation from plantation counties and the
prominence of political leaders more attuned to political equality and self-help formulas than to rural
freedmen's thirst for land.

Nonetheless, these early black conventions both
reflected and advanced the process of political mobilization. Some Tennessee delegates, for example, took
to heart their convention's instruction to "look after
the welfare" of their constituents. After returning
home, they actively promoted black education, protested to civil authorities and the Freedmen's Bureau
about violence and contract frauds, and struggled
against unequal odds to secure blacks a modicum of
justice in local courts. Chapters of the Georgia Equal
Rights and Educational Association, established at the
state's January 1866 convention, became "schools in
which the colored citizens learn their rights." Spreading into fifty counties by the end of the year, the
Association's local meetings attracted as many as 2,000
freedmen, who listened to speeches on issues of the
day and readings from Republican newspapers.

All in all, the most striking characteristic of this initial phase of black political mobilization was uneven-
ness. In some states, organization proceeded steadily
in 1865 and 1866; in others, such as Mississippi, little

activity occurred between an initial flurry in the summer of 1865 and the advent of black suffrage two years later. Large parts of the black belt remained untouched by organized politics, but many blacks were aware of Congressional debates on Reconstruction policy and quickly employed on their own behalf the Civil Rights Act of 1866. "The negro of today," remarked a correspondent of the New Orleans *Tribune* in September 1866, "is not the same as he was six years ago. . . . He has been told of his rights, which have long been robbed." Only in 1867 would blacks enter the "political nation," but in organization, leadership, and an ideology that drew on America's republican heritage to demand an equal place as citizens, the seeds that flowered then were planted in the first years of freedom.

QUESTIONS TO CONSIDER

1. What effects did emancipation have on the status and importance of the southern black family and on its various members? What changes occurred in the lines of African American women? How did southern whites react to those changes?

2. What do changes in African American churches after 1865 reveal about what their members most desired from freedom? What kinds of roles did the church and ministers play in the community? Why?

3. Describe what education meant to African Americans at the time of emancipation and why. What accomplishments did they achieve in this domain?

4. In what ways did the economic status of African Americans change as a result of emancipation, and how did they see themselves in economic terms? Why was their "quest for land" so intense? Did African Americans differ in this from freed slaves in other countries, and how does Eric Foner judge the importance of land distribution?

5. What were the principal political goals of African Americans and their delegates at the statewide conventions of 1865 and 1866? On what did they base these goals, and how did they feel about the United States?

30

Reconstruction:
The Revolution That Failed

JAMES MACGREGOR BURNS

For defeated southern whites, the loss of the Civil War was a monumental calamity. By turns, they were angry, helpless, vindictive, resigned, and heartsick. Their cherished South was not just defeated; it was annihilated. Some 260,000 rebel soldiers, the flower of southern manhood, were dead and thousands more were maimed and crippled for life. The South's major cities were in ruins, railroads and industry desolated, commerce paralyzed, and two-thirds of the assessed wealth, including billions of dollars in slaves, destroyed. As James MacGregor Burns says in The Workshop of Democracy *(1985), from which the following selection is excerpted, "Many [white southerners] were already grieving over sons, plantations, and fortunes taken by war; losing their blacks was the final blow." Some masters shot or hanged African Americans who proclaimed their freedom. That was a harbinger of the years of Reconstruction, for most white southerners were certain that their cause had been just and were entirely unrepentant about fighting against the Union. A popular ballad captured the current mood in conquered Dixie:*

> *Oh, I'm a good ole Rebel, now that's just what I am*
> *For this fair land of freedom I do not care a damn,*
> *I'm glad I fit against it, I only wish't we'd won*
> *And I don't want no pardon for nothin' what I done. . . .*
>
> *I hates the Yankee nation and everything they do*
> *I hates the Declaration of Independence too*

431

I hates the glorious Union, 'tis dripping with our blood
And I hate the striped banner, I fit it all I could. . . .

I can't take up my musket and fight 'em now no mo'
But I ain't gonna love 'em and that is certain sho'
And I don't want no pardon for what I was and am
And I won't be reconstructed and I don't care a damn.

In Washington, Republican leaders were jubilant in victory and determined to deal firmly with southern whites in order to preserve the fruits of the war. But what about the new president, Andrew Johnson? A profane, hard-drinking Tennessee Democrat who bragged about his plebeian origins, Johnson had been the only southern senator to oppose secession openly. He had sided with the Union, served as war governor of Tennessee, and become Lincoln's running mate in 1864, on a Union ticket comprising both Republicans and War Democrats. As a result of the assassination of Lincoln, Johnson was now president, and he faced one of the most difficult tasks ever to confront an American chief executive: how to bind the nation's wounds, preserve African American freedom, and restore the southern states to their proper places in the Union.

Lincoln had contemplated an army of occupation for the South, thinking that military force might be necessary to protect the former slaves and prevent the old southern leadership from returning to power. Now there was such an army in the South: some 200,000 Union troops had moved in to restore order there and to perform whatever reconstruction duties Johnson might ask of them.

Initially, Republican leaders were hopeful about Johnson, for in talking about his native region he seemed tough, even uncompromising. But as he set about restoring defeated Dixie, Johnson alarmed and then enraged congressional Republicans by adopting a soft, conciliatory reconstruction policy. The president not only opposed granting blacks the right to vote but allowed former Confederates to return to power in the southern states. He stood by as they adopted black codes that reduced blacks to a virtual condition of peonage, and he hotly opposed congressional interference in the reconstruction process. He even urged southern states to reject the Fourteenth Amendment, pushed through Congress by the Republicans, which would protect southern blacks. The amendment would prevent the states from enacting laws that abridged "the privileges or immunties of citizens of the United States." It would also bar the states from depriving "any person of life, liberty, or property, without due process of law," or from denying any person the "equal protection of the law." Johnson did more than just oppose the amendment; he damned Republican leaders like Charles Sumner of Massachusetts and Thaddeus Stevens of Pennsylvania, calling them tyrants and traitors. He even campaigned against the Republican party in the 1866 off-year elections. As a consequence, he alienated moderate as well as radical Republicans, who soon united against him. When the 1866 elections gave the Republicans huge majorities in both houses of Congress, they set out to take control of Reconstruction and to reform the South themselves.

This sets the scene for Burns's account of Republican Reconstruction. Burns believes that it was a revolutionary experiment that failed. He does not, of course, subscribe to the outmoded interpretation of Reconstruction as a misguided attempt to "put the colored people on top" in the South and turn the region over to hordes of beady-eyed carpetbaggers and roguish scalawags intent on "stealing the South blind." In the old view, Reconstruction was "a blackout of honest government," a time when the "Southern people were put to the torch," a period so rife with "political rancor, and social violence and disorder," that nothing good came out of it. Since the 1930s, modern scholarship has systematically rejected this interpretation and the bigotry that underlay it. Drawing on modern studies of the period, Burns argues that the Republican Congress did go too far in trying to centralize power in the legislative branch. But he is sympathetic to Republican efforts to bring southern blacks into the American mainstream, to grant them political, social, and educational opportunities for self-advancement. On this score, however, the Republicans did not go far enough, for they failed to provide blacks with the economic security they needed to be truly free in America. Alas, that failure was to plague black Americans for generations to come.

GLOSSARY

CARPETBAGGER   A northern white who migrated to the South and became politically active as a Republican.

ENFORCEMENT ACT OF 1870   Enacted in response to mob violence in the South, it prohibited the use of force, intimidation, and bribery to inhibit African American voting in local and state elections.

FIFTEENTH AMENDMENT   The right of United States citizens to vote could not be denied or abridged, the amendment said, "on account of race, color, or previous condition of servitude." Many white feminists pressed Congress to include "regardless of sex" in the amendment; this would have enfranchised women as well as black men. But Congress refused on the ground that the amendment was already controversial enough and would never be ratified if it enfranchised women, too. It was ratified in 1870.

GRANT, ULYSSES S.   Northern war hero elected president in 1868.

JOHNSON, ANDREW   United States president, 1865–1869; because he defied and obstructed congressional reconstruction measures, the Republican-controlled House of Representatives impeached him, but the Senate failed to convict him by just one vote; it was the first and last attempt to impeach an American president for political reasons.

KU KLUX KLAN   Southern white supremacist group organized in response to the Fifteenth Amendment; dressed in white sheets and hoods, Klansmen tried to prevent African Americans from voting by mob violence and other means of intimidation.

RECONSTRUCTION ACTS OF 1867   "The heart of congressional strategy to democratize the South," the measures divided the South into five military districts under army commanders and empowered them "to suppress disorder, protect life and property, remove civil officeholders [and] to initiate political reconstruction by enrolling qualified voters including blacks, and excluding the disloyal."

SCALAWAG   Native southern white who became a Republican during Reconstruction.

For a brief fleeting moment in history — from late 1866 to almost the end of the decade — radical senators and congressmen led the Republican party in an audacious venture in both the organization and the goals of political power. To a degree that would have astonished the constitution-makers of earlier years, they converted the eighty-year-old system of checks and balances into a highly centralized, majoritarian system that elevated the legislative branch, subordinated the executive and judicial branches, and suspended federalism and "states' rights" in the South. They turned the Constitution on its head. The aims of these leaders were indeed revolutionary — to reverse age-old human and class relationships in the South and to raise millions of people to a much higher level of economic, political, social, and educational self-fulfillment. That such potent means could not in the end produce such humane and democratic ends was the ultimate tragedy of this revolutionary experiment.

This heroic effort was not conducted by men on white horses, but rather by quarrelsome parliamentarians — by a Congress that seemed to one of its members as never "more querulous, distracted, incoherent and ignoble." In the Senate, [Charles] Sumner had good reason to be distracted, for he had married a woman half his age shortly before the [1866] election and was preoccupied first by marital bliss and very soon by marital distress as he and his wife found themselves hopelessly incompatible. His colleagues found him more remote and unpredictable than ever. In the House, [Thaddeus] Stevens worked closely with his Radical allies, but he was now desperately anxious to move swiftly ahead, for he knew that time was running out for him and perhaps for his cause. Rising on the House floor, he now presented the countenance of death, with his dourly twisted mouth, deeply sunken eyes, parchment skin, and a body so wasted that he often conducted business from a couch just outside the chamber. But the old man never lost his ferocious drive to dominate; as he spoke, his eyes lighted up in a fierce gleam and his croaking voice turned thunderous, while he stretched his bony arm out in a wide sweep and punctuated his arguments with sudden thrusts of his long yellow forefinger.

The strength of the Republican party lay in the advanced positions of these two men but even more in the quality and commitment of other party leaders in both houses. Some of these men — John Sherman, James A. Garfield, James G. Blaine — would gain fame in the decades ahead. Others . . . would fade into the mists of history. Occupying almost every hue on the party rainbow, these men differed sharply and disputed mightily, but they felt they had a clear election mandate to establish civil and other rights in the South; they had a strong sense of party solidarity; and they had the backing of rank-and-file senators and representatives and of party organizations throughout the North.

They also had a common adversary in Andrew Johnson. The President stewed over his election defeat, but he would make no fundamental change in his political and legislative strategy. Setbacks seemed only to mire him more deeply in his own resentments. . . . He received little independent advice from his Cabinet, which appeared to believe that the beleaguered President needed above all their loyalty. [Secretary of War Edwin] Stanton dissented on occasion but, characteristically, Johnson did not wholly trust him. As the President stuck to the disintegrating political center and the Republicans moved toward a radical posture, the legislative stage was set for drama and conflict.

The upshot was a burst of legislative creativity in the "hundred days" of winter 1866–67:

December 14, 1866: Congress enacts black suffrage for the District of Columbia, later reenacts it over Johnson's veto. *January 7, 1867:* the House adopts [James M.] Ashley's resolution instructing the Judi-

ciary Committee to "inquire into the conduct of Andrew Johnson." *January 22:* Congress grants itself authority to call itself into special session, a right recognized until now as belonging only to the President. *March 2:* all on the same day, Congress passes a basic act laying out its general plan of political reconstruction; in effect deprives the President of command of the army; and enacts the Tenure of Office Act barring the Chief Executive from removing officials appointed by and with the advice of the Senate, without Senate approval. *March 23:* Congress passes a supplementary Reconstruction Act requiring military commanders to start registering "loyal" voters.

The heart of congressional strategy to democratize the South lay in the first Reconstruction Act of March 2, 1867, as clarified, strengthened, and implemented in later acts. With the ostensible purpose of restoring social order and republican government in the South, and on the premise that the existing "Johnson" state regimes there could not realize these ends or even protect life or property, the South was divided into five military districts subject to martial law. The commanders were empowered not only to govern — to suppress disorder, protect life and property, remove civil officeholders — but to initiate political reconstruction by enrolling qualified voters including blacks, and excluding the disloyal. To be restored to the Union, the Southern states must call new constitutional conventions that, elected under universal manhood suffrage, in turn must establish new state governments that would guarantee black suffrage and ratify the Fourteenth Amendment. These states would be eligibile for representation in the national legislature only after Congress had approved their state constitutions and after the Fourteenth Amendment had become part of the Constitution.

It was a radical's dream, a centralist's heaven — and a states'-righter's nightmare. Congress held all the governmental strings in its hands. No more exquisite punishment could have been devised for secessionists than to make them conform to national standards in reconstructing their own state governments and gaining restoration to the Union. Congress did not stop with upsetting the division of powers between nation and states; it overturned the separation of powers [between the executive and legislative branches of the national government. In 1868, congressional Republicans sought to remove Johnson by a method never before used against an American president. The Republican-controlled House impeached Johnson on various partisan charges, including his defiance of the Tenure of Office Act and his efforts to undermine the Reconstruction Act, but the Senate failed to convict him by just one vote short of the two-thirds required for removal. Thus ended the first and last attempt to impeach an American president for political reasons. Even so, Johnson's presidency was irreparably damaged; he served out his last year in office, as truculent as ever. The Republicans, meanwhile, nominated war hero Ulysses S. Grant as their candidate in the 1868 presidential election. Because Grant had maintained ties with congressional Republicans and seemed genuinely militant in his stance on Reconstruction, congressional Republicans were certain that he would cooperate with them. That November, Grant defeated Democratic candidate Horatio Seymour by winning all but three northern states and polling 52.7 percent of the popular vote].

Some Radical Republicans now were more optimistic than ever. Grant's election, they felt, provided a supreme and perhaps final opportunity to reconstruct the South. Now the Republicans had their own men in the White House; they still controlled both houses of Congress; they had established their supremacy over the Supreme Court; they had considerable influence over the federal military and civilian bureaucracy in the South. They still had the power to discipline the Southern states, by admitting them to the Union or expelling them. The Republicans had pushed through the Thirteenth and Fourteenth Amendments. They still possessed the ablest, most experienced political leadership in the nation. Stevens had died during the campaign, but Sumner had been handsomely reelected in Massachusetts. "So at

last I have conquered; after a life of struggle," the senator said.

Other Radicals were less sanguine. They knew that far more than Andrew Johnson had thwarted Reconstruction. The national commitment to black equality was weak, the mechanisms of government faulty, and even with the best of intentions and machinery, the connecting line between a decision in Washington and an actual outcome affecting a black family in Virginia or Mississippi was long and fragile. Time and again, voters had opposed black wrongs without favoring black rights. Before the war, they had fought the extension of slavery but not slavery where it existed. During the war, they had come to approve emancipation only after Lincoln issued his proclamation. After the war, in a number of state elections — especially those of 1867 — Northerners had shown that they favored black suffrage in the South but not at home.

Spurred by effective leaders, Americans were moving toward racial justice, but the journey was agonizingly slow and meandering. "It took America three-quarters of a century of agitation and four years of war to learn the meaning of the word 'Liberty,'" the *American Freedman* editorialized. "God grant to teach us by easier lessons the meaning of the words 'equal rights.'" How quickly and firmly Americans moved ahead on black rights could turn significantly on continuing moral and political leadership.

The crucial issue after Grant's election was the right of blacks to vote. Republican leaders in Congress quickly pushed ahead with the Fifteenth Amendment, which declared in its final form that the "right of the citizens of the United States to vote shall not be denied or abridged by the United States or by any State on account of race, color, or previous condition of servitude." It was a noble sentiment that had emerged out of a set of highly mixed motives. Democrats charged, with some reason, that the majority party was far less interested in legalizing the freedman's vote in the South than in winning the black vote in the North. But the Republican leadership, knowing that countless whites in the North opposed black voting there, were responding to the demands of morality as well as practicality. Senator Henry Wilson reminded his colleagues that the "whole struggle in this country to give equal rights and equal privileges to all citizens of the United States has been an unpopular one; that we have been forced to struggle against passions and prejudices engendered by generations of wrong and oppression." He estimated that the struggle had cost his party a quarter of a million votes. Another Republican senator, however, contended that in the long run adherence to "equality of rights among men" had been not a source of party weakness but of its strength and power. . . .

If political morality in the long run meant political practicality, the Fifteenth Amendment nevertheless bore all the markings of compromise. To gain the two-thirds support constitutionally required in each chamber, the sponsors were compelled to jettison clauses that would have outlawed property qualifications and literacy tests. The amendment provided only that Congress and the states could not deny the vote, rather than requiring them to take positive action to secure black suffrage; nor was there any provision against denial of vote by mobs or other private groups. And of course the amendment did not provide for female voting — and so the National Woman Suffrage Association opposed it.

Still, radicals in and out of Congress were elated when the Fifteenth cleared Congress, elated even more when the measure became part of the Constitution in March 1870, after Republican state parties helped drive it through the required number of legislatures. . . .

The legal right of blacks to vote soon produced a phenomenon in Southern politics — black legislators, judges, superintendents of education, lieutenant governors and other state officials, members of Congress, and even two United States senators. These, however, made up only a fraction of Southern officeholders: in none of the legislatures did blacks hold a majority, except briefly in South Carolina's lower house.

Usually black leaders shared power with "carpetbaggers" — white Northerners who came south and became active in politics as Republicans — and "scalawags" — white Southerners who cooperated with Republicans and blacks. While many black leaders were men of "ability and integrity," in [historian] Kenneth Stampp's view, the whites and blacks together comprised a mixed lot of the corrupt and the incorruptible, moderate and extreme, opportunistic and principled, competent and ignorant. The quality of state government under such leadership also was mixed, but on the whole probably no worse than that of many state and local governments of the time. The state governments in the South bore unusually heavy burdens, moreover — demoralization and poverty in the wake of a devastating war, the need to build or rebuild public services throughout the region, the corrupting influence of contractors, speculators, and promoters seeking subsidies, grants, contracts, franchises, and land.

Far more important than the reality of black-and-white rule in the South was the perverted image of it refracted through the distorted lenses of Southern eyes. It was not easy for the white leadership to see newly freed men . . . occupy positions of prestige and power; and it was perhaps inevitable that they would caricature the new rulers to the world. A picture emerged of insolent boors indulging in legislative license, lording it over downtrodden whites, looting the public treasury, bankrupting the state, threatening white traditions, womanhood, and purity. . . .

The worse fear of the old white leadership — that black-and-white rule would produce a social revolution — turned out to be the least warranted of all. The mixed rule of blacks, scalawags, and carpetbaggers produced a few symbolic and actual changes: rhetoric drawn directly from the Declaration of Independence proclaiming liberty, "equality of all persons before the law," various civil and political rights; a mild effort in two or three states to integrate certain educational institutions; a feeble effort at land reform. [Southern state] constitutions were made somewhat more democratic, legislative apportionment less discriminatory, more offices elective; "rights of women were enlarged, tax systems were made more equitable, penal codes were reformed, and the number of crimes punishable by death was reduced," in Stampp's summation. The constitution of South Carolina — the state that had served as the South's political and ideological heartland, and the state that now paradoxically had elevated the most blacks to leadership positions — was converted almost into a model state charter, with provisions for manhood suffrage, public education, extension of women's rights, and even the state's first divorce law. . . .

But what the black-and-white leadership failed to do was of far more profound consequence than what it did. Both radicals and moderates understood that education was a fundamental need for Southern blacks, but the obstacles were formidable and progress slow. Even the best educational system could hardly have compensated for decades of illiteracy and ignorance. "The children," James McPherson noted, "came from a cultural environment almost entirely devoid of intellectual stimulus. Many of them had never heard of the alphabet, geography, or arithmetic when they first came to school. Few of them knew their right hand from their left, or could tell the date of their birth. Most of them realized only vaguely that there was a world outside their own plantation or town." In the early years, teachers sponsored by "Freedmen's Aid" and missionary groups met the challenge, often finding to their surprise that black children had a passion to learn, could be taught to read as quickly as white children, and might be found laboriously teaching their own parents the alphabet and the multiplication table.

These private educational efforts were never adequate, however, to teach more than a fraction of the South's black children. The question was whether the reconstructed black-and-white state governments would take over the task in a comprehensive way, and here they failed. The difficulties were at least as great as ever: inadequate facilities, insufficient money, lack of teachers, inadequate student motivation, discipline problems (black teachers tended to be the harsher disciplinarians). But the biggest hurdle was the constant, pervasive, and continuing hostility of many Southern whites to schooling for blacks. "I have seen many an absurdity in my lifetime," said a Louisiana legislator on observing black pupils for the first time, "but this is the climax of absurdities." A Southern white woman warned a teacher that "you might as well try to teach your horse or mule to read, as to teach these niggers. They *can't* learn."

Behind these white Southern attitudes toward schooling for black children lay a host of fears. One was their old worry that blacks would be educated above their station and out of the labor supply. "To talk about educating this drudge," opined the Paducah (Kentucky) *Herald,* "is to talk without thinking. Either to 'educate,' or to teach him merely to read and write, is to ruin him as a laborer. Thousands of them have already been ruined by it." Even more pervasive was the white fear of integration, although most black leaders made it clear that their main interest was education, whether segregated or not. Southern fears often took the form of harassing and humiliating teachers or, more ingeniously, depriving them of white housing so that some teachers lived with blacks — and hence could be arrested as vagrants. Defending the arrest of a freedmen's teacher, the mayor of Enterprise, Mississippi, said that the teacher had been "living on terms of equality with negroes, living in their houses, boarding with them, and at one time gave a party at which there were no persons present (except himself) but negroes, all of which are offenses against the laws of the state and declared acts of vagrancy." Black-and-white governments could not overcome such deep-seated attitudes.

To many blacks, even more important than education was land — "forty acres and a mule." During the war, when workers on a South Carolina plantation had rejected a wage offer from their master, one of them had said, "I mean to own my own manhood, and I'm goin' on to my own land, just as soon as when I git dis crop in. . . ." Declared a black preacher in Florida to a group of field hands: "It's de white man's turn ter labor now. He ain't got nothin' lef' but his lan', an' de lan' won't be his'n long, fur de Guverment is gwine ter gie ter ev'ry Nigger forty acres of lan' an' a mule." Black hopes for their own plots had dwindled sharply after the war, when Johnson's amnesty proclamation restored property as well as civil rights to most former rebels who would take an oath of allegiance. His expectations dashed, a Virginia black said now that he would ask for only a single acre of land — "ef you make it de acre dat Marsa's house sets on."

Black hopes for land soared again after the congressional Republicans took control of Reconstruction in the late 1860s, only to collapse when Republican moderates — and even some radicals — refused to support a program of land confiscation. Black hopes rose still again when black-and-white regimes took over state governments; some freedmen heard rumors that they need only go to the polls and vote and they would return home with a mule and a deed to a forty-acre lot. But, curiously, "radical" rule in no state produced systematic effort at land redistribution. Some delegates to the Louisiana constitutional convention proposed that purchases of more than 150 acres be prohibited when planters sold their estates, and the South Carolina convention authorized the creation of a commission to buy land for sale to blacks, but little came of these efforts. One reason was clear: Southern whites who had resisted black voting and black education would have reacted with even greater fury to as radical a program as land redistribution, with all its implications for white pride, white property — and the white labor supply.

Black leaders themselves were wary of the freedmen's lust for "forty acres and a mule." In part, this caution may have been due to the class divisions between the black Southern masses and their leaders, many of whom had been artisans or ministers, had been free before the war, and had never experienced plantation life and closeness to the soil. Some of these leaders were, indeed, virtually middle-class in their attitudes toward property, frugality, "negative" liberty, and hard work, and in their fear that radical blacks might infuriate white power elites by talking "confiscation." Such leaders preferred to bargain with the white power structure rather than threaten its control over land and other property. Prizing liberal values of individual liberty, the need for schooling, and above all the right to vote, they played down the economic and social needs of the blacks. And they based their whole strategy on the suffrage, arguing that all the other rights that blacks claimed — land, education, homes — were dependent on their using the potential power inherent in their right to vote.

Would black voting make the crucial difference? Of the three prongs of black advance in the South — schools, land, and the vote — the limited success of the first and the essential failure of the second left black suffrage as the great battlefield of Southern reform. Certainly Southern whites realized this and, as the Republican commitment faltered during the Grant Administration, they stepped up their efforts to thwart black voting. They used a battery of stratagems: opening polling places late or closing them early or changing their location; gerrymandering districts in order to neutralize the black vote; requiring the payment of a poll tax to vote; "losing" or disregarding black ballots; counting Democratic ballots more than once; making local offices appointive rather than elective; plying blacks with liquor. These devices had long been used against white Americans, and by no means did all Southern whites use them now, but fraud and trickery were especially effective against inexperienced and unlettered blacks.

When nonviolent methods failed, many Southern whites turned to other weapons against voting: intimidation, harassment, and terror. Mobs drove blacks away from the polls. Whites blocked polling entrances or crowded around ballot boxes so blacks could not vote. Rowdies with guns or whips followed black voters away from the polling place. When a group of black voters in Gibson County,

Tennessee, returned the fire of a band of masked men, the authorities put the blacks in jail, from which an armed mob took them by force to a nearby riverbank and shot them down. Fifty-three defendants were arrested by federal authorities and tried, none convicted.

Some of this violence erupted spontaneously as young firebrands, emboldened by liquor, rode into polling areas with their guns blazing. But as the stakes of voting rose, terrorists organized themselves. Most notable was the Ku Klux Klan, with its white robes and hoods, sheeted horses, and its weird hierarchies of wizards, genii, dragons, hydras, ghouls, and cyclopes. Proclaiming its devotion to "Chivalry, Humanity, Mercy, and Patriotism," the Klan proposed to protect the "weak, the innocent, and the defenseless" — and the "Constitution of the United States." The Klan had allies in the Knights of the White Camelia, the White Brotherhood, and other secret societies.

Incensed by mob violence, the Republicans in Washington tried to counter it with legislation. The Enforcement Act of May 1870 outlawed the use of force, bribery, or intimidation that hindered the right to vote because of race in state and local elections. Two more enforcement acts during the next twelve months extended and tightened enforcement machinery, and in April 1871 Congress in effect outlawed the Klan and similar groups. But actual enforcement in the thousands of far-flung polling places required an enormous number of marshals and soldiers. As army garrisons in the South thinned out, enforcement appropriations dwindled, and the number of both prosecutions by white prosecutors and convictions by white juries dropped, black voting was more and more choked off.

After his election to a second term Grant tried vigorously though spasmodically to support black rights for the sake of both Republican principle and Republican victories. In a final effort, the Republicans were able to push through the Civil Rights Act of 1875, designed to guarantee equal rights for blacks in public places, but the act was weak in coverage and

enforcement, and later would be struck down by the Supreme Court.

By the mid-seventies Republicanism, Reconstruction, and reform were all running out of steam. Southern Democrats were extending their grip over political machinery; the Republican leadership was shaken by an economic panic in 1873, and the party lost badly in the 1874 midterm elections. The *coup de grâce* for Reconstruction came after Rutherford Hayes's razor-thin electoral-college victory in 1876 over [Democrat] Samuel J. Tilden. Awarded the office as a result of Republican control over three Southern states where voting returns were in doubt, and as a result too of a Republican majority on the Electoral Commission, Hayes bolstered his position by offering assurances about future treatment of the South. While these were in the soft political currency of veiled promises and delphic utterances, the currency was hard enough for the Democrats — and for Hayes as well. Within two months of his inauguration, he ordered the last federal troops out of the South and turned over political control of Louisiana, South Carolina, and Florida to the Southern [Democrats].

*　　*　　*

And what of the objects of this long political struggle — the black people of the South? The vast majority were in the same socioeconomic situation as ten years before, at the end of the war. They had gained certain personal liberties, such as the right to marry, and a modicum of legal and civil and political rights, including the right to vote in certain areas; but their everyday lot was much the same as before. Most still lacked land, property, money, capital; they were still dependent on the planters, sometimes the same old "massa." It was not a black man but a prominent white Georgian who said of the freedman late in 1865: "The negro's first want is, not the ballot, but a chance to live, — yes, sir, *a chance to live*. Why, he can't even live without the consent of the white man!

When the war ended, most of the former slaves owned little more than the skin on their backs. To secure their liberty, they needed their own land, schools, and the right to vote. During Reconstruction, they did gain such personal liberties as the right to marry and a modicum of political, civil, and legal rights. But their everyday lot improved little. When Reconstruction ended, as James MacGregor Burns says, most African Americans in the South "still lacked land, property, money, capital; they were still dependent on the planters, sometimes the same old 'massa.'" (Collection of William Gladstone)

He has no land; he can make no crops except the white man gives him a chance. He hasn't any timber; he can't get a stick of wood without leave from a white man. We crowd him into the fewest possible employments, and then he can scarcely get work anywhere but in the rice-fields and cotton plantations of a white man who has owned him and given up slavery only at the point of the bayonet. . . . What sort of freedom is that?"

Many a freedman had exchanged bondage for a kind of bargaining relationship with employers, but his bargaining position was woefully weak. If he held out for better terms, he could be evicted; if he left, he might be denied work elsewhere and arrested for va-grancy; if he struck, he had no unions or money to sustain him. So the "bargains" were usually one-sided; contracts sometimes literally required "perfect obedience" from employees. Some blacks had had the worst of both worlds — they had left the security of old age and sickness in bondage, under masters who cared for them because they were valuable property, for a strange "free-market" world in which they developed new dependencies on old masters.

Could Reconstruction have turned out differently? Many have concluded that the impotence of the blacks was too deeply rooted, the white intransigence too powerful, the institutions of change too faulty, and the human mind too limited to begin to meet the requirements of a genuine Reconstruction. Yet the human mind had already conducted a stupendous social revolution with the blacks. For a hundred years and more, Southern planters, assisted by slave recruiters in Africa, masters of slaving ships, various middlemen, auctioneers, and drivers, had been uprooting blacks by the hundreds of thousands out of far-off tribal civilizations, bringing most of them safely across broad expanses of water, establishing them in a new and very different culture, and converting them into productive and profit-creating slaves. Somehow the human mind seemed wholly capable of malign "social engineering," incapable of benign.

Yet there were some Americans who did understand the kind of broad social planning and governmental action that was needed to reconstruct genuine democracy in the South and truly to liberate the freed people. [Abolitionist] Wendell Phillips understood the depth of the problem, the need for a "social revolution." He said: "You must plant at the South the elements which make a different society. You cannot enact four millions of slaves, ignorant, down-trodden, and despised, into personal equals of the old leaders of the South." He wanted to "give the negroes land, ballot and education and to hold the arm of the Federal government over the whole Southern Territory until these seeds have begun to bear fruit beyond any possibility of blighting." We must see to it, said Senator Henry Wilson, that "the man made free by the Constitution is a freeman indeed; that he can go where he pleases, work when and for whom he pleases; that he can sue and be sued; that he can lease and buy and sell and own property, real and personal; that he can go into the schools and educate himself and his children. . . ." [Black leader Frederick] Douglass and Stevens and Sumner took similar positions.

These men were not typical of Republicans or even of Radical Republicans, but many other radicals and moderates recognized that the freed people needed an array of economic, political, social, and legal supports, and that these were interrelated. Con-

gressman George Hoar lamented that blacks had been given universal suffrage without universal education. Some radicals believed that voting was the black's first need and others that land or sustenance came first, but most recognized that no single "solution" was adequate. Antislavery men, said Phillips, "will believe the negro safe when we see him with 40 acres under his feet, a schoolhouse behind him, a ballot in his right hand, the sceptre of the Federal Government over his head, and no State Government to interefere with him, until more than one-half of the white men of the Southern States are in their graves." . . .

The critical failure of Reconstruction probably lay . . . in the realm of leadership — especially that of opinion-makers. Editors, ministers, and others preached liberty and equality without always comprehending the full dimensions of these values and the means necessary — in the South of the 1870s — to accomplish such ends. The radicals "seemed to have little conception," according to Stampp, "of what might be called the sociology of freedom, the ease with which mere laws can be flouted when they alone support an economically dependent class, especially a minority group against whom is directed an intense racial prejudice." Reconstruction could have succeeded only through use of strategy employed in a number of successful postwar reconstructions of a comprehensive nature — a strategy of combining ideological, economic, political, educational, and institutional forces in such a firm and coordinated way as truly to transform the social environment in which Southerners, both black and white, were trying to remake their lives after the Civil War. And such a strategy, it should be noted, would have imposed heavy intellectual, economic, and psychological burdens on the North as well.

Not only would such a strategy have called for rare political leadership — especially for a leader, in William Gillette's words, able to "fashion a means and then persevere in it, bending men to his purpose by vigorous initiative, skillful influence, and masterful policy." Even more it called for a rare kind of *intellectual* leadership — political thinkers who could translate the component elements of values such as liberty and equality into policy priorities and operational guidelines. But aside from a few radicals such as Phillips, most of the liberals and many of the radicals had a stunted view of the necessary role of public authority in achieving libertarian and egalitarian purposes. *The Nation,* the most influential liberal weekly in the postwar period, under Edwin L. Godkin shrank from using the only means — government — that could have marshaled the resources necessary for genuine reconstruction. "To Govern Well," *The Nation* proclaimed, "Govern Little." A decisive number of otherwise liberal-minded and generously inclined intellectual leaders held similar views. . . . There were many reasons for the failure of Reconstruction, but the decisive one — because it occurred in people's conceptualizing and analyzing processes and not merely in ineluctable social and economic circumstances — took place in the liberal mind. Most of the liberals were effective transactional leaders, or brokers; few displayed transforming leadership.

That liberal mind seemed to have closed itself off even to the results of practical experimentation. During the war, General Sherman had set aside for freedmen several hundred thousand acres on the Sea Islands south of Charleston and on the abandoned rice lands inland for thirty miles along the coast. Each black family was to receive its forty acres until Congress should rule on their final disposition. Federal officials helped settle 40,000 blacks on these lands. When the whole enterprise was terminated by Johnson's pardon and amnesty program, and land turned back to former owners, the black farmers were incredulous. Some had to be driven off their land by force. The program had lasted long enough, however, to demonstrate that freed people could make a success of independent farming, and that "forty acres and a mule" could serve as the foundation of Reconstruction. But the lesson seemed lost on Northerners who shuddered at the thought of "land confiscation."

Thus the great majority of black people were left in a condition of dependency, a decade after war's end, that was not decisively different, in terms of everyday existence, from their prewar status. They were still landless farm laborers, lacking schooling, the suffrage, and self-respect. They achieved certain civil and legal rights, but their expectations had been greatly raised too, so the Golden Shore for many seemed more distant than ever. Said a black woman: "De slaves, where I lived, knowed after de war dat they had abundance of dat somethin' called freedom, what they could not eat, wear, and sleep in. Yes, sir, they soon found out dat freedom ain't nothin', 'less you is got somethin' to live on and a place to call home. Dis livin' on liberty is lak young folks livin' on love after they gits married. It just don't work."

Or as an Alabama freedman said more tersely when asked what price tag he bore — and perhaps with two meanings of the word in mind:

"I'se free. Ain't wuf nuffin."

QUESTIONS TO CONSIDER

1. Why does Burns call Reconstruction a revolution? Why does he consider the actions of federal officials, especially members of Congress, to be revolutionary? What happened to the Constitution during Reconstruction? Why was Reconstruction "a radicalist's dream, a centralist's heaven, and a states'-righter's nightmare"?

2. What compromises and weaknesses vitiated the strength of the Fifteenth (voting rights) Amendment?

3. Reconstructionists recognized that African Americans needed education, land, and the vote if equality was to become a reality in the South. What fundamental fears and racist attitudes in both the South and the North kept these goals from being realized? What practical steps does Burns feel ought to

have been taken to ensure the success of Reconstruction policies? Do you see any potential problems in aggressive governmental policies temporarily adopted to make Reconstruction work? Or do you think the Constitution is strong enough to protect us from government excesses?

4. Discuss Burns's contention that the failure of liberal intellectual leaders to shape public opinion was responsible for the failure of Reconstruction. Were the leaders more to blame than the weak enforcement policies of the federal government or the repressive, sometimes violent reactions of white southerners?

5. This selection deals with the harsh legacy of the Civil War and failed Reconstruction. Imagine for a moment that Reconstruction was a success, that African Americans in the late nineteenth century achieved lives founded on a sound economic and legal base, with equal access to land, education, and the franchise. How would the United States be different today? Would the nation have elected an African American president by now? How might other issues of social justice, such as women's rights, have been affected?

An Invitation to Respond

We would like to find out a little about your background and about your reactions to the sixth edition of *Portrait of America*. Your evaluation of the book will help us to meet the interests and needs of students in future editions. We invite you to share your reactions by completing the questionnaire below and returning it to *College Marketing. Houghton Mifflin Company, 222 Berkeley Street, Boston, MA 02116.*

1. How do you rate this textbook in the following areas?

	Excellent	Good	Adequate	Poor
a. Understandable style of writing	_____	_____	_____	_____
b. Physical appearance/ readability	_____	_____	_____	_____
c. Fair coverage of topics	_____	_____	_____	_____
d. Comprehensiveness (covered major issues and time periods)	_____	_____	_____	_____

2. Can you comment on or illustate your above ratings? _____
   _____
   _____
   _____

3. What chapters or features did you particularly like? _____
   _____
   _____
   _____

4. What chapters or features did you dislike or think should be changed?
   _____
   _____
   _____

5. What material would you suggest adding or deleting? _____
   _____
   _____
   _____

6. Are you a student at a community college or a four-year school? _____
   _____

7. Do you intend to major in history? _____

8. We would appreciate any other comments or reactions you are willing to share. _____
   _____
   _____